OUR CANCER YEAR

OUR CANCER YEAR

BY JOYCE BRABNER AND HARVEY PEKAR

ILLUSTRATIONS BY FRANK STACK

FOUR WALLS EIGHT WINDOWS, NEW YORK/LONDON

PUBLISHED IN THE UNITED STATES BY:
FOUR WALLS EIGHT WINDOWS
39 WEST 14TH STREET, ROOM 503
NEW YORK, N.Y., 10011

U.K. OFFICES:
FOUR WALLS EIGHT WINDOWS/TURNAROUND
27 HORSELL ROAD
LONDON, N51 XL, ENGLAND

FIRST PRINTING SEPTEMBER 1994.

LIBRARY OF CONGRESS CATALOGING-IN-PUBLICATION DATA:
BRABNER, JOYCE, AND PEKAR, HARVEY.
OUR CANCER YEAR/ BY HARVEY PEKAR AND JOYCE BRABNER. P.   CM.
ISBN: 1-56858-011-8
1. PEKAR, HARVEY--HEALTH--COMIC BOOKS, STRIPS, ETC. 2. CANCER--
PATIENTS--OHIO-- CLEVELAND--BIOGRAPHY--COMIC BOOKS, STRIPS, ETC.
I. BRABNER, JOYCE. II. TITLE.

RC265.6.P45A3	1994
1994 362.1'96994'0092--DC20	94-10523
[B]	CIP

PRINTED IN THE UNITED STATES

10 9 8 7 6 5 4 3 2 1

1

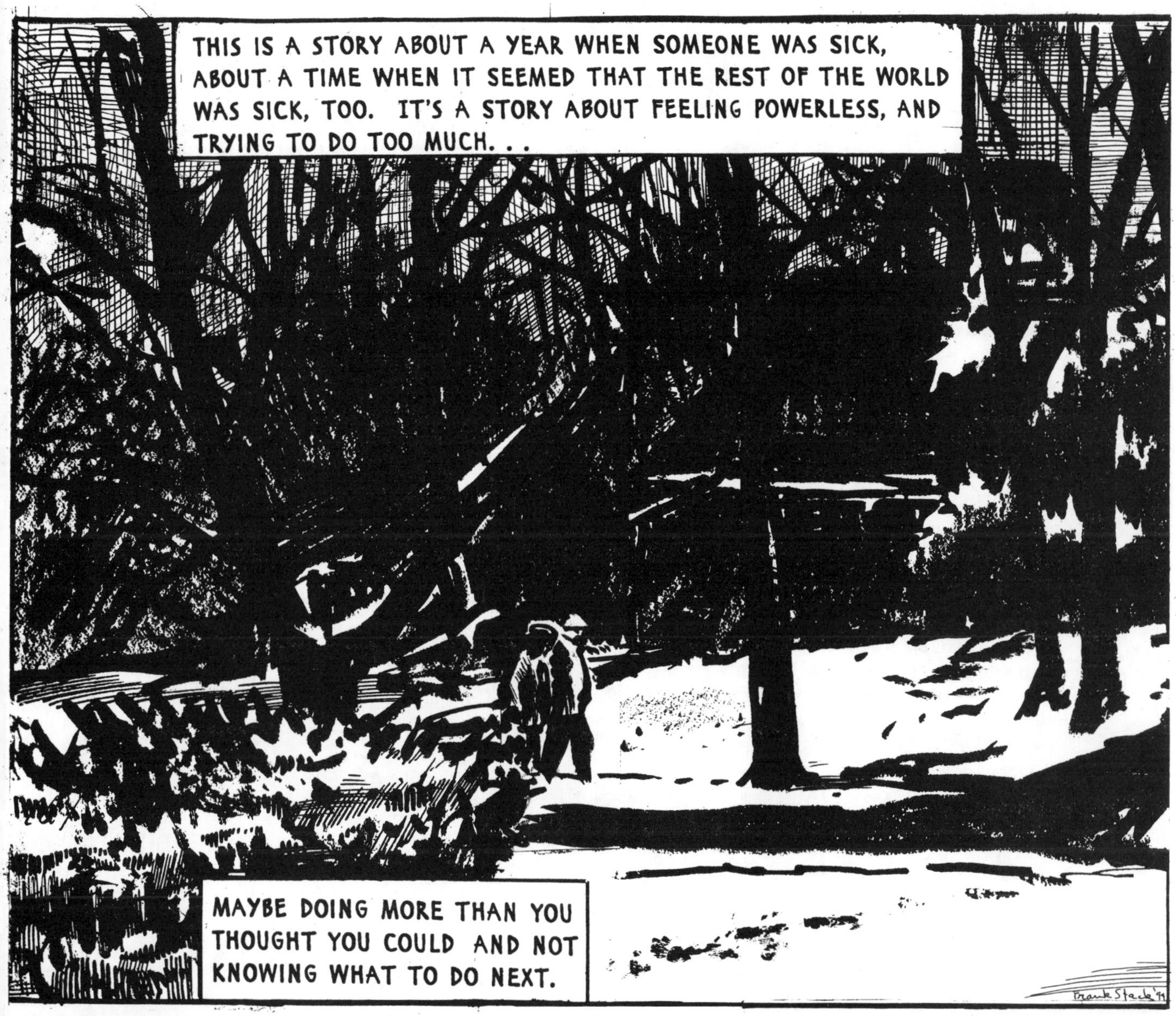
THIS IS A STORY ABOUT A YEAR WHEN SOMEONE WAS SICK, ABOUT A TIME WHEN IT SEEMED THAT THE REST OF THE WORLD WAS SICK, TOO. IT'S A STORY ABOUT FEELING POWERLESS, AND TRYING TO DO TOO MUCH. . .
MAYBE DOING MORE THAN YOU THOUGHT YOU COULD AND NOT KNOWING WHAT TO DO NEXT.
Frank Stack '94

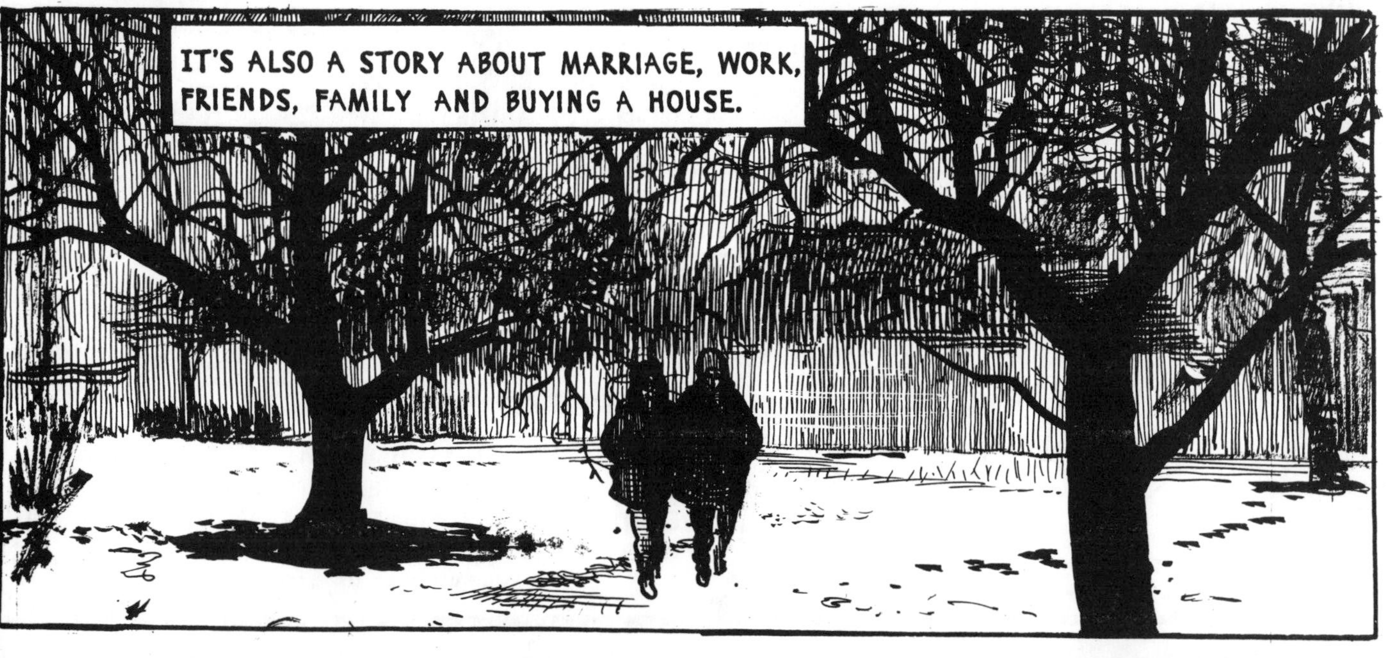
IT'S ALSO A STORY ABOUT MARRIAGE, WORK, FRIENDS, FAMILY AND BUYING A HOUSE.

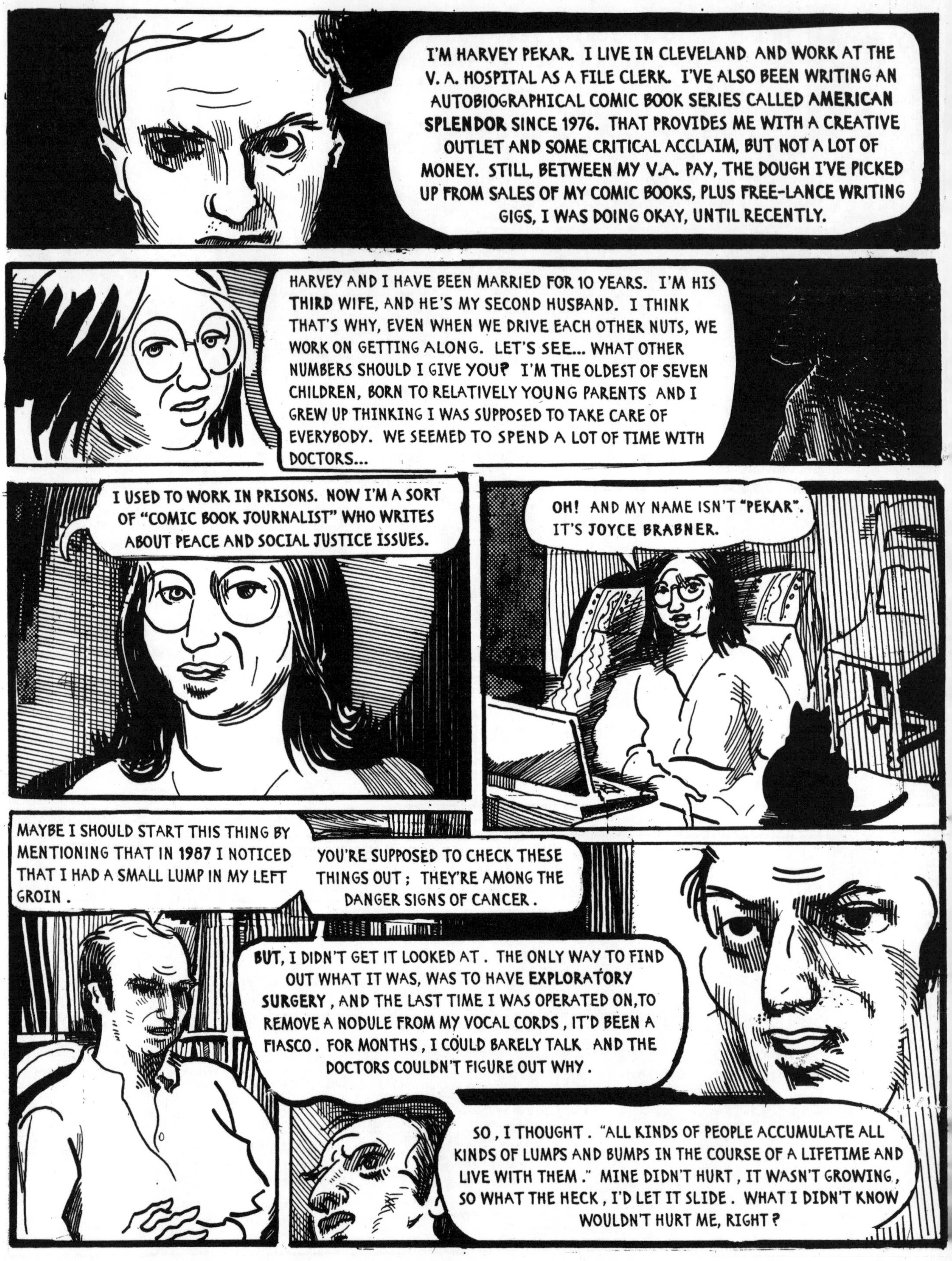
I'M HARVEY PEKAR. I LIVE IN CLEVELAND AND WORK AT THE V. A. HOSPITAL AS A FILE CLERK. I'VE ALSO BEEN WRITING AN AUTOBIOGRAPHICAL COMIC BOOK SERIES CALLED AMERICAN SPLENDOR SINCE 1976. THAT PROVIDES ME WITH A CREATIVE OUTLET AND SOME CRITICAL ACCLAIM, BUT NOT A LOT OF MONEY. STILL, BETWEEN MY V.A. PAY, THE DOUGH I'VE PICKED UP FROM SALES OF MY COMIC BOOKS, PLUS FREE-LANCE WRITING GIGS, I WAS DOING OKAY, UNTIL RECENTLY.
HARVEY AND I HAVE BEEN MARRIED FOR 10 YEARS. I'M HIS THIRD WIFE, AND HE'S MY SECOND HUSBAND. I THINK THAT'S WHY, EVEN WHEN WE DRIVE EACH OTHER NUTS, WE WORK ON GETTING ALONG. LET'S SEE... WHAT OTHER NUMBERS SHOULD I GIVE YOU? I'M THE OLDEST OF SEVEN CHILDREN, BORN TO RELATIVELY YOUNG PARENTS AND I GREW UP THINKING I WAS SUPPOSED TO TAKE CARE OF EVERYBODY. WE SEEMED TO SPEND A LOT OF TIME WITH DOCTORS...
I USED TO WORK IN PRISONS. NOW I'M A SORT OF "COMIC BOOK JOURNALIST" WHO WRITES ABOUT PEACE AND SOCIAL JUSTICE ISSUES.
OH! AND MY NAME ISN'T "PEKAR". IT'S JOYCE BRABNER.
MAYBE I SHOULD START THIS THING BY MENTIONING THAT IN 1987 I NOTICED THAT I HAD A SMALL LUMP IN MY LEFT GROIN.
YOU'RE SUPPOSED TO CHECK THESE THINGS OUT; THEY'RE AMONG THE DANGER SIGNS OF CANCER.
BUT, I DIDN'T GET IT LOOKED AT. THE ONLY WAY TO FIND OUT WHAT IT WAS, WAS TO HAVE EXPLORATORY SURGERY, AND THE LAST TIME I WAS OPERATED ON, TO REMOVE A NODULE FROM MY VOCAL CORDS, IT'D BEEN A FIASCO. FOR MONTHS, I COULD BARELY TALK AND THE DOCTORS COULDN'T FIGURE OUT WHY.
SO, I THOUGHT. "ALL KINDS OF PEOPLE ACCUMULATE ALL KINDS OF LUMPS AND BUMPS IN THE COURSE OF A LIFETIME AND LIVE WITH THEM." MINE DIDN'T HURT, IT WASN'T GROWING, SO WHAT THE HECK, I'D LET IT SLIDE. WHAT I DIDN'T KNOW WOULDN'T HURT ME, RIGHT?

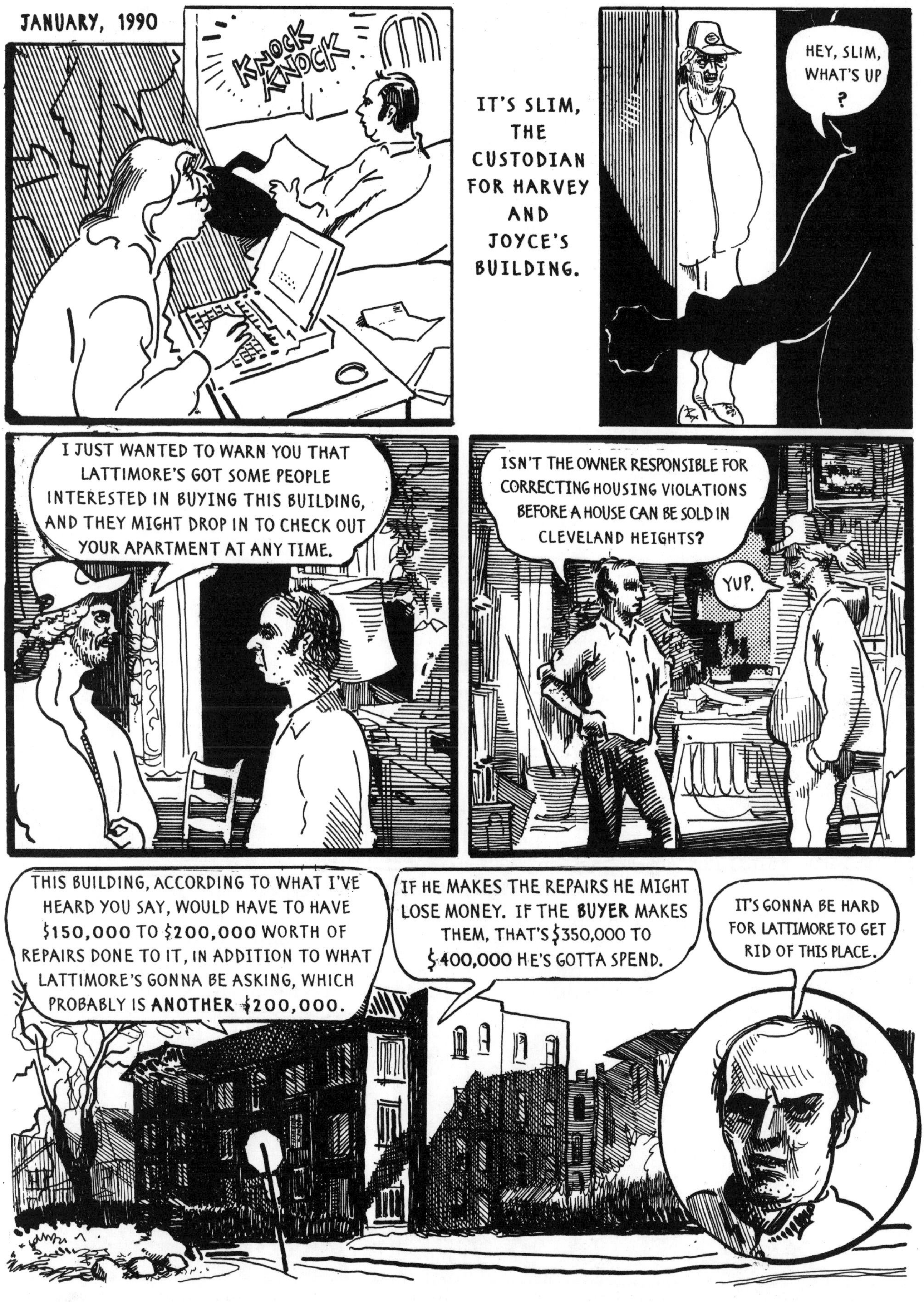
JANUARY, 1990
KNOCK KNOCK
IT'S SLIM, THE CUSTODIAN FOR HARVEY AND JOYCE'S BUILDING.
HEY, SLIM, WHAT'S UP ?
I JUST WANTED TO WARN YOU THAT LATTIMORE'S GOT SOME PEOPLE INTERESTED IN BUYING THIS BUILDING, AND THEY MIGHT DROP IN TO CHECK OUT YOUR APARTMENT AT ANY TIME.
ISN'T THE OWNER RESPONSIBLE FOR CORRECTING HOUSING VIOLATIONS BEFORE A HOUSE CAN BE SOLD IN CLEVELAND HEIGHTS?
YUP.
THIS BUILDING, ACCORDING TO WHAT I'VE HEARD YOU SAY, WOULD HAVE TO HAVE $150,000 TO $200,000 WORTH OF REPAIRS DONE TO IT, IN ADDITION TO WHAT LATTIMORE'S GONNA BE ASKING, WHICH PROBABLY IS ANOTHER $200,000.
IF HE MAKES THE REPAIRS HE MIGHT LOSE MONEY. IF THE BUYER MAKES THEM, THAT'S $350,000 TO $400,000 HE'S GOTTA SPEND.
IT'S GONNA BE HARD FOR LATTIMORE TO GET RID OF THIS PLACE.

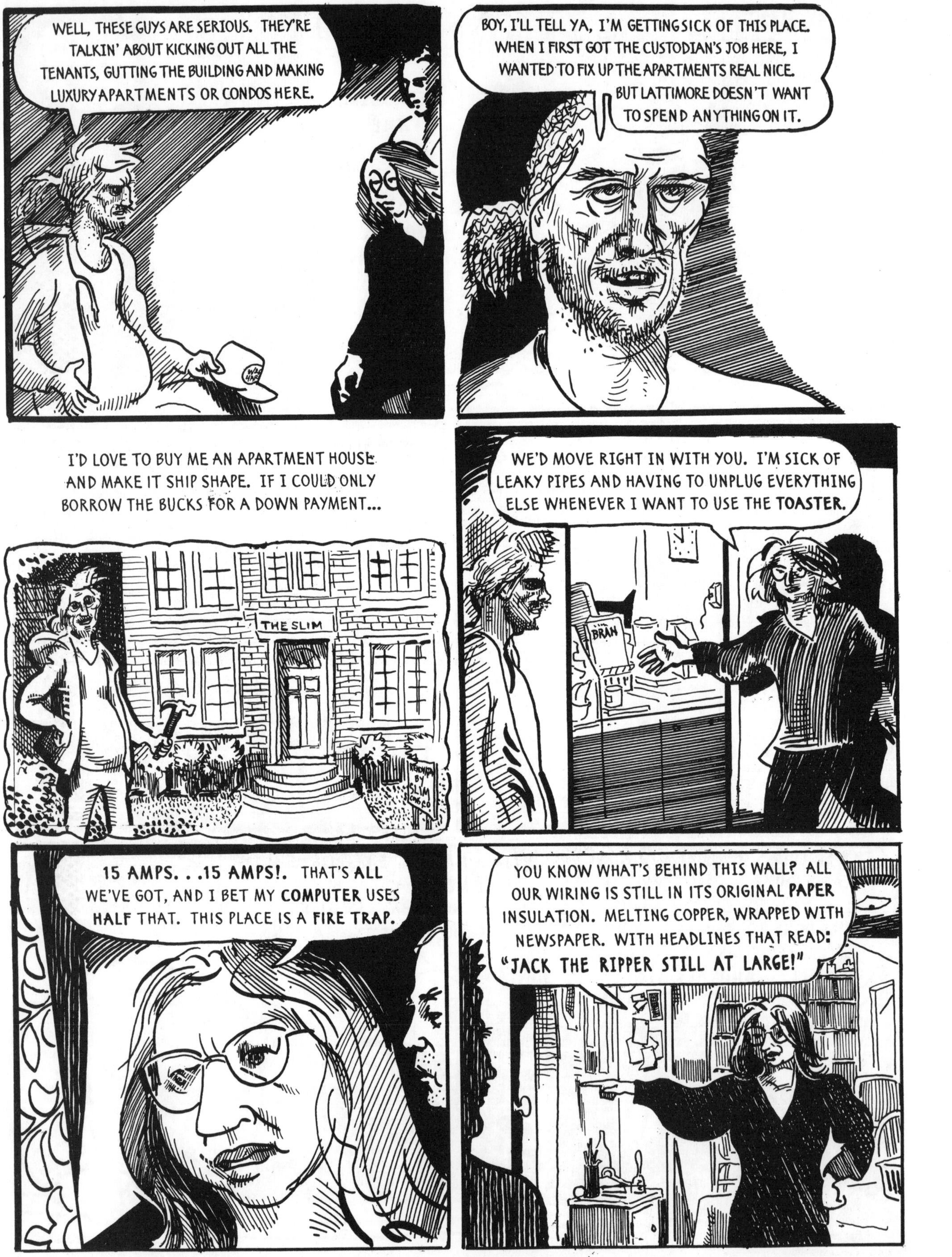
WELL, THESE GUYS ARE SERIOUS. THEY'RE TALKIN' ABOUT KICKING OUT ALL THE TENANTS, GUTTING THE BUILDING AND MAKING LUXURY APARTMENTS OR CONDOS HERE.
BOY, I'LL TELL YA, I'M GETTING SICK OF THIS PLACE. WHEN I FIRST GOT THE CUSTODIAN'S JOB HERE, I WANTED TO FIX UP THE APARTMENTS REAL NICE.
BUT LATTIMORE DOESN'T WANT TO SPEND ANYTHING ON IT.
I'D LOVE TO BUY ME AN APARTMENT HOUSE AND MAKE IT SHIP SHAPE. IF I COULD ONLY BORROW THE BUCKS FOR A DOWN PAYMENT...
THE SLIM
WE'D MOVE RIGHT IN WITH YOU. I'M SICK OF LEAKY PIPES AND HAVING TO UNPLUG EVERYTHING ELSE WHENEVER I WANT TO USE THE **TOASTER.**
BRAN
15 AMPS. . .15 AMPS!. THAT'S **ALL** WE'VE GOT, AND I BET MY **COMPUTER** USES **HALF** THAT. THIS PLACE IS A **FIRE TRAP.**
YOU KNOW WHAT'S BEHIND THIS WALL? ALL OUR WIRING IS STILL IN ITS ORIGINAL **PAPER** INSULATION. MELTING COPPER, WRAPPED WITH NEWSPAPER. WITH HEADLINES THAT READ: **"JACK THE RIPPER STILL AT LARGE!"**

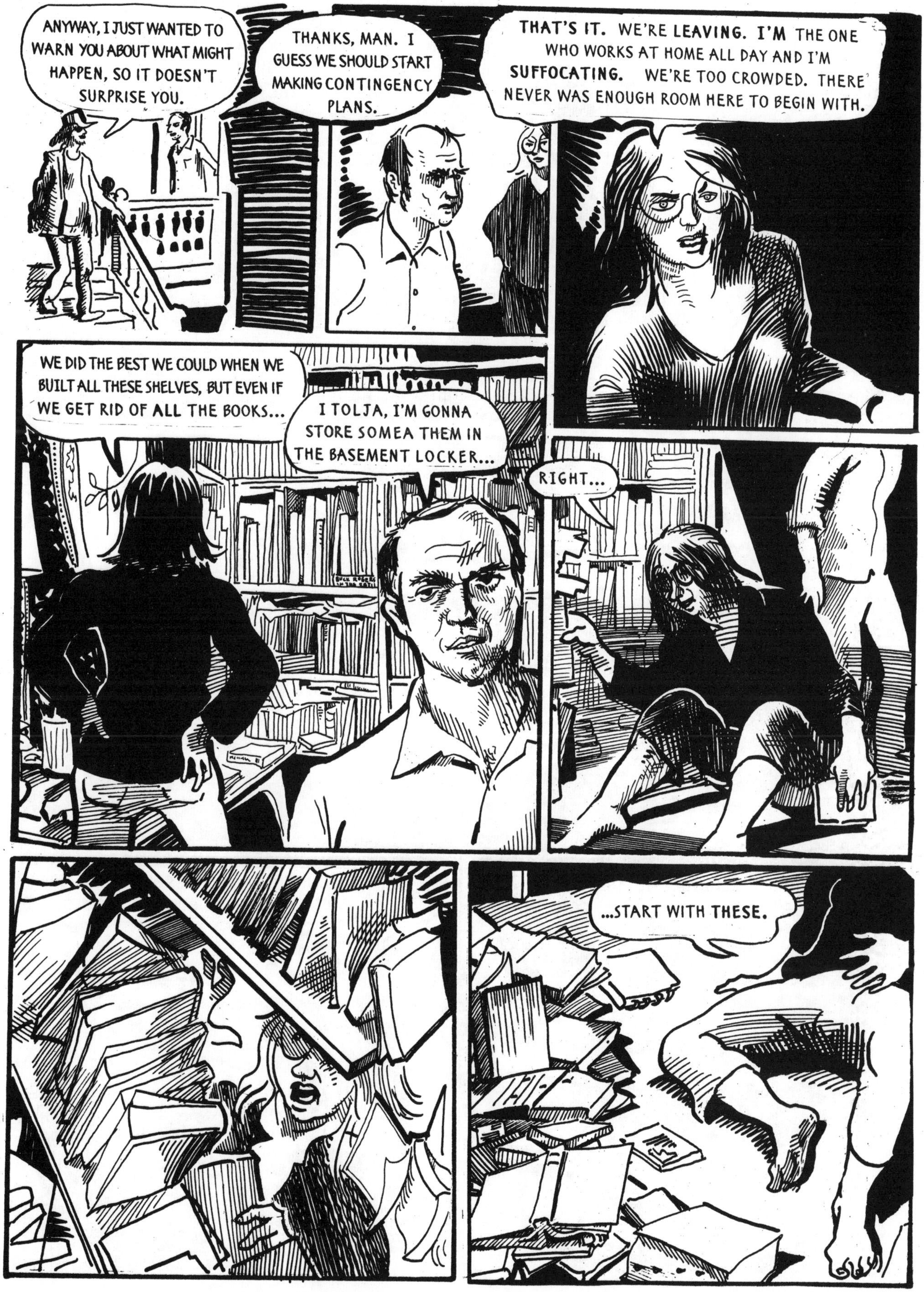
ANYWAY, I JUST WANTED TO WARN YOU ABOUT WHAT MIGHT HAPPEN, SO IT DOESN'T SURPRISE YOU.
THANKS, MAN. I GUESS WE SHOULD START MAKING CONTINGENCY PLANS.
THAT'S IT. WE'RE LEAVING. I'M THE ONE WHO WORKS AT HOME ALL DAY AND I'M SUFFOCATING. WE'RE TOO CROWDED. THERE NEVER WAS ENOUGH ROOM HERE TO BEGIN WITH.
WE DID THE BEST WE COULD WHEN WE BUILT ALL THESE SHELVES, BUT EVEN IF WE GET RID OF ALL THE BOOKS...
I TOLJA, I'M GONNA STORE SOMEA THEM IN THE BASEMENT LOCKER...
RIGHT...
...START WITH THESE.

WALKING TO WORK THE NEXT DAY WITH A FELLOW TENANT, TIM.

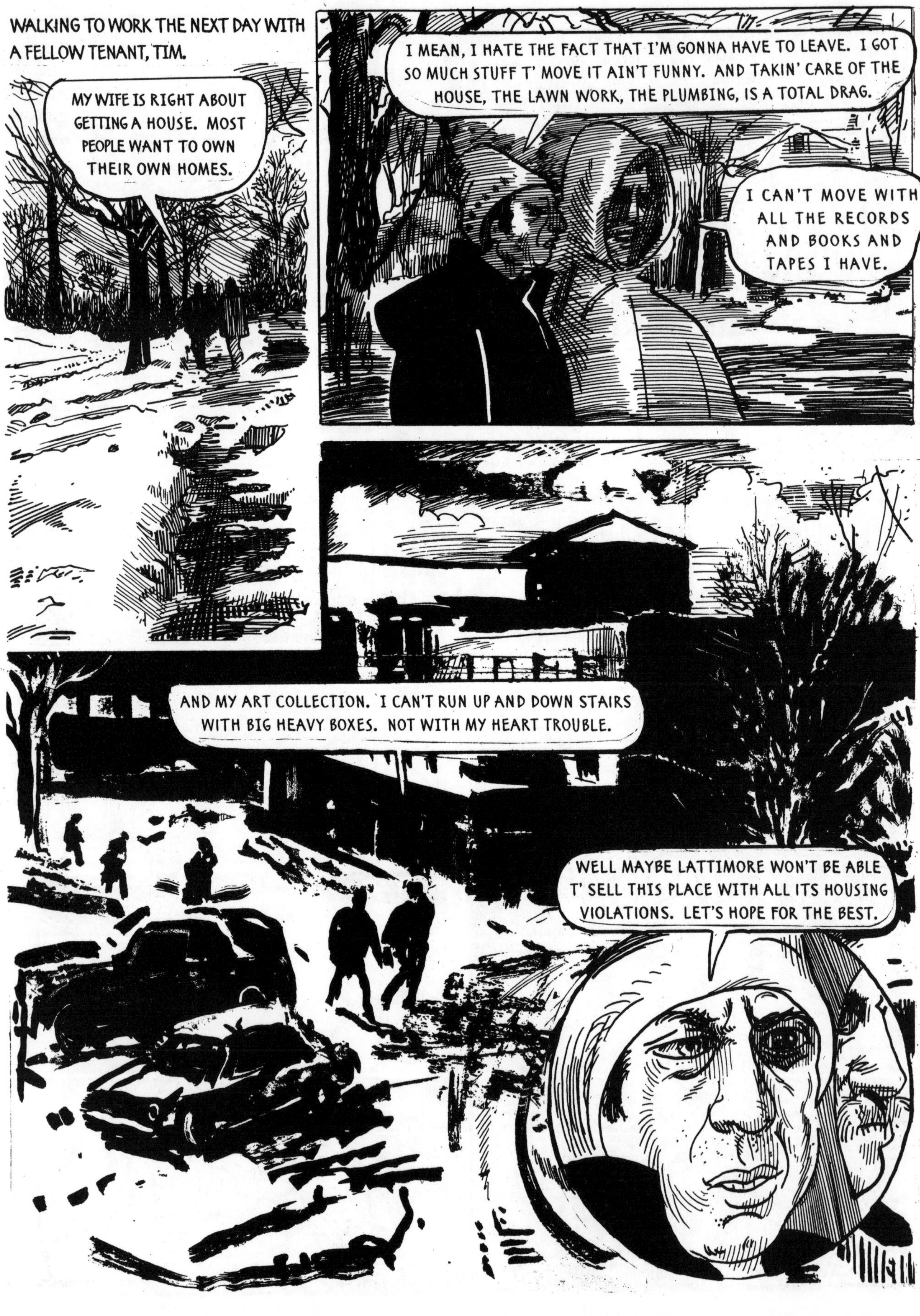
MY WIFE IS RIGHT ABOUT GETTING A HOUSE. MOST PEOPLE WANT TO OWN THEIR OWN HOMES.
I MEAN, I HATE THE FACT THAT I'M GONNA HAVE TO LEAVE. I GOT SO MUCH STUFF T' MOVE IT AIN'T FUNNY. AND TAKIN' CARE OF THE HOUSE, THE LAWN WORK, THE PLUMBING, IS A TOTAL DRAG.
I CAN'T MOVE WITH ALL THE RECORDS AND BOOKS AND TAPES I HAVE.
AND MY ART COLLECTION. I CAN'T RUN UP AND DOWN STAIRS WITH BIG HEAVY BOXES. NOT WITH MY HEART TROUBLE.
WELL MAYBE LATTIMORE WON'T BE ABLE T' SELL THIS PLACE WITH ALL ITS HOUSING VIOLATIONS. LET'S HOPE FOR THE BEST.

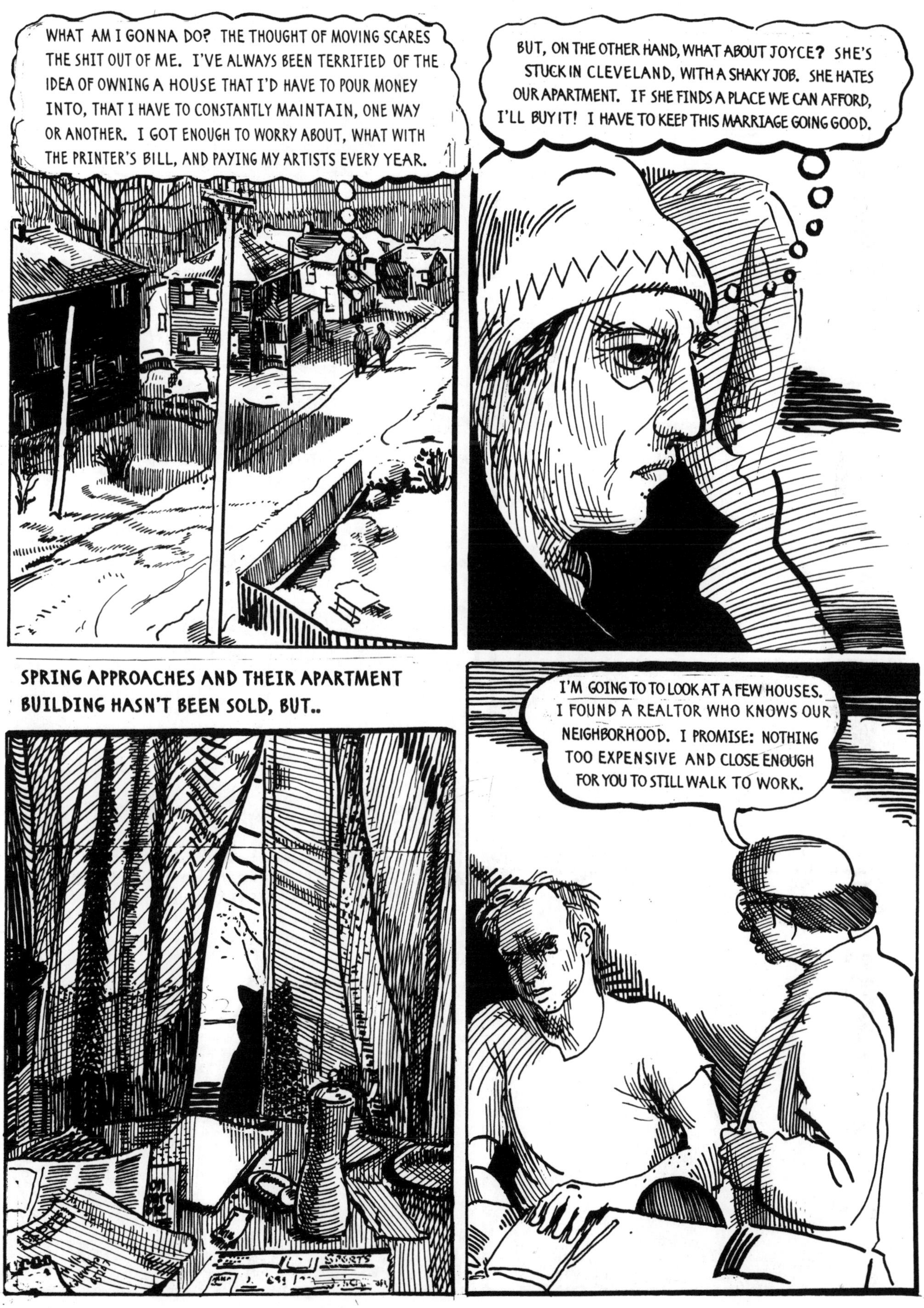
WHAT AM I GONNA DO? THE THOUGHT OF MOVING SCARES THE SHIT OUT OF ME. I'VE ALWAYS BEEN TERRIFIED OF THE IDEA OF OWNING A HOUSE THAT I'D HAVE TO POUR MONEY INTO, THAT I HAVE TO CONSTANTLY MAINTAIN, ONE WAY OR ANOTHER. I GOT ENOUGH TO WORRY ABOUT, WHAT WITH THE PRINTER'S BILL, AND PAYING MY ARTISTS EVERY YEAR.
BUT, ON THE OTHER HAND, WHAT ABOUT JOYCE? SHE'S STUCK IN CLEVELAND, WITH A SHAKY JOB. SHE HATES OUR APARTMENT. IF SHE FINDS A PLACE WE CAN AFFORD, I'LL BUY IT! I HAVE TO KEEP THIS MARRIAGE GOING GOOD.
SPRING APPROACHES AND THEIR APARTMENT BUILDING HASN'T BEEN SOLD, BUT..
I'M GOING TO TO LOOK AT A FEW HOUSES. I FOUND A REALTOR WHO KNOWS OUR NEIGHBORHOOD. I PROMISE: NOTHING TOO EXPENSIVE AND CLOSE ENOUGH FOR YOU TO STILL WALK TO WORK.

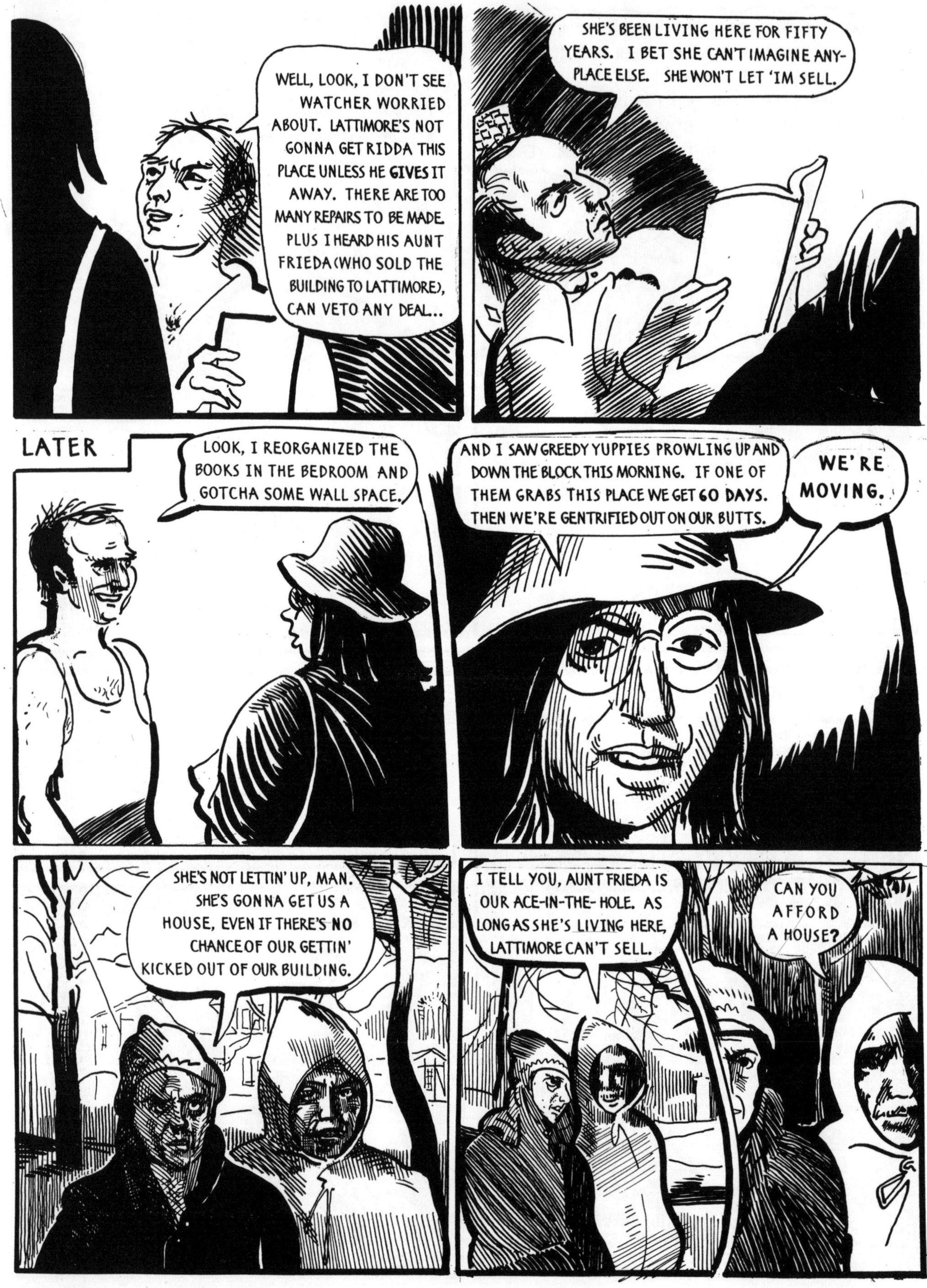
WELL, LOOK, I DON'T SEE WATCHER WORRIED ABOUT. LATTIMORE'S NOT GONNA GET RIDDA THIS PLACE UNLESS HE GIVES IT AWAY. THERE ARE TOO MANY REPAIRS TO BE MADE. PLUS I HEARD HIS AUNT FRIEDA (WHO SOLD THE BUILDING TO LATTIMORE), CAN VETO ANY DEAL...
SHE'S BEEN LIVING HERE FOR FIFTY YEARS. I BET SHE CAN'T IMAGINE ANY-PLACE ELSE. SHE WON'T LET 'IM SELL.
LATER
LOOK, I REORGANIZED THE BOOKS IN THE BEDROOM AND GOTCHA SOME WALL SPACE.
AND I SAW GREEDY YUPPIES PROWLING UP AND DOWN THE BLOCK THIS MORNING. IF ONE OF THEM GRABS THIS PLACE WE GET 60 DAYS. THEN WE'RE GENTRIFIED OUT ON OUR BUTTS.
WE'RE MOVING.
SHE'S NOT LETTIN' UP, MAN. SHE'S GONNA GET US A HOUSE, EVEN IF THERE'S NO CHANCE OF OUR GETTIN' KICKED OUT OF OUR BUILDING.
I TELL YOU, AUNT FRIEDA IS OUR ACE-IN-THE-HOLE. AS LONG AS SHE'S LIVING HERE, LATTIMORE CAN'T SELL.
CAN YOU AFFORD A HOUSE?

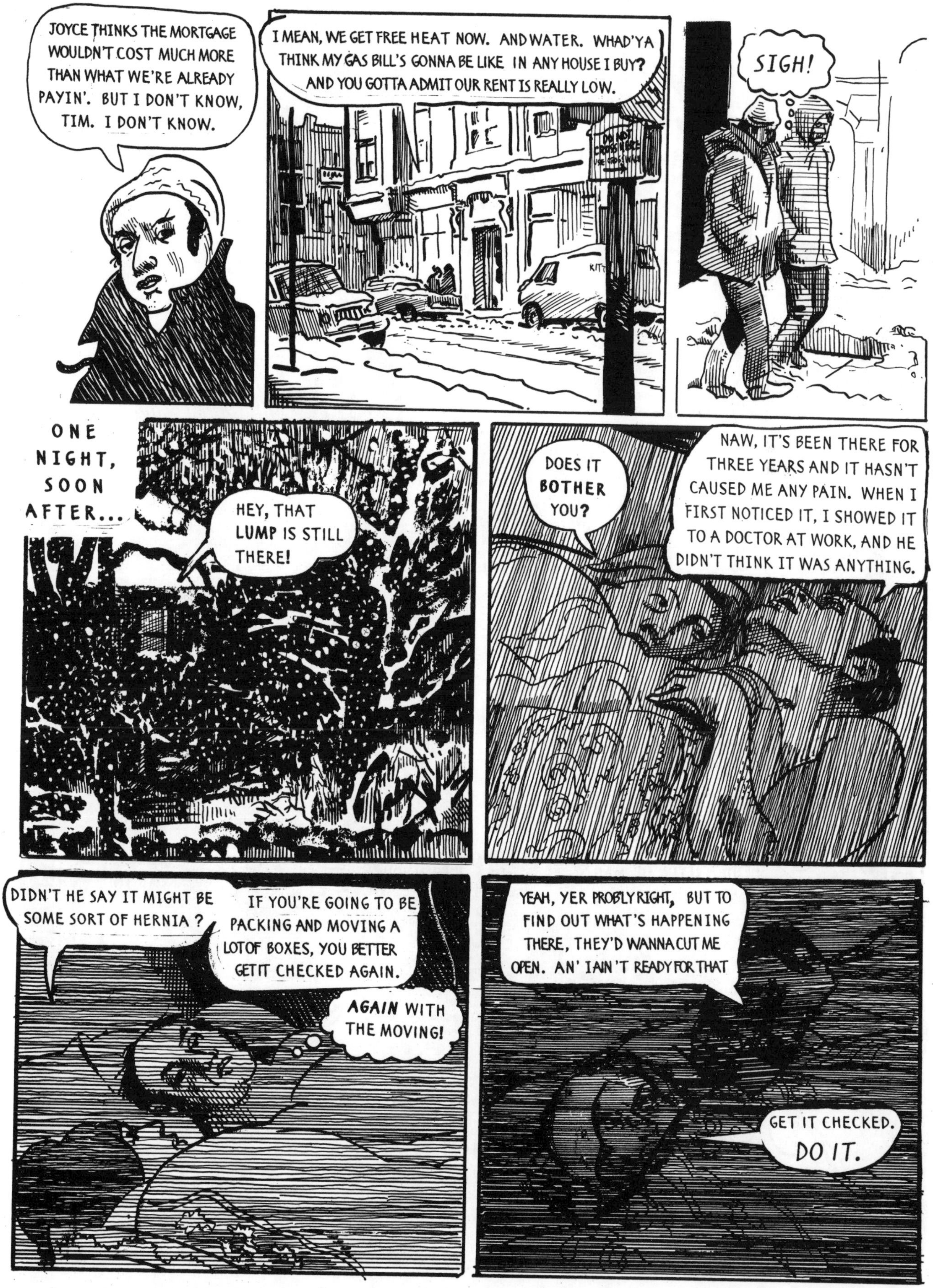
JOYCE THINKS THE MORTGAGE WOULDN'T COST MUCH MORE THAN WHAT WE'RE ALREADY PAYIN'. BUT I DON'T KNOW, TIM. I DON'T KNOW.
I MEAN, WE GET FREE HEAT NOW. AND WATER. WHAD'YA THINK MY GAS BILL'S GONNA BE LIKE IN ANY HOUSE I BUY? AND YOU GOTTA ADMIT OUR RENT IS REALLY LOW.
SIGH!
ONE NIGHT, SOON AFTER...
HEY, THAT LUMP IS STILL THERE!
DOES IT BOTHER YOU?
NAW, IT'S BEEN THERE FOR THREE YEARS AND IT HASN'T CAUSED ME ANY PAIN. WHEN I FIRST NOTICED IT, I SHOWED IT TO A DOCTOR AT WORK, AND HE DIDN'T THINK IT WAS ANYTHING.
DIDN'T HE SAY IT MIGHT BE SOME SORT OF HERNIA ?
IF YOU'RE GOING TO BE PACKING AND MOVING A LOTOF BOXES, YOU BETTER GETIT CHECKED AGAIN.
AGAIN WITH THE MOVING!
YEAH, YER PROBLY RIGHT, BUT TO FIND OUT WHAT'S HAPPENING THERE, THEY'D WANNA CUT ME OPEN. AN' IAIN'T READY FOR THAT
GET IT CHECKED. DO IT.

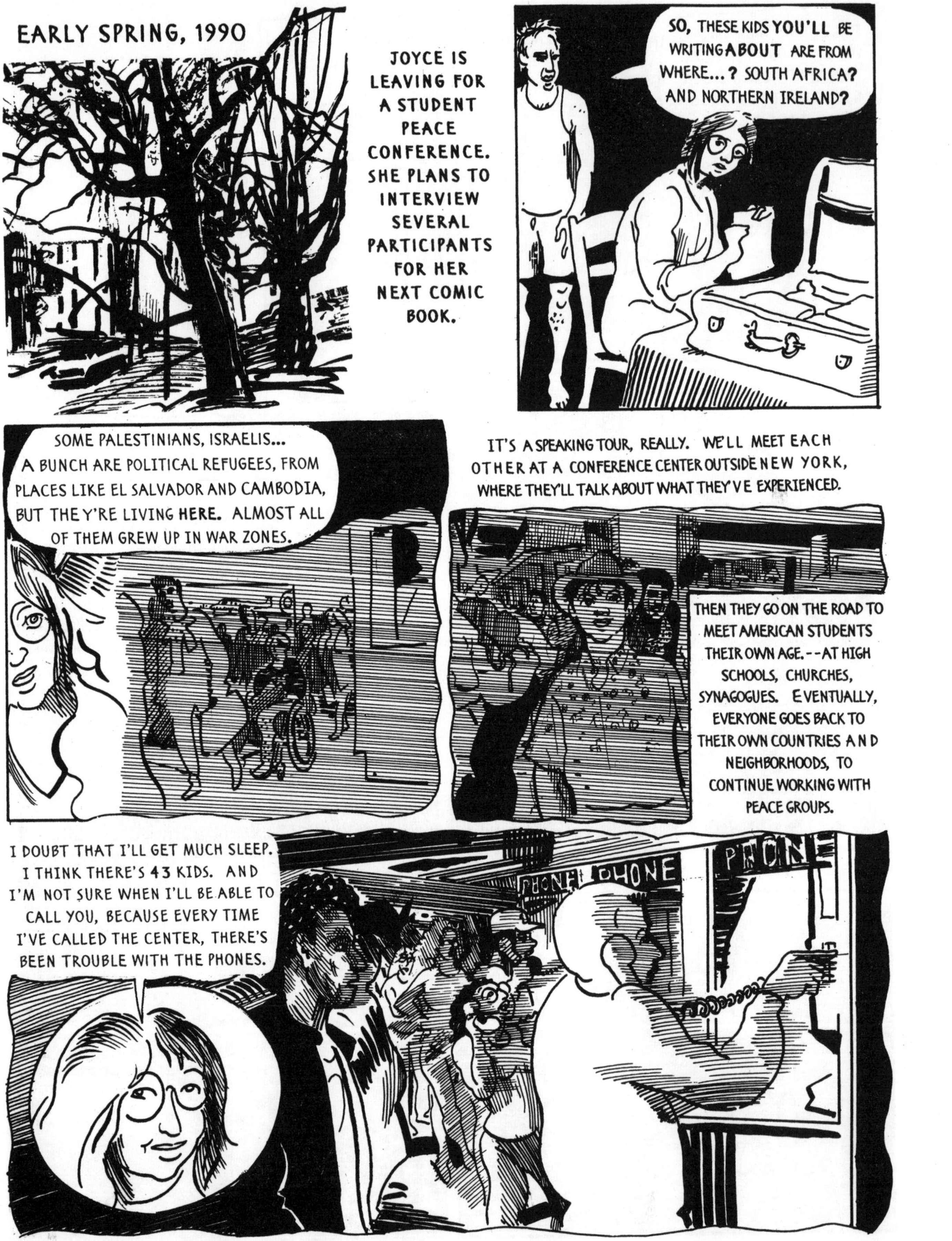
EARLY SPRING, 1990
JOYCE IS LEAVING FOR A STUDENT PEACE CONFERENCE. SHE PLANS TO INTERVIEW SEVERAL PARTICIPANTS FOR HER NEXT COMIC BOOK.
SO, THESE KIDS YOU'LL BE WRITING ABOUT ARE FROM WHERE...? SOUTH AFRICA? AND NORTHERN IRELAND?
SOME PALESTINIANS, ISRAELIS... A BUNCH ARE POLITICAL REFUGEES, FROM PLACES LIKE EL SALVADOR AND CAMBODIA, BUT THEY'RE LIVING HERE. ALMOST ALL OF THEM GREW UP IN WAR ZONES.
IT'S A SPEAKING TOUR, REALLY. WE'LL MEET EACH OTHER AT A CONFERENCE CENTER OUTSIDE NEW YORK, WHERE THEY'LL TALK ABOUT WHAT THEY'VE EXPERIENCED.
THEN THEY GO ON THE ROAD TO MEET AMERICAN STUDENTS THEIR OWN AGE.--AT HIGH SCHOOLS, CHURCHES, SYNAGOGUES. EVENTUALLY, EVERYONE GOES BACK TO THEIR OWN COUNTRIES AND NEIGHBORHOODS, TO CONTINUE WORKING WITH PEACE GROUPS.
I DOUBT THAT I'LL GET MUCH SLEEP. I THINK THERE'S 43 KIDS. AND I'M NOT SURE WHEN I'LL BE ABLE TO CALL YOU, BECAUSE EVERY TIME I'VE CALLED THE CENTER, THERE'S BEEN TROUBLE WITH THE PHONES.
PHONE
PHONE
PHONE

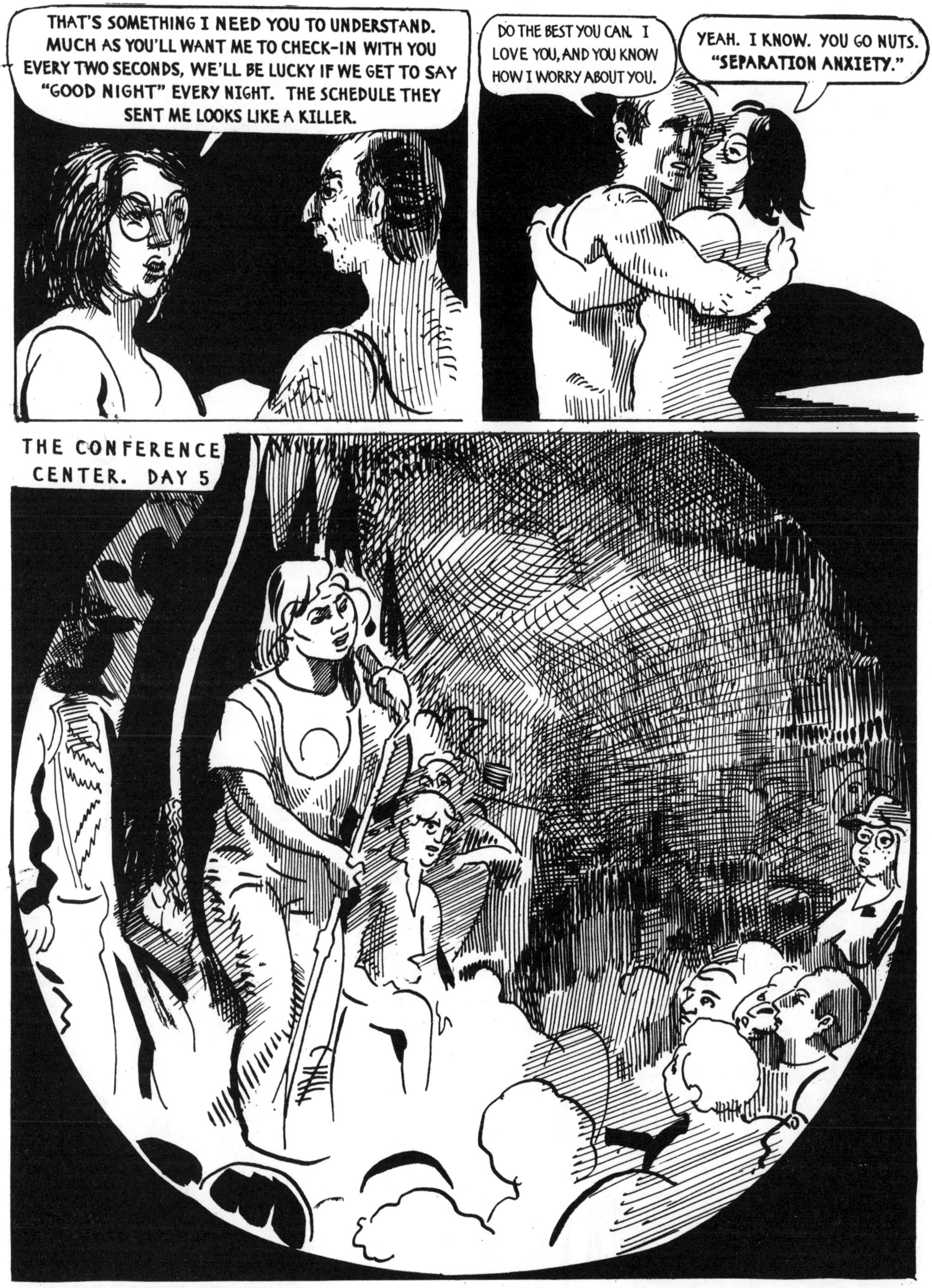
THAT'S SOMETHING I NEED YOU TO UNDERSTAND. MUCH AS YOU'LL WANT ME TO CHECK-IN WITH YOU EVERY TWO SECONDS, WE'LL BE LUCKY IF WE GET TO SAY "GOOD NIGHT" EVERY NIGHT. THE SCHEDULE THEY SENT ME LOOKS LIKE A KILLER.
DO THE BEST YOU CAN. I LOVE YOU, AND YOU KNOW HOW I WORRY ABOUT YOU.
YEAH. I KNOW. YOU GO NUTS. "SEPARATION ANXIETY."
THE CONFERENCE CENTER. DAY 5

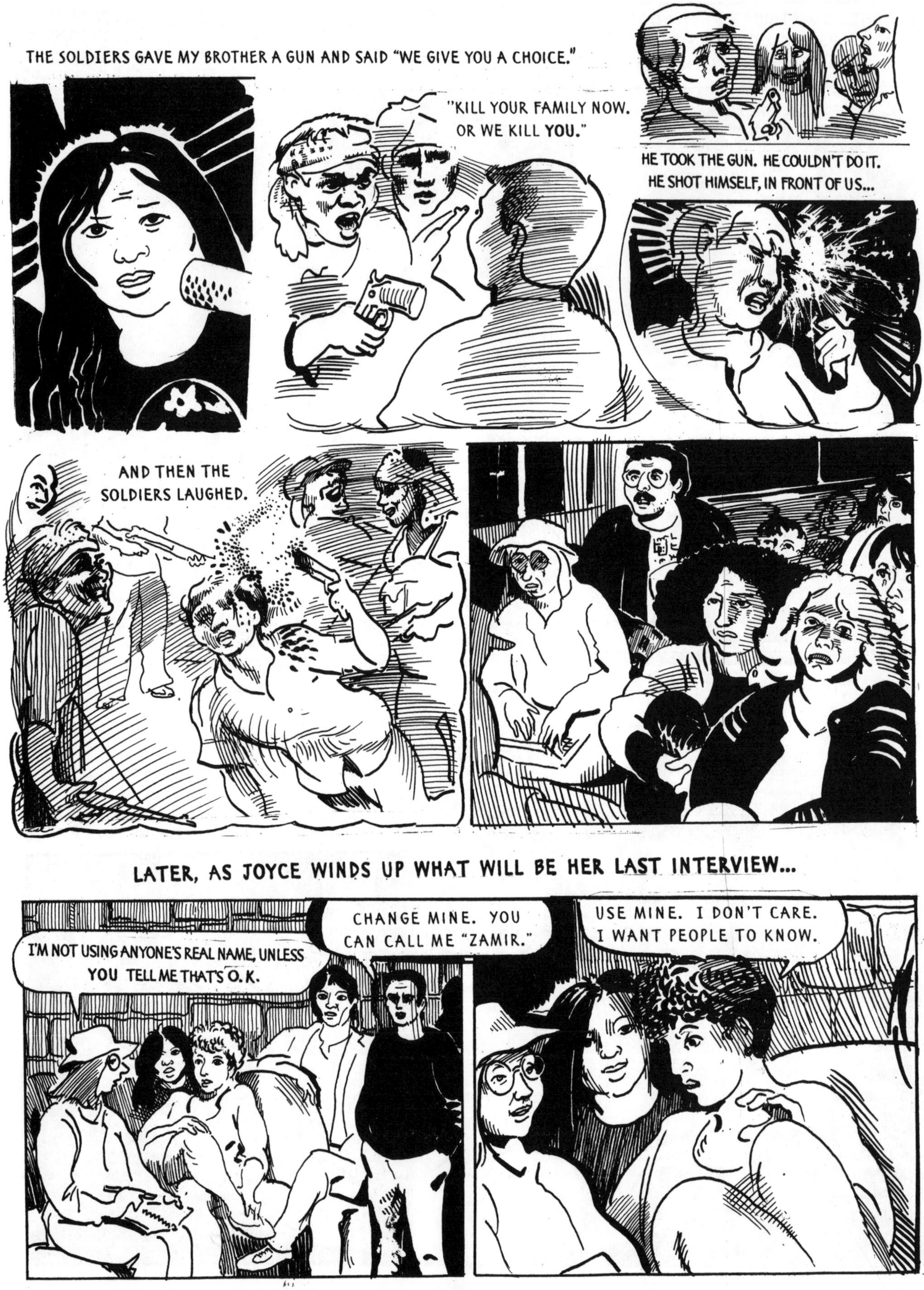
THE SOLDIERS GAVE MY BROTHER A GUN AND SAID "WE GIVE YOU A CHOICE."
"KILL YOUR FAMILY NOW. OR WE KILL YOU."
HE TOOK THE GUN. HE COULDN'T DO IT. HE SHOT HIMSELF, IN FRONT OF US...
AND THEN THE SOLDIERS LAUGHED.
LATER, AS JOYCE WINDS UP WHAT WILL BE HER LAST INTERVIEW...
I'M NOT USING ANYONE'S REAL NAME, UNLESS YOU TELL ME THAT'S O.K.
CHANGE MINE. YOU CAN CALL ME "ZAMIR."
USE MINE. I DON'T CARE. I WANT PEOPLE TO KNOW.

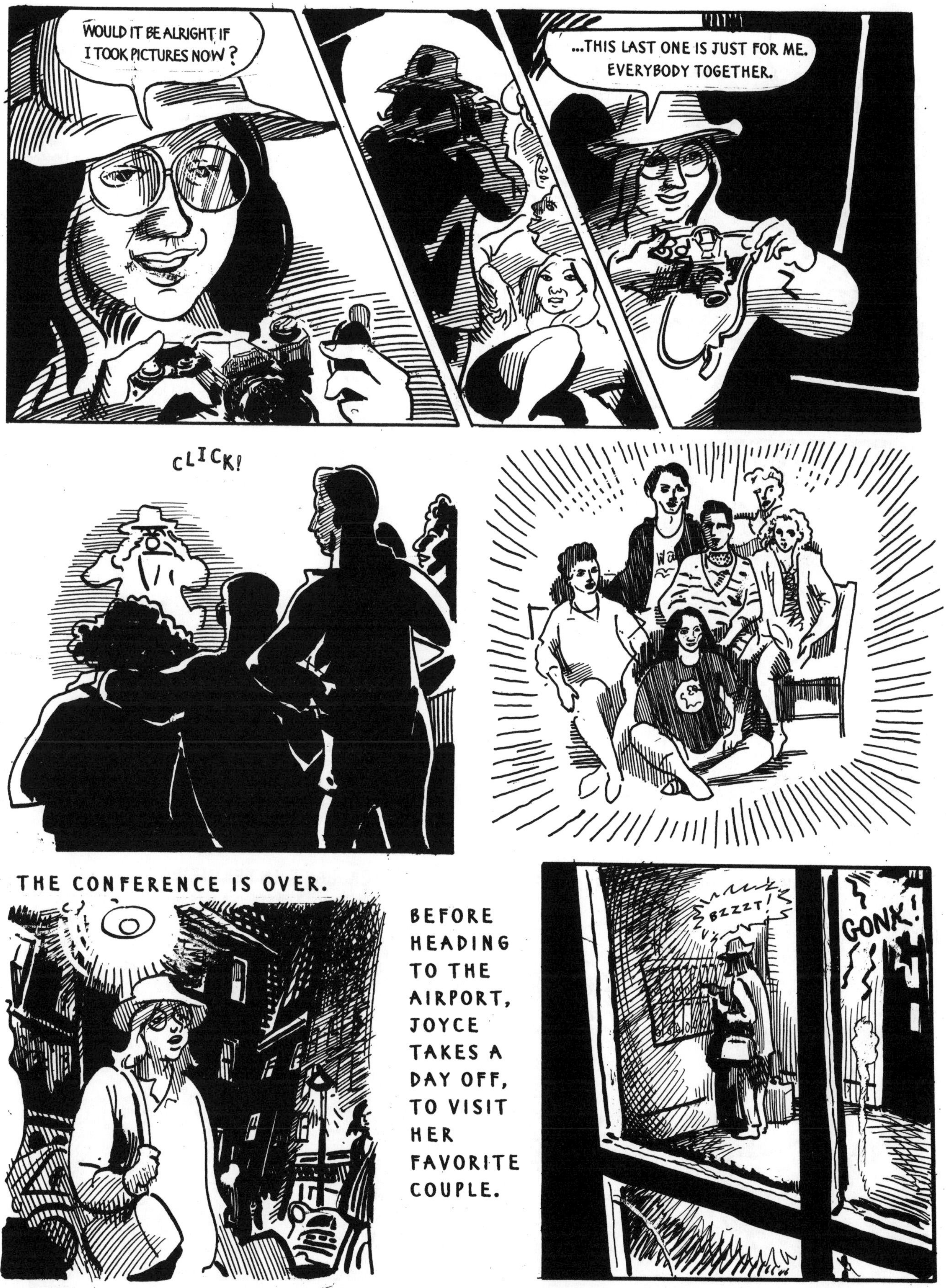
WOULD IT BE ALRIGHT IF I TOOK PICTURES NOW ?
...THIS LAST ONE IS JUST FOR ME. EVERYBODY TOGETHER.
CLICK!
THE CONFERENCE IS OVER.
BEFORE HEADING TO THE AIRPORT, JOYCE TAKES A DAY OFF, TO VISIT HER FAVORITE COUPLE.
BZZZT!
GONK!

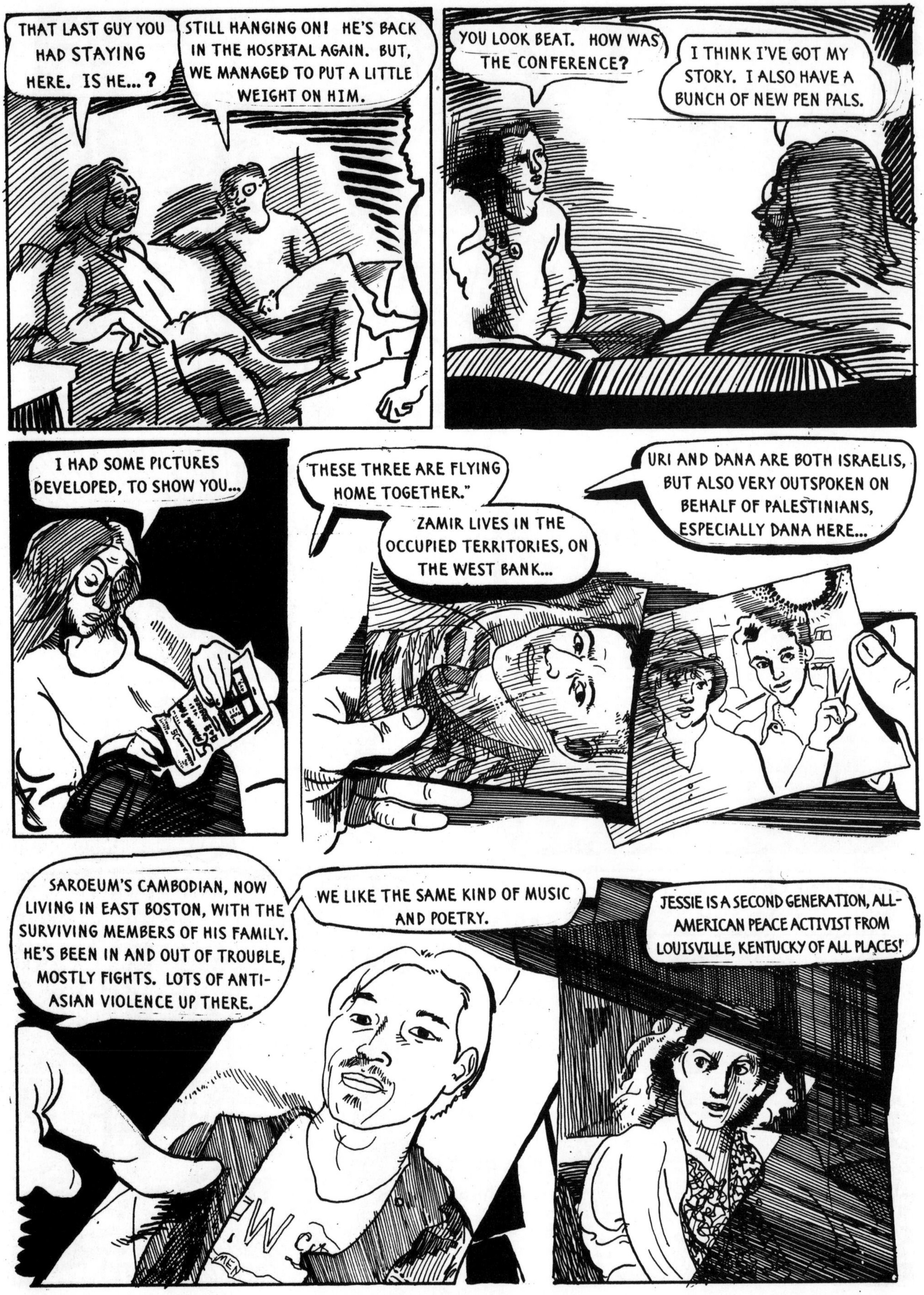

THAT LAST GUY YOU HAD STAYING HERE. IS HE...?
STILL HANGING ON! HE'S BACK IN THE HOSPITAL AGAIN. BUT, WE MANAGED TO PUT A LITTLE WEIGHT ON HIM.
YOU LOOK BEAT. HOW WAS THE CONFERENCE?
I THINK I'VE GOT MY STORY. I ALSO HAVE A BUNCH OF NEW PEN PALS.
I HAD SOME PICTURES DEVELOPED, TO SHOW YOU...
"THESE THREE ARE FLYING HOME TOGETHER."
ZAMIR LIVES IN THE OCCUPIED TERRITORIES, ON THE WEST BANK...
URI AND DANA ARE BOTH ISRAELIS, BUT ALSO VERY OUTSPOKEN ON BEHALF OF PALESTINIANS, ESPECIALLY DANA HERE...
SAROEUM'S CAMBODIAN, NOW LIVING IN EAST BOSTON, WITH THE SURVIVING MEMBERS OF HIS FAMILY. HE'S BEEN IN AND OUT OF TROUBLE, MOSTLY FIGHTS. LOTS OF ANTI-ASIAN VIOLENCE UP THERE.
WE LIKE THE SAME KIND OF MUSIC AND POETRY.
JESSIE IS A SECOND GENERATION, ALL-AMERICAN PEACE ACTIVIST FROM LOUISVILLE, KENTUCKY OF ALL PLACES!

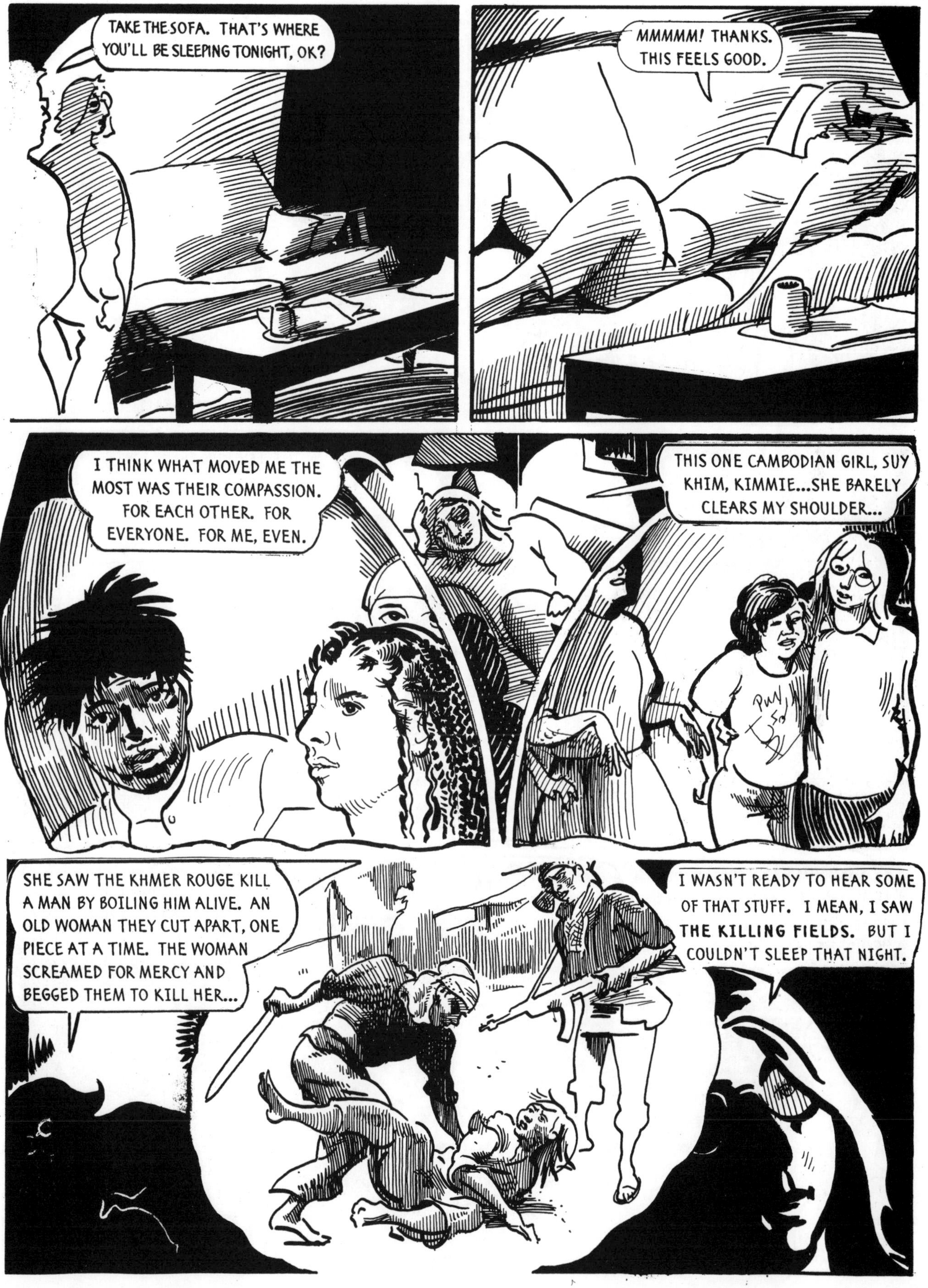
TAKE THE SOFA. THAT'S WHERE YOU'LL BE SLEEPING TONIGHT, OK?
MMMMM! THANKS. THIS FEELS GOOD.
I THINK WHAT MOVED ME THE MOST WAS THEIR COMPASSION. FOR EACH OTHER. FOR EVERYONE. FOR ME, EVEN.
THIS ONE CAMBODIAN GIRL, SUY KHIM, KIMMIE...SHE BARELY CLEARS MY SHOULDER...
SHE SAW THE KHMER ROUGE KILL A MAN BY BOILING HIM ALIVE. AN OLD WOMAN THEY CUT APART, ONE PIECE AT A TIME. THE WOMAN SCREAMED FOR MERCY AND BEGGED THEM TO KILL HER...
I WASN'T READY TO HEAR SOME OF THAT STUFF. I MEAN, I SAW THE KILLING FIELDS. BUT I COULDN'T SLEEP THAT NIGHT.

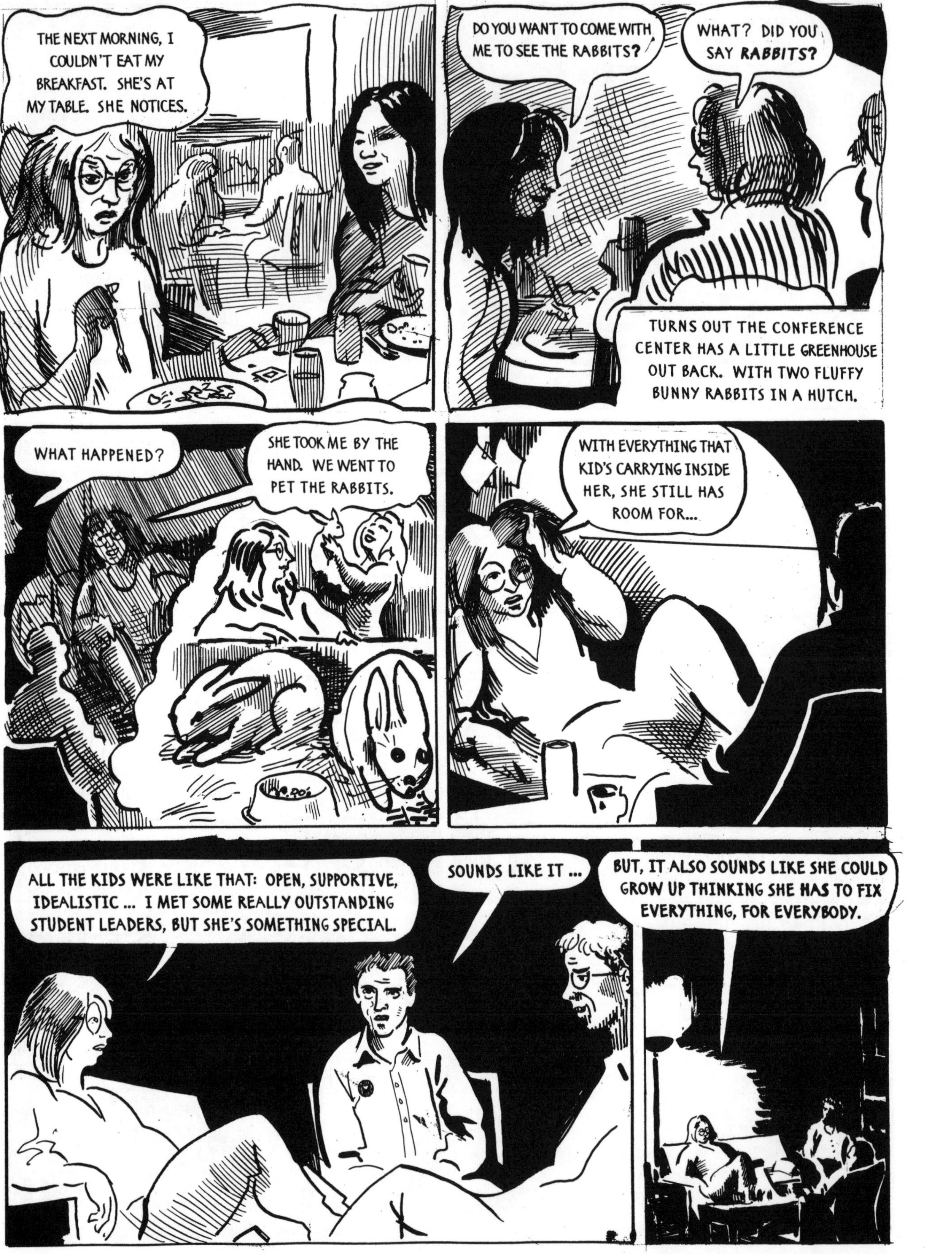
THE NEXT MORNING, I COULDN'T EAT MY BREAKFAST. SHE'S AT MY TABLE. SHE NOTICES.
DO YOU WANT TO COME WITH ME TO SEE THE RABBITS?
WHAT? DID YOU SAY RABBITS?
TURNS OUT THE CONFERENCE CENTER HAS A LITTLE GREENHOUSE OUT BACK. WITH TWO FLUFFY BUNNY RABBITS IN A HUTCH.
WHAT HAPPENED?
SHE TOOK ME BY THE HAND. WE WENT TO PET THE RABBITS.
WITH EVERYTHING THAT KID'S CARRYING INSIDE HER, SHE STILL HAS ROOM FOR...
ALL THE KIDS WERE LIKE THAT: OPEN, SUPPORTIVE, IDEALISTIC ... I MET SOME REALLY OUTSTANDING STUDENT LEADERS, BUT SHE'S SOMETHING SPECIAL.
SOUNDS LIKE IT ...
BUT, IT ALSO SOUNDS LIKE SHE COULD GROW UP THINKING SHE HAS TO FIX EVERYTHING, FOR EVERYBODY.

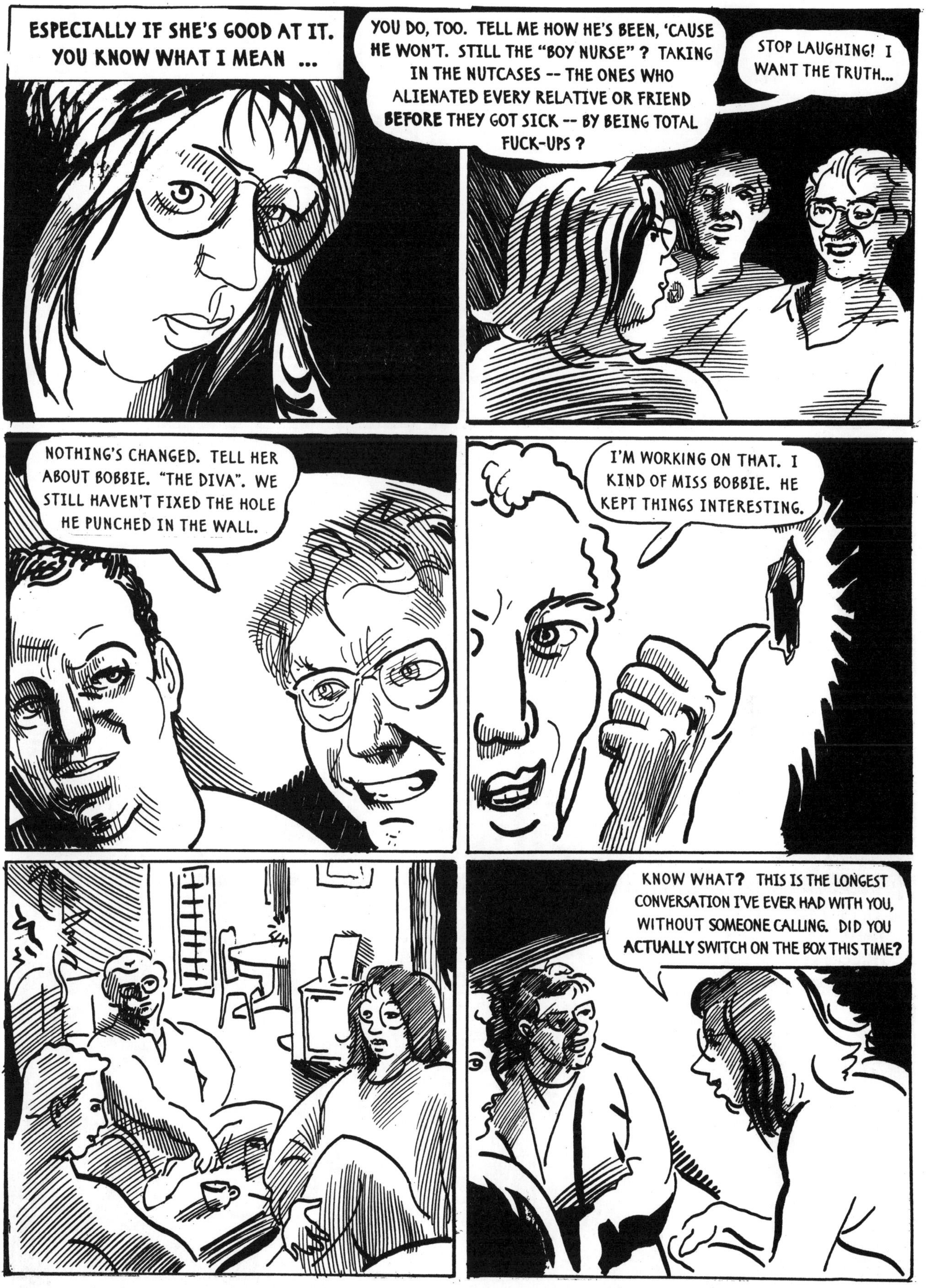
ESPECIALLY IF SHE'S GOOD AT IT. YOU KNOW WHAT I MEAN ...
YOU DO, TOO. TELL ME HOW HE'S BEEN, 'CAUSE HE WON'T. STILL THE "BOY NURSE" ? TAKING IN THE NUTCASES -- THE ONES WHO ALIENATED EVERY RELATIVE OR FRIEND BEFORE THEY GOT SICK -- BY BEING TOTAL FUCK-UPS ?
STOP LAUGHING! I WANT THE TRUTH...
NOTHING'S CHANGED. TELL HER ABOUT BOBBIE. "THE DIVA". WE STILL HAVEN'T FIXED THE HOLE HE PUNCHED IN THE WALL.
I'M WORKING ON THAT. I KIND OF MISS BOBBIE. HE KEPT THINGS INTERESTING.
KNOW WHAT? THIS IS THE LONGEST CONVERSATION I'VE EVER HAD WITH YOU, WITHOUT SOMEONE CALLING. DID YOU ACTUALLY SWITCH ON THE BOX THIS TIME?

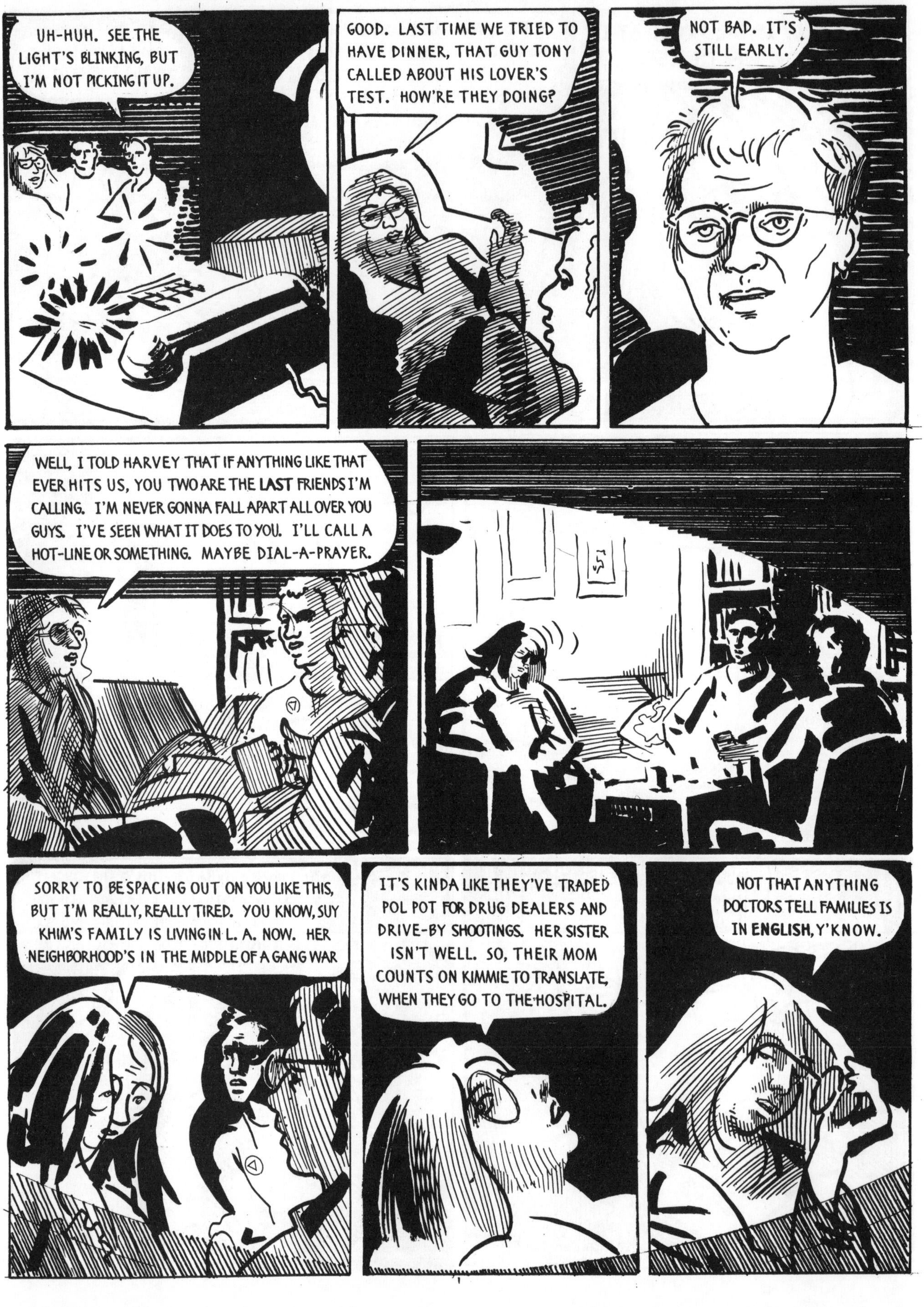
UH-HUH. SEE THE LIGHT'S BLINKING, BUT I'M NOT PICKING IT UP.
GOOD. LAST TIME WE TRIED TO HAVE DINNER, THAT GUY TONY CALLED ABOUT HIS LOVER'S TEST. HOW'RE THEY DOING?
NOT BAD. IT'S STILL EARLY.
WELL, I TOLD HARVEY THAT IF ANYTHING LIKE THAT EVER HITS US, YOU TWO ARE THE LAST FRIENDS I'M CALLING. I'M NEVER GONNA FALL APART ALL OVER YOU GUYS. I'VE SEEN WHAT IT DOES TO YOU. I'LL CALL A HOT-LINE OR SOMETHING. MAYBE DIAL-A-PRAYER.
SORRY TO BE SPACING OUT ON YOU LIKE THIS, BUT I'M REALLY, REALLY TIRED. YOU KNOW, SUY KHIM'S FAMILY IS LIVING IN L. A. NOW. HER NEIGHBORHOOD'S IN THE MIDDLE OF A GANG WAR
IT'S KINDA LIKE THEY'VE TRADED POL POT FOR DRUG DEALERS AND DRIVE-BY SHOOTINGS. HER SISTER ISN'T WELL. SO, THEIR MOM COUNTS ON KIMMIE TO TRANSLATE, WHEN THEY GO TO THE HOSPITAL.
NOT THAT ANYTHING DOCTORS TELL FAMILIES IS IN ENGLISH, Y'KNOW.

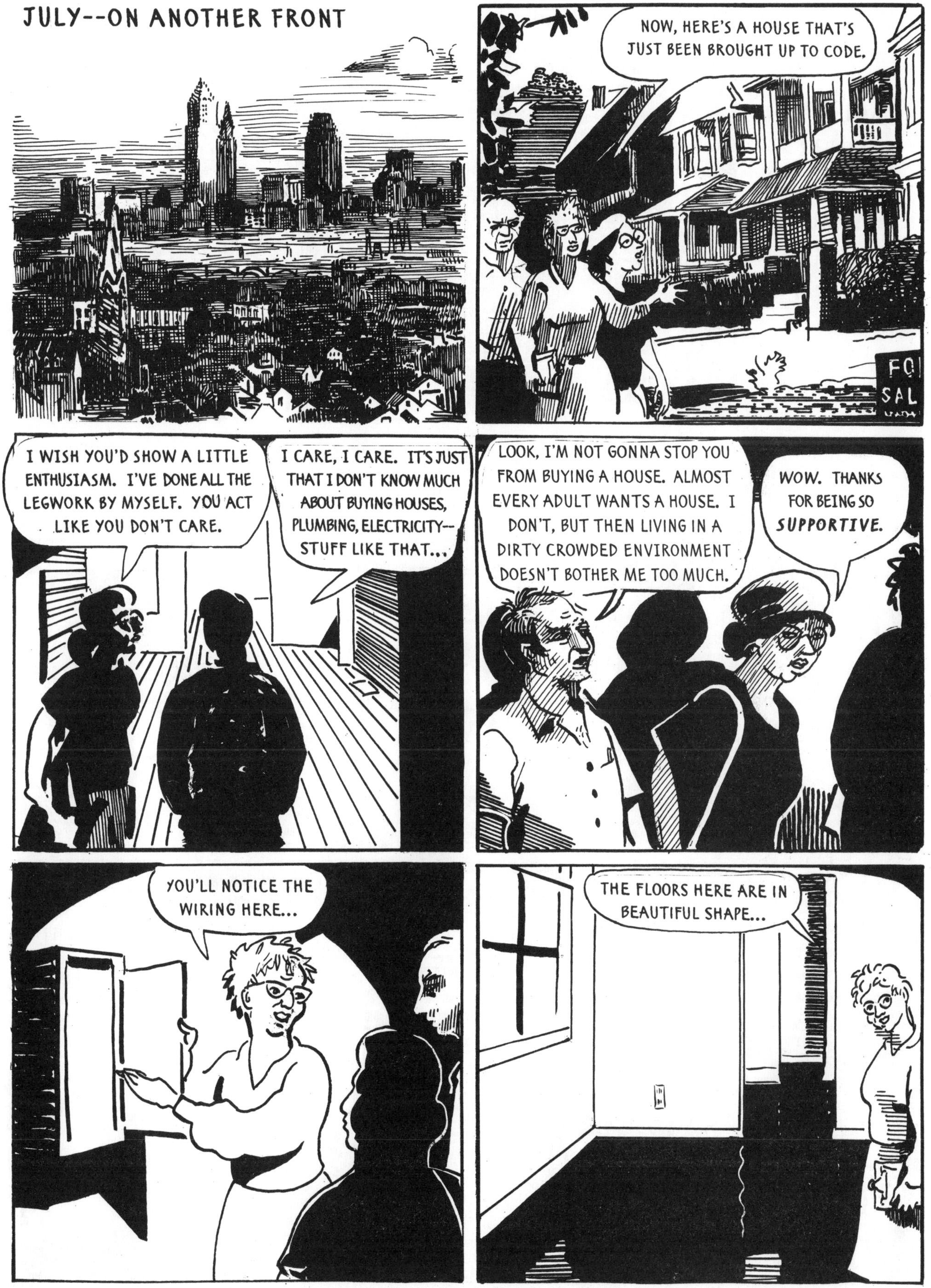
JULY--ON ANOTHER FRONT
NOW, HERE'S A HOUSE THAT'S JUST BEEN BROUGHT UP TO CODE.
I WISH YOU'D SHOW A LITTLE ENTHUSIASM. I'VE DONE ALL THE LEGWORK BY MYSELF. YOU ACT LIKE YOU DON'T CARE.
I CARE, I CARE. IT'S JUST THAT I DON'T KNOW MUCH ABOUT BUYING HOUSES, PLUMBING, ELECTRICITY--STUFF LIKE THAT...
LOOK, I'M NOT GONNA STOP YOU FROM BUYING A HOUSE. ALMOST EVERY ADULT WANTS A HOUSE. I DON'T, BUT THEN LIVING IN A DIRTY CROWDED ENVIRONMENT DOESN'T BOTHER ME TOO MUCH.
WOW. THANKS FOR BEING SO SUPPORTIVE.
YOU'LL NOTICE THE WIRING HERE...
THE FLOORS HERE ARE IN BEAUTIFUL SHAPE...

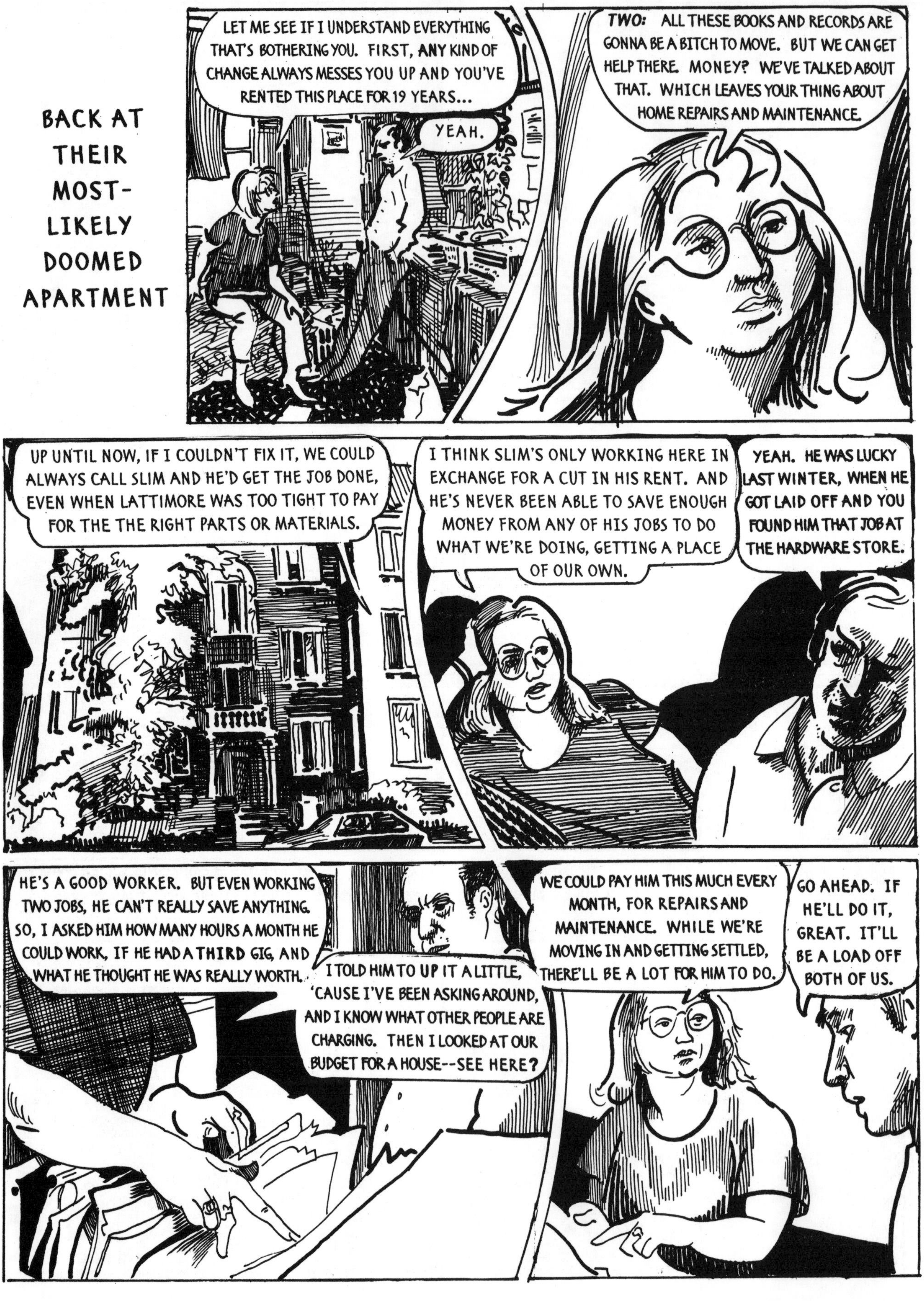
BACK AT THEIR MOST-LIKELY DOOMED APARTMENT
LET ME SEE IF I UNDERSTAND EVERYTHING THAT'S BOTHERING YOU. FIRST, ANY KIND OF CHANGE ALWAYS MESSES YOU UP AND YOU'VE RENTED THIS PLACE FOR 19 YEARS...
YEAH.
TWO: ALL THESE BOOKS AND RECORDS ARE GONNA BE A BITCH TO MOVE. BUT WE CAN GET HELP THERE. MONEY? WE'VE TALKED ABOUT THAT. WHICH LEAVES YOUR THING ABOUT HOME REPAIRS AND MAINTENANCE.
UP UNTIL NOW, IF I COULDN'T FIX IT, WE COULD ALWAYS CALL SLIM AND HE'D GET THE JOB DONE, EVEN WHEN LATTIMORE WAS TOO TIGHT TO PAY FOR THE THE RIGHT PARTS OR MATERIALS.
I THINK SLIM'S ONLY WORKING HERE IN EXCHANGE FOR A CUT IN HIS RENT. AND HE'S NEVER BEEN ABLE TO SAVE ENOUGH MONEY FROM ANY OF HIS JOBS TO DO WHAT WE'RE DOING, GETTING A PLACE OF OUR OWN.
YEAH. HE WAS LUCKY LAST WINTER, WHEN HE GOT LAID OFF AND YOU FOUND HIM THAT JOB AT THE HARDWARE STORE.
HE'S A GOOD WORKER. BUT EVEN WORKING TWO JOBS, HE CAN'T REALLY SAVE ANYTHING. SO, I ASKED HIM HOW MANY HOURS A MONTH HE COULD WORK, IF HE HAD A THIRD GIG, AND WHAT HE THOUGHT HE WAS REALLY WORTH.
I TOLD HIM TO UP IT A LITTLE, 'CAUSE I'VE BEEN ASKING AROUND, AND I KNOW WHAT OTHER PEOPLE ARE CHARGING. THEN I LOOKED AT OUR BUDGET FOR A HOUSE--SEE HERE?
WE COULD PAY HIM THIS MUCH EVERY MONTH, FOR REPAIRS AND MAINTENANCE. WHILE WE'RE MOVING IN AND GETTING SETTLED, THERE'LL BE A LOT FOR HIM TO DO.
GO AHEAD. IF HE'LL DO IT, GREAT. IT'LL BE A LOAD OFF BOTH OF US.

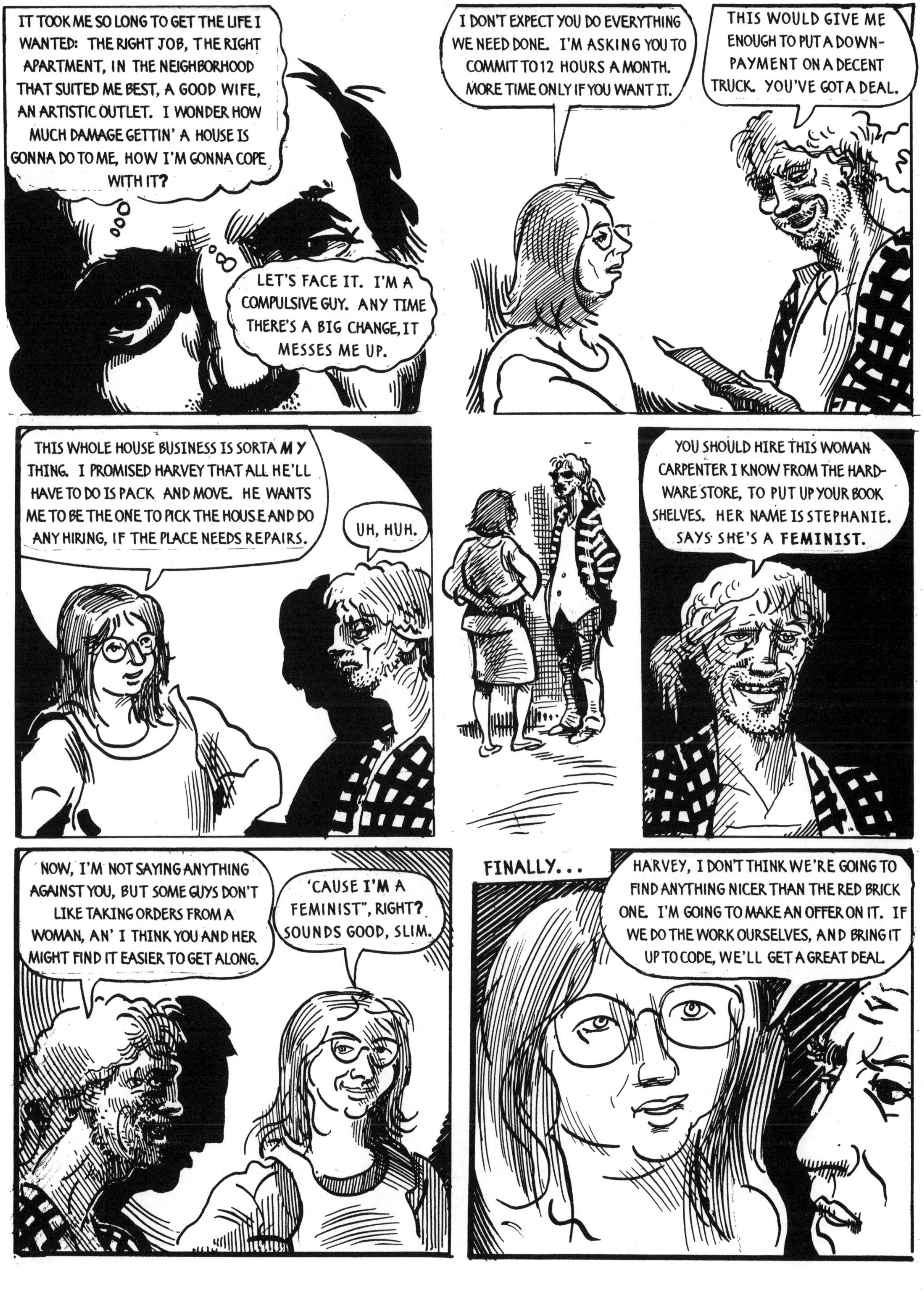
IT TOOK ME SO LONG TO GET THE LIFE I WANTED: THE RIGHT JOB, THE RIGHT APARTMENT, IN THE NEIGHBORHOOD THAT SUITED ME BEST, A GOOD WIFE, AN ARTISTIC OUTLET. I WONDER HOW MUCH DAMAGE GETTIN' A HOUSE IS GONNA DO TO ME, HOW I'M GONNA COPE WITH IT?
LET'S FACE IT. I'M A COMPULSIVE GUY. ANY TIME THERE'S A BIG CHANGE, IT MESSES ME UP.
I DON'T EXPECT YOU DO EVERYTHING WE NEED DONE. I'M ASKING YOU TO COMMIT TO 12 HOURS A MONTH. MORE TIME ONLY IF YOU WANT IT.
THIS WOULD GIVE ME ENOUGH TO PUT A DOWN-PAYMENT ON A DECENT TRUCK. YOU'VE GOT A DEAL.
THIS WHOLE HOUSE BUSINESS IS SORTA **MY** THING. I PROMISED HARVEY THAT ALL HE'LL HAVE TO DO IS PACK AND MOVE. HE WANTS ME TO BE THE ONE TO PICK THE HOUSE AND DO ANY HIRING, IF THE PLACE NEEDS REPAIRS.
UH, HUH.
YOU SHOULD HIRE THIS WOMAN CARPENTER I KNOW FROM THE HARD-WARE STORE, TO PUT UP YOUR BOOK SHELVES. HER NAME IS STEPHANIE. SAYS SHE'S A **FEMINIST**.
NOW, I'M NOT SAYING ANYTHING AGAINST YOU, BUT SOME GUYS DON'T LIKE TAKING ORDERS FROM A WOMAN, AN' I THINK YOU AND HER MIGHT FIND IT EASIER TO GET ALONG.
'CAUSE **I'M** A FEMINIST", RIGHT? SOUNDS GOOD, SLIM.
FINALLY...
HARVEY, I DON'T THINK WE'RE GOING TO FIND ANYTHING NICER THAN THE RED BRICK ONE. I'M GOING TO MAKE AN OFFER ON IT. IF WE DO THE WORK OURSELVES, AND BRING IT UP TO CODE, WE'LL GET A GREAT DEAL.

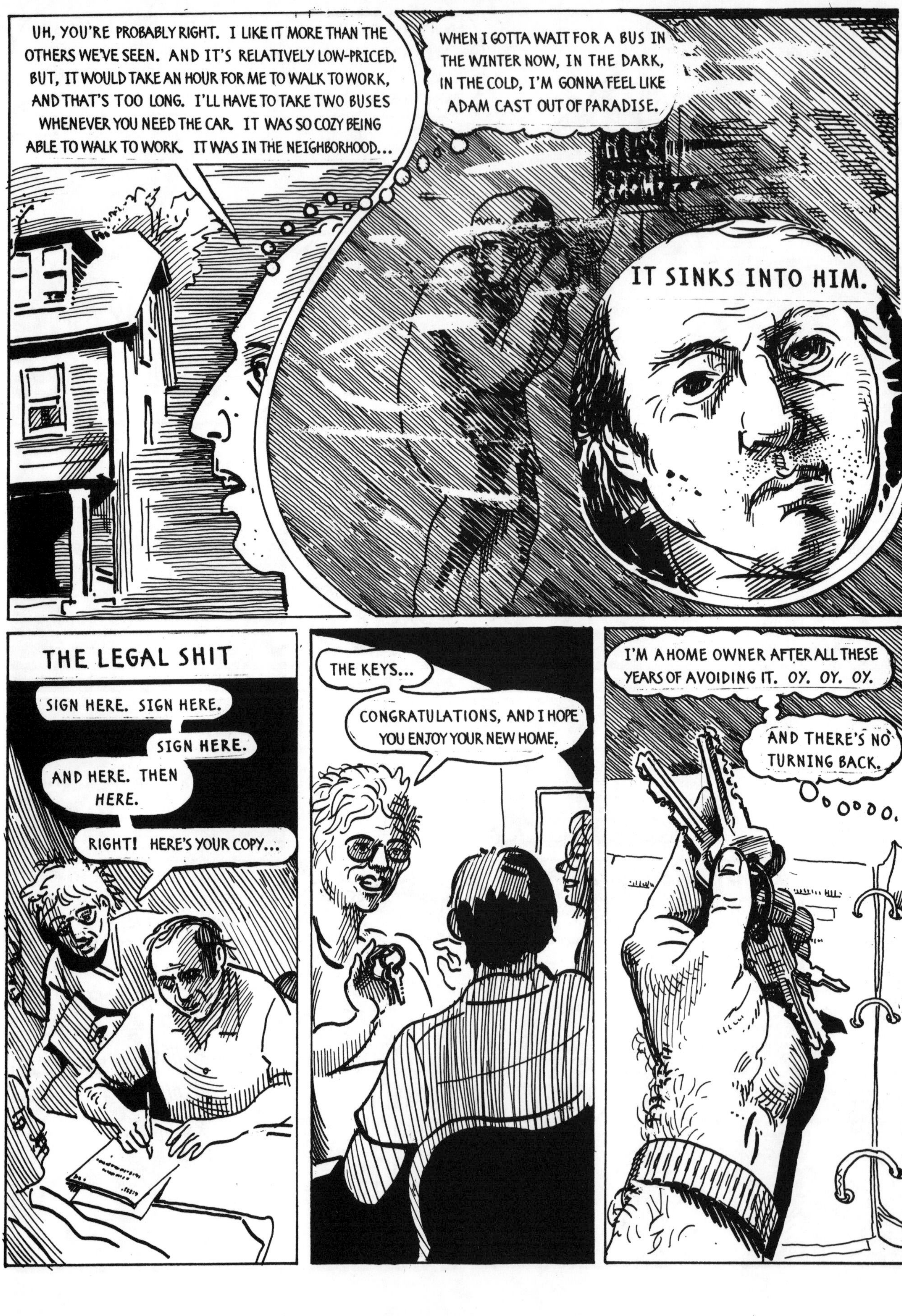
UH, YOU'RE PROBABLY RIGHT. I LIKE IT MORE THAN THE OTHERS WE'VE SEEN. AND IT'S RELATIVELY LOW-PRICED. BUT, IT WOULD TAKE AN HOUR FOR ME TO WALK TO WORK, AND THAT'S TOO LONG. I'LL HAVE TO TAKE TWO BUSES WHENEVER YOU NEED THE CAR. IT WAS SO COZY BEING ABLE TO WALK TO WORK. IT WAS IN THE NEIGHBORHOOD...
WHEN I GOTTA WAIT FOR A BUS IN THE WINTER NOW, IN THE DARK, IN THE COLD, I'M GONNA FEEL LIKE ADAM CAST OUT OF PARADISE.
IT SINKS INTO HIM.
THE LEGAL SHIT
SIGN HERE. SIGN HERE.
SIGN HERE.
AND HERE. THEN HERE.
RIGHT! HERE'S YOUR COPY...
THE KEYS...
CONGRATULATIONS, AND I HOPE YOU ENJOY YOUR NEW HOME.
I'M A HOME OWNER AFTER ALL THESE YEARS OF AVOIDING IT. OY. OY. OY.
AND THERE'S NO TURNING BACK.

2

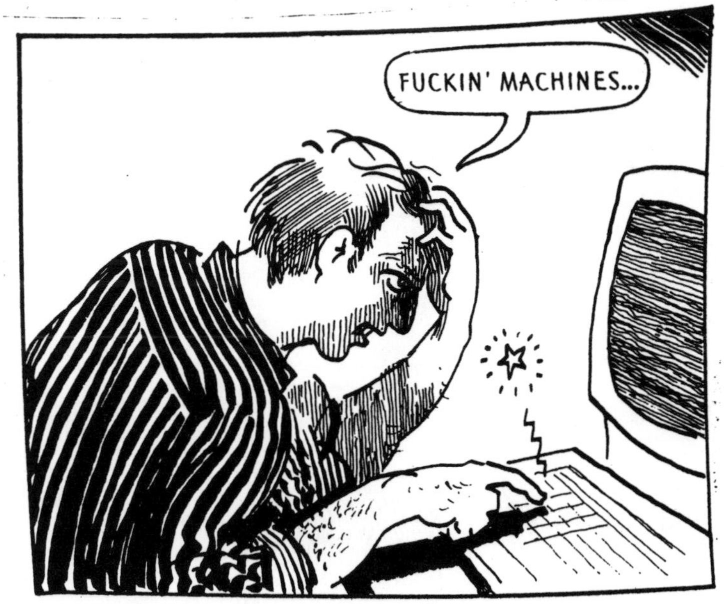
FUCKIN' MACHINES...

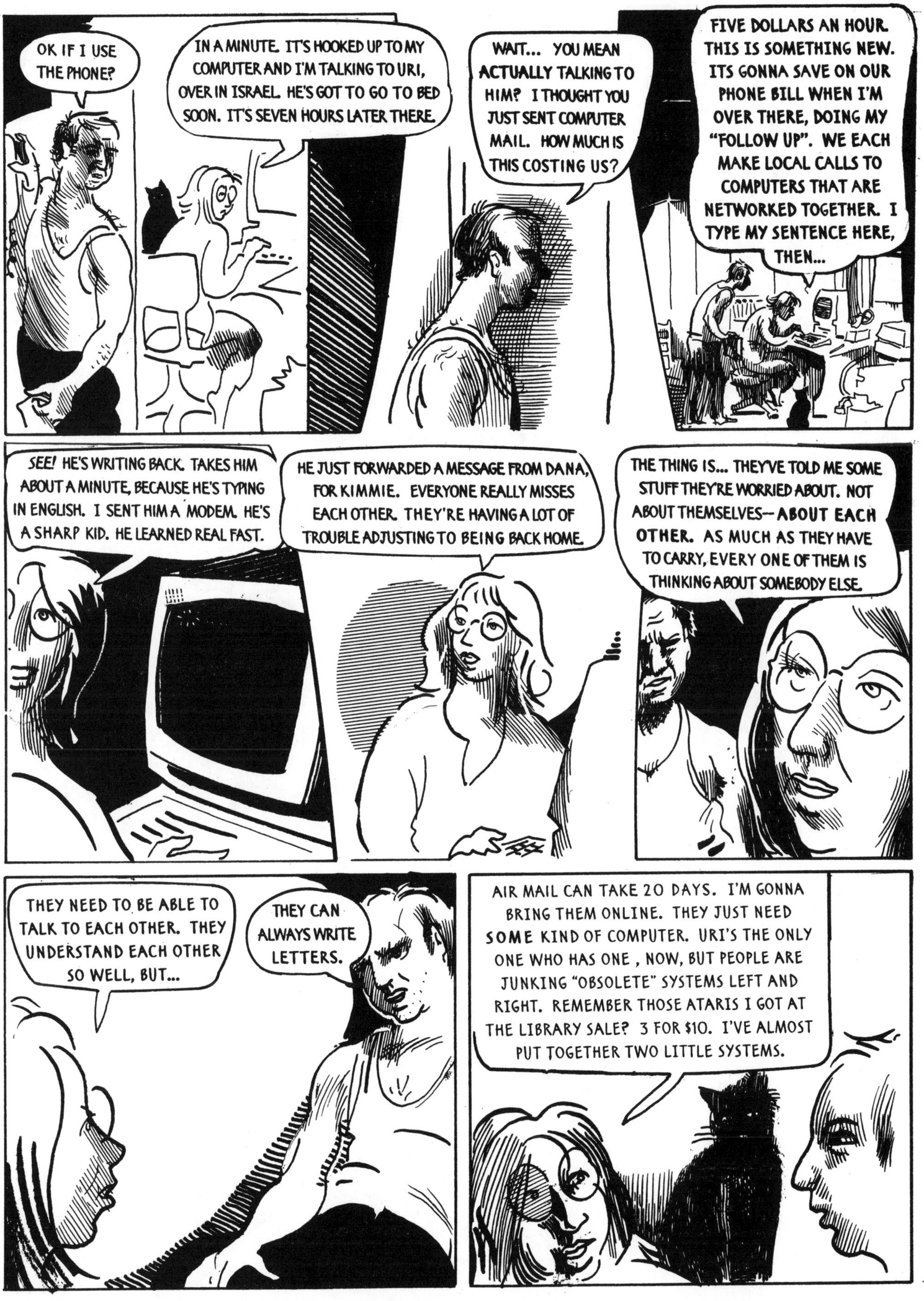

OK IF I USE THE PHONE?
IN A MINUTE. IT'S HOOKED UP TO MY COMPUTER AND I'M TALKING TO URI, OVER IN ISRAEL. HE'S GOT TO GO TO BED SOON. IT'S SEVEN HOURS LATER THERE.
WAIT... YOU MEAN ACTUALLY TALKING TO HIM? I THOUGHT YOU JUST SENT COMPUTER MAIL. HOW MUCH IS THIS COSTING US?
FIVE DOLLARS AN HOUR. THIS IS SOMETHING NEW. ITS GONNA SAVE ON OUR PHONE BILL WHEN I'M OVER THERE, DOING MY "FOLLOW UP". WE EACH MAKE LOCAL CALLS TO COMPUTERS THAT ARE NETWORKED TOGETHER. I TYPE MY SENTENCE HERE, THEN...
SEE! HE'S WRITING BACK. TAKES HIM ABOUT A MINUTE, BECAUSE HE'S TYPING IN ENGLISH. I SENT HIM A MODEM. HE'S A SHARP KID. HE LEARNED REAL FAST.
HE JUST FORWARDED A MESSAGE FROM DANA, FOR KIMMIE. EVERYONE REALLY MISSES EACH OTHER. THEY'RE HAVING A LOT OF TROUBLE ADJUSTING TO BEING BACK HOME.
THE THING IS... THEY'VE TOLD ME SOME STUFF THEY'RE WORRIED ABOUT. NOT ABOUT THEMSELVES-- ABOUT EACH OTHER. AS MUCH AS THEY HAVE TO CARRY, EVERY ONE OF THEM IS THINKING ABOUT SOMEBODY ELSE.
THEY NEED TO BE ABLE TO TALK TO EACH OTHER. THEY UNDERSTAND EACH OTHER SO WELL, BUT...
THEY CAN ALWAYS WRITE LETTERS.
AIR MAIL CAN TAKE 20 DAYS. I'M GONNA BRING THEM ONLINE. THEY JUST NEED SOME KIND OF COMPUTER. URI'S THE ONLY ONE WHO HAS ONE, NOW, BUT PEOPLE ARE JUNKING "OBSOLETE" SYSTEMS LEFT AND RIGHT. REMEMBER THOSE ATARIS I GOT AT THE LIBRARY SALE? 3 FOR $10. I'VE ALMOST PUT TOGETHER TWO LITTLE SYSTEMS.

I CAN SHARE MY ACCOUNT WITH THEM. OFF-PEAK HOURS ARE ONLY $1 PER. I CAN COVER THAT FOR NOW.

LATER, EVERYONE CAN SPLIT COSTS. JESSIE SAYS SHE'LL CHIP IN, ONCE HER SUMMER JOB STARTS.

JESSIE WON'T NEED A MONITOR, SHE HAS A TV. I FOUND A 300 BAUD MODEM FOR ONLY $15. WHEN SHE COMES UP TO VISIT FROM LOUISVILLE, I'LL GIVE HER A CRASH COURSE.

IT'S EASY. YOU JUST HAVE TO KNOW HOW TO TYPE. I COULD TEACH THE TWO OF YOU TOGETHER AND YOU COULD...

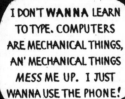

I DON'T WANNA LEARN TO TYPE. COMPUTERS ARE MECHANICAL THINGS, AN' MECHANICAL THINGS MESS ME UP. I JUST WANNA USE THE PHONE!

YEAH? THINK YOU'LL BE ABLE TO MANAGE? I KNOW USING *TOUCH TONE* IS A REAL STRETCH FOR YOU.

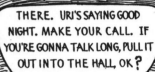

THERE. URI'S SAYING GOOD NIGHT. MAKE YOUR CALL. IF YOU'RE GONNA TALK LONG, PULL IT OUT IN TO THE HALL, OK?

TAP!

EVERY SO OFTEN, SOMEONE WHO READS *AMERICAN SPLENDOR* LOOKS HARVEY UP. THIS TIME, IT'S A MEDICAL STUDENT NAMED CHRISTIAN, WHO'S JUST STARTED WORKING AT THE V.A. HOSPITAL.

DIT DIT

HEY, I'M RETURNING YOUR CALL. WHAT'S UP?

SURE, WE CAN GET TOGETHER. WHYN'T YOU MEET ME IN THE RECORD ROOM, AROUND LUNCH TIME?

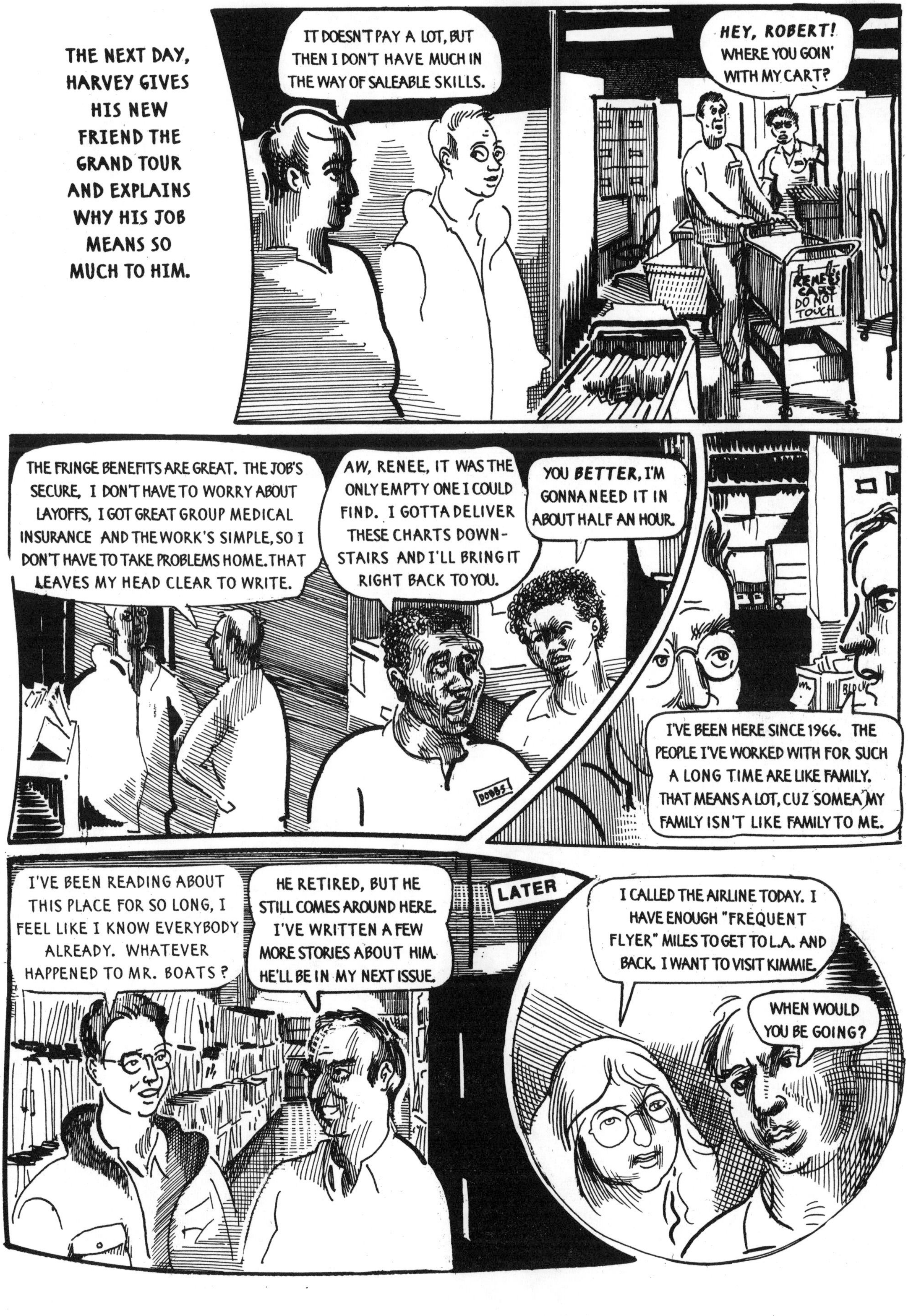
THE NEXT DAY, HARVEY GIVES HIS NEW FRIEND THE GRAND TOUR AND EXPLAINS WHY HIS JOB MEANS SO MUCH TO HIM.
IT DOESN'T PAY A LOT, BUT THEN I DON'T HAVE MUCH IN THE WAY OF SALEABLE SKILLS.
HEY, ROBERT! WHERE YOU GOIN' WITH MY CART?
RENEE'S CART DO NOT TOUCH
THE FRINGE BENEFITS ARE GREAT. THE JOB'S SECURE, I DON'T HAVE TO WORRY ABOUT LAYOFFS, I GOT GREAT GROUP MEDICAL INSURANCE AND THE WORK'S SIMPLE, SO I DON'T HAVE TO TAKE PROBLEMS HOME. THAT LEAVES MY HEAD CLEAR TO WRITE.
AW, RENEE, IT WAS THE ONLY EMPTY ONE I COULD FIND. I GOTTA DELIVER THESE CHARTS DOWN-STAIRS AND I'LL BRING IT RIGHT BACK TO YOU.
YOU BETTER, I'M GONNA NEED IT IN ABOUT HALF AN HOUR.
DOBBS
I'VE BEEN HERE SINCE 1966. THE PEOPLE I'VE WORKED WITH FOR SUCH A LONG TIME ARE LIKE FAMILY. THAT MEANS A LOT, CUZ SOMEA MY FAMILY ISN'T LIKE FAMILY TO ME.
I'VE BEEN READING ABOUT THIS PLACE FOR SO LONG, I FEEL LIKE I KNOW EVERYBODY ALREADY. WHATEVER HAPPENED TO MR. BOATS?
HE RETIRED, BUT HE STILL COMES AROUND HERE. I'VE WRITTEN A FEW MORE STORIES ABOUT HIM. HE'LL BE IN MY NEXT ISSUE.
LATER
I CALLED THE AIRLINE TODAY. I HAVE ENOUGH "FREQUENT FLYER" MILES TO GET TO L.A. AND BACK. I WANT TO VISIT KIMMIE.
WHEN WOULD YOU BE GOING?

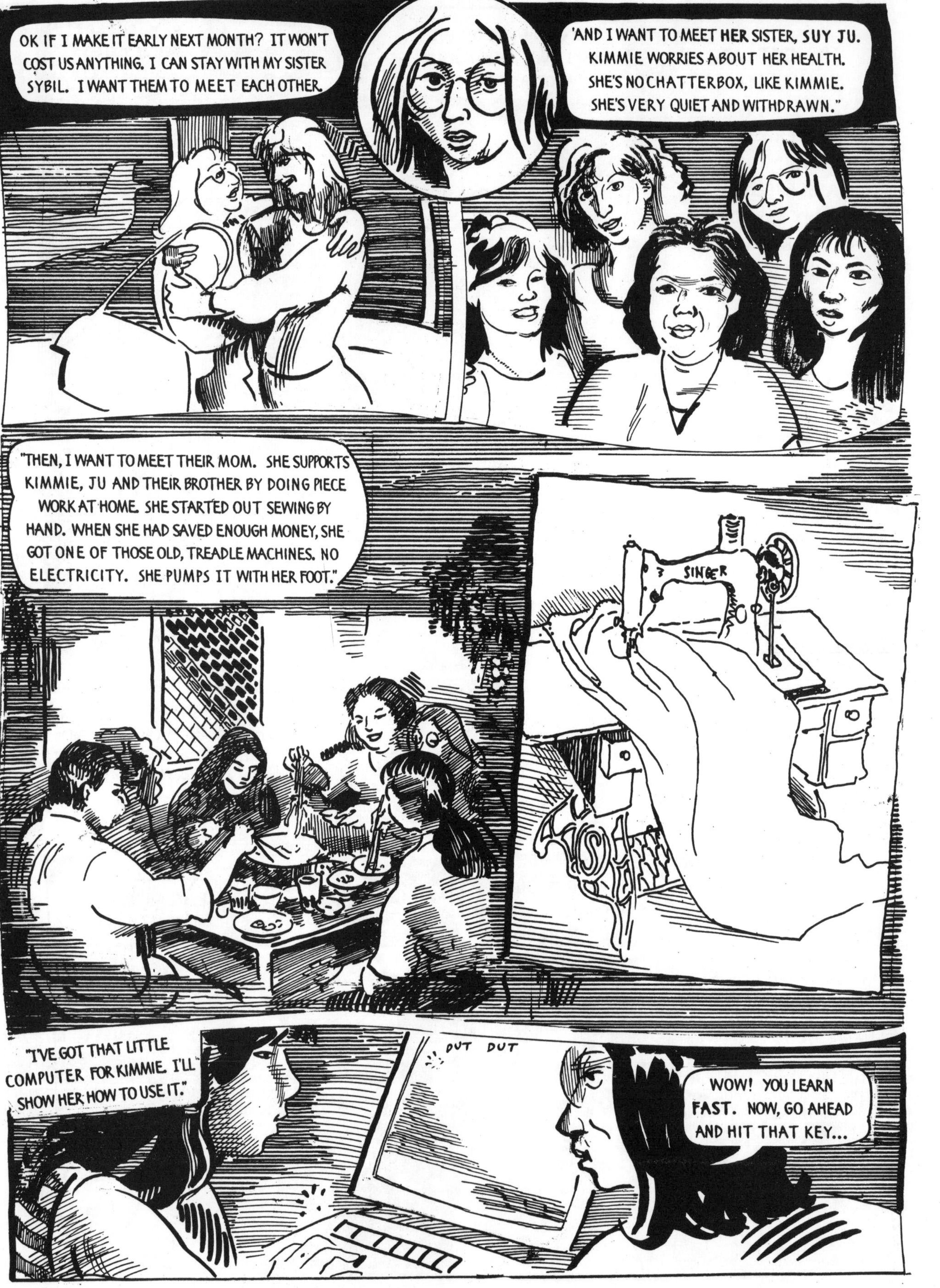
OK IF I MAKE IT EARLY NEXT MONTH? IT WON'T COST US ANYTHING. I CAN STAY WITH MY SISTER SYBIL. I WANT THEM TO MEET EACH OTHER.
"AND I WANT TO MEET HER SISTER, SUY JU. KIMMIE WORRIES ABOUT HER HEALTH. SHE'S NO CHATTERBOX, LIKE KIMMIE. SHE'S VERY QUIET AND WITHDRAWN."
"THEN, I WANT TO MEET THEIR MOM. SHE SUPPORTS KIMMIE, JU AND THEIR BROTHER BY DOING PIECE WORK AT HOME. SHE STARTED OUT SEWING BY HAND. WHEN SHE HAD SAVED ENOUGH MONEY, SHE GOT ONE OF THOSE OLD, TREADLE MACHINES. NO ELECTRICITY. SHE PUMPS IT WITH HER FOOT."
SINGER
"I'VE GOT THAT LITTLE COMPUTER FOR KIMMIE. I'LL SHOW HER HOW TO USE IT."
DUT DUT
WOW! YOU LEARN FAST. NOW, GO AHEAD AND HIT THAT KEY...

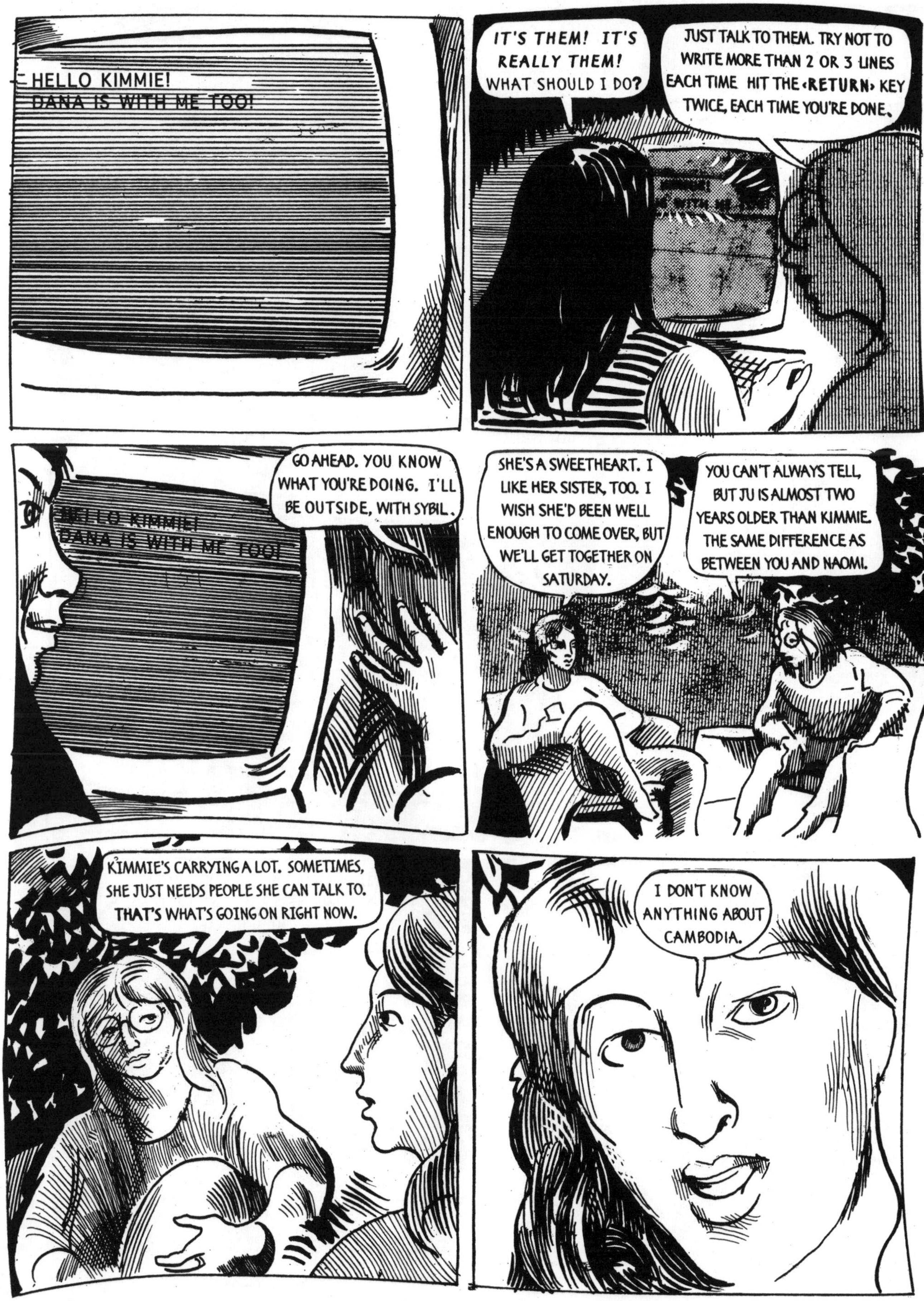
HELLO KIMMIE!
DANA IS WITH ME TOO!
IT'S THEM! IT'S REALLY THEM! WHAT SHOULD I DO?
JUST TALK TO THEM. TRY NOT TO WRITE MORE THAN 2 OR 3 LINES EACH TIME HIT THE ‹RETURN› KEY TWICE, EACH TIME YOU'RE DONE.
HELLO KIMMIE!
DANA IS WITH ME TOO!
GO AHEAD. YOU KNOW WHAT YOU'RE DOING. I'LL BE OUTSIDE, WITH SYBIL.
SHE'S A SWEETHEART. I LIKE HER SISTER, TOO. I WISH SHE'D BEEN WELL ENOUGH TO COME OVER, BUT WE'LL GET TOGETHER ON SATURDAY.
YOU CAN'T ALWAYS TELL, BUT JU IS ALMOST TWO YEARS OLDER THAN KIMMIE. THE SAME DIFFERENCE AS BETWEEN YOU AND NAOMI.
KIMMIE'S CARRYING A LOT. SOMETIMES, SHE JUST NEEDS PEOPLE SHE CAN TALK TO. THAT'S WHAT'S GOING ON RIGHT NOW.
I DON'T KNOW ANYTHING ABOUT CAMBODIA.

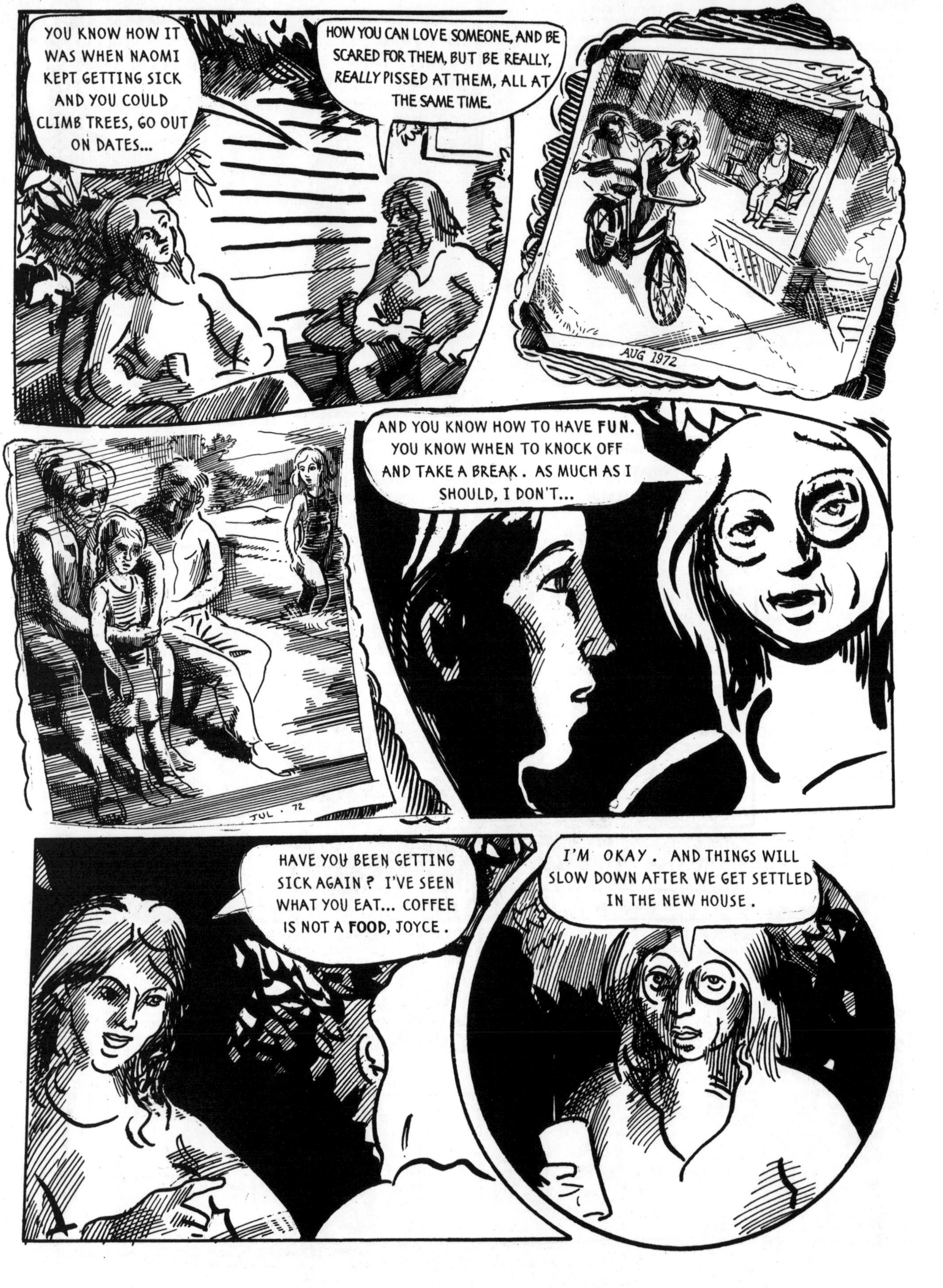
YOU KNOW HOW IT WAS WHEN NAOMI KEPT GETTING SICK AND YOU COULD CLIMB TREES, GO OUT ON DATES...
HOW YOU CAN LOVE SOMEONE, AND BE SCARED FOR THEM, BUT BE REALLY, REALLY PISSED AT THEM, ALL AT THE SAME TIME.
AUG 1972
JUL · 72
AND YOU KNOW HOW TO HAVE FUN. YOU KNOW WHEN TO KNOCK OFF AND TAKE A BREAK. AS MUCH AS I SHOULD, I DON'T...
HAVE YOU BEEN GETTING SICK AGAIN? I'VE SEEN WHAT YOU EAT... COFFEE IS NOT A FOOD, JOYCE.
I'M OKAY. AND THINGS WILL SLOW DOWN AFTER WE GET SETTLED IN THE NEW HOUSE.

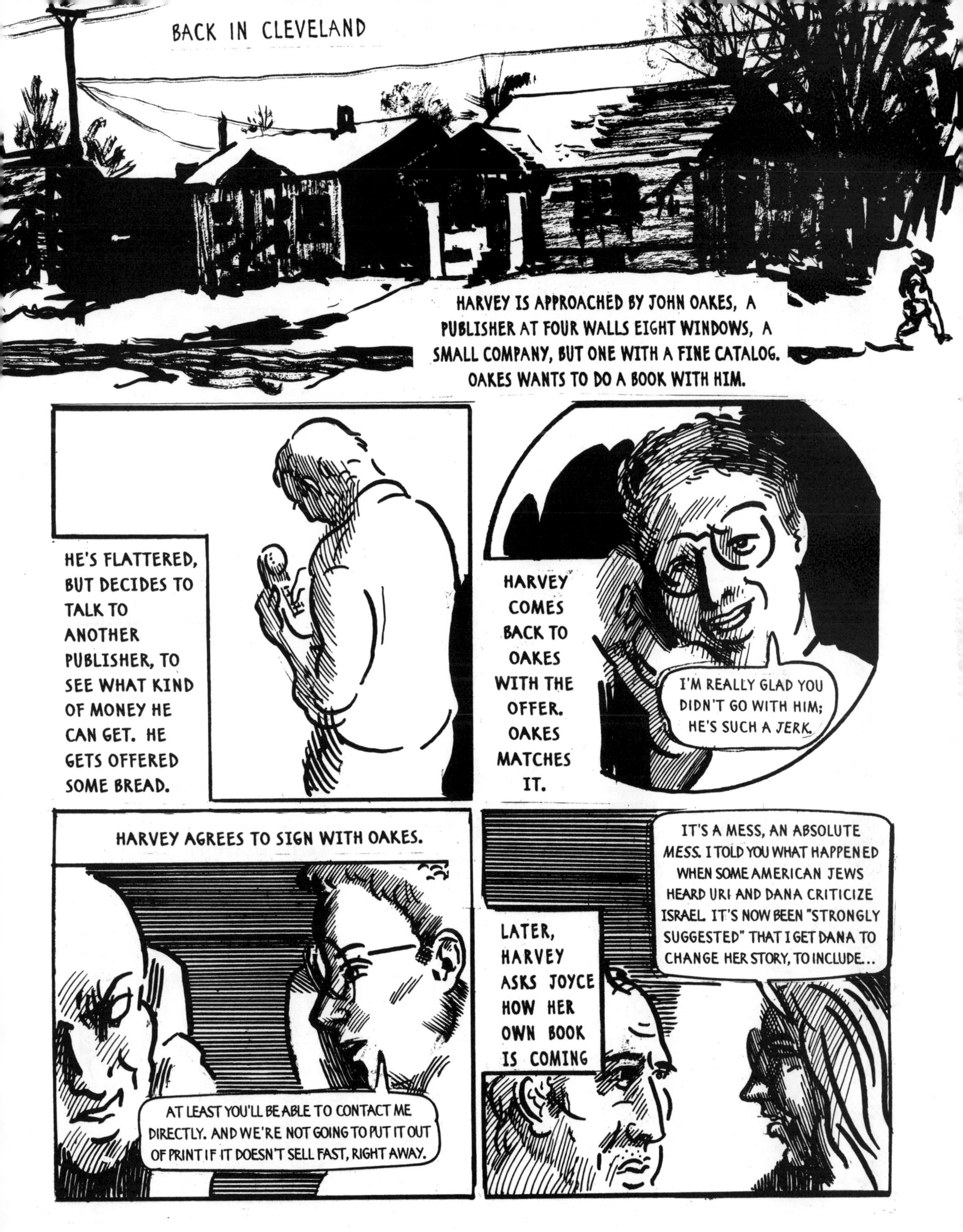
BACK IN CLEVELAND
HARVEY IS APPROACHED BY JOHN OAKES, A PUBLISHER AT FOUR WALLS EIGHT WINDOWS, A SMALL COMPANY, BUT ONE WITH A FINE CATALOG. OAKES WANTS TO DO A BOOK WITH HIM.
HE'S FLATTERED, BUT DECIDES TO TALK TO ANOTHER PUBLISHER, TO SEE WHAT KIND OF MONEY HE CAN GET. HE GETS OFFERED SOME BREAD.
HARVEY COMES BACK TO OAKES WITH THE OFFER. OAKES MATCHES IT.
I'M REALLY GLAD YOU DIDN'T GO WITH HIM; HE'S SUCH A JERK.
HARVEY AGREES TO SIGN WITH OAKES.
AT LEAST YOU'LL BE ABLE TO CONTACT ME DIRECTLY. AND WE'RE NOT GOING TO PUT IT OUT OF PRINT IF IT DOESN'T SELL FAST, RIGHT AWAY.
LATER, HARVEY ASKS JOYCE HOW HER OWN BOOK IS COMING
IT'S A MESS, AN ABSOLUTE MESS. I TOLD YOU WHAT HAPPENED WHEN SOME AMERICAN JEWS HEARD URI AND DANA CRITICIZE ISRAEL. IT'S NOW BEEN "STRONGLY SUGGESTED" THAT I GET DANA TO CHANGE HER STORY, TO INCLUDE...

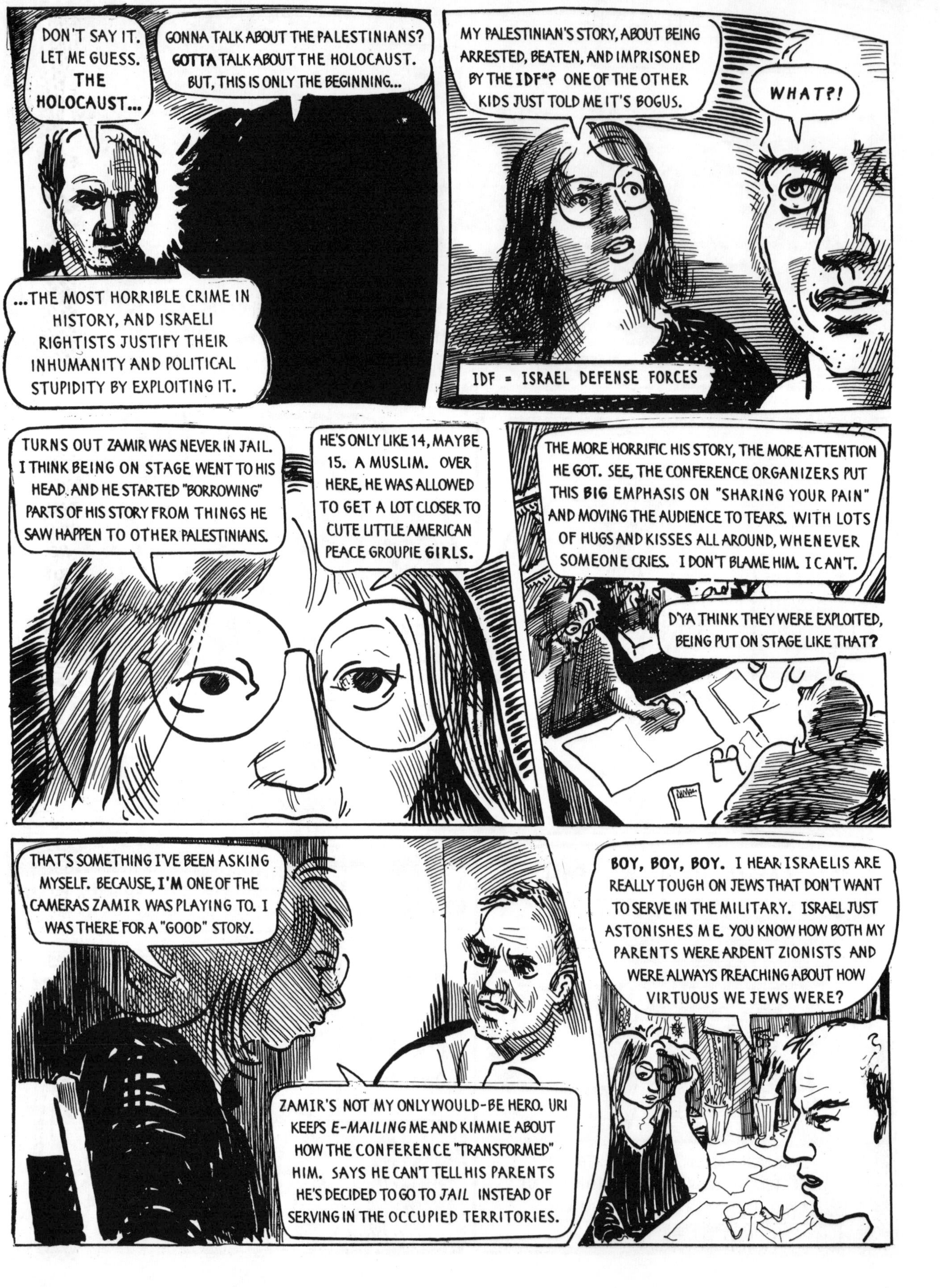
DON'T SAY IT. LET ME GUESS. **THE HOLOCAUST...**
GONNA TALK ABOUT THE PALESTINIANS? **GOTTA** TALK ABOUT THE HOLOCAUST. BUT, THIS IS ONLY THE BEGINNING...
...THE MOST HORRIBLE CRIME IN HISTORY, AND ISRAELI RIGHTISTS JUSTIFY THEIR INHUMANITY AND POLITICAL STUPIDITY BY EXPLOITING IT.
MY PALESTINIAN'S STORY, ABOUT BEING ARRESTED, BEATEN, AND IMPRISONED BY THE **IDF***? ONE OF THE OTHER KIDS JUST TOLD ME IT'S BOGUS.
WHAT?!
IDF = ISRAEL DEFENSE FORCES
TURNS OUT ZAMIR WAS NEVER IN JAIL. I THINK BEING ON STAGE WENT TO HIS HEAD. AND HE STARTED "BORROWING" PARTS OF HIS STORY FROM THINGS HE SAW HAPPEN TO OTHER PALESTINIANS.
HE'S ONLY LIKE 14, MAYBE 15. A MUSLIM. OVER HERE, HE WAS ALLOWED TO GET A LOT CLOSER TO CUTE LITTLE AMERICAN PEACE GROUPIE **GIRLS.**
THE MORE HORRIFIC HIS STORY, THE MORE ATTENTION HE GOT. SEE, THE CONFERENCE ORGANIZERS PUT THIS **BIG** EMPHASIS ON "SHARING YOUR PAIN" AND MOVING THE AUDIENCE TO TEARS. WITH LOTS OF HUGS AND KISSES ALL AROUND, WHENEVER SOMEONE CRIES. I DON'T BLAME HIM. I CAN'T.
D'YA THINK THEY WERE EXPLOITED, BEING PUT ON STAGE LIKE THAT?
THAT'S SOMETHING I'VE BEEN ASKING MYSELF. BECAUSE, **I'M** ONE OF THE CAMERAS ZAMIR WAS PLAYING TO. I WAS THERE FOR A "GOOD" STORY.
ZAMIR'S NOT MY ONLY WOULD-BE HERO. URI KEEPS *E-MAILING* ME AND KIMMIE ABOUT HOW THE CONFERENCE "TRANSFORMED" HIM. SAYS HE CAN'T TELL HIS PARENTS HE'S DECIDED TO GO TO *JAIL* INSTEAD OF SERVING IN THE OCCUPIED TERRITORIES.
BOY, BOY, BOY. I HEAR ISRAELIS ARE REALLY TOUGH ON JEWS THAT DON'T WANT TO SERVE IN THE MILITARY. ISRAEL JUST ASTONISHES ME. YOU KNOW HOW BOTH MY PARENTS WERE ARDENT ZIONISTS AND WERE ALWAYS PREACHING ABOUT HOW VIRTUOUS WE JEWS WERE?

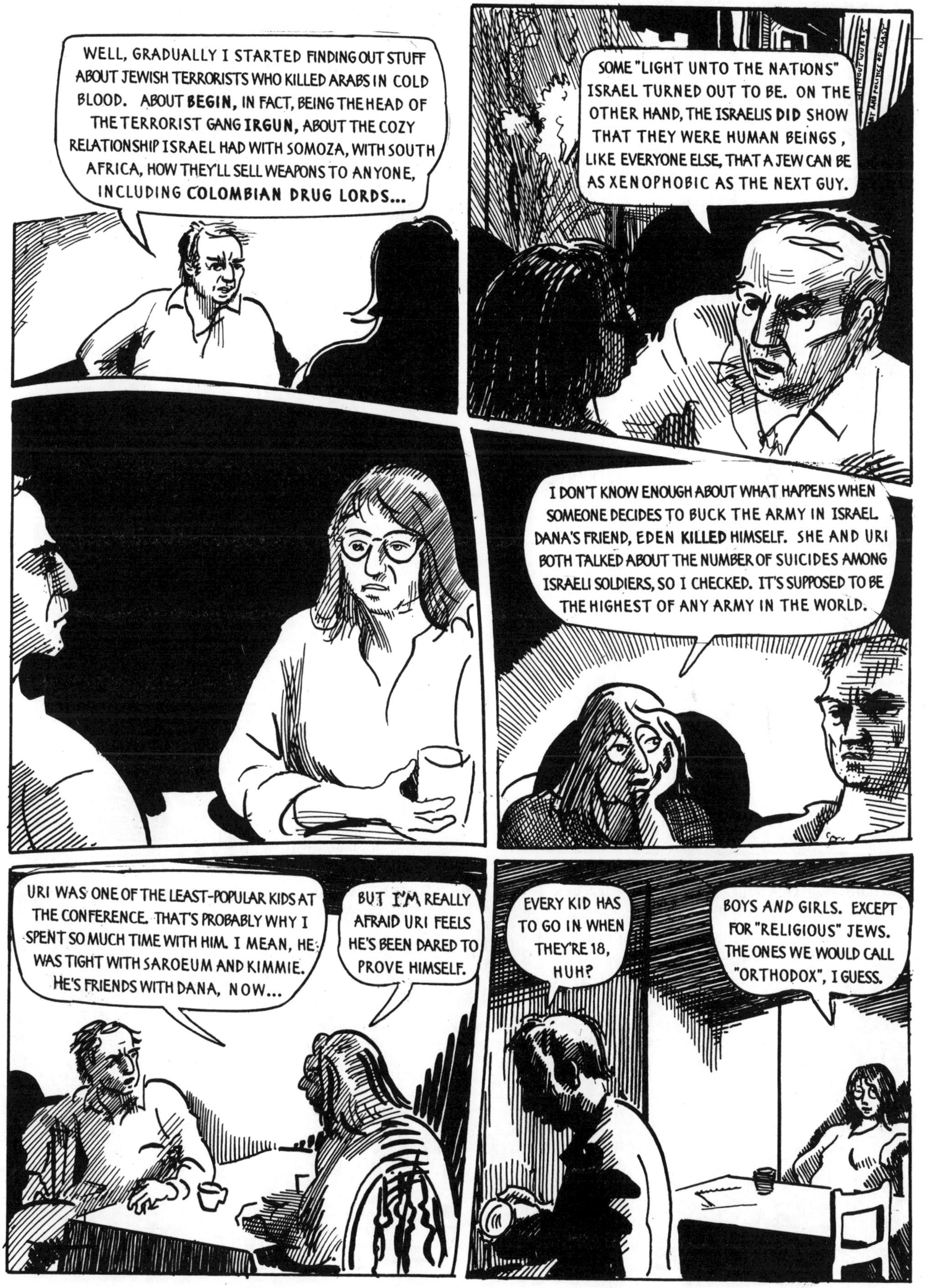
WELL, GRADUALLY I STARTED FINDING OUT STUFF ABOUT JEWISH TERRORISTS WHO KILLED ARABS IN COLD BLOOD. ABOUT **BEGIN**, IN FACT, BEING THE HEAD OF THE TERRORIST GANG **IRGUN**, ABOUT THE COZY RELATIONSHIP ISRAEL HAD WITH SOMOZA, WITH SOUTH AFRICA, HOW THEY'LL SELL WEAPONS TO ANYONE, INCLUDING **COLOMBIAN DRUG LORDS...**
SOME "LIGHT UNTO THE NATIONS" ISRAEL TURNED OUT TO BE. ON THE OTHER HAND, THE ISRAELIS **DID** SHOW THAT THEY WERE HUMAN BEINGS, LIKE EVERYONE ELSE, THAT A JEW CAN BE AS XENOPHOBIC AS THE NEXT GUY.
I DON'T KNOW ENOUGH ABOUT WHAT HAPPENS WHEN SOMEONE DECIDES TO BUCK THE ARMY IN ISRAEL. DANA'S FRIEND, EDEN **KILLED** HIMSELF. SHE AND URI BOTH TALKED ABOUT THE NUMBER OF SUICIDES AMONG ISRAELI SOLDIERS, SO I CHECKED. IT'S SUPPOSED TO BE THE HIGHEST OF ANY ARMY IN THE WORLD.
URI WAS ONE OF THE LEAST-POPULAR KIDS AT THE CONFERENCE. THAT'S PROBABLY WHY I SPENT SO MUCH TIME WITH HIM. I MEAN, HE WAS TIGHT WITH SAROEUM AND KIMMIE. HE'S FRIENDS WITH DANA, NOW...
BUT I'M REALLY AFRAID URI FEELS HE'S BEEN DARED TO PROVE HIMSELF.
EVERY KID HAS TO GO IN WHEN THEY'RE 18, HUH?
BOYS AND GIRLS. EXCEPT FOR "RELIGIOUS" JEWS. THE ONES WE WOULD CALL "ORTHODOX", I GUESS.

Y'KNOW... SAROEUM WON THIS SUMMER SCHOLARSHIP-- A CHANCE TO SPEND SIX WEEKS IN THE U.K. IT WOULDN'T COST US THAT MUCH TO RE-ROUTE HIS RETURN THROUGH TEL-AVIV.

HE WAS URI'S ROOM MATE. KIDS CAN USUALLY TALK EACH OTHER DOWN TO EARTH, GIVEN THE CHANCE.

I MEAN, IF ANYONE KNOWS THE DIFFERENCE BETWEEN MACHO POSTURING AND REAL TROUBLE, IT'S SAROEUM. HE USED TO RUN WITH A GANG IN L. A. HE'S BEEN IN JAIL.

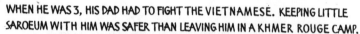

WHEN HE WAS 3, HIS DAD HAD TO FIGHT THE VIETNAMESE. KEEPING LITTLE SAROEUM WITH HIM WAS SAFER THAN LEAVING HIM IN A KHMER ROUGE CAMP.

ONCE, HIS DAD TOOK A BULLET IN HIS NECK. HE PASSED OUT. SAROEUM HID WITH HIM IN SOME BUSHES AND STAYED WITH HIM, PATTING HIS FACE, UNTIL HE CAME TO.

WITH SAROEUM UNDER ONE ARM, HE PICKED UP HIS GUN AND SOMEHOW STAGGERED TO SAFETY.

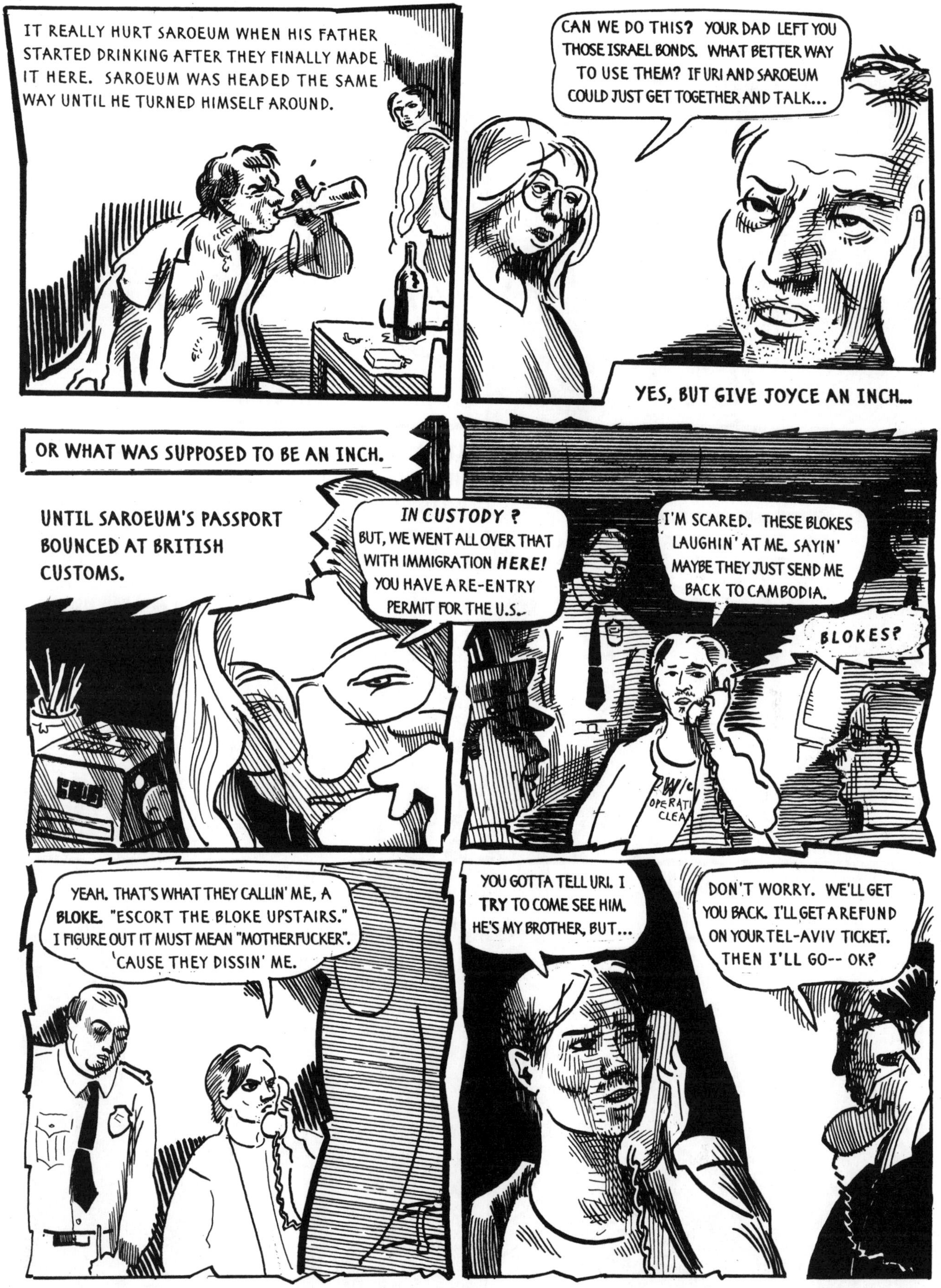
IT REALLY HURT SAROEUM WHEN HIS FATHER STARTED DRINKING AFTER THEY FINALLY MADE IT HERE. SAROEUM WAS HEADED THE SAME WAY UNTIL HE TURNED HIMSELF AROUND.
CAN WE DO THIS? YOUR DAD LEFT YOU THOSE ISRAEL BONDS. WHAT BETTER WAY TO USE THEM? IF URI AND SAROEUM COULD JUST GET TOGETHER AND TALK...
YES, BUT GIVE JOYCE AN INCH...
OR WHAT WAS SUPPOSED TO BE AN INCH.
UNTIL SAROEUM'S PASSPORT BOUNCED AT BRITISH CUSTOMS.
IN CUSTODY? BUT, WE WENT ALL OVER THAT WITH IMMIGRATION HERE! YOU HAVE A RE-ENTRY PERMIT FOR THE U.S..
I'M SCARED. THESE BLOKES LAUGHIN' AT ME. SAYIN' MAYBE THEY JUST SEND ME BACK TO CAMBODIA.
BLOKES?
YEAH. THAT'S WHAT THEY CALLIN' ME, A BLOKE. "ESCORT THE BLOKE UPSTAIRS." I FIGURE OUT IT MUST MEAN "MOTHERFUCKER". 'CAUSE THEY DISSIN' ME.
YOU GOTTA TELL URI. I TRY TO COME SEE HIM. HE'S MY BROTHER, BUT...
DON'T WORRY. WE'LL GET YOU BACK. I'LL GET A REFUND ON YOUR TEL-AVIV TICKET. THEN I'LL GO-- OK?

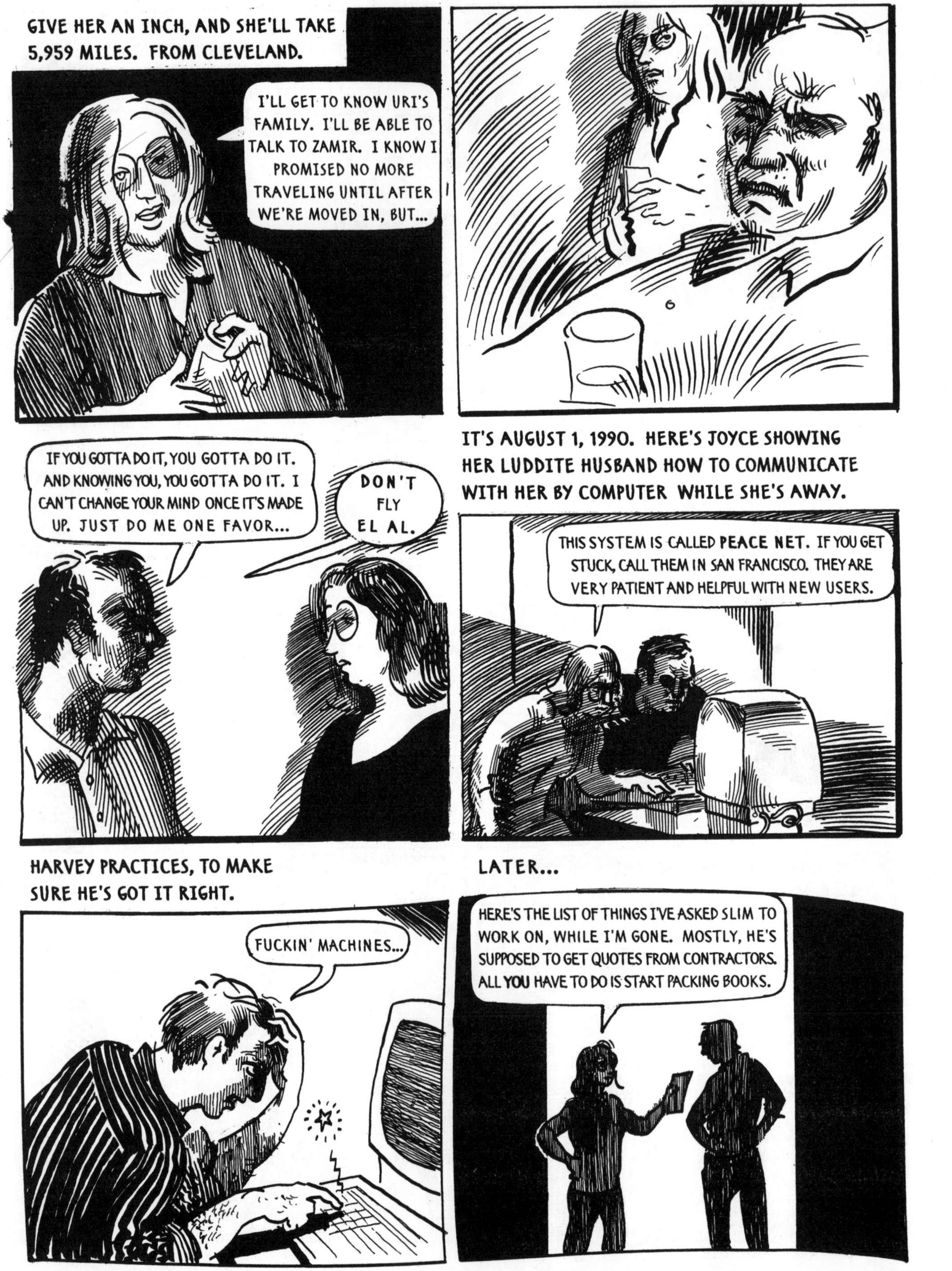
GIVE HER AN INCH, AND SHE'LL TAKE 5,959 MILES. FROM CLEVELAND.
I'LL GET TO KNOW URI'S FAMILY. I'LL BE ABLE TO TALK TO ZAMIR. I KNOW I PROMISED NO MORE TRAVELING UNTIL AFTER WE'RE MOVED IN, BUT...
IF YOU GOTTA DO IT, YOU GOTTA DO IT. AND KNOWING YOU, YOU GOTTA DO IT. I CAN'T CHANGE YOUR MIND ONCE IT'S MADE UP. JUST DO ME ONE FAVOR...
DON'T FLY EL AL.
IT'S AUGUST 1, 1990. HERE'S JOYCE SHOWING HER LUDDITE HUSBAND HOW TO COMMUNICATE WITH HER BY COMPUTER WHILE SHE'S AWAY.
THIS SYSTEM IS CALLED PEACE NET. IF YOU GET STUCK, CALL THEM IN SAN FRANCISCO. THEY ARE VERY PATIENT AND HELPFUL WITH NEW USERS.
HARVEY PRACTICES, TO MAKE SURE HE'S GOT IT RIGHT.
FUCKIN' MACHINES...
LATER...
HERE'S THE LIST OF THINGS I'VE ASKED SLIM TO WORK ON, WHILE I'M GONE. MOSTLY, HE'S SUPPOSED TO GET QUOTES FROM CONTRACTORS. ALL YOU HAVE TO DO IS START PACKING BOOKS.

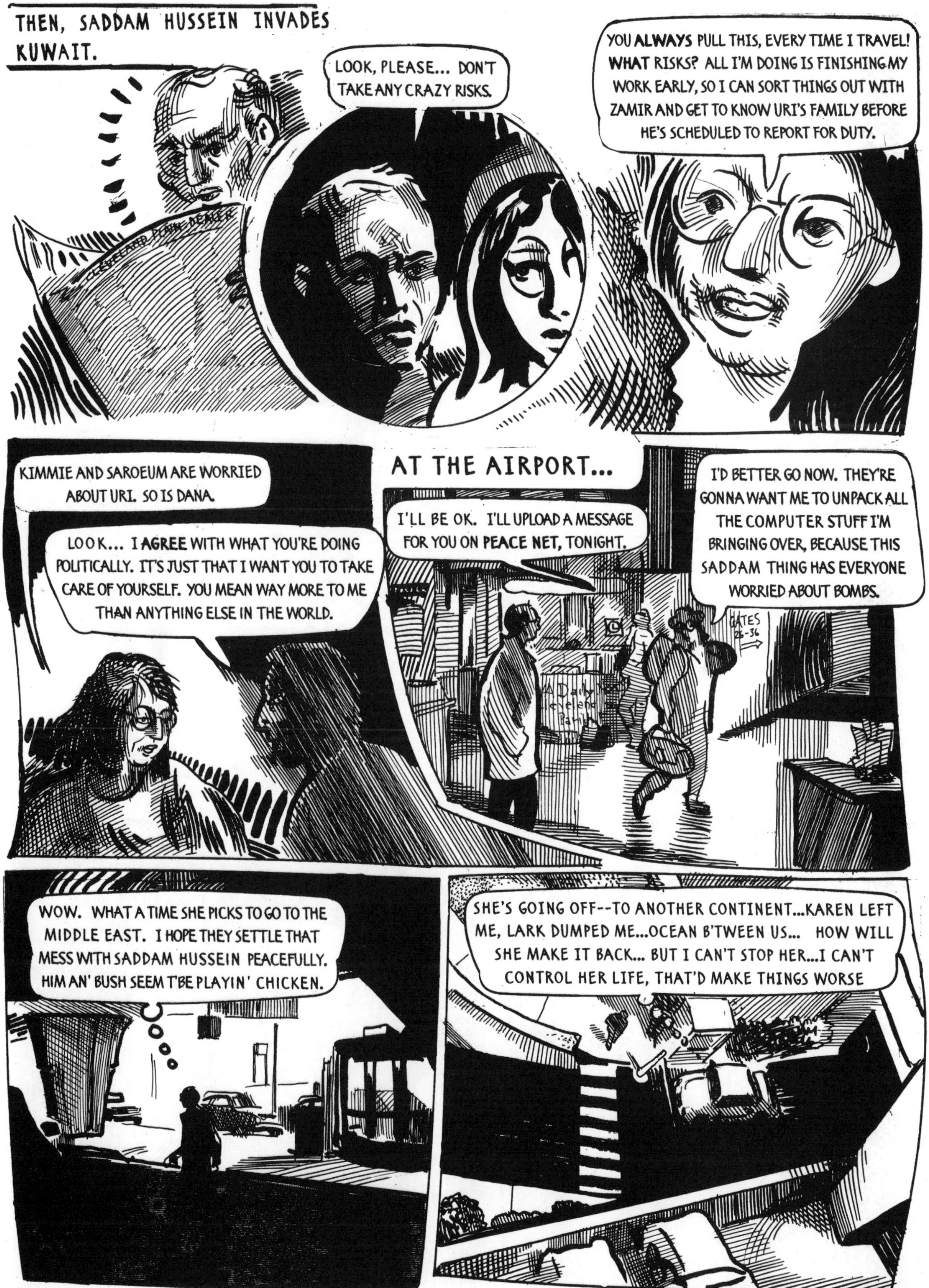
THEN, SADDAM HUSSEIN INVADES KUWAIT.
LOOK, PLEASE... DON'T TAKE ANY CRAZY RISKS.
YOU ALWAYS PULL THIS, EVERY TIME I TRAVEL! WHAT RISKS? ALL I'M DOING IS FINISHING MY WORK EARLY, SO I CAN SORT THINGS OUT WITH ZAMIR AND GET TO KNOW URI'S FAMILY BEFORE HE'S SCHEDULED TO REPORT FOR DUTY.
KIMMIE AND SAROEUM ARE WORRIED ABOUT URI. SO IS DANA.
LOOK... I AGREE WITH WHAT YOU'RE DOING POLITICALLY. IT'S JUST THAT I WANT YOU TO TAKE CARE OF YOURSELF. YOU MEAN WAY MORE TO ME THAN ANYTHING ELSE IN THE WORLD.
AT THE AIRPORT...
I'LL BE OK. I'LL UPLOAD A MESSAGE FOR YOU ON PEACE NET, TONIGHT.
I'D BETTER GO NOW. THEY'RE GONNA WANT ME TO UNPACK ALL THE COMPUTER STUFF I'M BRINGING OVER, BECAUSE THIS SADDAM THING HAS EVERYONE WORRIED ABOUT BOMBS.
GATES 26-36
WOW. WHAT A TIME SHE PICKS TO GO TO THE MIDDLE EAST. I HOPE THEY SETTLE THAT MESS WITH SADDAM HUSSEIN PEACEFULLY. HIM AN' BUSH SEEM T'BE PLAYIN' CHICKEN.
SHE'S GOING OFF--TO ANOTHER CONTINENT...KAREN LEFT ME, LARK DUMPED ME...OCEAN B'TWEEN US... HOW WILL SHE MAKE IT BACK... BUT I CAN'T STOP HER...I CAN'T CONTROL HER LIFE, THAT'D MAKE THINGS WORSE

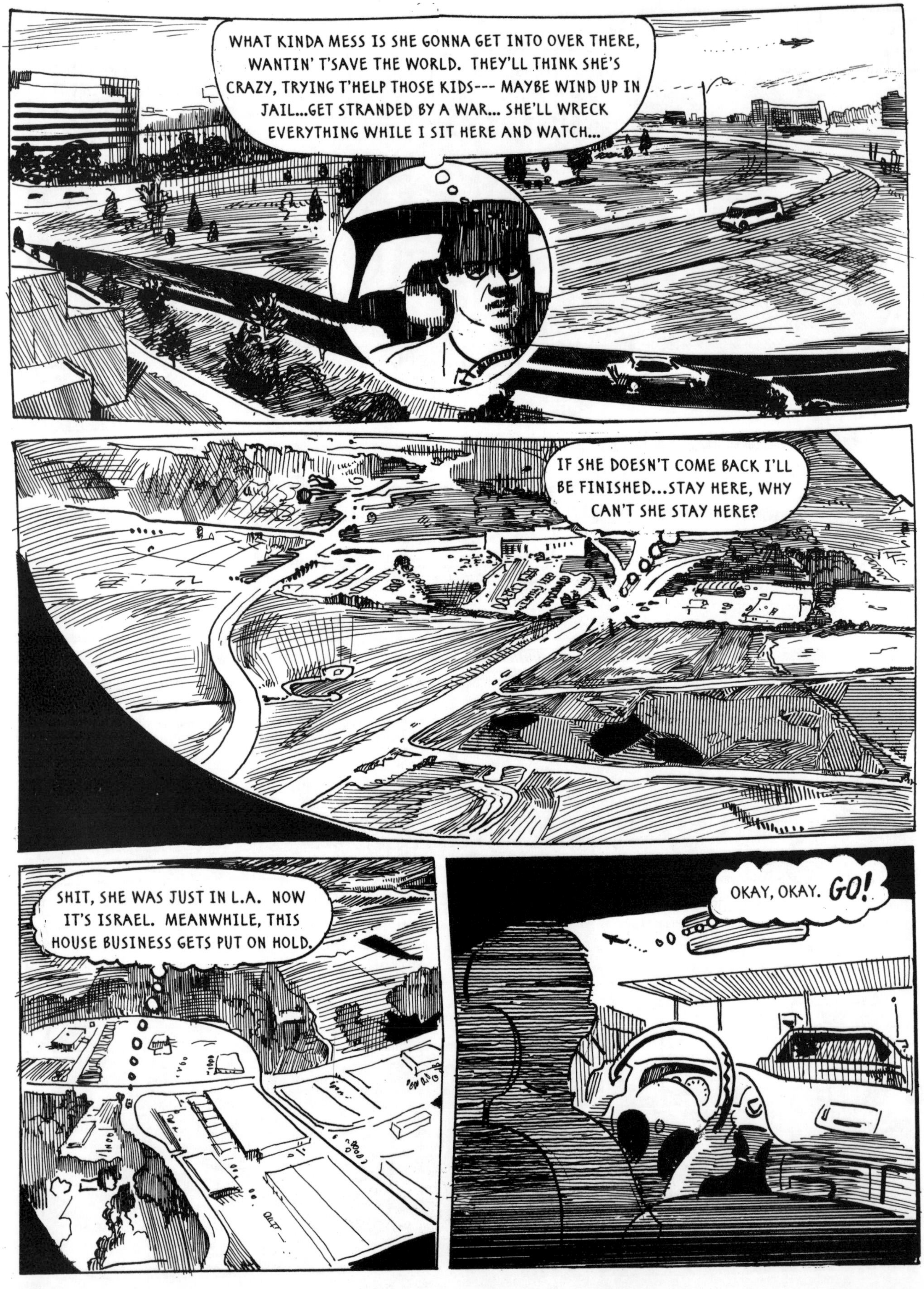
WHAT KINDA MESS IS SHE GONNA GET INTO OVER THERE, WANTIN' T'SAVE THE WORLD. THEY'LL THINK SHE'S CRAZY, TRYING T'HELP THOSE KIDS--- MAYBE WIND UP IN JAIL...GET STRANDED BY A WAR... SHE'LL WRECK EVERYTHING WHILE I SIT HERE AND WATCH...
IF SHE DOESN'T COME BACK I'LL BE FINISHED...STAY HERE, WHY CAN'T SHE STAY HERE?
SHIT, SHE WAS JUST IN L.A. NOW IT'S ISRAEL. MEANWHILE, THIS HOUSE BUSINESS GETS PUT ON HOLD.
OKAY, OKAY. GO!

3

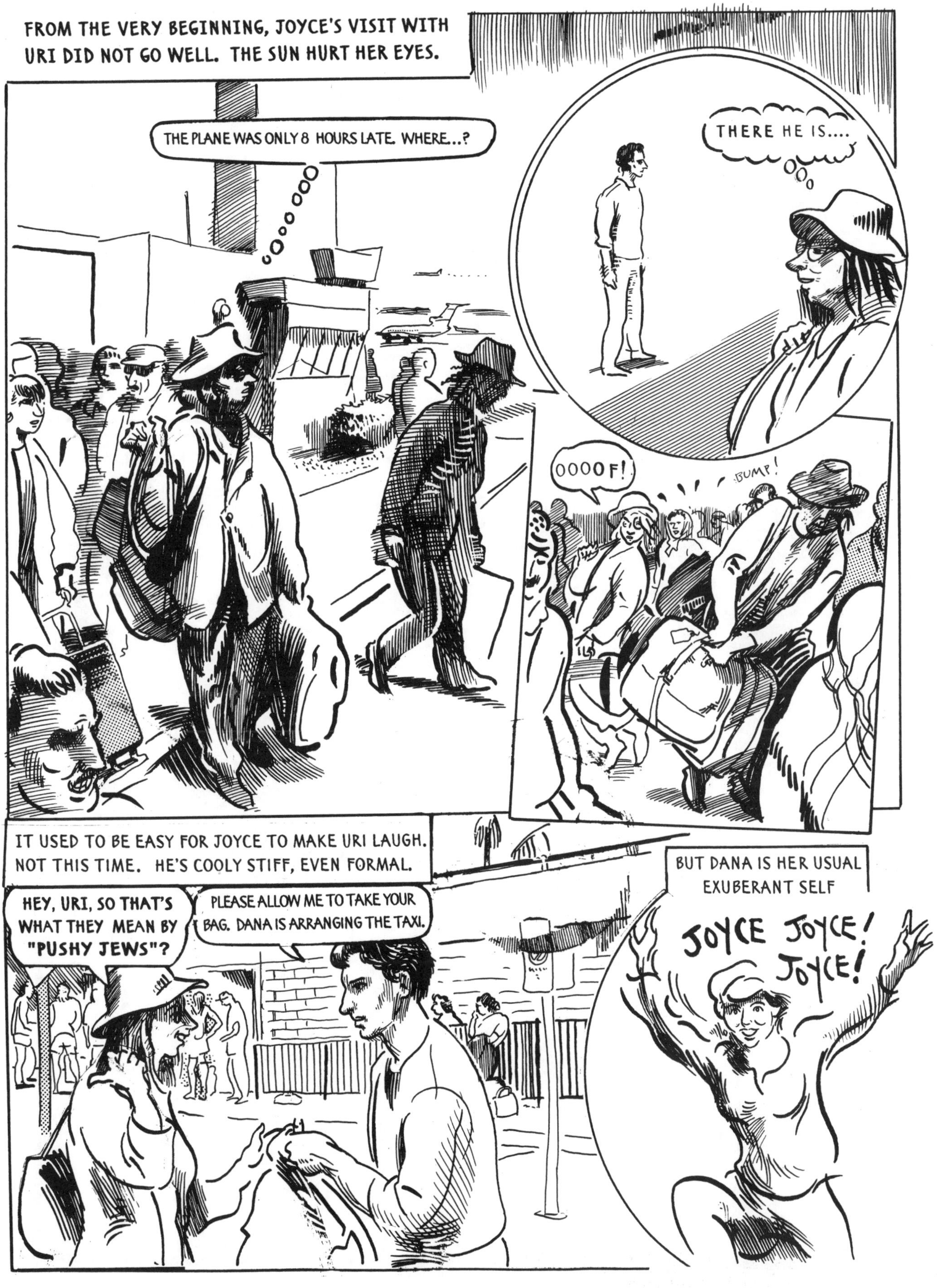
FROM THE VERY BEGINNING, JOYCE'S VISIT WITH URI DID NOT GO WELL. THE SUN HURT HER EYES.
THE PLANE WAS ONLY 8 HOURS LATE. WHERE...?
THERE HE IS....
OOOOF!
BUMP!
IT USED TO BE EASY FOR JOYCE TO MAKE URI LAUGH. NOT THIS TIME. HE'S COOLY STIFF, EVEN FORMAL.
HEY, URI, SO THAT'S WHAT THEY MEAN BY "PUSHY JEWS"?
PLEASE ALLOW ME TO TAKE YOUR BAG. DANA IS ARRANGING THE TAXI.
BUT DANA IS HER USUAL EXUBERANT SELF
JOYCE JOYCE! JOYCE!

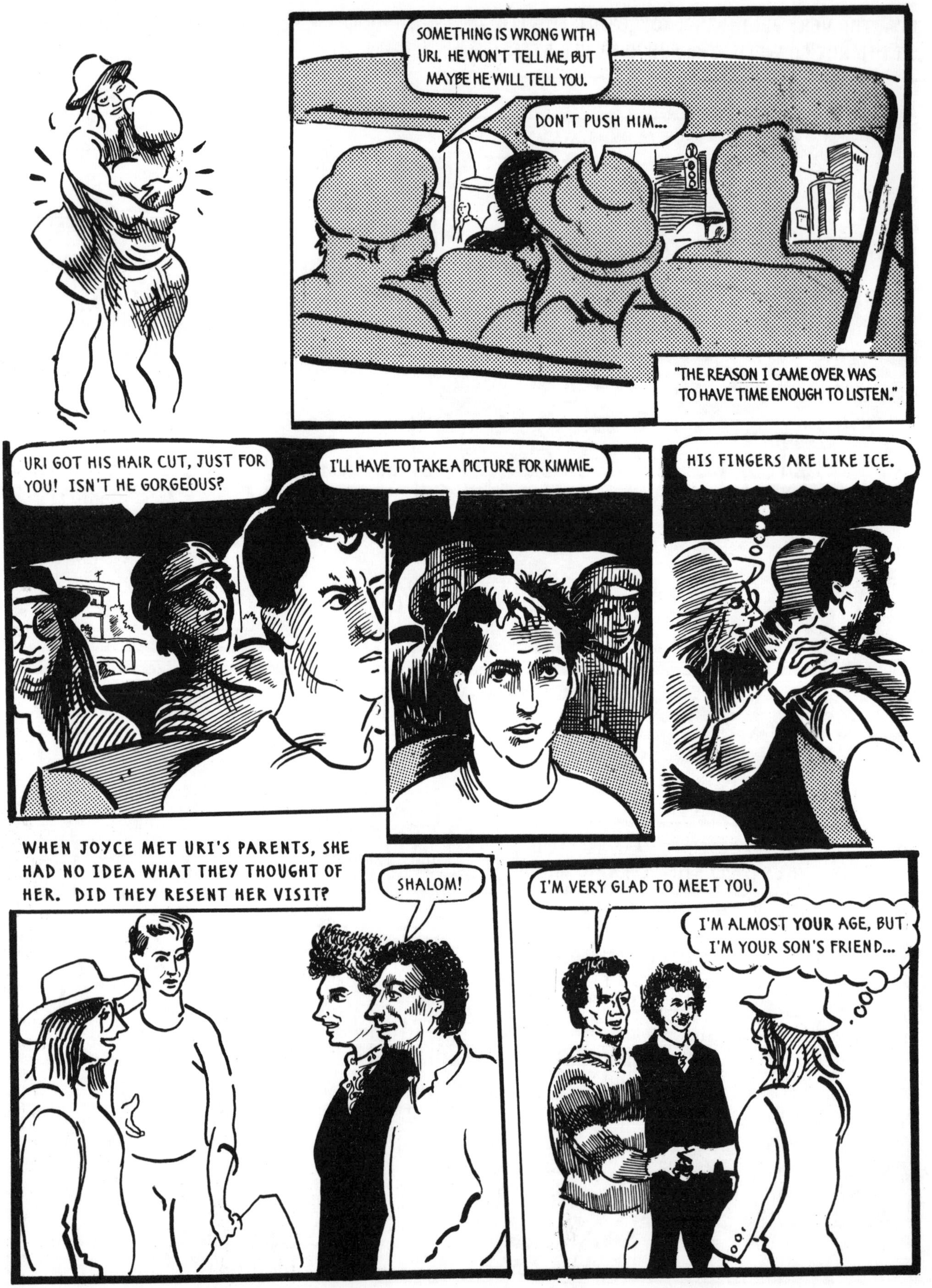
SOMETHING IS WRONG WITH URI. HE WON'T TELL ME, BUT MAYBE HE WILL TELL YOU.
DON'T PUSH HIM...
"THE REASON I CAME OVER WAS TO HAVE TIME ENOUGH TO LISTEN."
URI GOT HIS HAIR CUT, JUST FOR YOU! ISN'T HE GORGEOUS?
I'LL HAVE TO TAKE A PICTURE FOR KIMMIE.
HIS FINGERS ARE LIKE ICE.
WHEN JOYCE MET URI'S PARENTS, SHE HAD NO IDEA WHAT THEY THOUGHT OF HER. DID THEY RESENT HER VISIT?
SHALOM!
I'M VERY GLAD TO MEET YOU.
I'M ALMOST YOUR AGE, BUT I'M YOUR SON'S FRIEND...

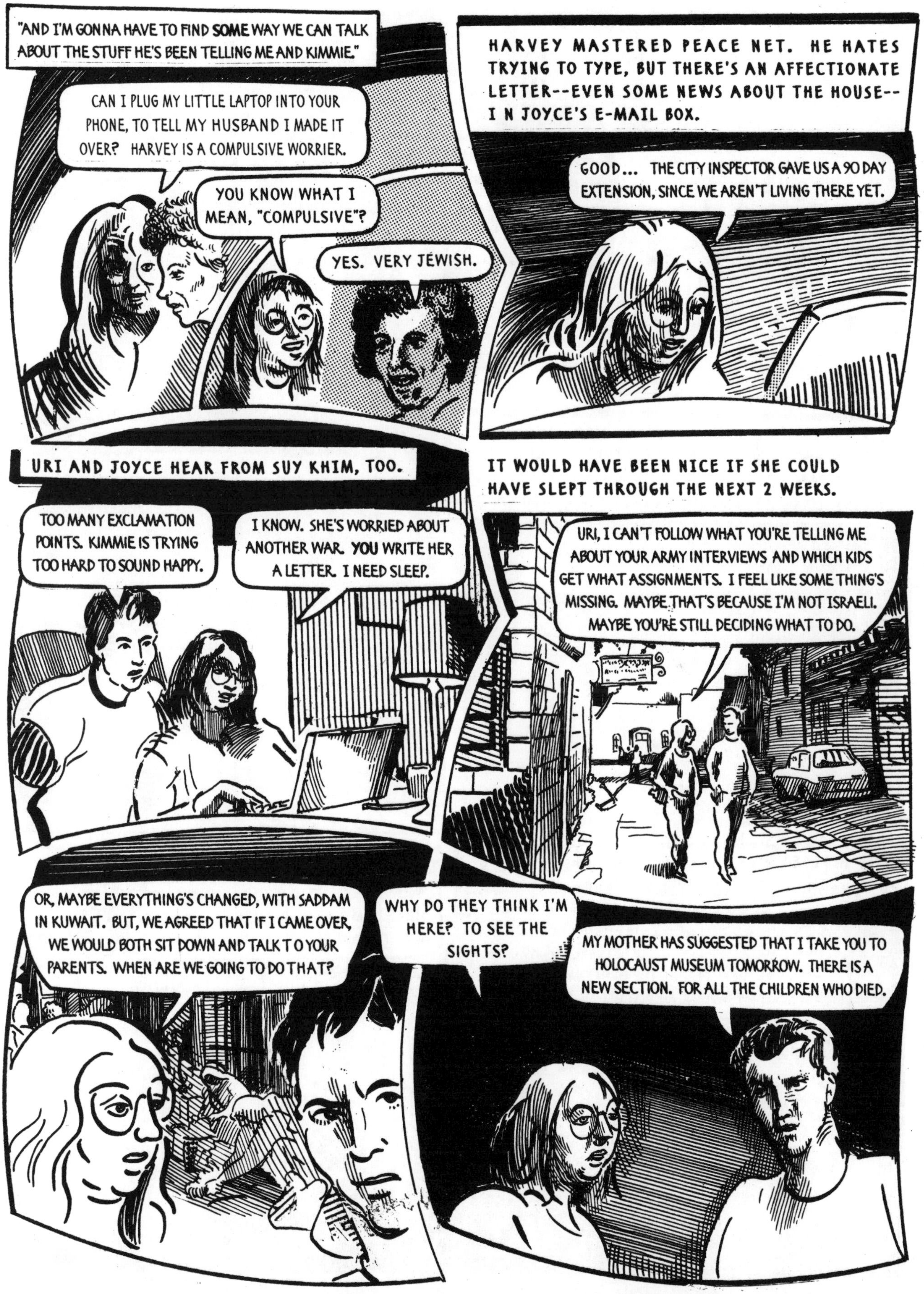
"AND I'M GONNA HAVE TO FIND SOME WAY WE CAN TALK ABOUT THE STUFF HE'S BEEN TELLING ME AND KIMMIE."
CAN I PLUG MY LITTLE LAPTOP INTO YOUR PHONE, TO TELL MY HUSBAND I MADE IT OVER? HARVEY IS A COMPULSIVE WORRIER.
YOU KNOW WHAT I MEAN, "COMPULSIVE"?
YES. VERY JEWISH.
HARVEY MASTERED PEACE NET. HE HATES TRYING TO TYPE, BUT THERE'S AN AFFECTIONATE LETTER--EVEN SOME NEWS ABOUT THE HOUSE--IN JOYCE'S E-MAIL BOX.
GOOD... THE CITY INSPECTOR GAVE US A 90 DAY EXTENSION, SINCE WE AREN'T LIVING THERE YET.
URI AND JOYCE HEAR FROM SUY KHIM, TOO.
TOO MANY EXCLAMATION POINTS. KIMMIE IS TRYING TOO HARD TO SOUND HAPPY.
I KNOW. SHE'S WORRIED ABOUT ANOTHER WAR. YOU WRITE HER A LETTER. I NEED SLEEP.
IT WOULD HAVE BEEN NICE IF SHE COULD HAVE SLEPT THROUGH THE NEXT 2 WEEKS.
URI, I CAN'T FOLLOW WHAT YOU'RE TELLING ME ABOUT YOUR ARMY INTERVIEWS AND WHICH KIDS GET WHAT ASSIGNMENTS. I FEEL LIKE SOME THING'S MISSING. MAYBE THAT'S BECAUSE I'M NOT ISRAELI. MAYBE YOU'RE STILL DECIDING WHAT TO DO.
OR, MAYBE EVERYTHING'S CHANGED, WITH SADDAM IN KUWAIT. BUT, WE AGREED THAT IF I CAME OVER, WE WOULD BOTH SIT DOWN AND TALK TO YOUR PARENTS. WHEN ARE WE GOING TO DO THAT?
WHY DO THEY THINK I'M HERE? TO SEE THE SIGHTS?
MY MOTHER HAS SUGGESTED THAT I TAKE YOU TO HOLOCAUST MUSEUM TOMORROW. THERE IS A NEW SECTION. FOR ALL THE CHILDREN WHO DIED.

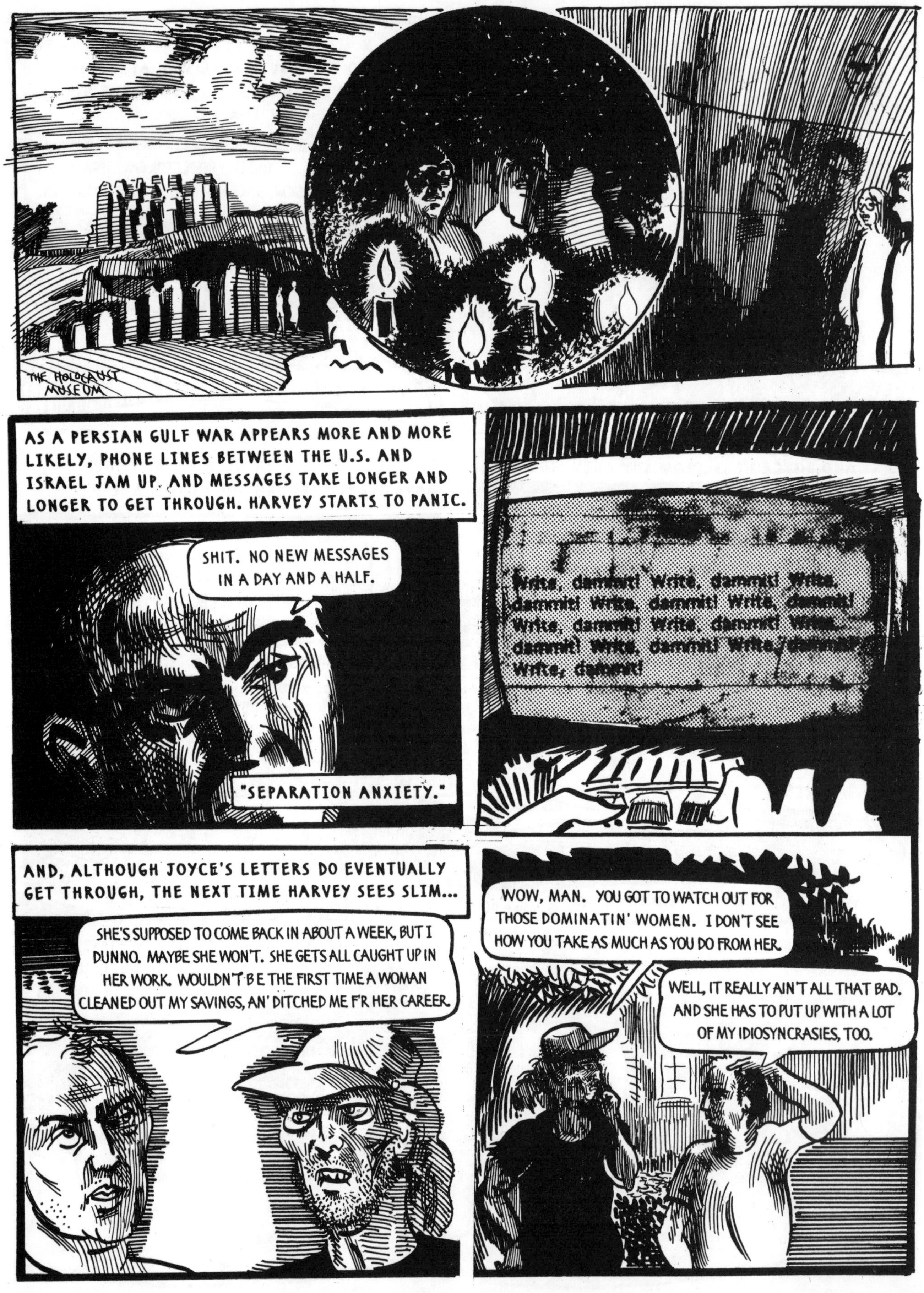
THE HOLOCAUST MUSEUM
AS A PERSIAN GULF WAR APPEARS MORE AND MORE LIKELY, PHONE LINES BETWEEN THE U.S. AND ISRAEL JAM UP, AND MESSAGES TAKE LONGER AND LONGER TO GET THROUGH. HARVEY STARTS TO PANIC.
SHIT. NO NEW MESSAGES IN A DAY AND A HALF.
"SEPARATION ANXIETY."
Write, dammit! Write, dammit! Write, dammit! Write, dammit! Write, dammit! Write, dammit! Write, dammit! Write, dammit! Write, dammit! Write, dammit! Write, dammit!
AND, ALTHOUGH JOYCE'S LETTERS DO EVENTUALLY GET THROUGH, THE NEXT TIME HARVEY SEES SLIM...
SHE'S SUPPOSED TO COME BACK IN ABOUT A WEEK, BUT I DUNNO. MAYBE SHE WON'T. SHE GETS ALL CAUGHT UP IN HER WORK. WOULDN'T BE THE FIRST TIME A WOMAN CLEANED OUT MY SAVINGS, AN' DITCHED ME F'R HER CAREER.
WOW, MAN. YOU GOT TO WATCH OUT FOR THOSE DOMINATIN' WOMEN. I DON'T SEE HOW YOU TAKE AS MUCH AS YOU DO FROM HER.
WELL, IT REALLY AIN'T ALL THAT BAD. AND SHE HAS TO PUT UP WITH A LOT OF MY IDIOSYNCRASIES, TOO.

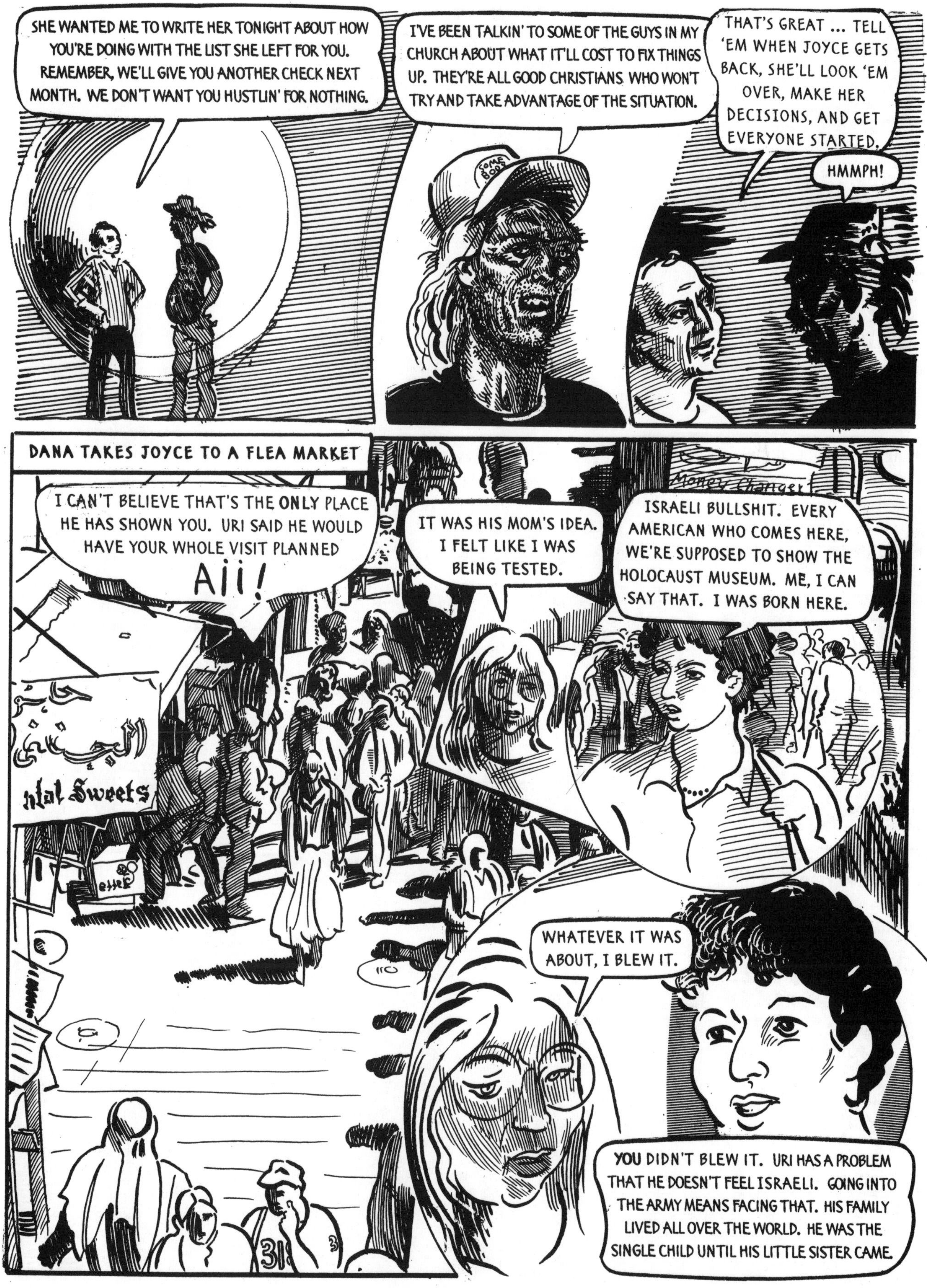
SHE WANTED ME TO WRITE HER TONIGHT ABOUT HOW YOU'RE DOING WITH THE LIST SHE LEFT FOR YOU. REMEMBER, WE'LL GIVE YOU ANOTHER CHECK NEXT MONTH. WE DON'T WANT YOU HUSTLIN' FOR NOTHING.
I'VE BEEN TALKIN' TO SOME OF THE GUYS IN MY CHURCH ABOUT WHAT IT'LL COST TO FIX THINGS UP. THEY'RE ALL GOOD CHRISTIANS WHO WON'T TRY AND TAKE ADVANTAGE OF THE SITUATION.
THAT'S GREAT ... TELL 'EM WHEN JOYCE GETS BACK, SHE'LL LOOK 'EM OVER, MAKE HER DECISIONS, AND GET EVERYONE STARTED.
HMMPH!
DANA TAKES JOYCE TO A FLEA MARKET
I CAN'T BELIEVE THAT'S THE ONLY PLACE HE HAS SHOWN YOU. URI SAID HE WOULD HAVE YOUR WHOLE VISIT PLANNED
Aii!
IT WAS HIS MOM'S IDEA. I FELT LIKE I WAS BEING TESTED.
ISRAELI BULLSHIT. EVERY AMERICAN WHO COMES HERE, WE'RE SUPPOSED TO SHOW THE HOLOCAUST MUSEUM. ME, I CAN SAY THAT. I WAS BORN HERE.
Money Changer
ntal Sweets
WHATEVER IT WAS ABOUT, I BLEW IT.
YOU DIDN'T BLEW IT. URI HAS A PROBLEM THAT HE DOESN'T FEEL ISRAELI. GOING INTO THE ARMY MEANS FACING THAT. HIS FAMILY LIVED ALL OVER THE WORLD. HE WAS THE SINGLE CHILD UNTIL HIS LITTLE SISTER CAME.

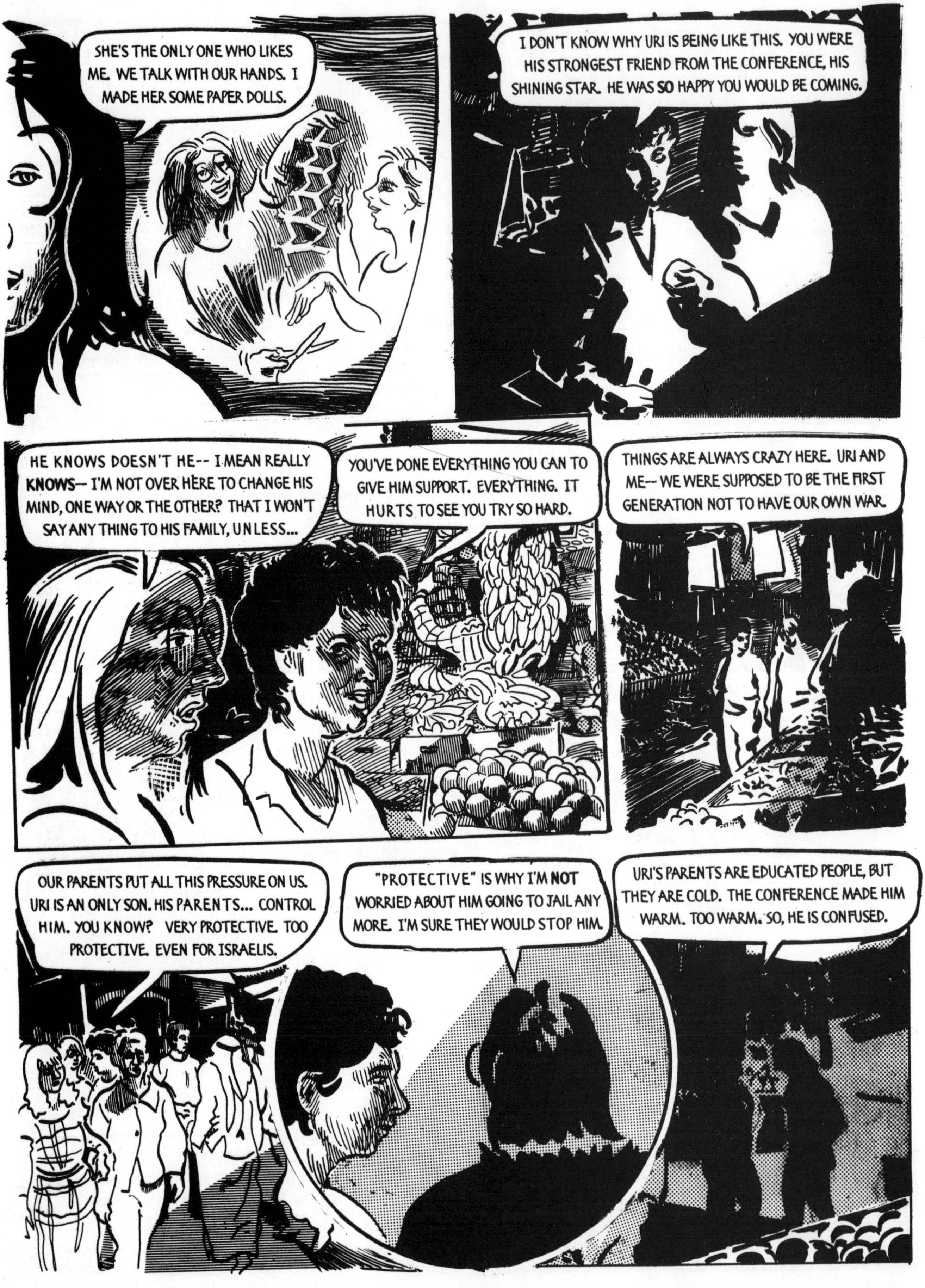
SHE'S THE ONLY ONE WHO LIKES ME. WE TALK WITH OUR HANDS. I MADE HER SOME PAPER DOLLS.
I DON'T KNOW WHY URI IS BEING LIKE THIS. YOU WERE HIS STRONGEST FRIEND FROM THE CONFERENCE, HIS SHINING STAR. HE WAS SO HAPPY YOU WOULD BE COMING.
HE KNOWS DOESN'T HE-- I MEAN REALLY KNOWS-- I'M NOT OVER HERE TO CHANGE HIS MIND, ONE WAY OR THE OTHER? THAT I WON'T SAY ANY THING TO HIS FAMILY, UNLESS...
YOU'VE DONE EVERYTHING YOU CAN TO GIVE HIM SUPPORT. EVERYTHING. IT HURTS TO SEE YOU TRY SO HARD.
THINGS ARE ALWAYS CRAZY HERE. URI AND ME-- WE WERE SUPPOSED TO BE THE FIRST GENERATION NOT TO HAVE OUR OWN WAR.
OUR PARENTS PUT ALL THIS PRESSURE ON US. URI IS AN ONLY SON. HIS PARENTS... CONTROL HIM. YOU KNOW? VERY PROTECTIVE. TOO PROTECTIVE. EVEN FOR ISRAELIS.
"PROTECTIVE" IS WHY I'M NOT WORRIED ABOUT HIM GOING TO JAIL ANY MORE. I'M SURE THEY WOULD STOP HIM.
URI'S PARENTS ARE EDUCATED PEOPLE, BUT THEY ARE COLD. THE CONFERENCE MADE HIM WARM. TOO WARM. SO, HE IS CONFUSED.

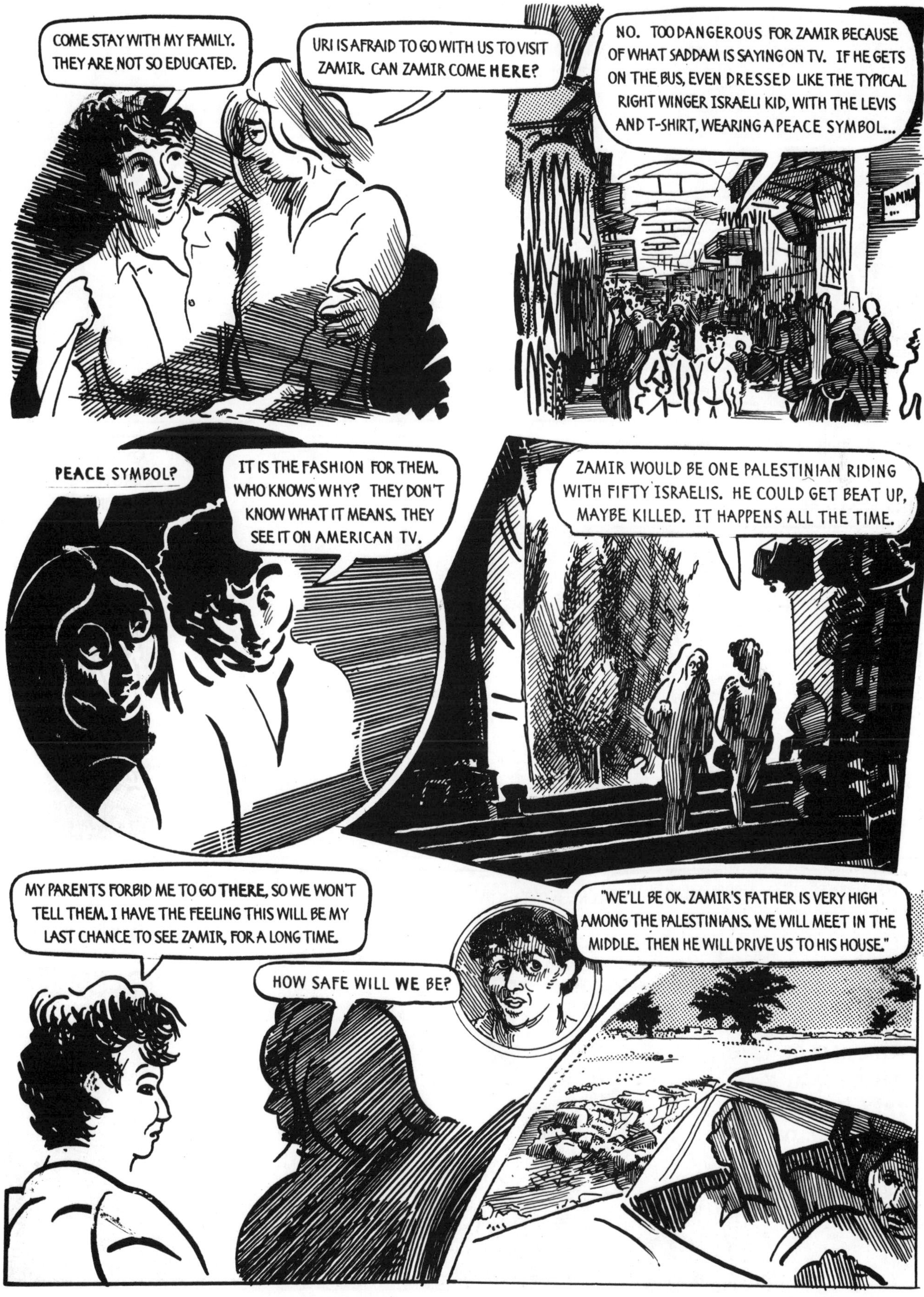
COME STAY WITH MY FAMILY. THEY ARE NOT SO EDUCATED.
URI IS AFRAID TO GO WITH US TO VISIT ZAMIR. CAN ZAMIR COME HERE?
NO. TOO DANGEROUS FOR ZAMIR BECAUSE OF WHAT SADDAM IS SAYING ON TV. IF HE GETS ON THE BUS, EVEN DRESSED LIKE THE TYPICAL RIGHT WINGER ISRAELI KID, WITH THE LEVIS AND T-SHIRT, WEARING A PEACE SYMBOL...
PEACE SYMBOL?
IT IS THE FASHION FOR THEM. WHO KNOWS WHY? THEY DON'T KNOW WHAT IT MEANS. THEY SEE IT ON AMERICAN TV.
ZAMIR WOULD BE ONE PALESTINIAN RIDING WITH FIFTY ISRAELIS. HE COULD GET BEAT UP, MAYBE KILLED. IT HAPPENS ALL THE TIME.
MY PARENTS FORBID ME TO GO THERE, SO WE WON'T TELL THEM. I HAVE THE FEELING THIS WILL BE MY LAST CHANCE TO SEE ZAMIR, FOR A LONG TIME.
HOW SAFE WILL WE BE?
"WE'LL BE OK. ZAMIR'S FATHER IS VERY HIGH AMONG THE PALESTINIANS. WE WILL MEET IN THE MIDDLE. THEN HE WILL DRIVE US TO HIS HOUSE."

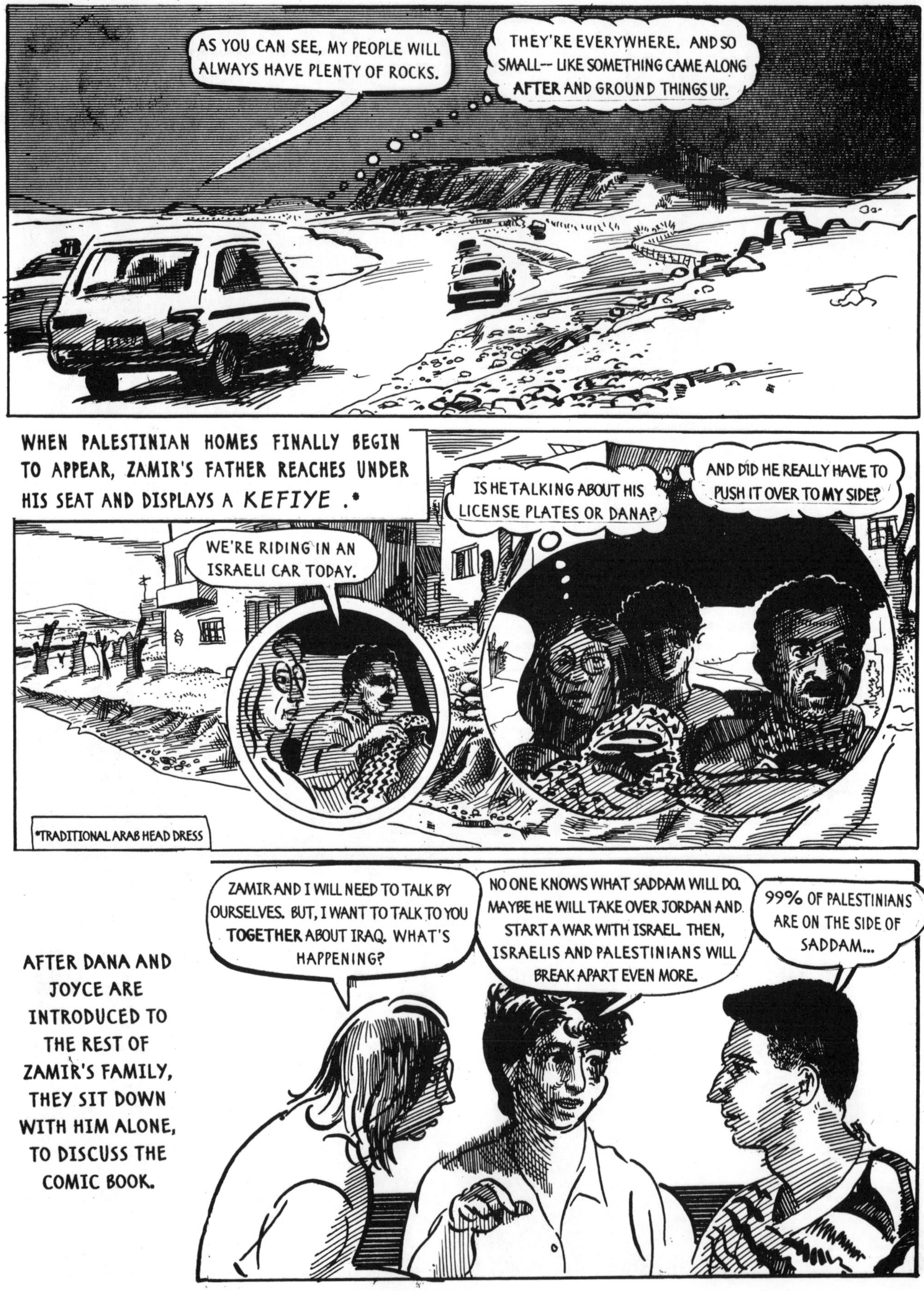
AS YOU CAN SEE, MY PEOPLE WILL ALWAYS HAVE PLENTY OF ROCKS.
THEY'RE EVERYWHERE. AND SO SMALL-- LIKE SOMETHING CAME ALONG AFTER AND GROUND THINGS UP.
WHEN PALESTINIAN HOMES FINALLY BEGIN TO APPEAR, ZAMIR'S FATHER REACHES UNDER HIS SEAT AND DISPLAYS A KEFIYE .*
WE'RE RIDING IN AN ISRAELI CAR TODAY.
IS HE TALKING ABOUT HIS LICENSE PLATES OR DANA?
AND DID HE REALLY HAVE TO PUSH IT OVER TO MY SIDE?
*TRADITIONAL ARAB HEAD DRESS
AFTER DANA AND JOYCE ARE INTRODUCED TO THE REST OF ZAMIR'S FAMILY, THEY SIT DOWN WITH HIM ALONE, TO DISCUSS THE COMIC BOOK.
ZAMIR AND I WILL NEED TO TALK BY OURSELVES. BUT, I WANT TO TALK TO YOU TOGETHER ABOUT IRAQ. WHAT'S HAPPENING?
NO ONE KNOWS WHAT SADDAM WILL DO. MAYBE HE WILL TAKE OVER JORDAN AND START A WAR WITH ISRAEL. THEN, ISRAELIS AND PALESTINIANS WILL BREAK APART EVEN MORE.
99% OF PALESTINIANS ARE ON THE SIDE OF SADDAM...

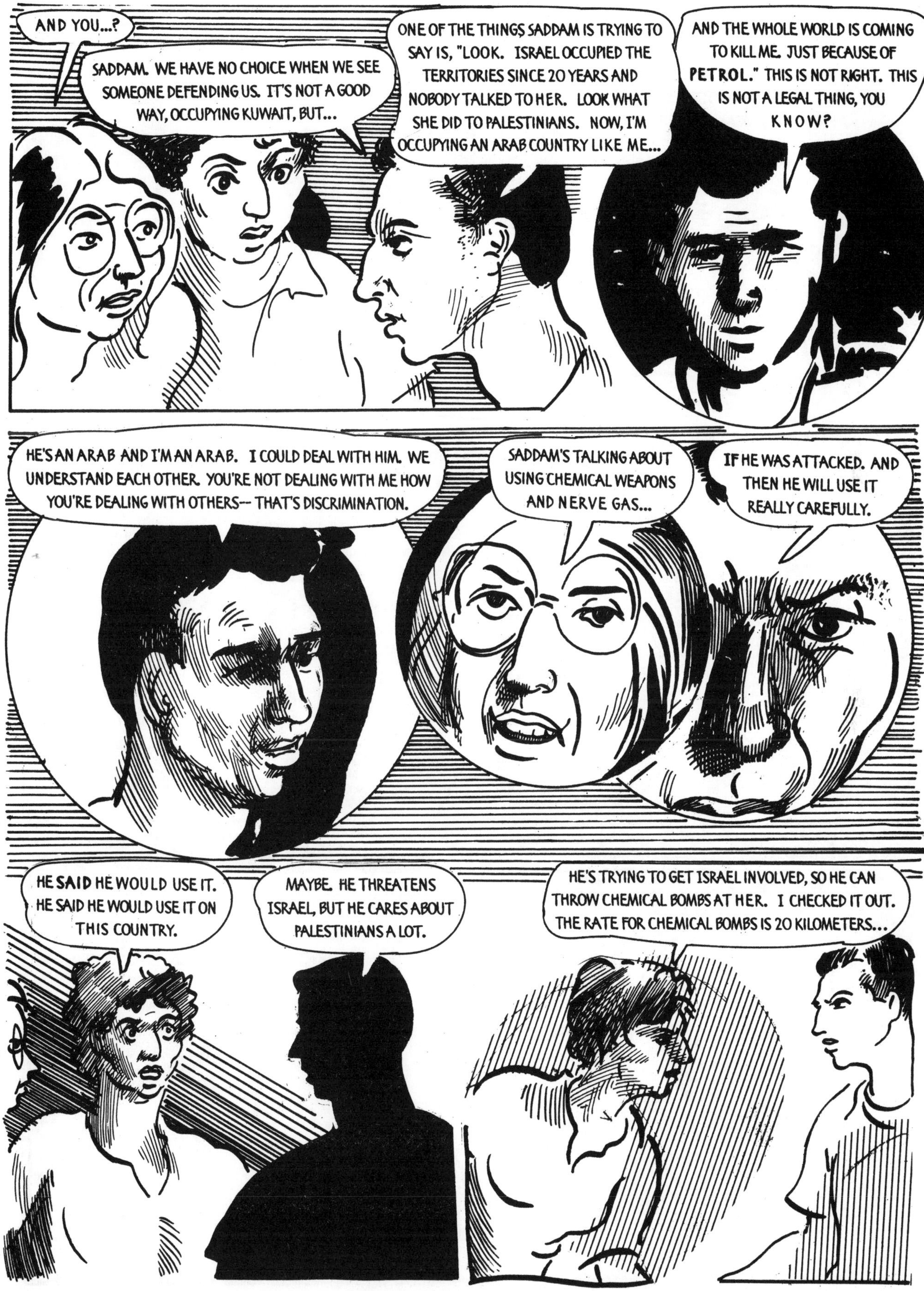
AND YOU...?
SADDAM. WE HAVE NO CHOICE WHEN WE SEE SOMEONE DEFENDING US. IT'S NOT A GOOD WAY, OCCUPYING KUWAIT, BUT...
ONE OF THE THINGS SADDAM IS TRYING TO SAY IS, "LOOK. ISRAEL OCCUPIED THE TERRITORIES SINCE 20 YEARS AND NOBODY TALKED TO HER. LOOK WHAT SHE DID TO PALESTINIANS. NOW, I'M OCCUPYING AN ARAB COUNTRY LIKE ME...
AND THE WHOLE WORLD IS COMING TO KILL ME. JUST BECAUSE OF PETROL." THIS IS NOT RIGHT. THIS IS NOT A LEGAL THING, YOU KNOW?
HE'S AN ARAB AND I'M AN ARAB. I COULD DEAL WITH HIM. WE UNDERSTAND EACH OTHER. YOU'RE NOT DEALING WITH ME HOW YOU'RE DEALING WITH OTHERS-- THAT'S DISCRIMINATION.
SADDAM'S TALKING ABOUT USING CHEMICAL WEAPONS AND NERVE GAS...
IF HE WAS ATTACKED. AND THEN HE WILL USE IT REALLY CAREFULLY.
HE SAID HE WOULD USE IT. HE SAID HE WOULD USE IT ON THIS COUNTRY.
MAYBE. HE THREATENS ISRAEL, BUT HE CARES ABOUT PALESTINIANS A LOT.
HE'S TRYING TO GET ISRAEL INVOLVED, SO HE CAN THROW CHEMICAL BOMBS AT HER. I CHECKED IT OUT. THE RATE FOR CHEMICAL BOMBS IS 20 KILOMETERS...

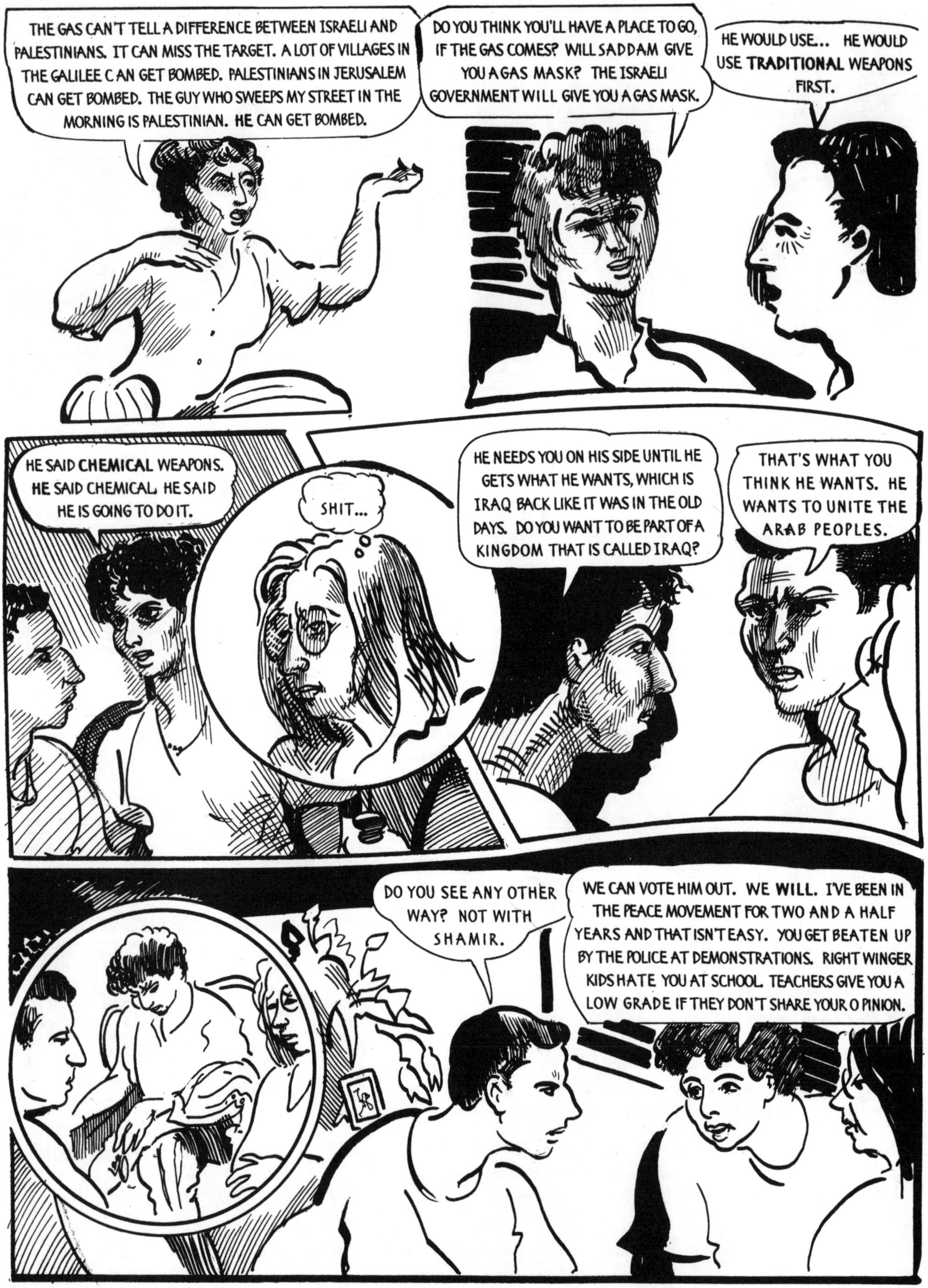
THE GAS CAN'T TELL A DIFFERENCE BETWEEN ISRAELI AND PALESTINIANS. IT CAN MISS THE TARGET. A LOT OF VILLAGES IN THE GALILEE CAN GET BOMBED. PALESTINIANS IN JERUSALEM CAN GET BOMBED. THE GUY WHO SWEEPS MY STREET IN THE MORNING IS PALESTINIAN. HE CAN GET BOMBED.
DO YOU THINK YOU'LL HAVE A PLACE TO GO, IF THE GAS COMES? WILL SADDAM GIVE YOU A GAS MASK? THE ISRAELI GOVERNMENT WILL GIVE YOU A GAS MASK.
HE WOULD USE... HE WOULD USE TRADITIONAL WEAPONS FIRST.
HE SAID CHEMICAL WEAPONS. HE SAID CHEMICAL. HE SAID HE IS GOING TO DO IT.
SHIT...
HE NEEDS YOU ON HIS SIDE UNTIL HE GETS WHAT HE WANTS, WHICH IS IRAQ BACK LIKE IT WAS IN THE OLD DAYS. DO YOU WANT TO BE PART OF A KINGDOM THAT IS CALLED IRAQ?
THAT'S WHAT YOU THINK HE WANTS. HE WANTS TO UNITE THE ARAB PEOPLES.
DO YOU SEE ANY OTHER WAY? NOT WITH SHAMIR.
WE CAN VOTE HIM OUT. WE WILL. I'VE BEEN IN THE PEACE MOVEMENT FOR TWO AND A HALF YEARS AND THAT ISN'T EASY. YOU GET BEATEN UP BY THE POLICE AT DEMONSTRATIONS. RIGHT WINGER KIDS HATE YOU AT SCHOOL. TEACHERS GIVE YOU A LOW GRADE IF THEY DON'T SHARE YOUR OPINION.

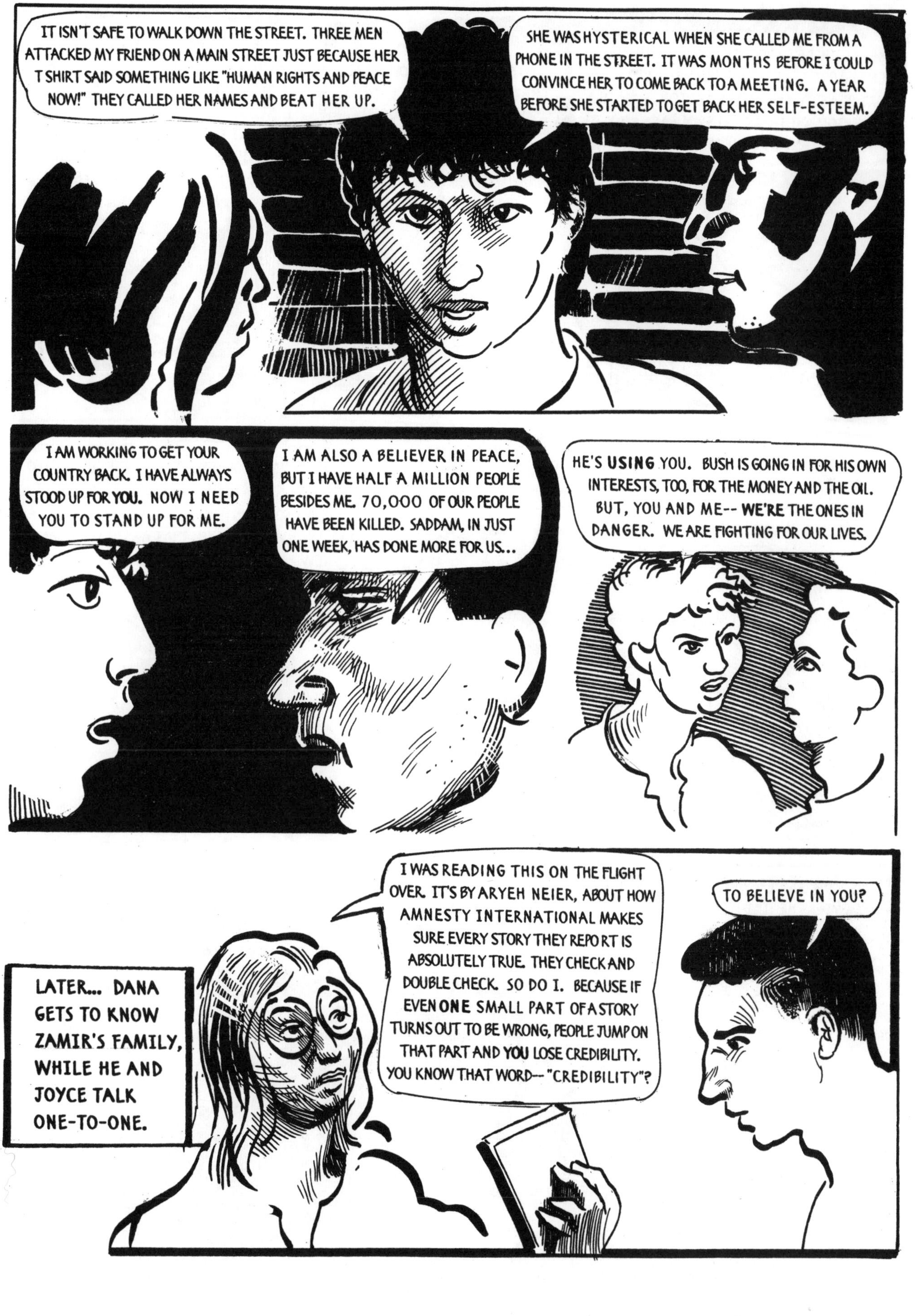
IT ISN'T SAFE TO WALK DOWN THE STREET. THREE MEN ATTACKED MY FRIEND ON A MAIN STREET JUST BECAUSE HER T SHIRT SAID SOMETHING LIKE "HUMAN RIGHTS AND PEACE NOW!" THEY CALLED HER NAMES AND BEAT HER UP.
SHE WAS HYSTERICAL WHEN SHE CALLED ME FROM A PHONE IN THE STREET. IT WAS MONTHS BEFORE I COULD CONVINCE HER TO COME BACK TO A MEETING. A YEAR BEFORE SHE STARTED TO GET BACK HER SELF-ESTEEM.
I AM WORKING TO GET YOUR COUNTRY BACK. I HAVE ALWAYS STOOD UP FOR **YOU**. NOW I NEED YOU TO STAND UP FOR ME.
I AM ALSO A BELIEVER IN PEACE, BUT I HAVE HALF A MILLION PEOPLE BESIDES ME. 70,000 OF OUR PEOPLE HAVE BEEN KILLED. SADDAM, IN JUST ONE WEEK, HAS DONE MORE FOR US...
HE'S **USING** YOU. BUSH IS GOING IN FOR HIS OWN INTERESTS, TOO, FOR THE MONEY AND THE OIL. BUT, YOU AND ME-- **WE'RE** THE ONES IN DANGER. WE ARE FIGHTING FOR OUR LIVES.
LATER... DANA GETS TO KNOW ZAMIR'S FAMILY, WHILE HE AND JOYCE TALK ONE-TO-ONE.
I WAS READING THIS ON THE FLIGHT OVER. IT'S BY ARYEH NEIER, ABOUT HOW AMNESTY INTERNATIONAL MAKES SURE EVERY STORY THEY REPORT IS ABSOLUTELY TRUE. THEY CHECK AND DOUBLE CHECK. SO DO I. BECAUSE IF EVEN **ONE** SMALL PART OF A STORY TURNS OUT TO BE WRONG, PEOPLE JUMP ON THAT PART AND **YOU** LOSE CREDIBILITY. YOU KNOW THAT WORD-- "CREDIBILITY"?
TO BELIEVE IN YOU?

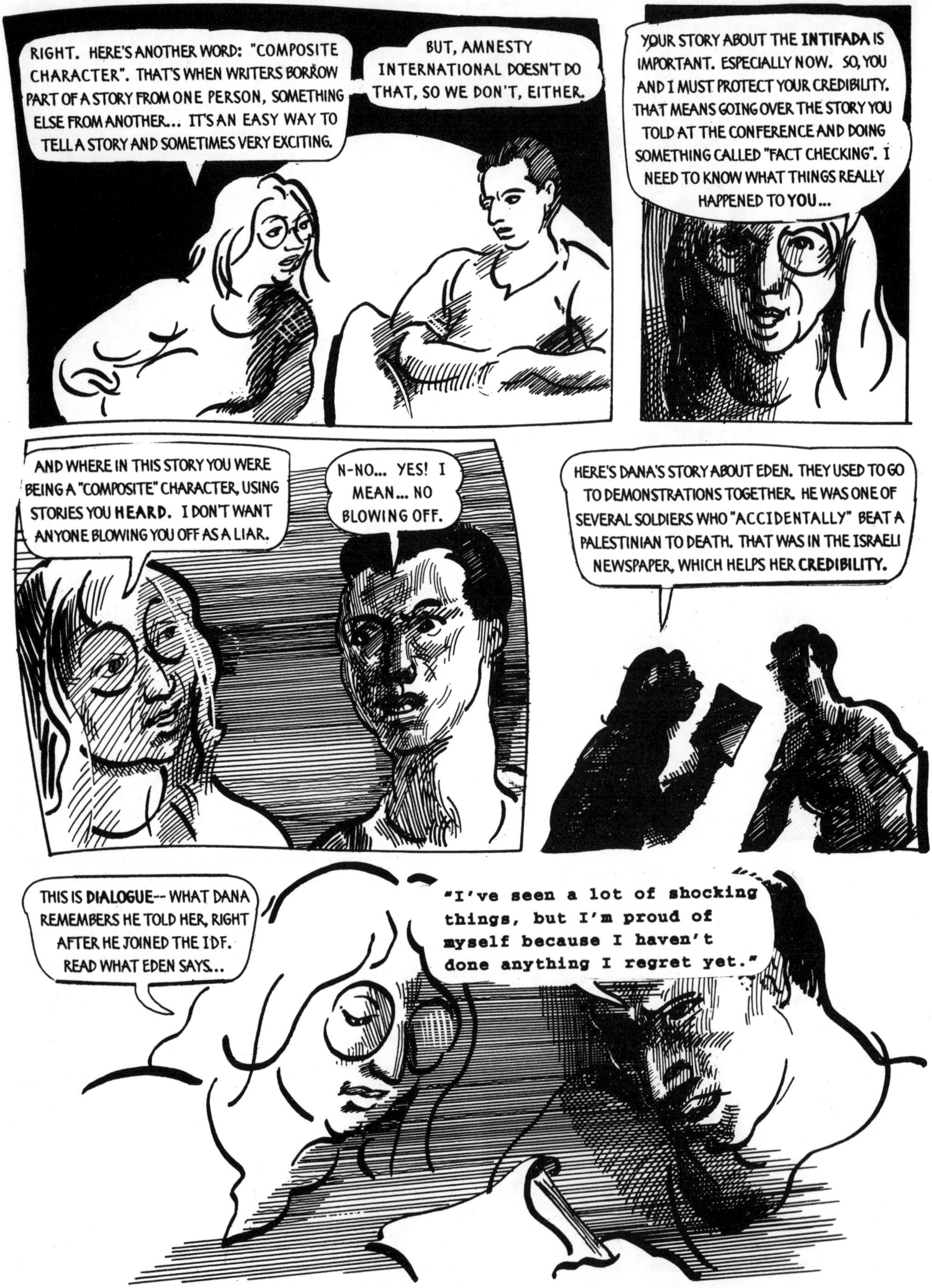

RIGHT. HERE'S ANOTHER WORD: "COMPOSITE CHARACTER". THAT'S WHEN WRITERS BORROW PART OF A STORY FROM ONE PERSON, SOMETHING ELSE FROM ANOTHER... IT'S AN EASY WAY TO TELL A STORY AND SOMETIMES VERY EXCITING.
BUT, AMNESTY INTERNATIONAL DOESN'T DO THAT, SO WE DON'T, EITHER.
YOUR STORY ABOUT THE INTIFADA IS IMPORTANT. ESPECIALLY NOW. SO, YOU AND I MUST PROTECT YOUR CREDIBILITY. THAT MEANS GOING OVER THE STORY YOU TOLD AT THE CONFERENCE AND DOING SOMETHING CALLED "FACT CHECKING". I NEED TO KNOW WHAT THINGS REALLY HAPPENED TO YOU...
AND WHERE IN THIS STORY YOU WERE BEING A "COMPOSITE" CHARACTER, USING STORIES YOU HEARD. I DON'T WANT ANYONE BLOWING YOU OFF AS A LIAR.
N-NO... YES! I MEAN... NO BLOWING OFF.
HERE'S DANA'S STORY ABOUT EDEN. THEY USED TO GO TO DEMONSTRATIONS TOGETHER. HE WAS ONE OF SEVERAL SOLDIERS WHO "ACCIDENTALLY" BEAT A PALESTINIAN TO DEATH. THAT WAS IN THE ISRAELI NEWSPAPER, WHICH HELPS HER CREDIBILITY.
THIS IS DIALOGUE-- WHAT DANA REMEMBERS HE TOLD HER, RIGHT AFTER HE JOINED THE IDF. READ WHAT EDEN SAYS...
"I've seen a lot of shocking things, but I'm proud of myself because I haven't done anything I regret yet."

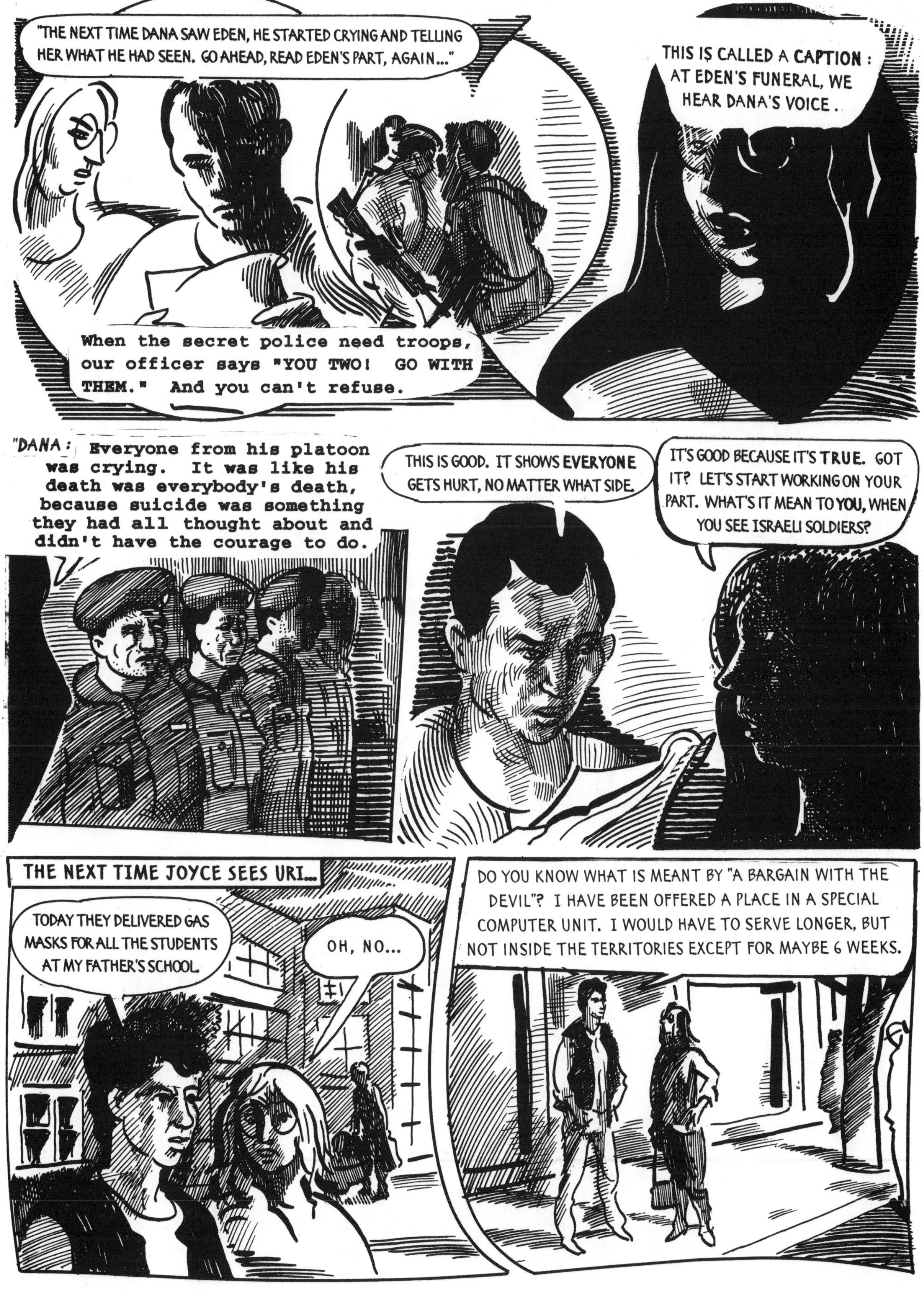

"THE NEXT TIME DANA SAW EDEN, HE STARTED CRYING AND TELLING HER WHAT HE HAD SEEN. GO AHEAD, READ EDEN'S PART, AGAIN..."
When the secret police need troops, our officer says "YOU TWO! GO WITH THEM." And you can't refuse.
THIS IS CALLED A CAPTION: AT EDEN'S FUNERAL, WE HEAR DANA'S VOICE.
"DANA: Everyone from his platoon was crying. It was like his death was everybody's death, because suicide was something they had all thought about and didn't have the courage to do.
THIS IS GOOD. IT SHOWS EVERYONE GETS HURT, NO MATTER WHAT SIDE.
IT'S GOOD BECAUSE IT'S TRUE. GOT IT? LET'S START WORKING ON YOUR PART. WHAT'S IT MEAN TO YOU, WHEN YOU SEE ISRAELI SOLDIERS?
THE NEXT TIME JOYCE SEES URI...
TODAY THEY DELIVERED GAS MASKS FOR ALL THE STUDENTS AT MY FATHER'S SCHOOL.
OH, NO...
DO YOU KNOW WHAT IS MEANT BY "A BARGAIN WITH THE DEVIL"? I HAVE BEEN OFFERED A PLACE IN A SPECIAL COMPUTER UNIT. I WOULD HAVE TO SERVE LONGER, BUT NOT INSIDE THE TERRITORIES EXCEPT FOR MAYBE 6 WEEKS.

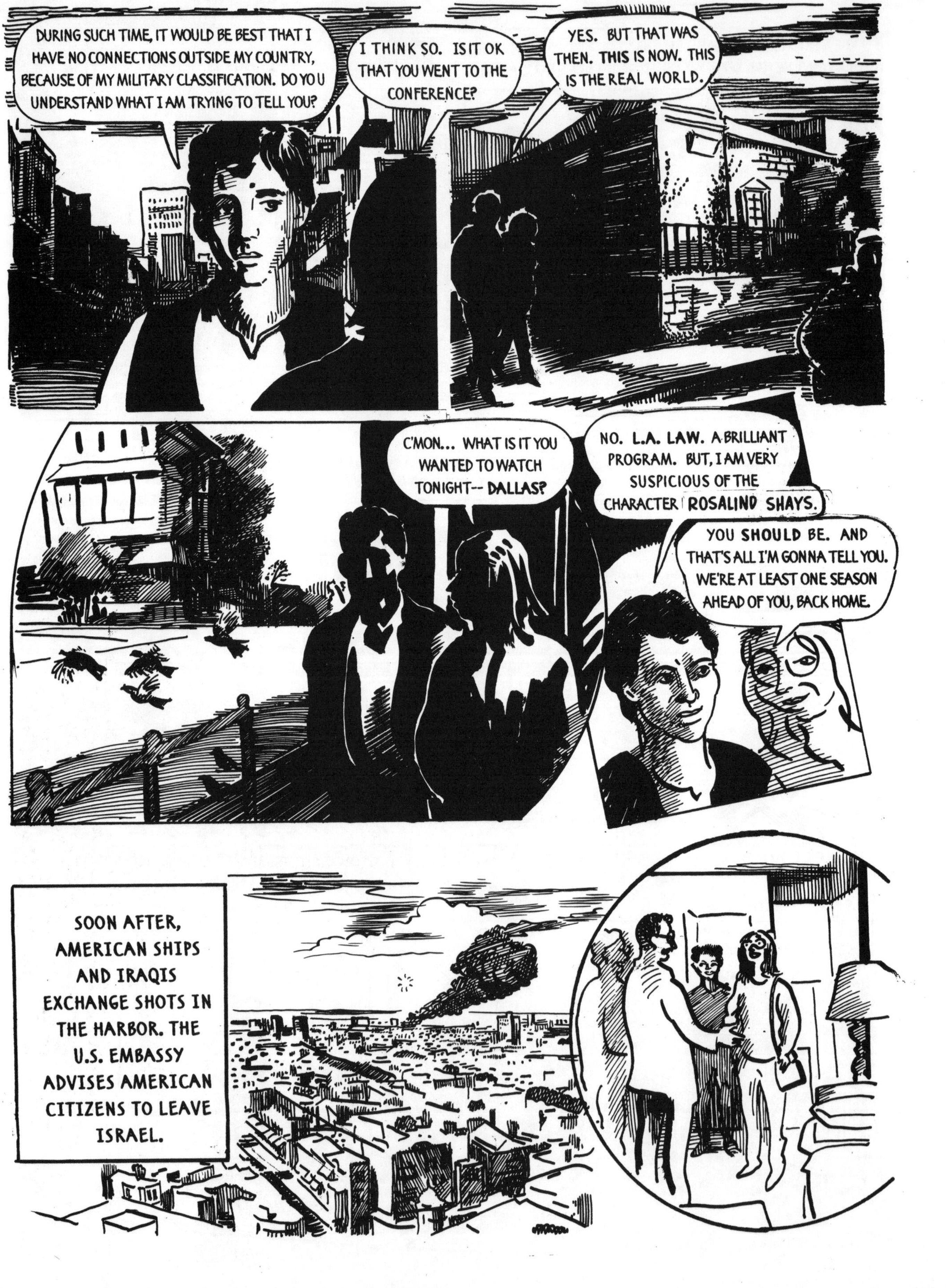
DURING SUCH TIME, IT WOULD BE BEST THAT I HAVE NO CONNECTIONS OUTSIDE MY COUNTRY, BECAUSE OF MY MILITARY CLASSIFICATION. DO YOU UNDERSTAND WHAT I AM TRYING TO TELL YOU?
I THINK SO. IS IT OK THAT YOU WENT TO THE CONFERENCE?
YES. BUT THAT WAS THEN. THIS IS NOW. THIS IS THE REAL WORLD.
C'MON... WHAT IS IT YOU WANTED TO WATCH TONIGHT-- DALLAS?
NO. L.A. LAW. A BRILLIANT PROGRAM. BUT, I AM VERY SUSPICIOUS OF THE CHARACTER ROSALIND SHAYS.
YOU SHOULD BE. AND THAT'S ALL I'M GONNA TELL YOU. WE'RE AT LEAST ONE SEASON AHEAD OF YOU, BACK HOME.
SOON AFTER, AMERICAN SHIPS AND IRAQIS EXCHANGE SHOTS IN THE HARBOR. THE U.S. EMBASSY ADVISES AMERICAN CITIZENS TO LEAVE ISRAEL.

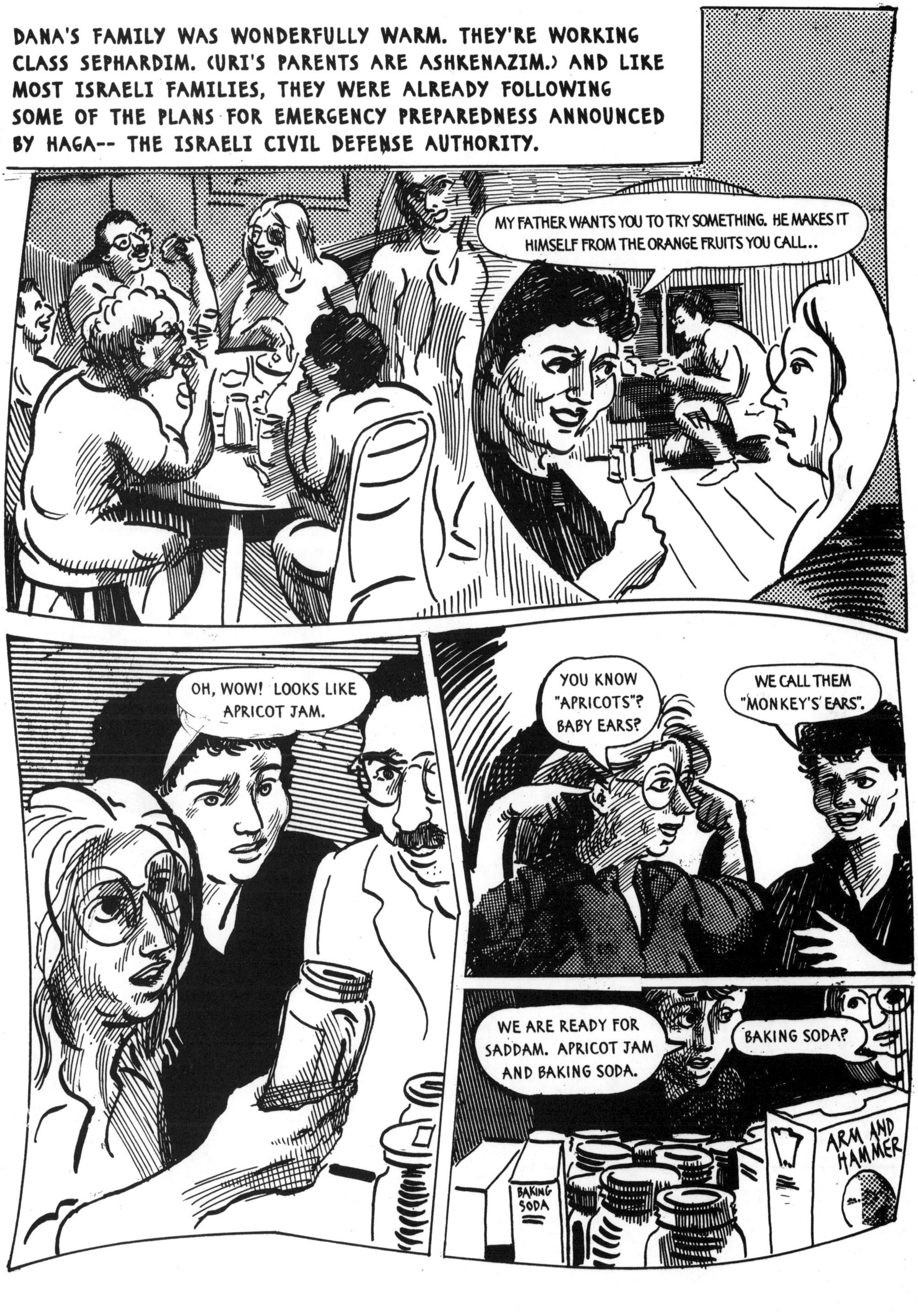
DANA'S FAMILY WAS WONDERFULLY WARM. THEY'RE WORKING CLASS SEPHARDIM. (URI'S PARENTS ARE ASHKENAZIM.) AND LIKE MOST ISRAELI FAMILIES, THEY WERE ALREADY FOLLOWING SOME OF THE PLANS FOR EMERGENCY PREPAREDNESS ANNOUNCED BY HAGA-- THE ISRAELI CIVIL DEFENSE AUTHORITY.
MY FATHER WANTS YOU TO TRY SOMETHING. HE MAKES IT HIMSELF FROM THE ORANGE FRUITS YOU CALL...
OH, WOW! LOOKS LIKE APRICOT JAM.
YOU KNOW "APRICOTS"? BABY EARS?
WE CALL THEM "MONKEY'S EARS".
WE ARE READY FOR SADDAM. APRICOT JAM AND BAKING SODA.
BAKING SODA?
BAKING SODA
ARM AND HAMMER

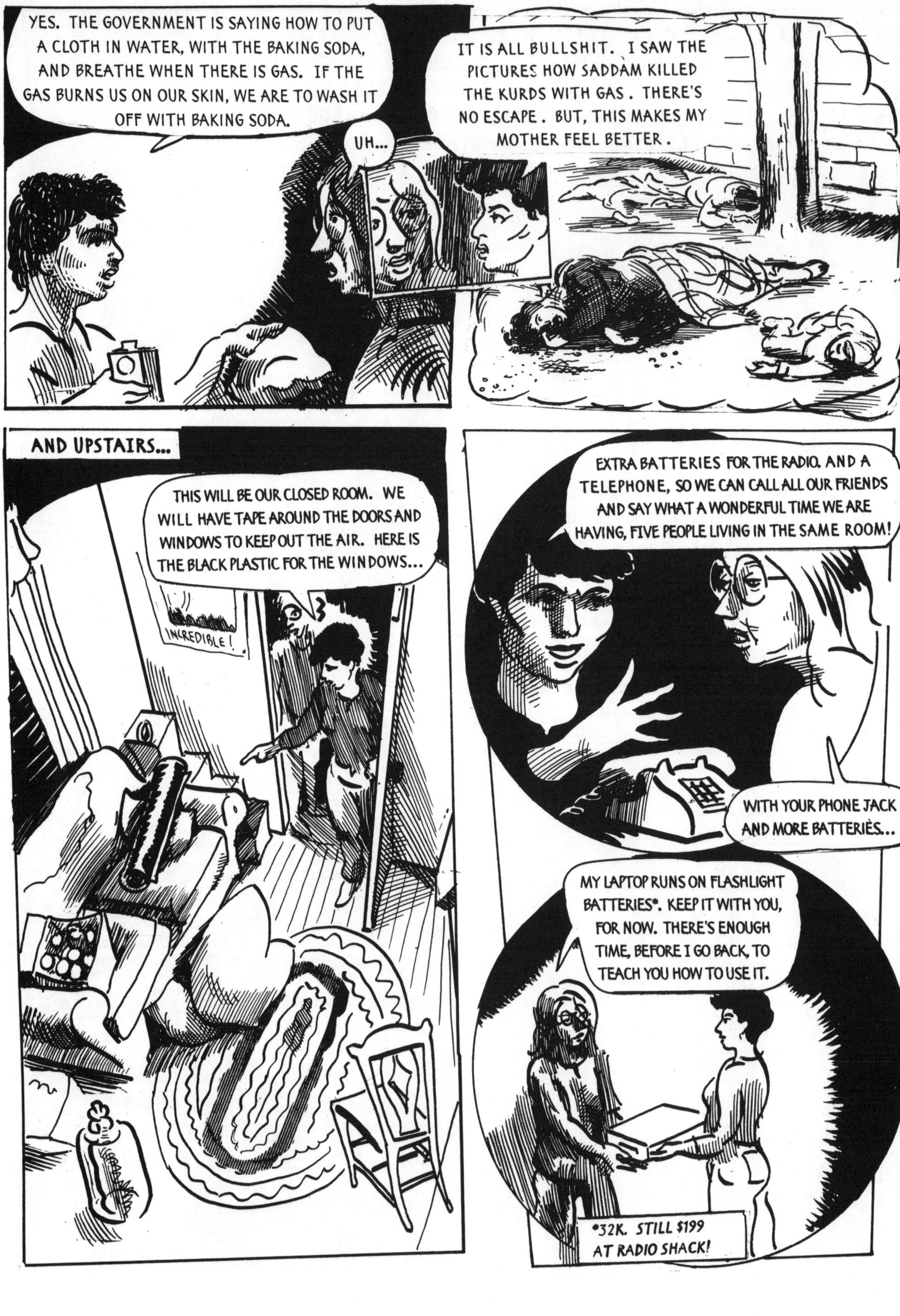
YES. THE GOVERNMENT IS SAYING HOW TO PUT A CLOTH IN WATER, WITH THE BAKING SODA, AND BREATHE WHEN THERE IS GAS. IF THE GAS BURNS US ON OUR SKIN, WE ARE TO WASH IT OFF WITH BAKING SODA.
UH...
IT IS ALL BULLSHIT. I SAW THE PICTURES HOW SADDAM KILLED THE KURDS WITH GAS. THERE'S NO ESCAPE. BUT, THIS MAKES MY MOTHER FEEL BETTER.
AND UPSTAIRS...
THIS WILL BE OUR CLOSED ROOM. WE WILL HAVE TAPE AROUND THE DOORS AND WINDOWS TO KEEP OUT THE AIR. HERE IS THE BLACK PLASTIC FOR THE WINDOWS...
INCREDIBLE!
EXTRA BATTERIES FOR THE RADIO. AND A TELEPHONE, SO WE CAN CALL ALL OUR FRIENDS AND SAY WHAT A WONDERFUL TIME WE ARE HAVING, FIVE PEOPLE LIVING IN THE SAME ROOM!
WITH YOUR PHONE JACK AND MORE BATTERIES...
MY LAPTOP RUNS ON FLASHLIGHT BATTERIES*. KEEP IT WITH YOU, FOR NOW. THERE'S ENOUGH TIME, BEFORE I GO BACK, TO TEACH YOU HOW TO USE IT.
*32K. STILL $199 AT RADIO SHACK!

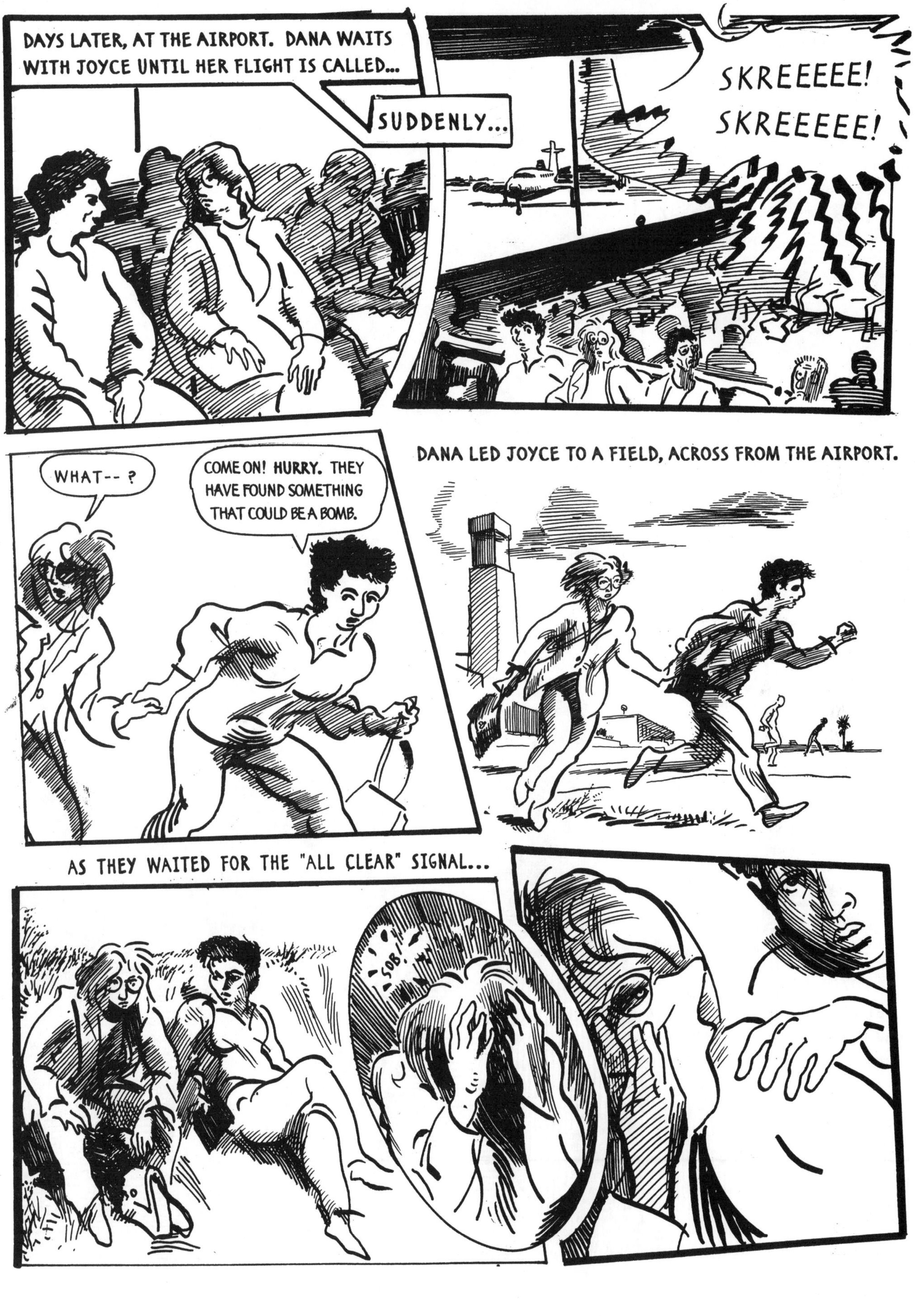
DAYS LATER, AT THE AIRPORT. DANA WAITS WITH JOYCE UNTIL HER FLIGHT IS CALLED...
SUDDENLY...
SKREEEEEE! SKREEEEEE!
WHAT-- ?
COME ON! HURRY. THEY HAVE FOUND SOMETHING THAT COULD BE A BOMB.
DANA LED JOYCE TO A FIELD, ACROSS FROM THE AIRPORT.
AS THEY WAITED FOR THE "ALL CLEAR" SIGNAL...
SOB!

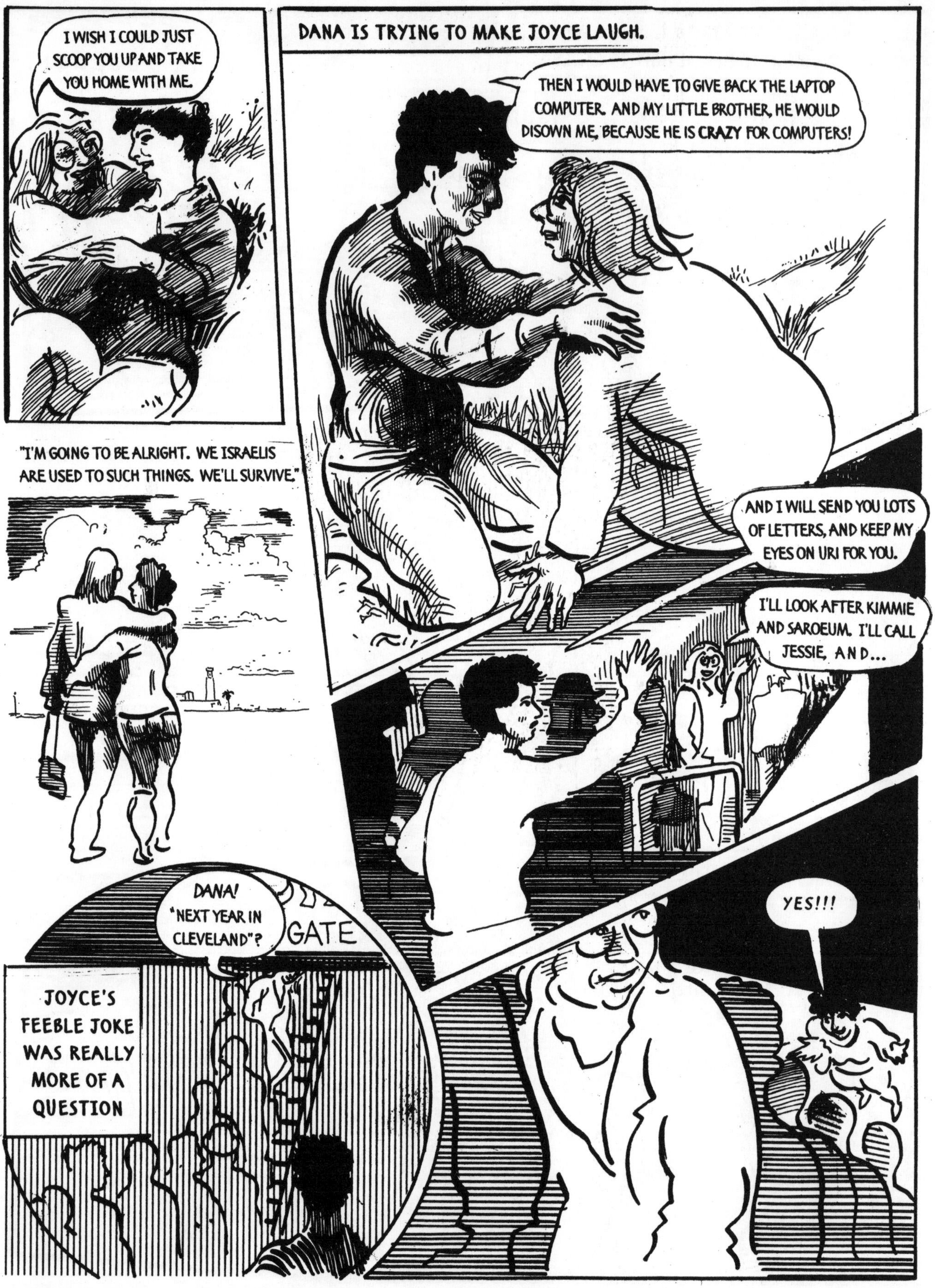
I WISH I COULD JUST SCOOP YOU UP AND TAKE YOU HOME WITH ME.
DANA IS TRYING TO MAKE JOYCE LAUGH.
THEN I WOULD HAVE TO GIVE BACK THE LAPTOP COMPUTER. AND MY LITTLE BROTHER, HE WOULD DISOWN ME, BECAUSE HE IS CRAZY FOR COMPUTERS!
"I'M GOING TO BE ALRIGHT. WE ISRAELIS ARE USED TO SUCH THINGS. WE'LL SURVIVE."
AND I WILL SEND YOU LOTS OF LETTERS, AND KEEP MY EYES ON URI FOR YOU.
I'LL LOOK AFTER KIMMIE AND SAROEUM. I'LL CALL JESSIE, AND...
DANA! "NEXT YEAR IN CLEVELAND"?
GATE
YES!!!
JOYCE'S FEEBLE JOKE WAS REALLY MORE OF A QUESTION

4

SYBIL CALLED NAOMI. NAOMI CALLED JOYCE.
SOON AFTER JOYCE RETURNED HOME, SHE BECAME VERY ILL. HARVEY HAD TO BRING HER IN TO THEIR HOSPITAL'S EMERGENCY ROOM. HE TOLD SYBIL...
IT'S JUST THAT EVERY SO OFTEN, WHEN I'VE BEEN UNDER A LITTLE STRESS, MY TEMPERATURE HEATS UP. NOTHING MAJOR.
JUST, PLEASE ... NO LECTURES.
THEY NEVER WORKED FOR ME.
BUT NO EXCUSES EITHER. WE BOTH KNOW WHAT'S GOING ON.
NAOMI WAS SERIOUSLY ILL DURING MUCH OF HER CHILDHOOD. JOYCE HELPED TAKE CARE OF HER. AS ADULTS, THEY SHARE SOME HEALTH PROBLEMS. IT'S SOMETIMES HARD FOR JOYCE TO TAKE ADVICE FROM HER "BABY SISTER".
WHEN'S THE LAST TIME YOU HAD A FLARE-UP, ANYHOW?
NOT SINCE I STARTED REALLY TAKING CARE OF MYSELF. WHICH MEANS KNOWING MY LIMITS. STOPPING FOR REST, WHEN I HAVE TO, NO MATTER WHAT I THINK I HAVE TO DO.
I'M HEALTHIER NOW THAN I'VE EVER BEEN. I FOUND A GOOD BOOK ABOUT HOW OUR ATTITUDE ABOUT ILLNESS INFLUENCES OUR HEALTH, PROBABLY BY AFFECTING OUR IMMUNE SYSTEMS.
IS THIS THAT NORMAN COUSINS THING? ABOUT HOW HE BEAT CANCER WITH LAUGHTER 'CAUSE HE KEPT WATCHING VIDEOS OF LAUREL & HARDY AND THE MARX BROTHERS?

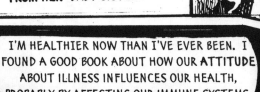

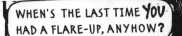

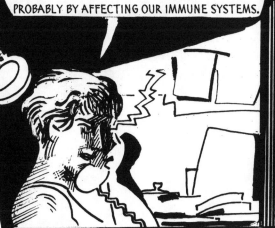

YOU MEAN *ANATOMY OF AN ILLNESS.* NO, I'M SENDING YOU SOMETHING BY A DOCTOR NAMED BERNIE SIEGEL.

THE BALD GUY, RIGHT? TALKS ABOUT MEDITATION AND "PROJECTING POSITIVE THOUGHTS"? I **HATE** GUIDED IMAGERY...

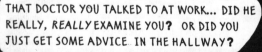

AND NOW THAT WE'VE GOT EVERYONE THINKING ABOUT DOCTORS...

HONEY, I THINK THAT LUMP'S GROWN BIGGER. IN FACT, I'M POSITIVE. IT WASN'T THIS BIG BEFORE I WENT AWAY. YOU SAID YOU WERE GONNA GET IT CHECKED. DID YOU?

NO.

THAT DOCTOR YOU TALKED TO AT WORK... DID HE REALLY, *REALLY* EXAMINE YOU? OR DID YOU JUST GET SOME ADVICE IN THE HALLWAY?

HARVEY KNOWS HE'S NOT GOING TO GET AWAY WITH THIS

OKAY... HE *DIDN'T* REALLY GIVE ME AN EXAMINATION.

YOU PROMISED TO GET IT CHECKED. I WANT YOU TO MAKE AN APPOINTMENT. YOU *SAID* YOU WOULD.

JOYCE AND SLIM BEGAN FIGHTING WHEN SHE FOUND OUT HE HADN'T DONE MUCH OF WHAT HE PROMISED HE'D DO-- GET PRICE QUOTES, START REPAIRS-- AT THE NEW HOUSE. AND WHY?

AS A CHRISTIAN MAN, AND A FRIEND TO BOTH YOU AND HARVEY, I FEEL THAT GOD WANTS ME TO SAVE YOUR MARRIAGE.

WHA-A-AT?

YOU TWO ARE HEADED DOWN THE PATH TOWARDS DIVORCE. HARVEY SAYS YOUR MIND IS ON YOUR CAREER, AND NOT YOUR HUSBAND, AND THAT YOU'RE SPENDING ALL HIS MONEY ON THIS HOUSE. A HOUSE THAT WOULD BE *YOURS* IN A DIVORCE SETTLEMENT. I CAN'T LET YOU DO THAT TO HIM.

I'M GETTING HARVEY!

DID YOU TELL SLIM I WAS GONNA STEAL ALL YOUR MONEY AND LEAVE YOU?

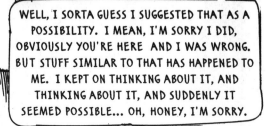

WELL, I SORTA GUESS I SUGGESTED THAT AS A POSSIBILITY. I MEAN, I'M SORRY I DID, OBVIOUSLY YOU'RE HERE AND I WAS WRONG. BUT STUFF SIMILAR TO THAT HAS HAPPENED TO ME. I KEPT ON THINKING ABOUT IT, AND THINKING ABOUT IT, AND SUDDENLY IT SEEMED POSSIBLE... OH, HONEY, I'M SORRY.

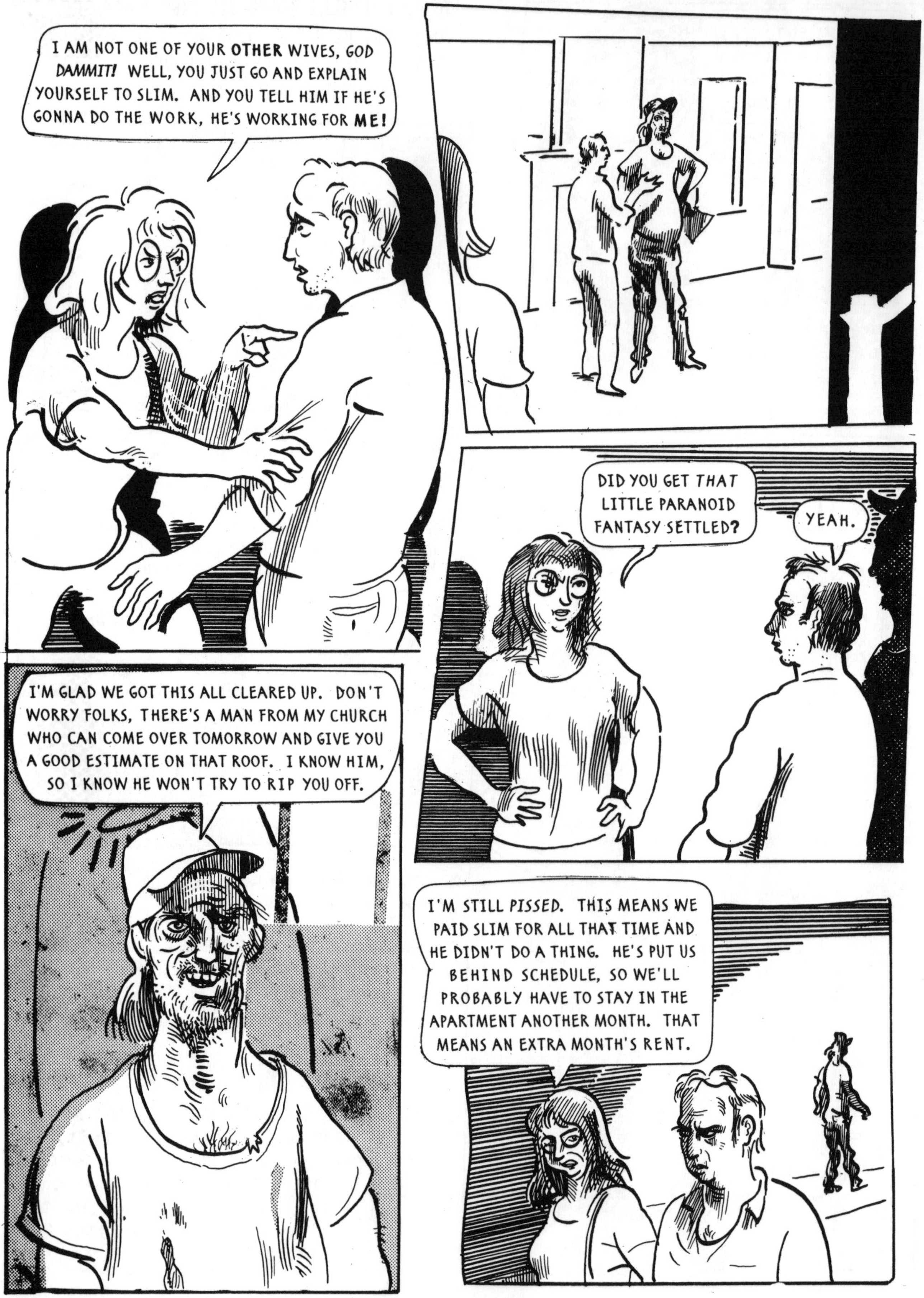
I AM NOT ONE OF YOUR **OTHER** WIVES, GOD *DAMMIT!* WELL, YOU JUST GO AND EXPLAIN YOURSELF TO SLIM. AND YOU TELL HIM IF HE'S GONNA DO THE WORK, HE'S WORKING FOR **ME!**
DID YOU GET *THAT* LITTLE PARANOID FANTASY SETTLED?
YEAH.
I'M GLAD WE GOT THIS ALL CLEARED UP. DON'T WORRY FOLKS, THERE'S A MAN FROM MY CHURCH WHO CAN COME OVER TOMORROW AND GIVE YOU A GOOD ESTIMATE ON THAT ROOF. I KNOW HIM, SO I KNOW HE WON'T TRY TO RIP YOU OFF.
I'M STILL *PISSED*. THIS MEANS WE PAID SLIM FOR ALL THAT TIME AND HE DIDN'T DO A THING. HE'S PUT US BEHIND SCHEDULE, SO WE'LL PROBABLY HAVE TO STAY IN THE APARTMENT ANOTHER MONTH. THAT MEANS AN EXTRA MONTH'S RENT.

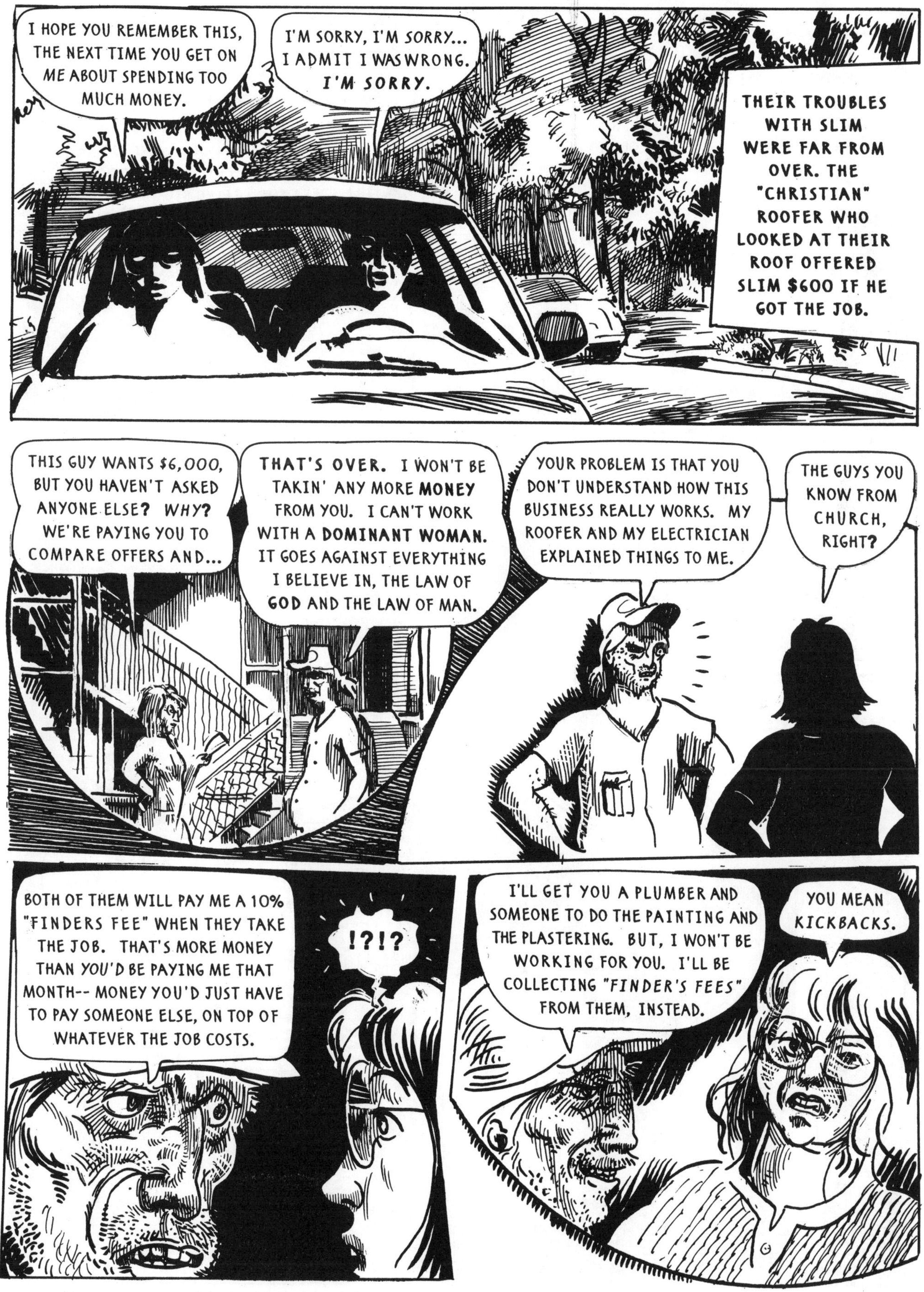
I HOPE YOU REMEMBER THIS, THE NEXT TIME YOU GET ON *ME* ABOUT SPENDING TOO MUCH MONEY.
I'M SORRY, I'M *SORRY*... I ADMIT I WAS WRONG. ***I'M SORRY.***
THEIR TROUBLES WITH SLIM WERE FAR FROM OVER. THE "CHRISTIAN" ROOFER WHO LOOKED AT THEIR ROOF OFFERED SLIM $600 IF HE GOT THE JOB.
THIS GUY WANTS $6,000, BUT YOU HAVEN'T ASKED ANYONE ELSE**?** *WHY***?** WE'RE PAYING YOU TO COMPARE OFFERS AND...
THAT'S OVER. I WON'T BE TAKIN' ANY MORE **MONEY** FROM YOU. I CAN'T WORK WITH A **DOMINANT WOMAN.** IT GOES AGAINST EVERYTHING I BELIEVE IN, THE LAW OF **GOD** AND THE LAW OF MAN.
YOUR PROBLEM IS THAT YOU DON'T UNDERSTAND HOW THIS BUSINESS REALLY WORKS. MY ROOFER AND MY ELECTRICIAN EXPLAINED THINGS TO ME.
THE GUYS YOU KNOW FROM CHURCH, RIGHT**?**
BOTH OF THEM WILL PAY ME A 10% "FINDERS FEE" WHEN THEY TAKE THE JOB. THAT'S MORE MONEY THAN *YOU'D* BE PAYING ME THAT MONTH-- MONEY YOU'D JUST HAVE TO PAY SOMEONE ELSE, ON TOP OF WHATEVER THE JOB COSTS.
!?!?
I'LL GET YOU A PLUMBER AND SOMEONE TO DO THE PAINTING AND THE PLASTERING. BUT, I WON'T BE WORKING FOR YOU. I'LL BE COLLECTING "*FINDER'S FEES*" FROM THEM, INSTEAD.
YOU MEAN *KICKBACKS.*

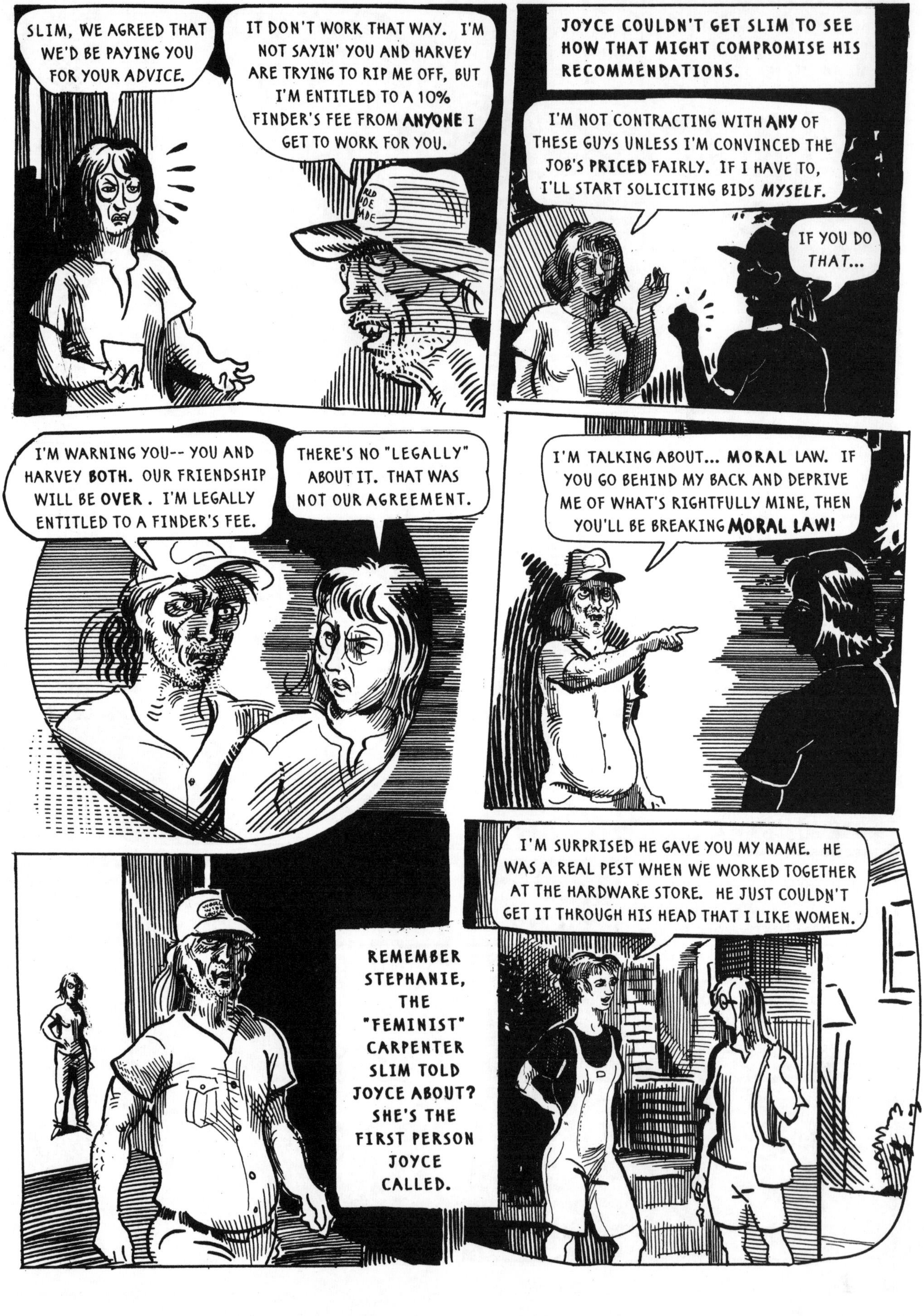
SLIM, WE AGREED THAT WE'D BE PAYING YOU FOR YOUR ADVICE.
IT DON'T WORK THAT WAY. I'M NOT SAYIN' YOU AND HARVEY ARE TRYING TO RIP ME OFF, BUT I'M ENTITLED TO A 10% FINDER'S FEE FROM ANYONE I GET TO WORK FOR YOU.
JOYCE COULDN'T GET SLIM TO SEE HOW THAT MIGHT COMPROMISE HIS RECOMMENDATIONS.
I'M NOT CONTRACTING WITH ANY OF THESE GUYS UNLESS I'M CONVINCED THE JOB'S PRICED FAIRLY. IF I HAVE TO, I'LL START SOLICITING BIDS MYSELF.
IF YOU DO THAT...
I'M WARNING YOU-- YOU AND HARVEY BOTH. OUR FRIENDSHIP WILL BE OVER . I'M LEGALLY ENTITLED TO A FINDER'S FEE.
THERE'S NO "LEGALLY" ABOUT IT. THAT WAS NOT OUR AGREEMENT.
I'M TALKING ABOUT... MORAL LAW. IF YOU GO BEHIND MY BACK AND DEPRIVE ME OF WHAT'S RIGHTFULLY MINE, THEN YOU'LL BE BREAKING MORAL LAW!
REMEMBER STEPHANIE, THE "FEMINIST" CARPENTER SLIM TOLD JOYCE ABOUT? SHE'S THE FIRST PERSON JOYCE CALLED.
I'M SURPRISED HE GAVE YOU MY NAME. HE WAS A REAL PEST WHEN WE WORKED TOGETHER AT THE HARDWARE STORE. HE JUST COULDN'T GET IT THROUGH HIS HEAD THAT I LIKE WOMEN.

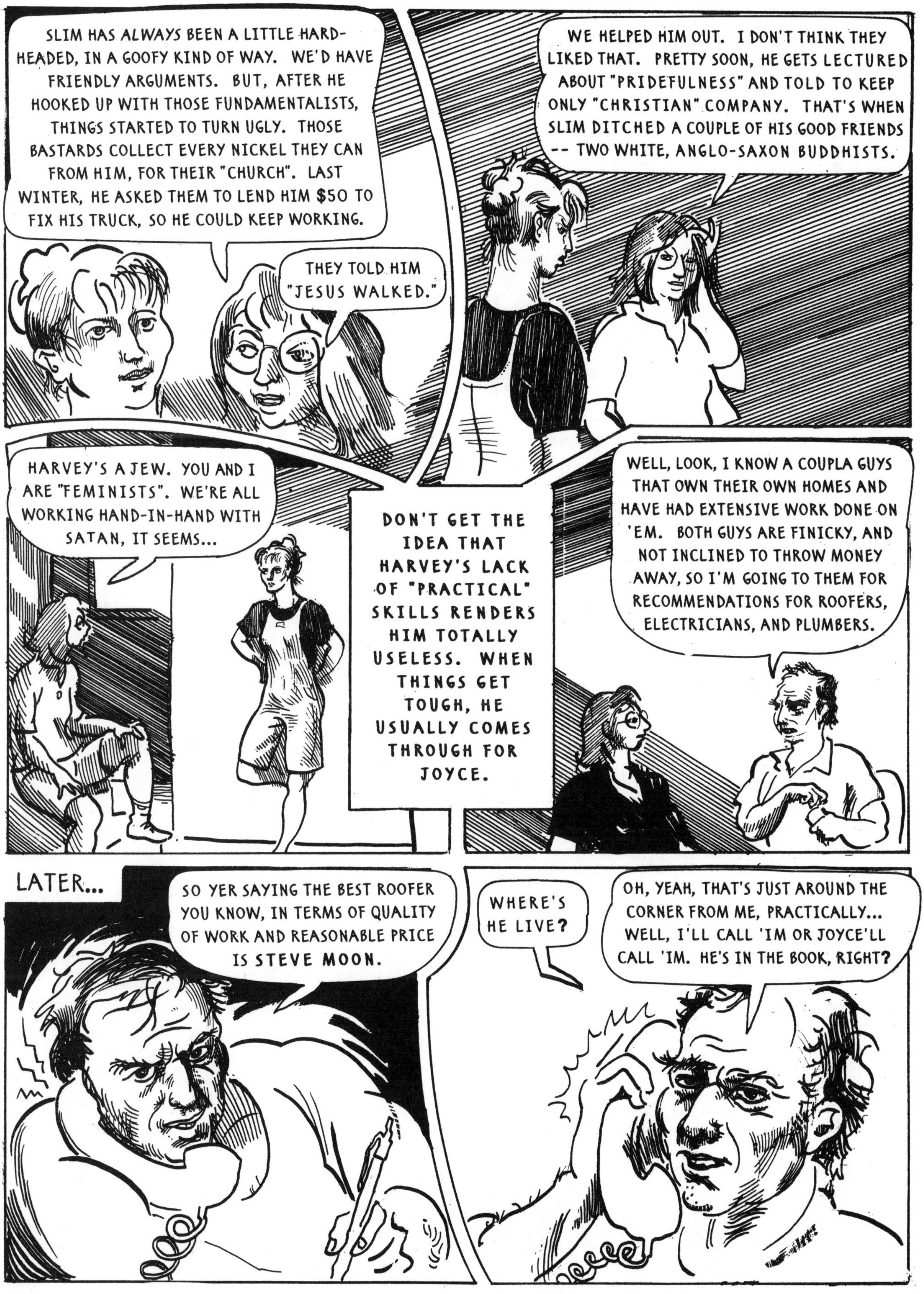
SLIM HAS ALWAYS BEEN A LITTLE HARD-HEADED, IN A GOOFY KIND OF WAY. WE'D HAVE FRIENDLY ARGUMENTS. BUT, AFTER HE HOOKED UP WITH THOSE FUNDAMENTALISTS, THINGS STARTED TO TURN UGLY. THOSE BASTARDS COLLECT EVERY NICKEL THEY CAN FROM HIM, FOR THEIR "CHURCH". LAST WINTER, HE ASKED THEM TO LEND HIM $50 TO FIX HIS TRUCK, SO HE COULD KEEP WORKING.
THEY TOLD HIM "JESUS WALKED."
WE HELPED HIM OUT. I DON'T THINK THEY LIKED THAT. PRETTY SOON, HE GETS LECTURED ABOUT "PRIDEFULNESS" AND TOLD TO KEEP ONLY "CHRISTIAN" COMPANY. THAT'S WHEN SLIM DITCHED A COUPLE OF HIS GOOD FRIENDS -- TWO WHITE, ANGLO-SAXON BUDDHISTS.
HARVEY'S A JEW. YOU AND I ARE "FEMINISTS". WE'RE ALL WORKING HAND-IN-HAND WITH SATAN, IT SEEMS...
DON'T GET THE IDEA THAT HARVEY'S LACK OF "PRACTICAL" SKILLS RENDERS HIM TOTALLY USELESS. WHEN THINGS GET TOUGH, HE USUALLY COMES THROUGH FOR JOYCE.
WELL, LOOK, I KNOW A COUPLA GUYS THAT OWN THEIR OWN HOMES AND HAVE HAD EXTENSIVE WORK DONE ON 'EM. BOTH GUYS ARE FINICKY, AND NOT INCLINED TO THROW MONEY AWAY, SO I'M GOING TO THEM FOR RECOMMENDATIONS FOR ROOFERS, ELECTRICIANS, AND PLUMBERS.
LATER...
SO YER SAYING THE BEST ROOFER YOU KNOW, IN TERMS OF QUALITY OF WORK AND REASONABLE PRICE IS STEVE MOON.
WHERE'S HE LIVE?
OH, YEAH, THAT'S JUST AROUND THE CORNER FROM ME, PRACTICALLY... WELL, I'LL CALL 'IM OR JOYCE'LL CALL 'IM. HE'S IN THE BOOK, RIGHT?

MOON LOOKED AT THEIR NEW HOUSE.

THE CITY HOUSING INSPECTOR DIDN'T CITE YOU FOR THE ROOF. AND FROM WHAT I'VE SEEN HERE, YOU CAN PROBABLY GET BY FOR ANOTHER 5-6 YEARS, BEFORE YOU'LL NEED MAJOR REPAIRS. ALL YOU NEED NOW IS WHAT WE CALL A ROOF "TUNE-UP", WHICH'LL COST YOU ABOUT $49.95.

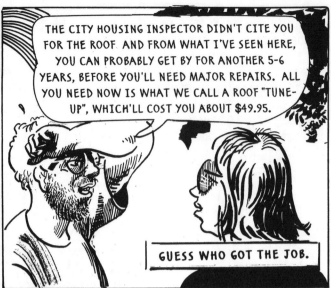

GUESS WHO GOT THE JOB.

HARVEY POLLED THE DOCTORS AT WORK...

YOU CAN GET CHEAPER GUYS THAN HIM, BUT HIS PRICES ARE FAIR, AND HE'S FAST. IN AND OUT. ALL THINGS CONSIDERED, HE'S THE BEST ELECTRICIAN I KNOW OF.

HE WAS RIGHT! AND IT TURNED OUT, THE NEW ELECTRICIAN CHARGED A LOT LESS THAN WHAT SLIM'S OTHER FRIEND WANTED.

WHICH LEFT SLIM NO LONGER SPEAKING TO JOYCE OR HARVEY. HE FIGURED JOYCE HAD CHEATED HIM, SOMEHOW.

SEPTEMBER, 1990

I'M GONNA DO ALL THE MOVING OF MY BOOKS, RECORDS AND PAPERS MYSELF. IT'S GONNA TAKE A COUPLE MONTHS TO GET THAT HOUSE IN SHAPE SO WE CAN MOVE INTO IT, SO I MIGHT AS WELL BE FILLIN' IT UP.

SO, ALMOST EVERY DAY, THROUGH SEPTEMBER AND OCTOBER

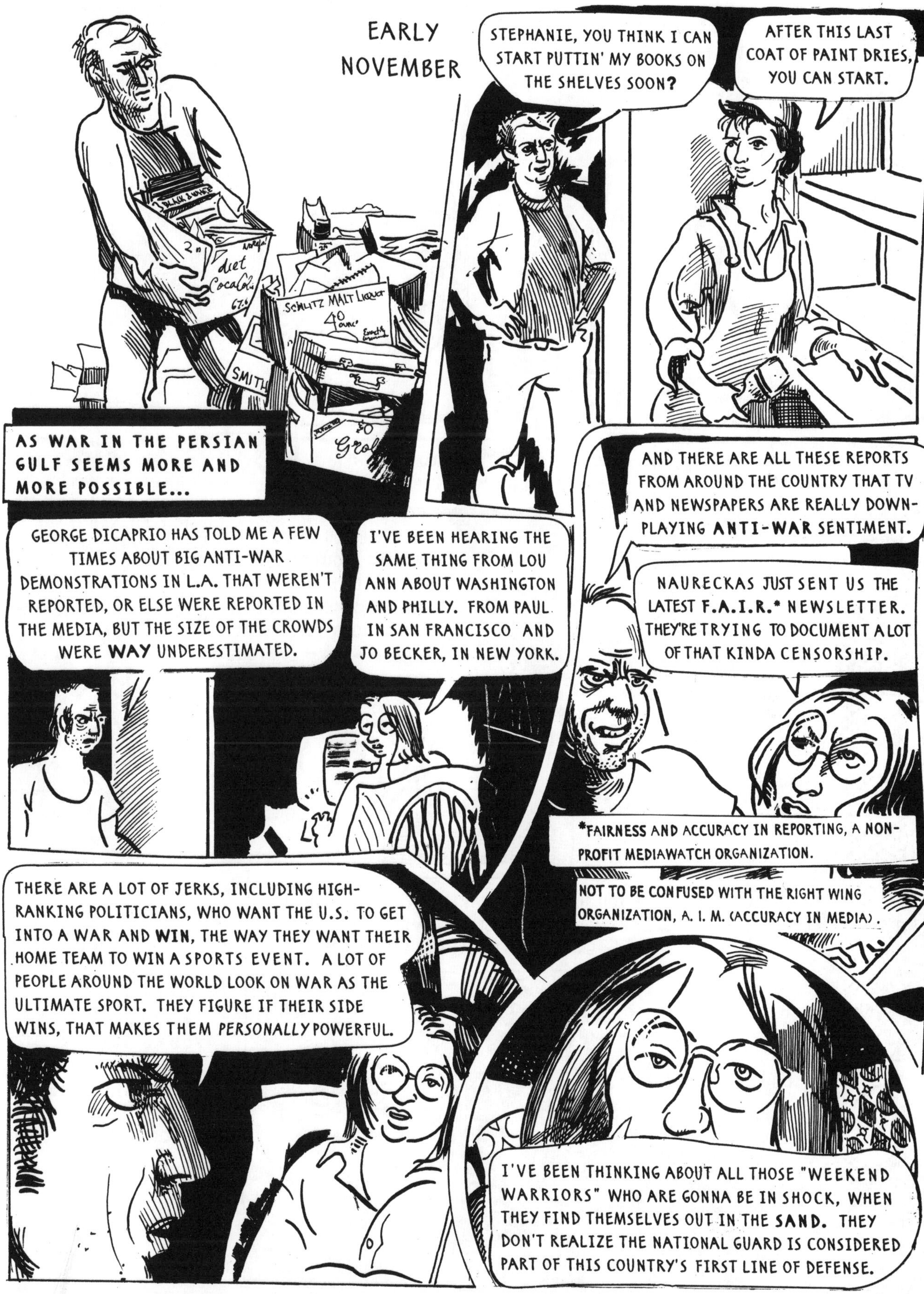
EARLY NOVEMBER
STEPHANIE, YOU THINK I CAN START PUTTIN' MY BOOKS ON THE SHELVES SOON?
AFTER THIS LAST COAT OF PAINT DRIES, YOU CAN START.
AS WAR IN THE PERSIAN GULF SEEMS MORE AND MORE POSSIBLE...
GEORGE DICAPRIO HAS TOLD ME A FEW TIMES ABOUT BIG ANTI-WAR DEMONSTRATIONS IN L.A. THAT WEREN'T REPORTED, OR ELSE WERE REPORTED IN THE MEDIA, BUT THE SIZE OF THE CROWDS WERE WAY UNDERESTIMATED.
I'VE BEEN HEARING THE SAME THING FROM LOU ANN ABOUT WASHINGTON AND PHILLY. FROM PAUL IN SAN FRANCISCO AND JO BECKER, IN NEW YORK.
AND THERE ARE ALL THESE REPORTS FROM AROUND THE COUNTRY THAT TV AND NEWSPAPERS ARE REALLY DOWN-PLAYING ANTI-WAR SENTIMENT.
NAURECKAS JUST SENT US THE LATEST F.A.I.R.* NEWSLETTER. THEY'RE TRYING TO DOCUMENT A LOT OF THAT KINDA CENSORSHIP.
*FAIRNESS AND ACCURACY IN REPORTING, A NON-PROFIT MEDIAWATCH ORGANIZATION.
NOT TO BE CONFUSED WITH THE RIGHT WING ORGANIZATION, A. I. M. (ACCURACY IN MEDIA).
THERE ARE A LOT OF JERKS, INCLUDING HIGH-RANKING POLITICIANS, WHO WANT THE U.S. TO GET INTO A WAR AND WIN, THE WAY THEY WANT THEIR HOME TEAM TO WIN A SPORTS EVENT. A LOT OF PEOPLE AROUND THE WORLD LOOK ON WAR AS THE ULTIMATE SPORT. THEY FIGURE IF THEIR SIDE WINS, THAT MAKES THEM PERSONALLY POWERFUL.
I'VE BEEN THINKING ABOUT ALL THOSE "WEEKEND WARRIORS" WHO ARE GONNA BE IN SHOCK, WHEN THEY FIND THEMSELVES OUT IN THE SAND. THEY DON'T REALIZE THE NATIONAL GUARD IS CONSIDERED PART OF THIS COUNTRY'S FIRST LINE OF DEFENSE.

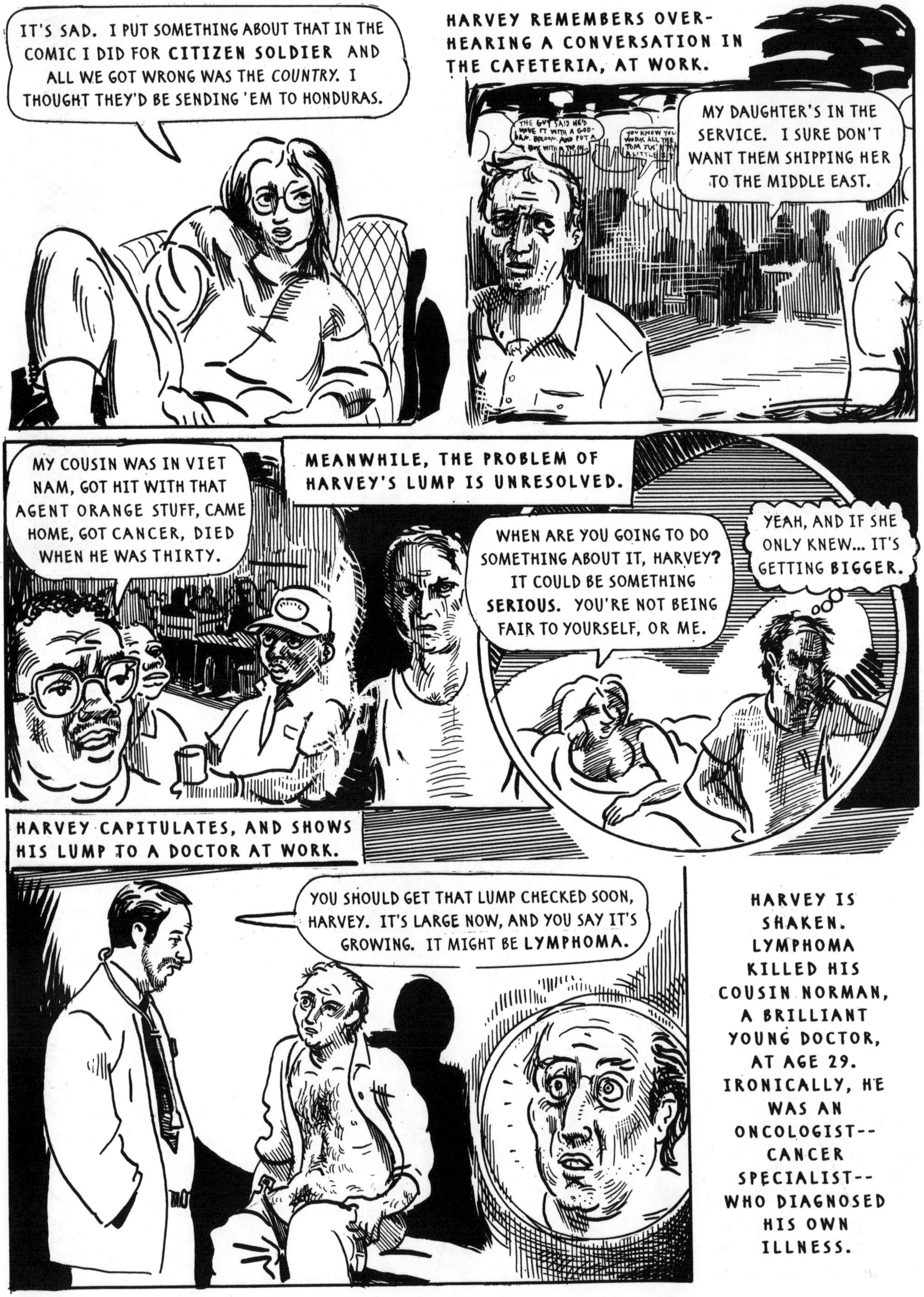

IT'S SAD. I PUT SOMETHING ABOUT THAT IN THE COMIC I DID FOR CITIZEN SOLDIER AND ALL WE GOT WRONG WAS THE COUNTRY. I THOUGHT THEY'D BE SENDING 'EM TO HONDURAS.
HARVEY REMEMBERS OVER-HEARING A CONVERSATION IN THE CAFETERIA, AT WORK.
THE GUY SAID HE'D MOVE IT WITH A GOD-DAM. BROOM. AND PUT A BOX WITH A TOP ON..
MY DAUGHTER'S IN THE SERVICE. I SURE DON'T WANT THEM SHIPPING HER TO THE MIDDLE EAST.
MY COUSIN WAS IN VIET NAM, GOT HIT WITH THAT AGENT ORANGE STUFF, CAME HOME, GOT CANCER, DIED WHEN HE WAS THIRTY.
MEANWHILE, THE PROBLEM OF HARVEY'S LUMP IS UNRESOLVED.
WHEN ARE YOU GOING TO DO SOMETHING ABOUT IT, HARVEY? IT COULD BE SOMETHING SERIOUS. YOU'RE NOT BEING FAIR TO YOURSELF, OR ME.
YEAH, AND IF SHE ONLY KNEW... IT'S GETTING BIGGER.
HARVEY CAPITULATES, AND SHOWS HIS LUMP TO A DOCTOR AT WORK.
YOU SHOULD GET THAT LUMP CHECKED SOON, HARVEY. IT'S LARGE NOW, AND YOU SAY IT'S GROWING. IT MIGHT BE LYMPHOMA.
HARVEY IS SHAKEN. LYMPHOMA KILLED HIS COUSIN NORMAN, A BRILLIANT YOUNG DOCTOR, AT AGE 29. IRONICALLY, HE WAS AN ONCOLOGIST--CANCER SPECIALIST--WHO DIAGNOSED HIS OWN ILLNESS.

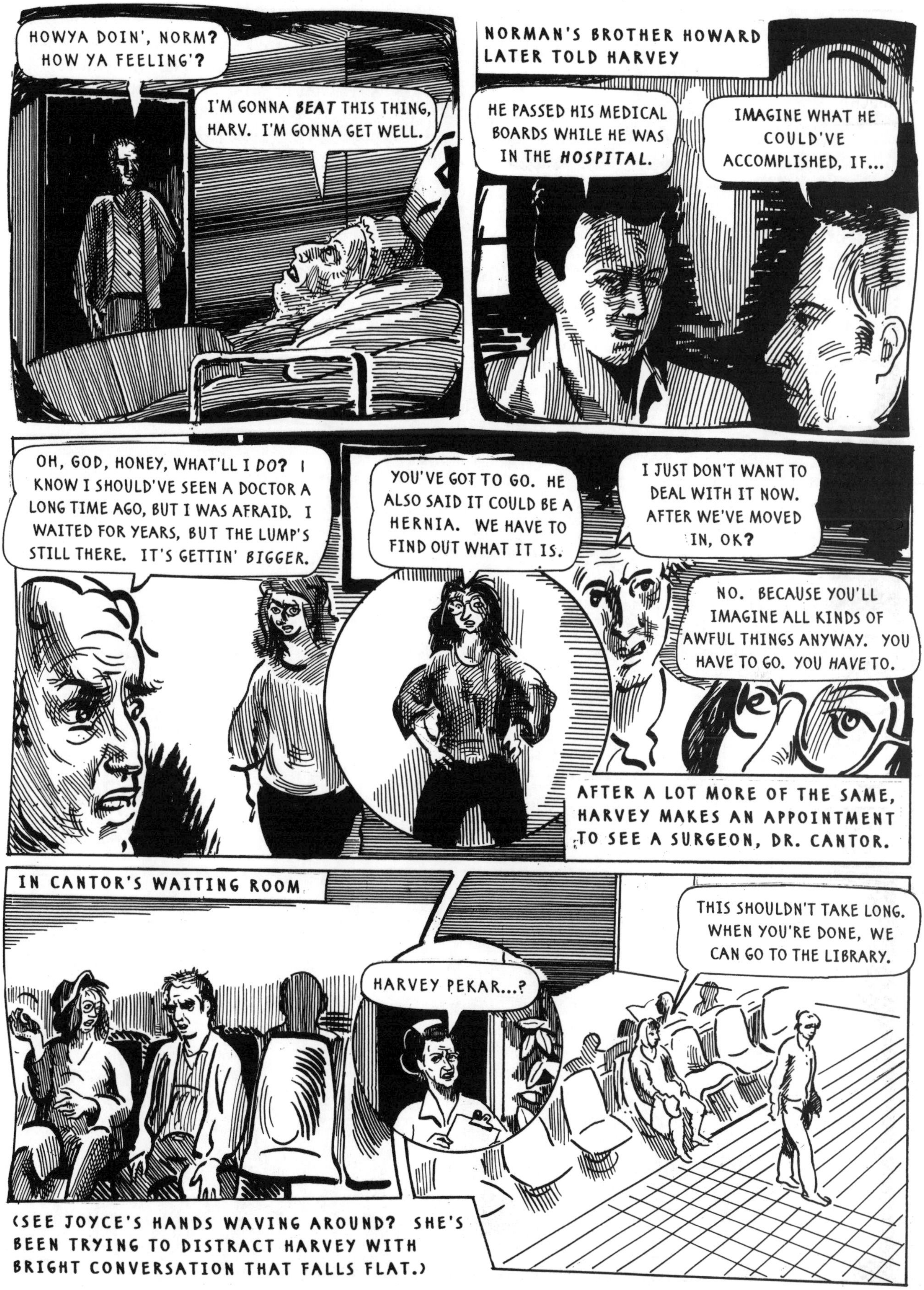
HOWYA DOIN', NORM? HOW YA FEELING'?
I'M GONNA BEAT THIS THING, HARV. I'M GONNA GET WELL.
NORMAN'S BROTHER HOWARD LATER TOLD HARVEY
HE PASSED HIS MEDICAL BOARDS WHILE HE WAS IN THE HOSPITAL.
IMAGINE WHAT HE COULD'VE ACCOMPLISHED, IF...
OH, GOD, HONEY, WHAT'LL I DO? I KNOW I SHOULD'VE SEEN A DOCTOR A LONG TIME AGO, BUT I WAS AFRAID. I WAITED FOR YEARS, BUT THE LUMP'S STILL THERE. IT'S GETTIN' BIGGER.
YOU'VE GOT TO GO. HE ALSO SAID IT COULD BE A HERNIA. WE HAVE TO FIND OUT WHAT IT IS.
I JUST DON'T WANT TO DEAL WITH IT NOW. AFTER WE'VE MOVED IN, OK?
NO. BECAUSE YOU'LL IMAGINE ALL KINDS OF AWFUL THINGS ANYWAY. YOU HAVE TO GO. YOU HAVE TO.
AFTER A LOT MORE OF THE SAME, HARVEY MAKES AN APPOINTMENT TO SEE A SURGEON, DR. CANTOR.
IN CANTOR'S WAITING ROOM
HARVEY PEKAR...?
THIS SHOULDN'T TAKE LONG. WHEN YOU'RE DONE, WE CAN GO TO THE LIBRARY.
(SEE JOYCE'S HANDS WAVING AROUND? SHE'S BEEN TRYING TO DISTRACT HARVEY WITH BRIGHT CONVERSATION THAT FALLS FLAT.)

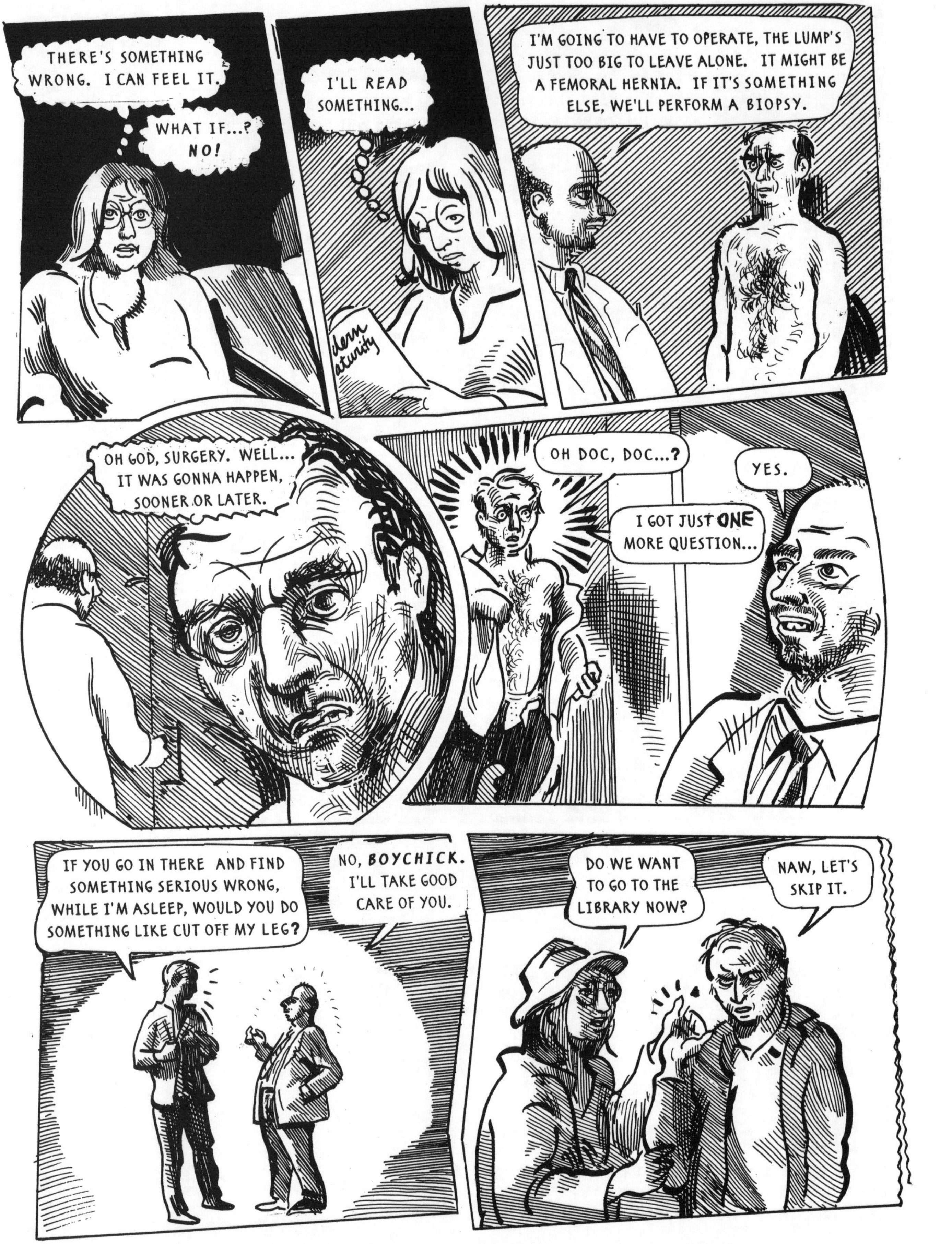
THERE'S SOMETHING WRONG. I CAN FEEL IT.
WHAT IF...? NO!
I'LL READ SOMETHING...
I'M GOING TO HAVE TO OPERATE, THE LUMP'S JUST TOO BIG TO LEAVE ALONE. IT MIGHT BE A FEMORAL HERNIA. IF IT'S SOMETHING ELSE, WE'LL PERFORM A BIOPSY.
OH GOD, SURGERY. WELL... IT WAS GONNA HAPPEN, SOONER OR LATER.
OH DOC, DOC...?
YES.
I GOT JUST ONE MORE QUESTION...
IF YOU GO IN THERE AND FIND SOMETHING SERIOUS WRONG, WHILE I'M ASLEEP, WOULD YOU DO SOMETHING LIKE CUT OFF MY LEG?
NO, BOYCHICK. I'LL TAKE GOOD CARE OF YOU.
DO WE WANT TO GO TO THE LIBRARY NOW?
NAW, LET'S SKIP IT.

5

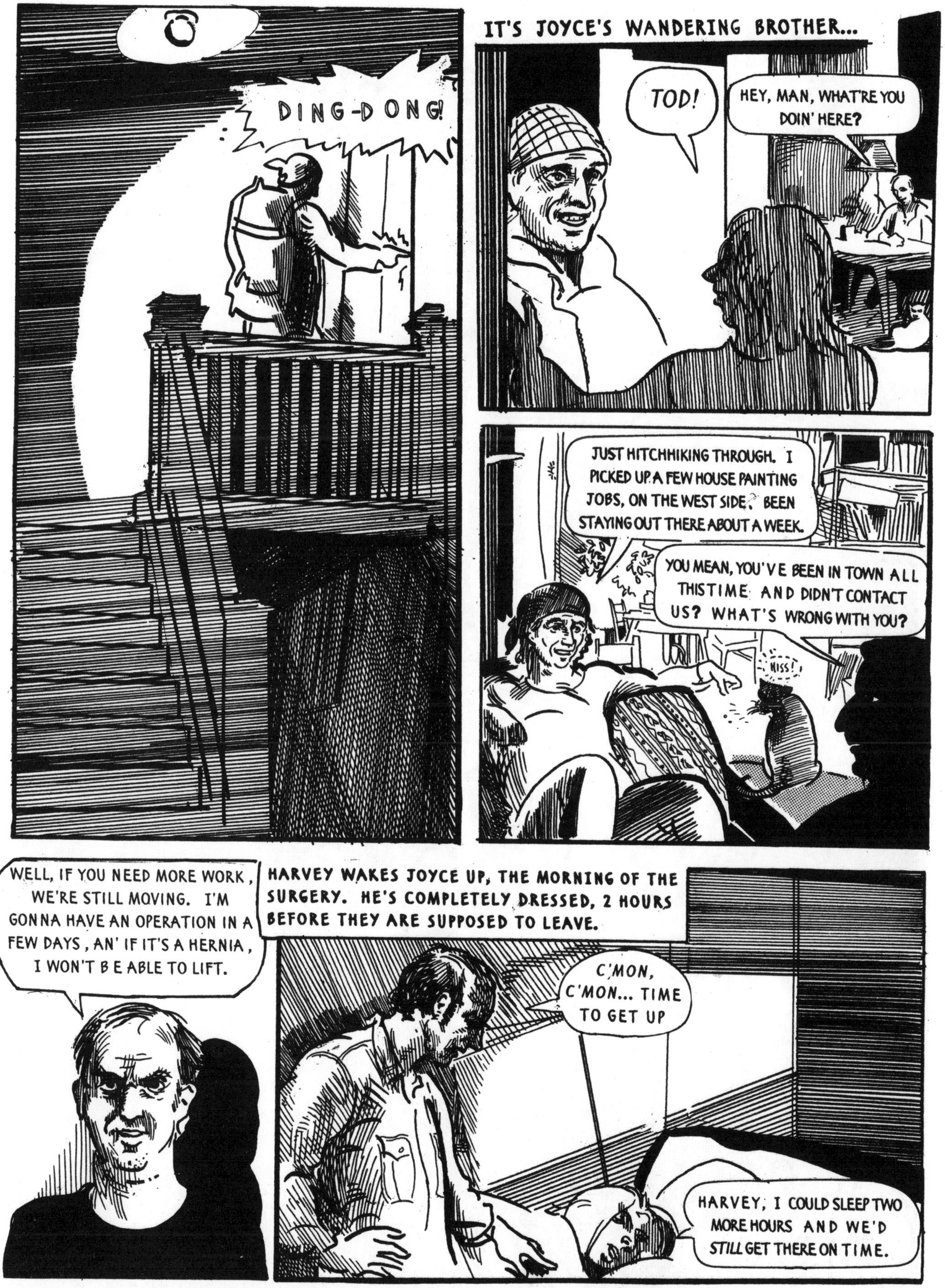
DING-DONG!
IT'S JOYCE'S WANDERING BROTHER...
TOD!
HEY, MAN, WHAT'RE YOU DOIN' HERE?
JUST HITCHHIKING THROUGH. I PICKED UP A FEW HOUSE PAINTING JOBS, ON THE WEST SIDE. BEEN STAYING OUT THERE ABOUT A WEEK.
YOU MEAN, YOU'VE BEEN IN TOWN ALL THIS TIME AND DIDN'T CONTACT US? WHAT'S WRONG WITH YOU?
HISS!
WELL, IF YOU NEED MORE WORK, WE'RE STILL MOVING. I'M GONNA HAVE AN OPERATION IN A FEW DAYS, AN' IF IT'S A HERNIA, I WON'T BE ABLE TO LIFT.
HARVEY WAKES JOYCE UP, THE MORNING OF THE SURGERY. HE'S COMPLETELY DRESSED, 2 HOURS BEFORE THEY ARE SUPPOSED TO LEAVE.
C'MON, C'MON... TIME TO GET UP
HARVEY, I COULD SLEEP TWO MORE HOURS AND WE'D *STILL* GET THERE ON TIME.

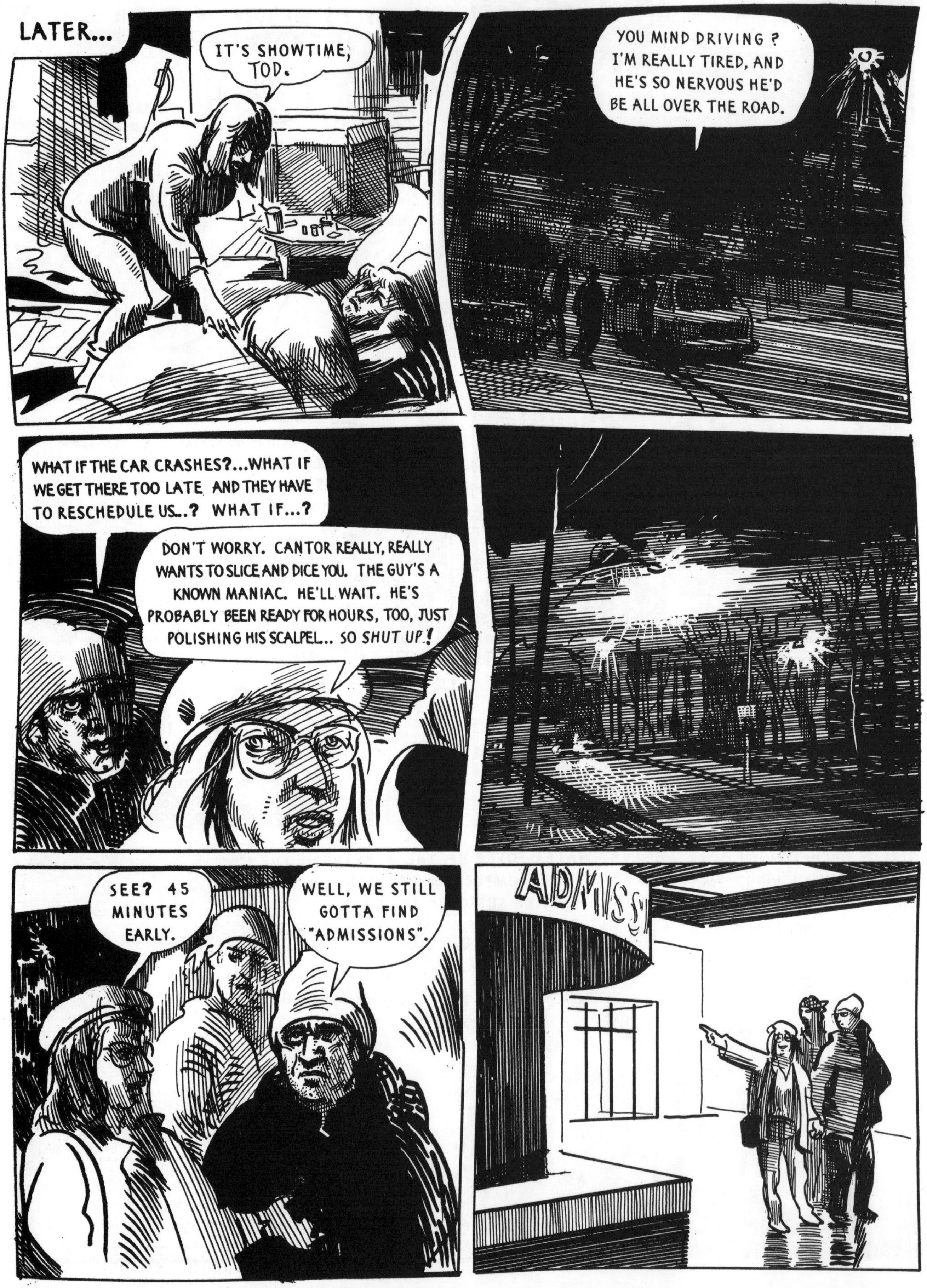
LATER...
IT'S SHOWTIME, TOD.
YOU MIND DRIVING? I'M REALLY TIRED, AND HE'S SO NERVOUS HE'D BE ALL OVER THE ROAD.
WHAT IF THE CAR CRASHES?...WHAT IF WE GET THERE TOO LATE AND THEY HAVE TO RESCHEDULE US..? WHAT IF...?
DON'T WORRY. CANTOR REALLY, REALLY WANTS TO SLICE AND DICE YOU. THE GUY'S A KNOWN MANIAC. HE'LL WAIT. HE'S PROBABLY BEEN READY FOR HOURS, TOO, JUST POLISHING HIS SCALPEL.. SO SHUT UP!
SEE? 45 MINUTES EARLY.
WELL, WE STILL GOTTA FIND "ADMISSIONS".

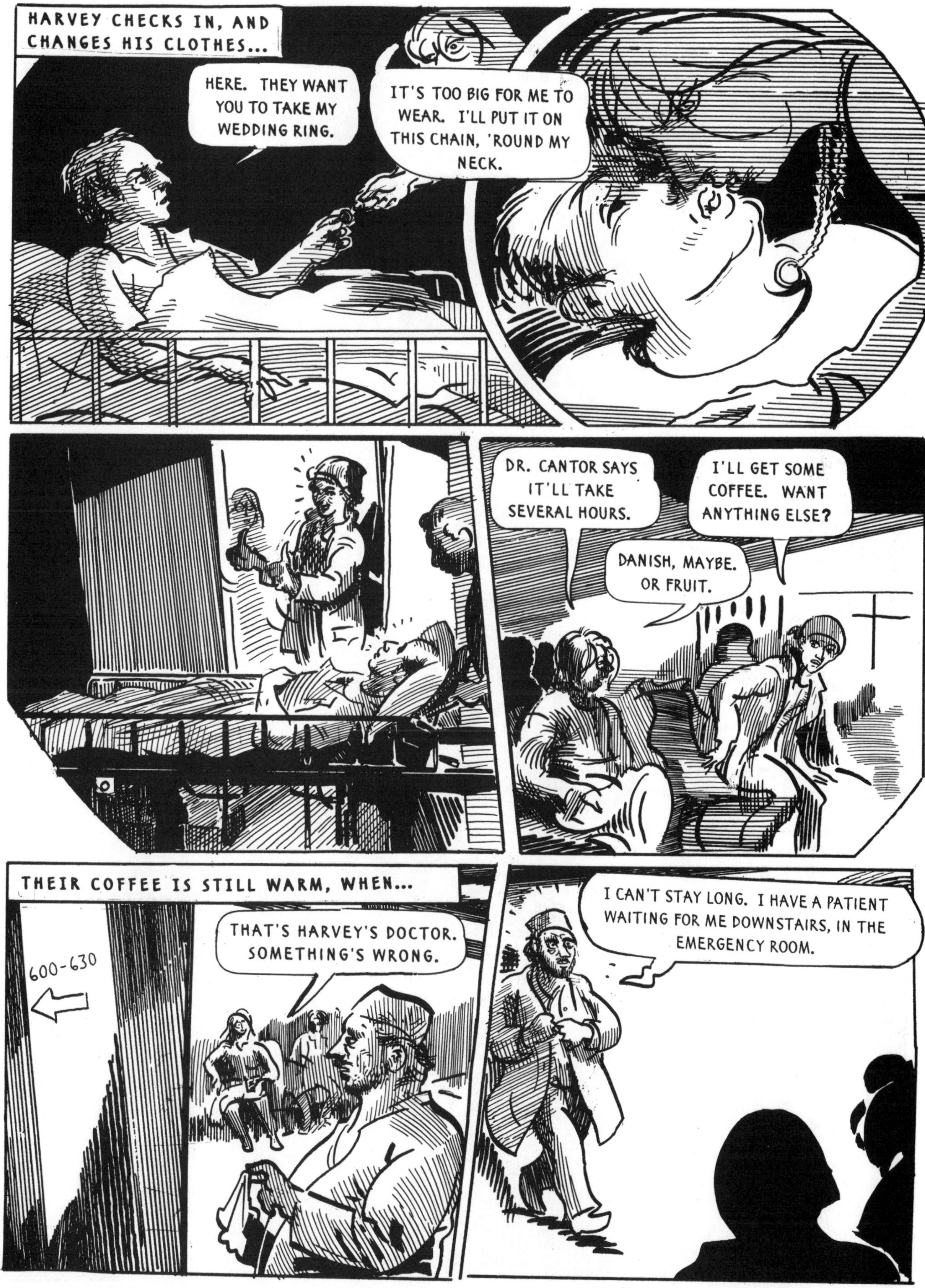
HARVEY CHECKS IN, AND CHANGES HIS CLOTHES...
HERE. THEY WANT YOU TO TAKE MY WEDDING RING.
IT'S TOO BIG FOR ME TO WEAR. I'LL PUT IT ON THIS CHAIN, 'ROUND MY NECK.
DR. CANTOR SAYS IT'LL TAKE SEVERAL HOURS.
I'LL GET SOME COFFEE. WANT ANYTHING ELSE?
DANISH, MAYBE. OR FRUIT.
THEIR COFFEE IS STILL WARM, WHEN...
600-630
THAT'S HARVEY'S DOCTOR. SOMETHING'S WRONG.
I CAN'T STAY LONG. I HAVE A PATIENT WAITING FOR ME DOWNSTAIRS, IN THE EMERGENCY ROOM.

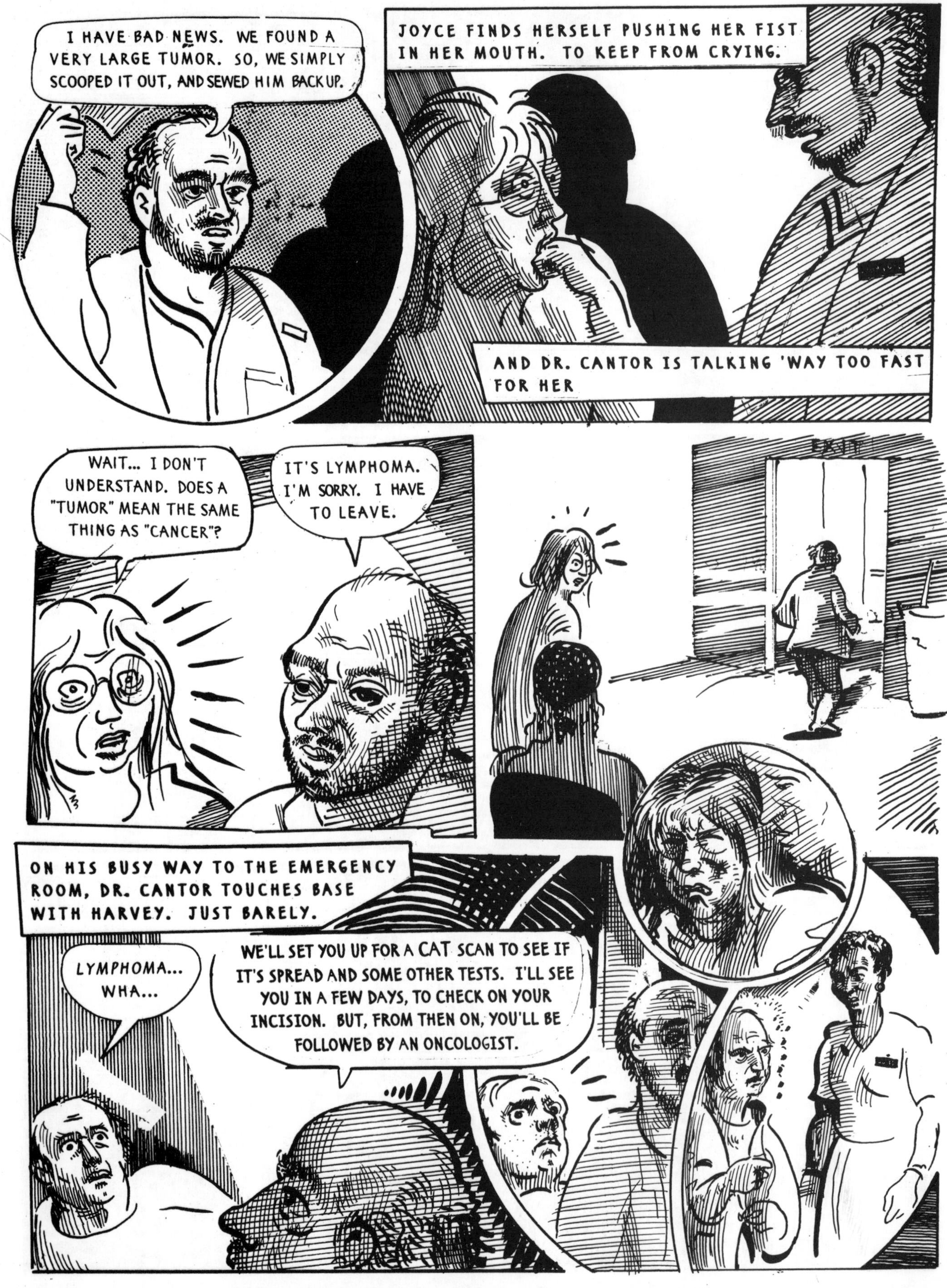
I HAVE BAD NEWS. WE FOUND A VERY LARGE TUMOR. SO, WE SIMPLY SCOOPED IT OUT, AND SEWED HIM BACK UP.
JOYCE FINDS HERSELF PUSHING HER FIST IN HER MOUTH. TO KEEP FROM CRYING.
AND DR. CANTOR IS TALKING 'WAY TOO FAST FOR HER
WAIT... I DON'T UNDERSTAND. DOES A "TUMOR" MEAN THE SAME THING AS "CANCER"?
IT'S LYMPHOMA. I'M SORRY. I HAVE TO LEAVE.
EXIT
ON HIS BUSY WAY TO THE EMERGENCY ROOM, DR. CANTOR TOUCHES BASE WITH HARVEY. JUST BARELY.
LYMPHOMA... WHA...
WE'LL SET YOU UP FOR A CAT SCAN TO SEE IF IT'S SPREAD AND SOME OTHER TESTS. I'LL SEE YOU IN A FEW DAYS, TO CHECK ON YOUR INCISION. BUT, FROM THEN ON, YOU'LL BE FOLLOWED BY AN ONCOLOGIST.

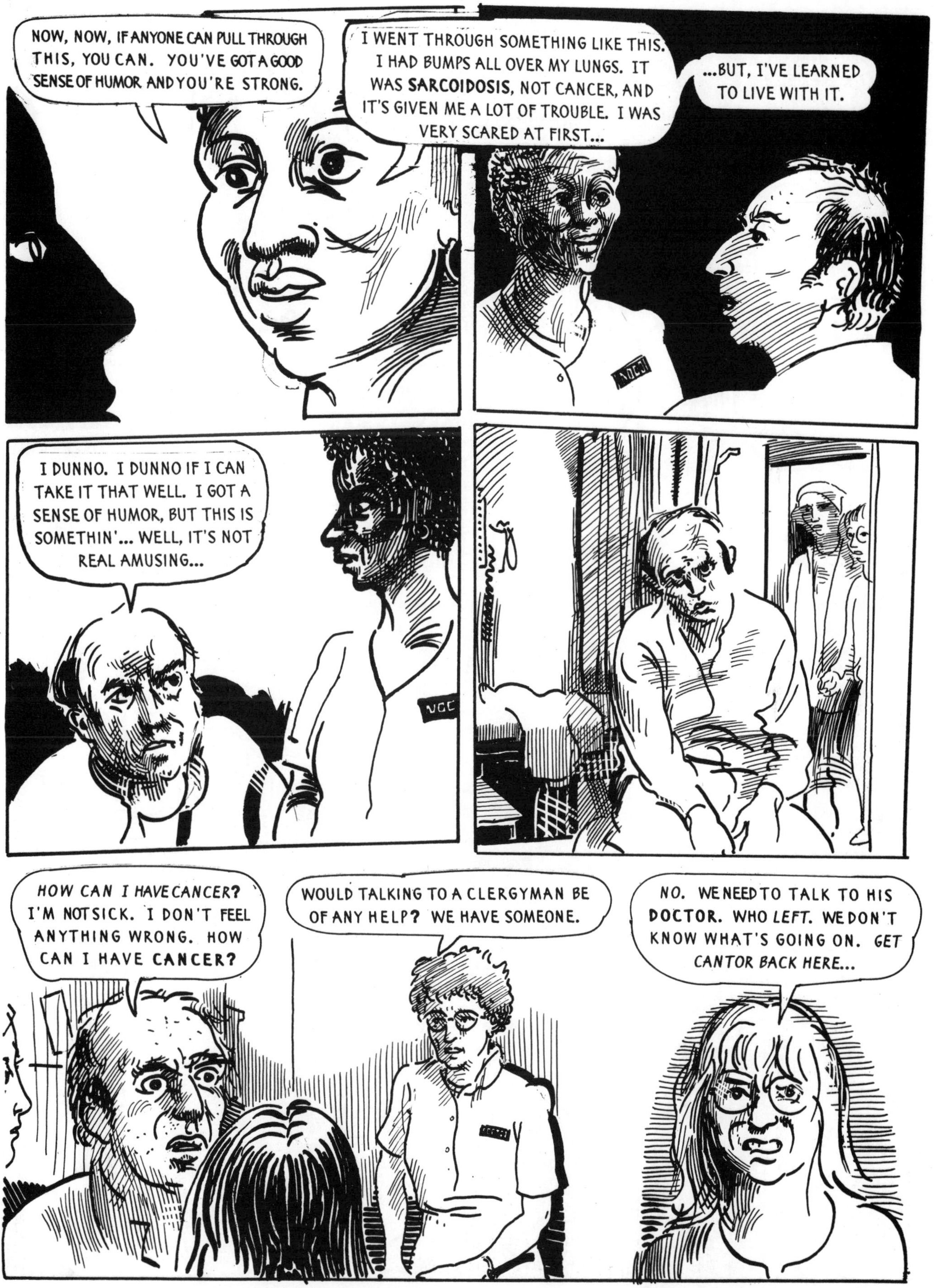
NOW, NOW, IF ANYONE CAN PULL THROUGH THIS, YOU CAN. YOU'VE GOT A GOOD SENSE OF HUMOR AND YOU'RE STRONG.
I WENT THROUGH SOMETHING LIKE THIS. I HAD BUMPS ALL OVER MY LUNGS. IT WAS **SARCOIDOSIS**, NOT CANCER, AND IT'S GIVEN ME A LOT OF TROUBLE. I WAS VERY SCARED AT FIRST...
...BUT, I'VE LEARNED TO LIVE WITH IT.
I DUNNO. I DUNNO IF I CAN TAKE IT THAT WELL. I GOT A SENSE OF HUMOR, BUT THIS IS SOMETHIN'... WELL, IT'S NOT REAL AMUSING...
HOW CAN I HAVE CANCER? I'M NOT SICK. I DON'T FEEL ANYTHING WRONG. HOW CAN I HAVE **CANCER?**
WOULD TALKING TO A CLERGYMAN BE OF ANY HELP? WE HAVE SOMEONE.
NO. WE NEED TO TALK TO HIS **DOCTOR**. WHO *LEFT*. WE DON'T KNOW WHAT'S GOING ON. GET CANTOR BACK HERE...

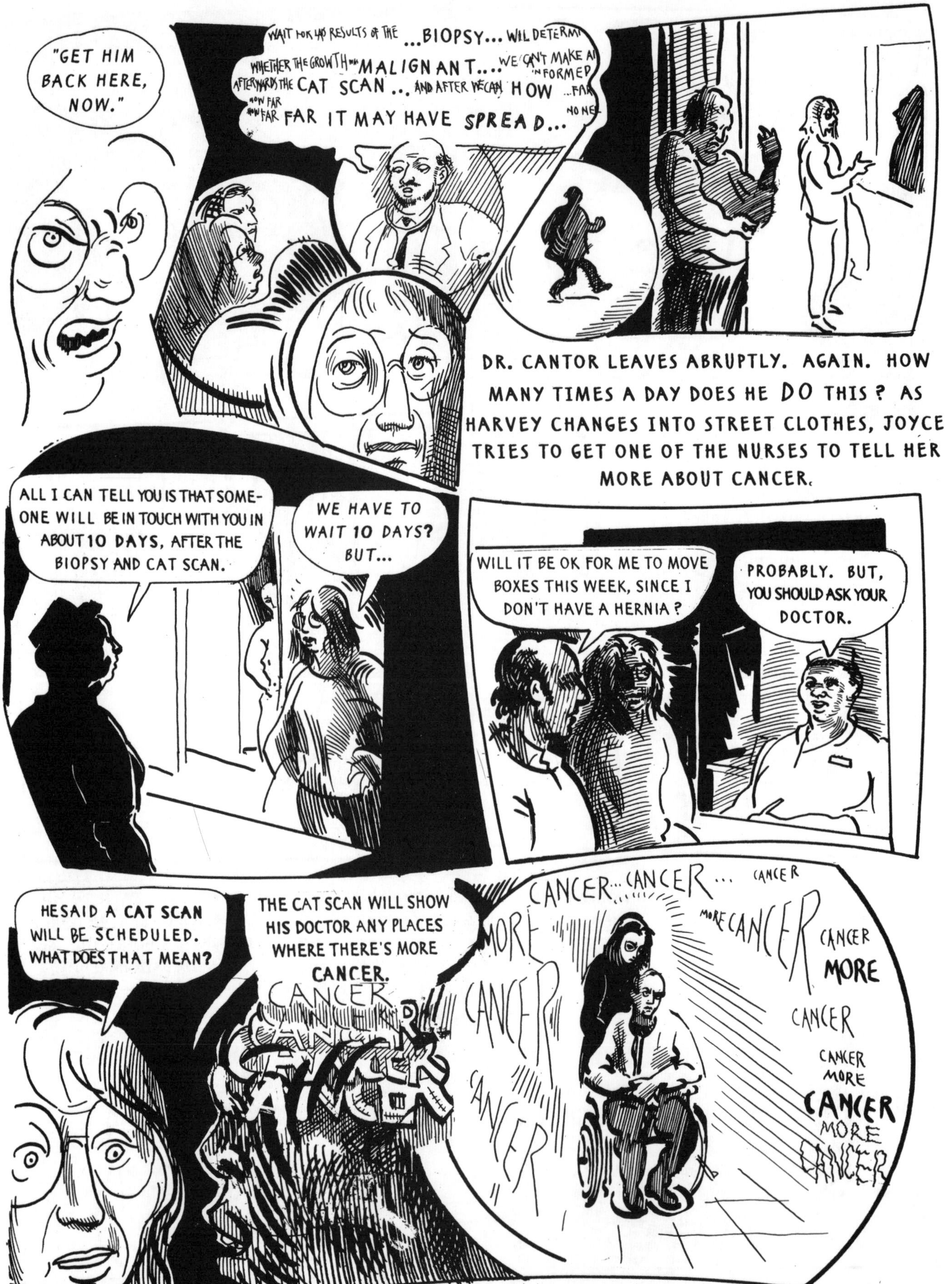
"GET HIM BACK HERE, NOW."
WAIT FOR LAB RESULTS OF THE ...BIOPSY... WIL DETERM
WHETHER THE GROWTH MALIGNANT.... WE CAN'T MAKE AI INFORMED
AFTERWARDS THE CAT SCAN ... AND AFTER WE CAN HOW ...FAR
HOW FAR HOW FAR FAR IT MAY HAVE SPREAD... NO NE
DR. CANTOR LEAVES ABRUPTLY. AGAIN. HOW MANY TIMES A DAY DOES HE DO THIS? AS HARVEY CHANGES INTO STREET CLOTHES, JOYCE TRIES TO GET ONE OF THE NURSES TO TELL HER MORE ABOUT CANCER.
ALL I CAN TELL YOU IS THAT SOMEONE WILL BE IN TOUCH WITH YOU IN ABOUT 10 DAYS, AFTER THE BIOPSY AND CAT SCAN.
WE HAVE TO WAIT 10 DAYS? BUT...
WILL IT BE OK FOR ME TO MOVE BOXES THIS WEEK, SINCE I DON'T HAVE A HERNIA?
PROBABLY. BUT, YOU SHOULD ASK YOUR DOCTOR.
HE SAID A CAT SCAN WILL BE SCHEDULED. WHAT DOES THAT MEAN?
THE CAT SCAN WILL SHOW HIS DOCTOR ANY PLACES WHERE THERE'S MORE CANCER.
CANCER
CANCER... CANCER... CANCER
MORE CANCER
MORE
CANCER
CANCER
CANCER MORE
CANCER
CANCER
CANCER MORE
CANCER MORE
CANCER

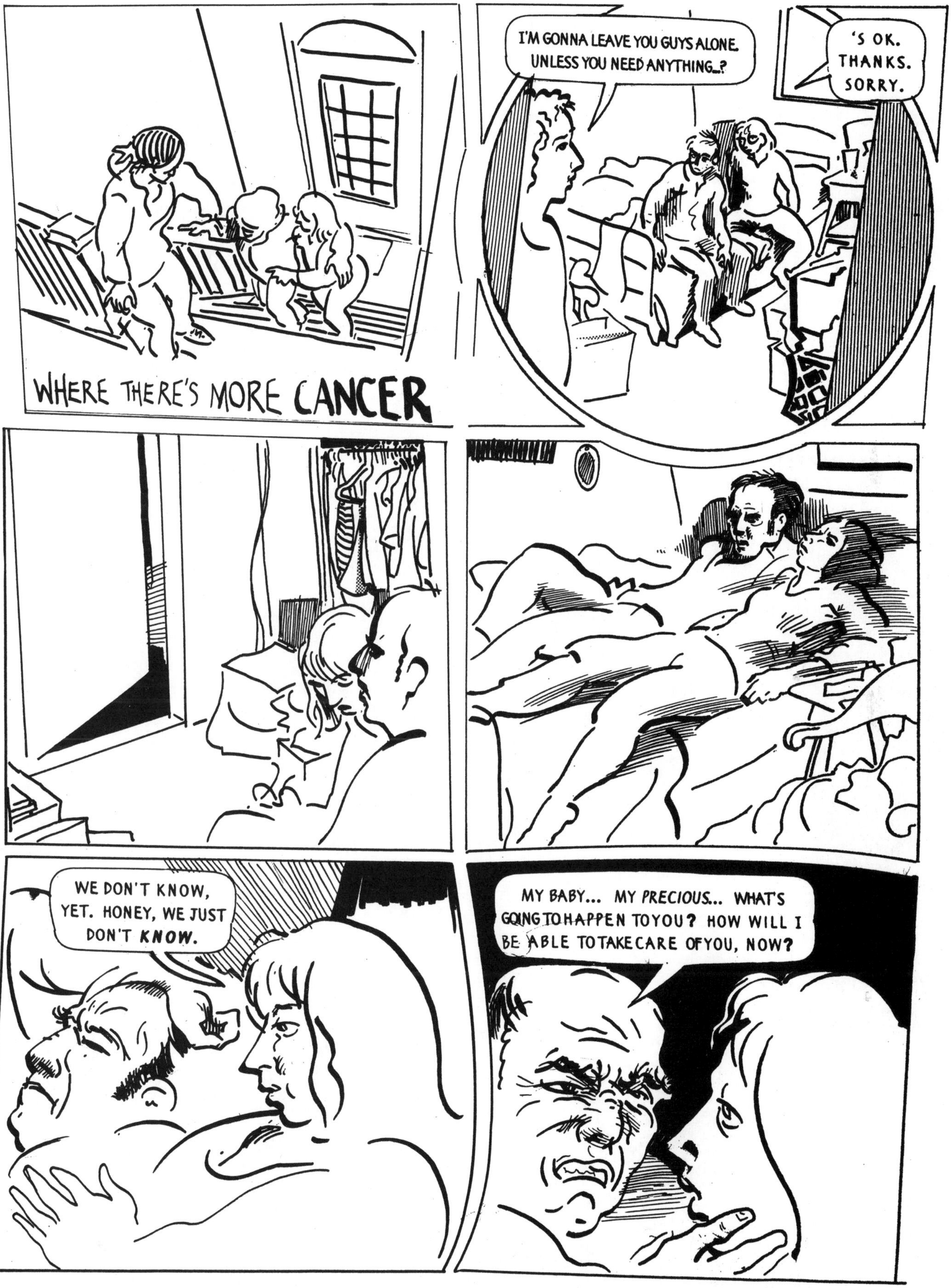
WHERE THERE'S MORE CANCER
I'M GONNA LEAVE YOU GUYS ALONE. UNLESS YOU NEED ANYTHING...?
'S OK. THANKS. SORRY.
WE DON'T KNOW, YET. HONEY, WE JUST DON'T KNOW.
MY BABY... MY PRECIOUS... WHAT'S GOING TO HAPPEN TO YOU? HOW WILL I BE ABLE TO TAKE CARE OF YOU, NOW?

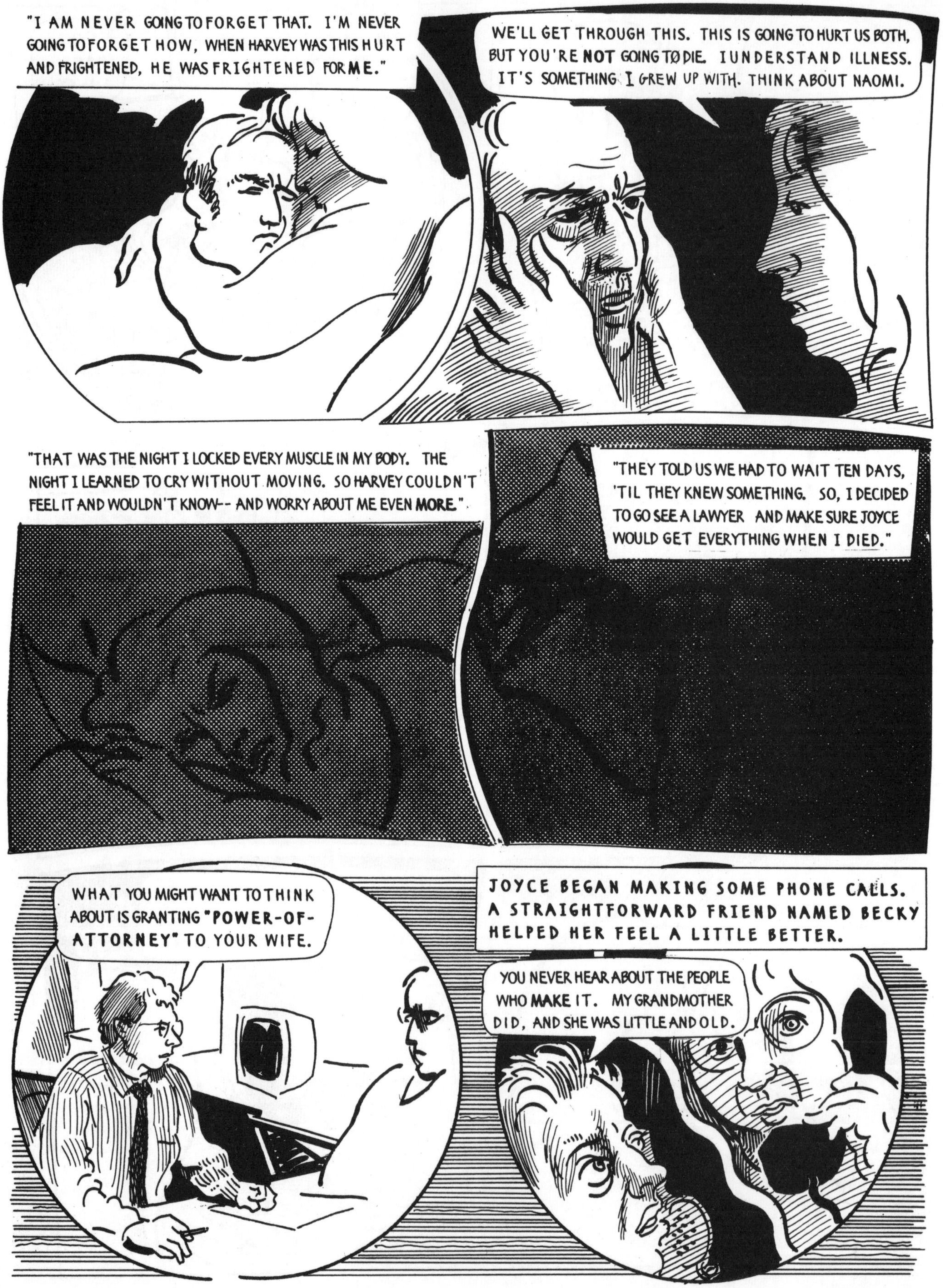
"I AM NEVER GOING TO FORGET THAT. I'M NEVER GOING TO FORGET HOW, WHEN HARVEY WAS THIS HURT AND FRIGHTENED, HE WAS FRIGHTENED FOR ME."
WE'LL GET THROUGH THIS. THIS IS GOING TO HURT US BOTH, BUT YOU'RE NOT GOING TO DIE. I UNDERSTAND ILLNESS. IT'S SOMETHING I GREW UP WITH. THINK ABOUT NAOMI.
"THAT WAS THE NIGHT I LOCKED EVERY MUSCLE IN MY BODY. THE NIGHT I LEARNED TO CRY WITHOUT MOVING. SO HARVEY COULDN'T FEEL IT AND WOULDN'T KNOW-- AND WORRY ABOUT ME EVEN MORE."
"THEY TOLD US WE HAD TO WAIT TEN DAYS, 'TIL THEY KNEW SOMETHING. SO, I DECIDED TO GO SEE A LAWYER AND MAKE SURE JOYCE WOULD GET EVERYTHING WHEN I DIED."
WHAT YOU MIGHT WANT TO THINK ABOUT IS GRANTING "POWER-OF-ATTORNEY" TO YOUR WIFE.
JOYCE BEGAN MAKING SOME PHONE CALLS. A STRAIGHTFORWARD FRIEND NAMED BECKY HELPED HER FEEL A LITTLE BETTER.
YOU NEVER HEAR ABOUT THE PEOPLE WHO MAKE IT. MY GRANDMOTHER DID, AND SHE WAS LITTLE AND OLD.

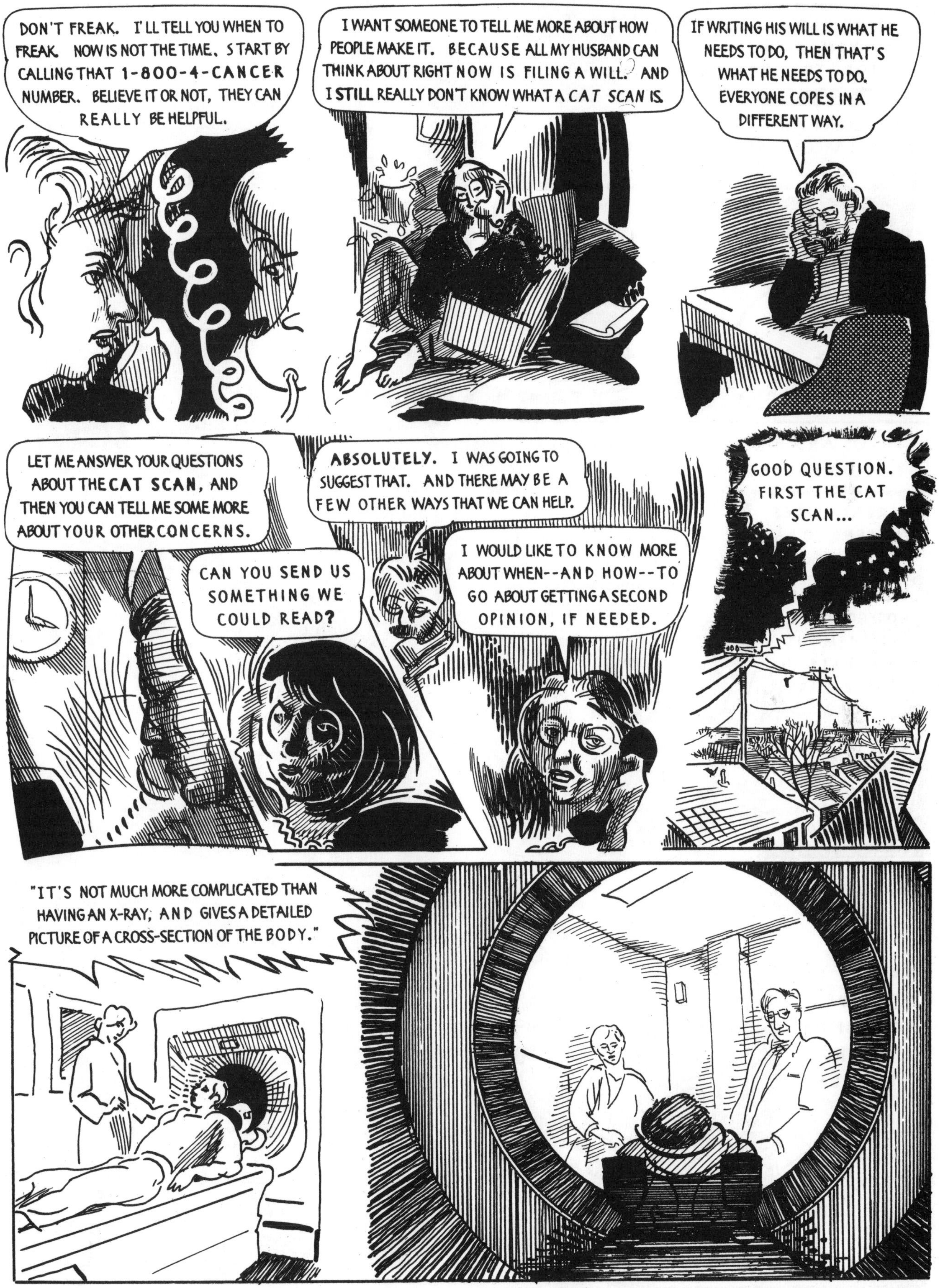

DON'T FREAK. I'LL TELL YOU WHEN TO FREAK. NOW IS NOT THE TIME. START BY CALLING THAT 1-800-4-CANCER NUMBER. BELIEVE IT OR NOT, THEY CAN REALLY BE HELPFUL.
I WANT SOMEONE TO TELL ME MORE ABOUT HOW PEOPLE MAKE IT. BECAUSE ALL MY HUSBAND CAN THINK ABOUT RIGHT NOW IS FILING A WILL. AND I STILL REALLY DON'T KNOW WHAT A CAT SCAN IS.
IF WRITING HIS WILL IS WHAT HE NEEDS TO DO, THEN THAT'S WHAT HE NEEDS TO DO. EVERYONE COPES IN A DIFFERENT WAY.
LET ME ANSWER YOUR QUESTIONS ABOUT THE CAT SCAN, AND THEN YOU CAN TELL ME SOME MORE ABOUT YOUR OTHER CONCERNS.
CAN YOU SEND US SOMETHING WE COULD READ?
ABSOLUTELY. I WAS GOING TO SUGGEST THAT. AND THERE MAY BE A FEW OTHER WAYS THAT WE CAN HELP.
I WOULD LIKE TO KNOW MORE ABOUT WHEN--AND HOW--TO GO ABOUT GETTING A SECOND OPINION, IF NEEDED.
GOOD QUESTION. FIRST THE CAT SCAN...
"IT'S NOT MUCH MORE COMPLICATED THAN HAVING AN X-RAY; AND GIVES A DETAILED PICTURE OF A CROSS-SECTION OF THE BODY."

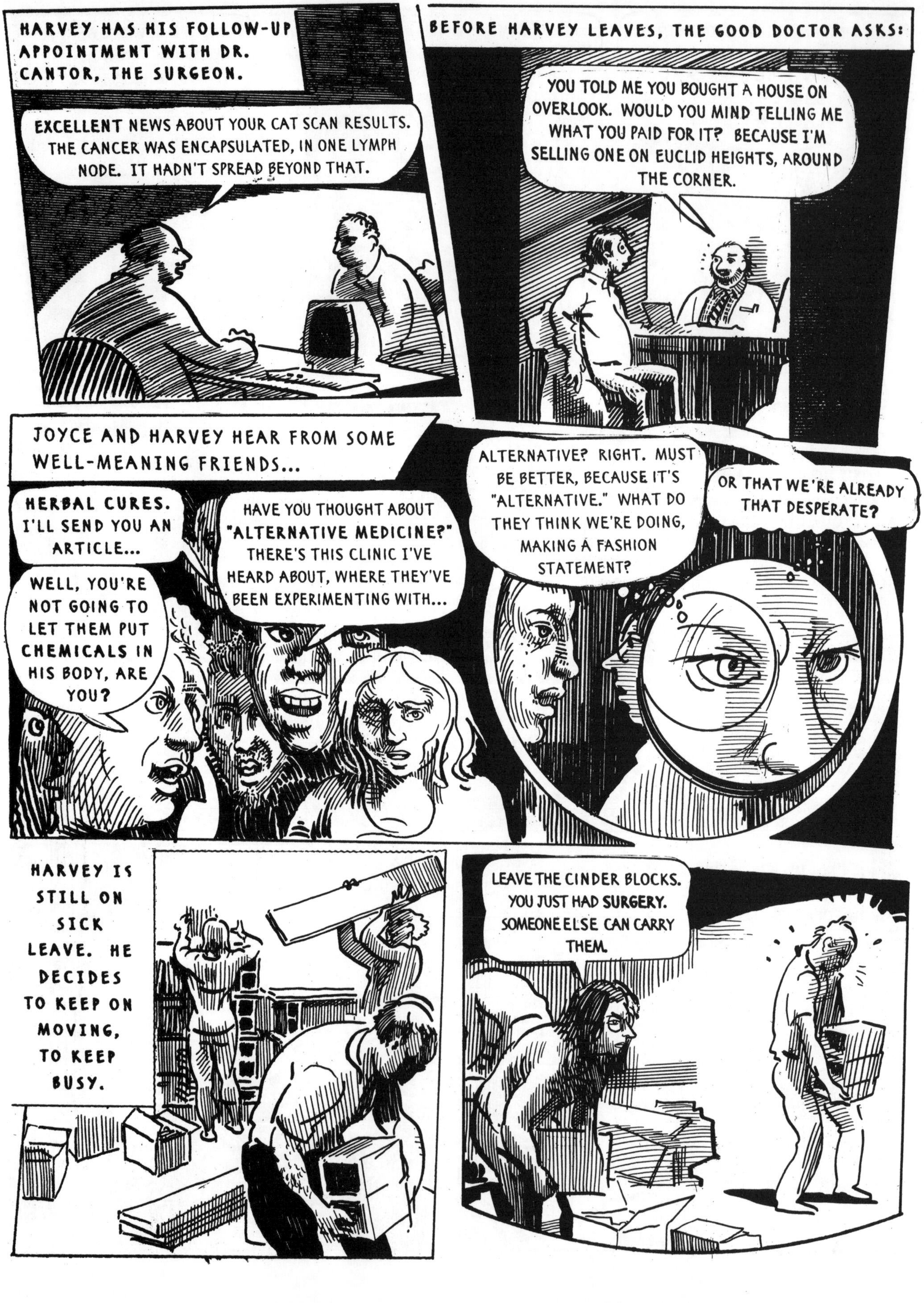
HARVEY HAS HIS FOLLOW-UP APPOINTMENT WITH DR. CANTOR, THE SURGEON.
EXCELLENT NEWS ABOUT YOUR CAT SCAN RESULTS. THE CANCER WAS ENCAPSULATED, IN ONE LYMPH NODE. IT HADN'T SPREAD BEYOND THAT.
BEFORE HARVEY LEAVES, THE GOOD DOCTOR ASKS:
YOU TOLD ME YOU BOUGHT A HOUSE ON OVERLOOK. WOULD YOU MIND TELLING ME WHAT YOU PAID FOR IT? BECAUSE I'M SELLING ONE ON EUCLID HEIGHTS, AROUND THE CORNER.
JOYCE AND HARVEY HEAR FROM SOME WELL-MEANING FRIENDS...
HERBAL CURES. I'LL SEND YOU AN ARTICLE...
WELL, YOU'RE NOT GOING TO LET THEM PUT CHEMICALS IN HIS BODY, ARE YOU?
HAVE YOU THOUGHT ABOUT "ALTERNATIVE MEDICINE?" THERE'S THIS CLINIC I'VE HEARD ABOUT, WHERE THEY'VE BEEN EXPERIMENTING WITH...
ALTERNATIVE? RIGHT. MUST BE BETTER, BECAUSE IT'S "ALTERNATIVE." WHAT DO THEY THINK WE'RE DOING, MAKING A FASHION STATEMENT?
OR THAT WE'RE ALREADY THAT DESPERATE?
HARVEY IS STILL ON SICK LEAVE. HE DECIDES TO KEEP ON MOVING, TO KEEP BUSY.
LEAVE THE CINDER BLOCKS. YOU JUST HAD SURGERY. SOMEONE ELSE CAN CARRY THEM.

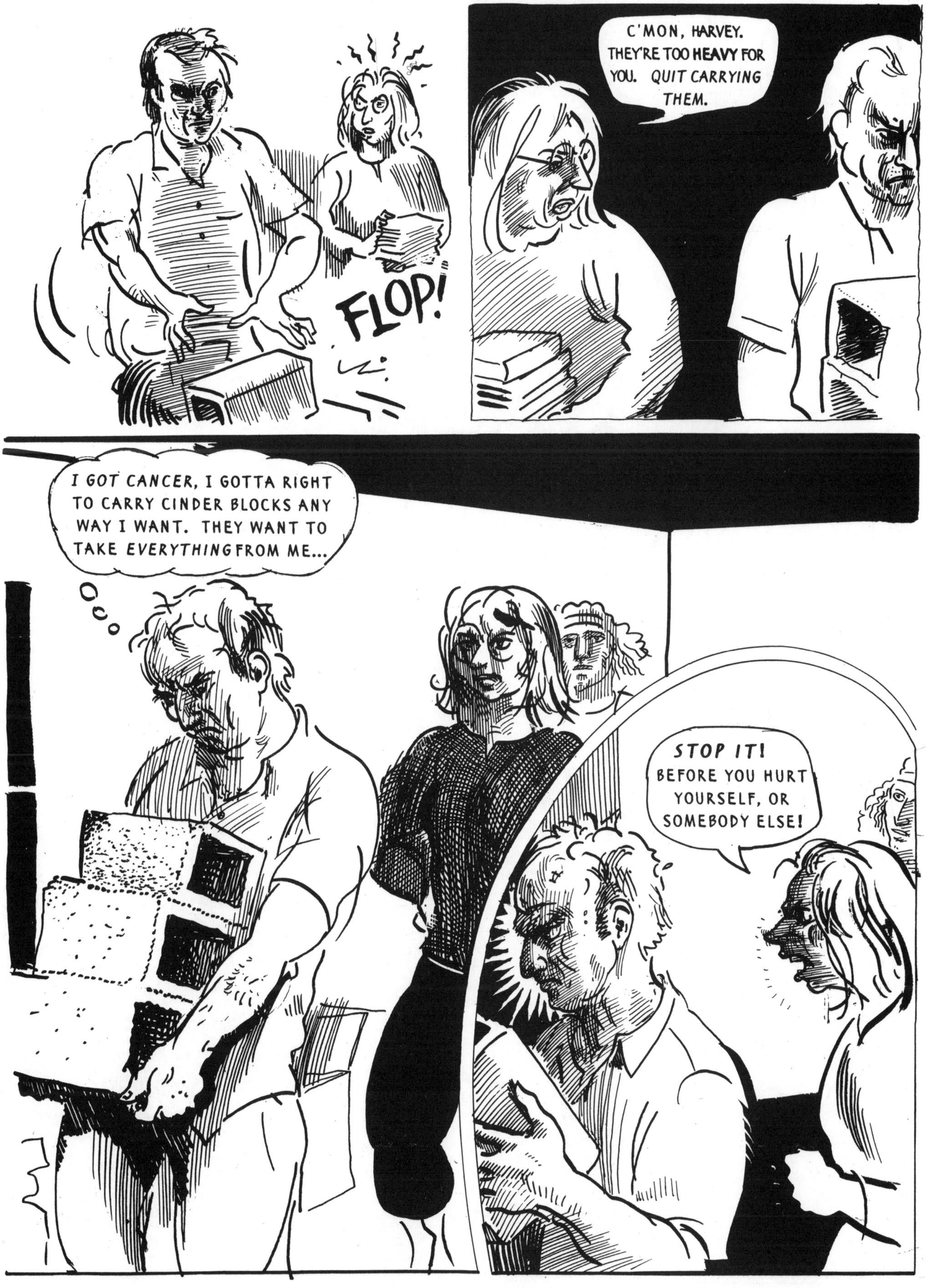
FLOP!
C'MON, HARVEY. THEY'RE TOO HEAVY FOR YOU. QUIT CARRYING THEM.
I GOT CANCER, I GOTTA RIGHT TO CARRY CINDER BLOCKS ANY WAY I WANT. THEY WANT TO TAKE EVERYTHING FROM ME...
STOP IT! BEFORE YOU HURT YOURSELF, OR SOMEBODY ELSE!

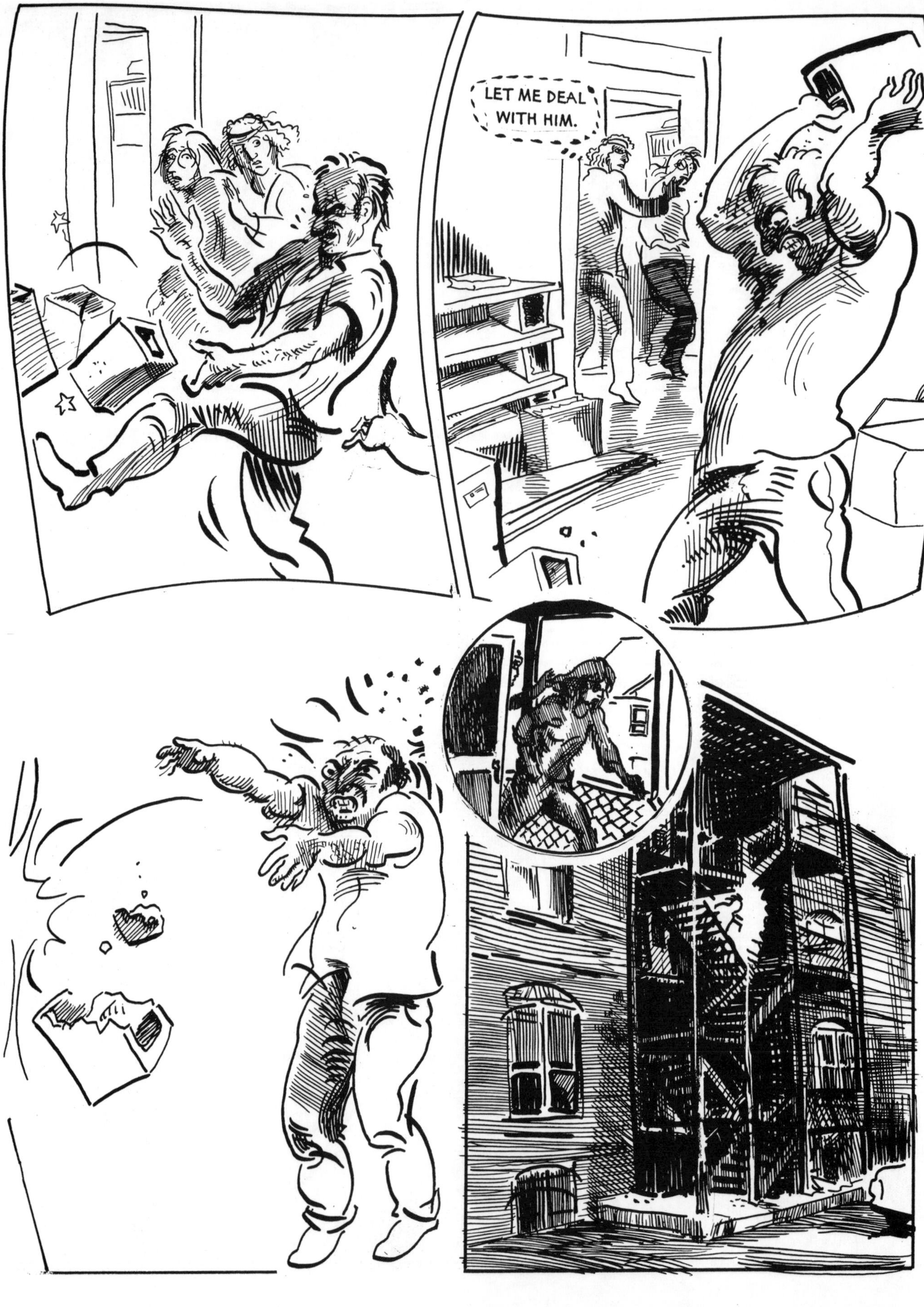
LET ME DEAL WITH HIM.

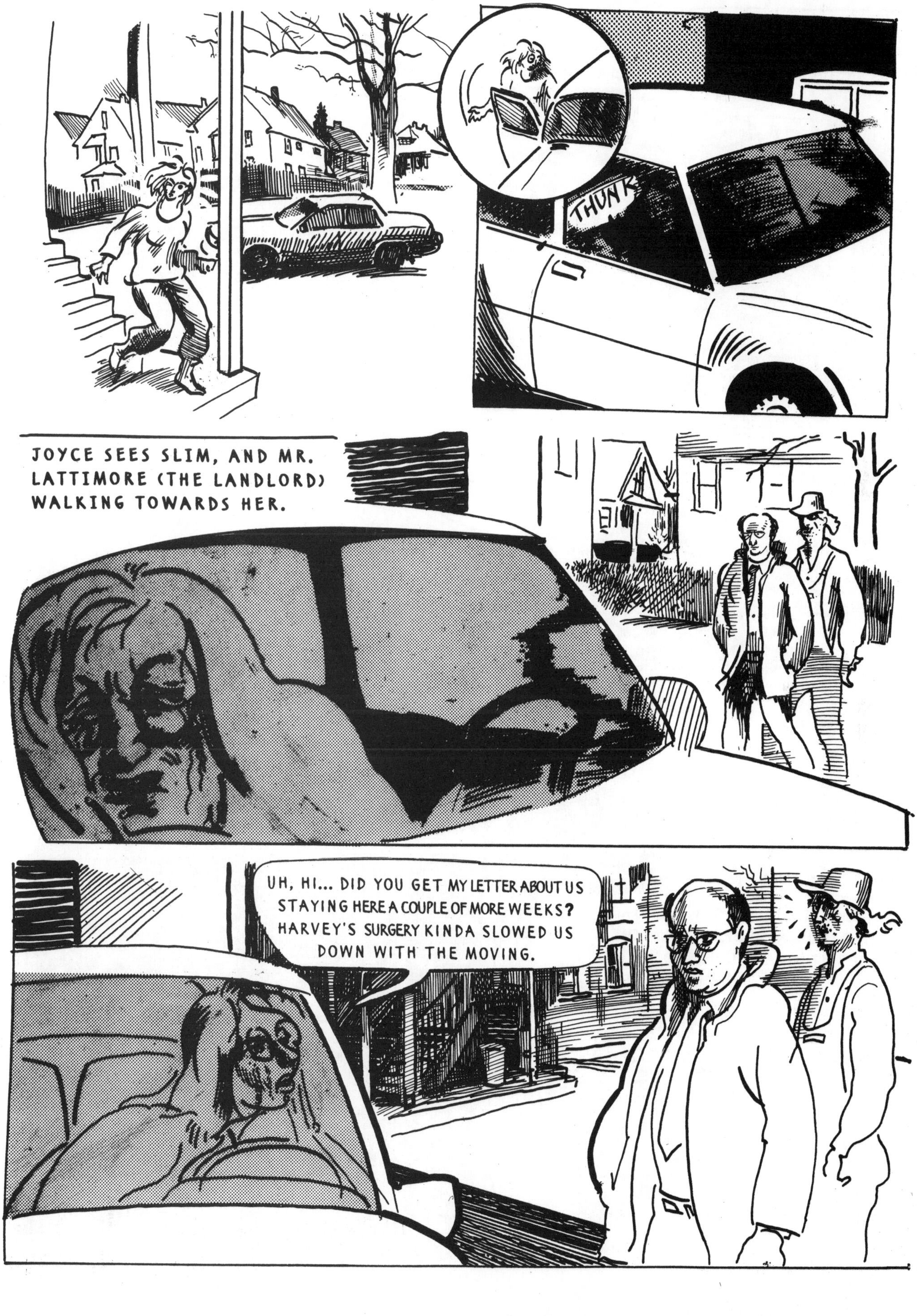
THUNK
JOYCE SEES SLIM, AND MR. LATTIMORE (THE LANDLORD) WALKING TOWARDS HER.
UH, HI... DID YOU GET MY LETTER ABOUT US STAYING HERE A COUPLE OF MORE WEEKS? HARVEY'S SURGERY KINDA SLOWED US DOWN WITH THE MOVING.

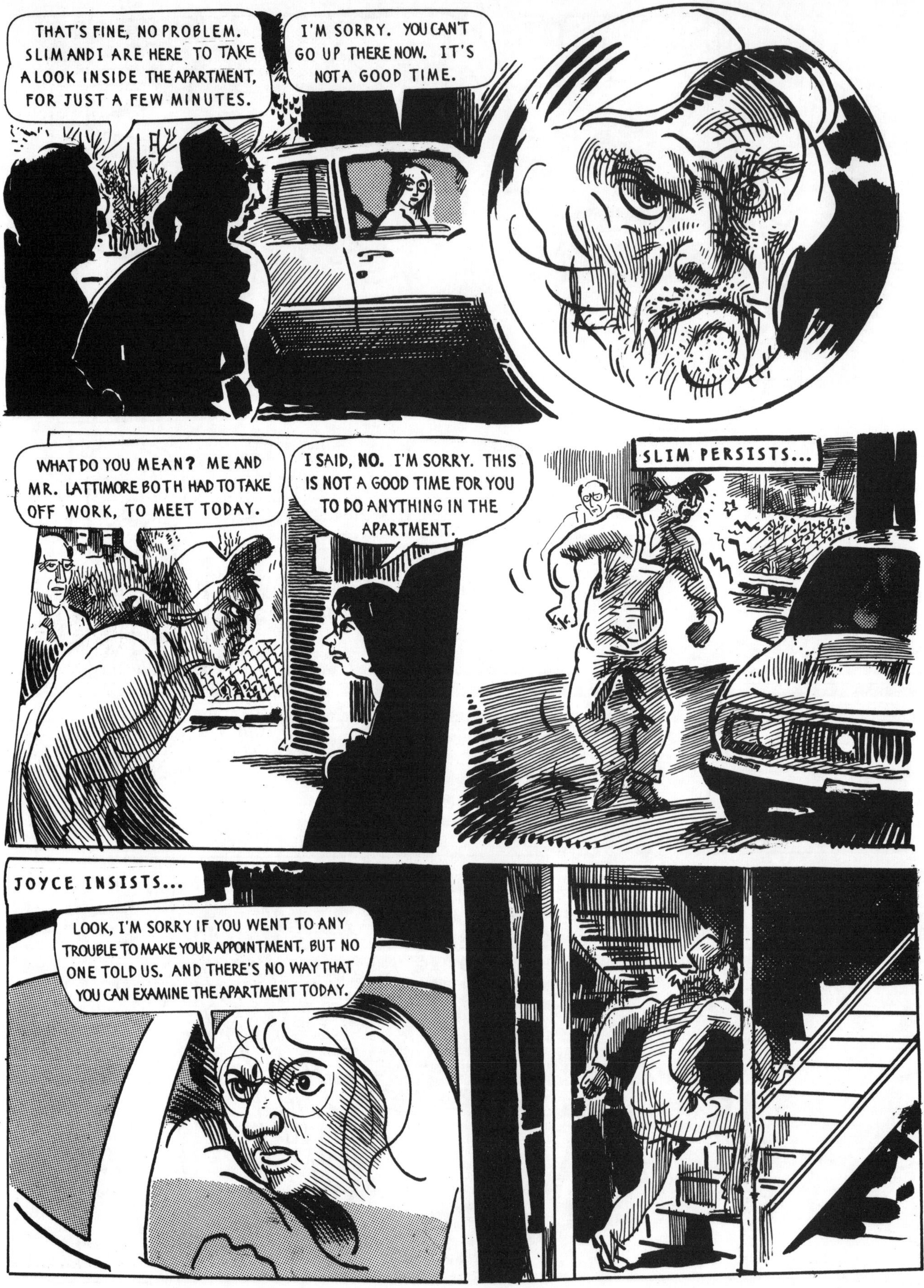
THAT'S FINE, NO PROBLEM. SLIM AND I ARE HERE TO TAKE A LOOK INSIDE THE APARTMENT, FOR JUST A FEW MINUTES.
I'M SORRY. YOU CAN'T GO UP THERE NOW. IT'S NOT A GOOD TIME.
WHAT DO YOU MEAN? ME AND MR. LATTIMORE BOTH HAD TO TAKE OFF WORK, TO MEET TODAY.
I SAID, NO. I'M SORRY. THIS IS NOT A GOOD TIME FOR YOU TO DO ANYTHING IN THE APARTMENT.
SLIM PERSISTS...
JOYCE INSISTS...
LOOK, I'M SORRY IF YOU WENT TO ANY TROUBLE TO MAKE YOUR APPOINTMENT, BUT NO ONE TOLD US. AND THERE'S NO WAY THAT YOU CAN EXAMINE THE APARTMENT TODAY.

LOOK, GOD DAMMIT! THIS IS A VERY DIFFICULT TIME FOR HARVEY AND ME, AND YOU ARE INVADING OUR PRIVACY.

IT'S NO PROBLEM. WE CAN COME BACK. I'M SORRY.

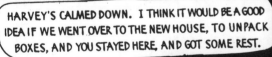

HARVEY'S CALMED DOWN. I THINK IT WOULD BE A GOOD IDEA IF WE WENT OVER TO THE NEW HOUSE, TO UNPACK BOXES, AND YOU STAYED HERE, AND GOT SOME REST.

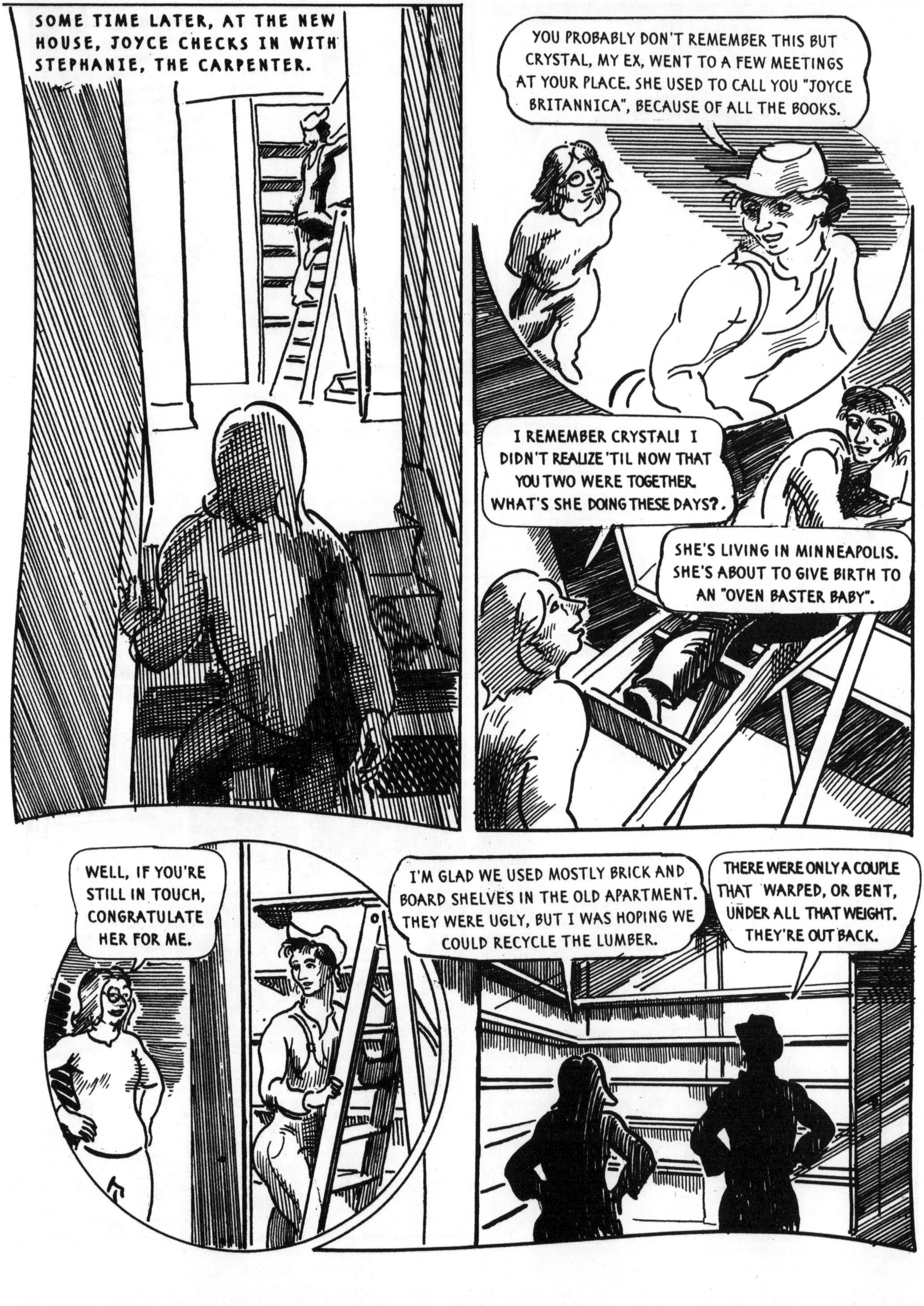
SOME TIME LATER, AT THE NEW HOUSE, JOYCE CHECKS IN WITH STEPHANIE, THE CARPENTER.
YOU PROBABLY DON'T REMEMBER THIS BUT CRYSTAL, MY EX, WENT TO A FEW MEETINGS AT YOUR PLACE. SHE USED TO CALL YOU "JOYCE BRITANNICA", BECAUSE OF ALL THE BOOKS.
I REMEMBER CRYSTAL! I DIDN'T REALIZE 'TIL NOW THAT YOU TWO WERE TOGETHER. WHAT'S SHE DOING THESE DAYS?.
SHE'S LIVING IN MINNEAPOLIS. SHE'S ABOUT TO GIVE BIRTH TO AN "OVEN BASTER BABY".
WELL, IF YOU'RE STILL IN TOUCH, CONGRATULATE HER FOR ME.
I'M GLAD WE USED MOSTLY BRICK AND BOARD SHELVES IN THE OLD APARTMENT. THEY WERE UGLY, BUT I WAS HOPING WE COULD RECYCLE THE LUMBER.
THERE WERE ONLY A COUPLE THAT WARPED, OR BENT, UNDER ALL THAT WEIGHT. THEY'RE OUT BACK.

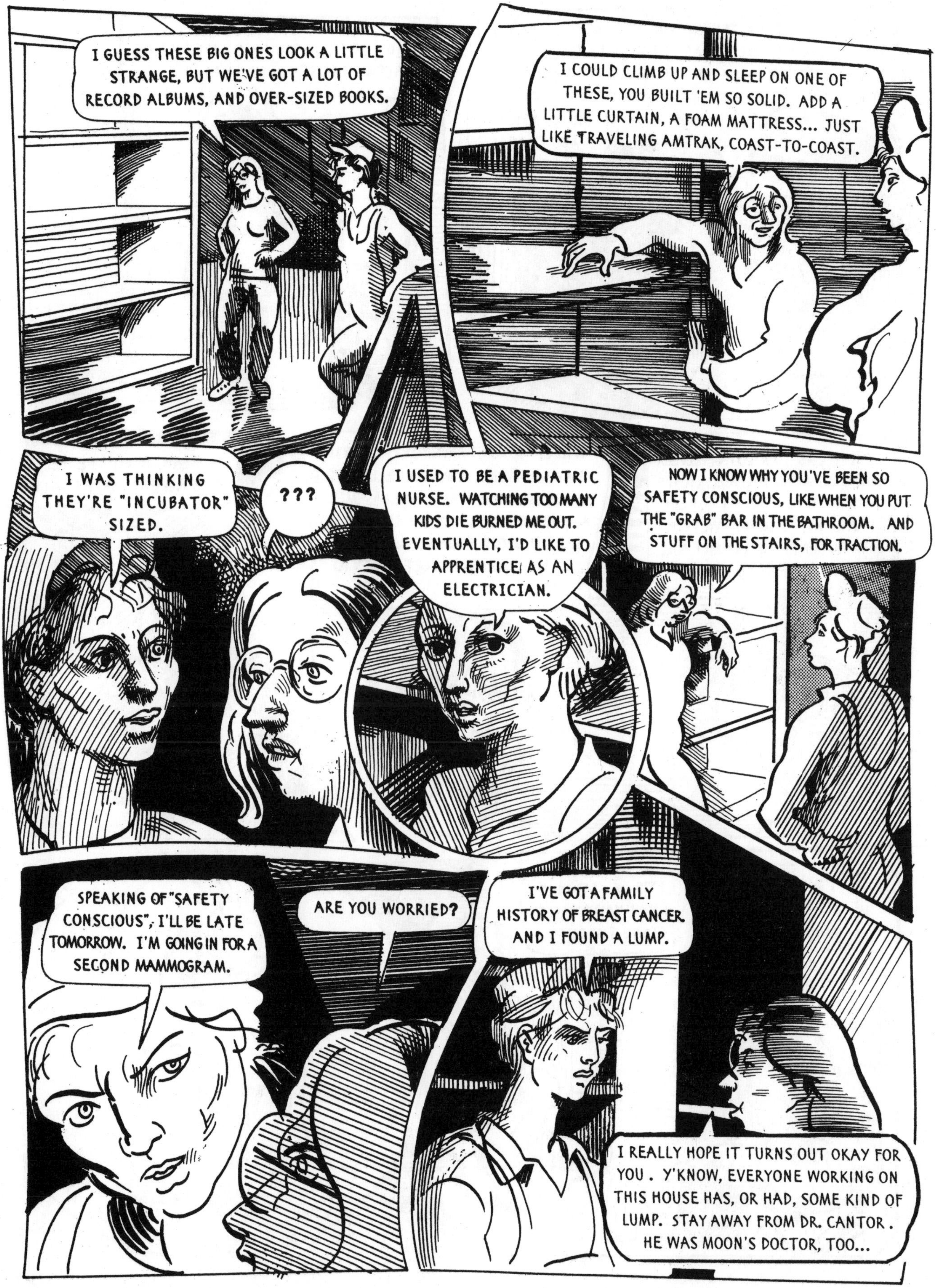
I GUESS THESE BIG ONES LOOK A LITTLE STRANGE, BUT WE'VE GOT A LOT OF RECORD ALBUMS, AND OVER-SIZED BOOKS.
I COULD CLIMB UP AND SLEEP ON ONE OF THESE, YOU BUILT 'EM SO SOLID. ADD A LITTLE CURTAIN, A FOAM MATTRESS... JUST LIKE TRAVELING AMTRAK, COAST-TO-COAST.
I WAS THINKING THEY'RE "INCUBATOR" SIZED.
???
I USED TO BE A PEDIATRIC NURSE. WATCHING TOO MANY KIDS DIE BURNED ME OUT. EVENTUALLY, I'D LIKE TO APPRENTICE AS AN ELECTRICIAN.
NOW I KNOW WHY YOU'VE BEEN SO SAFETY CONSCIOUS, LIKE WHEN YOU PUT THE "GRAB" BAR IN THE BATHROOM. AND STUFF ON THE STAIRS, FOR TRACTION.
SPEAKING OF "SAFETY CONSCIOUS", I'LL BE LATE TOMORROW. I'M GOING IN FOR A SECOND MAMMOGRAM.
ARE YOU WORRIED?
I'VE GOT A FAMILY HISTORY OF BREAST CANCER AND I FOUND A LUMP.
I REALLY HOPE IT TURNS OUT OKAY FOR YOU . Y'KNOW, EVERYONE WORKING ON THIS HOUSE HAS, OR HAD, SOME KIND OF LUMP. STAY AWAY FROM DR. CANTOR . HE WAS MOON'S DOCTOR, TOO...

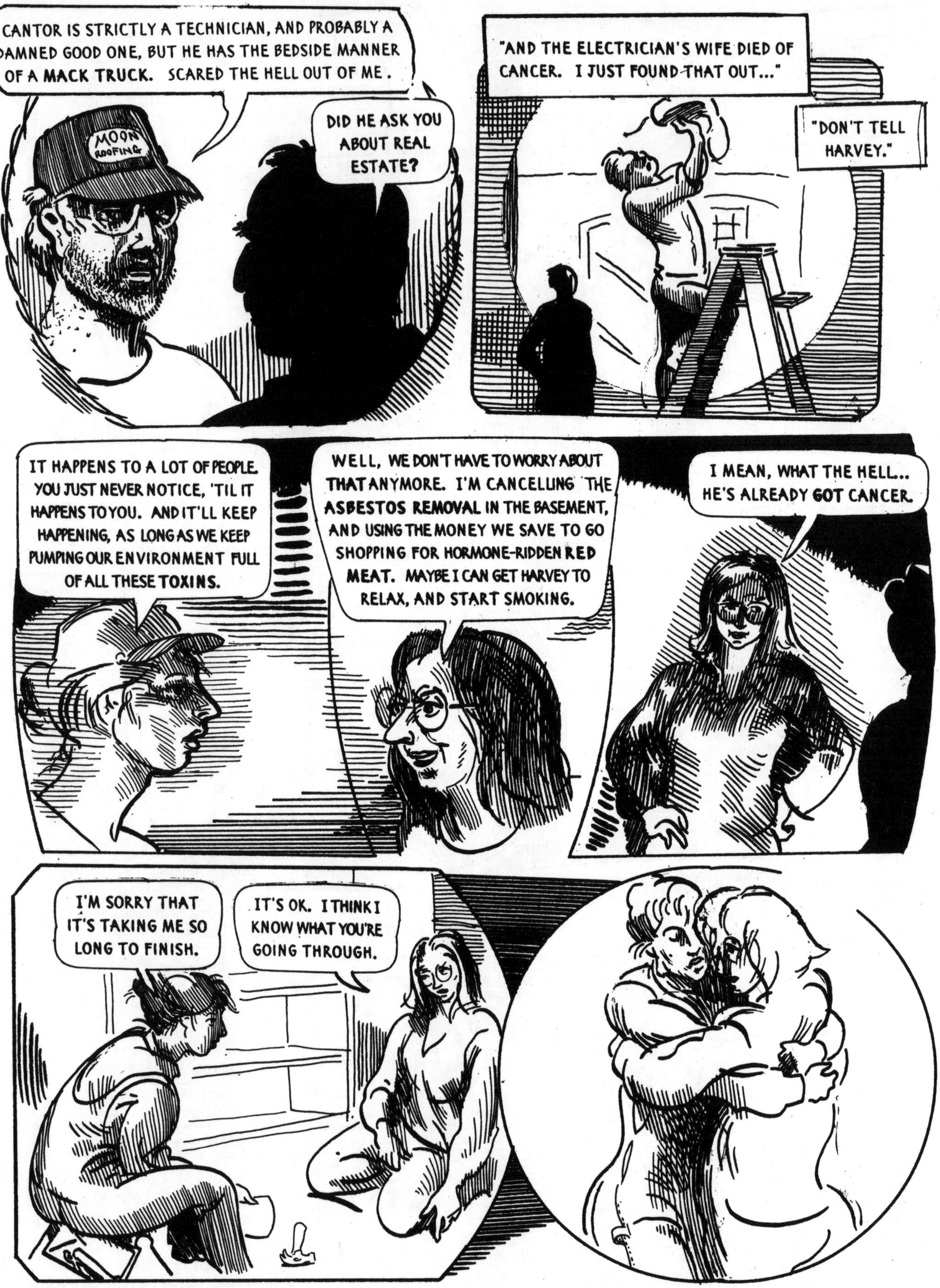
CANTOR IS STRICTLY A TECHNICIAN, AND PROBABLY A DAMNED GOOD ONE, BUT HE HAS THE BEDSIDE MANNER OF A MACK TRUCK. SCARED THE HELL OUT OF ME.
DID HE ASK YOU ABOUT REAL ESTATE?
"AND THE ELECTRICIAN'S WIFE DIED OF CANCER. I JUST FOUND THAT OUT..."
"DON'T TELL HARVEY."
IT HAPPENS TO A LOT OF PEOPLE. YOU JUST NEVER NOTICE, 'TIL IT HAPPENS TO YOU. AND IT'LL KEEP HAPPENING, AS LONG AS WE KEEP PUMPING OUR ENVIRONMENT FULL OF ALL THESE TOXINS.
WELL, WE DON'T HAVE TO WORRY ABOUT THAT ANYMORE. I'M CANCELLING THE ASBESTOS REMOVAL IN THE BASEMENT, AND USING THE MONEY WE SAVE TO GO SHOPPING FOR HORMONE-RIDDEN RED MEAT. MAYBE I CAN GET HARVEY TO RELAX, AND START SMOKING.
I MEAN, WHAT THE HELL... HE'S ALREADY GOT CANCER.
I'M SORRY THAT IT'S TAKING ME SO LONG TO FINISH.
IT'S OK. I THINK I KNOW WHAT YOU'RE GOING THROUGH.

6

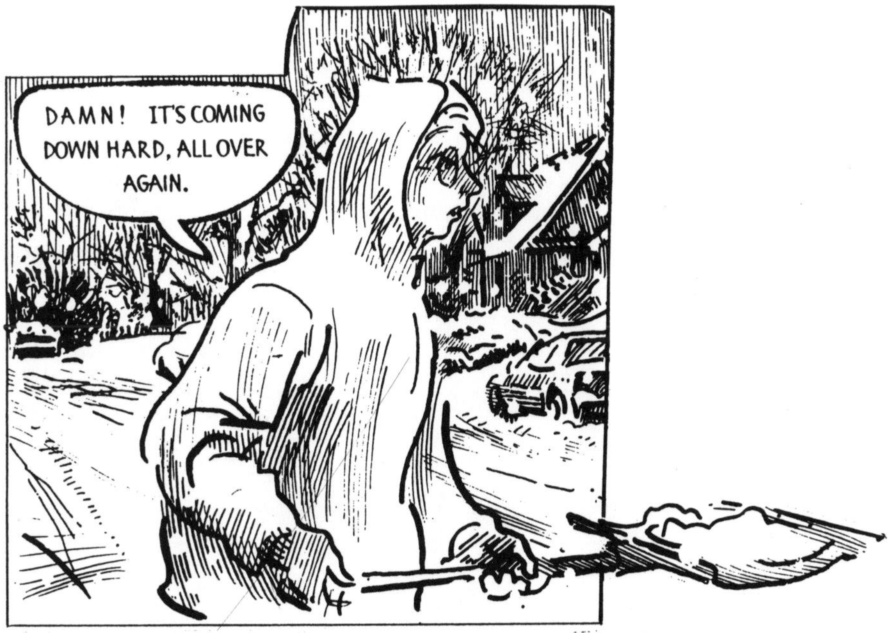
DAMN! IT'S COMING DOWN HARD, ALL OVER AGAIN.

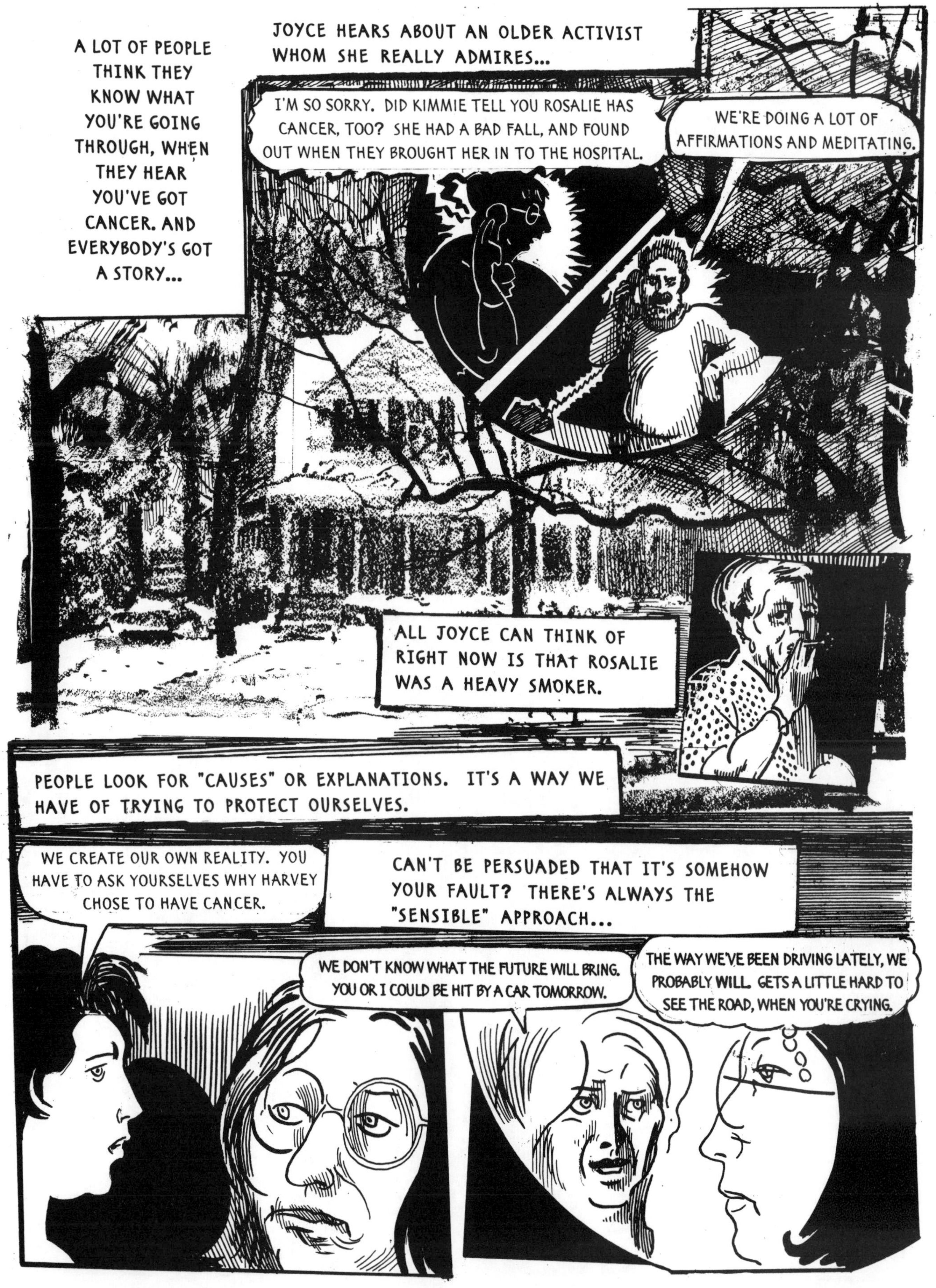
A LOT OF PEOPLE THINK THEY KNOW WHAT YOU'RE GOING THROUGH, WHEN THEY HEAR YOU'VE GOT CANCER. AND EVERYBODY'S GOT A STORY...
JOYCE HEARS ABOUT AN OLDER ACTIVIST WHOM SHE REALLY ADMIRES...
I'M SO SORRY. DID KIMMIE TELL YOU ROSALIE HAS CANCER, TOO? SHE HAD A BAD FALL, AND FOUND OUT WHEN THEY BROUGHT HER IN TO THE HOSPITAL.
WE'RE DOING A LOT OF AFFIRMATIONS AND MEDITATING.
ALL JOYCE CAN THINK OF RIGHT NOW IS THAT ROSALIE WAS A HEAVY SMOKER.
PEOPLE LOOK FOR "CAUSES" OR EXPLANATIONS. IT'S A WAY WE HAVE OF TRYING TO PROTECT OURSELVES.
WE CREATE OUR OWN REALITY. YOU HAVE TO ASK YOURSELVES WHY HARVEY CHOSE TO HAVE CANCER.
CAN'T BE PERSUADED THAT IT'S SOMEHOW YOUR FAULT? THERE'S ALWAYS THE "SENSIBLE" APPROACH...
WE DON'T KNOW WHAT THE FUTURE WILL BRING. YOU OR I COULD BE HIT BY A CAR TOMORROW.
THE WAY WE'VE BEEN DRIVING LATELY, WE PROBABLY WILL. GETS A LITTLE HARD TO SEE THE ROAD, WHEN YOU'RE CRYING.

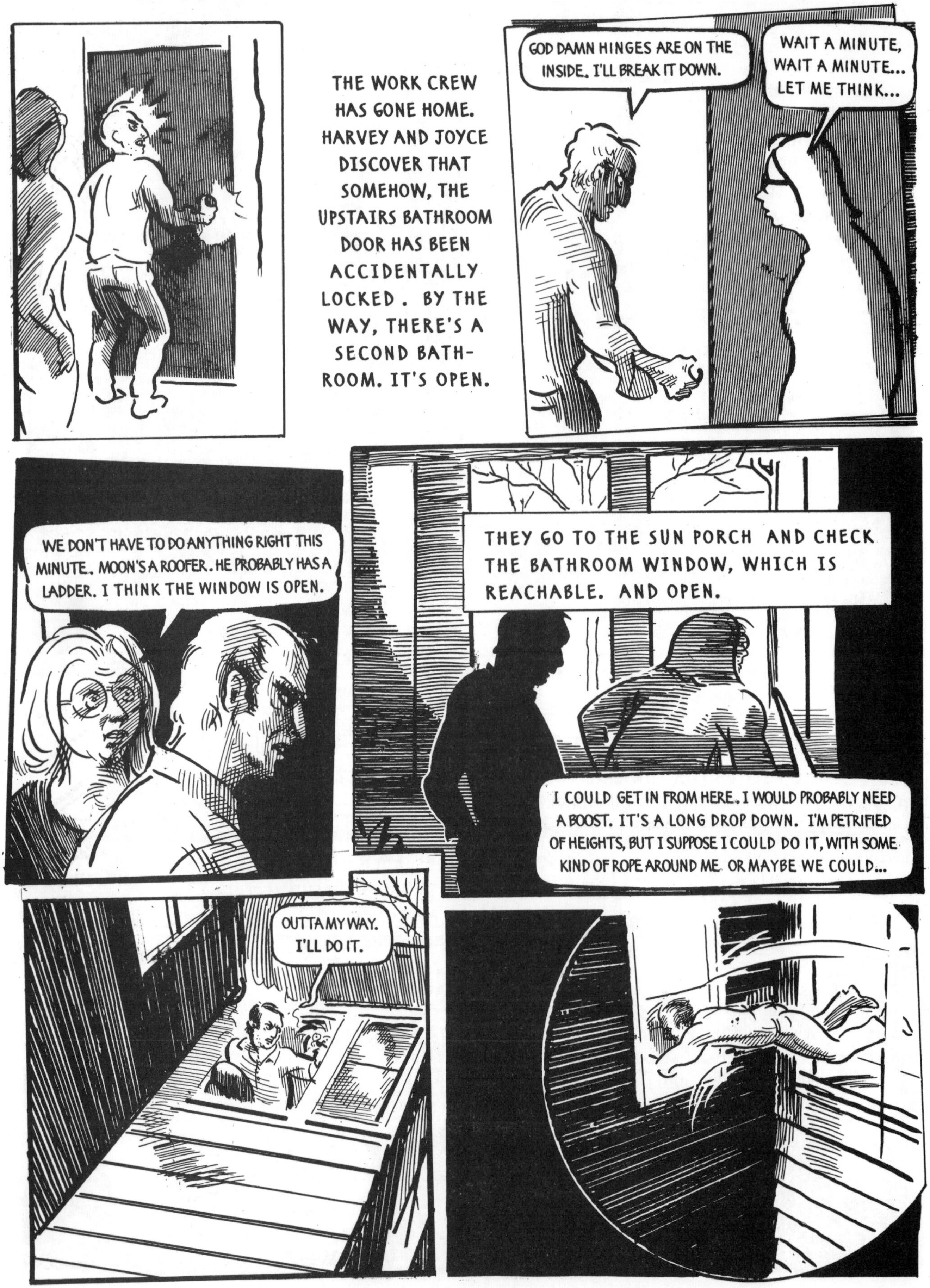
THE WORK CREW HAS GONE HOME. HARVEY AND JOYCE DISCOVER THAT SOMEHOW, THE UPSTAIRS BATHROOM DOOR HAS BEEN ACCIDENTALLY LOCKED. BY THE WAY, THERE'S A SECOND BATHROOM. IT'S OPEN.
GOD DAMN HINGES ARE ON THE INSIDE. I'LL BREAK IT DOWN.
WAIT A MINUTE, WAIT A MINUTE... LET ME THINK...
WE DON'T HAVE TO DO ANYTHING RIGHT THIS MINUTE. MOON'S A ROOFER. HE PROBABLY HAS A LADDER. I THINK THE WINDOW IS OPEN.
THEY GO TO THE SUN PORCH AND CHECK THE BATHROOM WINDOW, WHICH IS REACHABLE. AND OPEN.
I COULD GET IN FROM HERE. I WOULD PROBABLY NEED A BOOST. IT'S A LONG DROP DOWN. I'M PETRIFIED OF HEIGHTS, BUT I SUPPOSE I COULD DO IT, WITH SOME KIND OF ROPE AROUND ME. OR MAYBE WE COULD...
OUTTA MY WAY. I'LL DO IT.

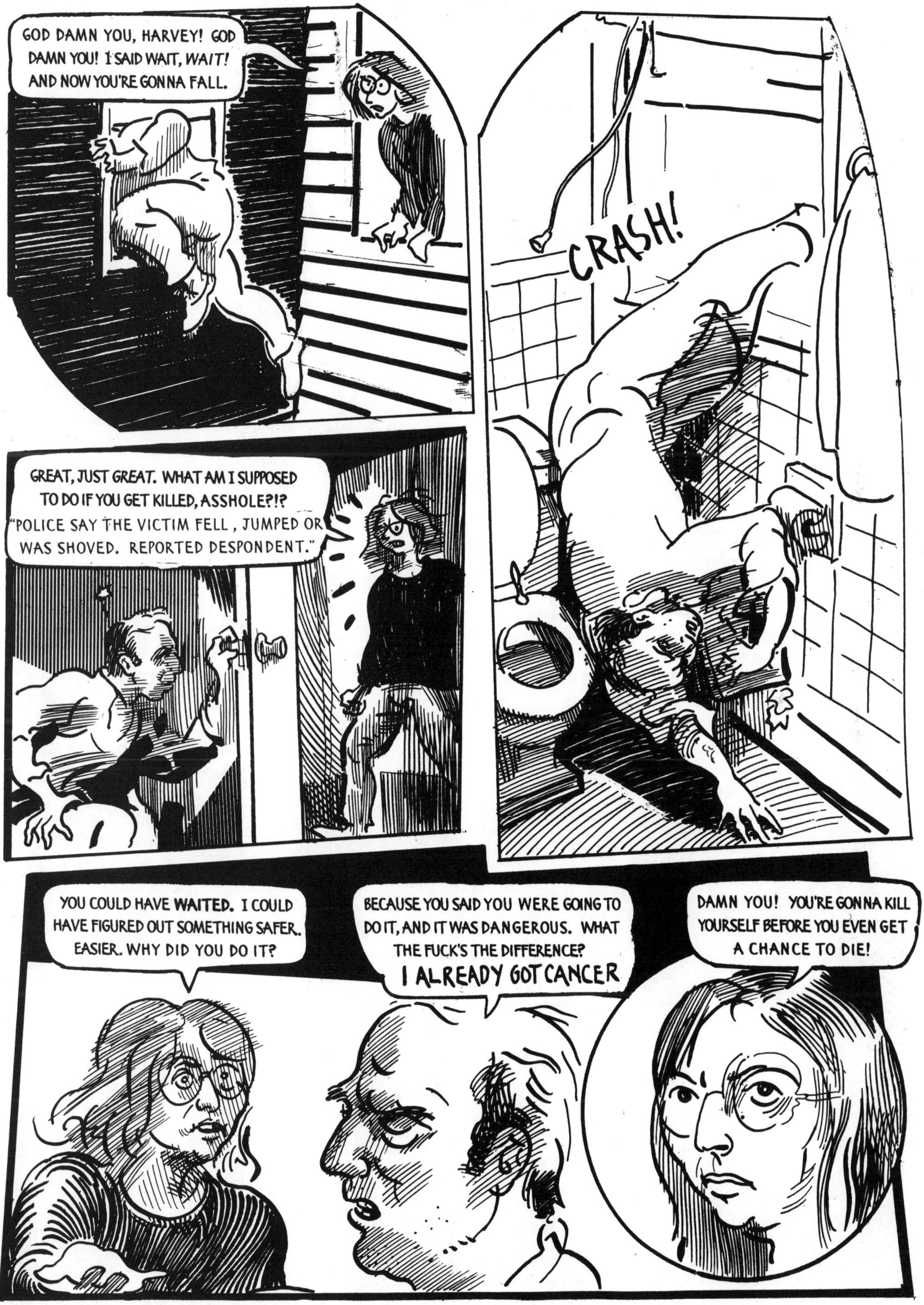
GOD DAMN YOU, HARVEY! GOD DAMN YOU! I SAID WAIT, WAIT! AND NOW YOU'RE GONNA FALL.
CRASH!
GREAT, JUST GREAT. WHAT AM I SUPPOSED TO DO IF YOU GET KILLED, ASSHOLE?!? "POLICE SAY THE VICTIM FELL, JUMPED OR WAS SHOVED. REPORTED DESPONDENT."
YOU COULD HAVE WAITED. I COULD HAVE FIGURED OUT SOMETHING SAFER. EASIER. WHY DID YOU DO IT?
BECAUSE YOU SAID YOU WERE GOING TO DO IT, AND IT WAS DANGEROUS. WHAT THE FUCK'S THE DIFFERENCE? I ALREADY GOT CANCER
DAMN YOU! YOU'RE GONNA KILL YOURSELF BEFORE YOU EVEN GET A CHANCE TO DIE!

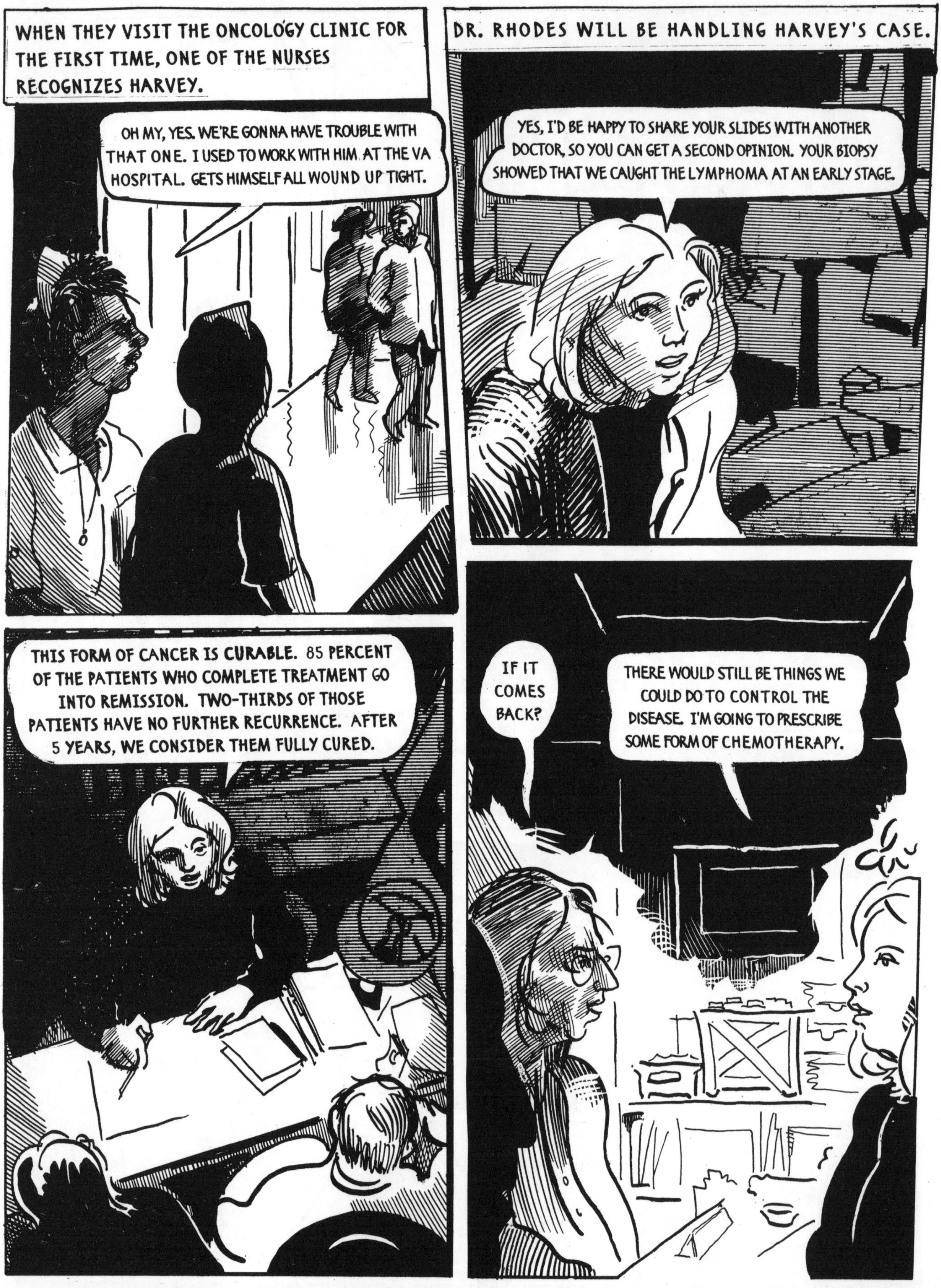
WHEN THEY VISIT THE ONCOLOGY CLINIC FOR THE FIRST TIME, ONE OF THE NURSES RECOGNIZES HARVEY.
OH MY, YES. WE'RE GONNA HAVE TROUBLE WITH THAT ONE. I USED TO WORK WITH HIM AT THE VA HOSPITAL. GETS HIMSELF ALL WOUND UP TIGHT.
DR. RHODES WILL BE HANDLING HARVEY'S CASE.
YES, I'D BE HAPPY TO SHARE YOUR SLIDES WITH ANOTHER DOCTOR, SO YOU CAN GET A SECOND OPINION. YOUR BIOPSY SHOWED THAT WE CAUGHT THE LYMPHOMA AT AN EARLY STAGE.
THIS FORM OF CANCER IS **CURABLE**. 85 PERCENT OF THE PATIENTS WHO COMPLETE TREATMENT GO INTO REMISSION. TWO-THIRDS OF THOSE PATIENTS HAVE NO FURTHER RECURRENCE. AFTER 5 YEARS, WE CONSIDER THEM FULLY CURED.
IF IT COMES BACK?
THERE WOULD STILL BE THINGS WE COULD DO TO CONTROL THE DISEASE. I'M GOING TO PRESCRIBE SOME FORM OF CHEMOTHERAPY.

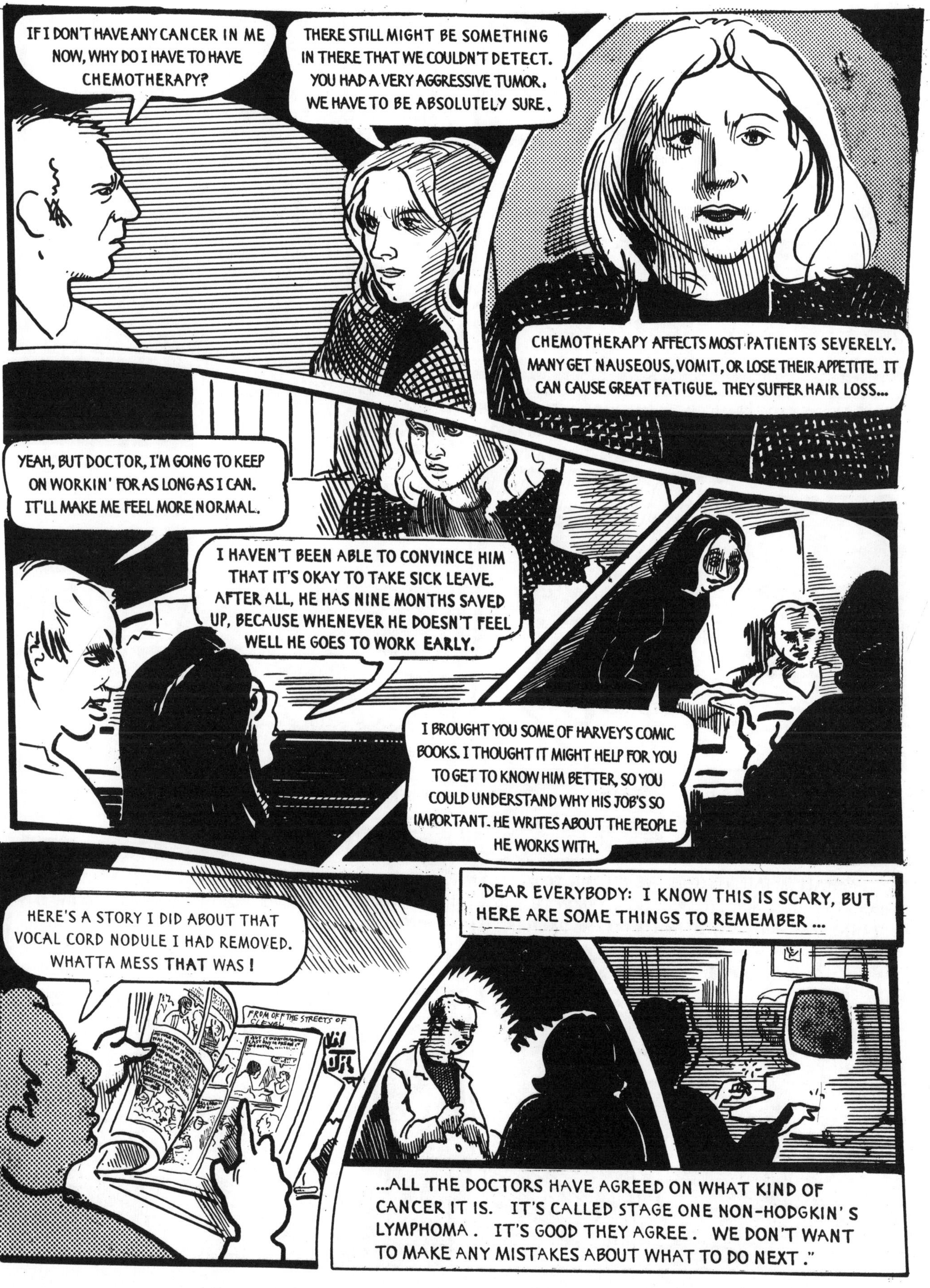
IF I DON'T HAVE ANY CANCER IN ME NOW, WHY DO I HAVE TO HAVE CHEMOTHERAPY?
THERE STILL MIGHT BE SOMETHING IN THERE THAT WE COULDN'T DETECT. YOU HAD A VERY AGGRESSIVE TUMOR. WE HAVE TO BE ABSOLUTELY SURE.
CHEMOTHERAPY AFFECTS MOST PATIENTS SEVERELY. MANY GET NAUSEOUS, VOMIT, OR LOSE THEIR APPETITE. IT CAN CAUSE GREAT FATIGUE. THEY SUFFER HAIR LOSS...
YEAH, BUT DOCTOR, I'M GOING TO KEEP ON WORKIN' FOR AS LONG AS I CAN. IT'LL MAKE ME FEEL MORE NORMAL.
I HAVEN'T BEEN ABLE TO CONVINCE HIM THAT IT'S OKAY TO TAKE SICK LEAVE. AFTER ALL, HE HAS NINE MONTHS SAVED UP, BECAUSE WHENEVER HE DOESN'T FEEL WELL HE GOES TO WORK EARLY.
I BROUGHT YOU SOME OF HARVEY'S COMIC BOOKS. I THOUGHT IT MIGHT HELP FOR YOU TO GET TO KNOW HIM BETTER, SO YOU COULD UNDERSTAND WHY HIS JOB'S SO IMPORTANT. HE WRITES ABOUT THE PEOPLE HE WORKS WITH.
HERE'S A STORY I DID ABOUT THAT VOCAL CORD NODULE I HAD REMOVED. WHATTA MESS THAT WAS!
FROM OFF THE STREETS OF CLEVEL
"DEAR EVERYBODY: I KNOW THIS IS SCARY, BUT HERE ARE SOME THINGS TO REMEMBER ...
...ALL THE DOCTORS HAVE AGREED ON WHAT KIND OF CANCER IT IS. IT'S CALLED STAGE ONE NON-HODGKIN'S LYMPHOMA. IT'S GOOD THEY AGREE. WE DON'T WANT TO MAKE ANY MISTAKES ABOUT WHAT TO DO NEXT."

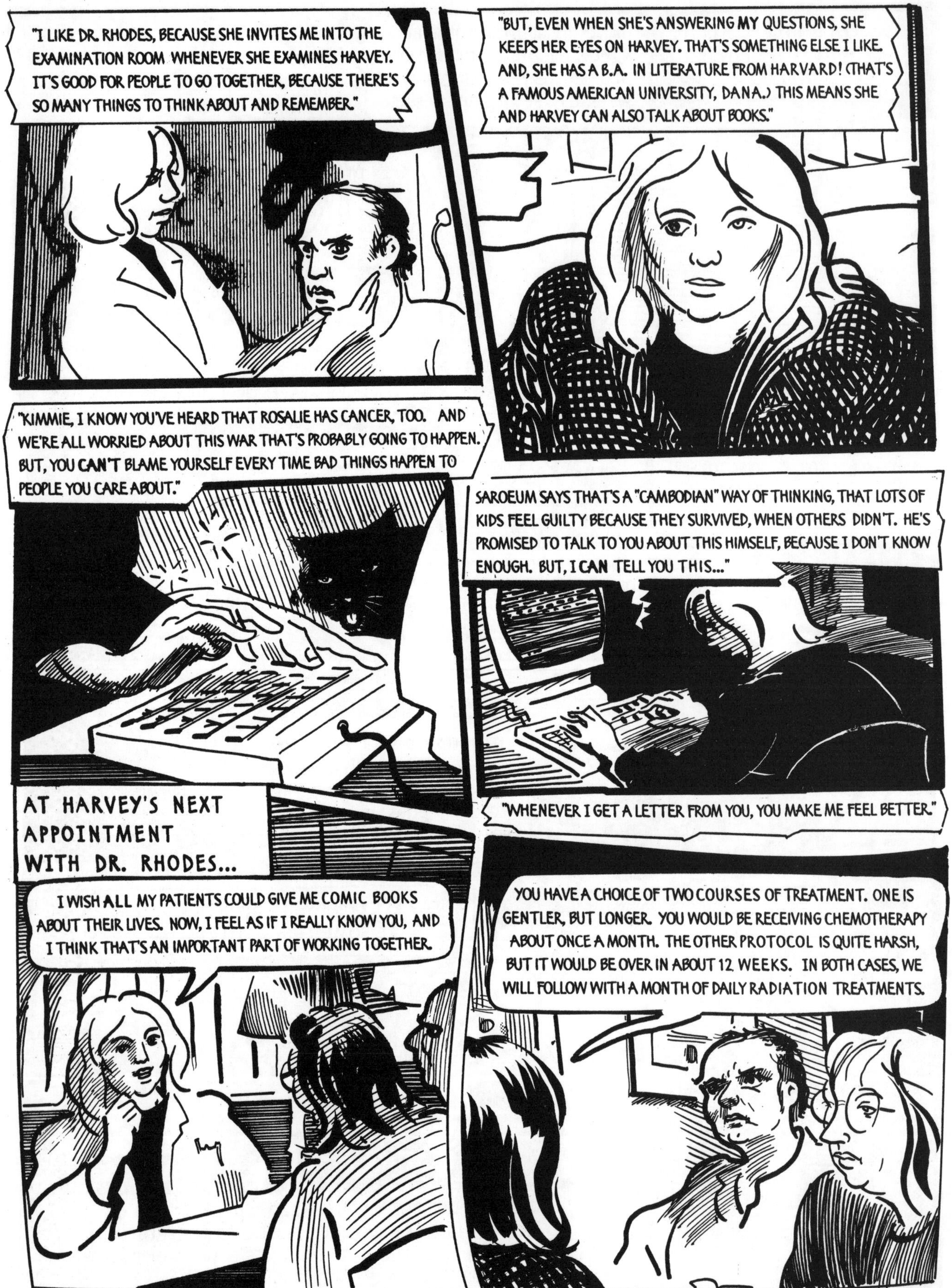
"I LIKE DR. RHODES, BECAUSE SHE INVITES ME INTO THE EXAMINATION ROOM WHENEVER SHE EXAMINES HARVEY. IT'S GOOD FOR PEOPLE TO GO TOGETHER, BECAUSE THERE'S SO MANY THINGS TO THINK ABOUT AND REMEMBER."
"BUT, EVEN WHEN SHE'S ANSWERING MY QUESTIONS, SHE KEEPS HER EYES ON HARVEY. THAT'S SOMETHING ELSE I LIKE. AND, SHE HAS A B.A. IN LITERATURE FROM HARVARD! (THAT'S A FAMOUS AMERICAN UNIVERSITY, DANA.) THIS MEANS SHE AND HARVEY CAN ALSO TALK ABOUT BOOKS."
"KIMMIE, I KNOW YOU'VE HEARD THAT ROSALIE HAS CANCER, TOO. AND WE'RE ALL WORRIED ABOUT THIS WAR THAT'S PROBABLY GOING TO HAPPEN. BUT, YOU CAN'T BLAME YOURSELF EVERY TIME BAD THINGS HAPPEN TO PEOPLE YOU CARE ABOUT."
SAROEUM SAYS THAT'S A "CAMBODIAN" WAY OF THINKING, THAT LOTS OF KIDS FEEL GUILTY BECAUSE THEY SURVIVED, WHEN OTHERS DIDN'T. HE'S PROMISED TO TALK TO YOU ABOUT THIS HIMSELF, BECAUSE I DON'T KNOW ENOUGH. BUT, I CAN TELL YOU THIS..."
"WHENEVER I GET A LETTER FROM YOU, YOU MAKE ME FEEL BETTER."
AT HARVEY'S NEXT APPOINTMENT WITH DR. RHODES...
I WISH ALL MY PATIENTS COULD GIVE ME COMIC BOOKS ABOUT THEIR LIVES. NOW, I FEEL AS IF I REALLY KNOW YOU, AND I THINK THAT'S AN IMPORTANT PART OF WORKING TOGETHER.
YOU HAVE A CHOICE OF TWO COURSES OF TREATMENT. ONE IS GENTLER, BUT LONGER. YOU WOULD BE RECEIVING CHEMOTHERAPY ABOUT ONCE A MONTH. THE OTHER PROTOCOL IS QUITE HARSH, BUT IT WOULD BE OVER IN ABOUT 12 WEEKS. IN BOTH CASES, WE WILL FOLLOW WITH A MONTH OF DAILY RADIATION TREATMENTS.

I'D LIKE TO TAKE THE 12 WEEK PROGRAM, GET IT OVER WITH AND GET BACK TO A NORMAL LIFE, AS SOON AS POSSIBLE.

I KNEW HE'D SAY THAT. ARE THEY BOTH EQUALLY EFFECTIVE?

YES. YOU SHOULD BE ABLE TO LIVE AT HOME DURING MOST, IF NOT ALL, OF THE TREATMENT. WE'LL CHECK YOUR WHITE BLOOD COUNT EVERY TIME YOU COME IN. TOWARDS THE END, THE CHEMOTHERAPY MAY CAUSE IT TO DROP SO FAR THAT YOU'LL HAVE TO BE HOSPITALIZED. YOUR NORMAL RESISTANCE TO COMMON COLDS OR VIRUSES WOULD BE GONE. WE WOULDN'T WANT TO RISK LOSING YOU TO SOMETHING LIKE PNEUMONIA, WHICH COULD DEVELOP QUICKLY.

YOU'LL RECEIVE MANY OF THE DRUGS BY I.V. HERE, BUT YOU WILL ALSO BE TAKING MEDICATION AT HOME ON AN AROUND-THE-CLOCK SCHEDULE. AT DIFFERENT TIMES, WE MAY ADD FOLLOW-UP MEDICATION OR REQUIRE YOU TO MONITOR YOUR TEMPERATURE CLOSELY.

BEFORE CERTAIN DRUGS CAN BE ADMINISTERED, YOU'LL HAVE TO PREPARE YOUR BODY BY DRINKING A SODIUM BICARBONATE SOLUTION--ORDINARY BAKING SODA AND WATER--EVERY FOUR HOURS. WILL ANY OF THIS PRESENT A PROBLEM?

NO.

WE CAN GET AN EXTRA ALARM CLOCK. I CAN GET UP.

THE DOCTORS WE WENT TO FOR A SECOND OPINION SAW HARVEY'S SLIDES. EVERYONE'S IN AGREEMENT ABOUT THE TYPE AND STAGE OF HIS TUMOR. CAN YOU WRITE DOWN THE NAME OF THIS 12 WEEK CHEMO-THERAPY? I'M GONNA ASK THEM ABOUT THAT, THEN IF EVERYTHING SEEMS OK, WE'LL BE READY TO GO.

SURE. IN FACT, I HAVE A HAND-OUT THAT DESCRIBES ALL THE DRUGS I WOULD BE PRESCRIBING.

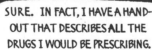

WHY DID YOU DECIDE TO ADD RADIATION TREATMENTS? WE DIDN'T TALK ABOUT THAT LAST WEEK.

THAT WAS A SUGGESTION OF THE TUMOR BOARD.

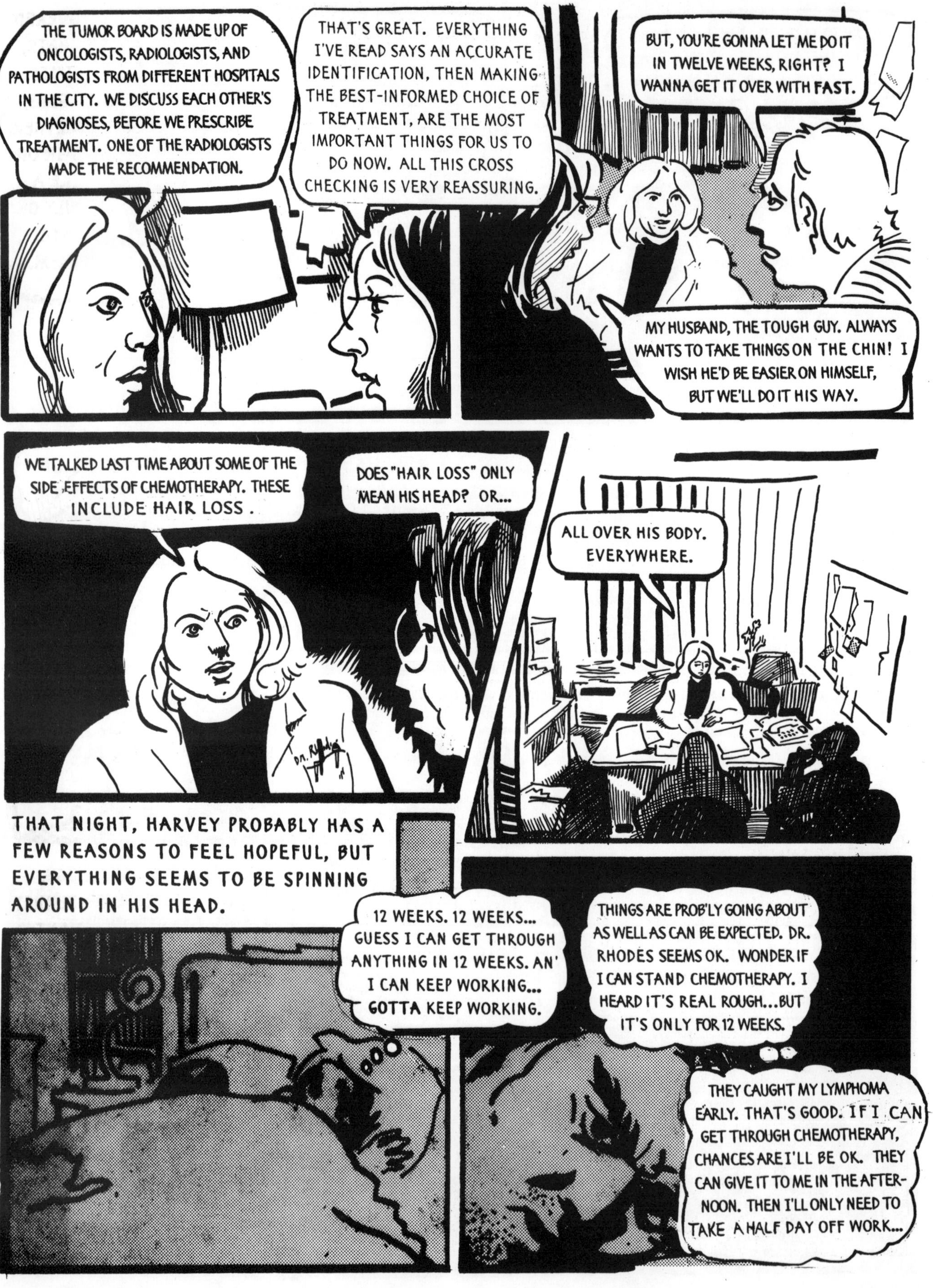
THE TUMOR BOARD IS MADE UP OF ONCOLOGISTS, RADIOLOGISTS, AND PATHOLOGISTS FROM DIFFERENT HOSPITALS IN THE CITY. WE DISCUSS EACH OTHER'S DIAGNOSES, BEFORE WE PRESCRIBE TREATMENT. ONE OF THE RADIOLOGISTS MADE THE RECOMMENDATION.
THAT'S GREAT. EVERYTHING I'VE READ SAYS AN ACCURATE IDENTIFICATION, THEN MAKING THE BEST-INFORMED CHOICE OF TREATMENT, ARE THE MOST IMPORTANT THINGS FOR US TO DO NOW. ALL THIS CROSS CHECKING IS VERY REASSURING.
BUT, YOU'RE GONNA LET ME DO IT IN TWELVE WEEKS, RIGHT? I WANNA GET IT OVER WITH FAST.
MY HUSBAND, THE TOUGH GUY. ALWAYS WANTS TO TAKE THINGS ON THE CHIN! I WISH HE'D BE EASIER ON HIMSELF, BUT WE'LL DO IT HIS WAY.
WE TALKED LAST TIME ABOUT SOME OF THE SIDE EFFECTS OF CHEMOTHERAPY. THESE INCLUDE HAIR LOSS.
DOES "HAIR LOSS" ONLY MEAN HIS HEAD? OR...
DR. RHODES
ALL OVER HIS BODY. EVERYWHERE.
THAT NIGHT, HARVEY PROBABLY HAS A FEW REASONS TO FEEL HOPEFUL, BUT EVERYTHING SEEMS TO BE SPINNING AROUND IN HIS HEAD.
12 WEEKS. 12 WEEKS... GUESS I CAN GET THROUGH ANYTHING IN 12 WEEKS. AN' I CAN KEEP WORKING... GOTTA KEEP WORKING.
THINGS ARE PROB'LY GOING ABOUT AS WELL AS CAN BE EXPECTED. DR. RHODES SEEMS OK. WONDER IF I CAN STAND CHEMOTHERAPY. I HEARD IT'S REAL ROUGH...BUT IT'S ONLY FOR 12 WEEKS.
THEY CAUGHT MY LYMPHOMA EARLY. THAT'S GOOD. IF I CAN GET THROUGH CHEMOTHERAPY, CHANCES ARE I'LL BE OK. THEY CAN GIVE IT TO ME IN THE AFTERNOON. THEN I'LL ONLY NEED TO TAKE A HALF DAY OFF WORK...

WHEN DR. RHODES SAID "ALL OVER HIS BODY. *EVERYWHERE.*" JOYCE FELT DEEP HURT. FOR SOME REASON, LOSING THE HAIR ON HARVEY'S HEAD SEEMS EASIER TO ACCEPT.

HARVEY'S BODY IS COVERED WITH THICK, SILKY HAIR, WHICH SHE SOMETIMES TWINES IN HER FINGERS, WHEN THEY SLEEP TOGETHER. LOSING ALL OF THE HAIR ON HIS BODY SEEMS LIKE A VIOLATION, AN ASSAULT ON SOMETHING INTIMATE, SHARED BETWEEN THEM.

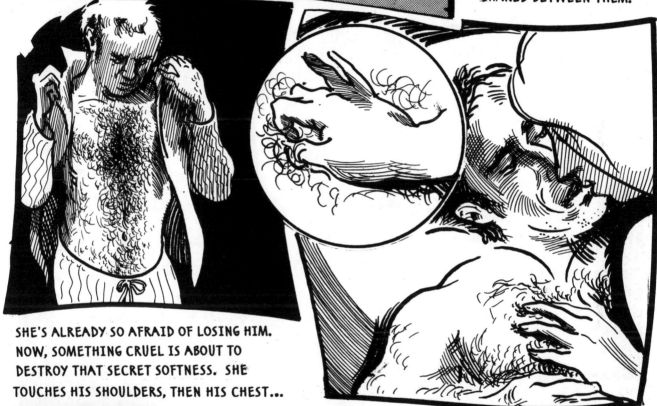

SHE'S ALREADY SO AFRAID OF LOSING HIM. NOW, SOMETHING CRUEL IS ABOUT TO DESTROY THAT SECRET SOFTNESS. SHE TOUCHES HIS SHOULDERS, THEN HIS CHEST...

AND THINKS ABOUT THE SCOTTISH LEGEND OF TAMLIN OF CARTERHAUGH, LONG HELD CAPTIVE BY A JEALOUS SPIRIT. WHEN HIS MORTAL WIFE JENNET FIRST LAY WITH HIM IN THEIR MARRIAGE BED, BOTH KNEW THE ENCHANTED TAMLIN WOULD DIE, IF SHE LACKED COURAGE.

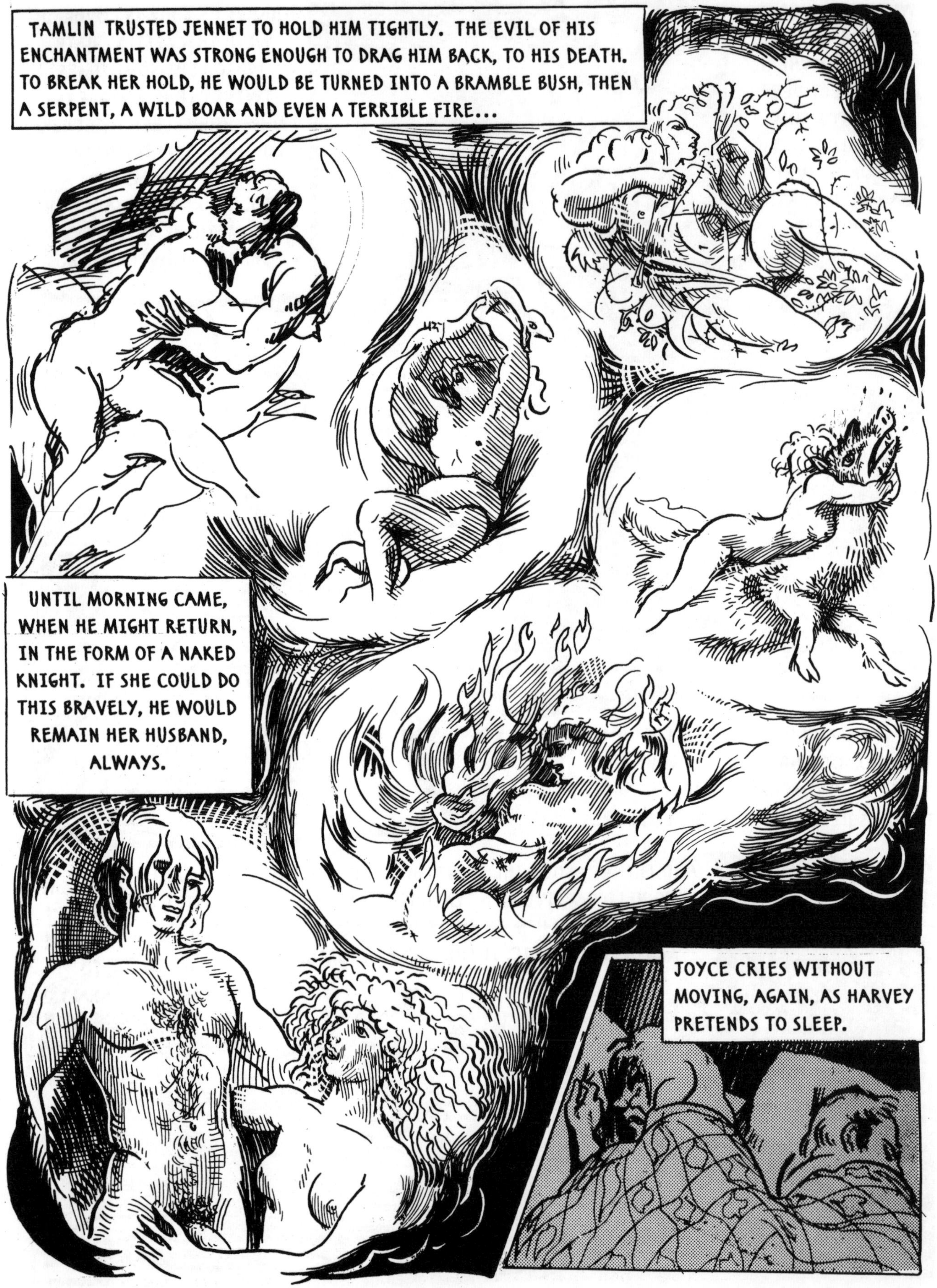
TAMLIN TRUSTED JENNET TO HOLD HIM TIGHTLY. THE EVIL OF HIS ENCHANTMENT WAS STRONG ENOUGH TO DRAG HIM BACK, TO HIS DEATH. TO BREAK HER HOLD, HE WOULD BE TURNED INTO A BRAMBLE BUSH, THEN A SERPENT, A WILD BOAR AND EVEN A TERRIBLE FIRE...
UNTIL MORNING CAME, WHEN HE MIGHT RETURN, IN THE FORM OF A NAKED KNIGHT. IF SHE COULD DO THIS BRAVELY, HE WOULD REMAIN HER HUSBAND, ALWAYS.
JOYCE CRIES WITHOUT MOVING, AGAIN, AS HARVEY PRETENDS TO SLEEP.

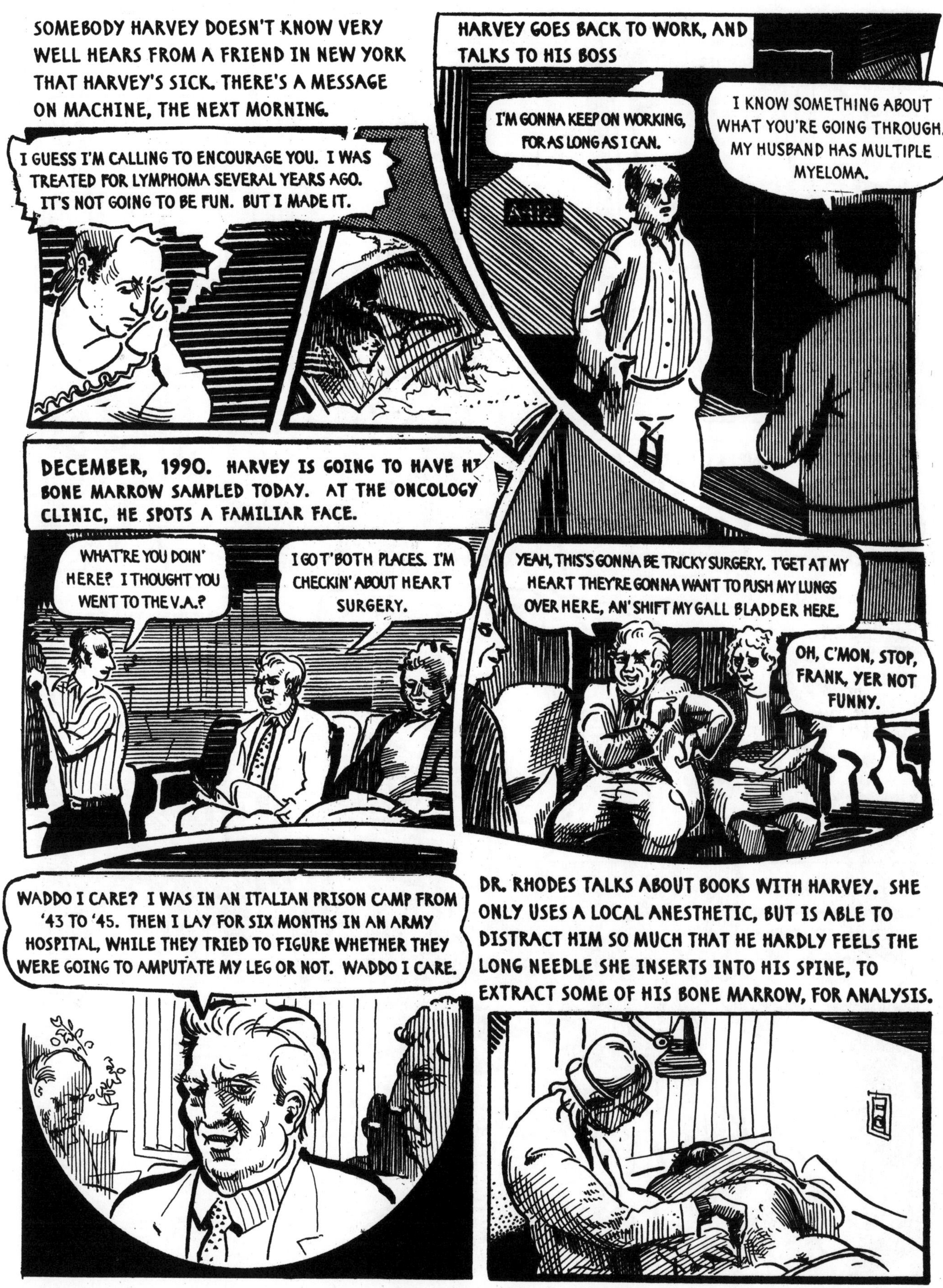
SOMEBODY HARVEY DOESN'T KNOW VERY WELL HEARS FROM A FRIEND IN NEW YORK THAT HARVEY'S SICK. THERE'S A MESSAGE ON MACHINE, THE NEXT MORNING.
I GUESS I'M CALLING TO ENCOURAGE YOU. I WAS TREATED FOR LYMPHOMA SEVERAL YEARS AGO. IT'S NOT GOING TO BE FUN. BUT I MADE IT.
HARVEY GOES BACK TO WORK, AND TALKS TO HIS BOSS
I'M GONNA KEEP ON WORKING, FOR AS LONG AS I CAN.
I KNOW SOMETHING ABOUT WHAT YOU'RE GOING THROUGH. MY HUSBAND HAS MULTIPLE MYELOMA.
DECEMBER, 1990. HARVEY IS GOING TO HAVE HIS BONE MARROW SAMPLED TODAY. AT THE ONCOLOGY CLINIC, HE SPOTS A FAMILIAR FACE.
WHAT'RE YOU DOIN' HERE? I THOUGHT YOU WENT TO THE V.A.?
I GOT'BOTH PLACES. I'M CHECKIN' ABOUT HEART SURGERY.
YEAH, THIS'S GONNA BE TRICKY SURGERY. T'GET AT MY HEART THEY'RE GONNA WANT TO PUSH MY LUNGS OVER HERE, AN' SHIFT MY GALL BLADDER HERE.
OH, C'MON, STOP, FRANK, YER NOT FUNNY.
WADDO I CARE? I WAS IN AN ITALIAN PRISON CAMP FROM '43 TO '45. THEN I LAY FOR SIX MONTHS IN AN ARMY HOSPITAL, WHILE THEY TRIED TO FIGURE WHETHER THEY WERE GOING TO AMPUTATE MY LEG OR NOT. WADDO I CARE.
DR. RHODES TALKS ABOUT BOOKS WITH HARVEY. SHE ONLY USES A LOCAL ANESTHETIC, BUT IS ABLE TO DISTRACT HIM SO MUCH THAT HE HARDLY FEELS THE LONG NEEDLE SHE INSERTS INTO HIS SPINE, TO EXTRACT SOME OF HIS BONE MARROW, FOR ANALYSIS.

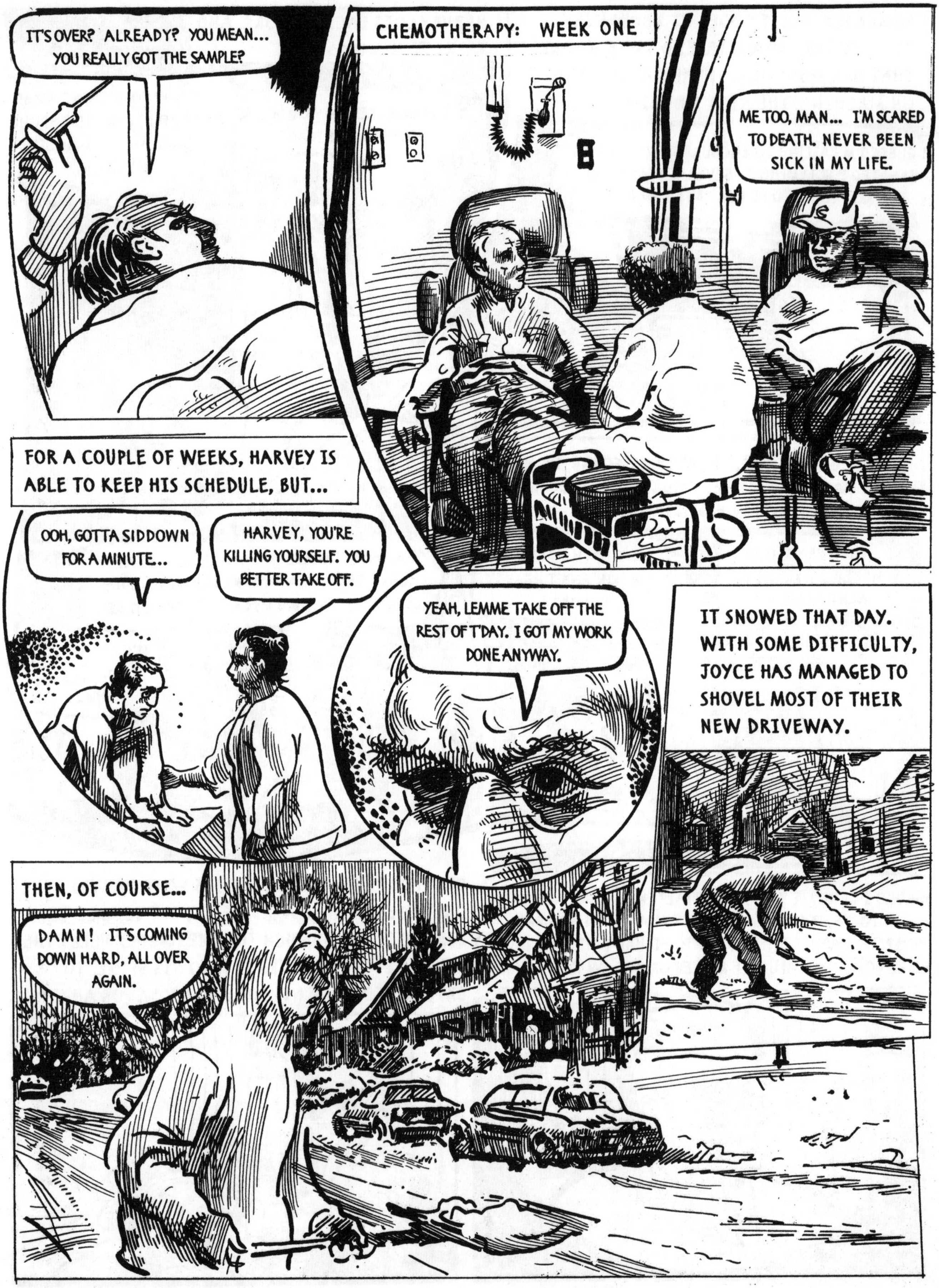

IT'S OVER? ALREADY? YOU MEAN... YOU REALLY GOT THE SAMPLE?
CHEMOTHERAPY: WEEK ONE
ME TOO, MAN... I'M SCARED TO DEATH. NEVER BEEN SICK IN MY LIFE.
FOR A COUPLE OF WEEKS, HARVEY IS ABLE TO KEEP HIS SCHEDULE, BUT...
OOH, GOTTA SIDDOWN FOR A MINUTE...
HARVEY, YOU'RE KILLING YOURSELF. YOU BETTER TAKE OFF.
YEAH, LEMME TAKE OFF THE REST OF T'DAY. I GOT MY WORK DONE ANYWAY.
IT SNOWED THAT DAY. WITH SOME DIFFICULTY, JOYCE HAS MANAGED TO SHOVEL MOST OF THEIR NEW DRIVEWAY.
THEN, OF COURSE...
DAMN! IT'S COMING DOWN HARD, ALL OVER AGAIN.

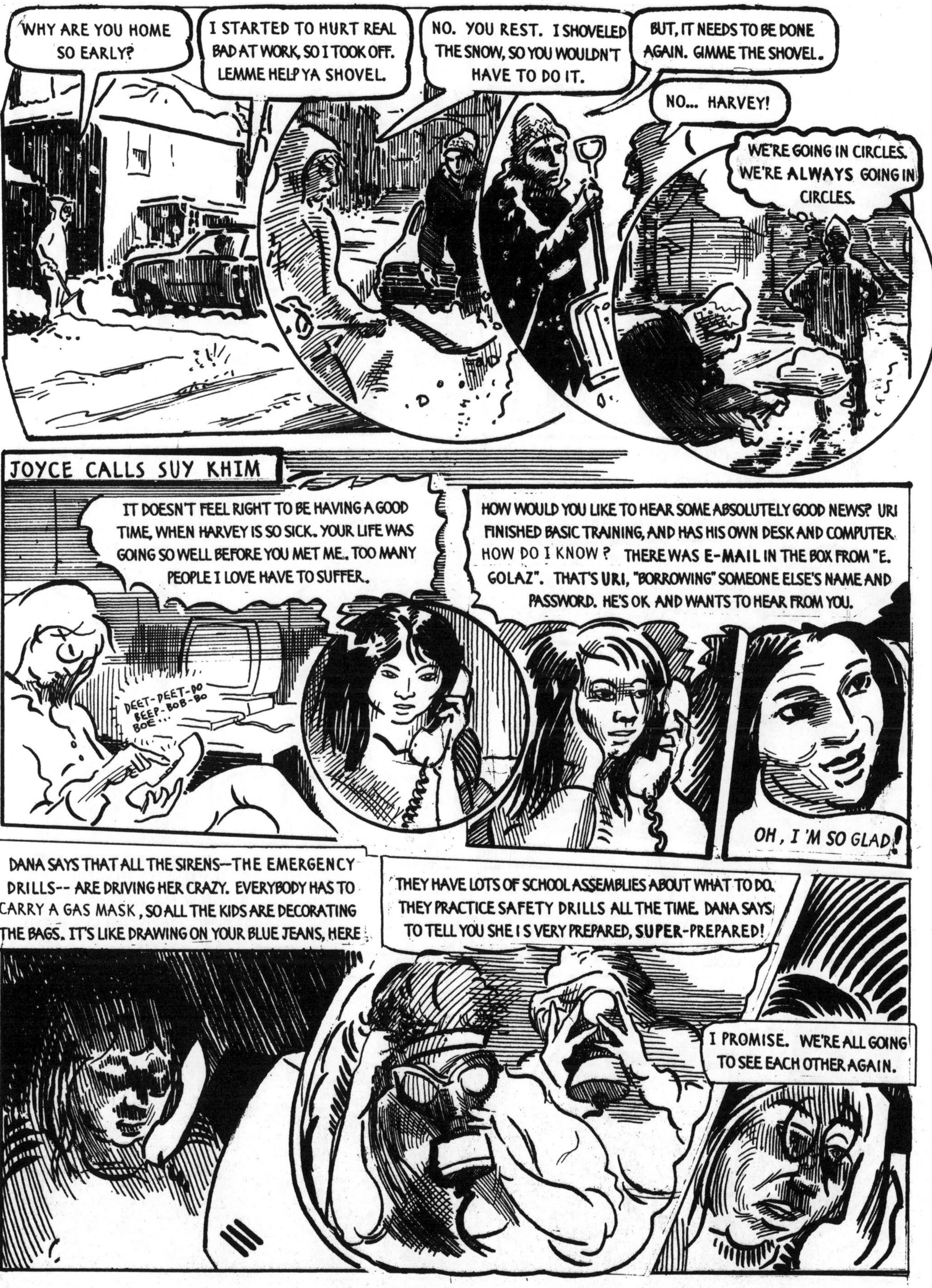
WHY ARE YOU HOME SO EARLY?
I STARTED TO HURT REAL BAD AT WORK, SO I TOOK OFF. LEMME HELP YA SHOVEL.
NO. YOU REST. I SHOVELED THE SNOW, SO YOU WOULDN'T HAVE TO DO IT.
BUT, IT NEEDS TO BE DONE AGAIN. GIMME THE SHOVEL.
NO... HARVEY!
WE'RE GOING IN CIRCLES. WE'RE ALWAYS GOING IN CIRCLES.
JOYCE CALLS SUY KHIM
IT DOESN'T FEEL RIGHT TO BE HAVING A GOOD TIME, WHEN HARVEY IS SO SICK. YOUR LIFE WAS GOING SO WELL BEFORE YOU MET ME.. TOO MANY PEOPLE I LOVE HAVE TO SUFFER.
DEET-DEET-DO BEEP-BOB-BO BOE...
HOW WOULD YOU LIKE TO HEAR SOME ABSOLUTELY GOOD NEWS? URI FINISHED BASIC TRAINING, AND HAS HIS OWN DESK AND COMPUTER. HOW DO I KNOW? THERE WAS E-MAIL IN THE BOX FROM "E. GOLAZ". THAT'S URI, "BORROWING" SOMEONE ELSE'S NAME AND PASSWORD. HE'S OK AND WANTS TO HEAR FROM YOU.
OH, I'M SO GLAD!
DANA SAYS THAT ALL THE SIRENS--THE EMERGENCY DRILLS-- ARE DRIVING HER CRAZY. EVERYBODY HAS TO CARRY A GAS MASK, SO ALL THE KIDS ARE DECORATING THE BAGS. IT'S LIKE DRAWING ON YOUR BLUE JEANS, HERE
THEY HAVE LOTS OF SCHOOL ASSEMBLIES ABOUT WHAT TO DO. THEY PRACTICE SAFETY DRILLS ALL THE TIME. DANA SAYS TO TELL YOU SHE IS VERY PREPARED, SUPER-PREPARED!
I PROMISE. WE'RE ALL GOING TO SEE EACH OTHER AGAIN.

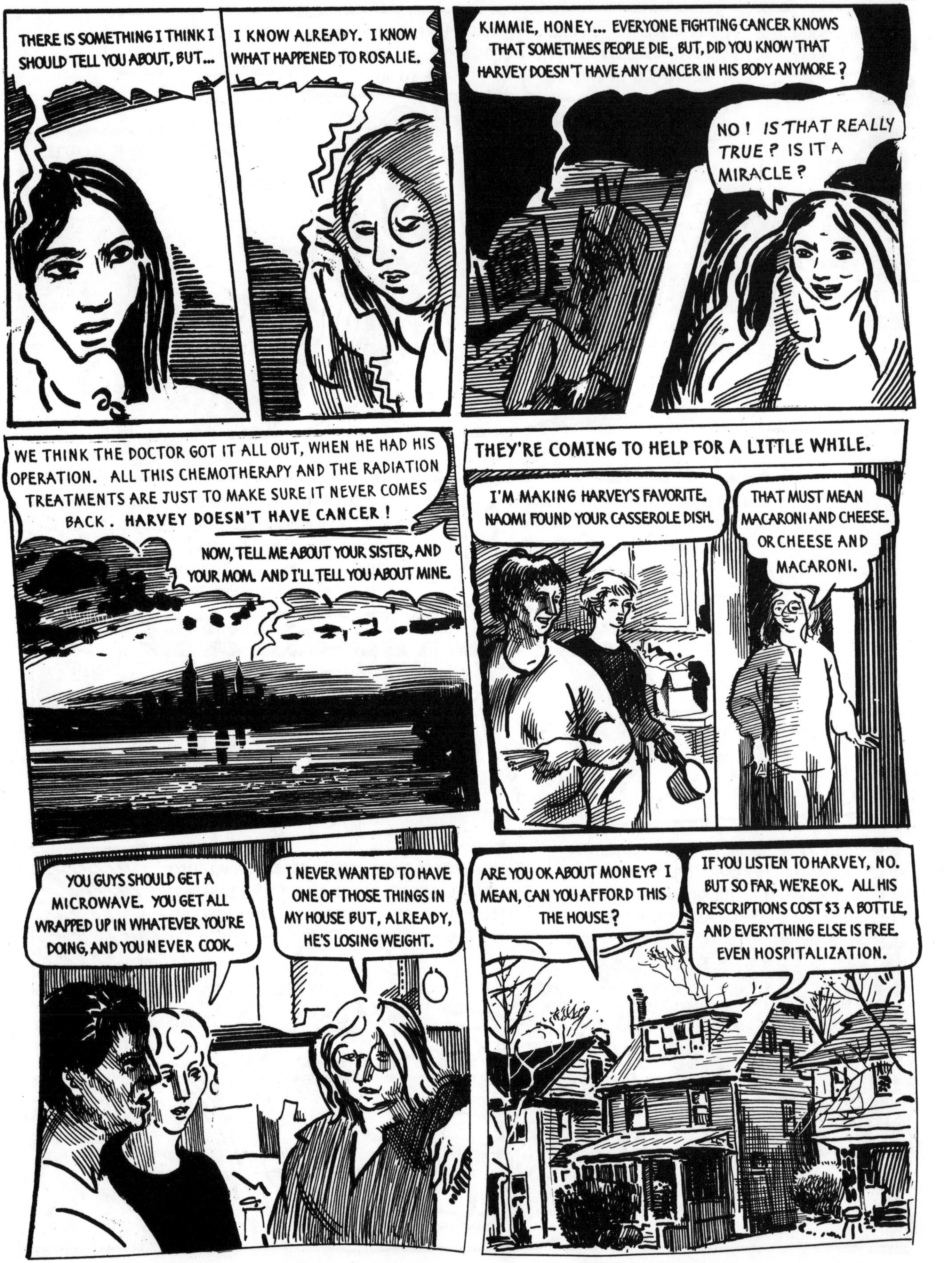
THERE IS SOMETHING I THINK I SHOULD TELL YOU ABOUT, BUT...
I KNOW ALREADY. I KNOW WHAT HAPPENED TO ROSALIE.
KIMMIE, HONEY... EVERYONE FIGHTING CANCER KNOWS THAT SOMETIMES PEOPLE DIE, BUT, DID YOU KNOW THAT HARVEY DOESN'T HAVE ANY CANCER IN HIS BODY ANYMORE ?
NO ! IS THAT REALLY TRUE ? IS IT A MIRACLE ?
WE THINK THE DOCTOR GOT IT ALL OUT, WHEN HE HAD HIS OPERATION. ALL THIS CHEMOTHERAPY AND THE RADIATION TREATMENTS ARE JUST TO MAKE SURE IT NEVER COMES BACK. HARVEY DOESN'T HAVE CANCER !
NOW, TELL ME ABOUT YOUR SISTER, AND YOUR MOM. AND I'LL TELL YOU ABOUT MINE.
THEY'RE COMING TO HELP FOR A LITTLE WHILE.
I'M MAKING HARVEY'S FAVORITE. NAOMI FOUND YOUR CASSEROLE DISH.
THAT MUST MEAN MACARONI AND CHEESE. OR CHEESE AND MACARONI.
YOU GUYS SHOULD GET A MICROWAVE. YOU GET ALL WRAPPED UP IN WHATEVER YOU'RE DOING, AND YOU NEVER COOK.
I NEVER WANTED TO HAVE ONE OF THOSE THINGS IN MY HOUSE BUT, ALREADY, HE'S LOSING WEIGHT.
ARE YOU OK ABOUT MONEY? I MEAN, CAN YOU AFFORD THIS THE HOUSE ?
IF YOU LISTEN TO HARVEY, NO. BUT SO FAR, WE'RE OK. ALL HIS PRESCRIPTIONS COST $3 A BOTTLE, AND EVERYTHING ELSE IS FREE. EVEN HOSPITALIZATION.

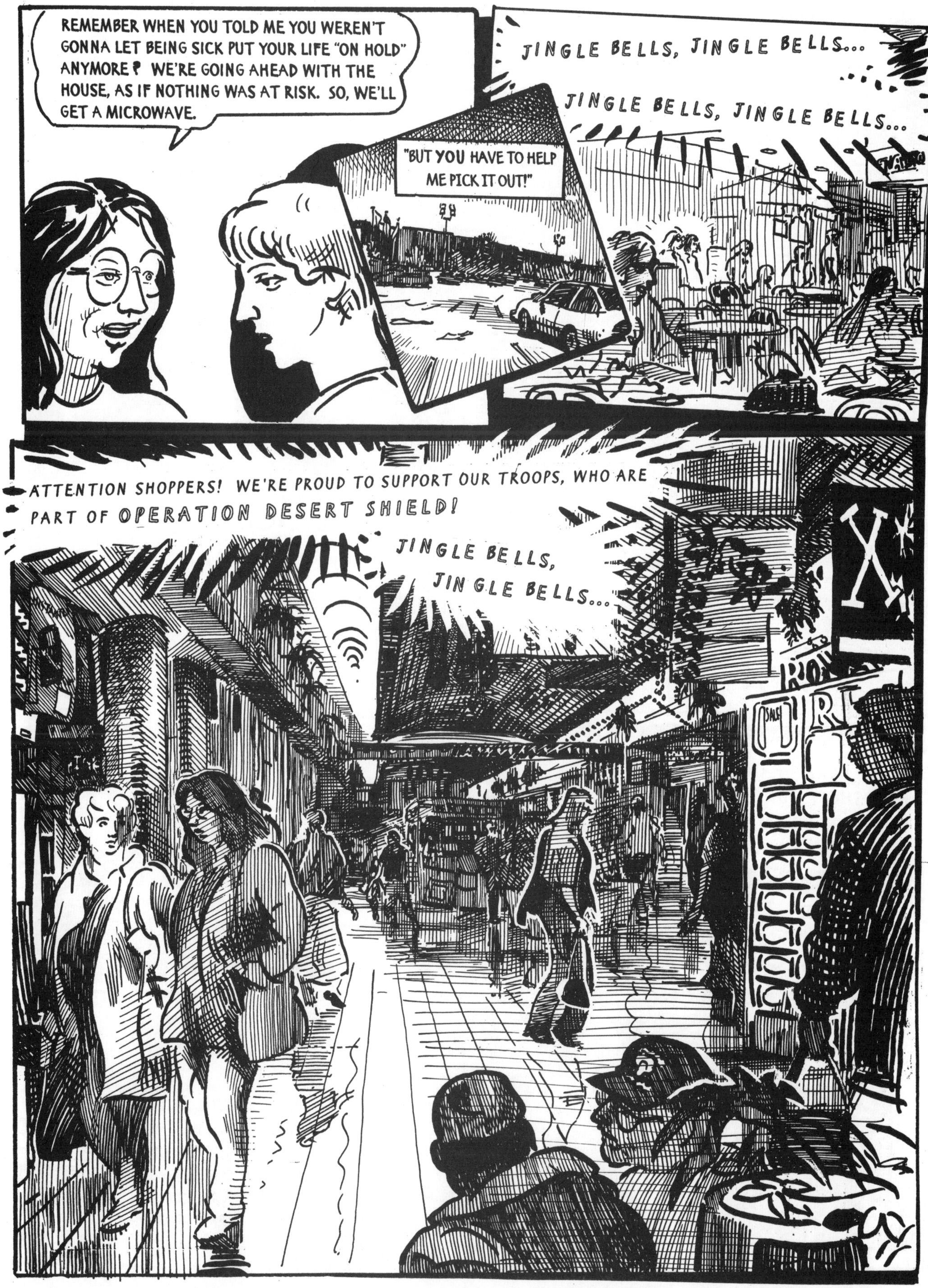
REMEMBER WHEN YOU TOLD ME YOU WEREN'T GONNA LET BEING SICK PUT YOUR LIFE "ON HOLD" ANYMORE? WE'RE GOING AHEAD WITH THE HOUSE, AS IF NOTHING WAS AT RISK. SO, WE'LL GET A MICROWAVE.
"BUT YOU HAVE TO HELP ME PICK IT OUT!"
JINGLE BELLS, JINGLE BELLS...
JINGLE BELLS, JINGLE BELLS...
ATTENTION SHOPPERS! WE'RE PROUD TO SUPPORT OUR TROOPS, WHO ARE PART OF OPERATION DESERT SHIELD!
JINGLE BELLS, JINGLE BELLS...

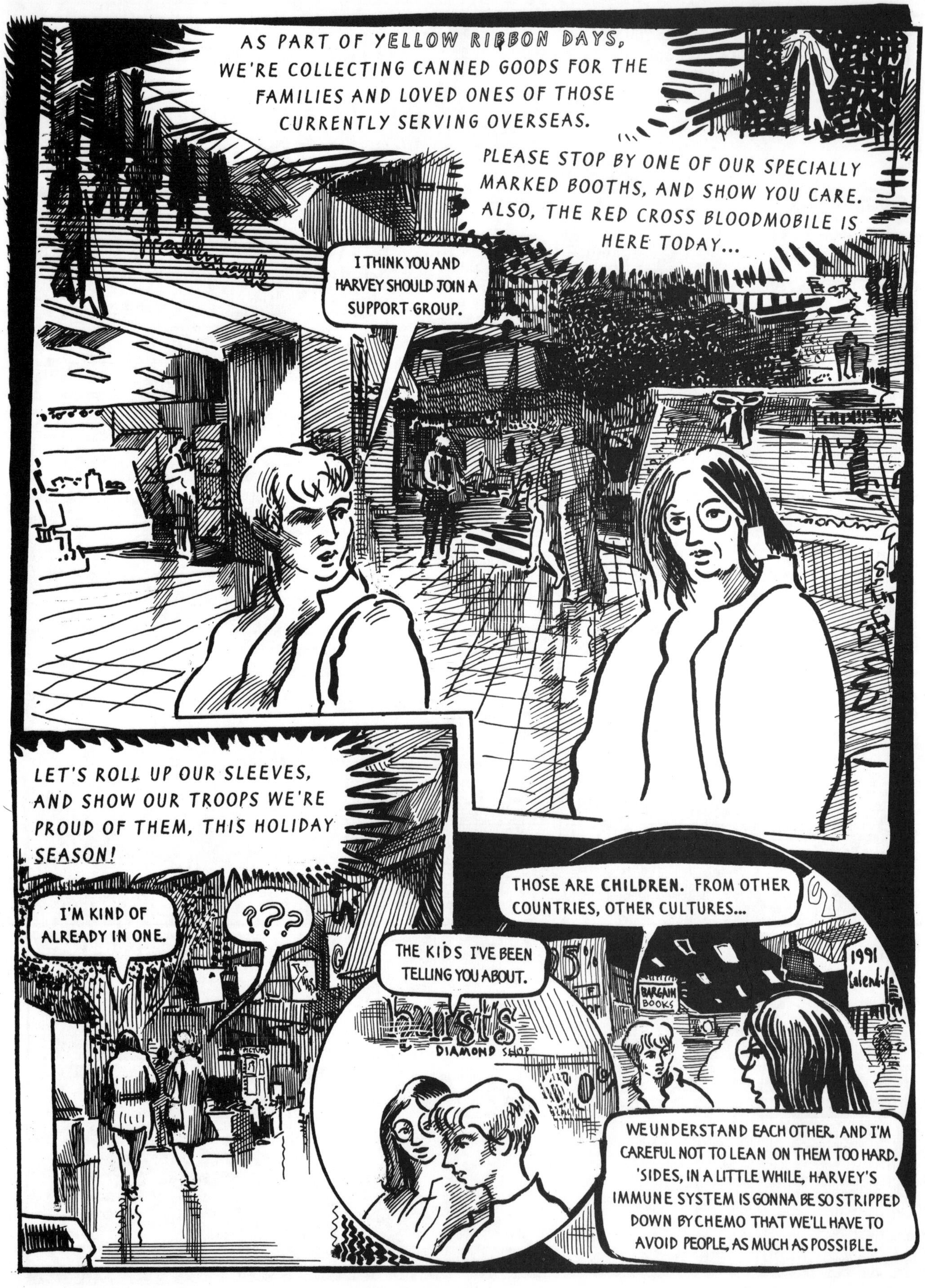
AS PART OF YELLOW RIBBON DAYS, WE'RE COLLECTING CANNED GOODS FOR THE FAMILIES AND LOVED ONES OF THOSE CURRENTLY SERVING OVERSEAS.
PLEASE STOP BY ONE OF OUR SPECIALLY MARKED BOOTHS, AND SHOW YOU CARE. ALSO, THE RED CROSS BLOODMOBILE IS HERE TODAY...
I THINK YOU AND HARVEY SHOULD JOIN A SUPPORT GROUP.
LET'S ROLL UP OUR SLEEVES, AND SHOW OUR TROOPS WE'RE PROUD OF THEM, THIS HOLIDAY SEASON!
I'M KIND OF ALREADY IN ONE.
???
THE KIDS I'VE BEEN TELLING YOU ABOUT.
THOSE ARE **CHILDREN.** FROM OTHER COUNTRIES, OTHER CULTURES...
DIAMOND SHOP
BARGAIN BOOKS
1991 Calendar
WE UNDERSTAND EACH OTHER. AND I'M CAREFUL NOT TO LEAN ON THEM TOO HARD. 'SIDES, IN A LITTLE WHILE, HARVEY'S IMMUNE SYSTEM IS GONNA BE SO STRIPPED DOWN BY CHEMO THAT WE'LL HAVE TO AVOID PEOPLE, AS MUCH AS POSSIBLE.

7

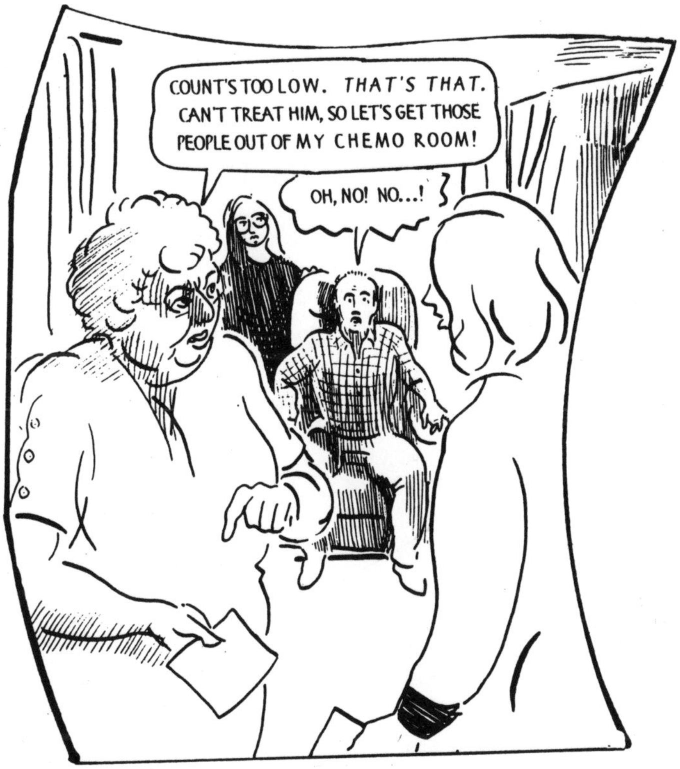
COUNT'S TOO LOW. THAT'S THAT. CAN'T TREAT HIM, SO LET'S GET THOSE PEOPLE OUT OF MY CHEMO ROOM!
OH, NO! NO...!

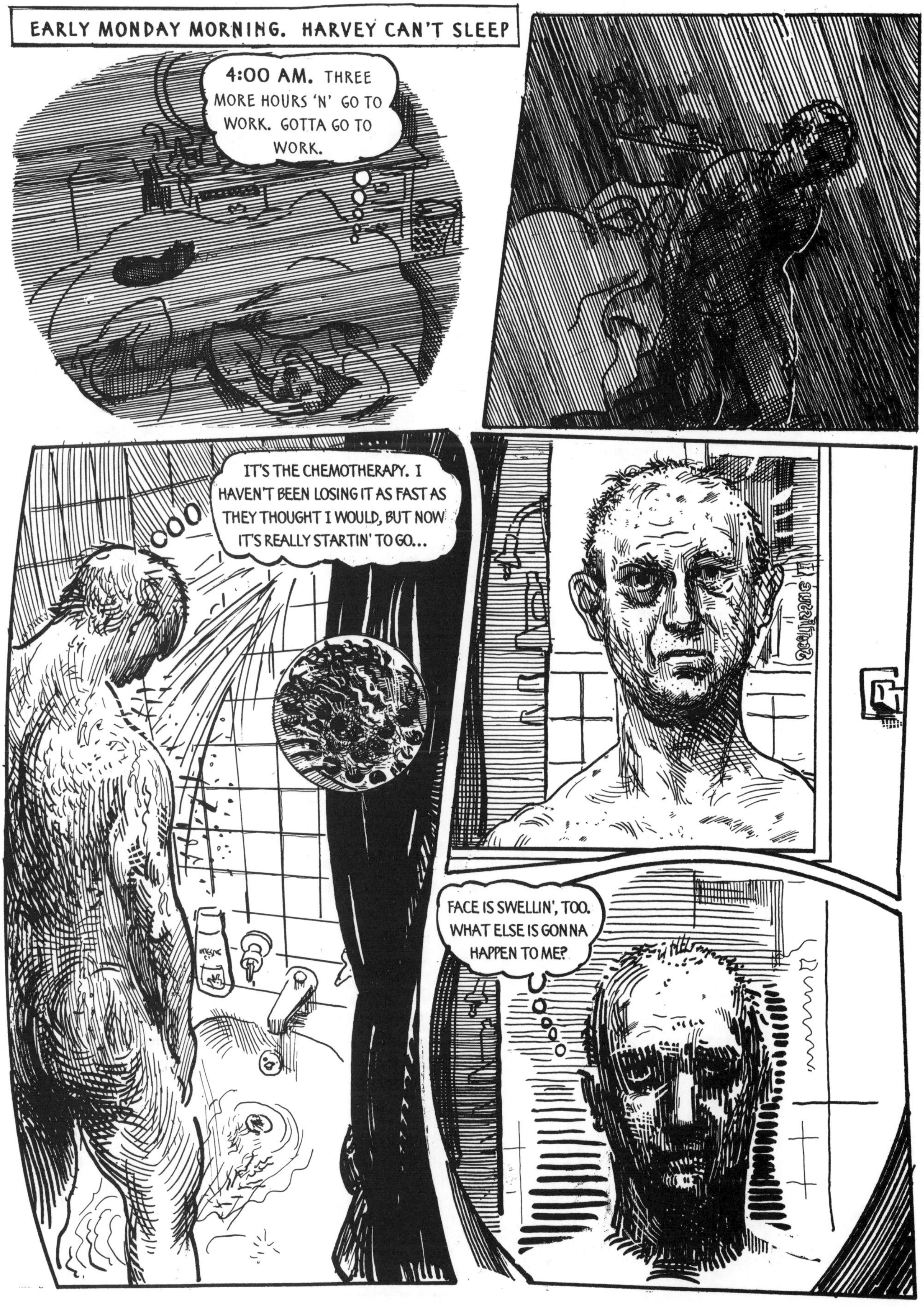
EARLY MONDAY MORNING. HARVEY CAN'T SLEEP
4:00 AM. THREE MORE HOURS 'N' GO TO WORK. GOTTA GO TO WORK.
IT'S THE CHEMOTHERAPY. I HAVEN'T BEEN LOSING IT AS FAST AS THEY THOUGHT I WOULD, BUT NOW IT'S REALLY STARTIN' TO GO...
FACE IS SWELLIN', TOO. WHAT ELSE IS GONNA HAPPEN TO ME?

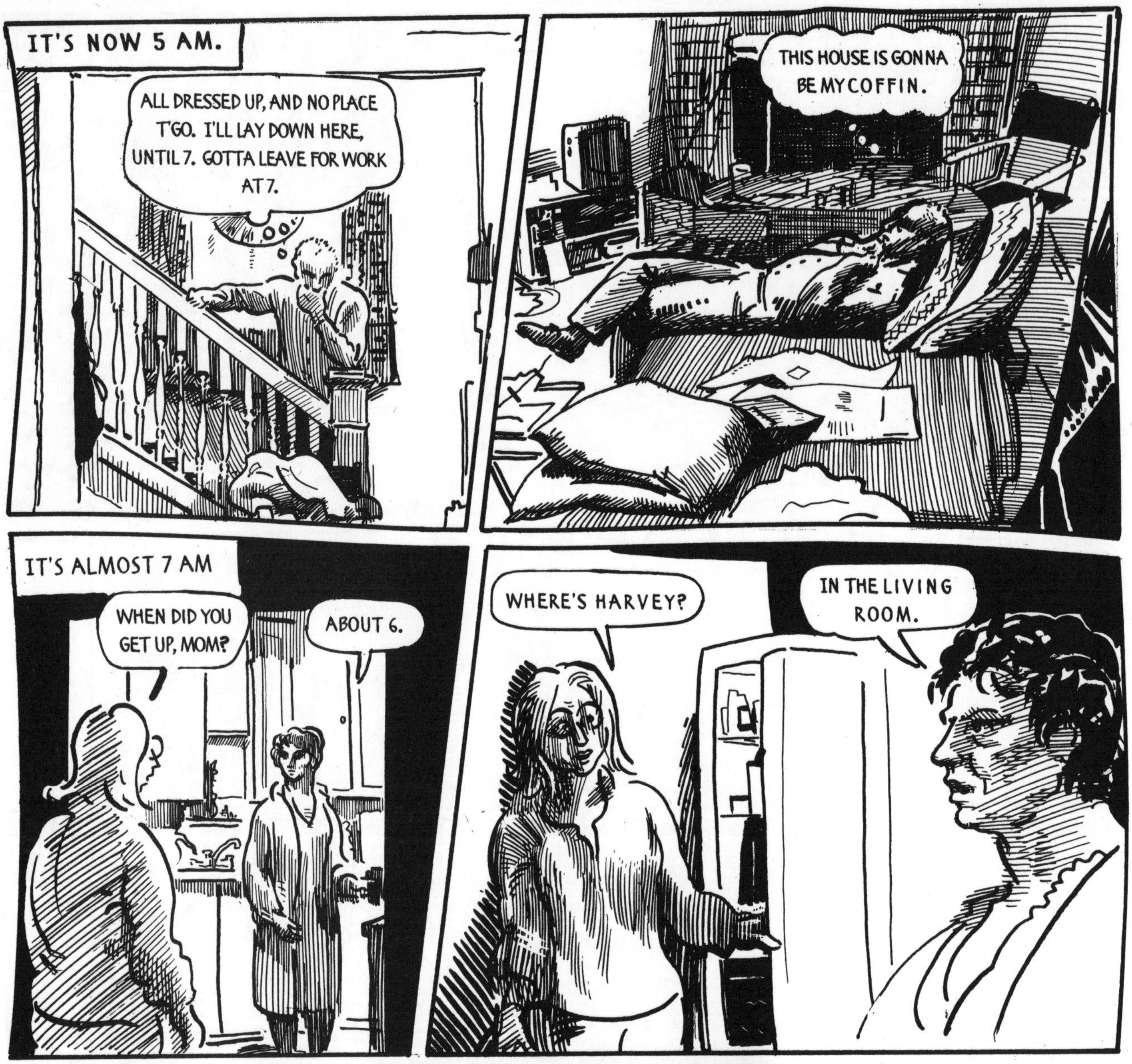
IT'S NOW 5 AM.
ALL DRESSED UP, AND NO PLACE T'GO. I'LL LAY DOWN HERE, UNTIL 7. GOTTA LEAVE FOR WORK AT 7.
THIS HOUSE IS GONNA BE MY COFFIN.
IT'S ALMOST 7 AM
WHEN DID YOU GET UP, MOM?
ABOUT 6.
WHERE'S HARVEY?
IN THE LIVING ROOM.

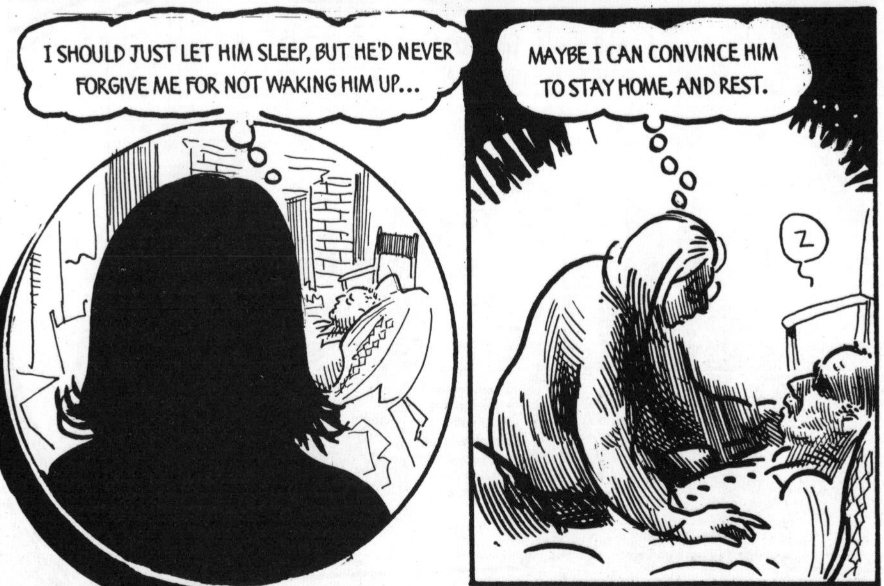
I SHOULD JUST LET HIM SLEEP, BUT HE'D NEVER FORGIVE ME FOR NOT WAKING HIM UP...
MAYBE I CAN CONVINCE HIM TO STAY HOME, AND REST.
Z

SHE COULDN'T CONVINCE HIM. THEY ENDED UP YELLING AT EACH OTHER AND YOU'VE HEARD *THAT* BEFORE. (MOM HASN'T.) SO, LETS SKIP MOST OF IT...

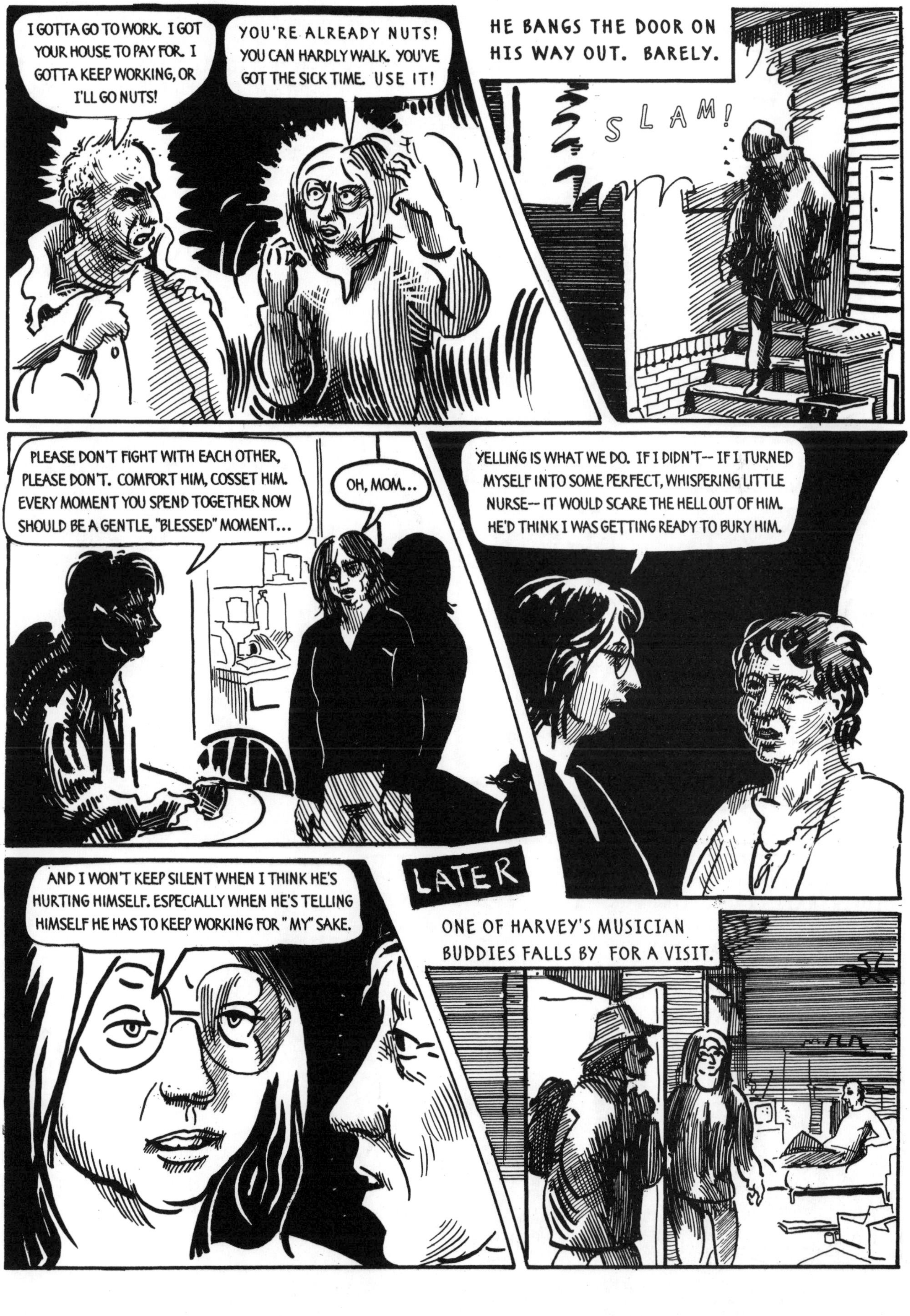
I GOTTA GO TO WORK. I GOT YOUR HOUSE TO PAY FOR. I GOTTA KEEP WORKING, OR I'LL GO NUTS!
YOU'RE ALREADY NUTS! YOU CAN HARDLY WALK. YOU'VE GOT THE SICK TIME. USE IT!
HE BANGS THE DOOR ON HIS WAY OUT. BARELY.
SLAM!
PLEASE DON'T FIGHT WITH EACH OTHER, PLEASE DON'T. COMFORT HIM, COSSET HIM. EVERY MOMENT YOU SPEND TOGETHER NOW SHOULD BE A GENTLE, "BLESSED" MOMENT...
OH, MOM...
YELLING IS WHAT WE DO. IF I DIDN'T-- IF I TURNED MYSELF INTO SOME PERFECT, WHISPERING LITTLE NURSE-- IT WOULD SCARE THE HELL OUT OF HIM. HE'D THINK I WAS GETTING READY TO BURY HIM.
AND I WON'T KEEP SILENT WHEN I THINK HE'S HURTING HIMSELF. ESPECIALLY WHEN HE'S TELLING HIMSELF HE HAS TO KEEP WORKING FOR "MY" SAKE.
LATER
ONE OF HARVEY'S MUSICIAN BUDDIES FALLS BY FOR A VISIT.

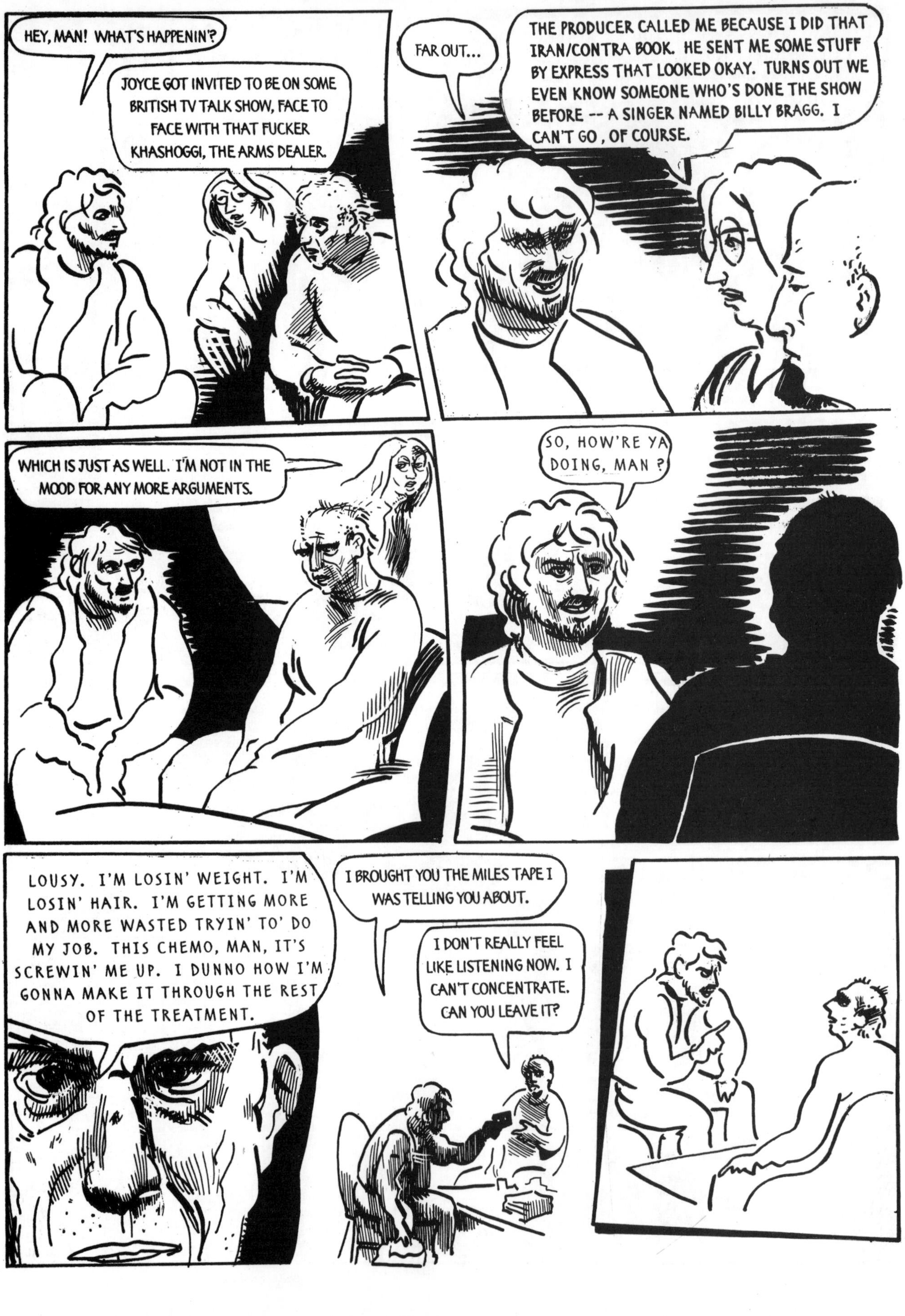
HEY, MAN! WHAT'S HAPPENIN'?
JOYCE GOT INVITED TO BE ON SOME BRITISH TV TALK SHOW, FACE TO FACE WITH THAT FUCKER KHASHOGGI, THE ARMS DEALER.
FAR OUT...
THE PRODUCER CALLED ME BECAUSE I DID THAT IRAN/CONTRA BOOK. HE SENT ME SOME STUFF BY EXPRESS THAT LOOKED OKAY. TURNS OUT WE EVEN KNOW SOMEONE WHO'S DONE THE SHOW BEFORE -- A SINGER NAMED BILLY BRAGG. I CAN'T GO, OF COURSE.
WHICH IS JUST AS WELL. I'M NOT IN THE MOOD FOR ANY MORE ARGUMENTS.
SO, HOW'RE YA DOING, MAN?
LOUSY. I'M LOSIN' WEIGHT. I'M LOSIN' HAIR. I'M GETTING MORE AND MORE WASTED TRYIN' TO' DO MY JOB. THIS CHEMO, MAN, IT'S SCREWIN' ME UP. I DUNNO HOW I'M GONNA MAKE IT THROUGH THE REST OF THE TREATMENT.
I BROUGHT YOU THE MILES TAPE I WAS TELLING YOU ABOUT.
I DON'T REALLY FEEL LIKE LISTENING NOW. I CAN'T CONCENTRATE. CAN YOU LEAVE IT?

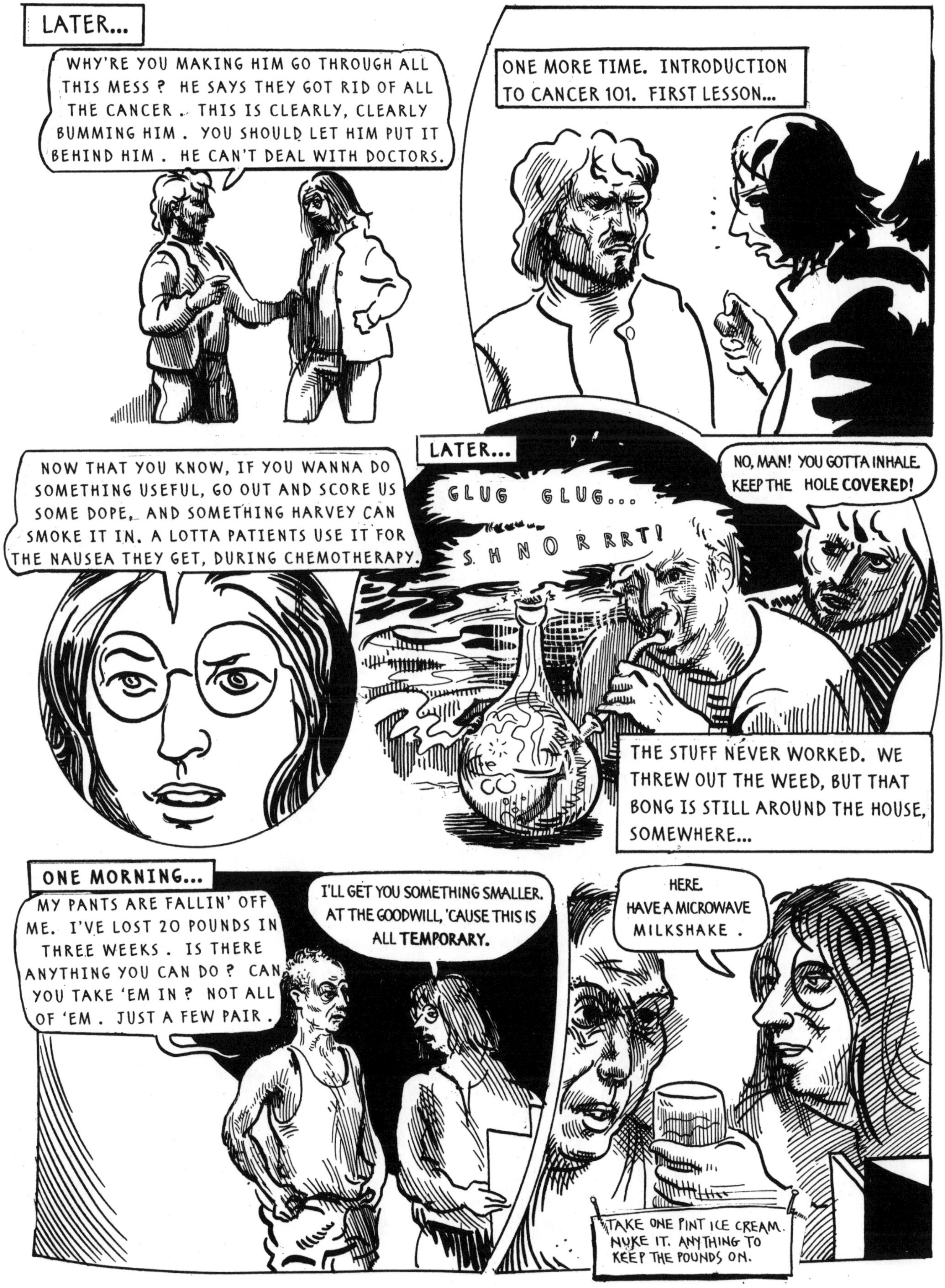
LATER...
WHY'RE YOU MAKING HIM GO THROUGH ALL THIS MESS ? HE SAYS THEY GOT RID OF ALL THE CANCER . THIS IS CLEARLY, CLEARLY BUMMING HIM . YOU SHOULD LET HIM PUT IT BEHIND HIM . HE CAN'T DEAL WITH DOCTORS.
ONE MORE TIME. INTRODUCTION TO CANCER 101. FIRST LESSON...
NOW THAT YOU KNOW, IF YOU WANNA DO SOMETHING USEFUL, GO OUT AND SCORE US SOME DOPE, AND SOMETHING HARVEY CAN SMOKE IT IN. A LOTTA PATIENTS USE IT FOR THE NAUSEA THEY GET, DURING CHEMOTHERAPY.
LATER...
GLUG GLUG...
SHNORRRT!
NO, MAN! YOU GOTTA INHALE. KEEP THE HOLE COVERED!
THE STUFF NEVER WORKED. WE THREW OUT THE WEED, BUT THAT BONG IS STILL AROUND THE HOUSE, SOMEWHERE...
ONE MORNING...
MY PANTS ARE FALLIN' OFF ME. I'VE LOST 20 POUNDS IN THREE WEEKS . IS THERE ANYTHING YOU CAN DO ? CAN YOU TAKE 'EM IN ? NOT ALL OF 'EM . JUST A FEW PAIR .
I'LL GET YOU SOMETHING SMALLER. AT THE GOODWILL, 'CAUSE THIS IS ALL TEMPORARY.
HERE. HAVE A MICROWAVE MILKSHAKE .
TAKE ONE PINT ICE CREAM. NUKE IT. ANYTHING TO KEEP THE POUNDS ON.

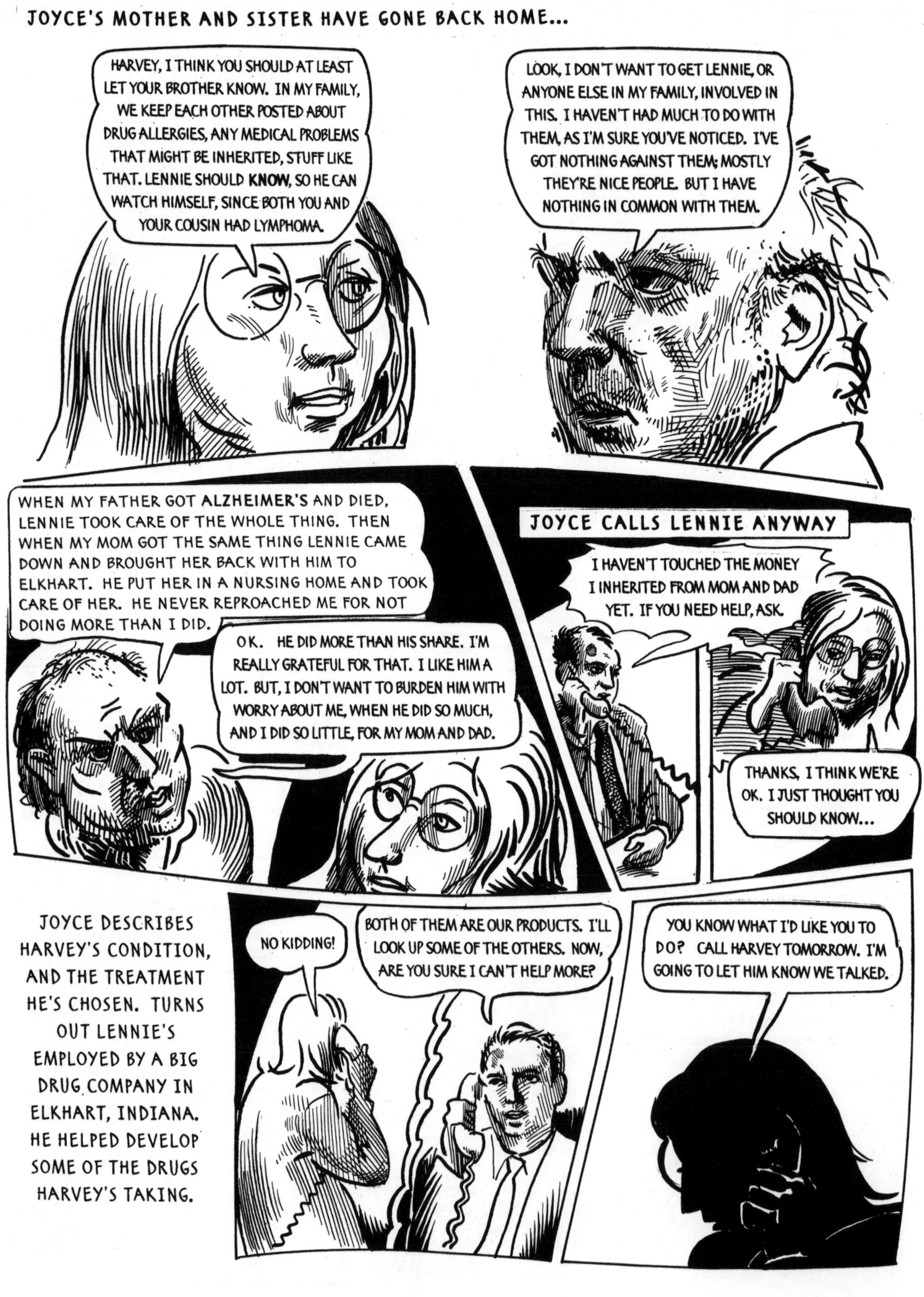
JOYCE'S MOTHER AND SISTER HAVE GONE BACK HOME...
HARVEY, I THINK YOU SHOULD AT LEAST LET YOUR BROTHER KNOW. IN MY FAMILY, WE KEEP EACH OTHER POSTED ABOUT DRUG ALLERGIES, ANY MEDICAL PROBLEMS THAT MIGHT BE INHERITED, STUFF LIKE THAT. LENNIE SHOULD KNOW, SO HE CAN WATCH HIMSELF, SINCE BOTH YOU AND YOUR COUSIN HAD LYMPHOMA.
LOOK, I DON'T WANT TO GET LENNIE, OR ANYONE ELSE IN MY FAMILY, INVOLVED IN THIS. I HAVEN'T HAD MUCH TO DO WITH THEM, AS I'M SURE YOU'VE NOTICED. I'VE GOT NOTHING AGAINST THEM; MOSTLY THEY'RE NICE PEOPLE. BUT I HAVE NOTHING IN COMMON WITH THEM.
WHEN MY FATHER GOT ALZHEIMER'S AND DIED, LENNIE TOOK CARE OF THE WHOLE THING. THEN WHEN MY MOM GOT THE SAME THING LENNIE CAME DOWN AND BROUGHT HER BACK WITH HIM TO ELKHART. HE PUT HER IN A NURSING HOME AND TOOK CARE OF HER. HE NEVER REPROACHED ME FOR NOT DOING MORE THAN I DID.
OK. HE DID MORE THAN HIS SHARE. I'M REALLY GRATEFUL FOR THAT. I LIKE HIM A LOT. BUT, I DON'T WANT TO BURDEN HIM WITH WORRY ABOUT ME, WHEN HE DID SO MUCH, AND I DID SO LITTLE, FOR MY MOM AND DAD.
JOYCE CALLS LENNIE ANYWAY
I HAVEN'T TOUCHED THE MONEY I INHERITED FROM MOM AND DAD YET. IF YOU NEED HELP, ASK.
THANKS. I THINK WE'RE OK. I JUST THOUGHT YOU SHOULD KNOW...
JOYCE DESCRIBES HARVEY'S CONDITION, AND THE TREATMENT HE'S CHOSEN. TURNS OUT LENNIE'S EMPLOYED BY A BIG DRUG COMPANY IN ELKHART, INDIANA. HE HELPED DEVELOP SOME OF THE DRUGS HARVEY'S TAKING.
NO KIDDING!
BOTH OF THEM ARE OUR PRODUCTS. I'LL LOOK UP SOME OF THE OTHERS. NOW, ARE YOU SURE I CAN'T HELP MORE?
YOU KNOW WHAT I'D LIKE YOU TO DO? CALL HARVEY TOMORROW. I'M GOING TO LET HIM KNOW WE TALKED.

BACK AT THE ONCOLOGY CLINIC...

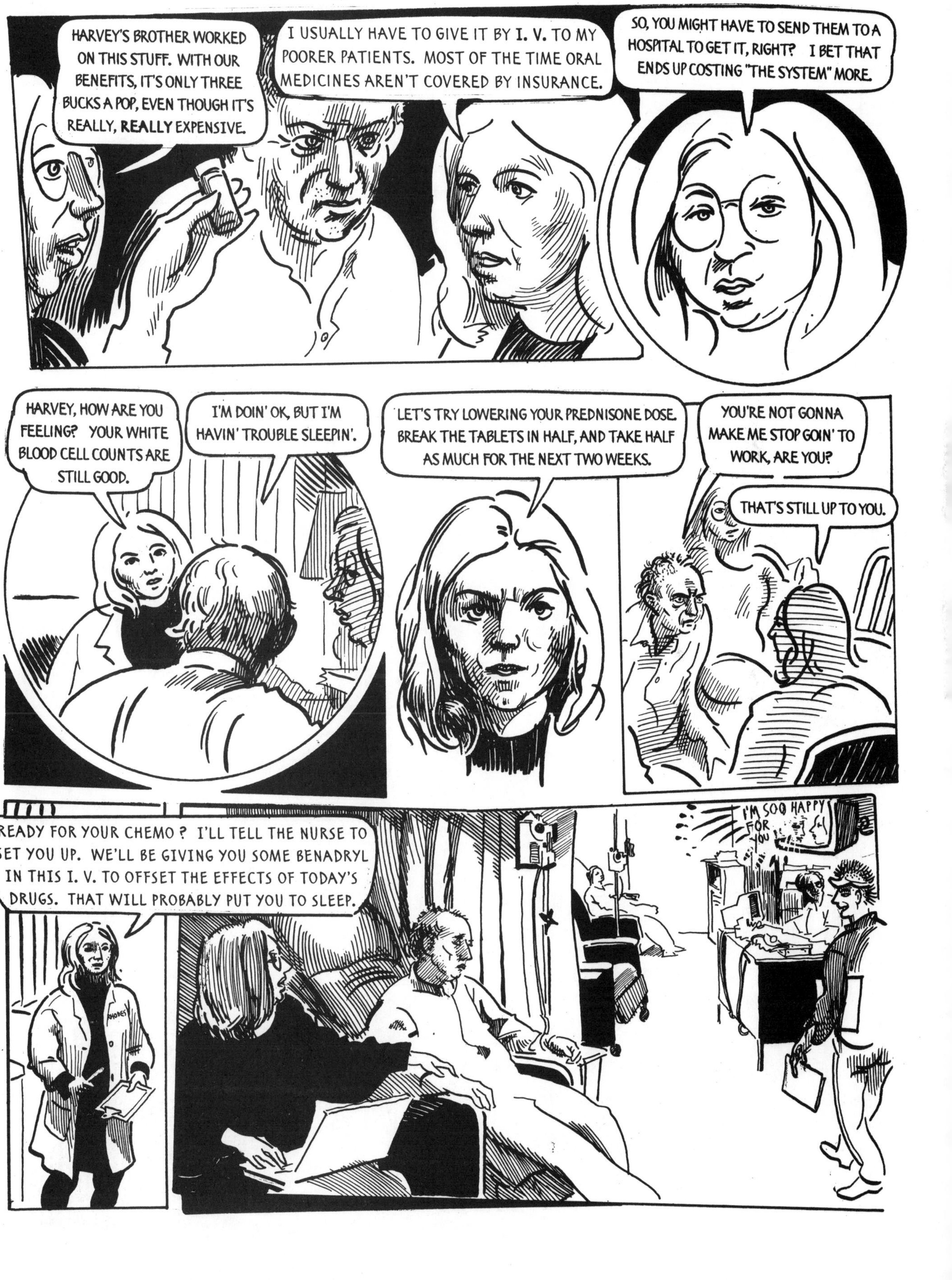
HARVEY'S BROTHER WORKED ON THIS STUFF. WITH OUR BENEFITS, IT'S ONLY THREE BUCKS A POP, EVEN THOUGH IT'S REALLY, **REALLY** EXPENSIVE.
I USUALLY HAVE TO GIVE IT BY **I. V.** TO MY POORER PATIENTS. MOST OF THE TIME ORAL MEDICINES AREN'T COVERED BY INSURANCE.
SO, YOU MIGHT HAVE TO SEND THEM TO A HOSPITAL TO GET IT, RIGHT? I BET THAT ENDS UP COSTING "THE SYSTEM" MORE.
HARVEY, HOW ARE YOU FEELING? YOUR WHITE BLOOD CELL COUNTS ARE STILL GOOD.
I'M DOIN' OK, BUT I'M HAVIN' TROUBLE SLEEPIN'.
LET'S TRY LOWERING YOUR PREDNISONE DOSE. BREAK THE TABLETS IN HALF, AND TAKE HALF AS MUCH FOR THE NEXT TWO WEEKS.
YOU'RE NOT GONNA MAKE ME STOP GOIN' TO WORK, ARE YOU?
THAT'S STILL UP TO YOU.
READY FOR YOUR CHEMO? I'LL TELL THE NURSE TO SET YOU UP. WE'LL BE GIVING YOU SOME BENADRYL IN THIS I. V. TO OFFSET THE EFFECTS OF TODAY'S DRUGS. THAT WILL PROBABLY PUT YOU TO SLEEP.
I'M SOO HAPPY FOR YOU

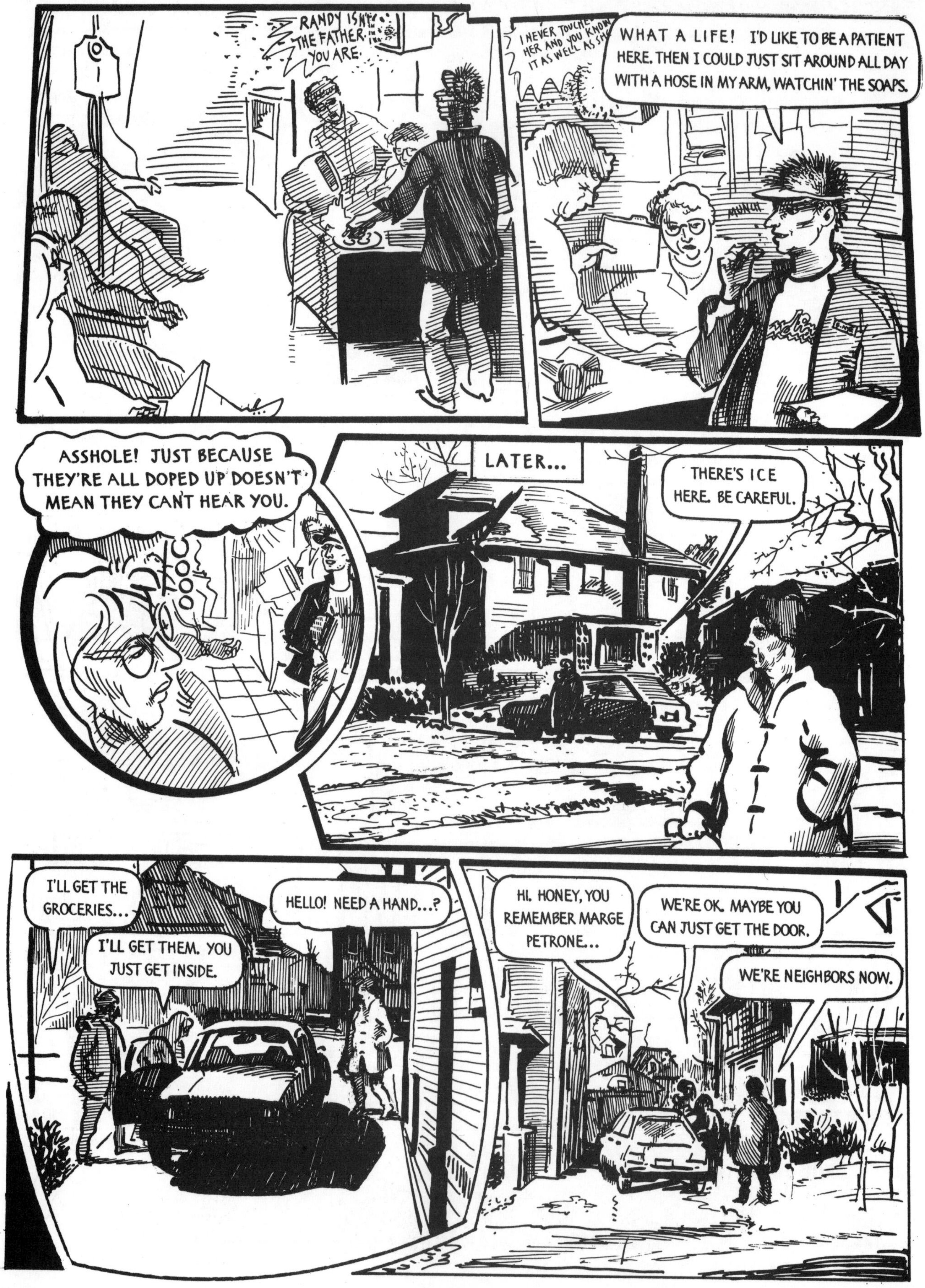
RANDY ISN'T THE FATHER. YOU ARE.
I NEVER TOUCHE HER AND YOU KNOW IT AS WELL AS SH
WHAT A LIFE! I'D LIKE TO BE A PATIENT HERE. THEN I COULD JUST SIT AROUND ALL DAY WITH A HOSE IN MY ARM, WATCHIN' THE SOAPS.
MUNCH
ASSHOLE! JUST BECAUSE THEY'RE ALL DOPED UP DOESN'T MEAN THEY CAN'T HEAR YOU.
LATER...
THERE'S ICE HERE. BE CAREFUL.
I'LL GET THE GROCERIES...
I'LL GET THEM. YOU JUST GET INSIDE.
HELLO! NEED A HAND...?
HI. HONEY, YOU REMEMBER MARGE PETRONE...
WE'RE OK. MAYBE YOU CAN JUST GET THE DOOR.
WE'RE NEIGHBORS NOW.

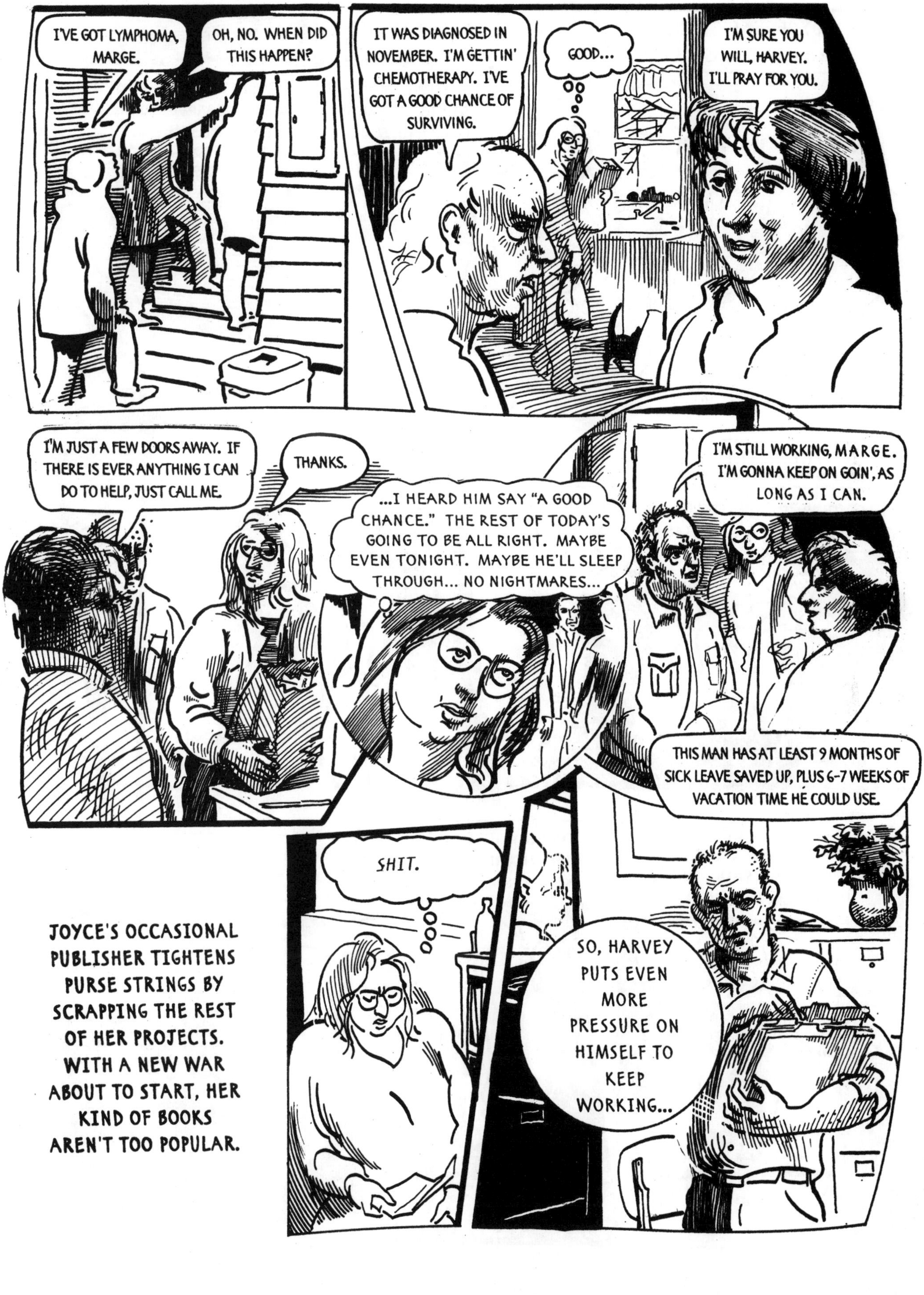
I'VE GOT LYMPHOMA, MARGE.
OH, NO. WHEN DID THIS HAPPEN?
IT WAS DIAGNOSED IN NOVEMBER. I'M GETTIN' CHEMOTHERAPY. I'VE GOT A GOOD CHANCE OF SURVIVING.
GOOD...
I'M SURE YOU WILL, HARVEY. I'LL PRAY FOR YOU.
I'M JUST A FEW DOORS AWAY. IF THERE IS EVER ANYTHING I CAN DO TO HELP, JUST CALL ME.
THANKS.
...I HEARD HIM SAY "A GOOD CHANCE." THE REST OF TODAY'S GOING TO BE ALL RIGHT. MAYBE EVEN TONIGHT. MAYBE HE'LL SLEEP THROUGH... NO NIGHTMARES...
I'M STILL WORKING, MARGE. I'M GONNA KEEP ON GOIN', AS LONG AS I CAN.
THIS MAN HAS AT LEAST 9 MONTHS OF SICK LEAVE SAVED UP, PLUS 6-7 WEEKS OF VACATION TIME HE COULD USE.
JOYCE'S OCCASIONAL PUBLISHER TIGHTENS PURSE STRINGS BY SCRAPPING THE REST OF HER PROJECTS. WITH A NEW WAR ABOUT TO START, HER KIND OF BOOKS AREN'T TOO POPULAR.
SHIT.
SO, HARVEY PUTS EVEN MORE PRESSURE ON HIMSELF TO KEEP WORKING...

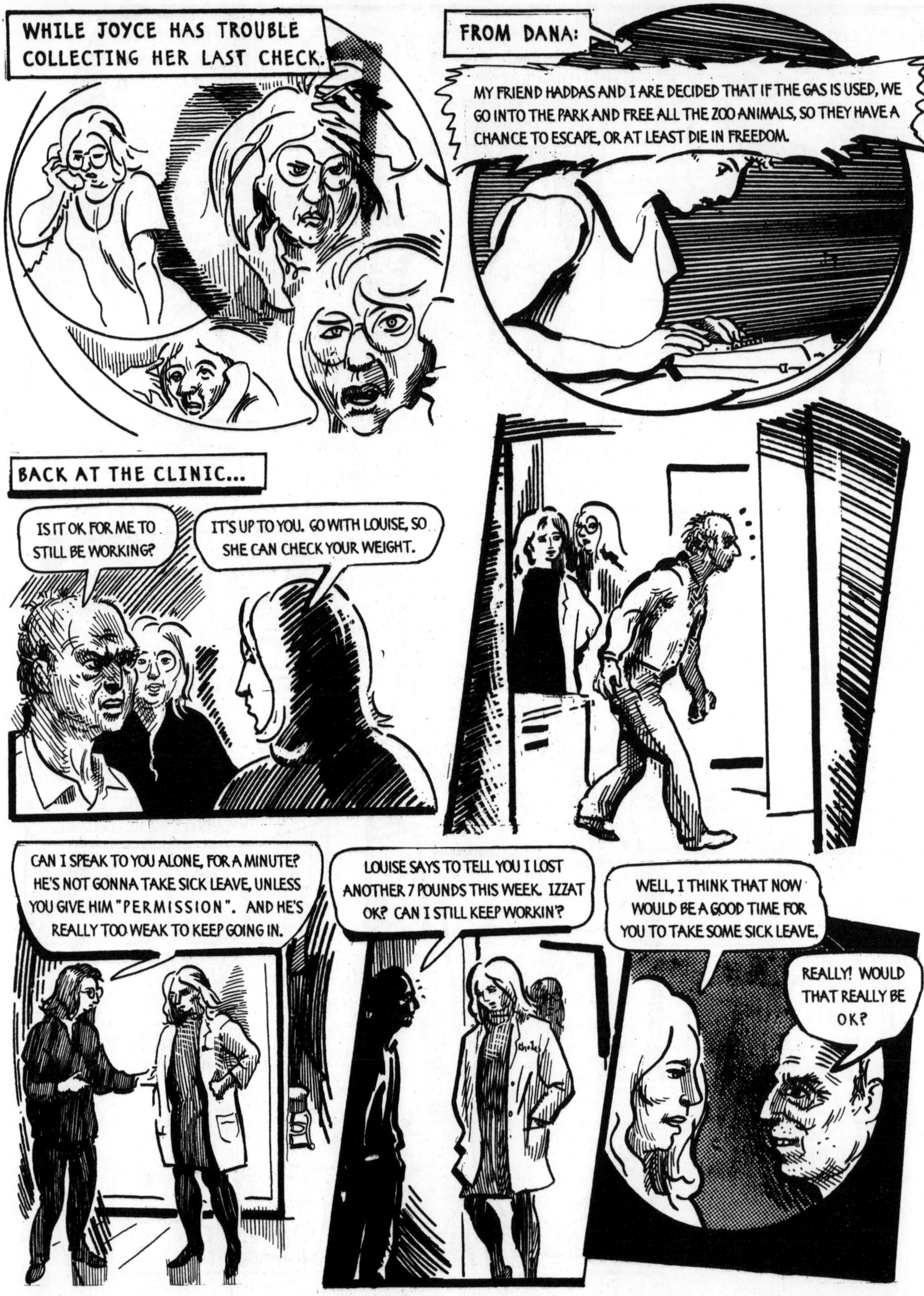

WHILE JOYCE HAS TROUBLE COLLECTING HER LAST CHECK.
FROM DANA:
MY FRIEND HADDAS AND I ARE DECIDED THAT IF THE GAS IS USED, WE GO INTO THE PARK AND FREE ALL THE ZOO ANIMALS, SO THEY HAVE A CHANCE TO ESCAPE, OR AT LEAST DIE IN FREEDOM.
BACK AT THE CLINIC...
IS IT OK FOR ME TO STILL BE WORKING?
IT'S UP TO YOU. GO WITH LOUISE, SO SHE CAN CHECK YOUR WEIGHT.
CAN I SPEAK TO YOU ALONE, FOR A MINUTE? HE'S NOT GONNA TAKE SICK LEAVE, UNLESS YOU GIVE HIM "PERMISSION". AND HE'S REALLY TOO WEAK TO KEEP GOING IN.
LOUISE SAYS TO TELL YOU I LOST ANOTHER 7 POUNDS THIS WEEK. IZZAT OK? CAN I STILL KEEP WORKIN'?
WELL, I THINK THAT NOW WOULD BE A GOOD TIME FOR YOU TO TAKE SOME SICK LEAVE.
REALLY! WOULD THAT REALLY BE OK?

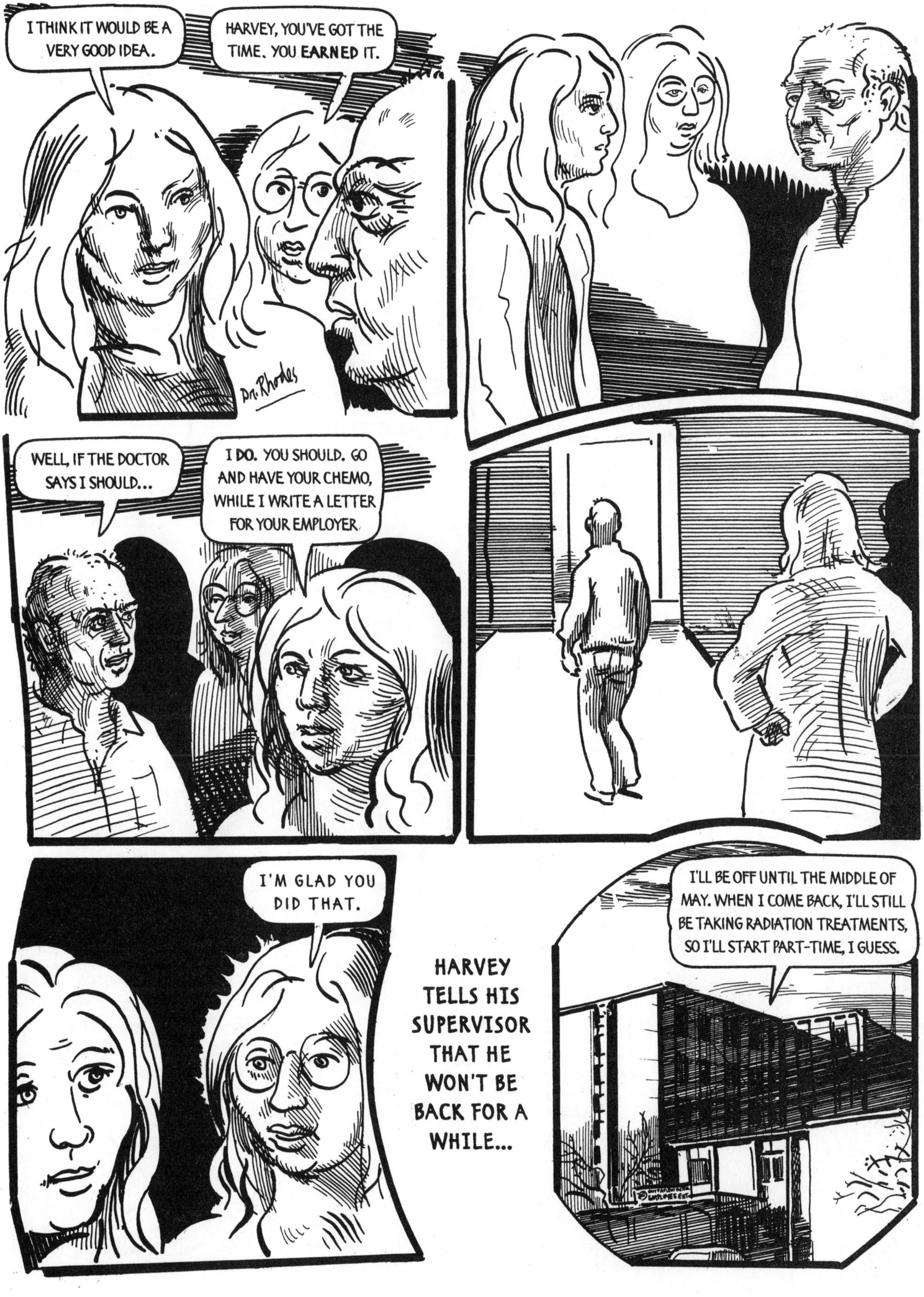
I THINK IT WOULD BE A VERY GOOD IDEA.
HARVEY, YOU'VE GOT THE TIME. YOU EARNED IT.
Dr. Rhodes
WELL, IF THE DOCTOR SAYS I SHOULD...
I DO. YOU SHOULD. GO AND HAVE YOUR CHEMO, WHILE I WRITE A LETTER FOR YOUR EMPLOYER
I'M GLAD YOU DID THAT.
HARVEY TELLS HIS SUPERVISOR THAT HE WON'T BE BACK FOR A WHILE...
I'LL BE OFF UNTIL THE MIDDLE OF MAY. WHEN I COME BACK, I'LL STILL BE TAKING RADIATION TREATMENTS, SO I'LL START PART-TIME, I GUESS.

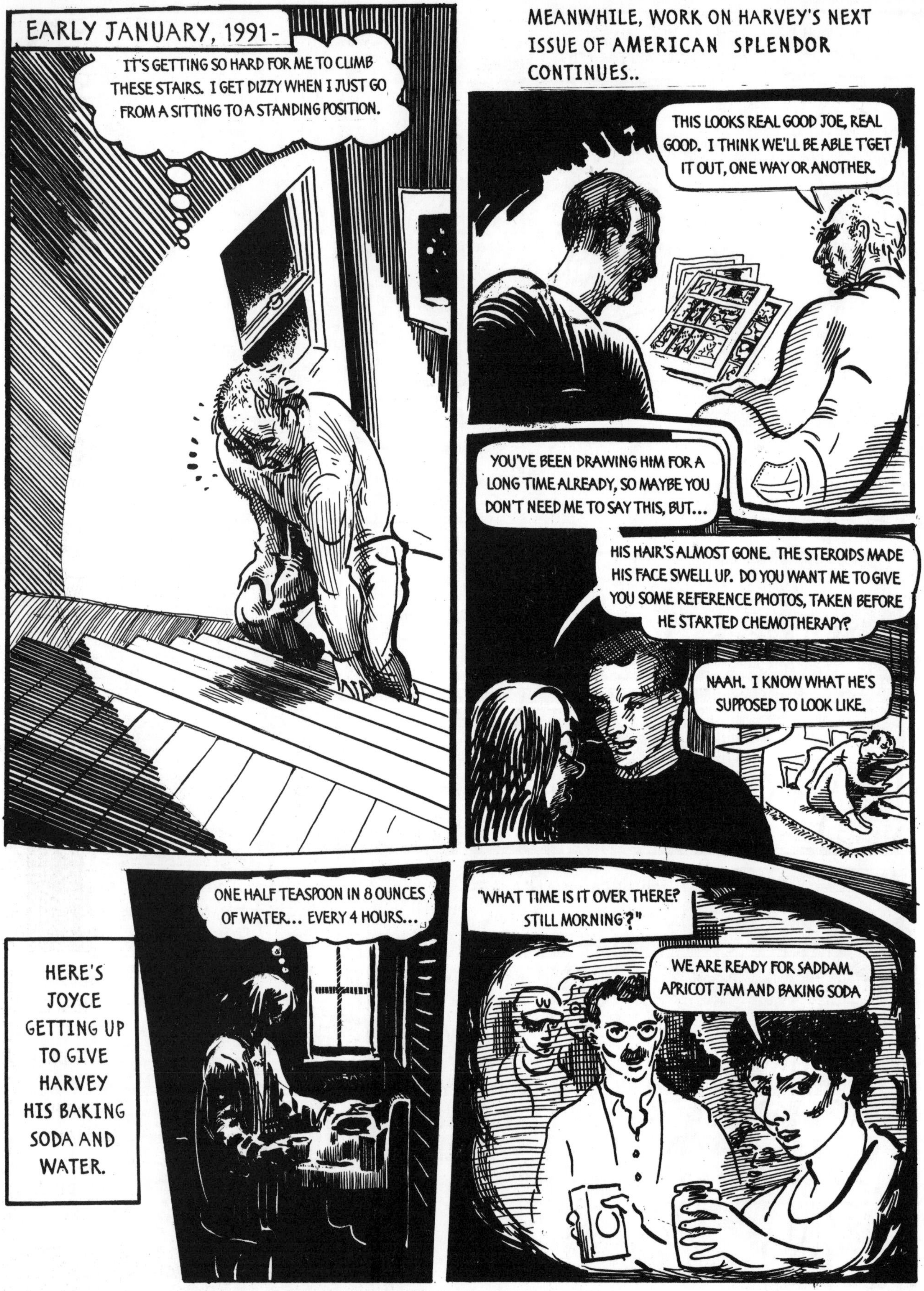
EARLY JANUARY, 1991-
IT'S GETTING SO HARD FOR ME TO CLIMB THESE STAIRS. I GET DIZZY WHEN I JUST GO FROM A SITTING TO A STANDING POSITION.
MEANWHILE, WORK ON HARVEY'S NEXT ISSUE OF AMERICAN SPLENDOR CONTINUES..
THIS LOOKS REAL GOOD JOE, REAL GOOD. I THINK WE'LL BE ABLE T'GET IT OUT, ONE WAY OR ANOTHER.
YOU'VE BEEN DRAWING HIM FOR A LONG TIME ALREADY, SO MAYBE YOU DON'T NEED ME TO SAY THIS, BUT...
HIS HAIR'S ALMOST GONE. THE STEROIDS MADE HIS FACE SWELL UP. DO YOU WANT ME TO GIVE YOU SOME REFERENCE PHOTOS, TAKEN BEFORE HE STARTED CHEMOTHERAPY?
NAAH. I KNOW WHAT HE'S SUPPOSED TO LOOK LIKE.
HERE'S JOYCE GETTING UP TO GIVE HARVEY HIS BAKING SODA AND WATER.
ONE HALF TEASPOON IN 8 OUNCES OF WATER... EVERY 4 HOURS...
"WHAT TIME IS IT OVER THERE? STILL MORNING?"
WE ARE READY FOR SADDAM. APRICOT JAM AND BAKING SODA

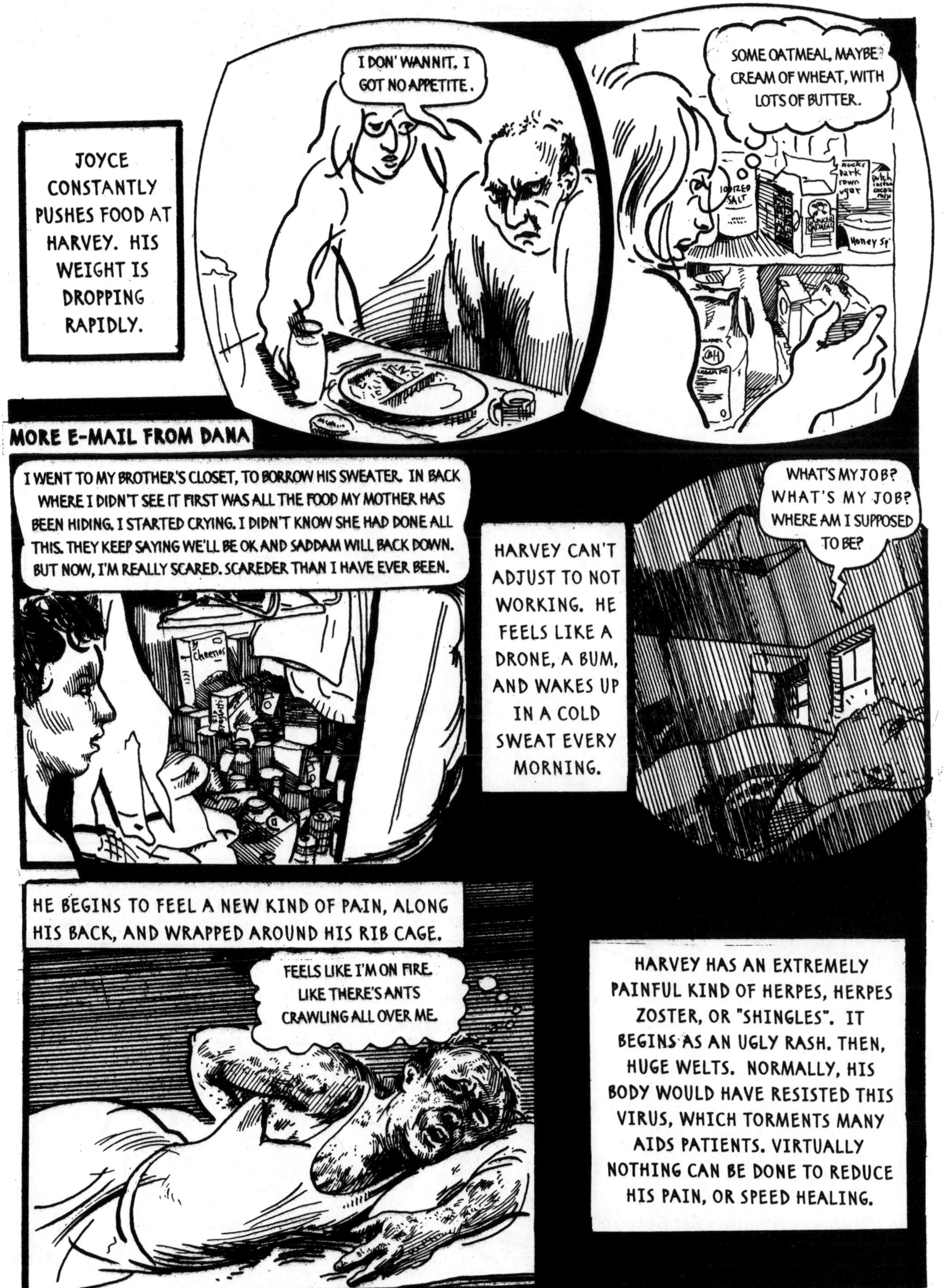

JOYCE CONSTANTLY PUSHES FOOD AT HARVEY. HIS WEIGHT IS DROPPING RAPIDLY.
I DON' WANNIT, I GOT NO APPETITE.
SOME OATMEAL, MAYBE CREAM OF WHEAT, WITH LOTS OF BUTTER.
MORE E-MAIL FROM DANA
I WENT TO MY BROTHER'S CLOSET, TO BORROW HIS SWEATER. IN BACK WHERE I DIDN'T SEE IT FIRST WAS ALL THE FOOD MY MOTHER HAS BEEN HIDING. I STARTED CRYING. I DIDN'T KNOW SHE HAD DONE ALL THIS. THEY KEEP SAYING WE'LL BE OK AND SADDAM WILL BACK DOWN. BUT NOW, I'M REALLY SCARED. SCAREDER THAN I HAVE EVER BEEN.
HARVEY CAN'T ADJUST TO NOT WORKING. HE FEELS LIKE A DRONE, A BUM, AND WAKES UP IN A COLD SWEAT EVERY MORNING.
WHAT'S MY JOB? WHAT'S MY JOB? WHERE AM I SUPPOSED TO BE?
HE BEGINS TO FEEL A NEW KIND OF PAIN, ALONG HIS BACK, AND WRAPPED AROUND HIS RIB CAGE.
FEELS LIKE I'M ON FIRE. LIKE THERE'S ANTS CRAWLING ALL OVER ME.
HARVEY HAS AN EXTREMELY PAINFUL KIND OF HERPES, HERPES ZOSTER, OR "SHINGLES". IT BEGINS AS AN UGLY RASH. THEN, HUGE WELTS. NORMALLY, HIS BODY WOULD HAVE RESISTED THIS VIRUS, WHICH TORMENTS MANY AIDS PATIENTS. VIRTUALLY NOTHING CAN BE DONE TO REDUCE HIS PAIN, OR SPEED HEALING.

THE PAIN ONLY INCREASES. THERE'S NO RELIEF. YOU SEE, IT'S HIS NERVOUS SYSTEM THAT'S BEING ATTACKED.

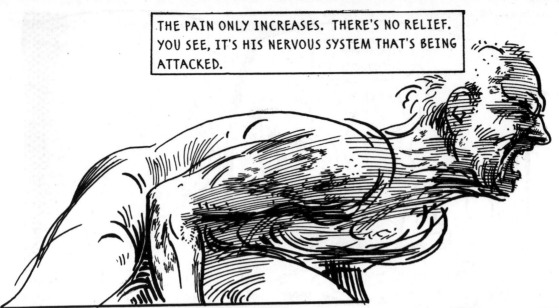

JOYCE IS DESPERATE. SHE GOES THROUGH CLOSETS AND CUPBOARDS UNTIL SHE FINDS AN OLD PAIR OF MEN'S SILK PAJAMAS AND THOSE SLIPPERY SATIN SHEETS THAT NEVER *WOULD* STAY ON THE BED. IN THE SAME DRAWER, SHE FINDS A LITTLE PLASTIC BOTTLE.

MASSAGE OIL GOD. I'VE ALMOST FORGOTTEN WHAT ALL THIS STUFF IS *FOR.*

I HURT. I HURT. BUT, I CAN'T BE SICK. I'VE GOT TO GO TO WORK...

DAMN IT, HARVEY. WORKING IS PROBABLY HOW YOU GOT THIS. YOU CAN'T WORK AT A HOSPITAL NOW. NOT WHEN YOUR IMMUNE SYSTEM'S BEEN SHOT TO HELL BY CHEMO.

SHE'S ABLE TO REMAKE THE BED AROUND HARVEY. HE'S HALF OUT OF HIS HEAD, MOANING.

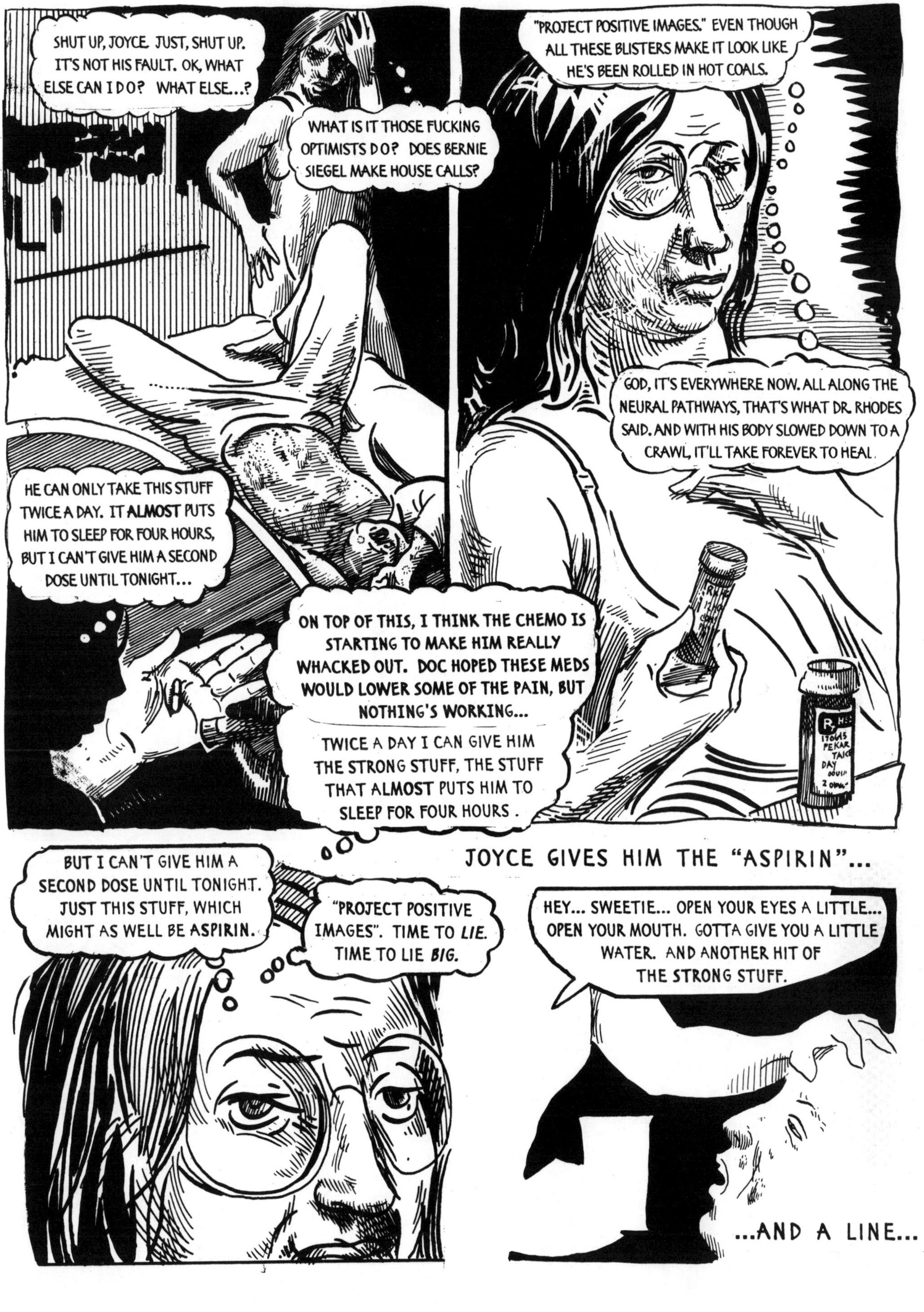

SHUT UP, JOYCE. JUST, SHUT UP. IT'S NOT HIS FAULT. OK, WHAT ELSE CAN I DO? WHAT ELSE...?
WHAT IS IT THOSE FUCKING OPTIMISTS DO? DOES BERNIE SIEGEL MAKE HOUSE CALLS?
HE CAN ONLY TAKE THIS STUFF TWICE A DAY. IT ALMOST PUTS HIM TO SLEEP FOR FOUR HOURS, BUT I CAN'T GIVE HIM A SECOND DOSE UNTIL TONIGHT...
"PROJECT POSITIVE IMAGES." EVEN THOUGH ALL THESE BLISTERS MAKE IT LOOK LIKE HE'S BEEN ROLLED IN HOT COALS.
GOD, IT'S EVERYWHERE NOW. ALL ALONG THE NEURAL PATHWAYS, THAT'S WHAT DR. RHODES SAID. AND WITH HIS BODY SLOWED DOWN TO A CRAWL, IT'LL TAKE FOREVER TO HEAL.
ON TOP OF THIS, I THINK THE CHEMO IS STARTING TO MAKE HIM REALLY WHACKED OUT. DOC HOPED THESE MEDS WOULD LOWER SOME OF THE PAIN, BUT NOTHING'S WORKING...
TWICE A DAY I CAN GIVE HIM THE STRONG STUFF, THE STUFF THAT ALMOST PUTS HIM TO SLEEP FOR FOUR HOURS.
BUT I CAN'T GIVE HIM A SECOND DOSE UNTIL TONIGHT. JUST THIS STUFF, WHICH MIGHT AS WELL BE ASPIRIN.
"PROJECT POSITIVE IMAGES". TIME TO LIE. TIME TO LIE BIG.
JOYCE GIVES HIM THE "ASPIRIN"...
HEY... SWEETIE... OPEN YOUR EYES A LITTLE... OPEN YOUR MOUTH. GOTTA GIVE YOU A LITTLE WATER. AND ANOTHER HIT OF THE STRONG STUFF.
...AND A LINE...

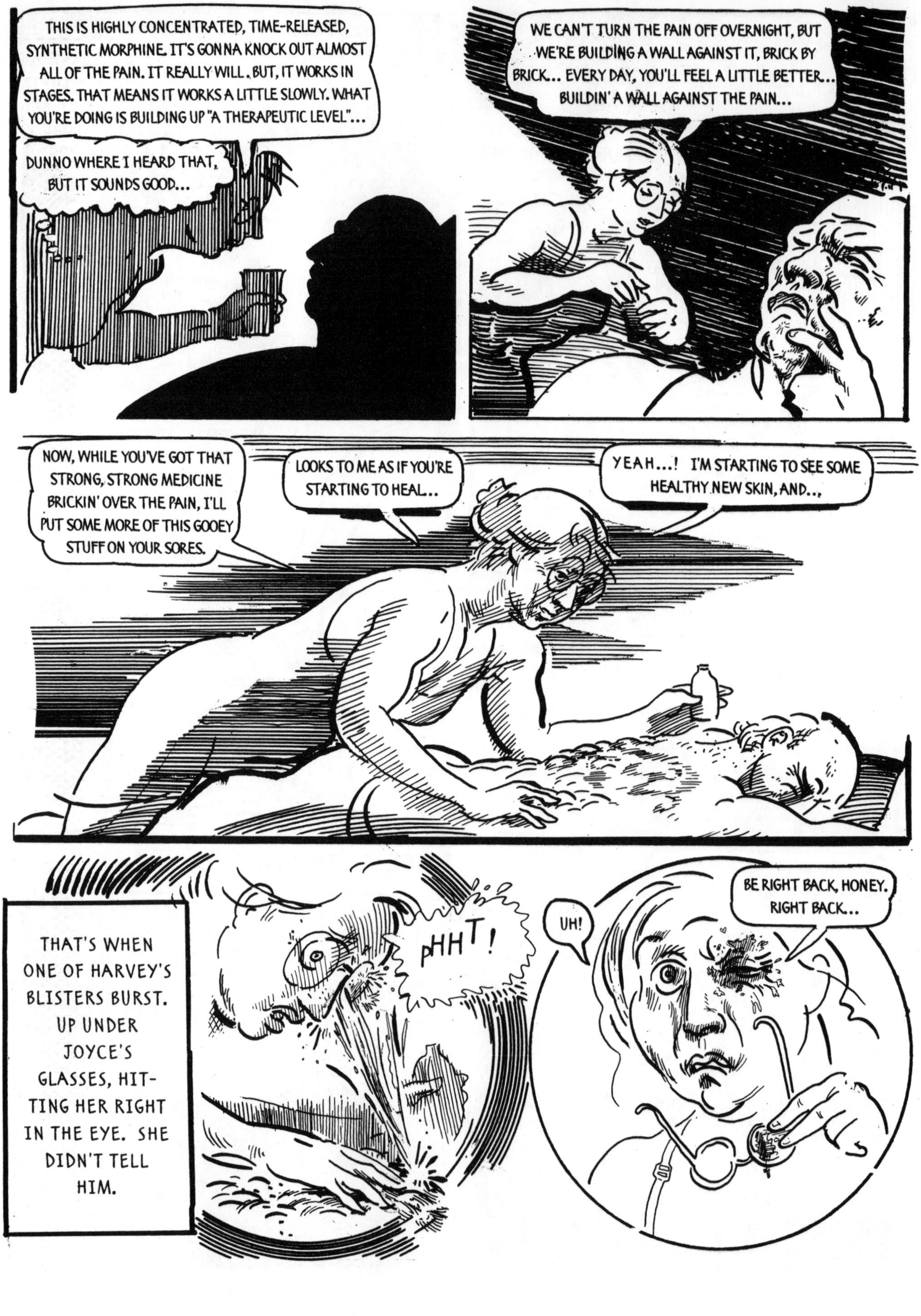
THIS IS HIGHLY CONCENTRATED, TIME-RELEASED, SYNTHETIC MORPHINE. IT'S GONNA KNOCK OUT ALMOST ALL OF THE PAIN. IT REALLY WILL. BUT, IT WORKS IN STAGES. THAT MEANS IT WORKS A LITTLE SLOWLY. WHAT YOU'RE DOING IS BUILDING UP "A THERAPEUTIC LEVEL"...
DUNNO WHERE I HEARD THAT, BUT IT SOUNDS GOOD...
WE CAN'T TURN THE PAIN OFF OVERNIGHT, BUT WE'RE BUILDING A WALL AGAINST IT, BRICK BY BRICK... EVERY DAY, YOU'LL FEEL A LITTLE BETTER... BUILDIN' A WALL AGAINST THE PAIN...
NOW, WHILE YOU'VE GOT THAT STRONG, STRONG MEDICINE BRICKIN' OVER THE PAIN, I'LL PUT SOME MORE OF THIS GOOEY STUFF ON YOUR SORES.
LOOKS TO ME AS IF YOU'RE STARTING TO HEAL...
YEAH...! I'M STARTING TO SEE SOME HEALTHY NEW SKIN, AND...
THAT'S WHEN ONE OF HARVEY'S BLISTERS BURST. UP UNDER JOYCE'S GLASSES, HITTING HER RIGHT IN THE EYE. SHE DIDN'T TELL HIM.
pHHT!
UH!
BE RIGHT BACK, HONEY. RIGHT BACK...

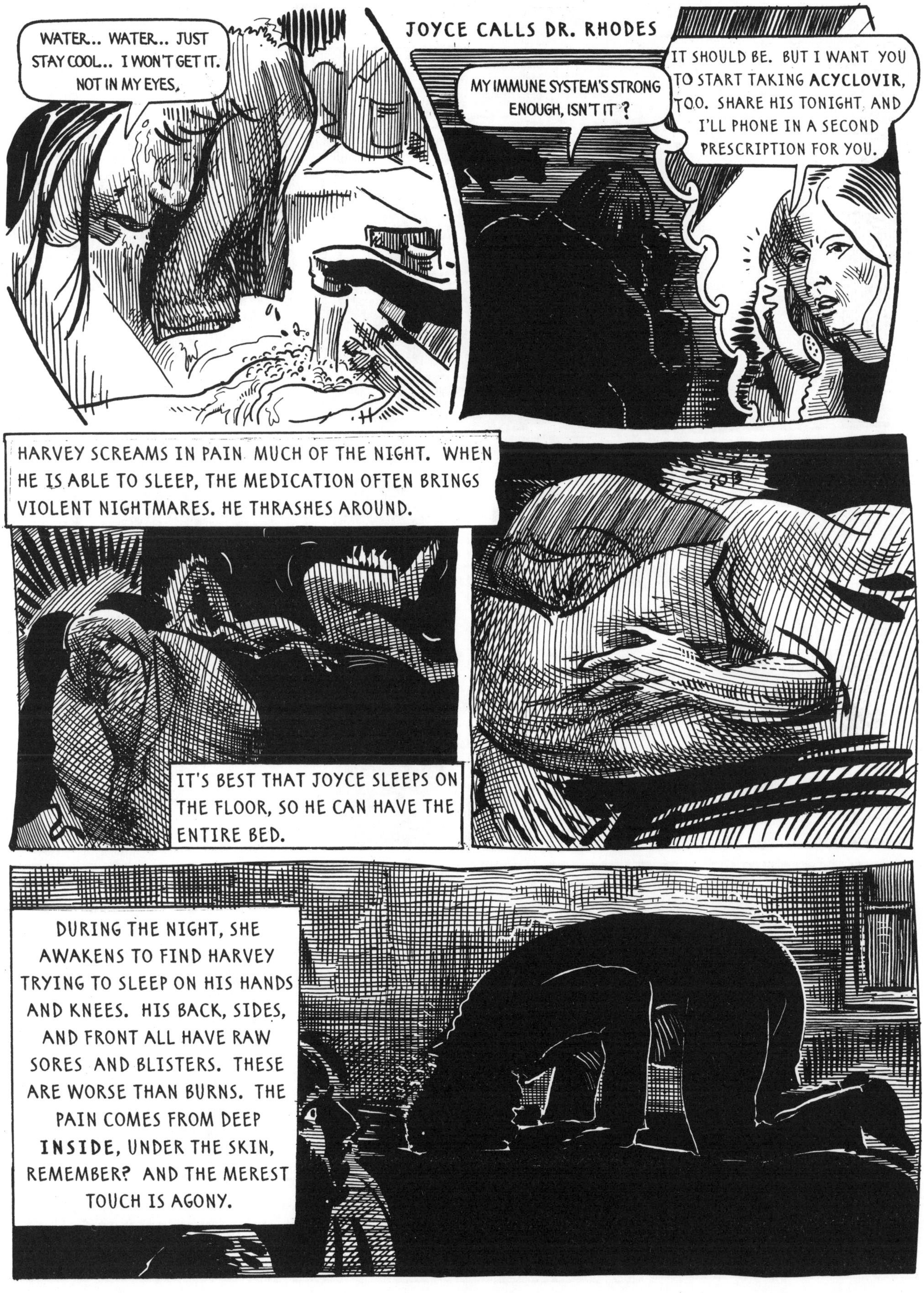
WATER.. WATER.. JUST STAY COOL.. I WON'T GET IT. NOT IN MY EYES,
JOYCE CALLS DR. RHODES
MY IMMUNE SYSTEM'S STRONG ENOUGH, ISN'T IT ?
IT SHOULD BE. BUT I WANT YOU TO START TAKING ACYCLOVIR, TOO. SHARE HIS TONIGHT AND I'LL PHONE IN A SECOND PRESCRIPTION FOR YOU.
HARVEY SCREAMS IN PAIN MUCH OF THE NIGHT. WHEN HE IS ABLE TO SLEEP, THE MEDICATION OFTEN BRINGS VIOLENT NIGHTMARES. HE THRASHES AROUND.
SOB!
IT'S BEST THAT JOYCE SLEEPS ON THE FLOOR, SO HE CAN HAVE THE ENTIRE BED.
DURING THE NIGHT, SHE AWAKENS TO FIND HARVEY TRYING TO SLEEP ON HIS HANDS AND KNEES. HIS BACK, SIDES, AND FRONT ALL HAVE RAW SORES AND BLISTERS. THESE ARE WORSE THAN BURNS. THE PAIN COMES FROM DEEP INSIDE, UNDER THE SKIN, REMEMBER? AND THE MEREST TOUCH IS AGONY.

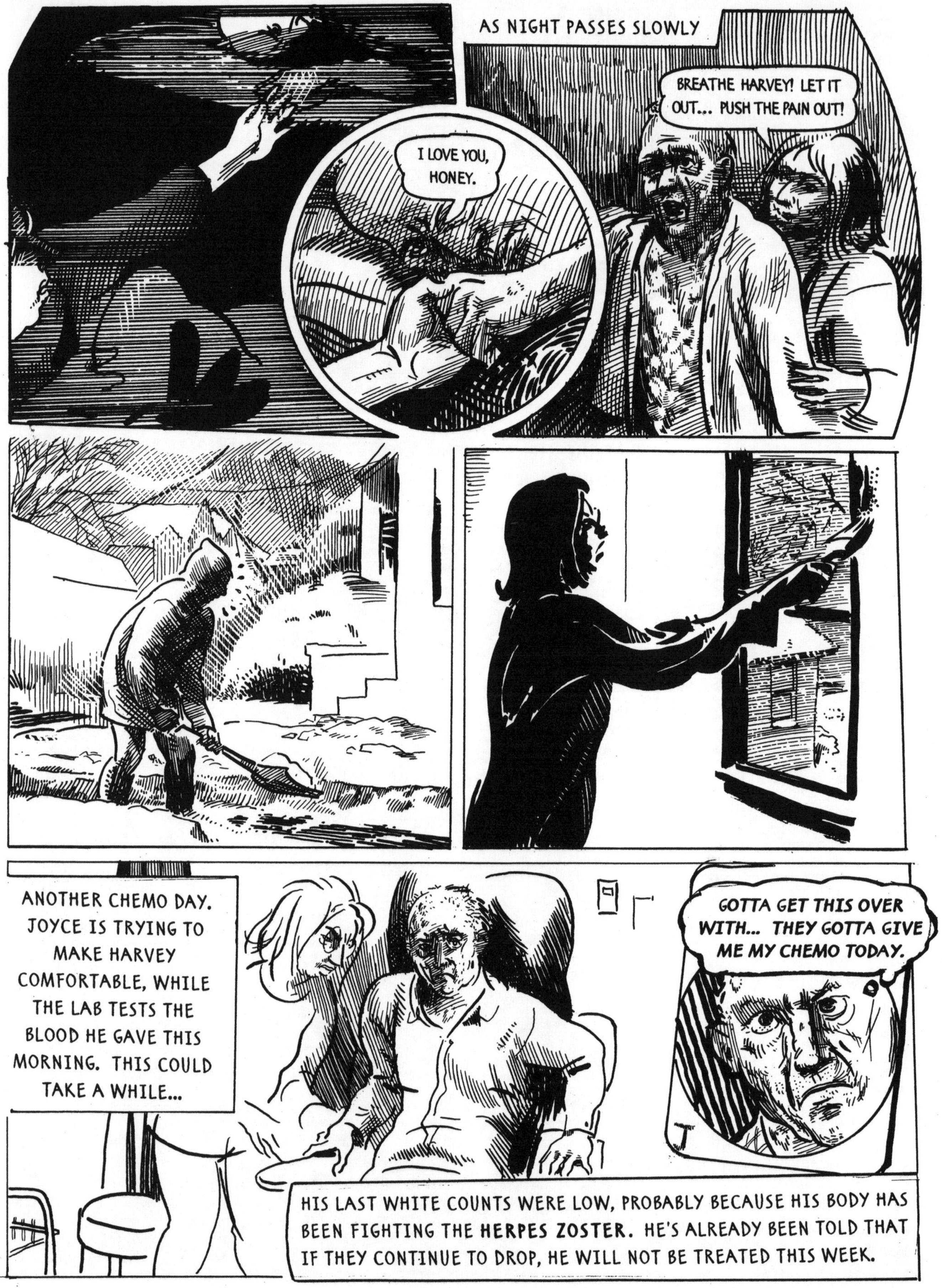
AS NIGHT PASSES SLOWLY
BREATHE HARVEY! LET IT OUT... PUSH THE PAIN OUT!
I LOVE YOU, HONEY.
ANOTHER CHEMO DAY. JOYCE IS TRYING TO MAKE HARVEY COMFORTABLE, WHILE THE LAB TESTS THE BLOOD HE GAVE THIS MORNING. THIS COULD TAKE A WHILE...
GOTTA GET THIS OVER WITH... THEY GOTTA GIVE ME MY CHEMO TODAY.
HIS LAST WHITE COUNTS WERE LOW, PROBABLY BECAUSE HIS BODY HAS BEEN FIGHTING THE HERPES ZOSTER. HE'S ALREADY BEEN TOLD THAT IF THEY CONTINUE TO DROP, HE WILL NOT BE TREATED THIS WEEK.

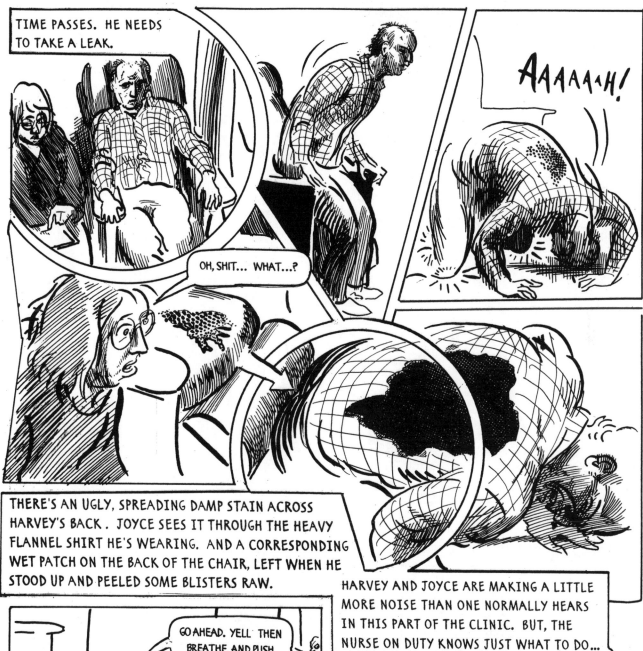

TIME PASSES. HE NEEDS TO TAKE A LEAK.

OH, SHIT... WHAT...?

AAAAAAH!

THERE'S AN UGLY, SPREADING DAMP STAIN ACROSS HARVEY'S BACK. JOYCE SEES IT THROUGH THE HEAVY FLANNEL SHIRT HE'S WEARING. AND A CORRESPONDING WET PATCH ON THE BACK OF THE CHAIR, LEFT WHEN HE STOOD UP AND PEELED SOME BLISTERS RAW.

HARVEY AND JOYCE ARE MAKING A LITTLE MORE NOISE THAN ONE NORMALLY HEARS IN THIS PART OF THE CLINIC. BUT, THE NURSE ON DUTY KNOWS JUST WHAT TO DO...

GO AHEAD. YELL THEN BREATHE, AND PUSH THE PAIN OUT.

PEKAR, AGAIN...!

GIUSEPPE

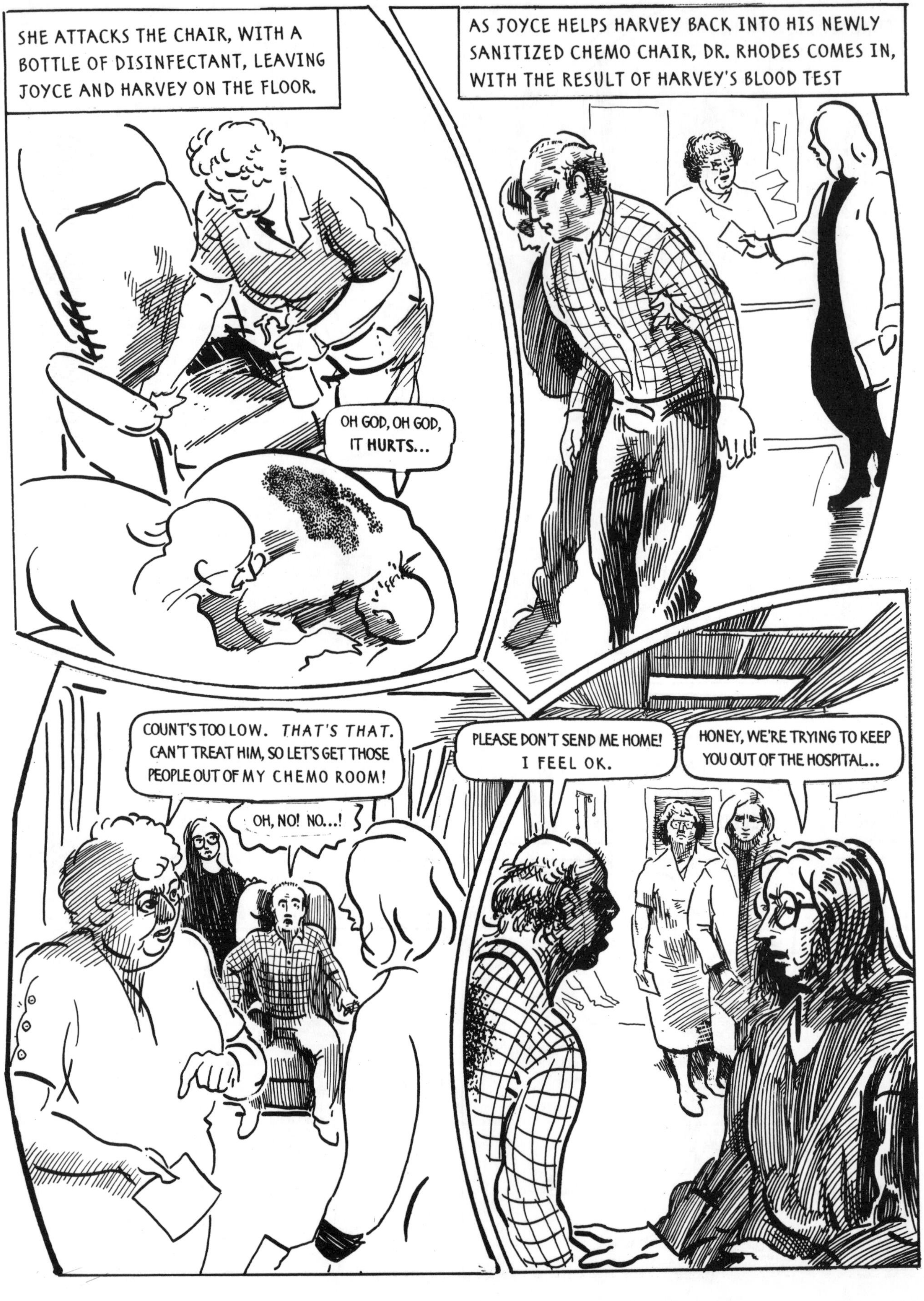
SHE ATTACKS THE CHAIR, WITH A BOTTLE OF DISINFECTANT, LEAVING JOYCE AND HARVEY ON THE FLOOR.
OH GOD, OH GOD, IT HURTS...
AS JOYCE HELPS HARVEY BACK INTO HIS NEWLY SANITIZED CHEMO CHAIR, DR. RHODES COMES IN, WITH THE RESULT OF HARVEY'S BLOOD TEST
COUNT'S TOO LOW. THAT'S THAT. CAN'T TREAT HIM, SO LET'S GET THOSE PEOPLE OUT OF MY CHEMO ROOM!
OH, NO! NO...!
PLEASE DON'T SEND ME HOME! I FEEL OK.
HONEY, WE'RE TRYING TO KEEP YOU OUT OF THE HOSPITAL...

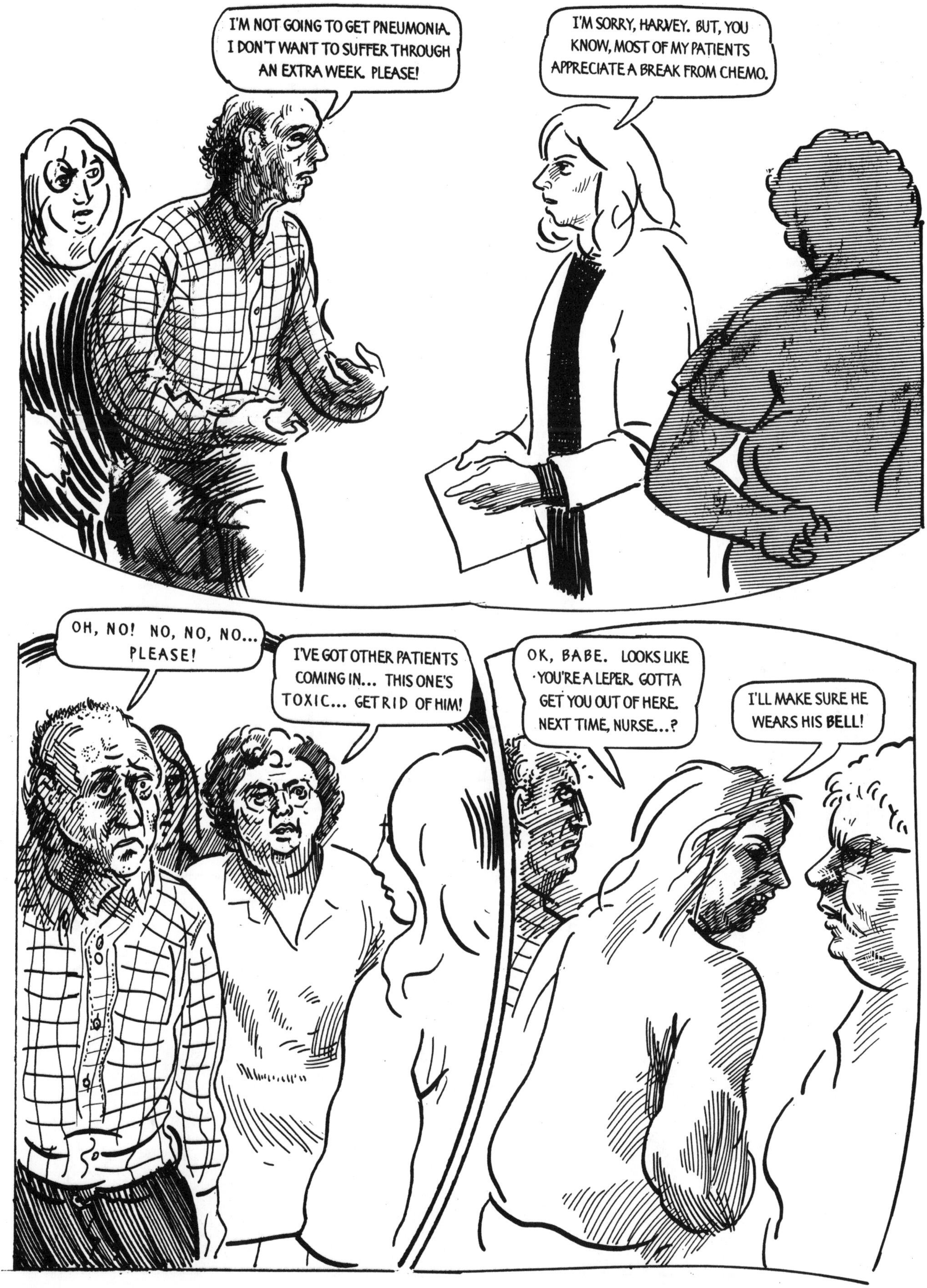
I'M NOT GOING TO GET PNEUMONIA. I DON'T WANT TO SUFFER THROUGH AN EXTRA WEEK. PLEASE!
I'M SORRY, HARVEY. BUT, YOU KNOW, MOST OF MY PATIENTS APPRECIATE A BREAK FROM CHEMO.
OH, NO! NO, NO, NO... PLEASE!
I'VE GOT OTHER PATIENTS COMING IN... THIS ONE'S TOXIC... GET RID OF HIM!
OK, BABE. LOOKS LIKE YOU'RE A LEPER. GOTTA GET YOU OUT OF HERE. NEXT TIME, NURSE...?
I'LL MAKE SURE HE WEARS HIS BELL!

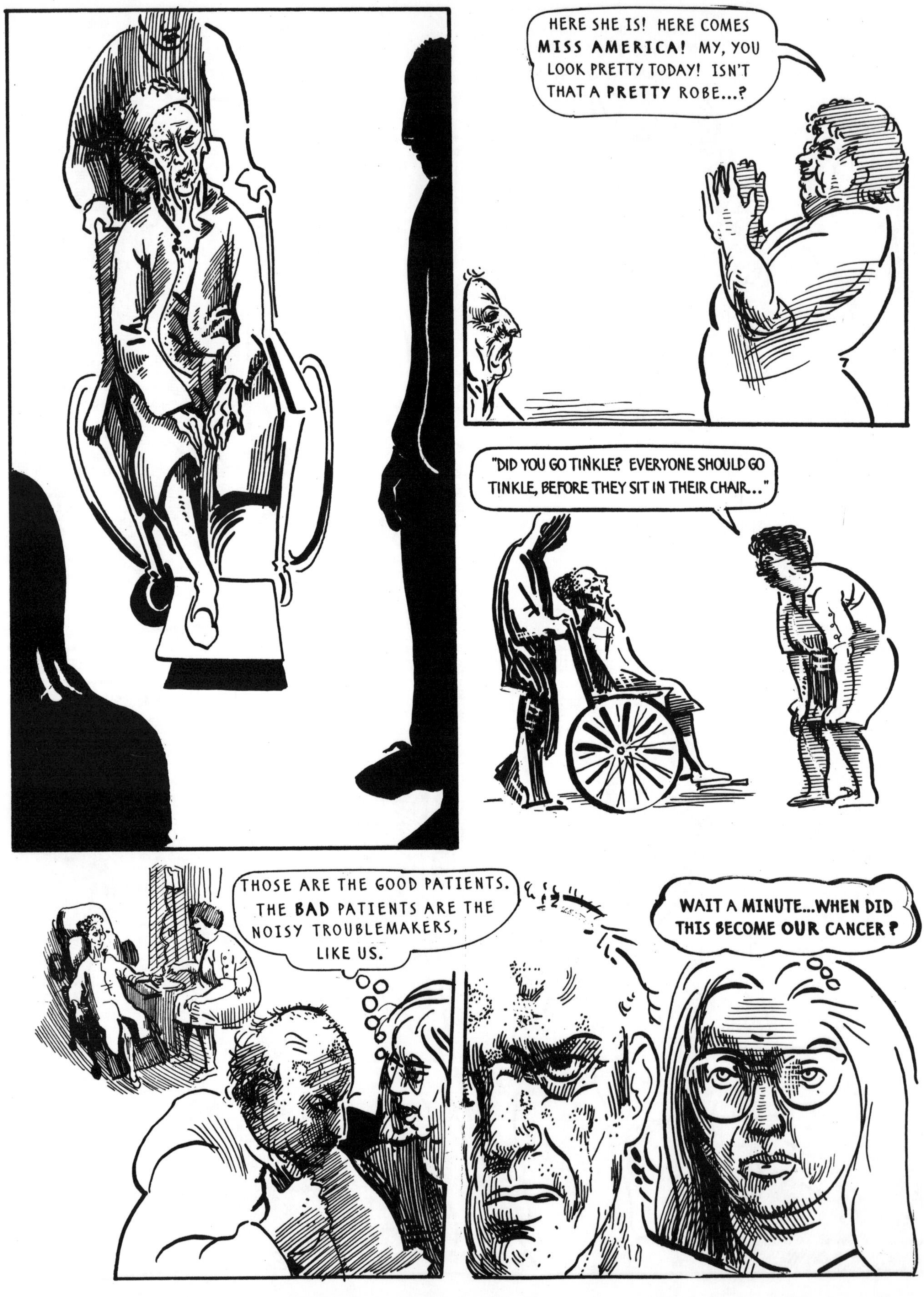
HERE SHE IS! HERE COMES MISS AMERICA! MY, YOU LOOK PRETTY TODAY! ISN'T THAT A PRETTY ROBE...?
"DID YOU GO TINKLE? EVERYONE SHOULD GO TINKLE, BEFORE THEY SIT IN THEIR CHAIR..."
THOSE ARE THE GOOD PATIENTS. THE BAD PATIENTS ARE THE NOISY TROUBLEMAKERS, LIKE US.
WAIT A MINUTE...WHEN DID THIS BECOME OUR CANCER?

8

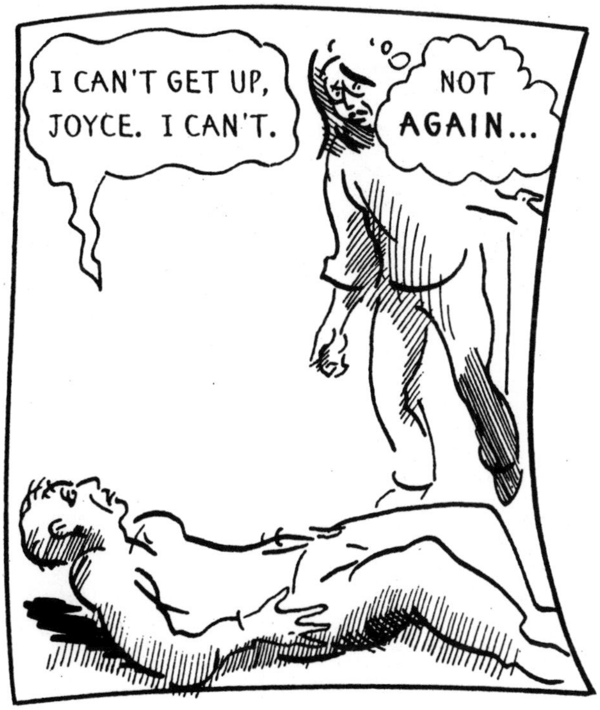
I CAN'T GET UP, JOYCE. I CAN'T.
NOT AGAIN...

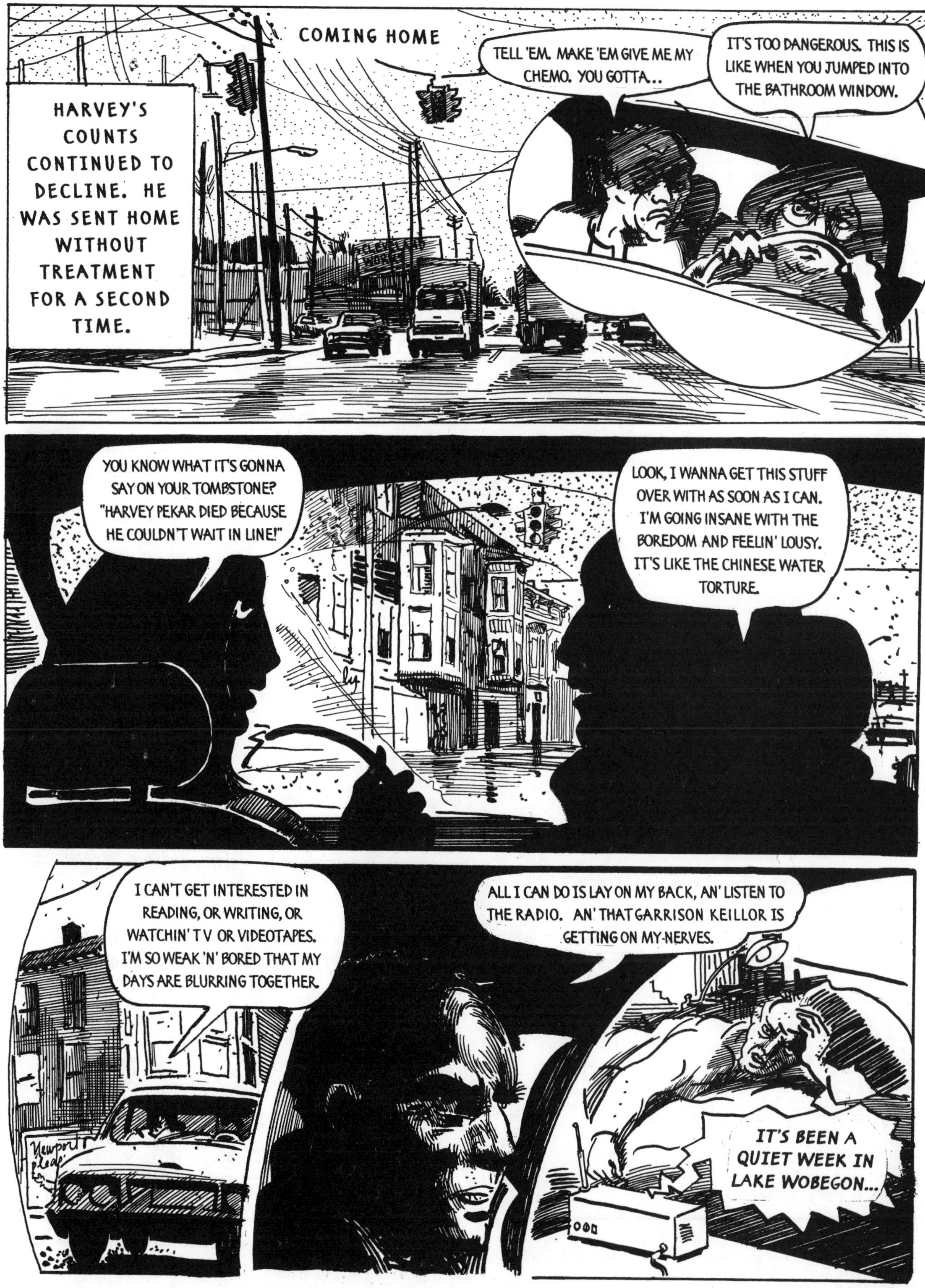
COMING HOME
HARVEY'S COUNTS CONTINUED TO DECLINE. HE WAS SENT HOME WITHOUT TREATMENT FOR A SECOND TIME.
TELL 'EM. MAKE 'EM GIVE ME MY CHEMO. YOU GOTTA...
IT'S TOO DANGEROUS. THIS IS LIKE WHEN YOU JUMPED INTO THE BATHROOM WINDOW.
YOU KNOW WHAT IT'S GONNA SAY ON YOUR TOMBSTONE? "HARVEY PEKAR DIED BECAUSE HE COULDN'T WAIT IN LINE!"
LOOK, I WANNA GET THIS STUFF OVER WITH AS SOON AS I CAN. I'M GOING INSANE WITH THE BOREDOM AND FEELIN' LOUSY. IT'S LIKE THE CHINESE WATER TORTURE.
I CAN'T GET INTERESTED IN READING, OR WRITING, OR WATCHIN' TV OR VIDEOTAPES. I'M SO WEAK 'N' BORED THAT MY DAYS ARE BLURRING TOGETHER.
ALL I CAN DO IS LAY ON MY BACK, AN' LISTEN TO THE RADIO. AN' THAT GARRISON KEILLOR IS GETTING ON MY NERVES.
IT'S BEEN A QUIET WEEK IN LAKE WOBEGON...

WHEN HARVEY IS FINALLY ALLOWED TO CONTINUE HIS CHEMOTHERAPY, THE NURSE TELLS JOYCE THAT SHE MAY NO LONGER SIT WITH HARVEY DURING HIS TREATMENT. IT SEEMS THERE'S SUDDENLY "NO ROOM" FOR HER.

SHE'S BANISHED TO THE CORRIDOR

I KNOW WHAT THIS IS ABOUT. BUT, DAMN! THE OTHER NURSES ARE SO NICE ...

EVERY NIGHT THIS WEEK, HE'S BEEN WAKING UP, YELLING, TRYING TO FIGHT SOMETHING ... I JUST WANNA BE THERE IN CASE HE TRIES TO PULL HIS TUBES OUT, AGAIN. WHY CAN'T WE WORK TOGETHER? ONE TIME, SHE WAS SO BUSY SHE LET HIM PEE HIMSELF. I DON'T WANT HIM TO WAKE UP TO THAT ...

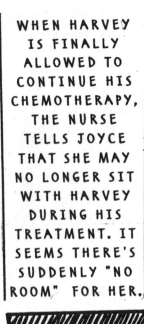

AT LEAST SHE'S GOOD AT HITTING VEINS. HE'S BLACK AND BLUE, BUT SHE STILL FINDS 'EM ... I LOOKED THE STUFF IN HIS BAG UP: SPILL IT ON THE FLOOR, IT'LL EAT THROUGH TILE. A "BURNING DRUG." SO BAD THEY HAD TO GIVE A PATIENT A SKIN GRAFT, WHEN SOMEONE SCREWED UP. A TUBE PULLED OUT, THE SYRINGE SPLASHED ...

I.V. LIQUID DRIPS INTO MY ARM. DRIP. DRIP. DRIP ... ONE DRIP AT A TIME. HOW DOES THIS TREATMENT EVER END? GOT SOME BENADRYL IN ME TO CALM ME DOWN, THOUGH ... KINDA SLEEPY... GO HOME ... IN TWO DAYS I'LL BE ROLLIN' AROUND ON THE FLOOR ... SHAKIN', TREMBLIN' ... NEVER BE OVER ...NEVER GET MY STRENGTH BACK ... CHEMO IS SLOWLY KILLIN' ME.

THE NURSE WHO USED TO WORK WITH HARVEY STOPS TO TALK WITH JOYCE

HEY, THERE! HOW ARE YOU DOING?

WELL, HARVEY IS STILL IN A LOT OF PAIN, BUT HE'S FINALLY STARTING TO FORM SOME SCAR TISSUE ON HIS BACK.

I WASN'T ASKING ABOUT HARVEY. I WAS ASKING ABOUT YOU.

I GUESS I'M TIRED. I HAD TO DIG US OUT OF THE SNOW AGAIN, TO GET HERE.

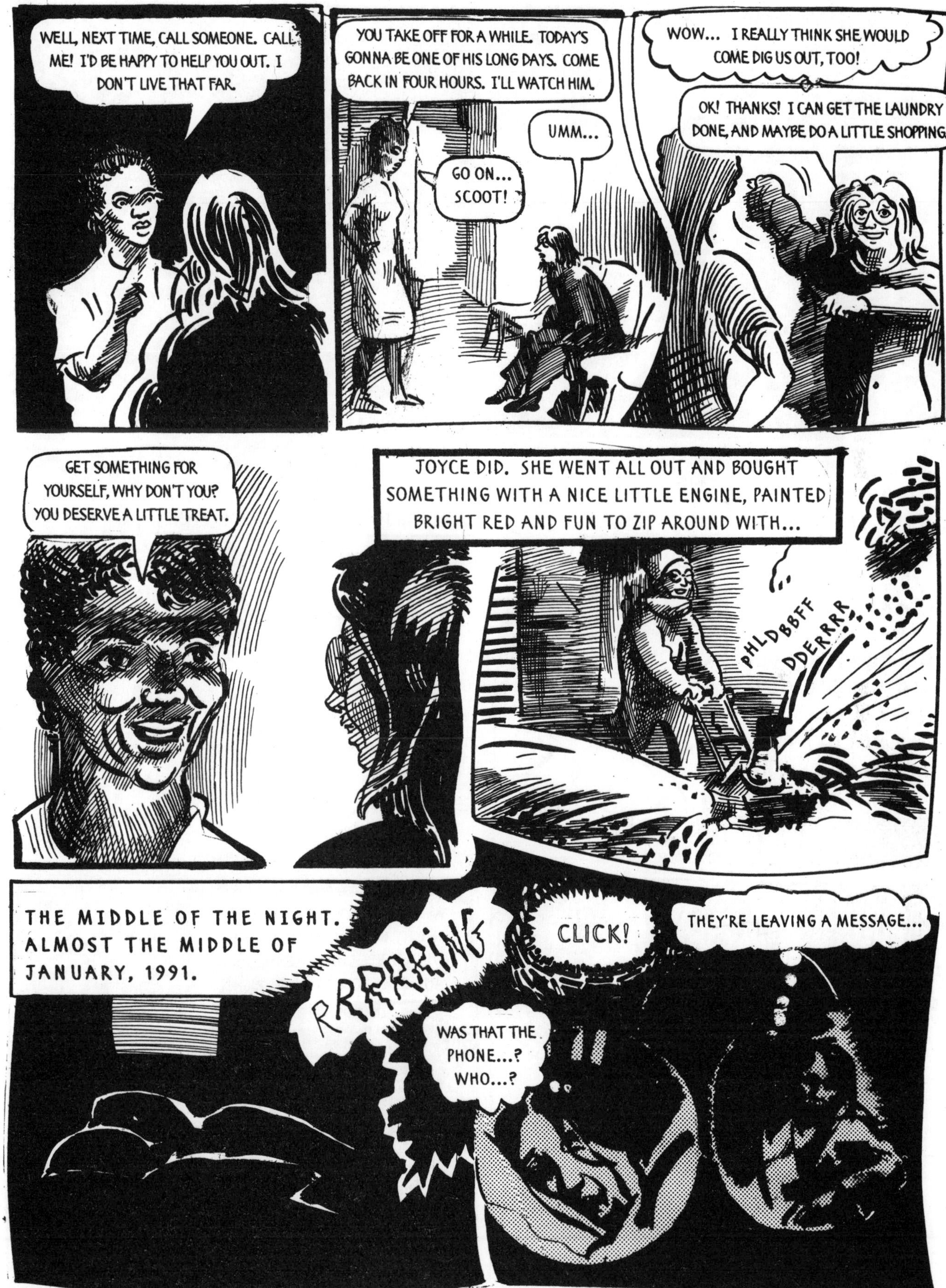
WELL, NEXT TIME, CALL SOMEONE. CALL ME! I'D BE HAPPY TO HELP YOU OUT. I DON'T LIVE THAT FAR.
YOU TAKE OFF FOR A WHILE. TODAY'S GONNA BE ONE OF HIS LONG DAYS. COME BACK IN FOUR HOURS. I'LL WATCH HIM.
UMM...
GO ON... SCOOT!
WOW... I REALLY THINK SHE WOULD COME DIG US OUT, TOO!
OK! THANKS! I CAN GET THE LAUNDRY DONE, AND MAYBE DO A LITTLE SHOPPING.
GET SOMETHING FOR YOURSELF, WHY DON'T YOU? YOU DESERVE A LITTLE TREAT.
JOYCE DID. SHE WENT ALL OUT AND BOUGHT SOMETHING WITH A NICE LITTLE ENGINE, PAINTED BRIGHT RED AND FUN TO ZIP AROUND WITH...
PHLDBBFF
DDERRRR
THE MIDDLE OF THE NIGHT. ALMOST THE MIDDLE OF JANUARY, 1991.
RRRRRING
CLICK!
THEY'RE LEAVING A MESSAGE...
WAS THAT THE PHONE...? WHO...?

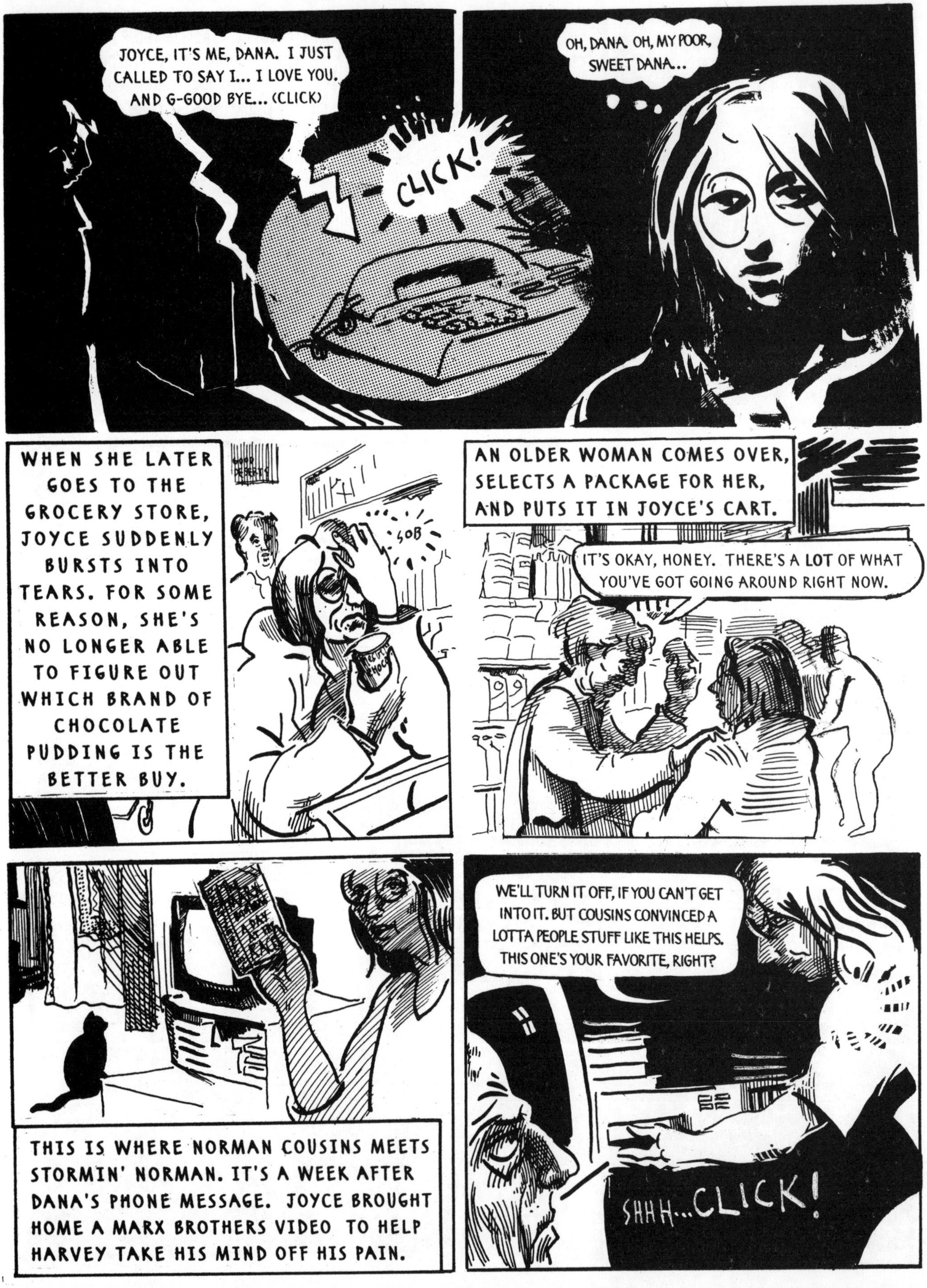
JOYCE, IT'S ME, DANA. I JUST CALLED TO SAY I... I LOVE YOU. AND G-GOOD BYE... (CLICK)
CLICK!
OH, DANA. OH, MY POOR, SWEET DANA...
WHEN SHE LATER GOES TO THE GROCERY STORE, JOYCE SUDDENLY BURSTS INTO TEARS. FOR SOME REASON, SHE'S NO LONGER ABLE TO FIGURE OUT WHICH BRAND OF CHOCOLATE PUDDING IS THE BETTER BUY.
SOB
AN OLDER WOMAN COMES OVER, SELECTS A PACKAGE FOR HER, AND PUTS IT IN JOYCE'S CART.
IT'S OKAY, HONEY. THERE'S A LOT OF WHAT YOU'VE GOT GOING AROUND RIGHT NOW.
THIS IS WHERE NORMAN COUSINS MEETS STORMIN' NORMAN. IT'S A WEEK AFTER DANA'S PHONE MESSAGE. JOYCE BROUGHT HOME A MARX BROTHERS VIDEO TO HELP HARVEY TAKE HIS MIND OFF HIS PAIN.
WE'LL TURN IT OFF, IF YOU CAN'T GET INTO IT. BUT COUSINS CONVINCED A LOTTA PEOPLE STUFF LIKE THIS HELPS. THIS ONE'S YOUR FAVORITE, RIGHT?
SHHH...CLICK!

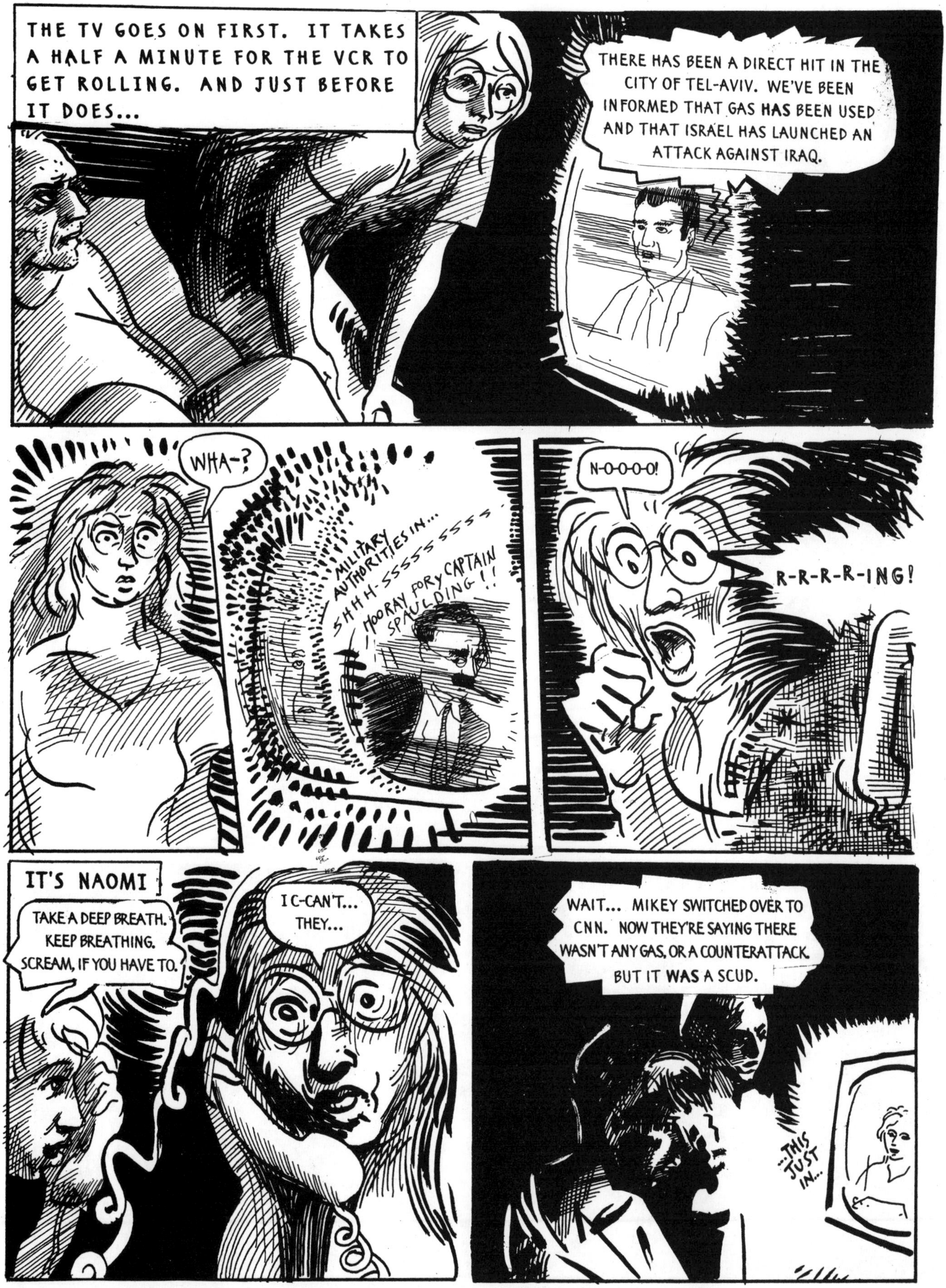
THE TV GOES ON FIRST. IT TAKES A HALF A MINUTE FOR THE VCR TO GET ROLLING. AND JUST BEFORE IT DOES...
THERE HAS BEEN A DIRECT HIT IN THE CITY OF TEL-AVIV. WE'VE BEEN INFORMED THAT GAS HAS BEEN USED AND THAT ISRAEL HAS LAUNCHED AN ATTACK AGAINST IRAQ.
WHA-?
MILITARY AUTHORITIES IN...
SHHH-SSSSSSSSSS
HOORAY FOR Y CAPTAIN SPAULDING!!
N-O-O-O-O!
R-R-R-R-ING!
IT'S NAOMI
TAKE A DEEP BREATH. KEEP BREATHING. SCREAM, IF YOU HAVE TO.
I C-CAN'T... THEY...
WAIT... MIKEY SWITCHED OVER TO CNN. NOW THEY'RE SAYING THERE WASN'T ANY GAS, OR A COUNTERATTACK. BUT IT WAS A SCUD.
...THIS JUST IN...

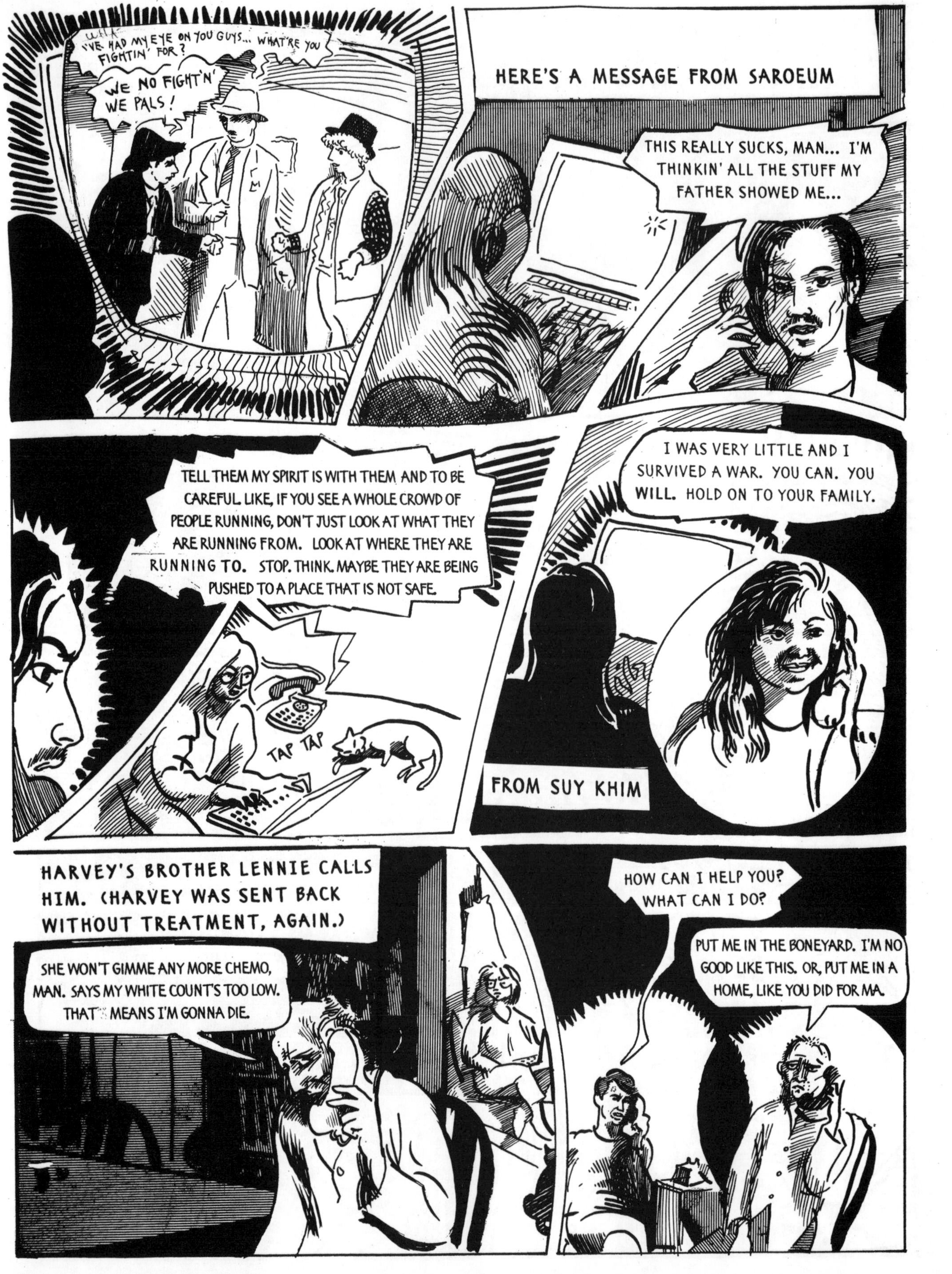

I'VE HAD MY EYE ON YOU GUYS... WHAT'RE YOU FIGHTIN' FOR?
WE NO FIGHT'N' WE PALS!
HERE'S A MESSAGE FROM SAROEUM
THIS REALLY SUCKS, MAN... I'M THINKIN' ALL THE STUFF MY FATHER SHOWED ME...
TELL THEM MY SPIRIT IS WITH THEM AND TO BE CAREFUL. LIKE, IF YOU SEE A WHOLE CROWD OF PEOPLE RUNNING, DON'T JUST LOOK AT WHAT THEY ARE RUNNING FROM. LOOK AT WHERE THEY ARE RUNNING TO. STOP. THINK. MAYBE THEY ARE BEING PUSHED TO A PLACE THAT IS NOT SAFE.
TAP TAP
I WAS VERY LITTLE AND I SURVIVED A WAR. YOU CAN. YOU WILL. HOLD ON TO YOUR FAMILY.
FROM SUY KHIM
HARVEY'S BROTHER LENNIE CALLS HIM. (HARVEY WAS SENT BACK WITHOUT TREATMENT, AGAIN.)
SHE WON'T GIMME ANY MORE CHEMO, MAN. SAYS MY WHITE COUNT'S TOO LOW. THAT MEANS I'M GONNA DIE.
HOW CAN I HELP YOU? WHAT CAN I DO?
PUT ME IN THE BONEYARD. I'M NO GOOD LIKE THIS. OR, PUT ME IN A HOME, LIKE YOU DID FOR MA.

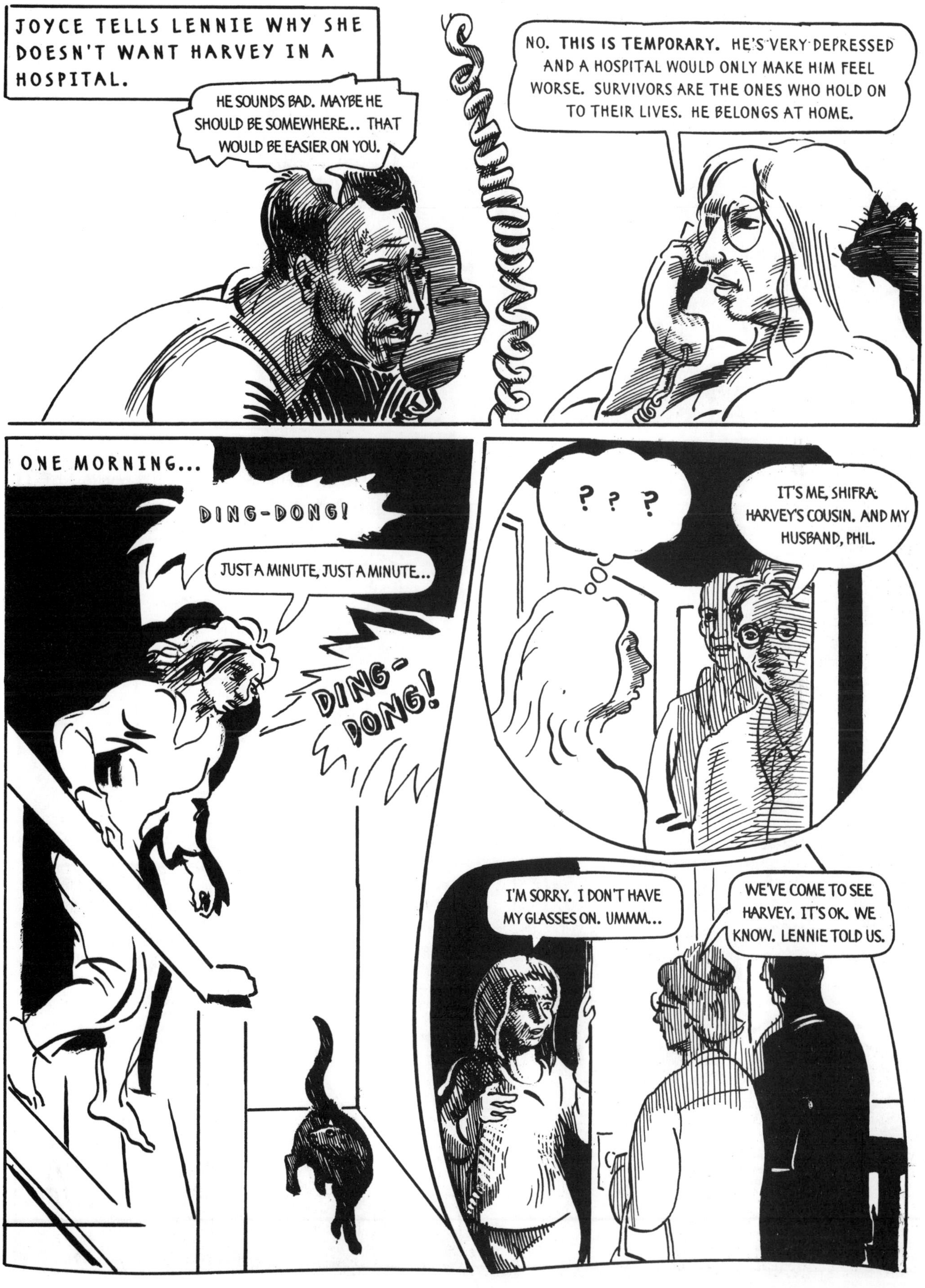

JOYCE TELLS LENNIE WHY SHE DOESN'T WANT HARVEY IN A HOSPITAL.
HE SOUNDS BAD. MAYBE HE SHOULD BE SOMEWHERE... THAT WOULD BE EASIER ON YOU.
NO. THIS IS TEMPORARY. HE'S VERY DEPRESSED AND A HOSPITAL WOULD ONLY MAKE HIM FEEL WORSE. SURVIVORS ARE THE ONES WHO HOLD ON TO THEIR LIVES. HE BELONGS AT HOME.
ONE MORNING...
DING-DONG!
JUST A MINUTE, JUST A MINUTE...
DING-DONG!
? ? ?
IT'S ME, SHIFRA. HARVEY'S COUSIN. AND MY HUSBAND, PHIL.
I'M SORRY. I DON'T HAVE MY GLASSES ON. UMMM...
WE'VE COME TO SEE HARVEY. IT'S OK. WE KNOW. LENNIE TOLD US.

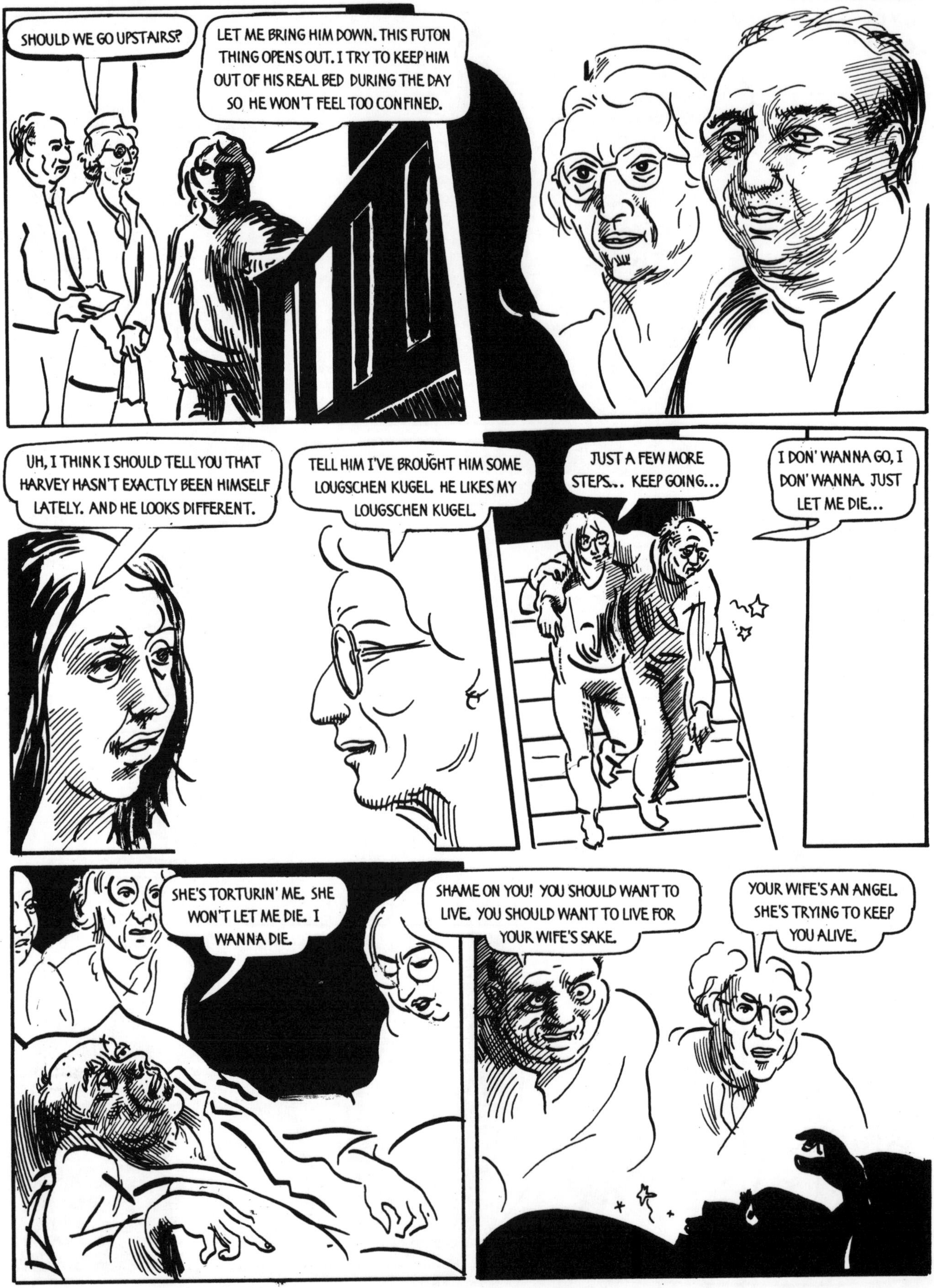
SHOULD WE GO UPSTAIRS?
LET ME BRING HIM DOWN. THIS FUTON THING OPENS OUT. I TRY TO KEEP HIM OUT OF HIS REAL BED DURING THE DAY SO HE WON'T FEEL TOO CONFINED.
UH, I THINK I SHOULD TELL YOU THAT HARVEY HASN'T EXACTLY BEEN HIMSELF LATELY. AND HE LOOKS DIFFERENT.
TELL HIM I'VE BROUGHT HIM SOME LOUGSCHEN KUGEL. HE LIKES MY LOUGSCHEN KUGEL.
JUST A FEW MORE STEPS... KEEP GOING...
I DON' WANNA GO, I DON' WANNA. JUST LET ME DIE...
SHE'S TORTURIN' ME. SHE WON'T LET ME DIE. I WANNA DIE.
SHAME ON YOU! YOU SHOULD WANT TO LIVE. YOU SHOULD WANT TO LIVE FOR YOUR WIFE'S SAKE.
YOUR WIFE'S AN ANGEL. SHE'S TRYING TO KEEP YOU ALIVE.

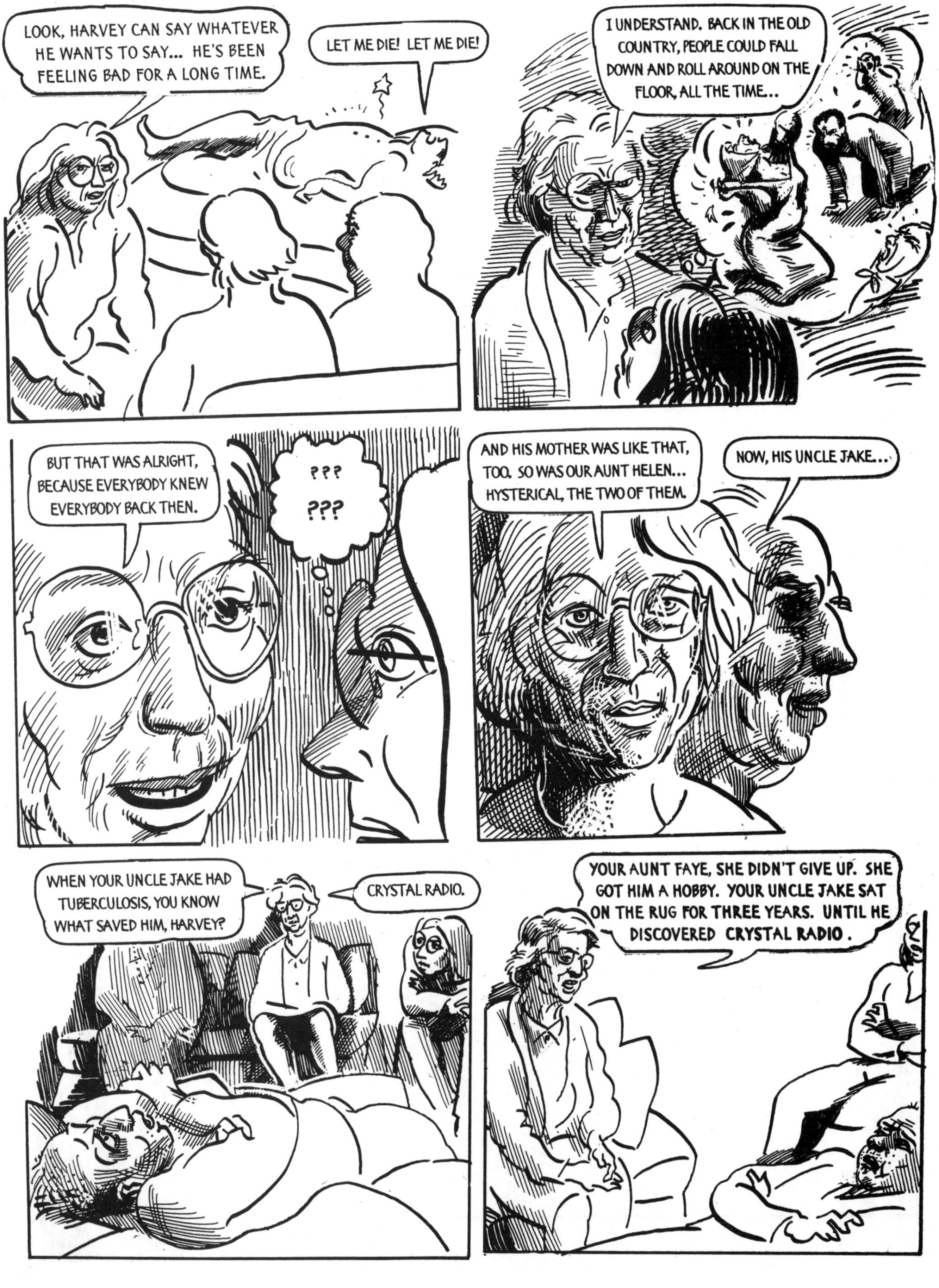
LOOK, HARVEY CAN SAY WHATEVER HE WANTS TO SAY... HE'S BEEN FEELING BAD FOR A LONG TIME.
LET ME DIE! LET ME DIE!
I UNDERSTAND. BACK IN THE OLD COUNTRY, PEOPLE COULD FALL DOWN AND ROLL AROUND ON THE FLOOR, ALL THE TIME...
BUT THAT WAS ALRIGHT, BECAUSE EVERYBODY KNEW EVERYBODY BACK THEN.
??? ???
AND HIS MOTHER WAS LIKE THAT, TOO. SO WAS OUR AUNT HELEN... HYSTERICAL, THE TWO OF THEM.
NOW, HIS UNCLE JAKE...
WHEN YOUR UNCLE JAKE HAD TUBERCULOSIS, YOU KNOW WHAT SAVED HIM, HARVEY?
CRYSTAL RADIO.
YOUR AUNT FAYE, SHE DIDN'T GIVE UP. SHE GOT HIM A HOBBY. YOUR UNCLE JAKE SAT ON THE RUG FOR THREE YEARS. UNTIL HE DISCOVERED CRYSTAL RADIO.

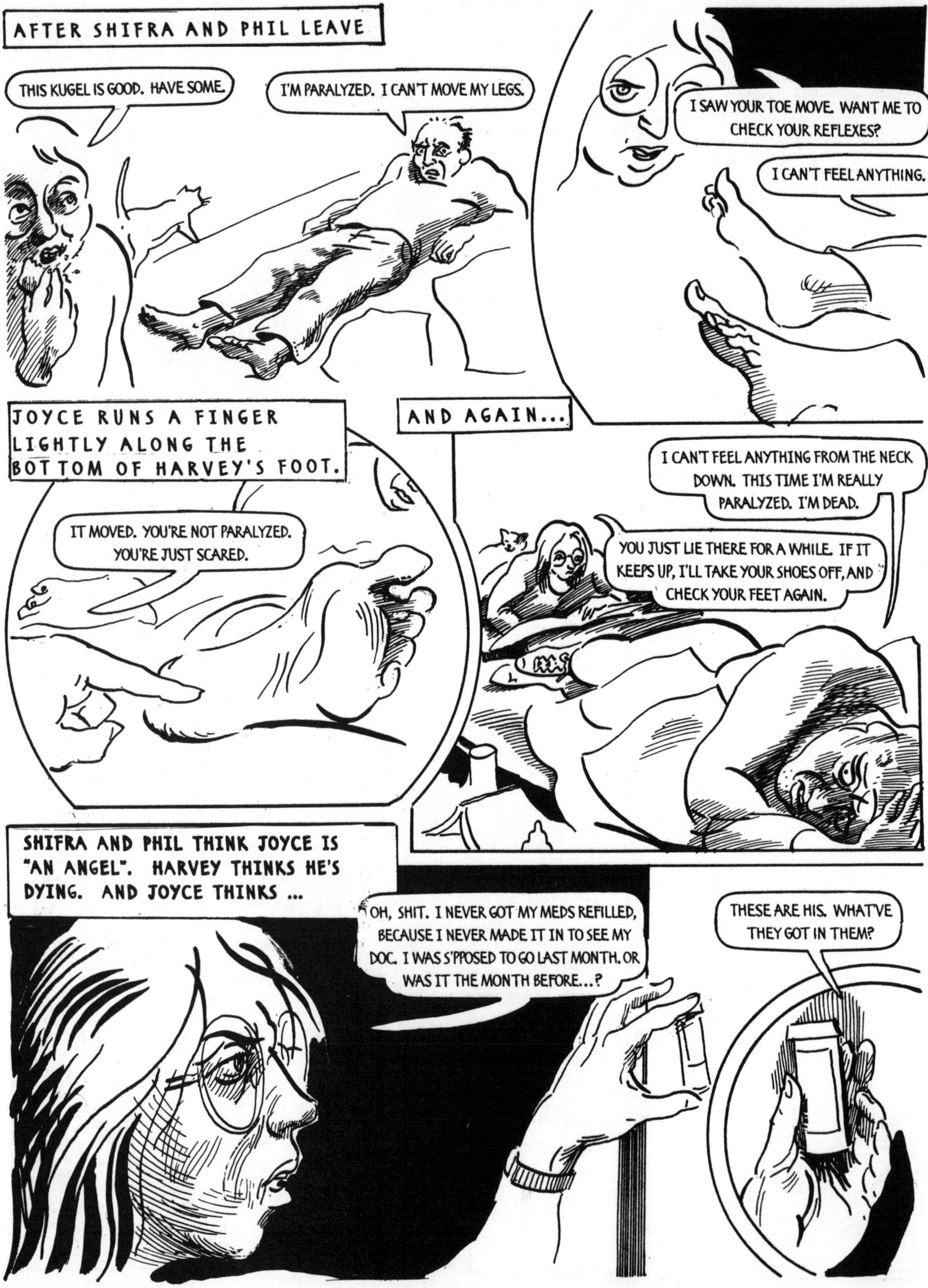
AFTER SHIFRA AND PHIL LEAVE
THIS KUGEL IS GOOD. HAVE SOME.
I'M PARALYZED. I CAN'T MOVE MY LEGS.
I SAW YOUR TOE MOVE. WANT ME TO CHECK YOUR REFLEXES?
I CAN'T FEEL ANYTHING.
JOYCE RUNS A FINGER LIGHTLY ALONG THE BOTTOM OF HARVEY'S FOOT.
IT MOVED. YOU'RE NOT PARALYZED. YOU'RE JUST SCARED.
AND AGAIN...
I CAN'T FEEL ANYTHING FROM THE NECK DOWN. THIS TIME I'M REALLY PARALYZED. I'M DEAD.
YOU JUST LIE THERE FOR A WHILE. IF IT KEEPS UP, I'LL TAKE YOUR SHOES OFF, AND CHECK YOUR FEET AGAIN.
SHIFRA AND PHIL THINK JOYCE IS "AN ANGEL". HARVEY THINKS HE'S DYING. AND JOYCE THINKS ...
OH, SHIT. I NEVER GOT MY MEDS REFILLED, BECAUSE I NEVER MADE IT IN TO SEE MY DOC. I WAS S'PPOSED TO GO LAST MONTH. OR WAS IT THE MONTH BEFORE...?
THESE ARE HIS. WHAT'VE THEY GOT IN THEM?

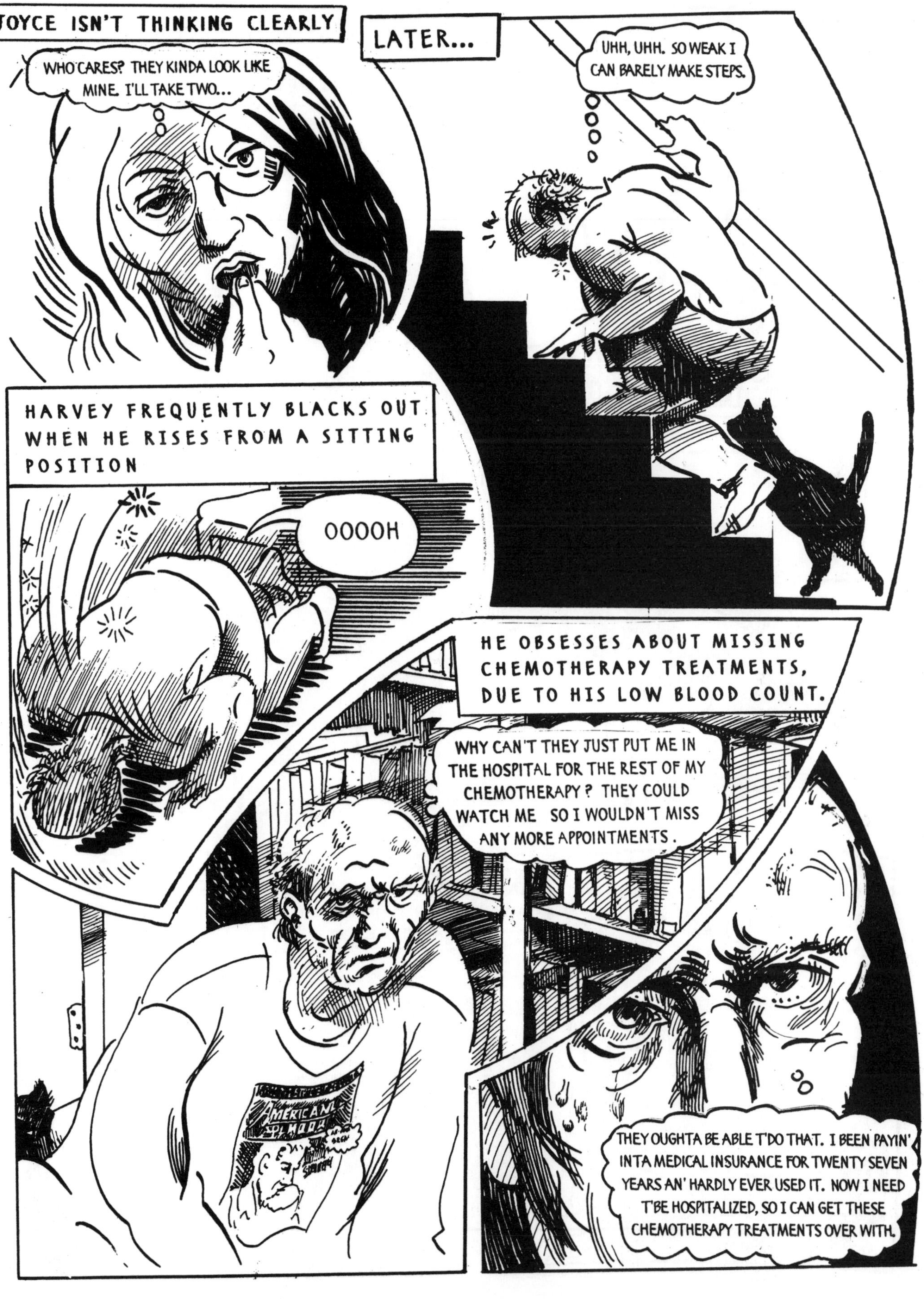
JOYCE ISN'T THINKING CLEARLY
WHO CARES? THEY KINDA LOOK LIKE MINE. I'LL TAKE TWO...
LATER...
UHH, UHH. SO WEAK I CAN BARELY MAKE STEPS.
HARVEY FREQUENTLY BLACKS OUT WHEN HE RISES FROM A SITTING POSITION
OOOOH
HE OBSESSES ABOUT MISSING CHEMOTHERAPY TREATMENTS, DUE TO HIS LOW BLOOD COUNT.
WHY CAN'T THEY JUST PUT ME IN THE HOSPITAL FOR THE REST OF MY CHEMOTHERAPY? THEY COULD WATCH ME SO I WOULDN'T MISS ANY MORE APPOINTMENTS.
THEY OUGHTA BE ABLE T'DO THAT. I BEEN PAYIN' INTA MEDICAL INSURANCE FOR TWENTY SEVEN YEARS AN' HARDLY EVER USED IT. NOW I NEED T'BE HOSPITALIZED, SO I CAN GET THESE CHEMOTHERAPY TREATMENTS OVER WITH.

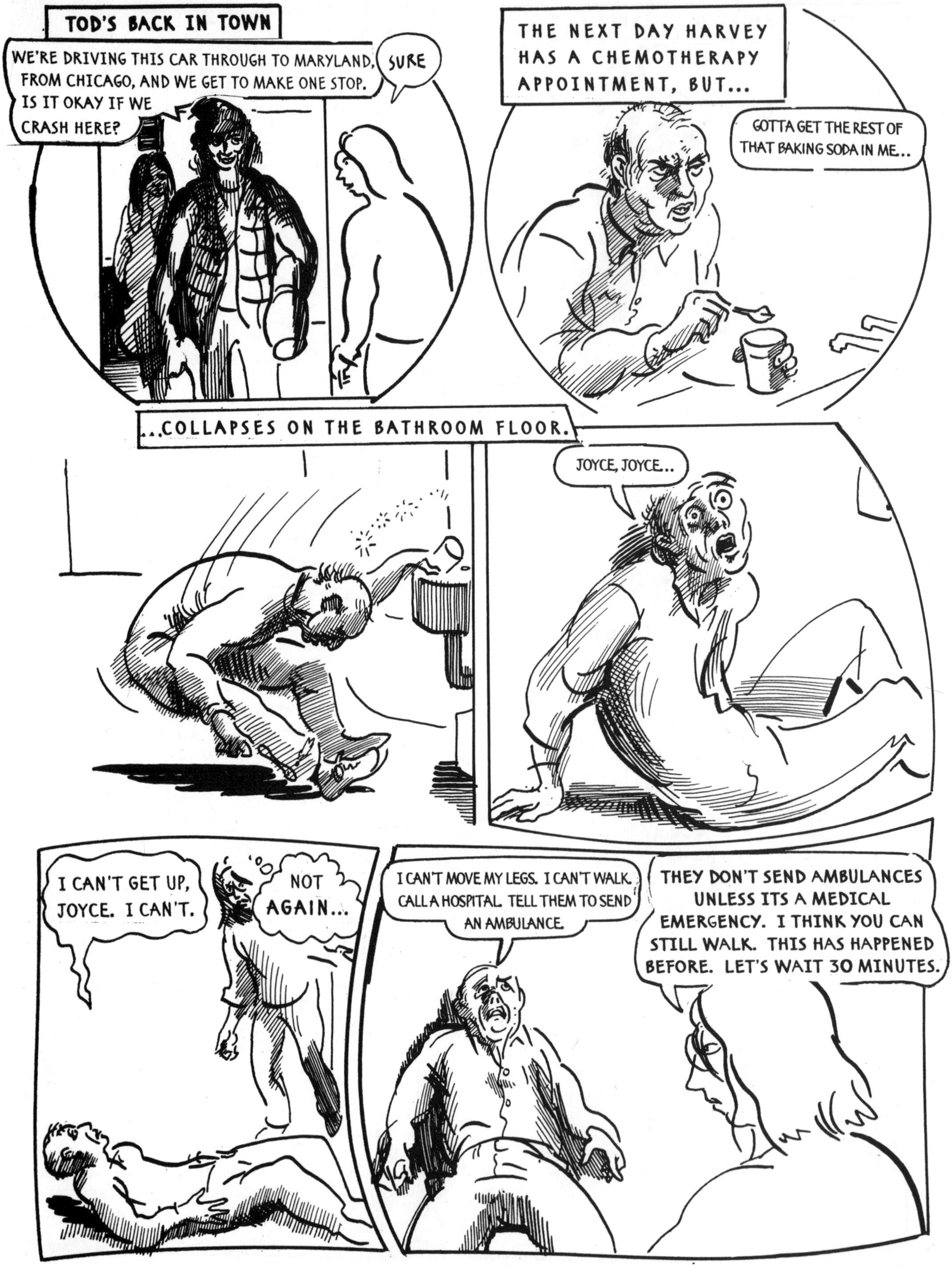
TOD'S BACK IN TOWN
WE'RE DRIVING THIS CAR THROUGH TO MARYLAND, FROM CHICAGO, AND WE GET TO MAKE ONE STOP. IS IT OKAY IF WE CRASH HERE?
SURE
THE NEXT DAY HARVEY HAS A CHEMOTHERAPY APPOINTMENT, BUT...
GOTTA GET THE REST OF THAT BAKING SODA IN ME...
...COLLAPSES ON THE BATHROOM FLOOR.
JOYCE, JOYCE...
I CAN'T GET UP, JOYCE. I CAN'T.
NOT AGAIN...
I CAN'T MOVE MY LEGS. I CAN'T WALK. CALL A HOSPITAL. TELL THEM TO SEND AN AMBULANCE.
THEY DON'T SEND AMBULANCES UNLESS ITS A MEDICAL EMERGENCY. I THINK YOU CAN STILL WALK. THIS HAS HAPPENED BEFORE. LET'S WAIT 30 MINUTES.

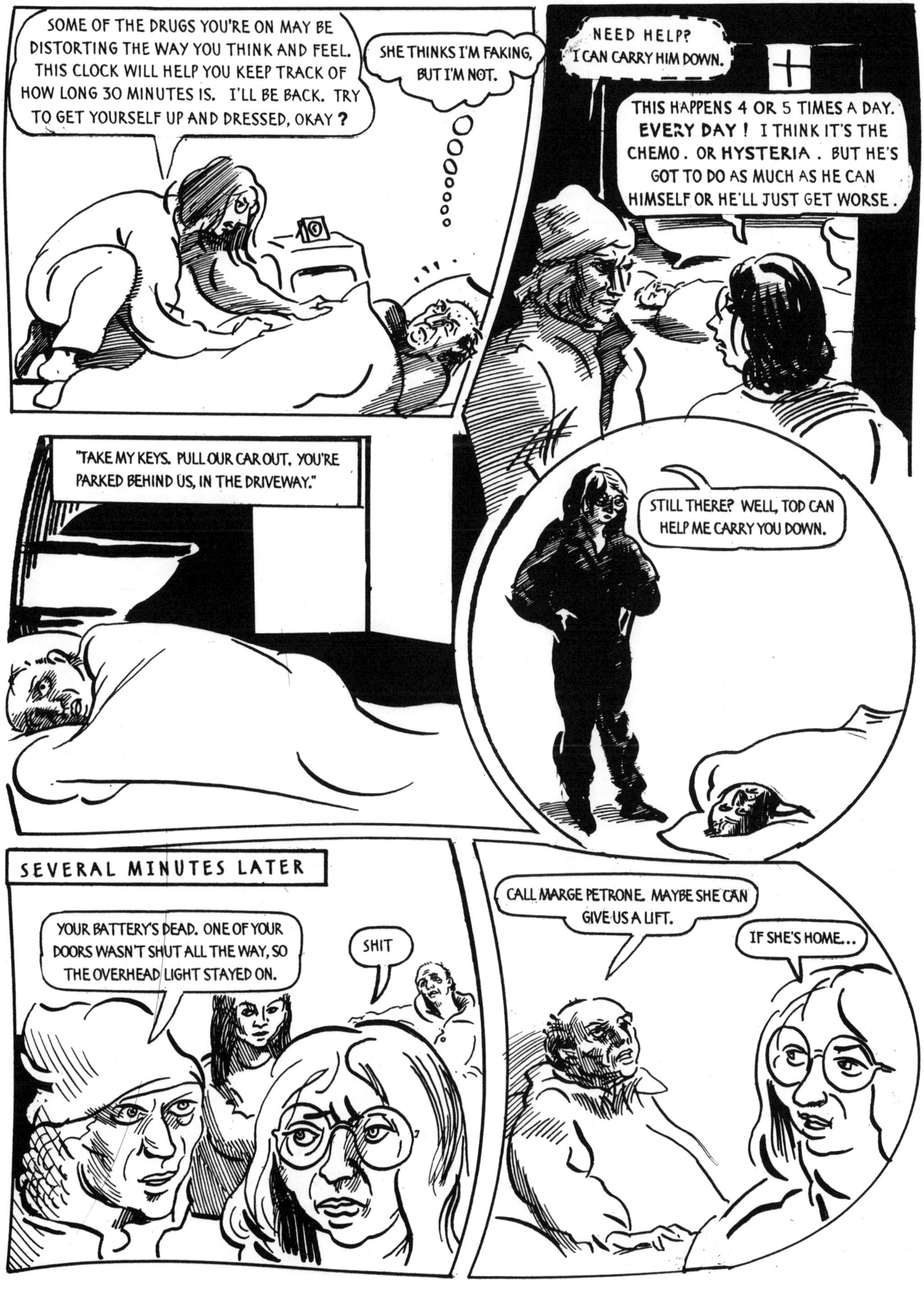
SOME OF THE DRUGS YOU'RE ON MAY BE DISTORTING THE WAY YOU THINK AND FEEL. THIS CLOCK WILL HELP YOU KEEP TRACK OF HOW LONG 30 MINUTES IS. I'LL BE BACK. TRY TO GET YOURSELF UP AND DRESSED, OKAY ?
SHE THINKS I'M FAKING, BUT I'M NOT.
NEED HELP? I CAN CARRY HIM DOWN.
THIS HAPPENS 4 OR 5 TIMES A DAY. EVERY DAY ! I THINK IT'S THE CHEMO. OR HYSTERIA. BUT HE'S GOT TO DO AS MUCH AS HE CAN HIMSELF OR HE'LL JUST GET WORSE.
"TAKE MY KEYS. PULL OUR CAR OUT. YOU'RE PARKED BEHIND US, IN THE DRIVEWAY."
STILL THERE? WELL, TOD CAN HELP ME CARRY YOU DOWN.
SEVERAL MINUTES LATER
YOUR BATTERY'S DEAD. ONE OF YOUR DOORS WASN'T SHUT ALL THE WAY, SO THE OVERHEAD LIGHT STAYED ON.
SHIT
CALL MARGE PETRONE. MAYBE SHE CAN GIVE US A LIFT.
IF SHE'S HOME...

SHE WAS.

MARGE SAYS SHE'LL PICK US UP IN A FEW MINUTES. TOD AND I WILL DRESS YOU.

OOH, MARGE IS REALLY GREAT.

TOD'S GOING TO TRY TO GET OUR CAR RUNNING WHILE WE GO SEE DR. RHODES. WE HAVE TO CHECK OUT ALL THIS "PARALYSIS."

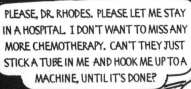

PLEASE, DR. RHODES. PLEASE LET ME STAY IN A HOSPITAL. I DON'T WANT TO MISS ANY MORE CHEMOTHERAPY. CAN'T THEY JUST STICK A TUBE IN ME AND HOOK ME UP TO A MACHINE, UNTIL IT'S DONE?

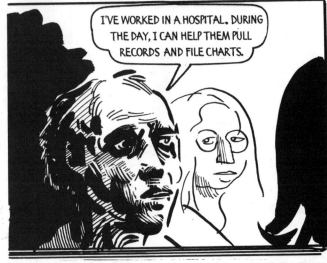

I'VE WORKED IN A HOSPITAL. DURING THE DAY, I CAN HELP THEM PULL RECORDS AND FILE CHARTS.

I THINK I WILL ADMIT YOU, AND ORDER SOME TESTS. YOU MAY BE EXPERIENCING SOME PERIPHERAL NEUROPATHY. CHEMO CAN MAKE YOUR HANDS OR FEET FEEL NUMB. SOMETIMES THERE ARE PROBLEMS AFTER A BONE MARROW SAMPLING, AND YOU DID HAVE THAT NEEDLE IN YOUR S PINE.

AND JOYCE NEEDS REST AS BADLY AS YOU DO.

9

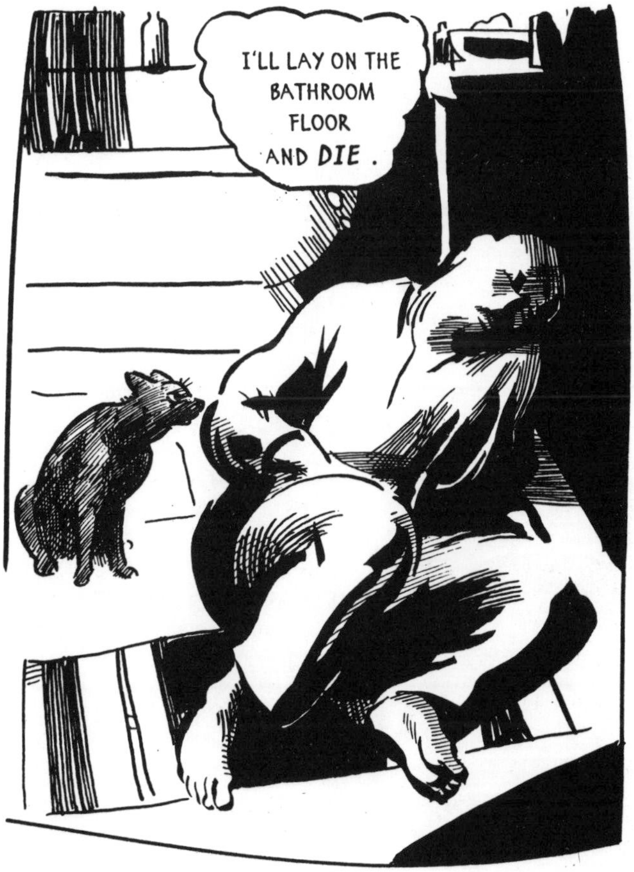
I'LL LAY ON THE BATHROOM FLOOR AND DIE.

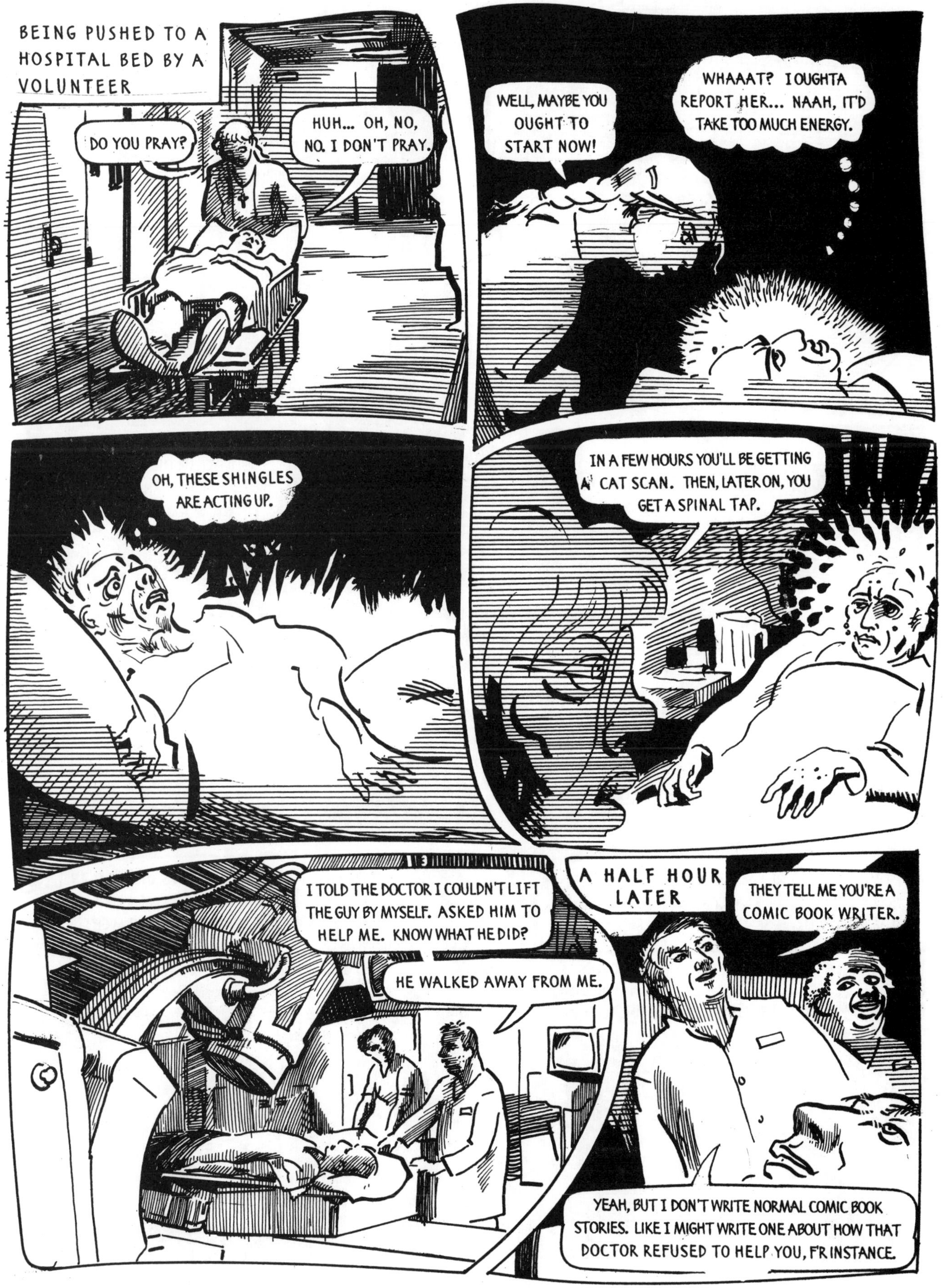
BEING PUSHED TO A HOSPITAL BED BY A VOLUNTEER
DO YOU PRAY?
HUH... OH, NO, NO. I DON'T PRAY.
WELL, MAYBE YOU OUGHT TO START NOW!
WHAAAT? I OUGHTA REPORT HER... NAAH, IT'D TAKE TOO MUCH ENERGY.
OH, THESE SHINGLES ARE ACTING UP.
IN A FEW HOURS YOU'LL BE GETTING A CAT SCAN. THEN, LATER ON, YOU GET A SPINAL TAP.
I TOLD THE DOCTOR I COULDN'T LIFT THE GUY BY MYSELF. ASKED HIM TO HELP ME. KNOW WHAT HE DID?
HE WALKED AWAY FROM ME.
A HALF HOUR LATER
THEY TELL ME YOU'RE A COMIC BOOK WRITER.
YEAH, BUT I DON'T WRITE NORMAL COMIC BOOK STORIES. LIKE I MIGHT WRITE ONE ABOUT HOW THAT DOCTOR REFUSED TO HELP YOU, F'RINSTANCE.

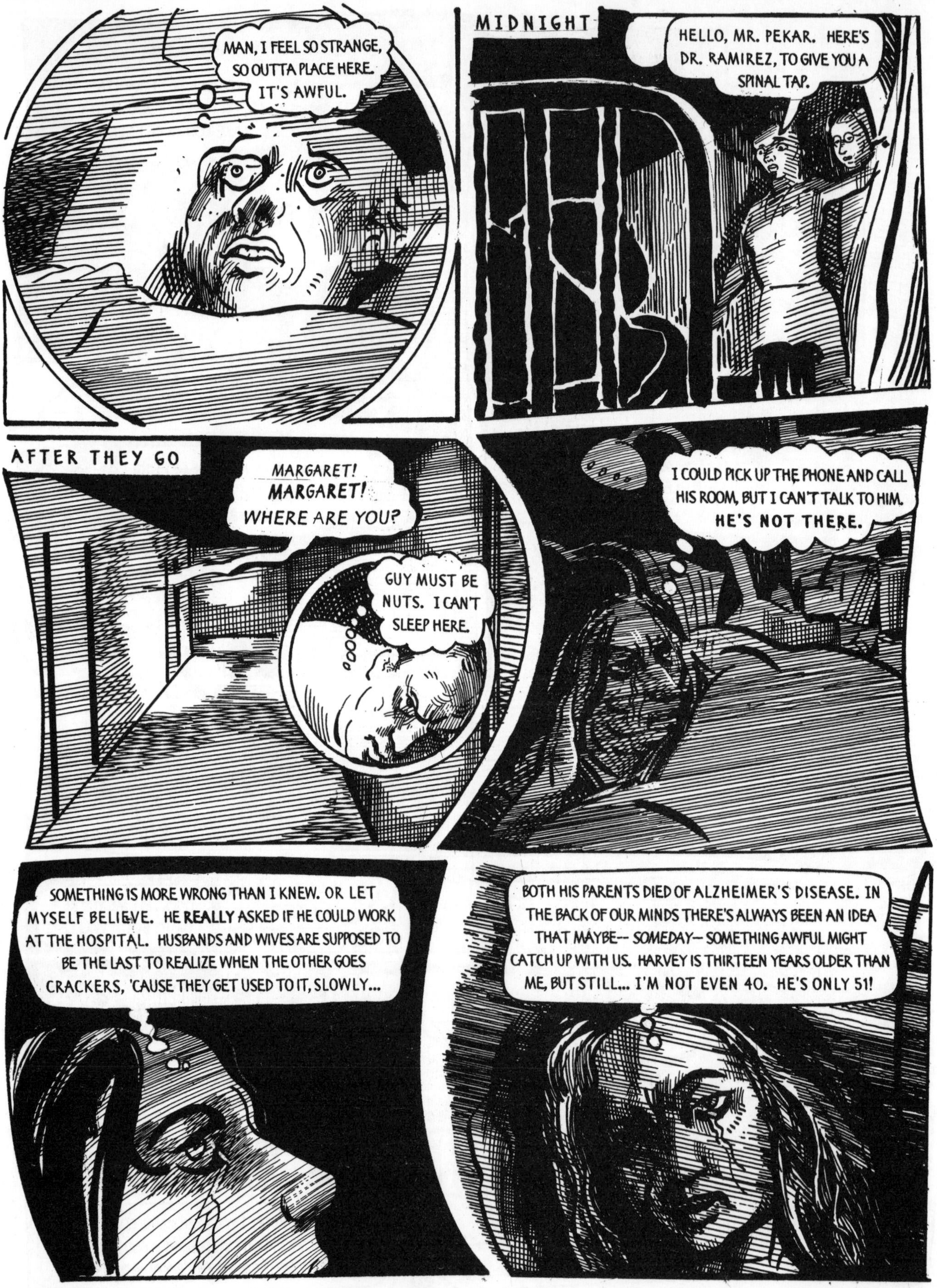

MAN, I FEEL SO STRANGE, SO OUTTA PLACE HERE. IT'S AWFUL.
MIDNIGHT
HELLO, MR. PEKAR. HERE'S DR. RAMIREZ, TO GIVE YOU A SPINAL TAP.
AFTER THEY GO
MARGARET! MARGARET! WHERE ARE YOU?
GUY MUST BE NUTS. I CAN'T SLEEP HERE.
I COULD PICK UP THE PHONE AND CALL HIS ROOM, BUT I CAN'T TALK TO HIM. HE'S NOT THERE.
SOMETHING IS MORE WRONG THAN I KNEW. OR LET MYSELF BELIEVE. HE REALLY ASKED IF HE COULD WORK AT THE HOSPITAL. HUSBANDS AND WIVES ARE SUPPOSED TO BE THE LAST TO REALIZE WHEN THE OTHER GOES CRACKERS, 'CAUSE THEY GET USED TO IT, SLOWLY...
BOTH HIS PARENTS DIED OF ALZHEIMER'S DISEASE. IN THE BACK OF OUR MINDS THERE'S ALWAYS BEEN AN IDEA THAT MAYBE-- SOMEDAY-- SOMETHING AWFUL MIGHT CATCH UP WITH US. HARVEY IS THIRTEEN YEARS OLDER THAN ME, BUT STILL... I'M NOT EVEN 40. HE'S ONLY 51!

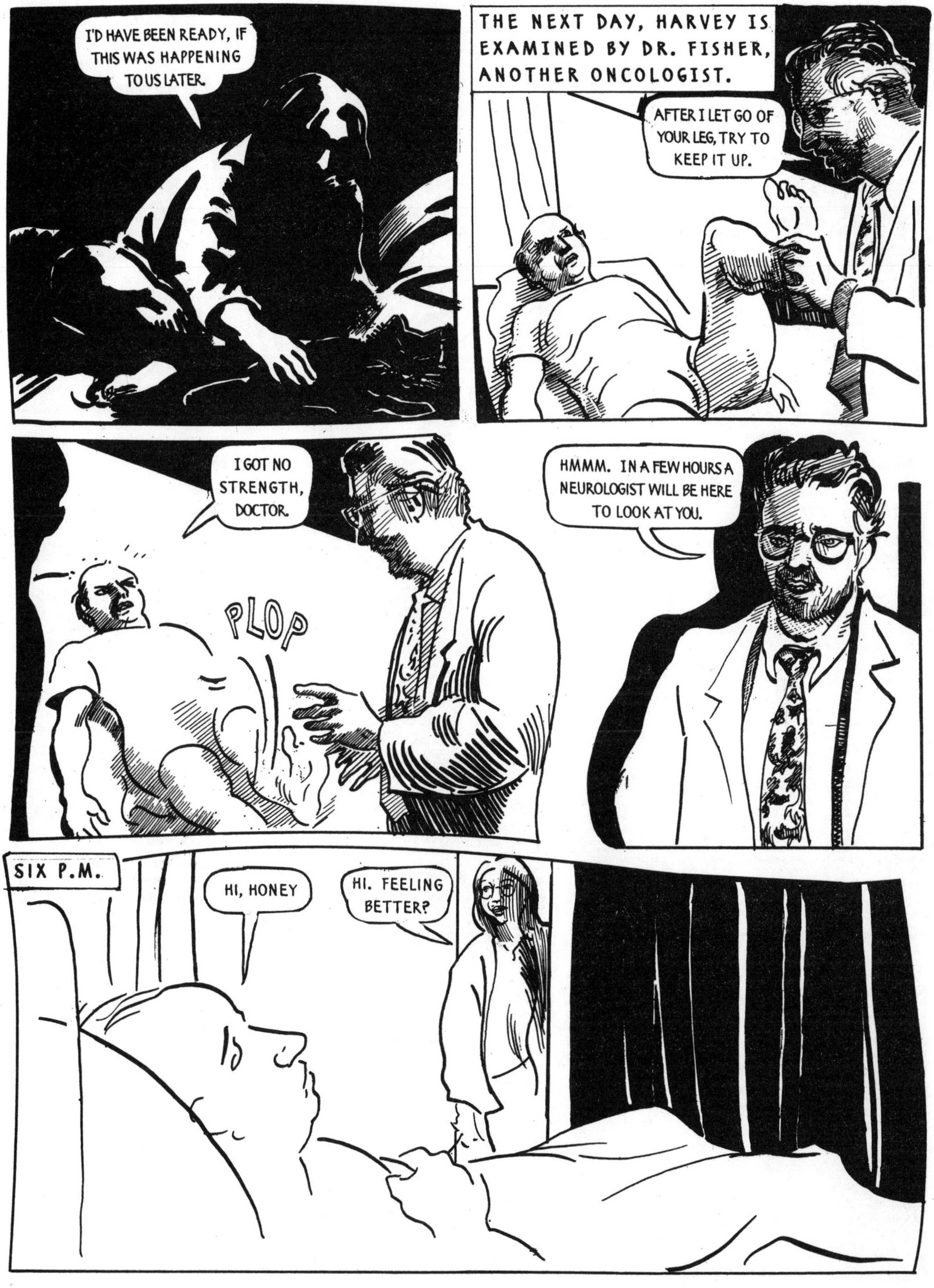
I'D HAVE BEEN READY, IF THIS WAS HAPPENING TO US LATER.
THE NEXT DAY, HARVEY IS EXAMINED BY DR. FISHER, ANOTHER ONCOLOGIST.
AFTER I LET GO OF YOUR LEG, TRY TO KEEP IT UP.
I GOT NO STRENGTH, DOCTOR.
PLOP
HMMM. IN A FEW HOURS A NEUROLOGIST WILL BE HERE TO LOOK AT YOU.
SIX P.M.
HI, HONEY
HI. FEELING BETTER?

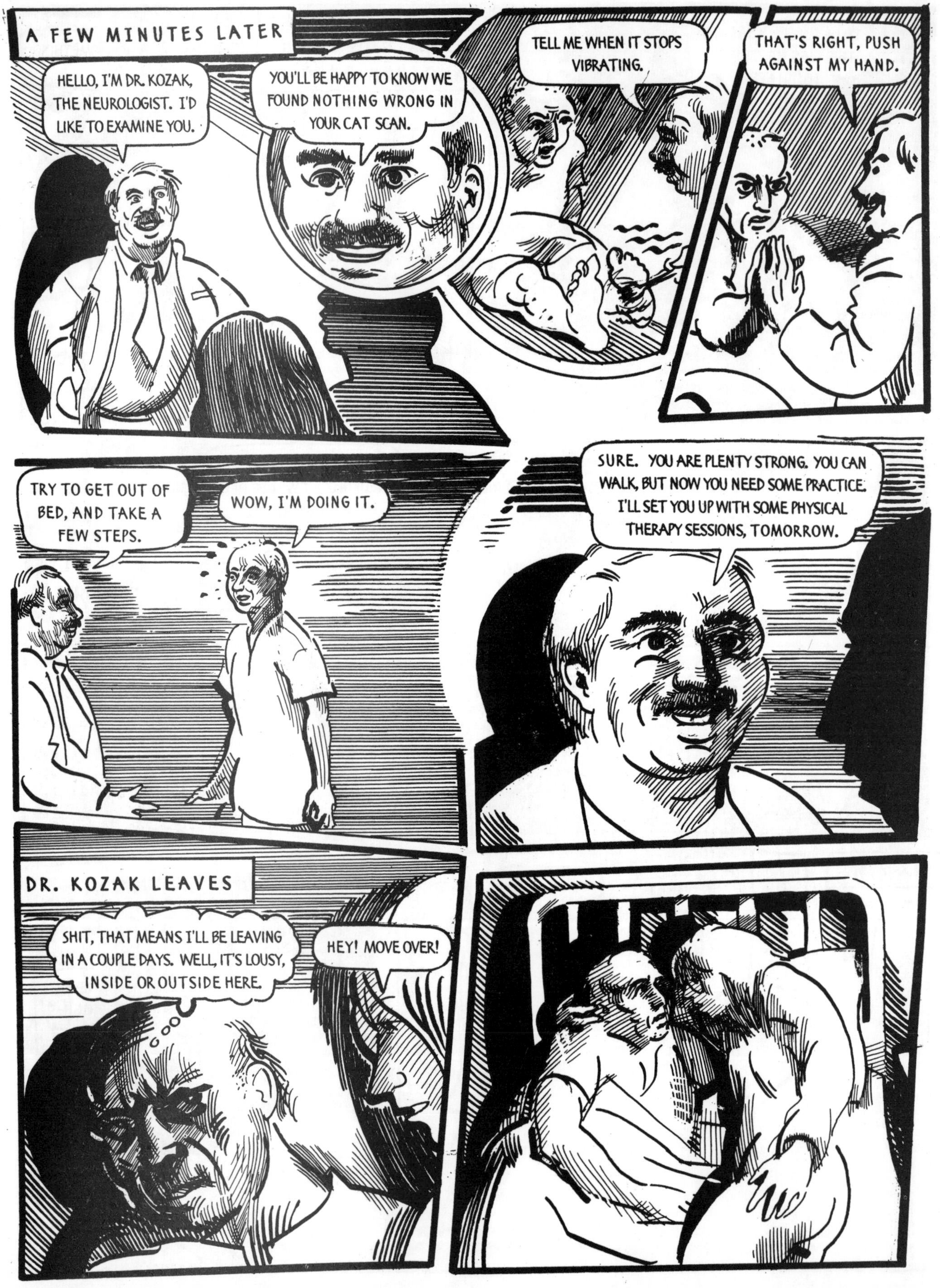
A FEW MINUTES LATER
HELLO, I'M DR. KOZAK, THE NEUROLOGIST. I'D LIKE TO EXAMINE YOU.
YOU'LL BE HAPPY TO KNOW WE FOUND NOTHING WRONG IN YOUR CAT SCAN.
TELL ME WHEN IT STOPS VIBRATING.
THAT'S RIGHT, PUSH AGAINST MY HAND.
TRY TO GET OUT OF BED, AND TAKE A FEW STEPS.
WOW, I'M DOING IT.
SURE. YOU ARE PLENTY STRONG. YOU CAN WALK, BUT NOW YOU NEED SOME PRACTICE. I'LL SET YOU UP WITH SOME PHYSICAL THERAPY SESSIONS, TOMORROW.
DR. KOZAK LEAVES
SHIT, THAT MEANS I'LL BE LEAVING IN A COUPLE DAYS. WELL, IT'S LOUSY, INSIDE OR OUTSIDE HERE.
HEY! MOVE OVER!

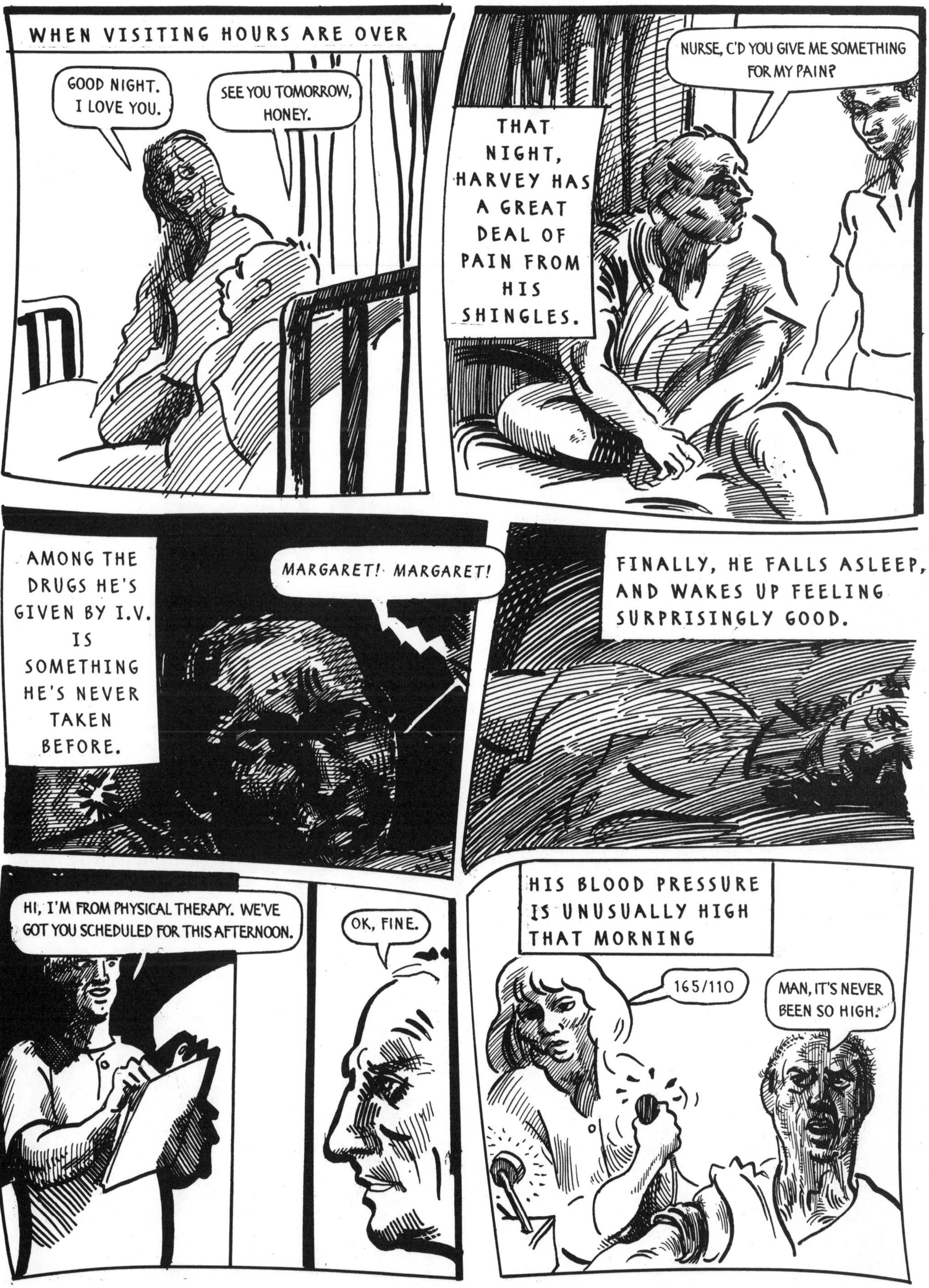
WHEN VISITING HOURS ARE OVER
GOOD NIGHT. I LOVE YOU.
SEE YOU TOMORROW, HONEY.
THAT NIGHT, HARVEY HAS A GREAT DEAL OF PAIN FROM HIS SHINGLES.
NURSE, C'D YOU GIVE ME SOMETHING FOR MY PAIN?
AMONG THE DRUGS HE'S GIVEN BY I.V. IS SOMETHING HE'S NEVER TAKEN BEFORE.
MARGARET! MARGARET!
FINALLY, HE FALLS ASLEEP, AND WAKES UP FEELING SURPRISINGLY GOOD.
HI, I'M FROM PHYSICAL THERAPY. WE'VE GOT YOU SCHEDULED FOR THIS AFTERNOON.
OK, FINE.
HIS BLOOD PRESSURE IS UNUSUALLY HIGH THAT MORNING
165/110
MAN, IT'S NEVER BEEN SO HIGH.

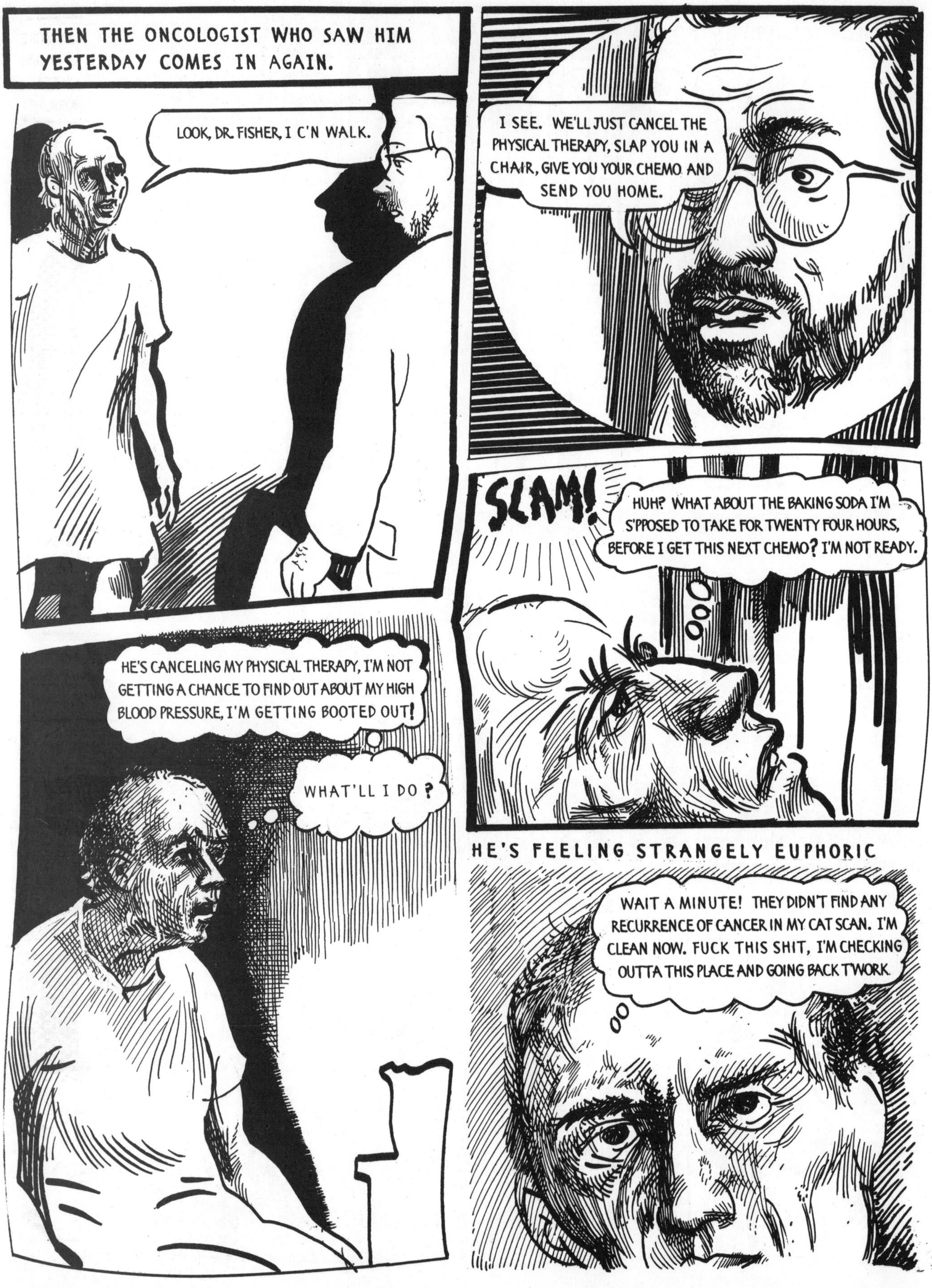
THEN THE ONCOLOGIST WHO SAW HIM YESTERDAY COMES IN AGAIN.
LOOK, DR. FISHER, I C'N WALK.
I SEE. WE'LL JUST CANCEL THE PHYSICAL THERAPY, SLAP YOU IN A CHAIR, GIVE YOU YOUR CHEMO AND SEND YOU HOME.
SLAM!
HUH? WHAT ABOUT THE BAKING SODA I'M S'PPOSED TO TAKE FOR TWENTY FOUR HOURS, BEFORE I GET THIS NEXT CHEMO? I'M NOT READY.
HE'S CANCELING MY PHYSICAL THERAPY, I'M NOT GETTING A CHANCE TO FIND OUT ABOUT MY HIGH BLOOD PRESSURE, I'M GETTING BOOTED OUT!
WHAT'LL I DO?
HE'S FEELING STRANGELY EUPHORIC
WAIT A MINUTE! THEY DIDN'T FIND ANY RECURRENCE OF CANCER IN MY CAT SCAN. I'M CLEAN NOW. FUCK THIS SHIT, I'M CHECKING OUTTA THIS PLACE AND GOING BACK TWORK.

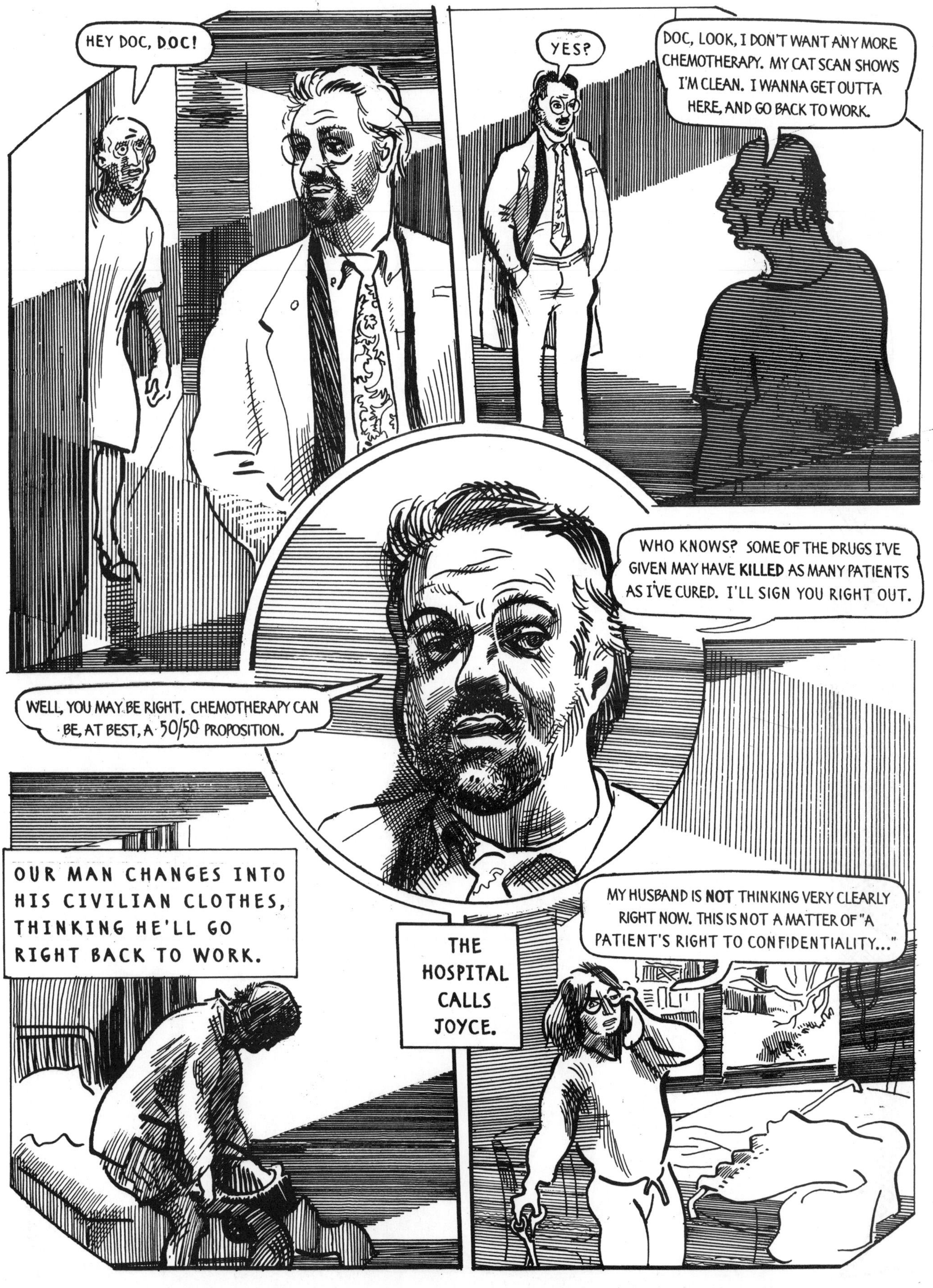
HEY DOC, DOC!
YES?
DOC, LOOK, I DON'T WANT ANY MORE CHEMOTHERAPY. MY CAT SCAN SHOWS I'M CLEAN. I WANNA GET OUTTA HERE, AND GO BACK TO WORK.
WELL, YOU MAY BE RIGHT. CHEMOTHERAPY CAN BE, AT BEST, A 50/50 PROPOSITION.
WHO KNOWS? SOME OF THE DRUGS I'VE GIVEN MAY HAVE KILLED AS MANY PATIENTS AS I'VE CURED. I'LL SIGN YOU RIGHT OUT.
OUR MAN CHANGES INTO HIS CIVILIAN CLOTHES, THINKING HE'LL GO RIGHT BACK TO WORK.
THE HOSPITAL CALLS JOYCE.
MY HUSBAND IS NOT THINKING VERY CLEARLY RIGHT NOW. THIS IS NOT A MATTER OF "A PATIENT'S RIGHT TO CONFIDENTIALITY..."

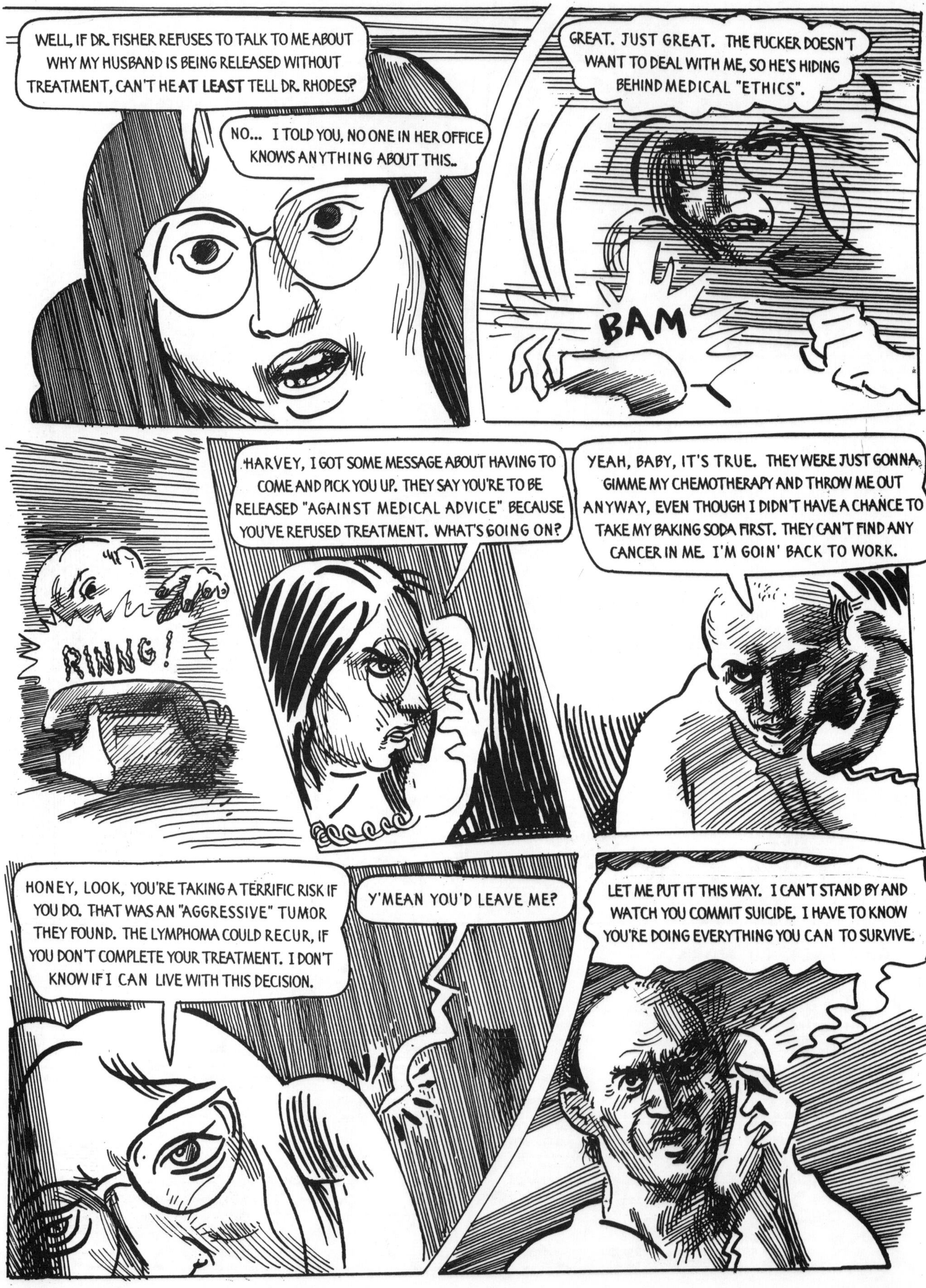
WELL, IF DR. FISHER REFUSES TO TALK TO ME ABOUT WHY MY HUSBAND IS BEING RELEASED WITHOUT TREATMENT, CAN'T HE AT LEAST TELL DR. RHODES?
NO... I TOLD YOU, NO ONE IN HER OFFICE KNOWS ANYTHING ABOUT THIS..
GREAT. JUST GREAT. THE FUCKER DOESN'T WANT TO DEAL WITH ME, SO HE'S HIDING BEHIND MEDICAL "ETHICS".
BAM
RINNG!
HARVEY, I GOT SOME MESSAGE ABOUT HAVING TO COME AND PICK YOU UP. THEY SAY YOU'RE TO BE RELEASED "AGAINST MEDICAL ADVICE" BECAUSE YOU'VE REFUSED TREATMENT. WHAT'S GOING ON?
YEAH, BABY, IT'S TRUE. THEY WERE JUST GONNA GIMME MY CHEMOTHERAPY AND THROW ME OUT ANYWAY, EVEN THOUGH I DIDN'T HAVE A CHANCE TO TAKE MY BAKING SODA FIRST. THEY CAN'T FIND ANY CANCER IN ME. I'M GOIN' BACK TO WORK.
HONEY, LOOK, YOU'RE TAKING A TERRIFIC RISK IF YOU DO. THAT WAS AN "AGGRESSIVE" TUMOR THEY FOUND. THE LYMPHOMA COULD RECUR, IF YOU DON'T COMPLETE YOUR TREATMENT. I DON'T KNOW IF I CAN LIVE WITH THIS DECISION.
Y'MEAN YOU'D LEAVE ME?
LET ME PUT IT THIS WAY. I CAN'T STAND BY AND WATCH YOU COMMIT SUICIDE. I HAVE TO KNOW YOU'RE DOING EVERYTHING YOU CAN TO SURVIVE.

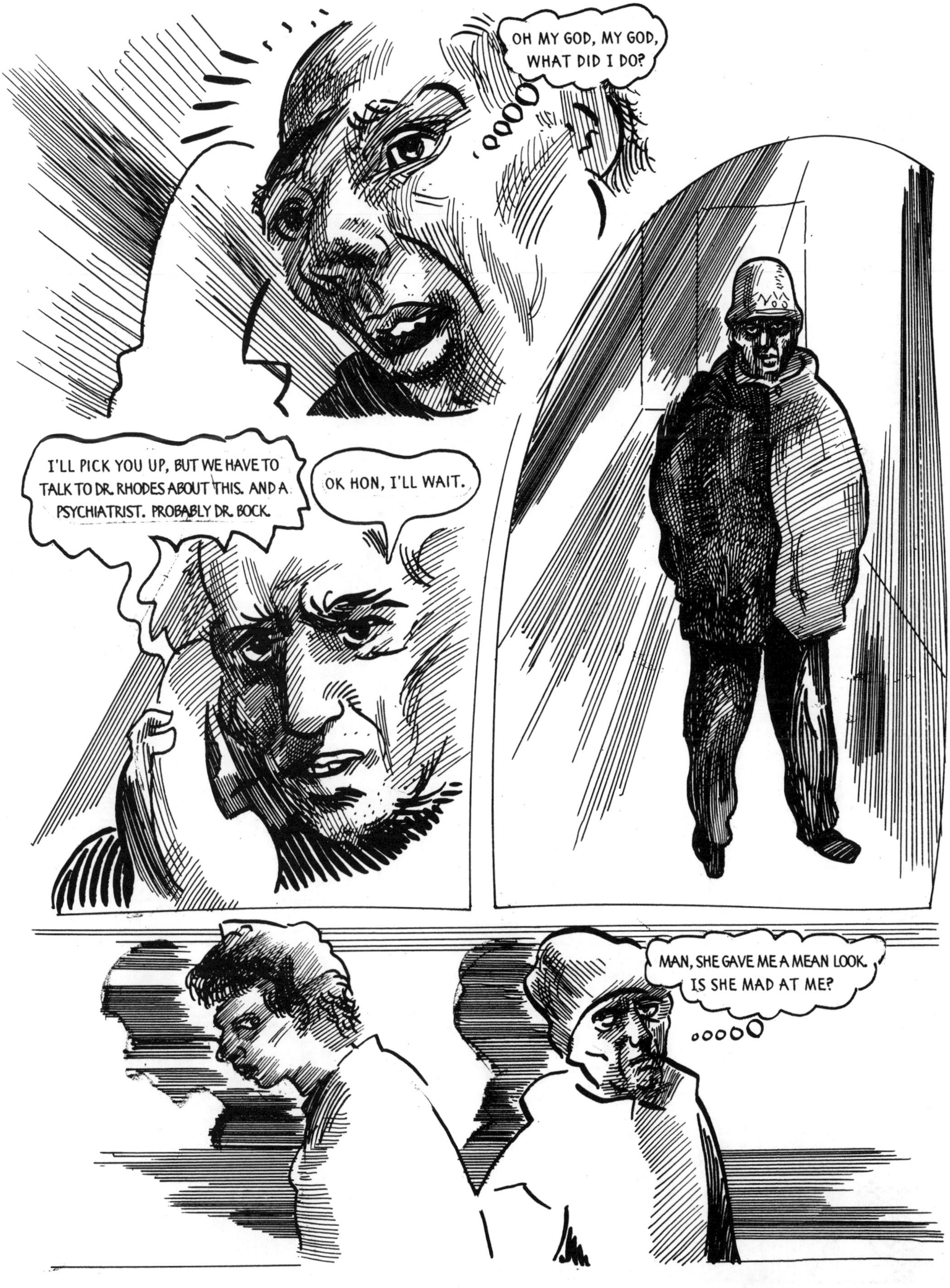
OH MY GOD, MY GOD, WHAT DID I DO?
I'LL PICK YOU UP, BUT WE HAVE TO TALK TO DR. RHODES ABOUT THIS. AND A PSYCHIATRIST. PROBABLY DR. BOCK.
OK HON, I'LL WAIT.
MAN, SHE GAVE ME A MEAN LOOK. IS SHE MAD AT ME?

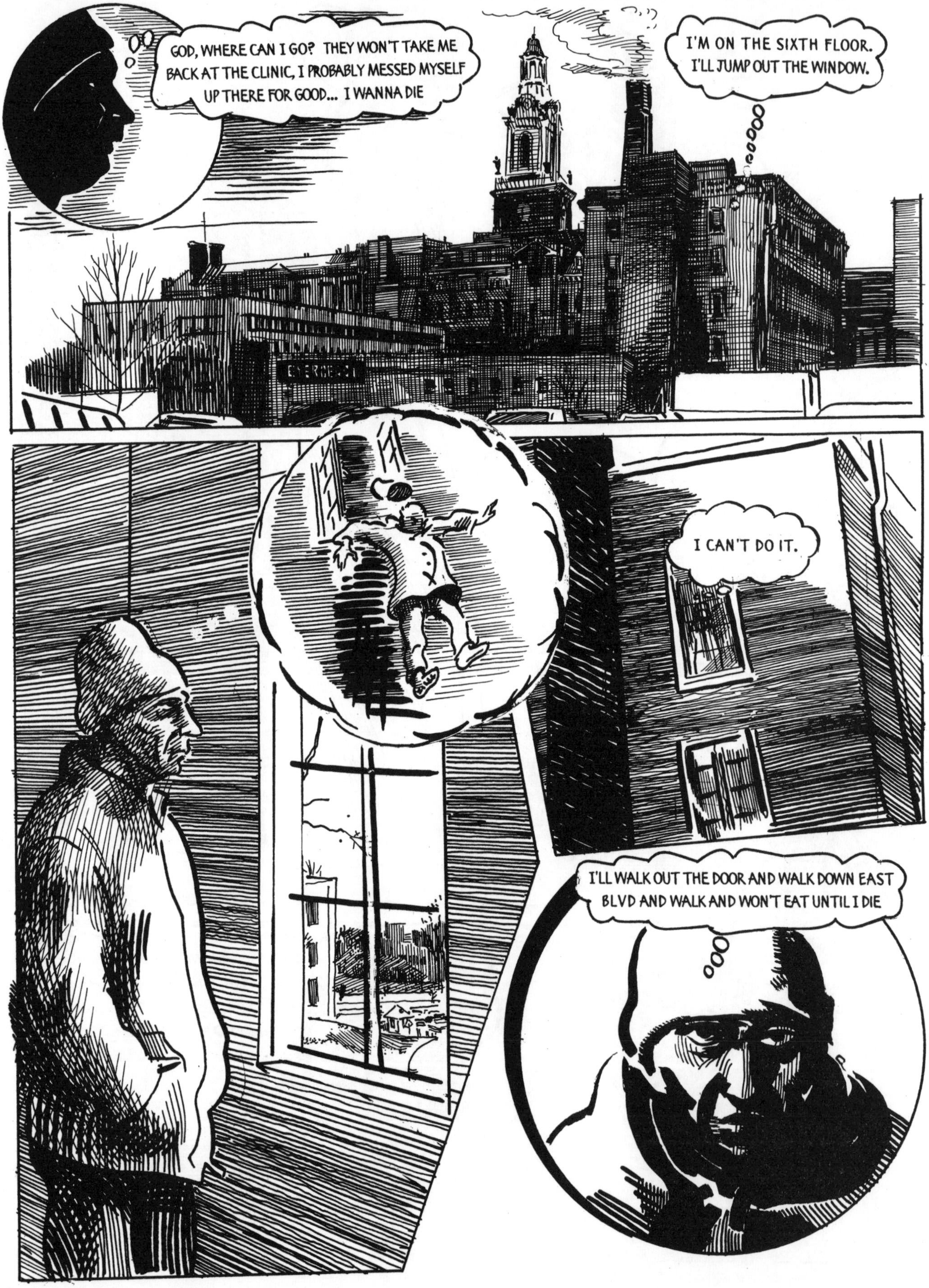
GOD, WHERE CAN I GO? THEY WON'T TAKE ME BACK AT THE CLINIC, I PROBABLY MESSED MYSELF UP THERE FOR GOOD... I WANNA DIE
I'M ON THE SIXTH FLOOR. I'LL JUMP OUT THE WINDOW.
I CAN'T DO IT.
I'LL WALK OUT THE DOOR AND WALK DOWN EAST BLVD AND WALK AND WON'T EAT UNTIL I DIE

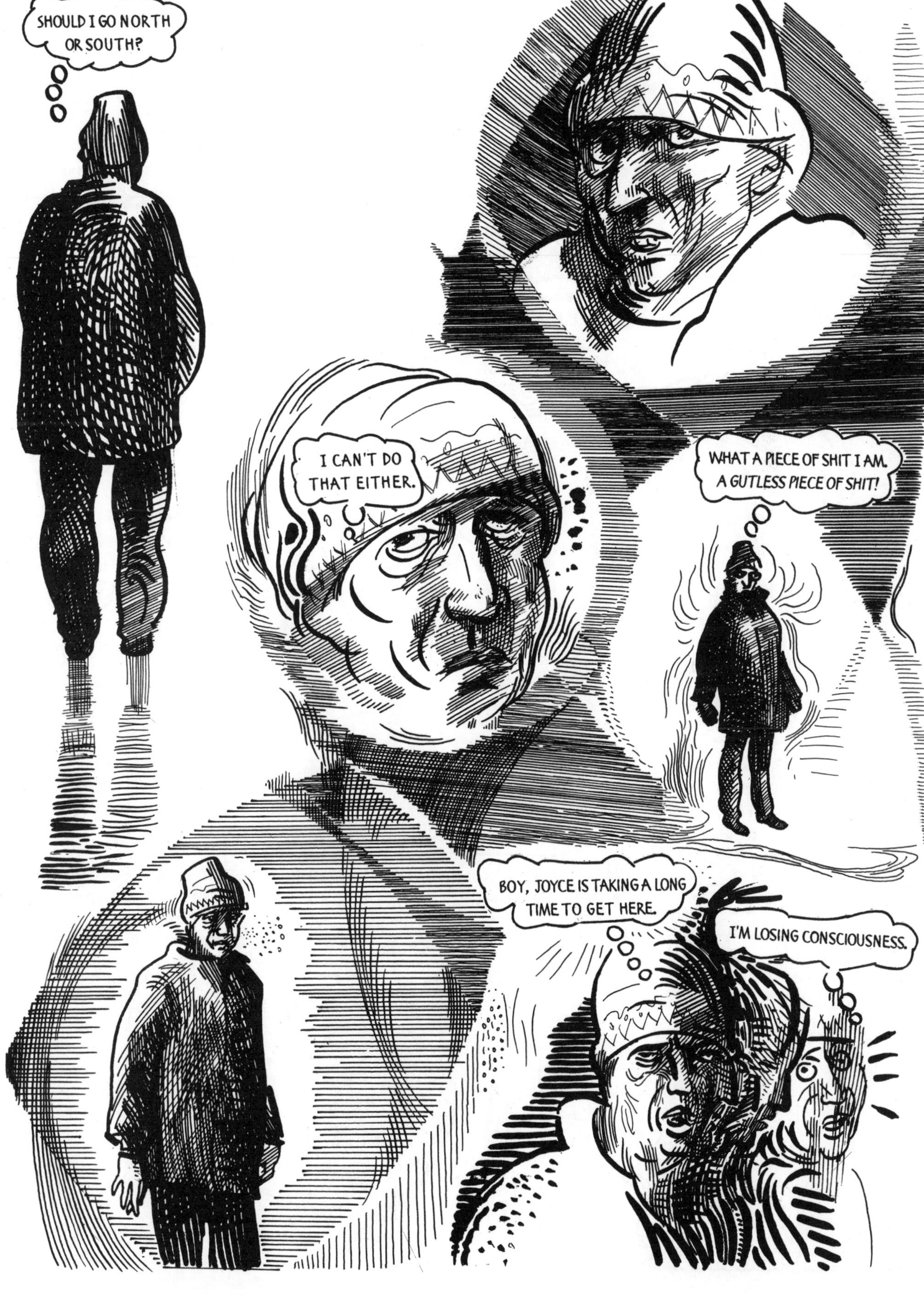
SHOULD I GO NORTH OR SOUTH?
I CAN'T DO THAT EITHER.
WHAT A PIECE OF SHIT I AM. A GUTLESS PIECE OF SHIT!
BOY, JOYCE IS TAKING A LONG TIME TO GET HERE.
I'M LOSING CONSCIOUSNESS.

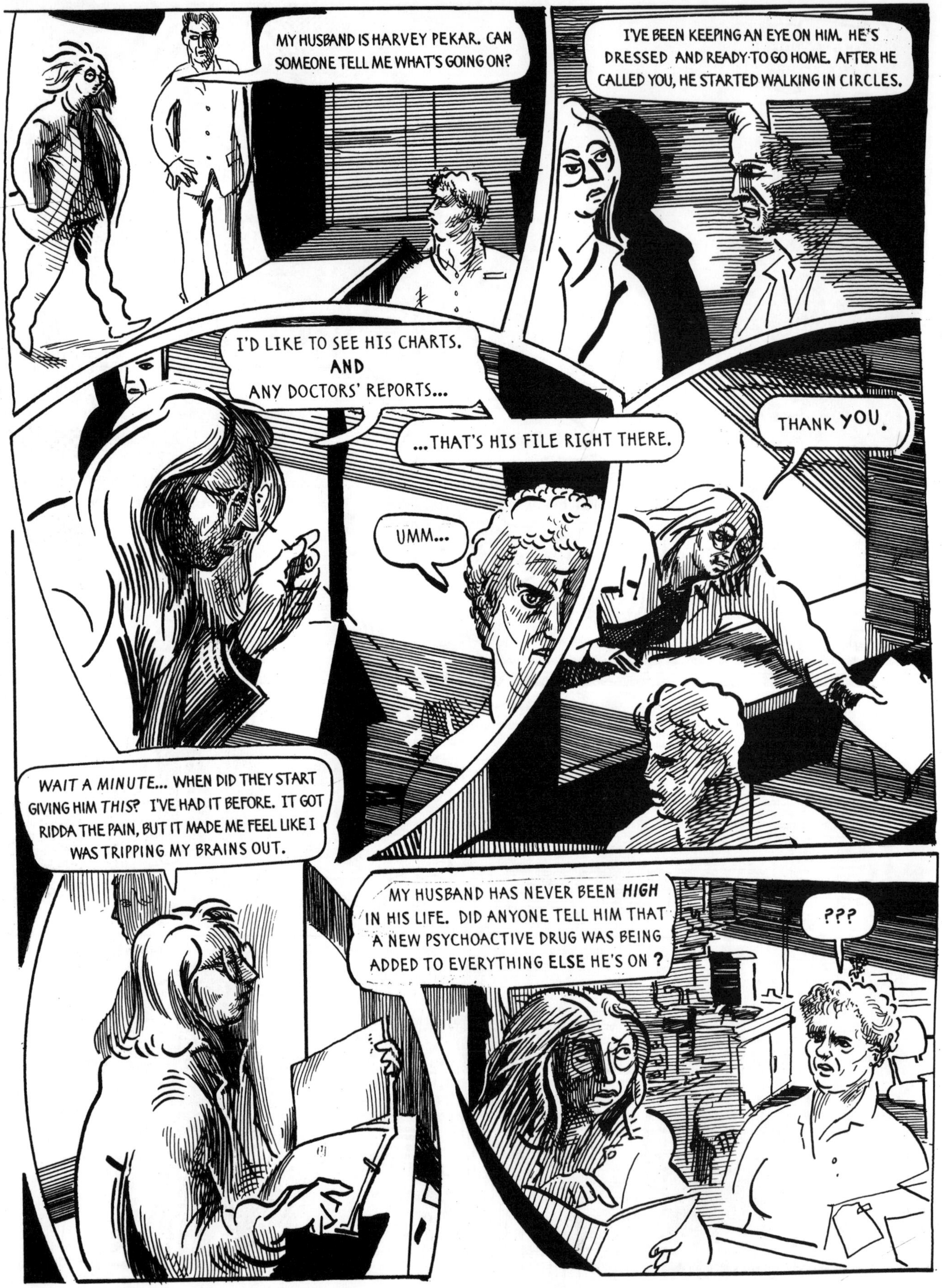
MY HUSBAND IS HARVEY PEKAR. CAN SOMEONE TELL ME WHAT'S GOING ON?
I'VE BEEN KEEPING AN EYE ON HIM. HE'S DRESSED AND READY TO GO HOME. AFTER HE CALLED YOU, HE STARTED WALKING IN CIRCLES.
I'D LIKE TO SEE HIS CHARTS. AND ANY DOCTORS' REPORTS...
UMM...
...THAT'S HIS FILE RIGHT THERE.
THANK YOU.
WAIT A MINUTE... WHEN DID THEY START GIVING HIM THIS? I'VE HAD IT BEFORE. IT GOT RIDDA THE PAIN, BUT IT MADE ME FEEL LIKE I WAS TRIPPING MY BRAINS OUT.
MY HUSBAND HAS NEVER BEEN HIGH IN HIS LIFE. DID ANYONE TELL HIM THAT A NEW PSYCHOACTIVE DRUG WAS BEING ADDED TO EVERYTHING ELSE HE'S ON?
???

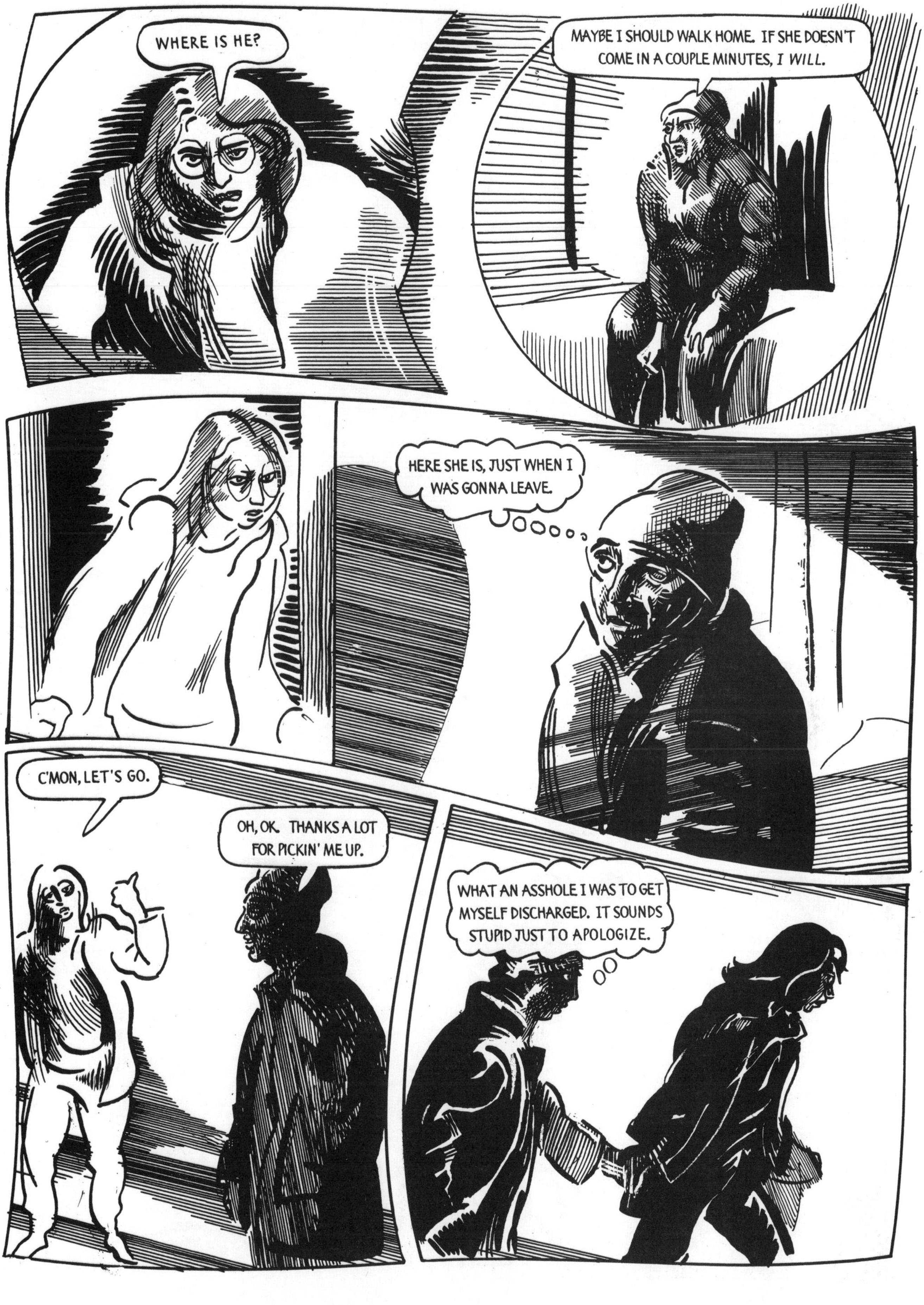
WHERE IS HE?
MAYBE I SHOULD WALK HOME. IF SHE DOESN'T COME IN A COUPLE MINUTES, *I WILL.*
HERE SHE IS, JUST WHEN I WAS GONNA LEAVE.
C'MON, LET'S GO.
OH, OK. THANKS A LOT FOR PICKIN' ME UP.
WHAT AN ASSHOLE I WAS TO GET MYSELF DISCHARGED. IT SOUNDS STUPID JUST TO APOLOGIZE.

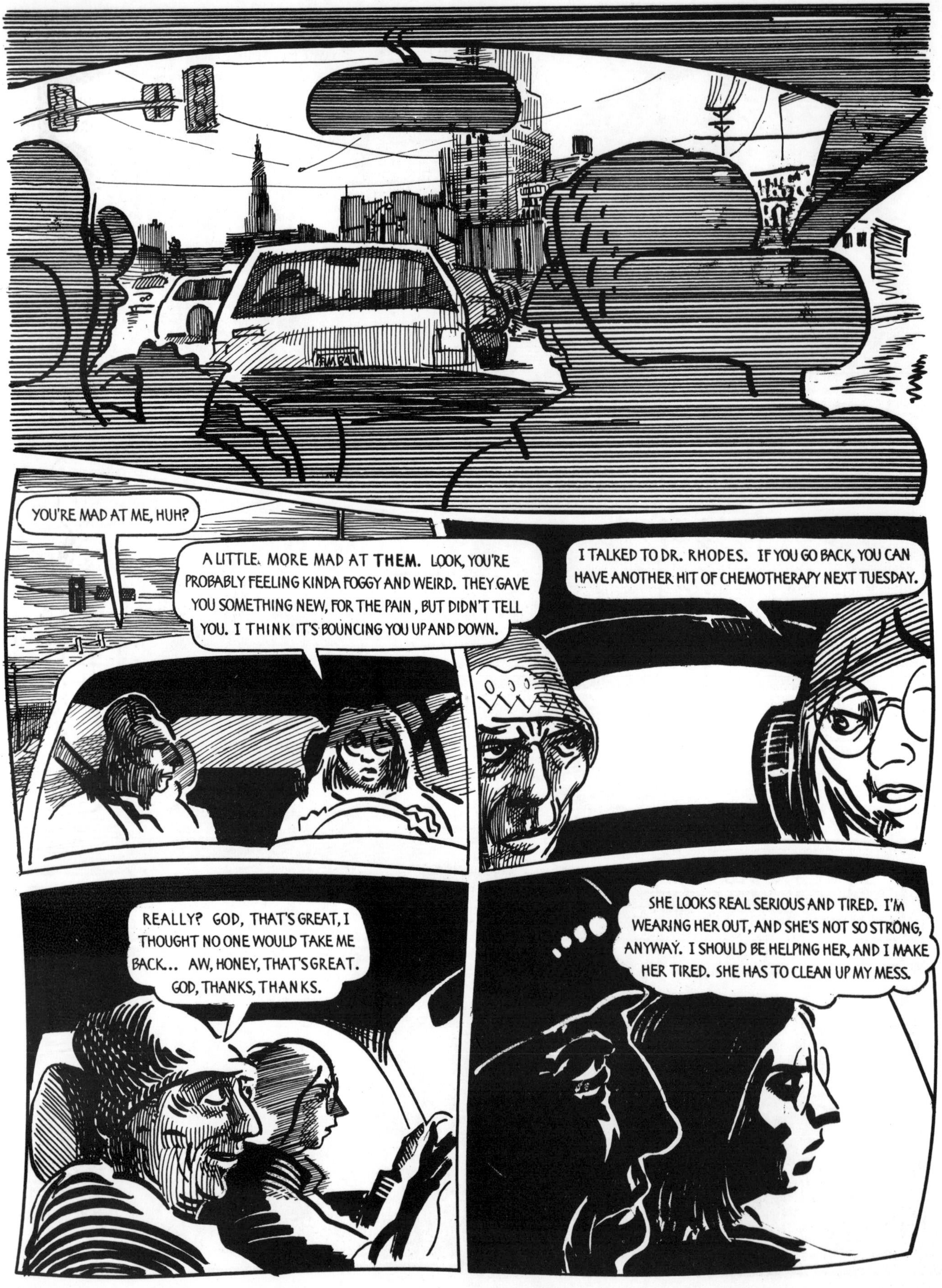
YOU'RE MAD AT ME, HUH?
A LITTLE. MORE MAD AT THEM. LOOK, YOU'RE PROBABLY FEELING KINDA FOGGY AND WEIRD. THEY GAVE YOU SOMETHING NEW, FOR THE PAIN, BUT DIDN'T TELL YOU. I THINK IT'S BOUNCING YOU UP AND DOWN.
I TALKED TO DR. RHODES. IF YOU GO BACK, YOU CAN HAVE ANOTHER HIT OF CHEMOTHERAPY NEXT TUESDAY.
REALLY? GOD, THAT'S GREAT, I THOUGHT NO ONE WOULD TAKE ME BACK... AW, HONEY, THAT'S GREAT. GOD, THANKS, THANKS.
SHE LOOKS REAL SERIOUS AND TIRED. I'M WEARING HER OUT, AND SHE'S NOT SO STRONG, ANYWAY. I SHOULD BE HELPING HER, AND I MAKE HER TIRED. SHE HAS TO CLEAN UP MY MESS.

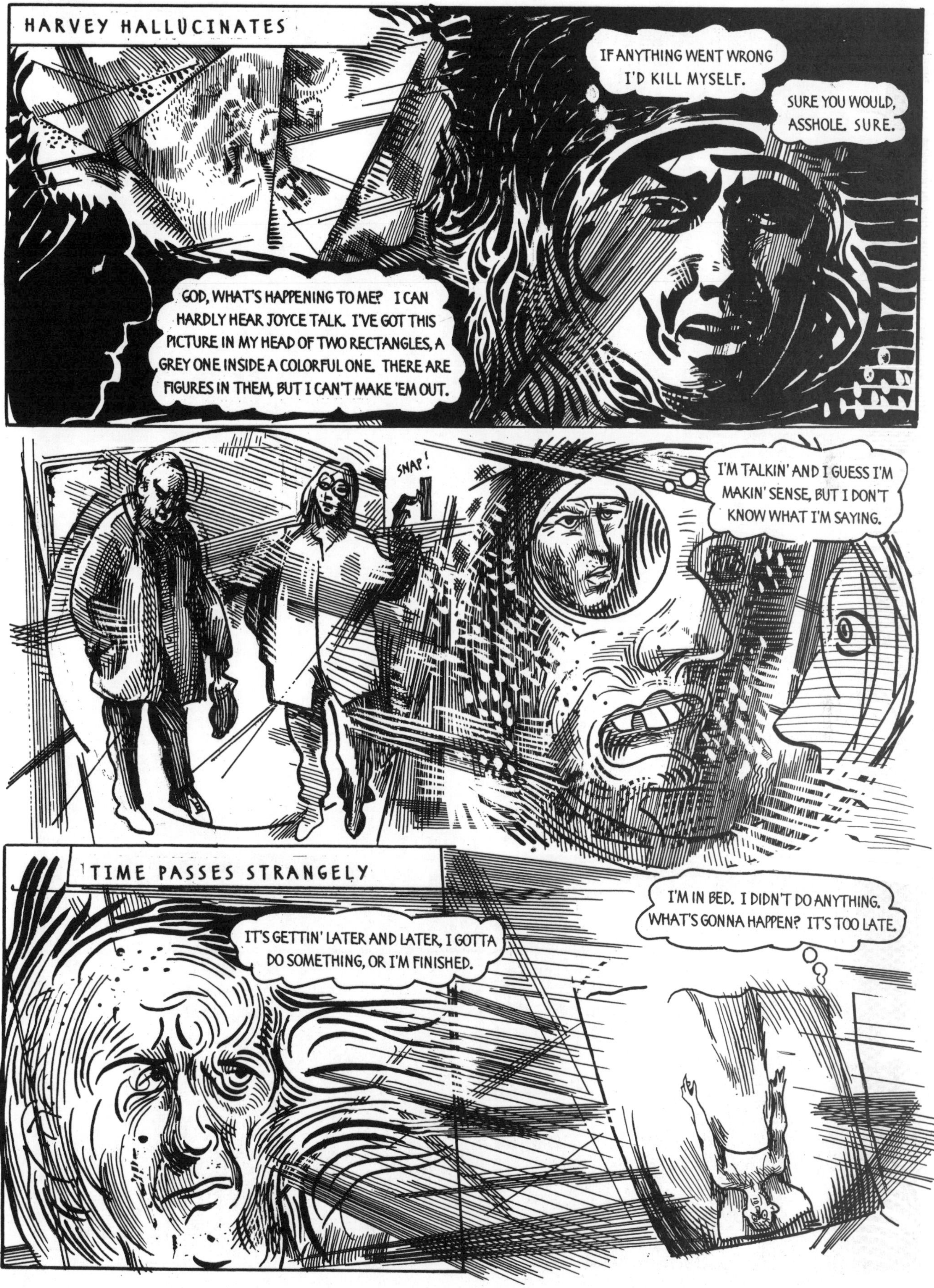
HARVEY HALLUCINATES
IF ANYTHING WENT WRONG I'D KILL MYSELF.
SURE YOU WOULD, ASSHOLE. SURE.
GOD, WHAT'S HAPPENING TO ME? I CAN HARDLY HEAR JOYCE TALK. I'VE GOT THIS PICTURE IN MY HEAD OF TWO RECTANGLES, A GREY ONE INSIDE A COLORFUL ONE. THERE ARE FIGURES IN THEM, BUT I CAN'T MAKE 'EM OUT.
SNAP!
I'M TALKIN' AND I GUESS I'M MAKIN' SENSE, BUT I DON'T KNOW WHAT I'M SAYING.
TIME PASSES STRANGELY
IT'S GETTIN' LATER AND LATER, I GOTTA DO SOMETHING, OR I'M FINISHED.
I'M IN BED. I DIDN'T DO ANYTHING. WHAT'S GONNA HAPPEN? IT'S TOO LATE.

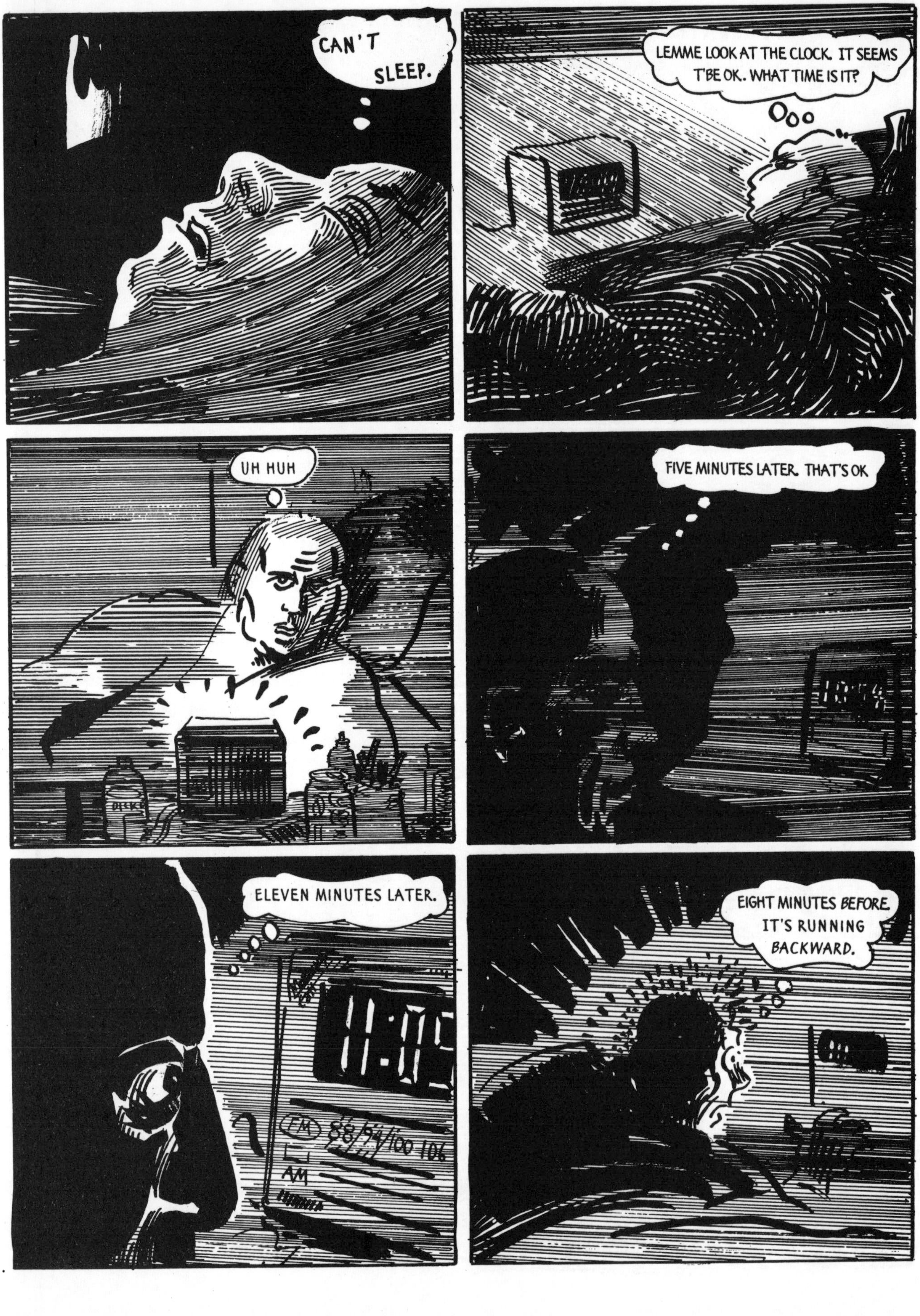
CAN'T SLEEP.
LEMME LOOK AT THE CLOCK. IT SEEMS T'BE OK. WHAT TIME IS IT?
OOO
UH HUH
FIVE MINUTES LATER. THAT'S OK
ELEVEN MINUTES LATER.
EIGHT MINUTES BEFORE. IT'S RUNNING BACKWARD.

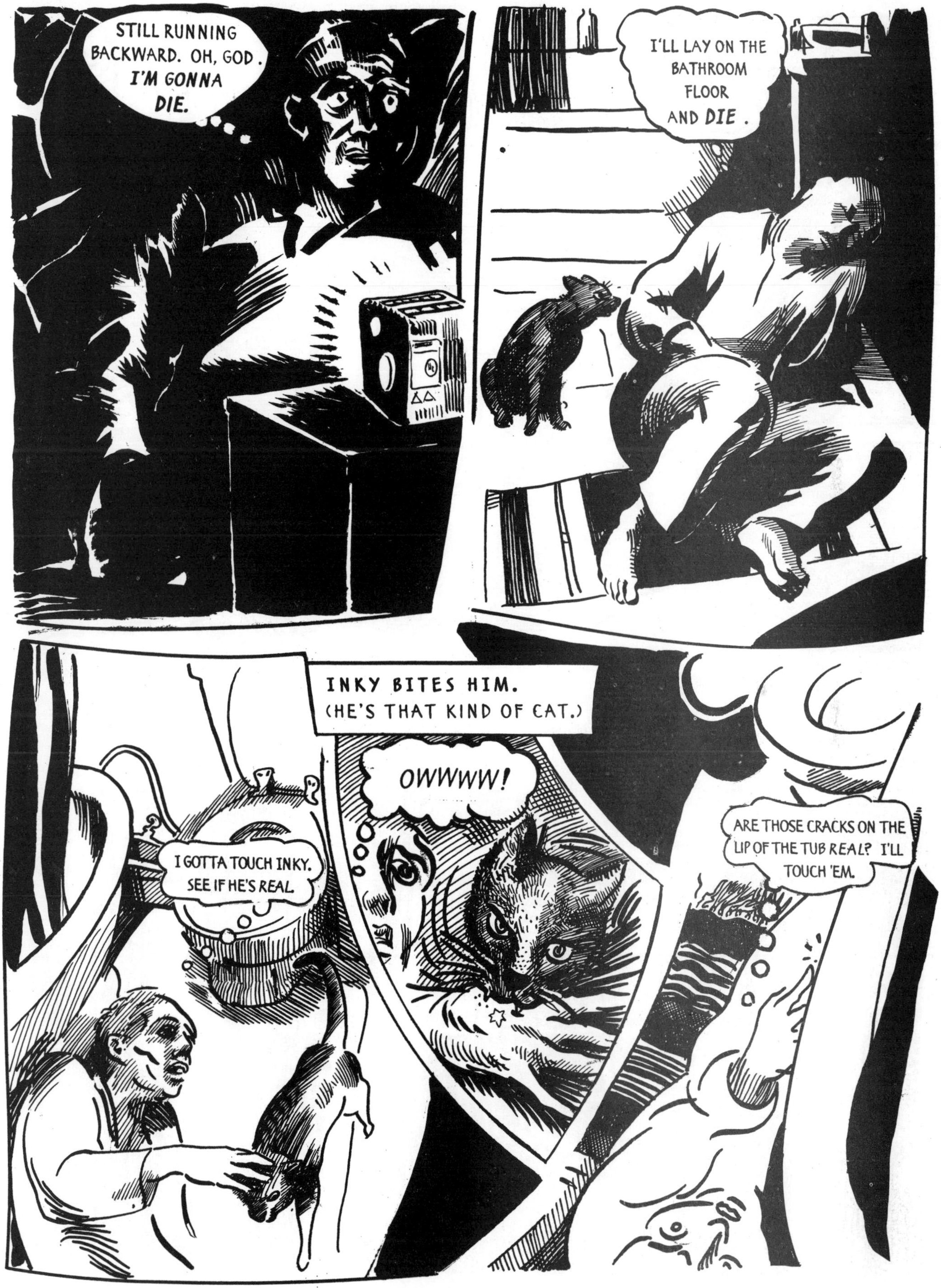
STILL RUNNING BACKWARD. OH, GOD. I'M GONNA DIE.
I'LL LAY ON THE BATHROOM FLOOR AND DIE.
INKY BITES HIM. (HE'S THAT KIND OF CAT.)
I GOTTA TOUCH INKY. SEE IF HE'S REAL
OWWWW!
ARE THOSE CRACKS ON THE LIP OF THE TUB REAL? I'LL TOUCH 'EM.

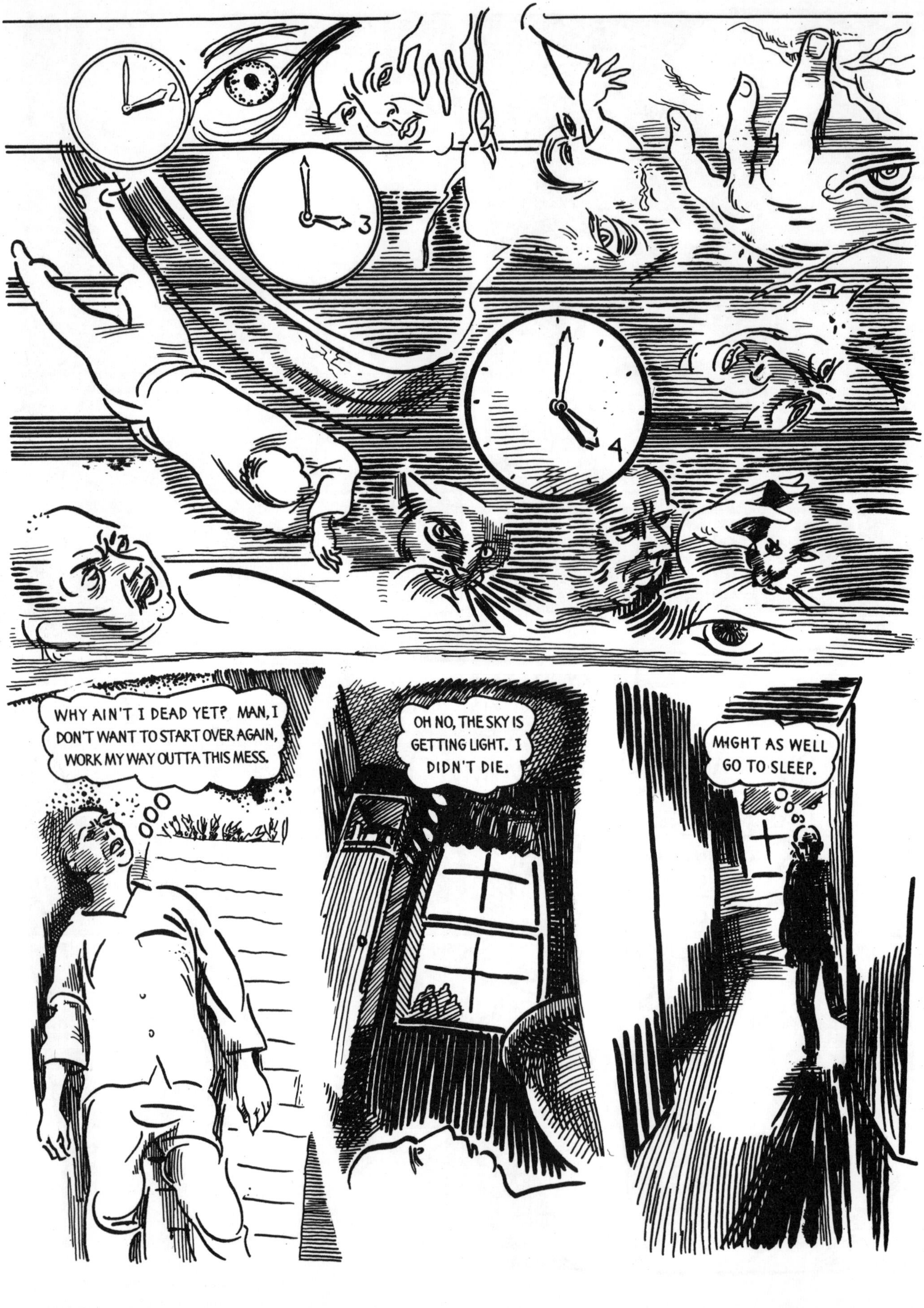

WHY AIN'T I DEAD YET? MAN, I DON'T WANT TO START OVER AGAIN, WORK MY WAY OUTTA THIS MESS.
OH NO, THE SKY IS GETTING LIGHT. I DIDN'T DIE.
MIGHT AS WELL GO TO SLEEP.

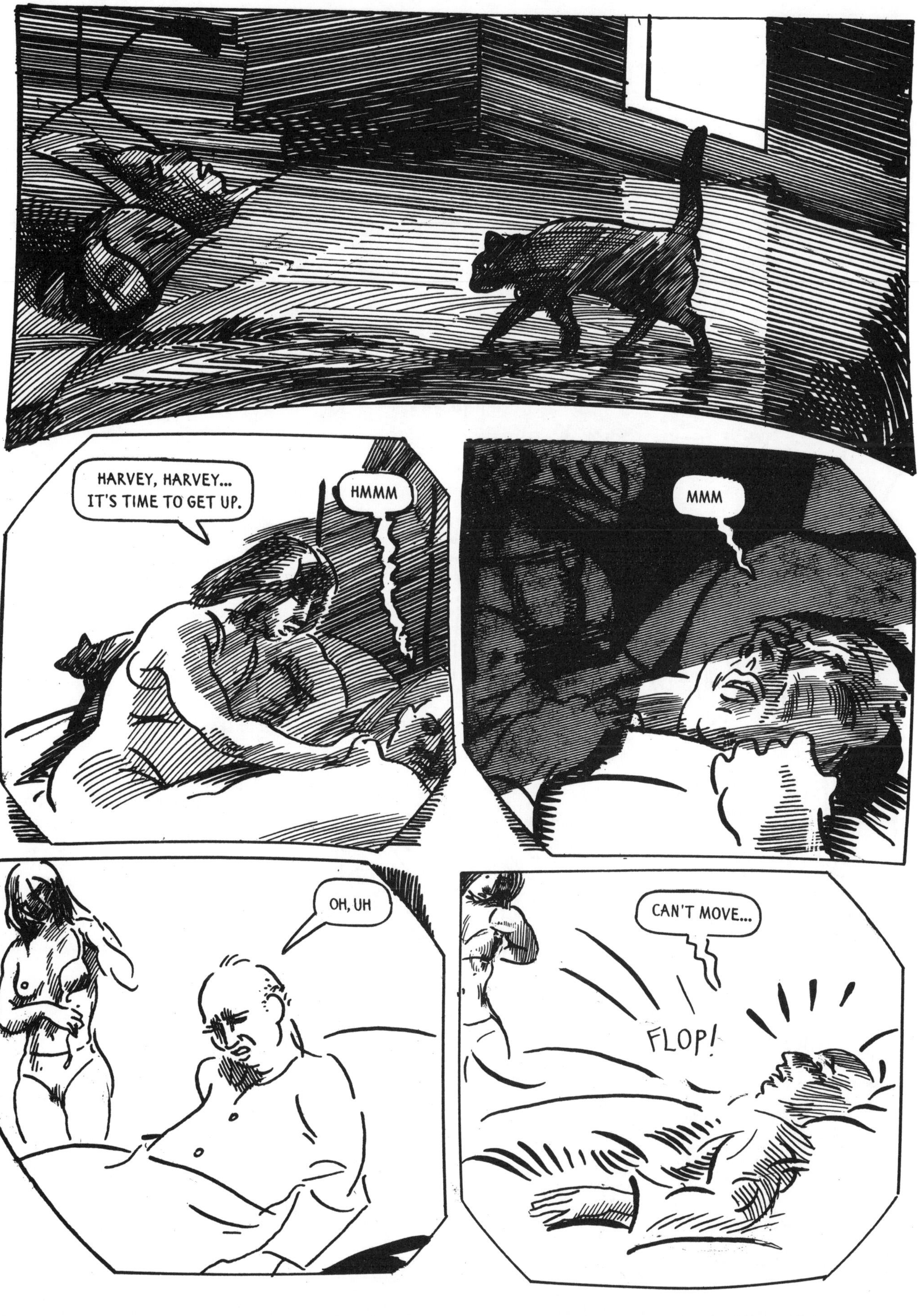
HARVEY, HARVEY... IT'S TIME TO GET UP.
HMMM
MMM
OH, UH
CAN'T MOVE...
FLOP!

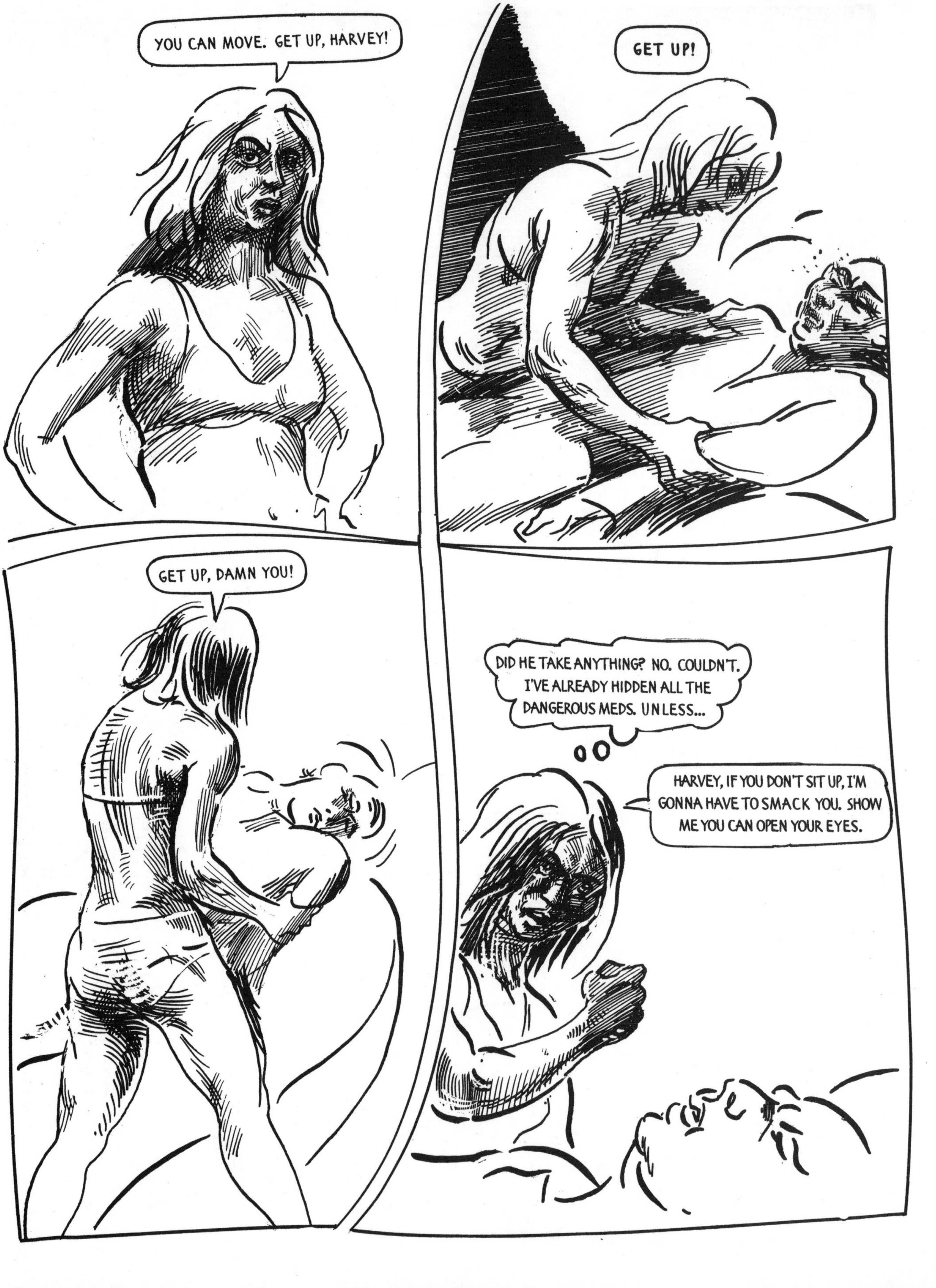
YOU CAN MOVE. GET UP, HARVEY!
GET UP!
GET UP, DAMN YOU!
DID HE TAKE ANYTHING? NO. COULDN'T. I'VE ALREADY HIDDEN ALL THE DANGEROUS MEDS. UNLESS...
HARVEY, IF YOU DON'T SIT UP, I'M GONNA HAVE TO SMACK YOU. SHOW ME YOU CAN OPEN YOUR EYES.

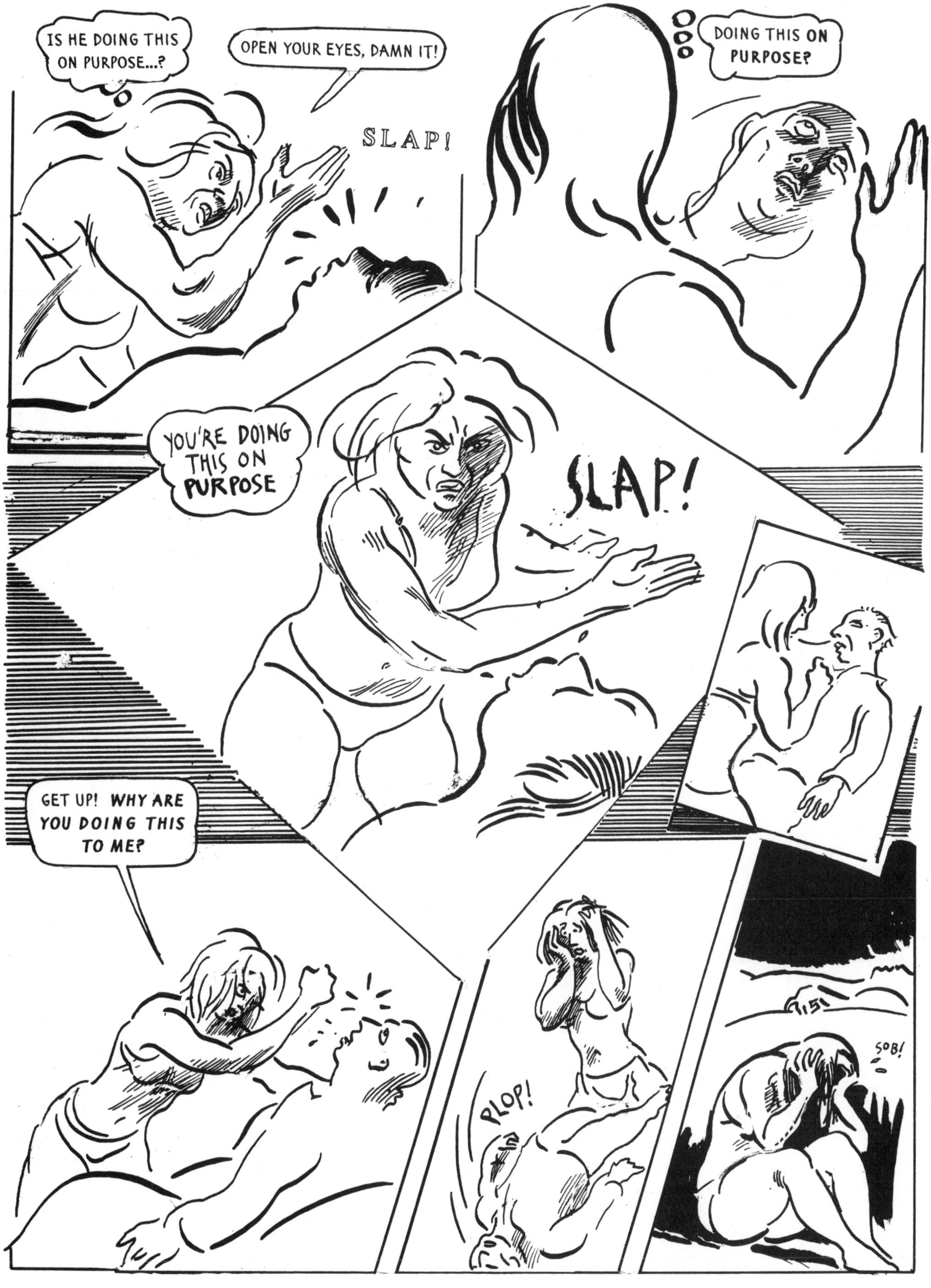

IS HE DOING THIS ON PURPOSE...?
OPEN YOUR EYES, DAMN IT!
SLAP!
DOING THIS ON PURPOSE?
YOU'RE DOING THIS ON PURPOSE
SLAP!
GET UP! WHY ARE YOU DOING THIS TO ME?
PLOP!
SOB!

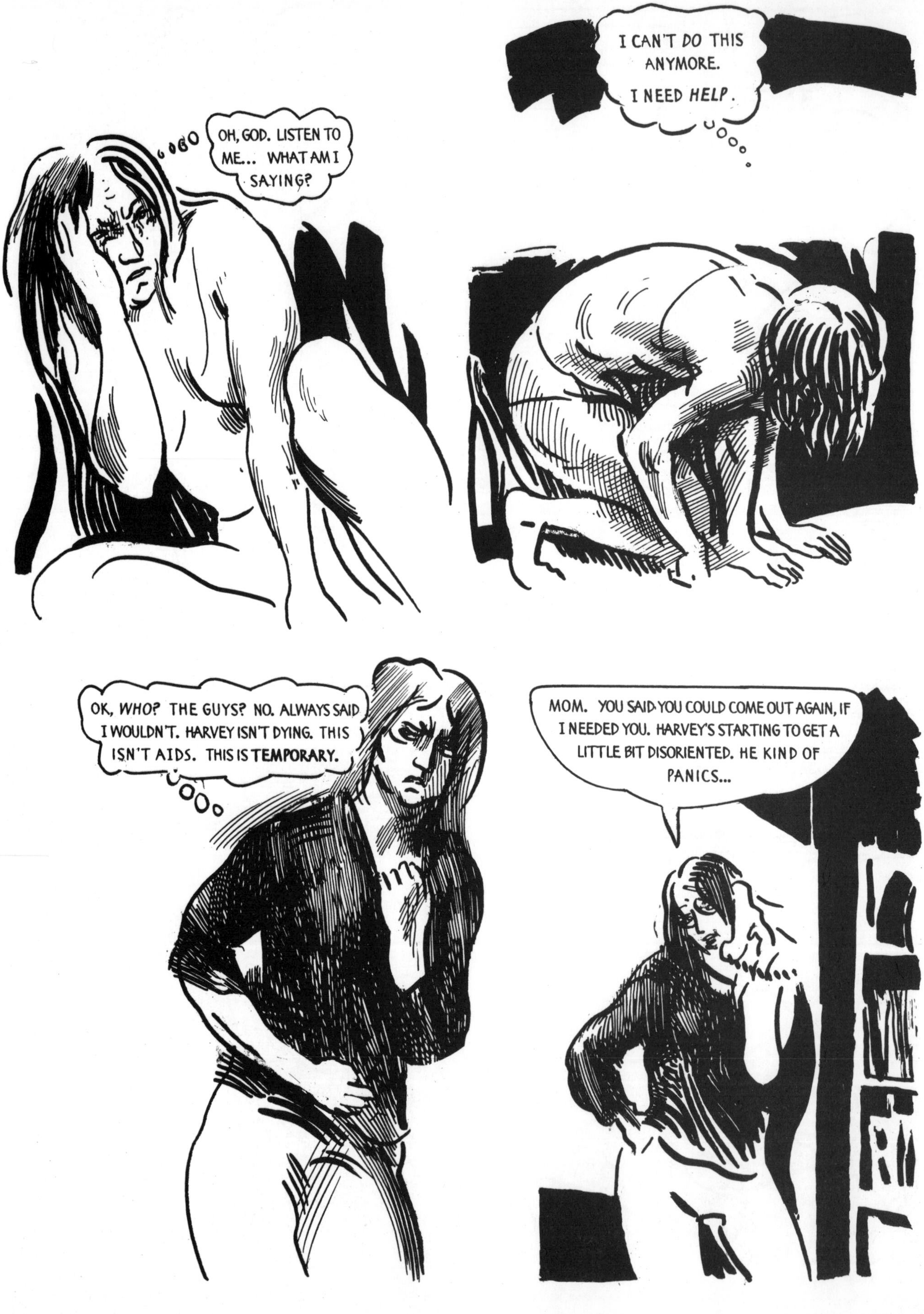
OH, GOD. LISTEN TO ME... WHAT AM I SAYING?
I CAN'T DO THIS ANYMORE. I NEED HELP.
OK, WHO? THE GUYS? NO. ALWAYS SAID I WOULDN'T. HARVEY ISN'T DYING. THIS ISN'T AIDS. THIS IS TEMPORARY.
MOM. YOU SAID YOU COULD COME OUT AGAIN, IF I NEEDED YOU. HARVEY'S STARTING TO GET A LITTLE BIT DISORIENTED. HE KIND OF PANICS...

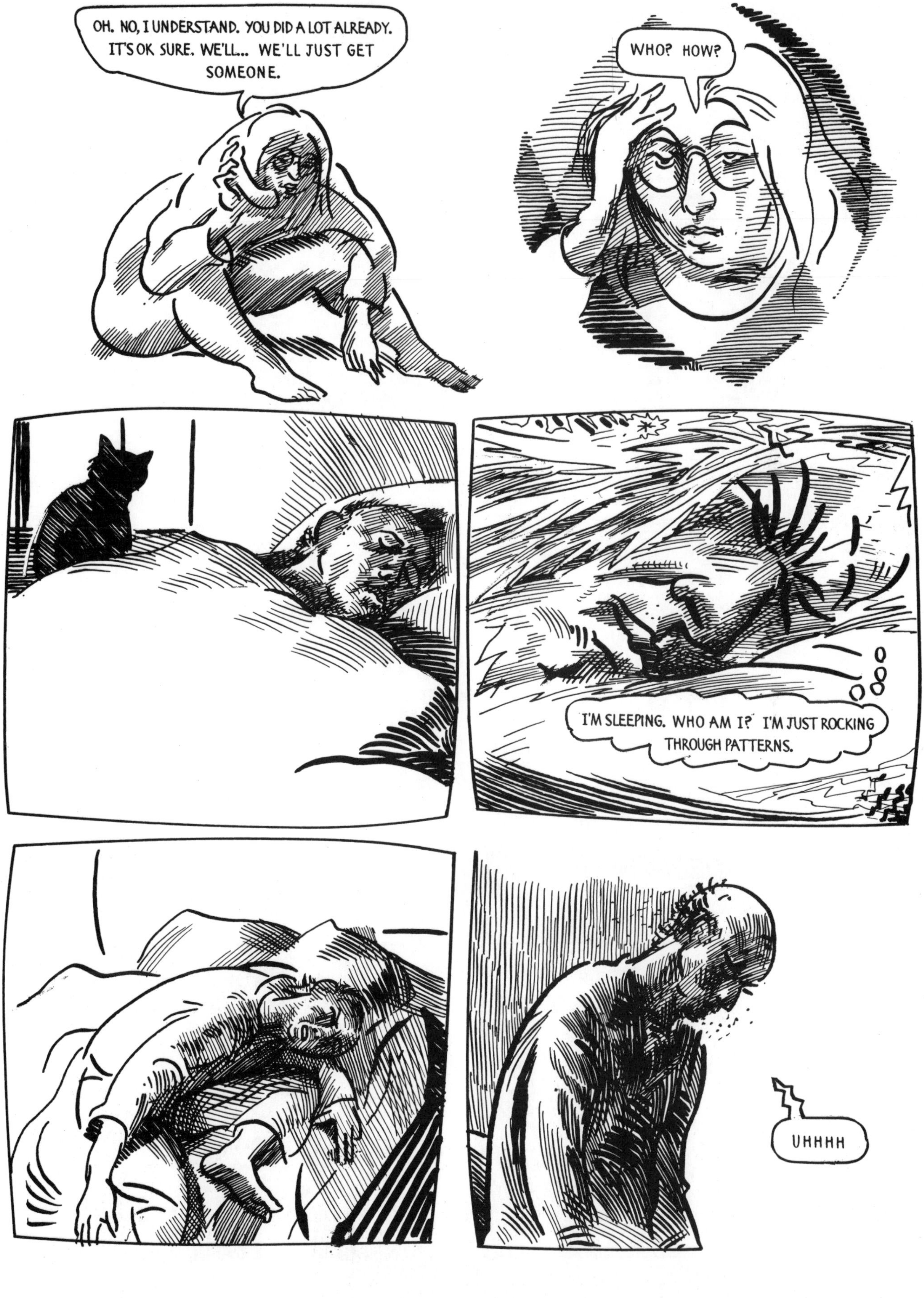
OH. NO, I UNDERSTAND. YOU DID A LOT ALREADY. IT'S OK SURE. WE'LL... WE'LL JUST GET SOMEONE.
WHO? HOW?
I'M SLEEPING. WHO AM I? I'M JUST ROCKING THROUGH PATTERNS.
UHHHH

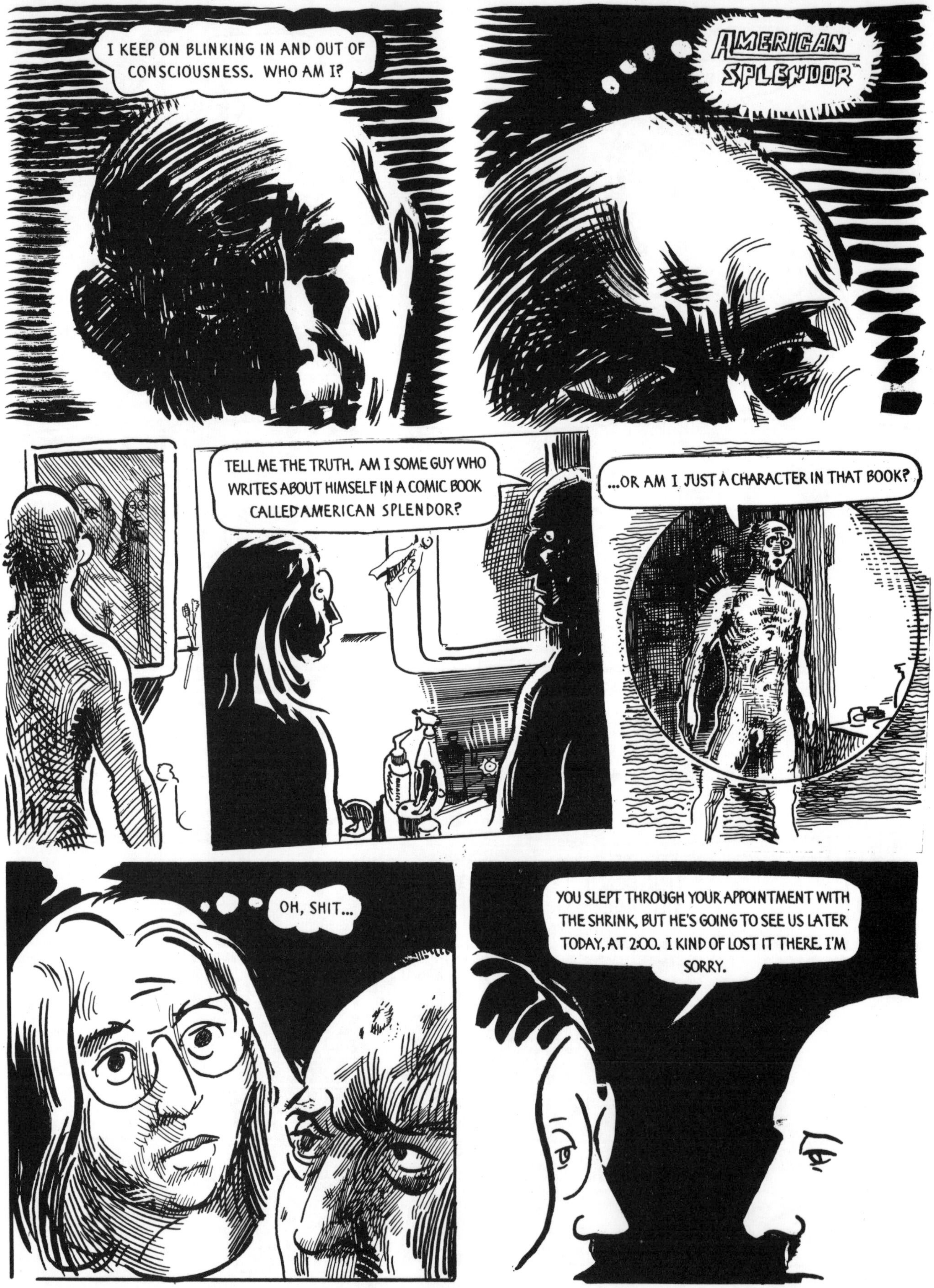
I KEEP ON BLINKING IN AND OUT OF CONSCIOUSNESS. WHO AM I?
AMERICAN SPLENDOR™
TELL ME THE TRUTH. AM I SOME GUY WHO WRITES ABOUT HIMSELF IN A COMIC BOOK CALLED AMERICAN SPLENDOR?
...OR AM I JUST A CHARACTER IN THAT BOOK?
OH, SHIT...
YOU SLEPT THROUGH YOUR APPOINTMENT WITH THE SHRINK, BUT HE'S GOING TO SEE US LATER TODAY, AT 2:00. I KIND OF LOST IT THERE. I'M SORRY.

10

JOYCE AND HARVEY MEET WITH DR. BOCK, THE PSYCHIATRIST WHO HAS BEEN TREATING HARVEY FOR DEPRESSION AND PAIN MANAGEMENT.

THIS MUST BE AN EXTREMELY PAINFUL AND TRYING TIME FOR BOTH OF YOU.

I JUST DON'T KNOW WHAT TO DO.

SOMETHING IS **NOT** WORKING. SOMETHING MORE THAN HYSTERIA OR PANIC OR HARVEY'S USUAL WAY OF MAKING THE WORST OF A BAD SITUATION.

WHEN I WAS IN THE HOSPITAL, I STARTED TO FEEL LIKE NOTHIN' WAS WRONG. I WAS GONNA WALK OUT, T'WORK. THEN I KINDA HALLUCINATED.

I KNOW I ACTED PRETTY IRRESPONSIBLY, BUT THE DOCTOR WANTED TO GIVE ME CHEMOTHERAPY RIGHT AWAY, EVEN THOUGH I HADN'T BEEN TAKIN' MY BAKING SODA. I'M S'PPOSED TO HAVE THAT IN ME FOR 24 HOURS BEFORE THEY GIVE ME THIS ONE REALLY HARSH DRUG.

MAYBE DR. FISHER WOULD HAVE CAUGHT THAT. BUT, HARVEY DIDN'T KNOW.

THEN, HE WANTED TO KICK ME OUT, BEFORE I HAD PHYSICAL THERAPY. AN' HE SAID HE MIGHTA KILLED PATIENTS IN THE PROCESS OF TREATING THEM. HE ACTED LIKE I WAS A NUISANCE, AND HE WANTED T'GET RIDDA ME. SO, I SIGNED MYSELF OUT, T'GET OUTTA HIS CONTROL.

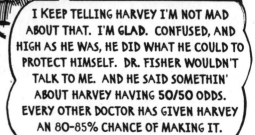

I KEEP TELLING HARVEY I'M NOT MAD ABOUT THAT. I'M GLAD. CONFUSED, AND HIGH AS HE WAS, HE DID WHAT HE COULD TO PROTECT HIMSELF. DR. FISHER WOULDN'T TALK TO ME. AND HE SAID SOMETHIN' ABOUT HARVEY HAVING 50/50 ODDS. EVERY OTHER DOCTOR HAS GIVEN HARVEY AN 80-85% CHANCE OF MAKING IT.

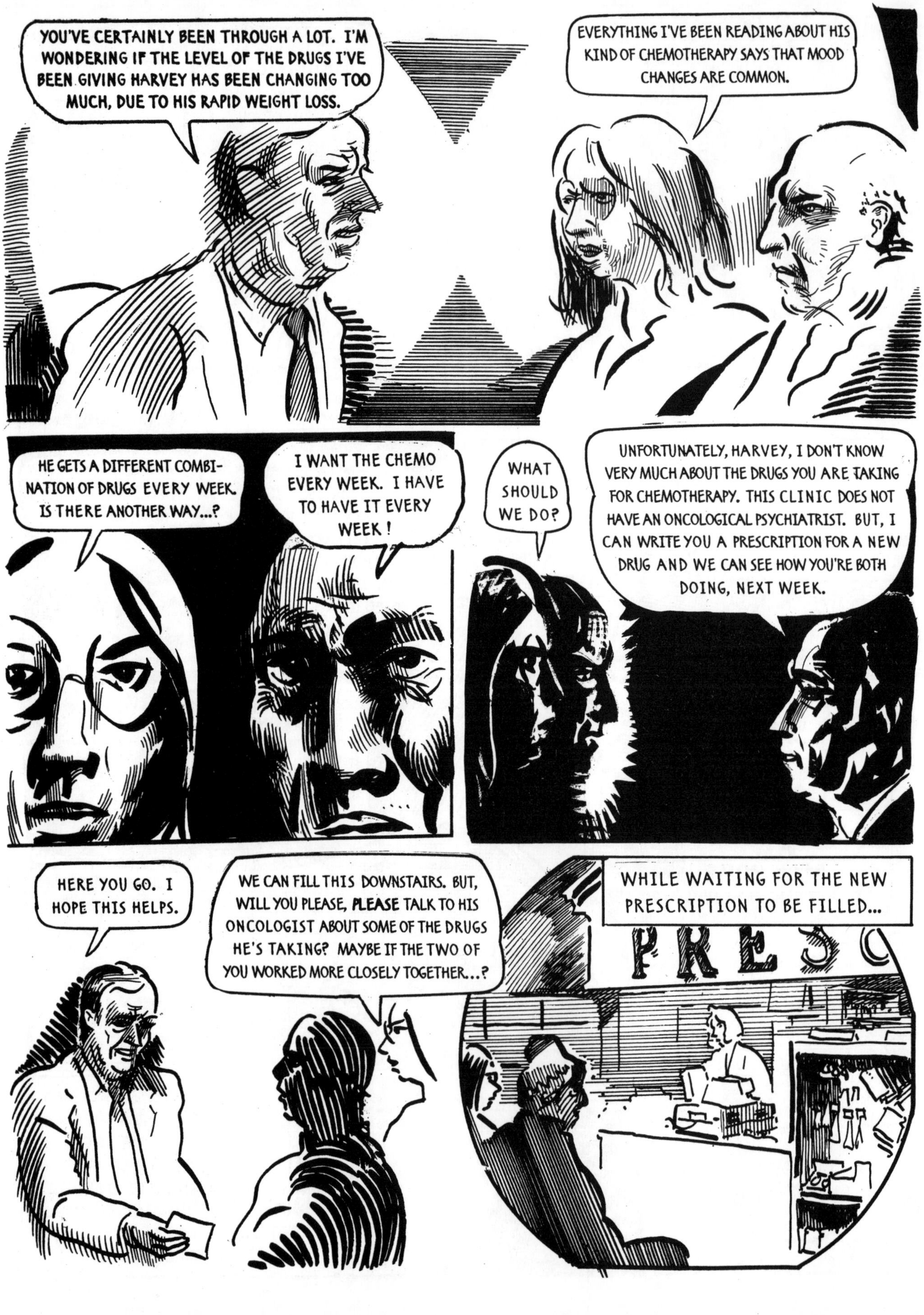

YOU'VE CERTAINLY BEEN THROUGH A LOT. I'M WONDERING IF THE LEVEL OF THE DRUGS I'VE BEEN GIVING HARVEY HAS BEEN CHANGING TOO MUCH, DUE TO HIS RAPID WEIGHT LOSS.
EVERYTHING I'VE BEEN READING ABOUT HIS KIND OF CHEMOTHERAPY SAYS THAT MOOD CHANGES ARE COMMON.
HE GETS A DIFFERENT COMBI-NATION OF DRUGS EVERY WEEK. IS THERE ANOTHER WAY...?
I WANT THE CHEMO EVERY WEEK. I HAVE TO HAVE IT EVERY WEEK!
WHAT SHOULD WE DO?
UNFORTUNATELY, HARVEY, I DON'T KNOW VERY MUCH ABOUT THE DRUGS YOU ARE TAKING FOR CHEMOTHERAPY. THIS CLINIC DOES NOT HAVE AN ONCOLOGICAL PSYCHIATRIST. BUT, I CAN WRITE YOU A PRESCRIPTION FOR A NEW DRUG AND WE CAN SEE HOW YOU'RE BOTH DOING, NEXT WEEK.
HERE YOU GO. I HOPE THIS HELPS.
WE CAN FILL THIS DOWNSTAIRS. BUT, WILL YOU PLEASE, PLEASE TALK TO HIS ONCOLOGIST ABOUT SOME OF THE DRUGS HE'S TAKING? MAYBE IF THE TWO OF YOU WORKED MORE CLOSELY TOGETHER...?
WHILE WAITING FOR THE NEW PRESCRIPTION TO BE FILLED...
PRES

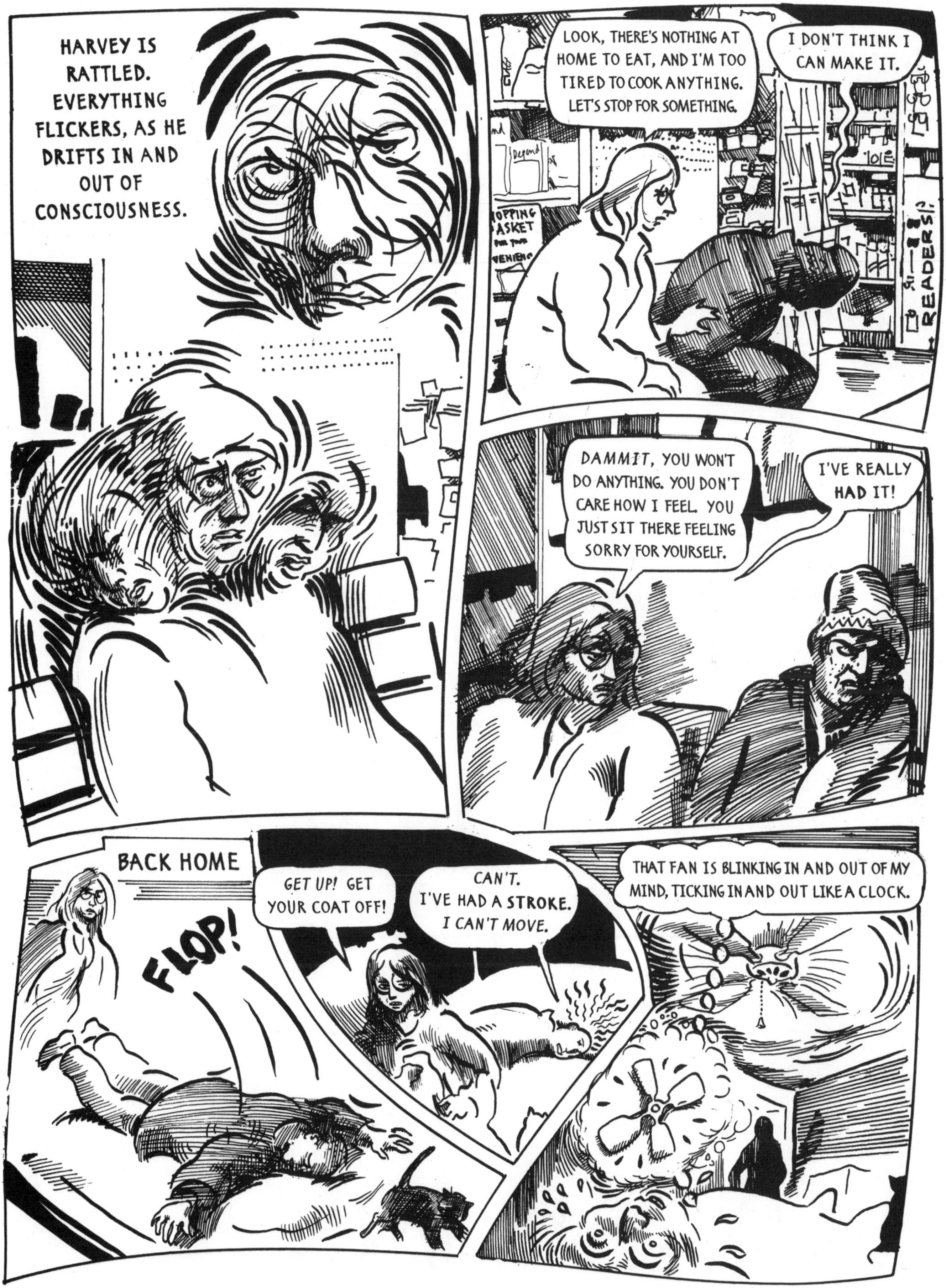
HARVEY IS RATTLED. EVERYTHING FLICKERS, AS HE DRIFTS IN AND OUT OF CONSCIOUSNESS.
LOOK, THERE'S NOTHING AT HOME TO EAT, AND I'M TOO TIRED TO COOK ANYTHING. LET'S STOP FOR SOMETHING.
I DON'T THINK I CAN MAKE IT.
DAMMIT, YOU WON'T DO ANYTHING. YOU DON'T CARE HOW I FEEL. YOU JUST SIT THERE FEELING SORRY FOR YOURSELF.
I'VE REALLY HAD IT!
BACK HOME
FLOP!
GET UP! GET YOUR COAT OFF!
CAN'T. I'VE HAD A STROKE. I CAN'T MOVE.
THAT FAN IS BLINKING IN AND OUT OF MY MIND, TICKING IN AND OUT LIKE A CLOCK.

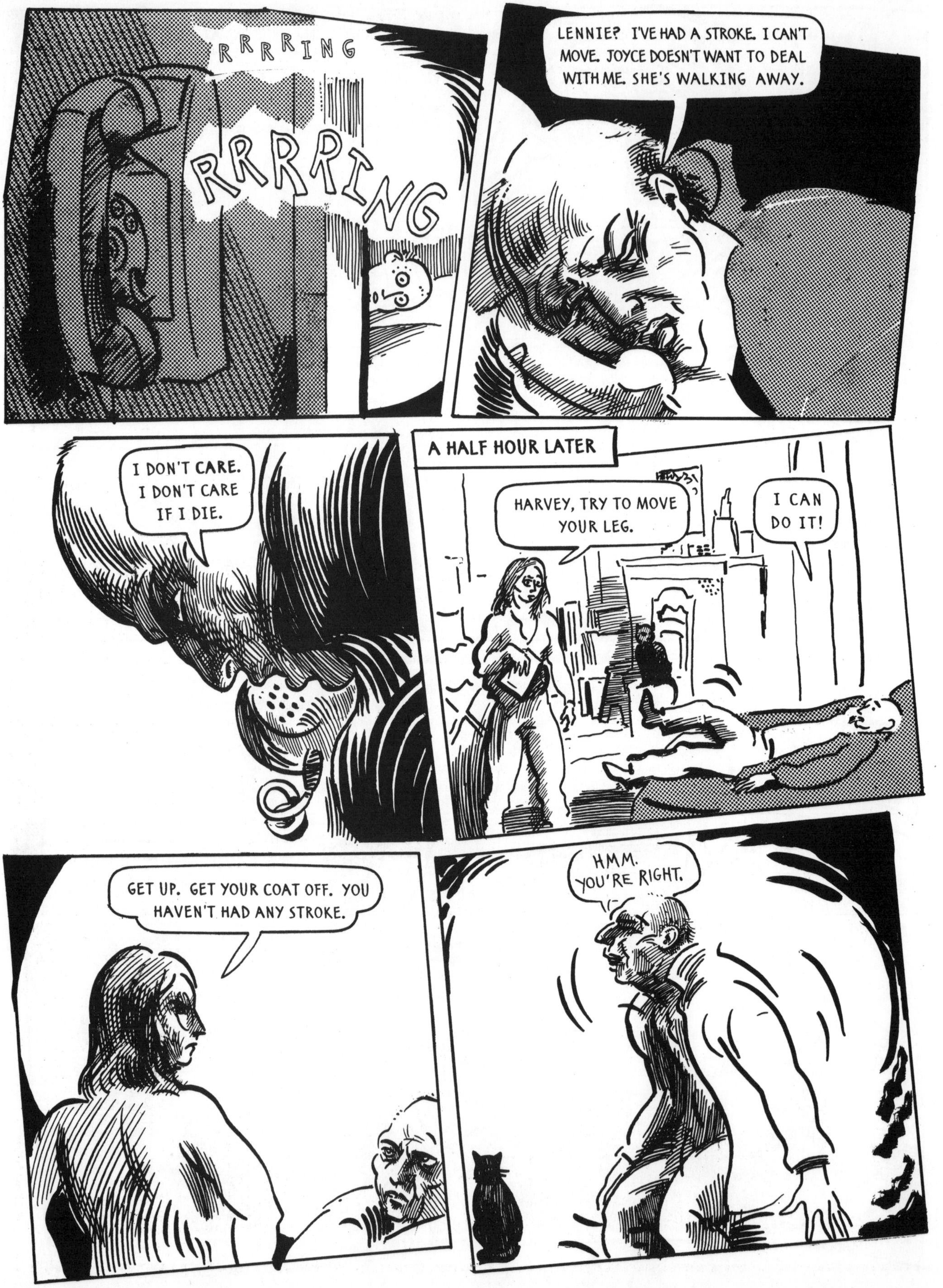
RRRRING
RRRRING
LENNIE? I'VE HAD A STROKE. I CAN'T MOVE. JOYCE DOESN'T WANT TO DEAL WITH ME. SHE'S WALKING AWAY.
I DON'T CARE. I DON'T CARE IF I DIE.
A HALF HOUR LATER
HARVEY, TRY TO MOVE YOUR LEG.
I CAN DO IT!
GET UP. GET YOUR COAT OFF. YOU HAVEN'T HAD ANY STROKE.
HMM. YOU'RE RIGHT.

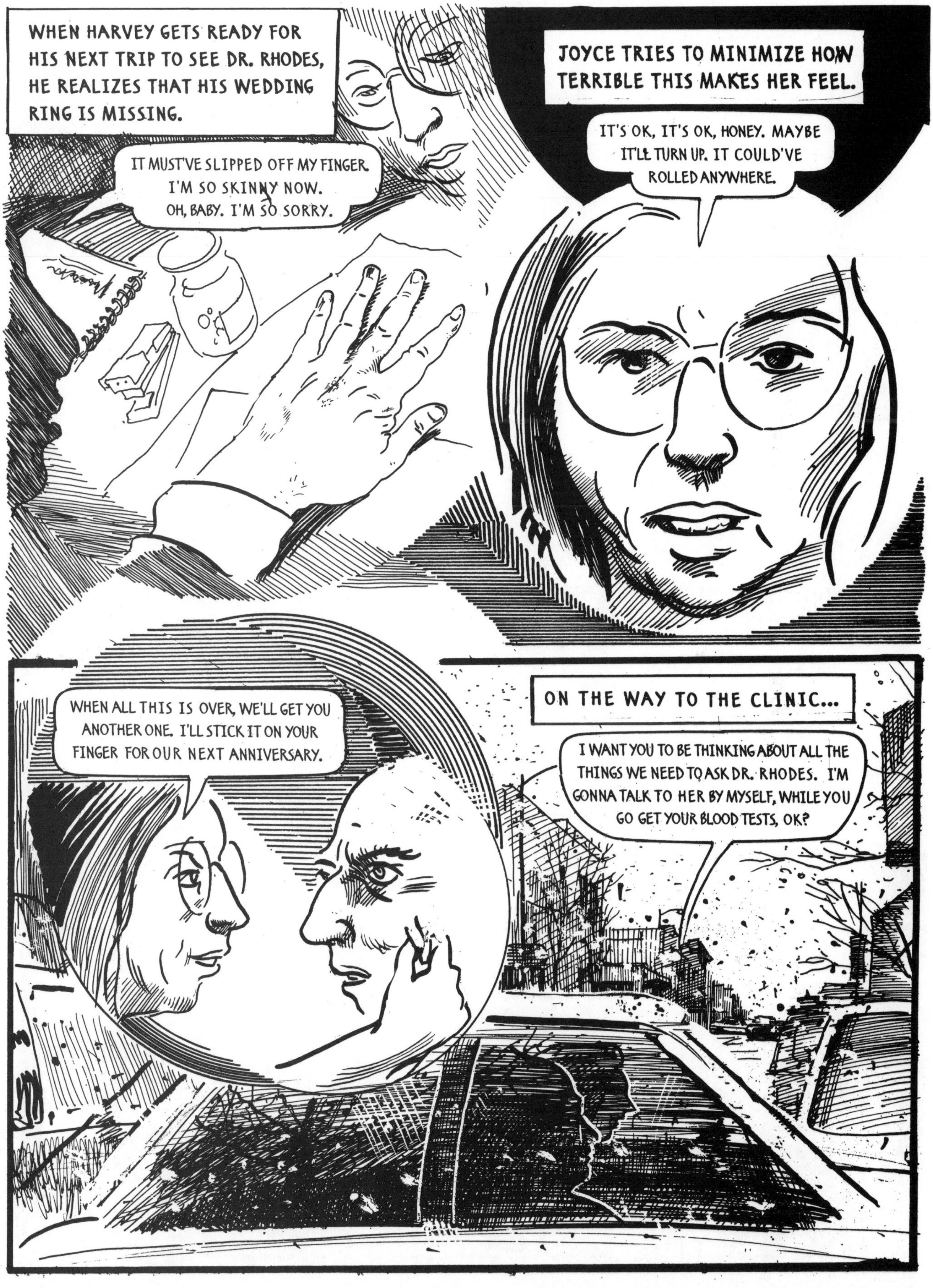
WHEN HARVEY GETS READY FOR HIS NEXT TRIP TO SEE DR. RHODES, HE REALIZES THAT HIS WEDDING RING IS MISSING.
IT MUST'VE SLIPPED OFF MY FINGER. I'M SO SKINNY NOW. OH, BABY. I'M SO SORRY.
JOYCE TRIES TO MINIMIZE HOW TERRIBLE THIS MAKES HER FEEL.
IT'S OK, IT'S OK, HONEY. MAYBE IT'LL TURN UP. IT COULD'VE ROLLED ANYWHERE.
WHEN ALL THIS IS OVER, WE'LL GET YOU ANOTHER ONE. I'LL STICK IT ON YOUR FINGER FOR OUR NEXT ANNIVERSARY.
ON THE WAY TO THE CLINIC...
I WANT YOU TO BE THINKING ABOUT ALL THE THINGS WE NEED TO ASK DR. RHODES. I'M GONNA TALK TO HER BY MYSELF, WHILE YOU GO GET YOUR BLOOD TESTS, OK?

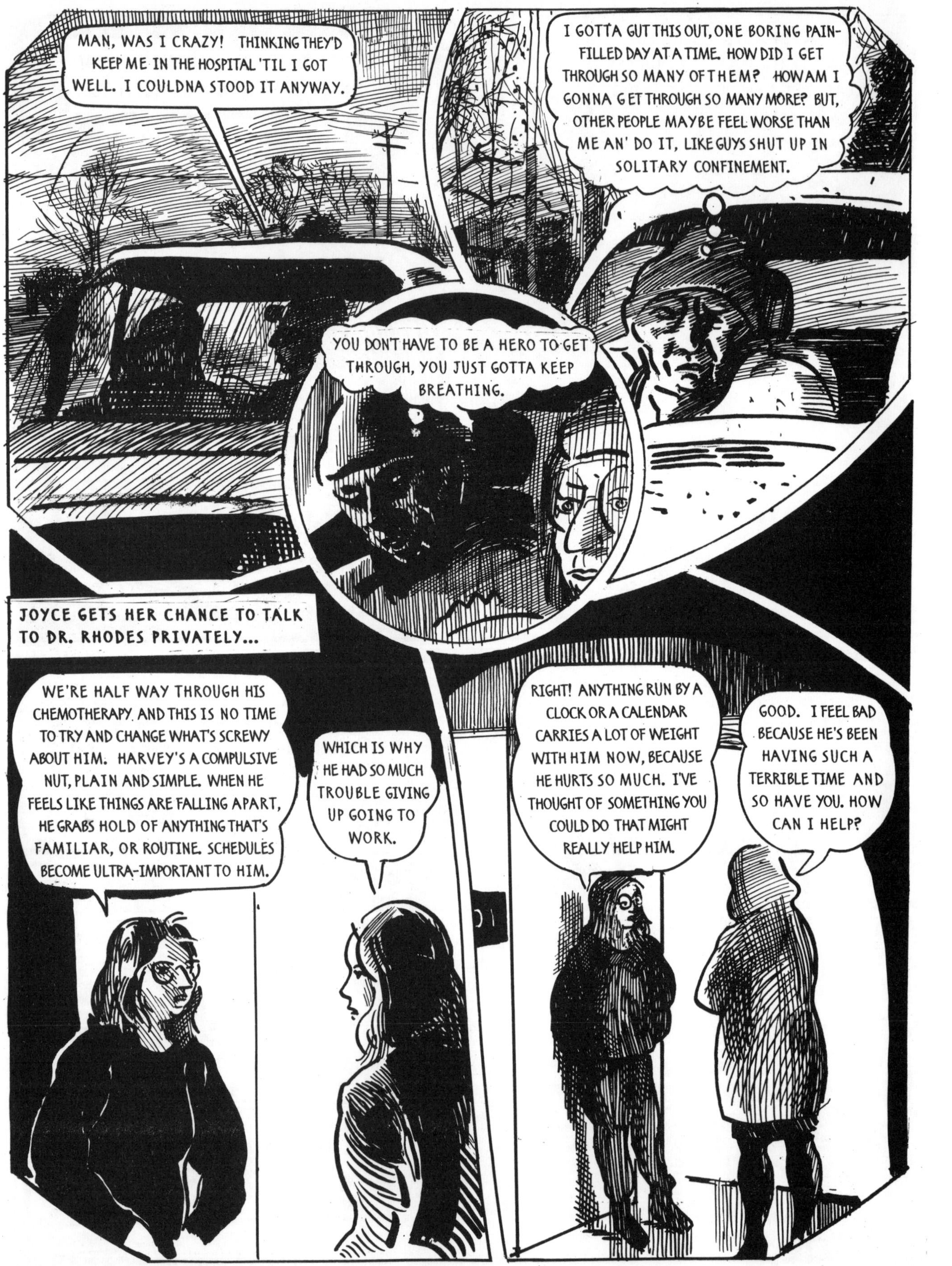

MAN, WAS I CRAZY! THINKING THEY'D KEEP ME IN THE HOSPITAL 'TIL I GOT WELL. I COULDNA STOOD IT ANYWAY.
I GOTTA GUT THIS OUT, ONE BORING PAIN-FILLED DAY AT A TIME. HOW DID I GET THROUGH SO MANY OF THEM? HOW AM I GONNA GET THROUGH SO MANY MORE? BUT, OTHER PEOPLE MAYBE FEEL WORSE THAN ME AN' DO IT, LIKE GUYS SHUT UP IN SOLITARY CONFINEMENT.
YOU DON'T HAVE TO BE A HERO TO GET THROUGH, YOU JUST GOTTA KEEP BREATHING.
JOYCE GETS HER CHANCE TO TALK TO DR. RHODES PRIVATELY...
WE'RE HALF WAY THROUGH HIS CHEMOTHERAPY. AND THIS IS NO TIME TO TRY AND CHANGE WHAT'S SCREWY ABOUT HIM. HARVEY'S A COMPULSIVE NUT, PLAIN AND SIMPLE. WHEN HE FEELS LIKE THINGS ARE FALLING APART, HE GRABS HOLD OF ANYTHING THAT'S FAMILIAR, OR ROUTINE. SCHEDULES BECOME ULTRA-IMPORTANT TO HIM.
WHICH IS WHY HE HAD SO MUCH TROUBLE GIVING UP GOING TO WORK.
RIGHT! ANYTHING RUN BY A CLOCK OR A CALENDAR CARRIES A LOT OF WEIGHT WITH HIM NOW, BECAUSE HE HURTS SO MUCH. I'VE THOUGHT OF SOMETHING YOU COULD DO THAT MIGHT REALLY HELP HIM.
GOOD. I FEEL BAD BECAUSE HE'S BEEN HAVING SUCH A TERRIBLE TIME AND SO HAVE YOU. HOW CAN I HELP?

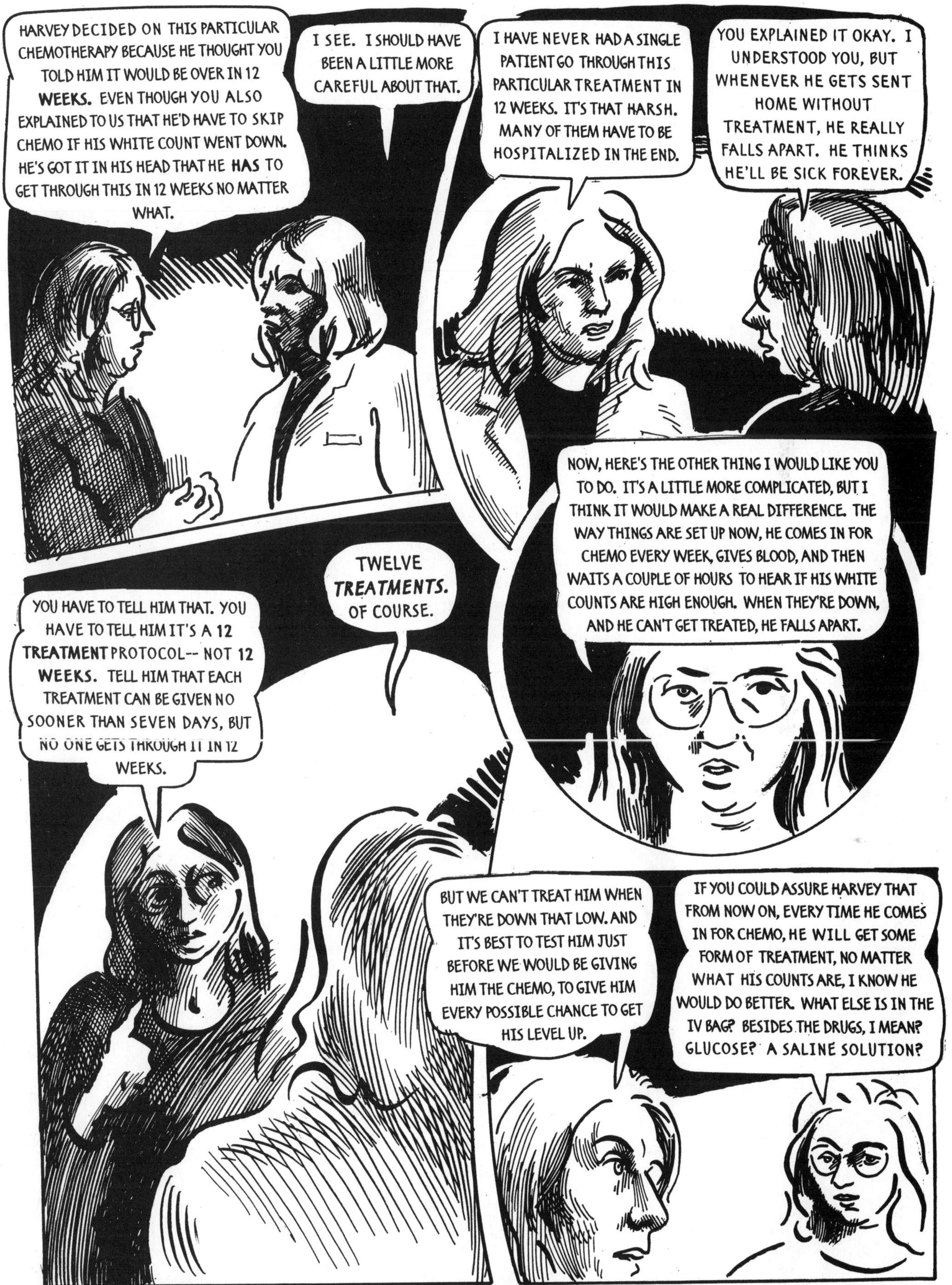
HARVEY DECIDED ON THIS PARTICULAR CHEMOTHERAPY BECAUSE HE THOUGHT YOU TOLD HIM IT WOULD BE OVER IN 12 **WEEKS.** EVEN THOUGH YOU ALSO EXPLAINED TO US THAT HE'D HAVE TO SKIP CHEMO IF HIS WHITE COUNT WENT DOWN. HE'S GOT IT IN HIS HEAD THAT HE **HAS** TO GET THROUGH THIS IN 12 WEEKS NO MATTER WHAT.
I SEE. I SHOULD HAVE BEEN A LITTLE MORE CAREFUL ABOUT THAT.
I HAVE NEVER HAD A SINGLE PATIENT GO THROUGH THIS PARTICULAR TREATMENT IN 12 WEEKS. IT'S THAT HARSH. MANY OF THEM HAVE TO BE HOSPITALIZED IN THE END.
YOU EXPLAINED IT OKAY. I UNDERSTOOD YOU, BUT WHENEVER HE GETS SENT HOME WITHOUT TREATMENT, HE REALLY FALLS APART. HE THINKS HE'LL BE SICK FOREVER.
NOW, HERE'S THE OTHER THING I WOULD LIKE YOU TO DO. IT'S A LITTLE MORE COMPLICATED, BUT I THINK IT WOULD MAKE A REAL DIFFERENCE. THE WAY THINGS ARE SET UP NOW, HE COMES IN FOR CHEMO EVERY WEEK, GIVES BLOOD, AND THEN WAITS A COUPLE OF HOURS TO HEAR IF HIS WHITE COUNTS ARE HIGH ENOUGH. WHEN THEY'RE DOWN, AND HE CAN'T GET TREATED, HE FALLS APART.
YOU HAVE TO TELL HIM THAT. YOU HAVE TO TELL HIM IT'S A 12 **TREATMENT** PROTOCOL-- NOT 12 **WEEKS.** TELL HIM THAT EACH TREATMENT CAN BE GIVEN NO SOONER THAN SEVEN DAYS, BUT NO ONE GETS THROUGH IT IN 12 WEEKS.
TWELVE ***TREATMENTS.*** OF COURSE.
BUT WE CAN'T TREAT HIM WHEN THEY'RE DOWN THAT LOW. AND IT'S BEST TO TEST HIM JUST BEFORE WE WOULD BE GIVING HIM THE CHEMO, TO GIVE HIM EVERY POSSIBLE CHANCE TO GET HIS LEVEL UP.
IF YOU COULD ASSURE HARVEY THAT FROM NOW ON, EVERY TIME HE COMES IN FOR CHEMO, HE WILL GET SOME FORM OF TREATMENT, NO MATTER WHAT HIS COUNTS ARE, I KNOW HE WOULD DO BETTER. WHAT ELSE IS IN THE IV BAG? BESIDES THE DRUGS, I MEAN? GLUCOSE? A SALINE SOLUTION?

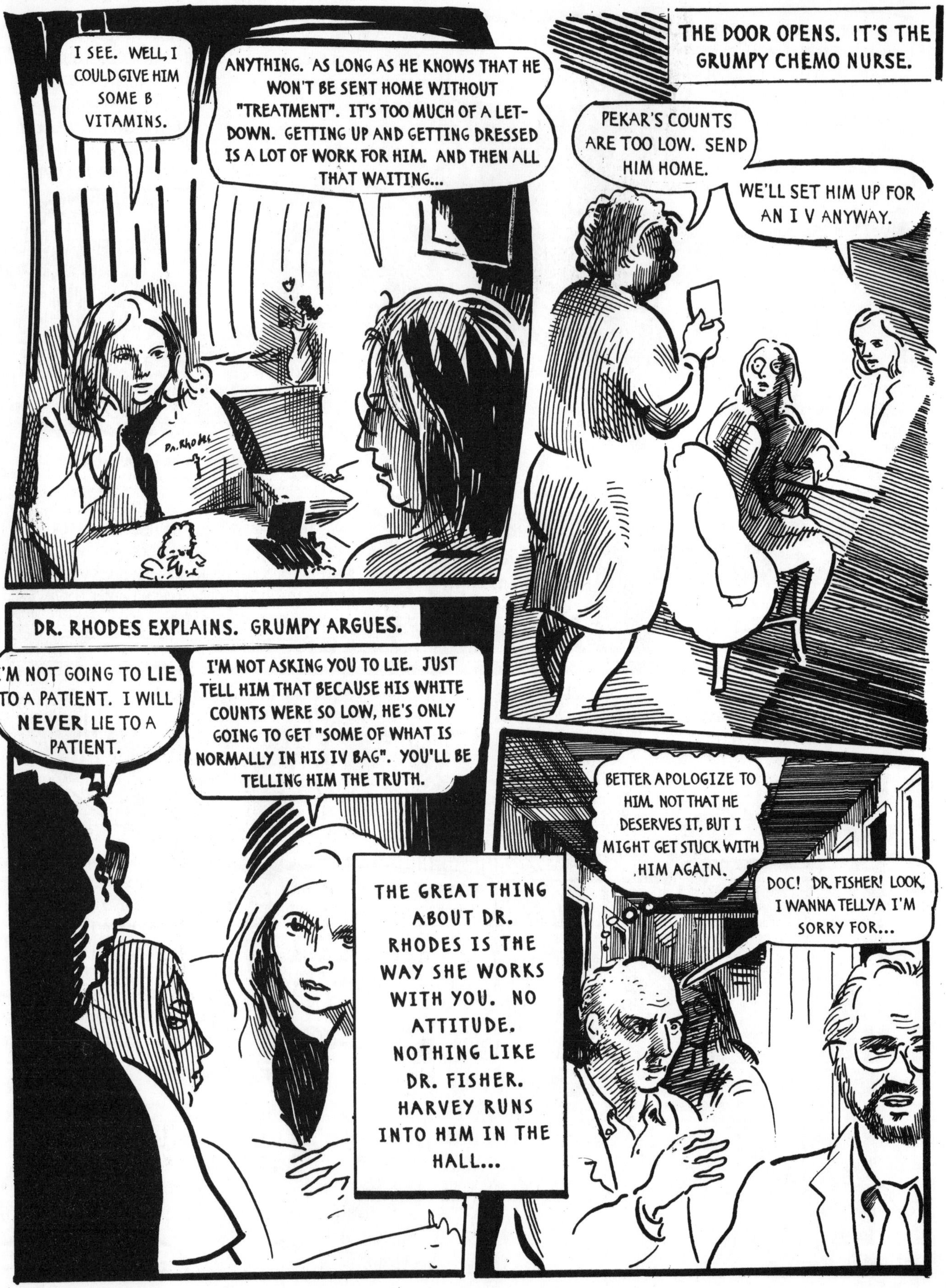
I SEE. WELL, I COULD GIVE HIM SOME B VITAMINS.
ANYTHING. AS LONG AS HE KNOWS THAT HE WON'T BE SENT HOME WITHOUT "TREATMENT". IT'S TOO MUCH OF A LET-DOWN. GETTING UP AND GETTING DRESSED IS A LOT OF WORK FOR HIM. AND THEN ALL THAT WAITING...
Dr. Rhodes
THE DOOR OPENS. IT'S THE GRUMPY CHEMO NURSE.
PEKAR'S COUNTS ARE TOO LOW. SEND HIM HOME.
WE'LL SET HIM UP FOR AN I V ANYWAY.
DR. RHODES EXPLAINS. GRUMPY ARGUES.
I'M NOT GOING TO LIE TO A PATIENT. I WILL NEVER LIE TO A PATIENT.
I'M NOT ASKING YOU TO LIE. JUST TELL HIM THAT BECAUSE HIS WHITE COUNTS WERE SO LOW, HE'S ONLY GOING TO GET "SOME OF WHAT IS NORMALLY IN HIS IV BAG". YOU'LL BE TELLING HIM THE TRUTH.
THE GREAT THING ABOUT DR. RHODES IS THE WAY SHE WORKS WITH YOU. NO ATTITUDE. NOTHING LIKE DR. FISHER. HARVEY RUNS INTO HIM IN THE HALL...
BETTER APOLOGIZE TO HIM. NOT THAT HE DESERVES IT, BUT I MIGHT GET STUCK WITH HIM AGAIN.
DOC! DR. FISHER! LOOK, I WANNA TELLYA I'M SORRY FOR...

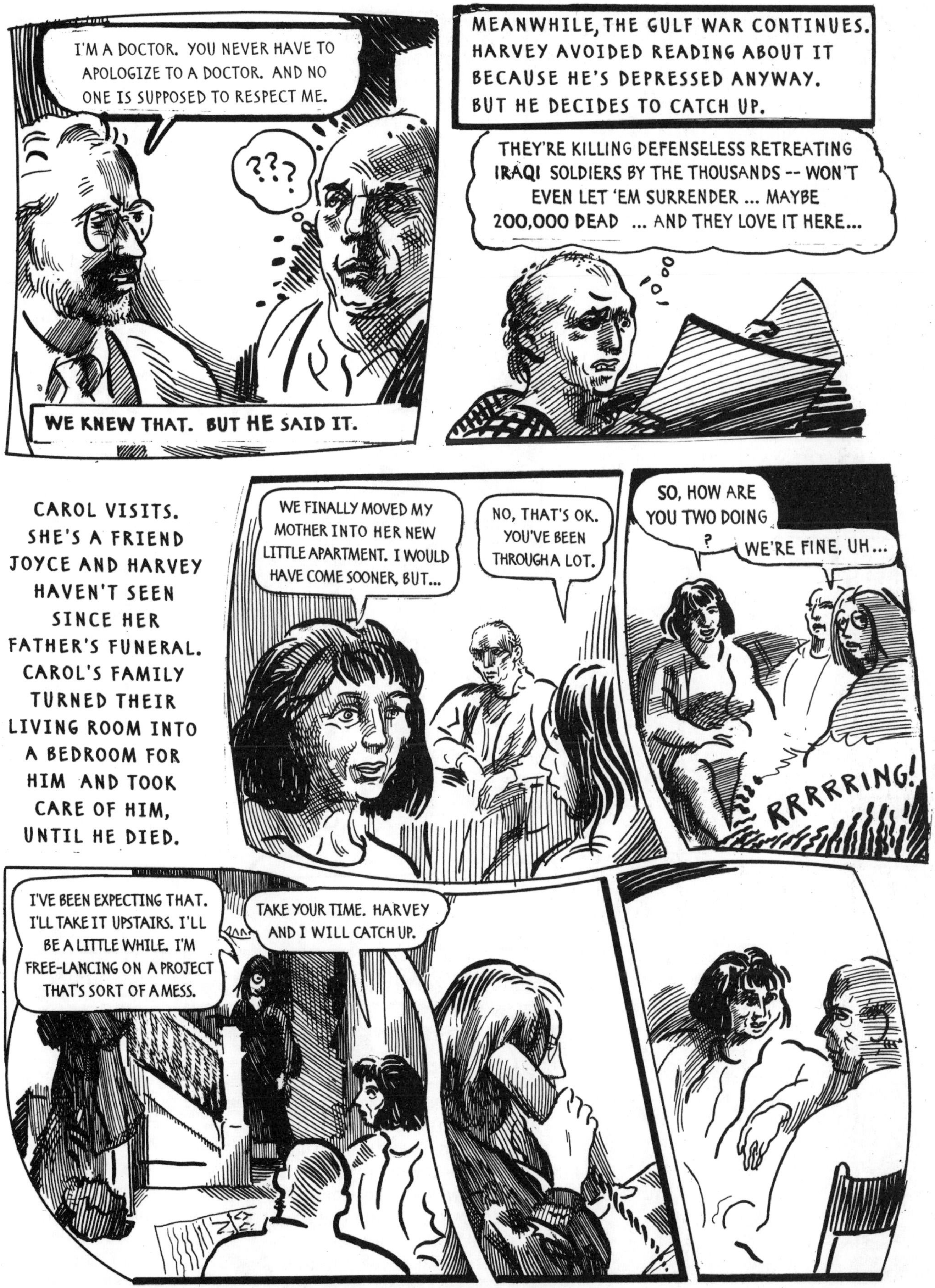
I'M A DOCTOR. YOU NEVER HAVE TO APOLOGIZE TO A DOCTOR. AND NO ONE IS SUPPOSED TO RESPECT ME.
???
WE KNEW THAT. BUT HE SAID IT.
MEANWHILE, THE GULF WAR CONTINUES. HARVEY AVOIDED READING ABOUT IT BECAUSE HE'S DEPRESSED ANYWAY. BUT HE DECIDES TO CATCH UP.
THEY'RE KILLING DEFENSELESS RETREATING IRAQI SOLDIERS BY THE THOUSANDS -- WON'T EVEN LET 'EM SURRENDER ... MAYBE 200,000 DEAD ... AND THEY LOVE IT HERE...
CAROL VISITS. SHE'S A FRIEND JOYCE AND HARVEY HAVEN'T SEEN SINCE HER FATHER'S FUNERAL. CAROL'S FAMILY TURNED THEIR LIVING ROOM INTO A BEDROOM FOR HIM AND TOOK CARE OF HIM, UNTIL HE DIED.
WE FINALLY MOVED MY MOTHER INTO HER NEW LITTLE APARTMENT. I WOULD HAVE COME SOONER, BUT...
NO, THAT'S OK. YOU'VE BEEN THROUGH A LOT.
SO, HOW ARE YOU TWO DOING ?
WE'RE FINE, UH...
RRRRRING!
I'VE BEEN EXPECTING THAT. I'LL TAKE IT UPSTAIRS. I'LL BE A LITTLE WHILE. I'M FREE-LANCING ON A PROJECT THAT'S SORT OF A MESS.
TAKE YOUR TIME. HARVEY AND I WILL CATCH UP.

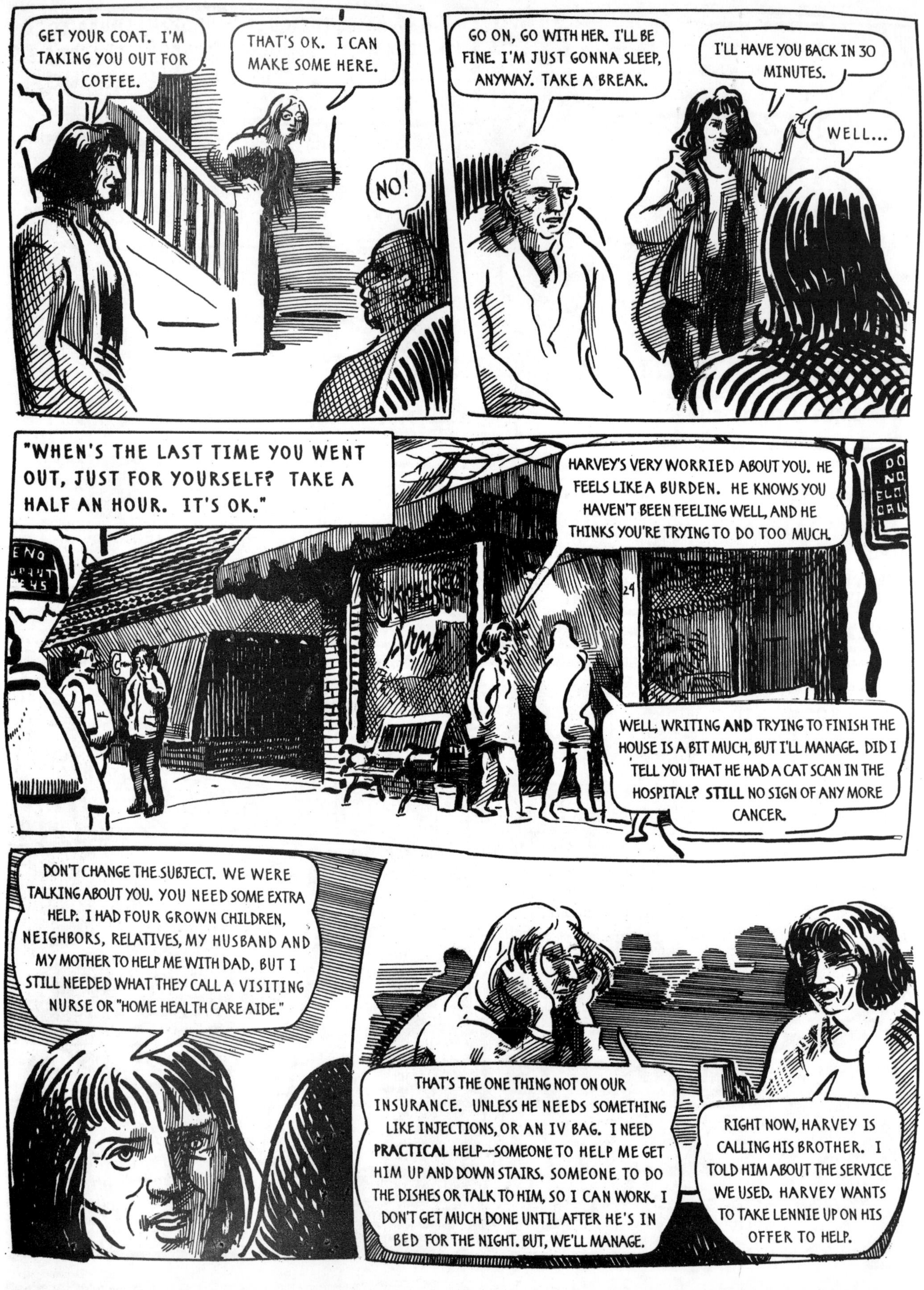
GET YOUR COAT. I'M TAKING YOU OUT FOR COFFEE.
THAT'S OK. I CAN MAKE SOME HERE.
NO!
GO ON, GO WITH HER. I'LL BE FINE. I'M JUST GONNA SLEEP, ANYWAY. TAKE A BREAK.
I'LL HAVE YOU BACK IN 30 MINUTES.
WELL...
"WHEN'S THE LAST TIME YOU WENT OUT, JUST FOR YOURSELF? TAKE A HALF AN HOUR. IT'S OK."
HARVEY'S VERY WORRIED ABOUT YOU. HE FEELS LIKE A BURDEN. HE KNOWS YOU HAVEN'T BEEN FEELING WELL, AND HE THINKS YOU'RE TRYING TO DO TOO MUCH.
WELL, WRITING **AND** TRYING TO FINISH THE HOUSE IS A BIT MUCH, BUT I'LL MANAGE. DID I TELL YOU THAT HE HAD A CAT SCAN IN THE HOSPITAL? **STILL** NO SIGN OF ANY MORE CANCER.
DON'T CHANGE THE SUBJECT. WE WERE TALKING ABOUT YOU. YOU NEED SOME EXTRA HELP. I HAD FOUR GROWN CHILDREN, NEIGHBORS, RELATIVES, MY HUSBAND AND MY MOTHER TO HELP ME WITH DAD, BUT I STILL NEEDED WHAT THEY CALL A VISITING NURSE OR "HOME HEALTH CARE AIDE."
THAT'S THE ONE THING NOT ON OUR INSURANCE. UNLESS HE NEEDS SOMETHING LIKE INJECTIONS, OR AN IV BAG. I NEED **PRACTICAL** HELP--SOMEONE TO HELP ME GET HIM UP AND DOWN STAIRS. SOMEONE TO DO THE DISHES OR TALK TO HIM, SO I CAN WORK. I DON'T GET MUCH DONE UNTIL AFTER HE'S IN BED FOR THE NIGHT. BUT, WE'LL MANAGE.
RIGHT NOW, HARVEY IS CALLING HIS BROTHER. I TOLD HIM ABOUT THE SERVICE WE USED. HARVEY WANTS TO TAKE LENNIE UP ON HIS OFFER TO HELP.

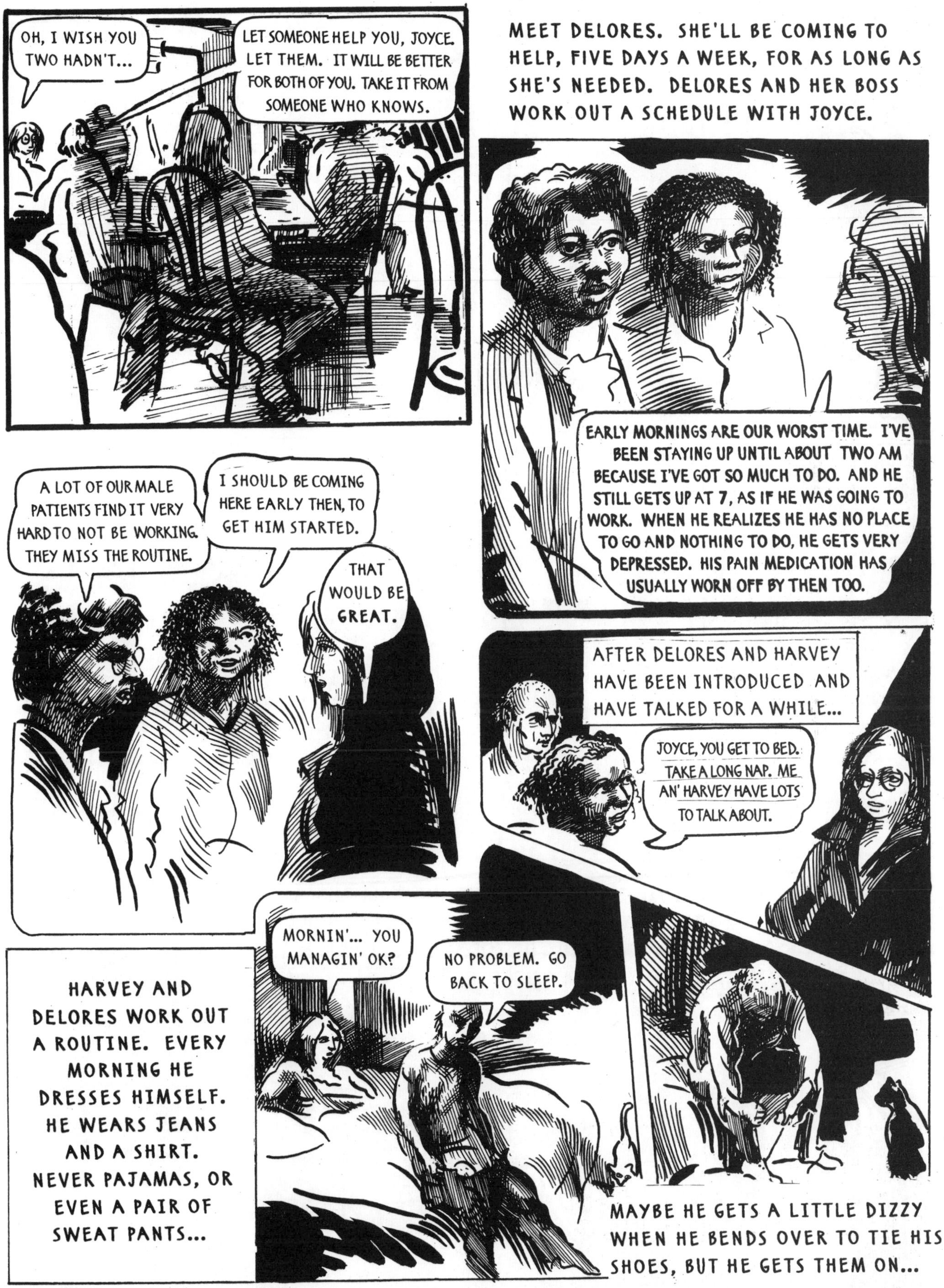
OH, I WISH YOU TWO HADN'T...
LET SOMEONE HELP YOU, JOYCE. LET THEM. IT WILL BE BETTER FOR BOTH OF YOU. TAKE IT FROM SOMEONE WHO KNOWS.
MEET DELORES. SHE'LL BE COMING TO HELP, FIVE DAYS A WEEK, FOR AS LONG AS SHE'S NEEDED. DELORES AND HER BOSS WORK OUT A SCHEDULE WITH JOYCE.
EARLY MORNINGS ARE OUR WORST TIME. I'VE BEEN STAYING UP UNTIL ABOUT TWO AM BECAUSE I'VE GOT SO MUCH TO DO. AND HE STILL GETS UP AT 7, AS IF HE WAS GOING TO WORK. WHEN HE REALIZES HE HAS NO PLACE TO GO AND NOTHING TO DO, HE GETS VERY DEPRESSED. HIS PAIN MEDICATION HAS USUALLY WORN OFF BY THEN TOO.
A LOT OF OUR MALE PATIENTS FIND IT VERY HARD TO NOT BE WORKING. THEY MISS THE ROUTINE.
I SHOULD BE COMING HERE EARLY THEN, TO GET HIM STARTED.
THAT WOULD BE GREAT.
AFTER DELORES AND HARVEY HAVE BEEN INTRODUCED AND HAVE TALKED FOR A WHILE...
JOYCE, YOU GET TO BED. TAKE A LONG NAP. ME AN' HARVEY HAVE LOTS TO TALK ABOUT.
HARVEY AND DELORES WORK OUT A ROUTINE. EVERY MORNING HE DRESSES HIMSELF. HE WEARS JEANS AND A SHIRT. NEVER PAJAMAS, OR EVEN A PAIR OF SWEAT PANTS...
MORNIN'... YOU MANAGIN' OK?
NO PROBLEM. GO BACK TO SLEEP.
MAYBE HE GETS A LITTLE DIZZY WHEN HE BENDS OVER TO TIE HIS SHOES, BUT HE GETS THEM ON...

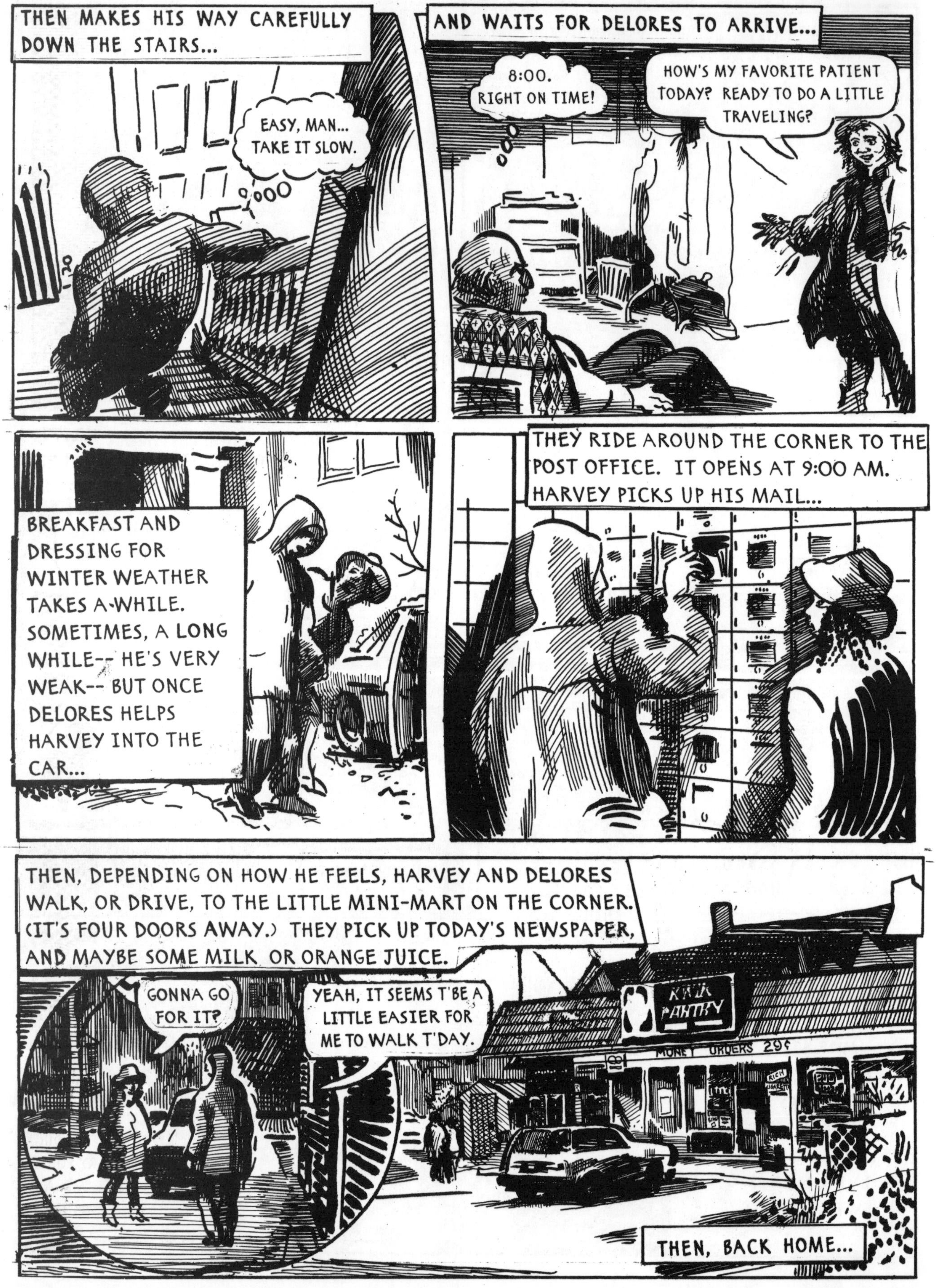
THEN MAKES HIS WAY CAREFULLY DOWN THE STAIRS...
EASY, MAN... TAKE IT SLOW.
AND WAITS FOR DELORES TO ARRIVE...
8:00. RIGHT ON TIME!
HOW'S MY FAVORITE PATIENT TODAY? READY TO DO A LITTLE TRAVELING?
BREAKFAST AND DRESSING FOR WINTER WEATHER TAKES A-WHILE. SOMETIMES, A LONG WHILE-- HE'S VERY WEAK-- BUT ONCE DELORES HELPS HARVEY INTO THE CAR...
THEY RIDE AROUND THE CORNER TO THE POST OFFICE. IT OPENS AT 9:00 AM. HARVEY PICKS UP HIS MAIL...
THEN, DEPENDING ON HOW HE FEELS, HARVEY AND DELORES WALK, OR DRIVE, TO THE LITTLE MINI-MART ON THE CORNER. (IT'S FOUR DOORS AWAY.) THEY PICK UP TODAY'S NEWSPAPER, AND MAYBE SOME MILK OR ORANGE JUICE.
GONNA GO FOR IT?
YEAH, IT SEEMS T'BE A LITTLE EASIER FOR ME TO WALK T'DAY.
MONEY ORDERS 29¢
THEN, BACK HOME...

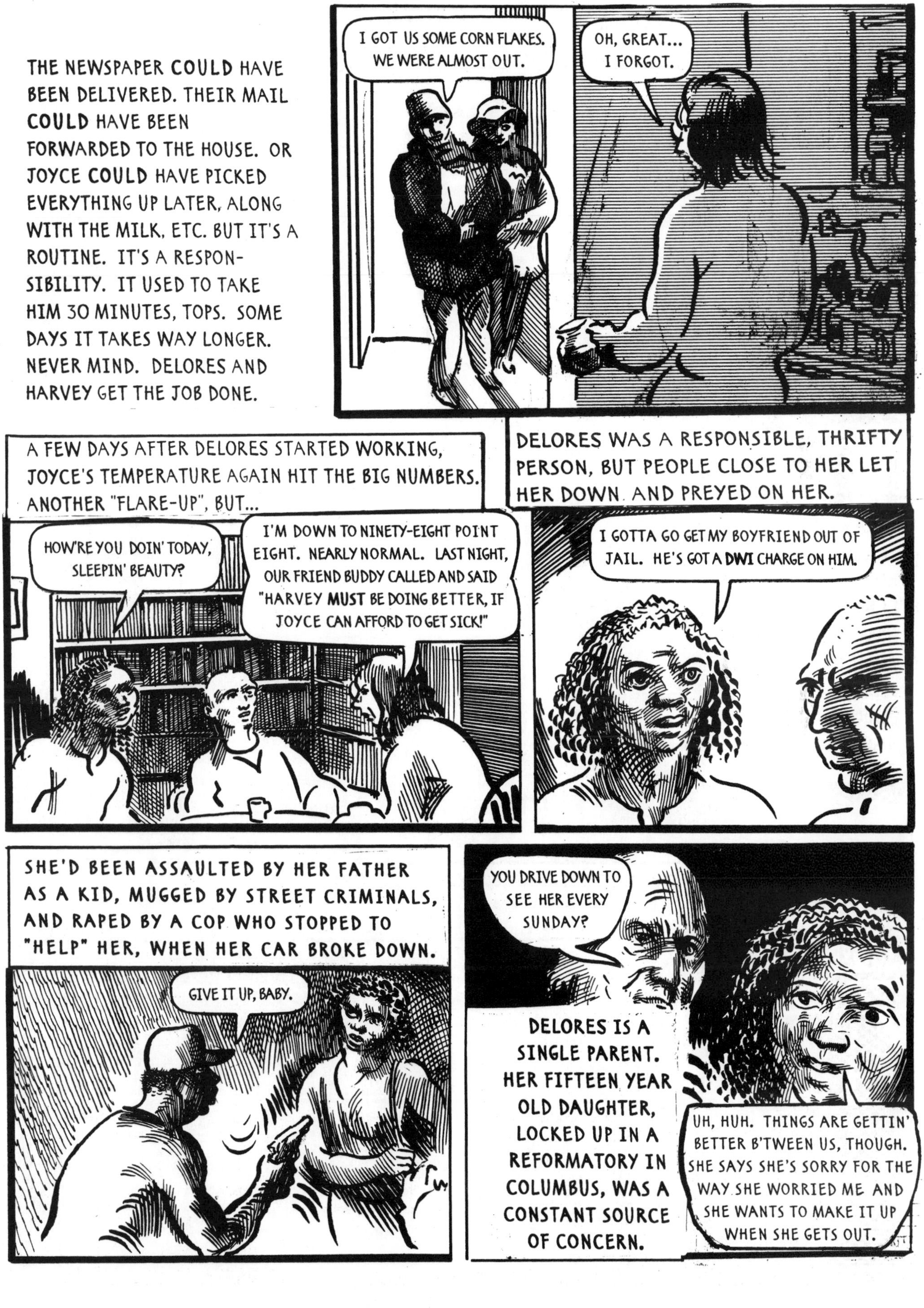
THE NEWSPAPER COULD HAVE BEEN DELIVERED. THEIR MAIL COULD HAVE BEEN FORWARDED TO THE HOUSE. OR JOYCE COULD HAVE PICKED EVERYTHING UP LATER, ALONG WITH THE MILK, ETC. BUT IT'S A ROUTINE. IT'S A RESPONSIBILITY. IT USED TO TAKE HIM 30 MINUTES, TOPS. SOME DAYS IT TAKES WAY LONGER. NEVER MIND. DELORES AND HARVEY GET THE JOB DONE.
I GOT US SOME CORN FLAKES. WE WERE ALMOST OUT.
OH, GREAT... I FORGOT.
A FEW DAYS AFTER DELORES STARTED WORKING, JOYCE'S TEMPERATURE AGAIN HIT THE BIG NUMBERS. ANOTHER "FLARE-UP", BUT...
HOW'RE YOU DOIN' TODAY, SLEEPIN' BEAUTY?
I'M DOWN TO NINETY-EIGHT POINT EIGHT. NEARLY NORMAL. LAST NIGHT, OUR FRIEND BUDDY CALLED AND SAID "HARVEY MUST BE DOING BETTER, IF JOYCE CAN AFFORD TO GET SICK!"
DELORES WAS A RESPONSIBLE, THRIFTY PERSON, BUT PEOPLE CLOSE TO HER LET HER DOWN AND PREYED ON HER.
I GOTTA GO GET MY BOYFRIEND OUT OF JAIL. HE'S GOT A DWI CHARGE ON HIM.
SHE'D BEEN ASSAULTED BY HER FATHER AS A KID, MUGGED BY STREET CRIMINALS, AND RAPED BY A COP WHO STOPPED TO "HELP" HER, WHEN HER CAR BROKE DOWN.
GIVE IT UP, BABY.
YOU DRIVE DOWN TO SEE HER EVERY SUNDAY?
DELORES IS A SINGLE PARENT. HER FIFTEEN YEAR OLD DAUGHTER, LOCKED UP IN A REFORMATORY IN COLUMBUS, WAS A CONSTANT SOURCE OF CONCERN.
UH, HUH. THINGS ARE GETTIN' BETTER B'TWEEN US, THOUGH. SHE SAYS SHE'S SORRY FOR THE WAY SHE WORRIED ME AND SHE WANTS TO MAKE IT UP WHEN SHE GETS OUT.

BUT, WHEN SHE DOES GET OUT...
HARVEY, I DON'T KNOW WHAT TO DO ABOUT HER. SHE WON'T GO TO SCHOOL, WON'T WORK... SHE THINKS SHE'S GONNA FIND SOME MAN T'TAKE CARE OF HER.
ALL WE BEEN DOIN' IS FIGHTIN'
DELORES WAS ONCE A HOTEL MAID, WHO WORKED HER WAY UP TO "HOUSEKEEPING SUPERVISOR". SHE WAS ABLE TO COMPLETE A COMMUNITY COLLEGE HEALTH CARE TRAINING PROGRAM AND WAS GOOD AT HER JOB.
SHE HELPED HARVEY GET THROUGH THE REST OF HIS CHEMOTHERAPY TREATMENTS.
TODAY IS GONNA BE A PIECE OF CAKE!
WHEN HARVEY'S BLOOD COUNTS WERE DOWN, HE HAD A FEW OF THOSE SPECIAL, "PARTIAL" CHEMOTHERAPY TREATMENTS. (JOYCE LET DELORES IN ON THE SECRET.)
IS THAT THE HARVEY PEKAR? FROM THE LETTERMAN SHOW?
OOOH. YOU'RE FAMOUS! HOW'S IT FEEL TO BE SO FAMOUS?
FAMOUS FOR BEIN' KICKED OFF. I WAS ON SIX TIMES, THEN WE GOT SICKA EACH OTHER.
IT WAS AROUND THEN WHEN ONE OF THAT LATE NIGHT TV SHOW'S ASSISTANTS CALLED. IT SEEMS SOMEBODY WAS IN A "FORGIVING" MOOD...
DAVE AND THE GANG HAVE BEEN TALKING ABOUT HARVEY. WE THINK IT'S TIME TO GIVE HIM ANOTHER CHANCE. LET'S TALK ABOUT BRINGING HIM BACK ON.
THE ROCKY HORROR PICTURE
GRIESS FLANNEL
WELL, RIGHT NOW HARVEY IS NEARLY BALD. HIS FACE IS ALL BLOWN UP, AND HE'S KINDA ORANGE COLORED. HE CAN'T WALK MORE THAN A FEW STEPS, 'CAUSE HE'S IN THE MIDDLE OF CHEMOTHERAPY. I DON'T THINK YOUR AUDIENCE WOULD FIND CANCER REAL ENTERTAINING.

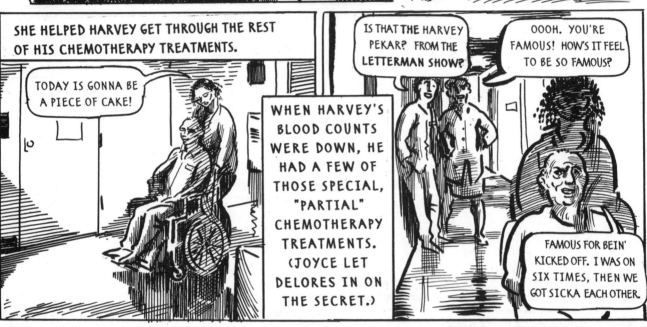

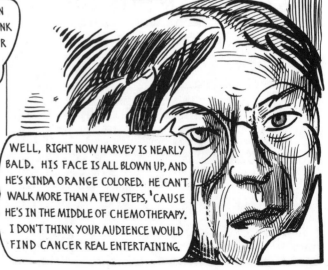

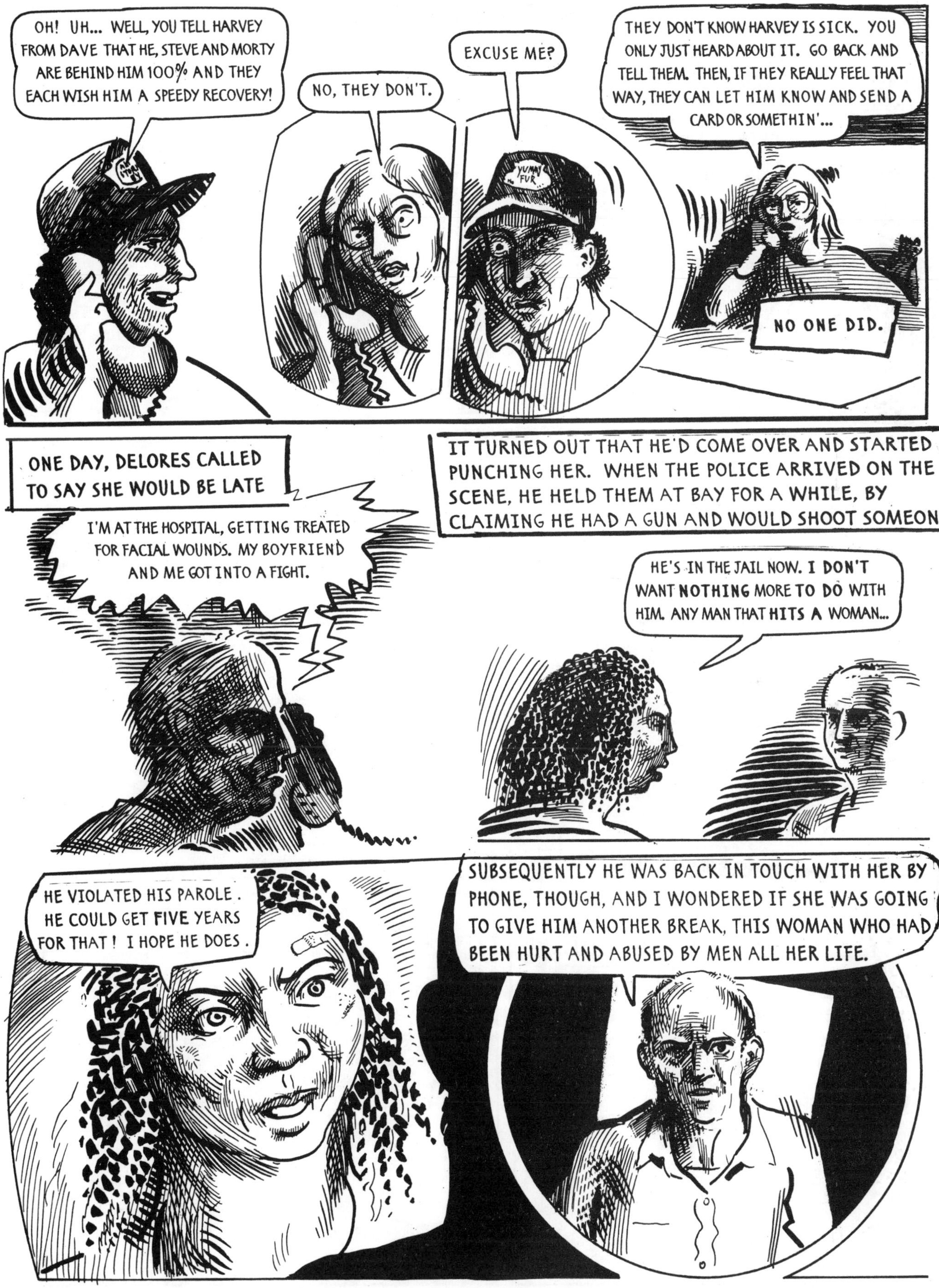
OH! UH... WELL, YOU TELL HARVEY FROM DAVE THAT HE, STEVE AND MORTY ARE BEHIND HIM 100% AND THEY EACH WISH HIM A SPEEDY RECOVERY!
NO, THEY DON'T.
EXCUSE ME?
THEY DON'T KNOW HARVEY IS SICK. YOU ONLY JUST HEARD ABOUT IT. GO BACK AND TELL THEM. THEN, IF THEY REALLY FEEL THAT WAY, THEY CAN LET HIM KNOW AND SEND A CARD OR SOMETHIN'...
NO ONE DID.
ONE DAY, DELORES CALLED TO SAY SHE WOULD BE LATE
I'M AT THE HOSPITAL, GETTING TREATED FOR FACIAL WOUNDS. MY BOYFRIEND AND ME GOT INTO A FIGHT.
IT TURNED OUT THAT HE'D COME OVER AND STARTED PUNCHING HER. WHEN THE POLICE ARRIVED ON THE SCENE, HE HELD THEM AT BAY FOR A WHILE, BY CLAIMING HE HAD A GUN AND WOULD SHOOT SOMEONE.
HE'S IN THE JAIL NOW. I DON'T WANT NOTHING MORE TO DO WITH HIM. ANY MAN THAT HITS A WOMAN...
HE VIOLATED HIS PAROLE. HE COULD GET FIVE YEARS FOR THAT! I HOPE HE DOES.
SUBSEQUENTLY HE WAS BACK IN TOUCH WITH HER BY PHONE, THOUGH, AND I WONDERED IF SHE WAS GOING TO GIVE HIM ANOTHER BREAK, THIS WOMAN WHO HAD BEEN HURT AND ABUSED BY MEN ALL HER LIFE.

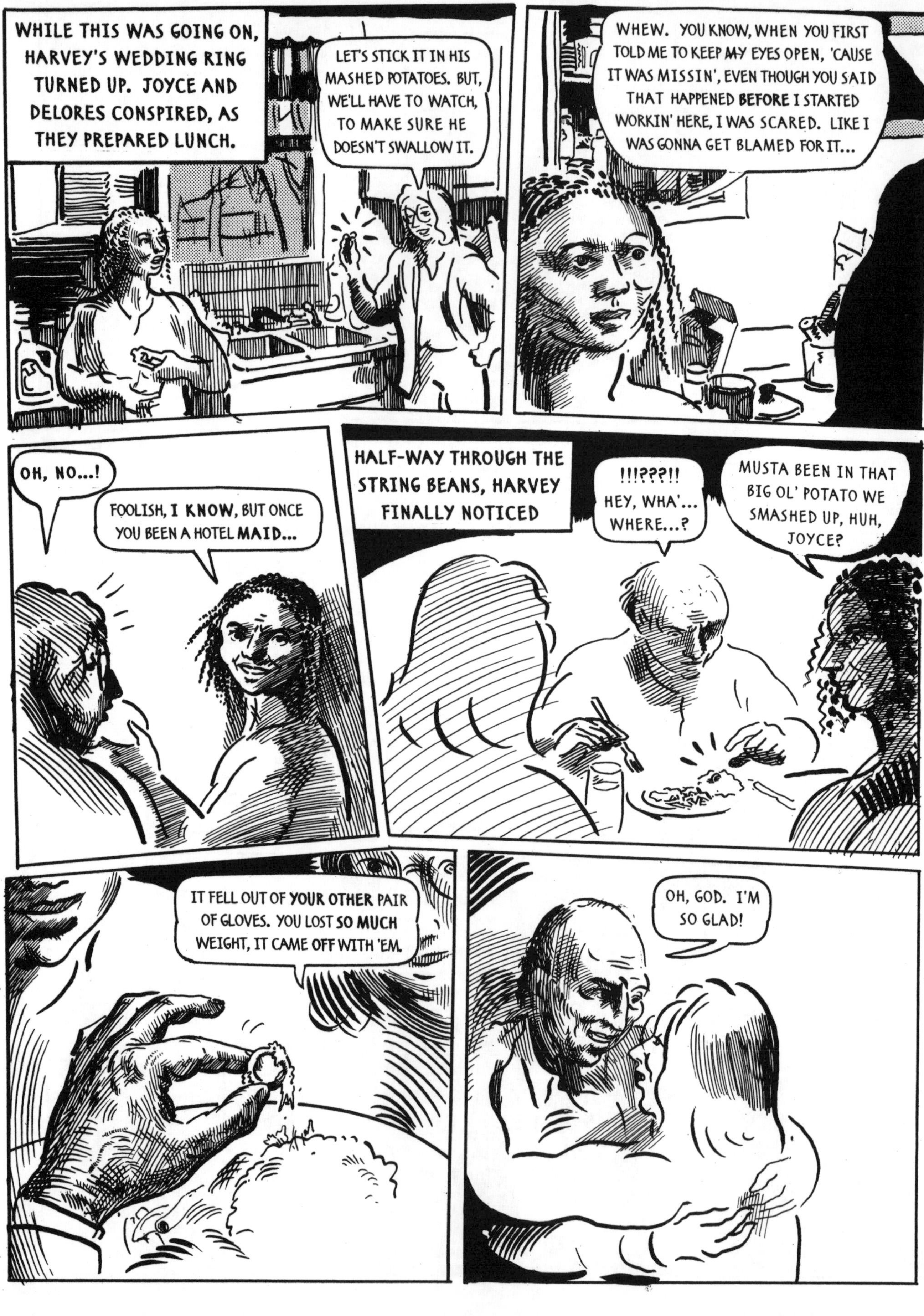

WHILE THIS WAS GOING ON, HARVEY'S WEDDING RING TURNED UP. JOYCE AND DELORES CONSPIRED, AS THEY PREPARED LUNCH.
LET'S STICK IT IN HIS MASHED POTATOES. BUT, WE'LL HAVE TO WATCH, TO MAKE SURE HE DOESN'T SWALLOW IT.
WHEW. YOU KNOW, WHEN YOU FIRST TOLD ME TO KEEP MY EYES OPEN, 'CAUSE IT WAS MISSIN', EVEN THOUGH YOU SAID THAT HAPPENED BEFORE I STARTED WORKIN' HERE, I WAS SCARED. LIKE I WAS GONNA GET BLAMED FOR IT...
OH, NO...!
FOOLISH, I KNOW, BUT ONCE YOU BEEN A HOTEL MAID...
HALF-WAY THROUGH THE STRING BEANS, HARVEY FINALLY NOTICED
!!!???!!
HEY, WHA'... WHERE...?
MUSTA BEEN IN THAT BIG OL' POTATO WE SMASHED UP, HUH, JOYCE?
IT FELL OUT OF YOUR OTHER PAIR OF GLOVES. YOU LOST SO MUCH WEIGHT, IT CAME OFF WITH 'EM.
OH, GOD. I'M SO GLAD!

11

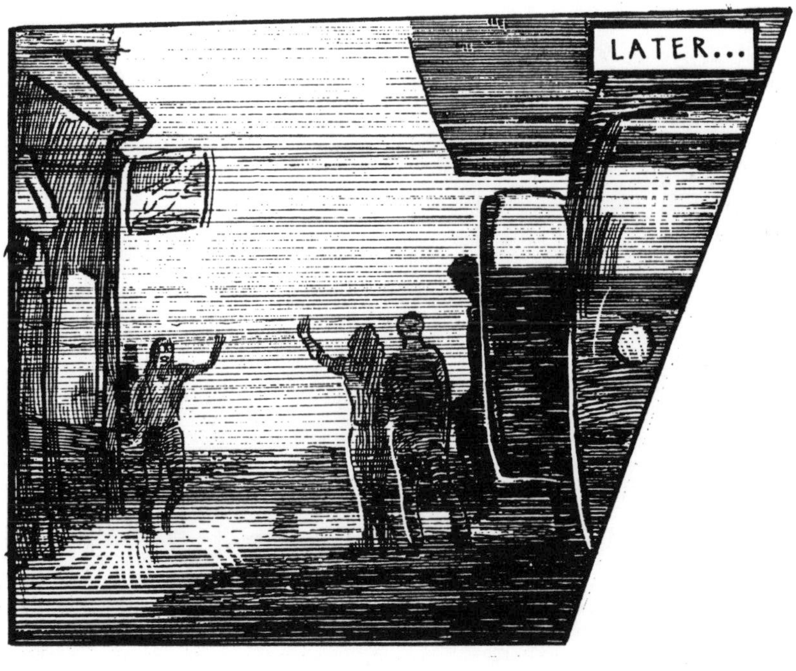
LATER...

IT'S DARK OUT. JOYCE IS SLEEPING. HARVEY MAKES HIS WAY INTO THE BATHROOM, WHERE HE STOPS TO CATCH HIS BREATH...

HE FAINTS. ON THE WAY DOWN HE BOUNCES OFF THE TUB, THEN SMASHES HIS HEAD AGAINST THE STEAMING RADIATOR. THAT PROBABLY KNOCKED HIM OUT A *SECOND* TIME, BECAUSE HE WAKES UP WITH A DEEP BURN ON HIS FOREHEAD.

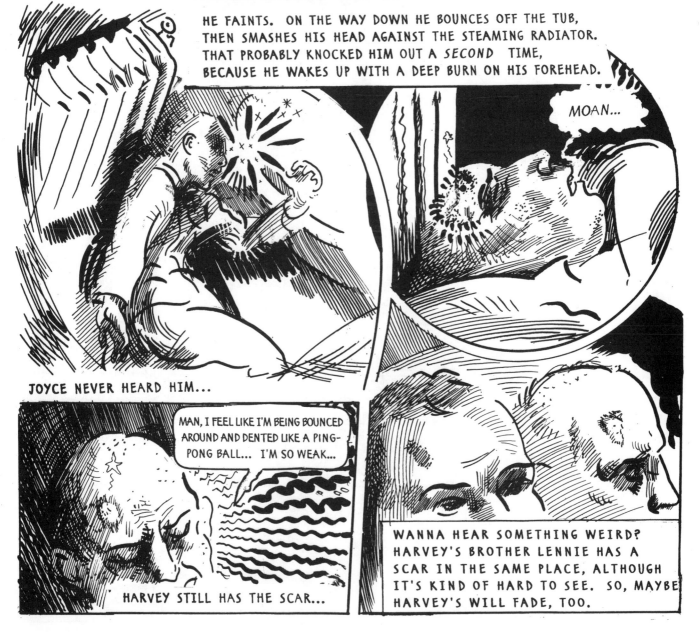

MOAN...

JOYCE NEVER HEARD HIM...

MAN, I FEEL LIKE I'M BEING BOUNCED AROUND AND DENTED LIKE A PING-PONG BALL... I'M SO WEAK...

HARVEY STILL HAS THE SCAR...

WANNA HEAR SOMETHING WEIRD? HARVEY'S BROTHER LENNIE HAS A SCAR IN THE SAME PLACE, ALTHOUGH IT'S KIND OF HARD TO SEE. SO, MAYBE HARVEY'S WILL FADE, TOO.

LENNIE COMES TO VISIT, AND IT'S GREAT FOR HARVEY TO SEE HIM, THIS BROTHER WITH WHOM HE'S BEEN OUT OF TOUCH FOR SO LONG, WHO'S BEEN SO GOOD TO HIM.

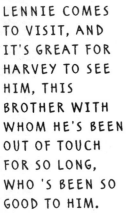

MAN, IT'S SO GOOD TO SEE YOU!

THAT NIGHT, HARVEY DREAMS THAT HE'S VISITING LENNIE IN INDIANA, SHOOTING HOOPS IN THAT BASKETBALL-CRAZY STATE.

SWITCH OFF!

YOUR MAN

DUNK!

BLOCK OUT... AH!

SHIT!

WHAT A WONDERFUL DREAM! HOW GREAT TO BE ABLE TO RUN AND JUMP, DRIBBLE AND SHOOT.

CONGRATULATIONS HARVEY

WHEN HARVEY FINISHES HIS CHEMOTHERAPY, DELORES' ASSIGNMENT WITH HIM IS OVER. THEY CELEBRATE WITH CAKE AND ICE CREAM.

YOU DID IT!

FINISHED THE JOB AT HOME! NO OXYGEN TANKS, NO I.C.U.*, NO HOSPITAL FOR YOU...

SMOOCH!

HA!

*Intensive Care Unit

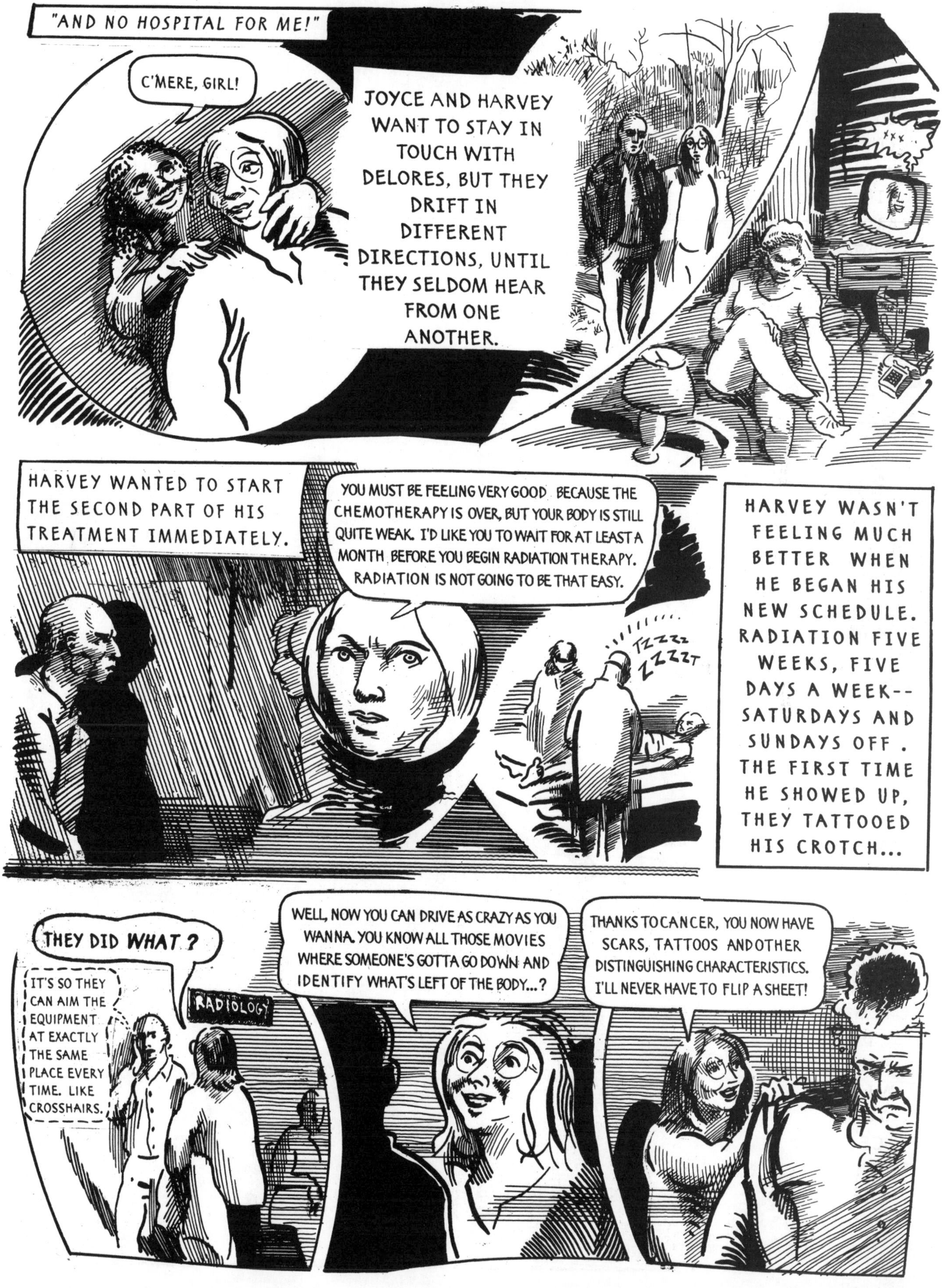
"AND NO HOSPITAL FOR ME!"
C'MERE, GIRL!
JOYCE AND HARVEY WANT TO STAY IN TOUCH WITH DELORES, BUT THEY DRIFT IN DIFFERENT DIRECTIONS, UNTIL THEY SELDOM HEAR FROM ONE ANOTHER.
HARVEY WANTED TO START THE SECOND PART OF HIS TREATMENT IMMEDIATELY.
YOU MUST BE FEELING VERY GOOD BECAUSE THE CHEMOTHERAPY IS OVER, BUT YOUR BODY IS STILL QUITE WEAK. I'D LIKE YOU TO WAIT FOR AT LEAST A MONTH BEFORE YOU BEGIN RADIATION THERAPY. RADIATION IS NOT GOING TO BE THAT EASY.
TZZZZ ZZZZT
HARVEY WASN'T FEELING MUCH BETTER WHEN HE BEGAN HIS NEW SCHEDULE. RADIATION FIVE WEEKS, FIVE DAYS A WEEK-- SATURDAYS AND SUNDAYS OFF. THE FIRST TIME HE SHOWED UP, THEY TATTOOED HIS CROTCH...
THEY DID WHAT?
IT'S SO THEY CAN AIM THE EQUIPMENT AT EXACTLY THE SAME PLACE EVERY TIME. LIKE CROSSHAIRS.
RADIOLOGY
WELL, NOW YOU CAN DRIVE AS CRAZY AS YOU WANNA. YOU KNOW ALL THOSE MOVIES WHERE SOMEONE'S GOTTA GO DOWN AND IDENTIFY WHAT'S LEFT OF THE BODY...?
THANKS TO CANCER, YOU NOW HAVE SCARS, TATTOOS AND OTHER DISTINGUISHING CHARACTERISTICS. I'LL NEVER HAVE TO FLIP A SHEET!

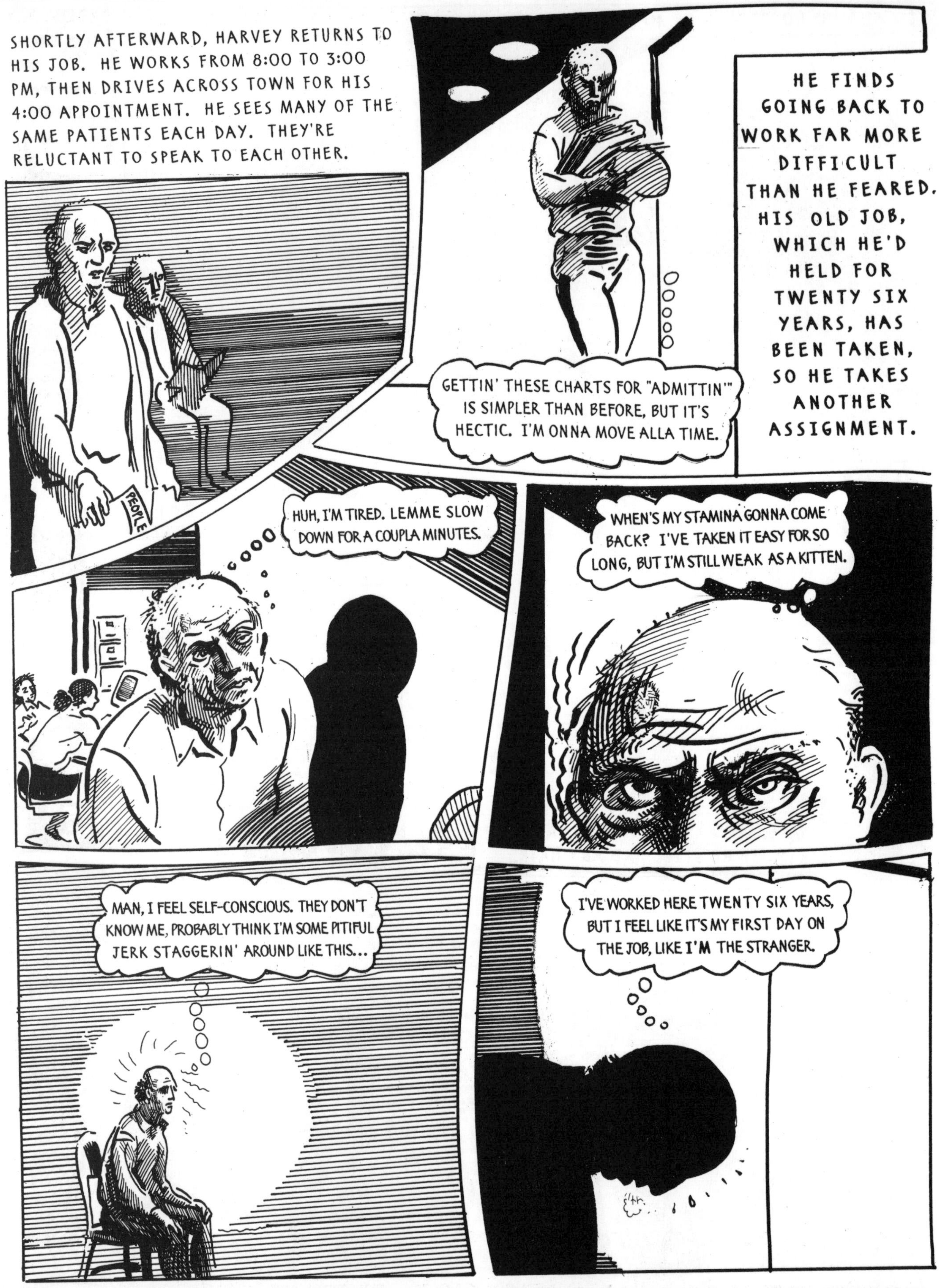
SHORTLY AFTERWARD, HARVEY RETURNS TO HIS JOB. HE WORKS FROM 8:00 TO 3:00 PM, THEN DRIVES ACROSS TOWN FOR HIS 4:00 APPOINTMENT. HE SEES MANY OF THE SAME PATIENTS EACH DAY. THEY'RE RELUCTANT TO SPEAK TO EACH OTHER.
PEOPLE
GETTIN' THESE CHARTS FOR "ADMITTIN'" IS SIMPLER THAN BEFORE, BUT IT'S HECTIC. I'M ONNA MOVE ALLA TIME.
HE FINDS GOING BACK TO WORK FAR MORE DIFFICULT THAN HE FEARED. HIS OLD JOB, WHICH HE'D HELD FOR TWENTY SIX YEARS, HAS BEEN TAKEN, SO HE TAKES ANOTHER ASSIGNMENT.
HUH, I'M TIRED. LEMME SLOW DOWN FOR A COUPLA MINUTES.
WHEN'S MY STAMINA GONNA COME BACK? I'VE TAKEN IT EASY FOR SO LONG, BUT I'M STILL WEAK AS A KITTEN.
MAN, I FEEL SELF-CONSCIOUS. THEY DON'T KNOW ME, PROBABLY THINK I'M SOME PITIFUL JERK STAGGERIN' AROUND LIKE THIS...
I'VE WORKED HERE TWENTY SIX YEARS, BUT I FEEL LIKE IT'S MY FIRST DAY ON THE JOB, LIKE I'M THE STRANGER.

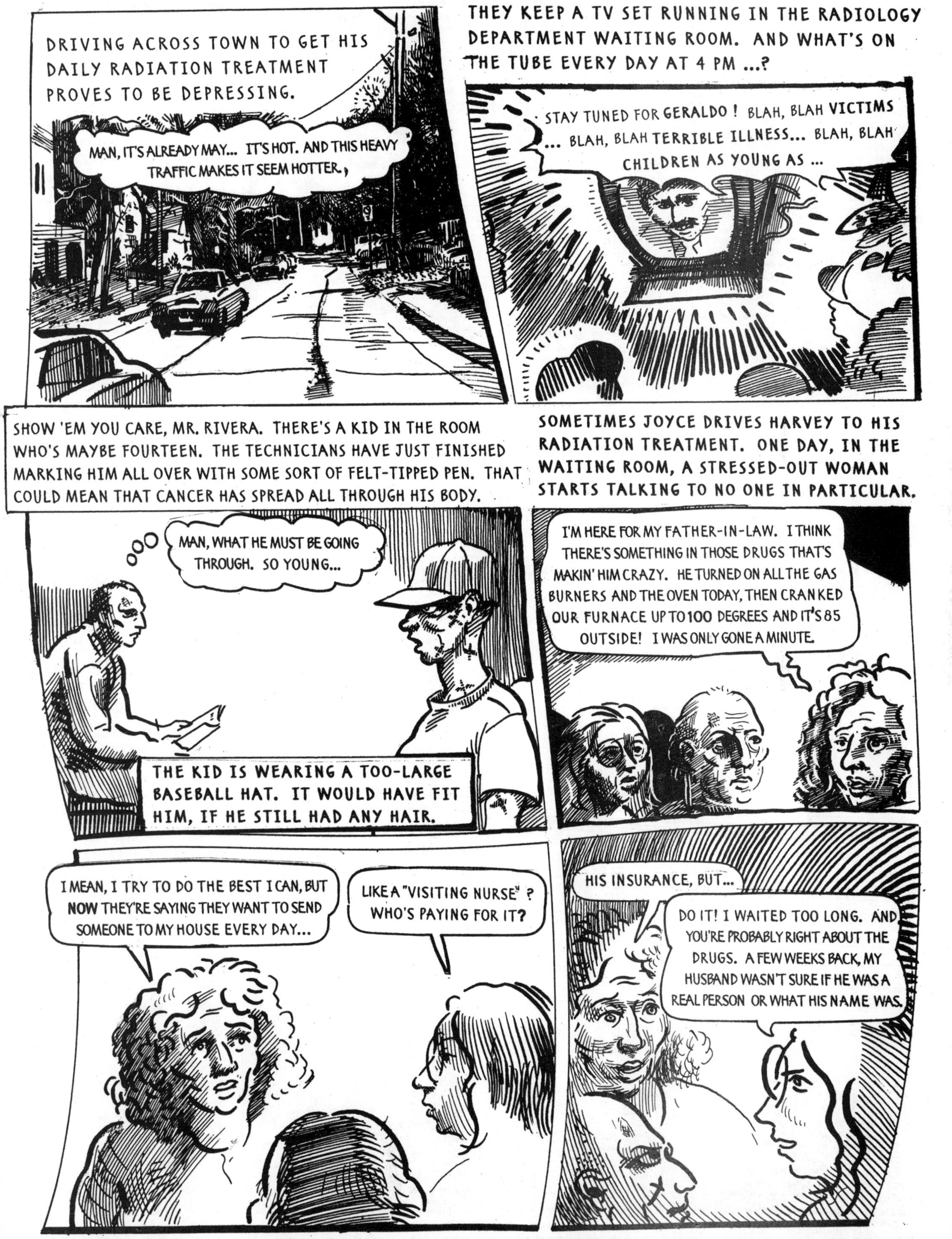

DRIVING ACROSS TOWN TO GET HIS DAILY RADIATION TREATMENT PROVES TO BE DEPRESSING.
MAN, IT'S ALREADY MAY... IT'S HOT. AND THIS HEAVY TRAFFIC MAKES IT SEEM HOTTER,
THEY KEEP A TV SET RUNNING IN THE RADIOLOGY DEPARTMENT WAITING ROOM. AND WHAT'S ON THE TUBE EVERY DAY AT 4 PM ...?
STAY TUNED FOR GERALDO! BLAH, BLAH VICTIMS ... BLAH, BLAH TERRIBLE ILLNESS... BLAH, BLAH CHILDREN AS YOUNG AS ...
SHOW 'EM YOU CARE, MR. RIVERA. THERE'S A KID IN THE ROOM WHO'S MAYBE FOURTEEN. THE TECHNICIANS HAVE JUST FINISHED MARKING HIM ALL OVER WITH SOME SORT OF FELT-TIPPED PEN. THAT COULD MEAN THAT CANCER HAS SPREAD ALL THROUGH HIS BODY.
MAN, WHAT HE MUST BE GOING THROUGH. SO YOUNG...
THE KID IS WEARING A TOO-LARGE BASEBALL HAT. IT WOULD HAVE FIT HIM, IF HE STILL HAD ANY HAIR.
SOMETIMES JOYCE DRIVES HARVEY TO HIS RADIATION TREATMENT. ONE DAY, IN THE WAITING ROOM, A STRESSED-OUT WOMAN STARTS TALKING TO NO ONE IN PARTICULAR.
I'M HERE FOR MY FATHER-IN-LAW. I THINK THERE'S SOMETHING IN THOSE DRUGS THAT'S MAKIN' HIM CRAZY. HE TURNED ON ALL THE GAS BURNERS AND THE OVEN TODAY, THEN CRANKED OUR FURNACE UP TO 100 DEGREES AND IT'S 85 OUTSIDE! I WAS ONLY GONE A MINUTE.
I MEAN, I TRY TO DO THE BEST I CAN, BUT NOW THEY'RE SAYING THEY WANT TO SEND SOMEONE TO MY HOUSE EVERY DAY...
LIKE A "VISITING NURSE"? WHO'S PAYING FOR IT?
HIS INSURANCE, BUT...
DO IT! I WAITED TOO LONG. AND YOU'RE PROBABLY RIGHT ABOUT THE DRUGS. A FEW WEEKS BACK, MY HUSBAND WASN'T SURE IF HE WAS A REAL PERSON OR WHAT HIS NAME WAS.

LET'S CATCH UP WITH THE REST OF THE WORLD. BY NOW, SOME 600 KUWAITI OIL WELLS ARE SMOKING WITH FIRES THAT MAY BURN UNTIL 1993.

JOYCE AND HARVEY COULDN'T FOLLOW THE COURSE OF THE PERSIAN GULF WAR VERY CLOSELY BECAUSE, WELL, YOU KNOW... BUT, JOYCE AND HER YOUNG FRIENDS HAVE BEEN STICKING TOGETHER.

BESIDES COMPUTER MAIL AND OCCASIONAL PHONE CALLS, THEY SEND EACH OTHER PHOTOS AND TAPES. NO ONE HAS BEEN HAVING AN EASY TIME. THERE ARE PROBLEMS WITH FAMILIES, FRIENDS, SCHOOL AND THE LIKE...

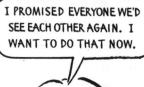

WHAT'S THAT YOU'RE PLAYING?

MUSIC FROM DANA'S PART OF THE WORLD.

HARVEY, I'VE BEEN THINKING... WE HAVE THIS BIG HOUSE, NOW. DANA HAS BEEN TRYING TO SAVE ENOUGH MONEY TO COME OVER HERE FOR THE REST OF THE SUMMER AND KIMMIE AND JU ARE STUCK IN LOS ANGELES. YOU REALLY LIKED JESSIE, WHEN SHE CAME UP LAST SUMMER. SHE SAYS HER PARENTS WILL LET HER USE THEIR VAN, IF...

I WANT TO HELP DANA WITH THE REST OF HER TICKET MONEY. I'LL USE THE LAST OF HER DISCOUNT COUPONS TO GET HER A GOOD FARE. GREYHOUND HAS THIRTY-DAY COAST-TO-COAST ANYWHERE TICKETS FOR SIXTY-EIGHT BUCKS. WE CAN COVER A COUPLE OF THOSE AND KNOCK OFF EVEN MORE MONEY BY BRINGING DANA IN BY WAY OF BOSTON. SHE AND SAROEUM CAN RIDE DOWN TOGETHER.

I MEAN, THEY'VE ALL GOT STURDY TEENAGED BUTTS AND ARE YOUNG ENOUGH TO THINK "RIDING THE DOG" IS AN ADVENTURE. THEY CAN PACK SANDWICHES, AND BESIDES...

I PROMISED EVERYONE WE'D SEE EACH OTHER AGAIN. I WANT TO DO THAT NOW.

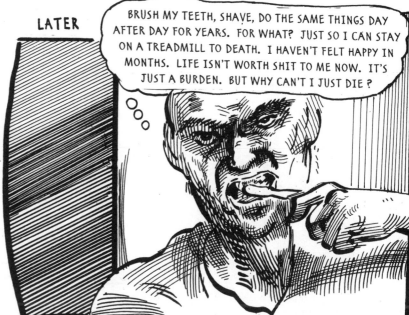

OK, OK... BUT, JUST REMEMBER I'M REALLY FUCKED. I'M NOT GONNA BE A LOT OF FUN FOR THE KIDS TO BE AROUND IF I'M A BASKET CASE. I JUST DON'T WANNA RUIN IT FOR EVERYONE, AFTER THEY'VE TRAVELED SO FAR TO GET HERE.

LATER

BRUSH MY TEETH, SHAVE, DO THE SAME THINGS DAY AFTER DAY FOR YEARS. FOR WHAT? JUST SO I CAN STAY ON A TREADMILL TO DEATH. I HAVEN'T FELT HAPPY IN MONTHS. LIFE ISN'T WORTH SHIT TO ME NOW. IT'S JUST A BURDEN. BUT WHY CAN'T I JUST DIE?

A **FEW DAYS** AFTER, JOYCE PUTS HARVEY ON THE PHONE TO TALK TO SUY KHIM

I'M PRETTY SICK NOW, KIMMIE, AND I SUPPOSE I MIGHT STILL BE WHEN YOU VISIT. I HOPE YOU AND JU DON'T TAKE IT PERSONALLY IF I'M NOT MUCH FUN.

OH, NO, HARVEY. YOU HAVE A PROBLEM NOW AND I HAVE PROBLEMS, TOO. MAYBE OUR PROBLEMS ARE DIFFERENT, BUT...

WHEN YOU HAVE A FRIEND, OR TALK TO SOMEONE YOU CAN COUNT ON, THEN YOUR PROBLEM GETS SMALLER. YES, YOU WILL STILL HAVE **SOME** PROBLEM, BUT YOU'LL FEEL RELIEF. WE CAN HELP EACH OTHER.

AFTER HARVEY HAS HANDED THE PHONE BACK TO JOYCE

I DON'T KNOW WHAT YOU SAID, BUT HE'S GOT THE BIGGEST SMILE ON HIS FACE... I THINK YOU'LL LIKE EACH OTHER. SO, WHAT'S GOING ON WITH YOU?

I NEED YOUR ADVICE ABOUT SOMETHING.

SURE, GO AHEAD...

I'VE BEEN THINKING ABOUT WHEN I WAS LITTLE, HOW I HAD NO DOLL, NO TOY, NO PLAY. AND I WANT TO KNOW...

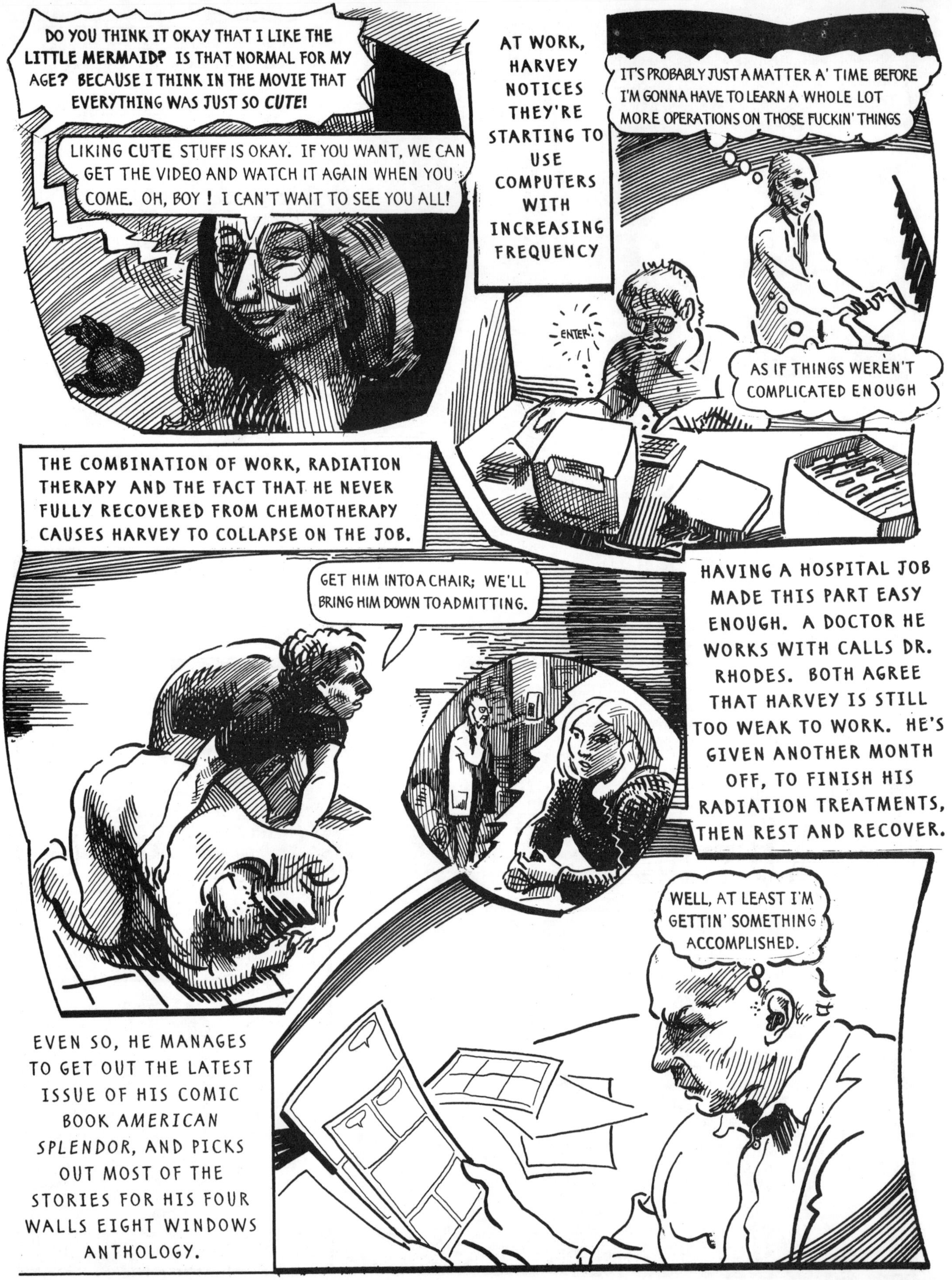

DO YOU THINK IT OKAY THAT I LIKE THE LITTLE MERMAID? IS THAT NORMAL FOR MY AGE? BECAUSE I THINK IN THE MOVIE THAT EVERYTHING WAS JUST SO CUTE!
LIKING CUTE STUFF IS OKAY. IF YOU WANT, WE CAN GET THE VIDEO AND WATCH IT AGAIN WHEN YOU COME. OH, BOY ! I CAN'T WAIT TO SEE YOU ALL!
AT WORK, HARVEY NOTICES THEY'RE STARTING TO USE COMPUTERS WITH INCREASING FREQUENCY
IT'S PROBABLY JUST A MATTER A' TIME BEFORE I'M GONNA HAVE TO LEARN A WHOLE LOT MORE OPERATIONS ON THOSE FUCKIN' THINGS
ENTER!
AS IF THINGS WEREN'T COMPLICATED ENOUGH
THE COMBINATION OF WORK, RADIATION THERAPY AND THE FACT THAT HE NEVER FULLY RECOVERED FROM CHEMOTHERAPY CAUSES HARVEY TO COLLAPSE ON THE JOB.
GET HIM INTO A CHAIR; WE'LL BRING HIM DOWN TO ADMITTING.
HAVING A HOSPITAL JOB MADE THIS PART EASY ENOUGH. A DOCTOR HE WORKS WITH CALLS DR. RHODES. BOTH AGREE THAT HARVEY IS STILL TOO WEAK TO WORK. HE'S GIVEN ANOTHER MONTH OFF, TO FINISH HIS RADIATION TREATMENTS, THEN REST AND RECOVER.
WELL, AT LEAST I'M GETTIN' SOMETHING ACCOMPLISHED.
EVEN SO, HE MANAGES TO GET OUT THE LATEST ISSUE OF HIS COMIC BOOK AMERICAN SPLENDOR, AND PICKS OUT MOST OF THE STORIES FOR HIS FOUR WALLS EIGHT WINDOWS ANTHOLOGY.

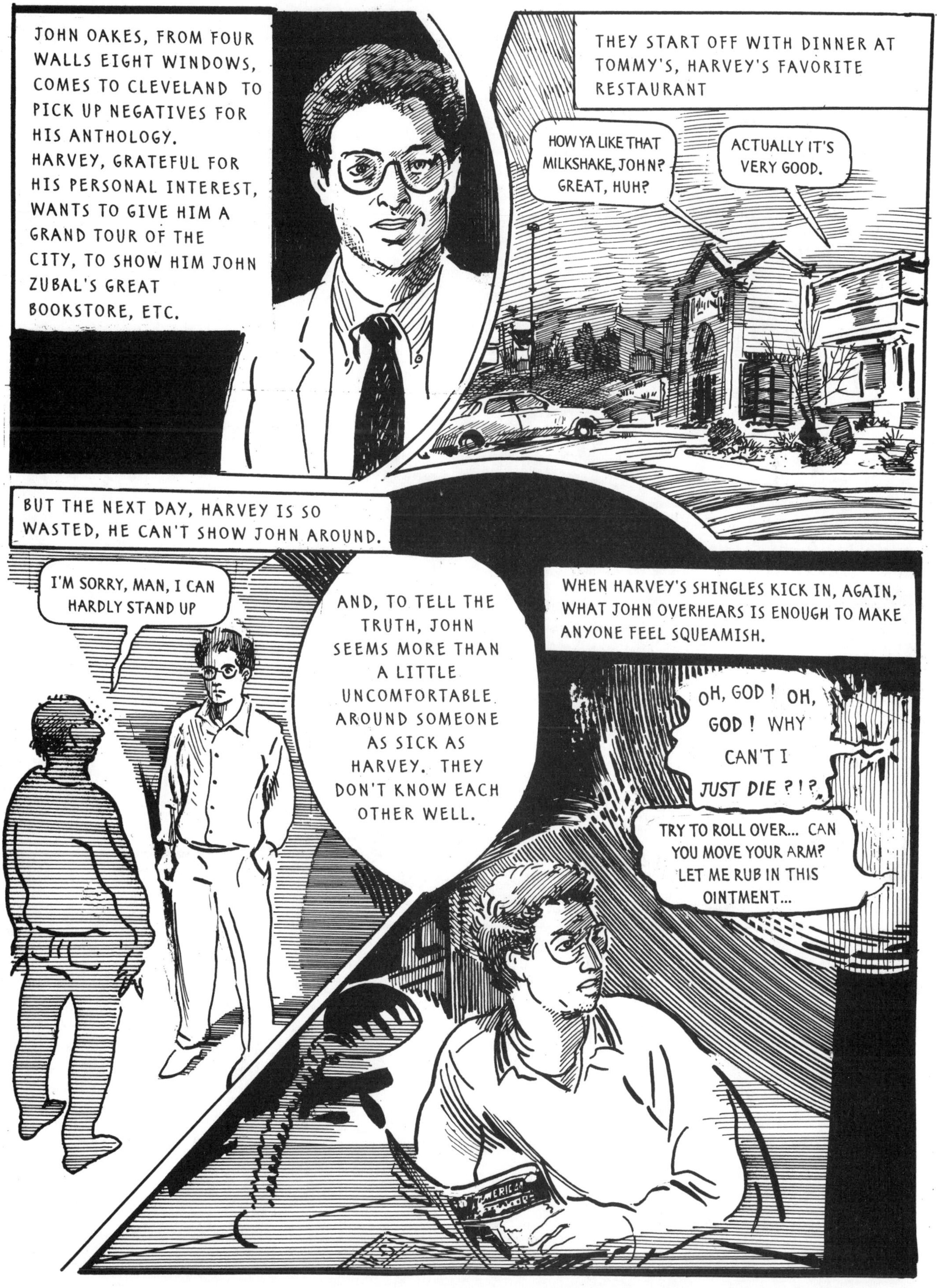
JOHN OAKES, FROM FOUR WALLS EIGHT WINDOWS, COMES TO CLEVELAND TO PICK UP NEGATIVES FOR HIS ANTHOLOGY. HARVEY, GRATEFUL FOR HIS PERSONAL INTEREST, WANTS TO GIVE HIM A GRAND TOUR OF THE CITY, TO SHOW HIM JOHN ZUBAL'S GREAT BOOKSTORE, ETC.
THEY START OFF WITH DINNER AT TOMMY'S, HARVEY'S FAVORITE RESTAURANT
HOW YA LIKE THAT MILKSHAKE, JOHN? GREAT, HUH?
ACTUALLY IT'S VERY GOOD.
BUT THE NEXT DAY, HARVEY IS SO WASTED, HE CAN'T SHOW JOHN AROUND.
I'M SORRY, MAN, I CAN HARDLY STAND UP
AND, TO TELL THE TRUTH, JOHN SEEMS MORE THAN A LITTLE UNCOMFORTABLE AROUND SOMEONE AS SICK AS HARVEY. THEY DON'T KNOW EACH OTHER WELL.
WHEN HARVEY'S SHINGLES KICK IN, AGAIN, WHAT JOHN OVERHEARS IS ENOUGH TO MAKE ANYONE FEEL SQUEAMISH.
OH, GOD! OH, GOD! WHY CAN'T I JUST DIE?!?
TRY TO ROLL OVER... CAN YOU MOVE YOUR ARM? LET ME RUB IN THIS OINTMENT...

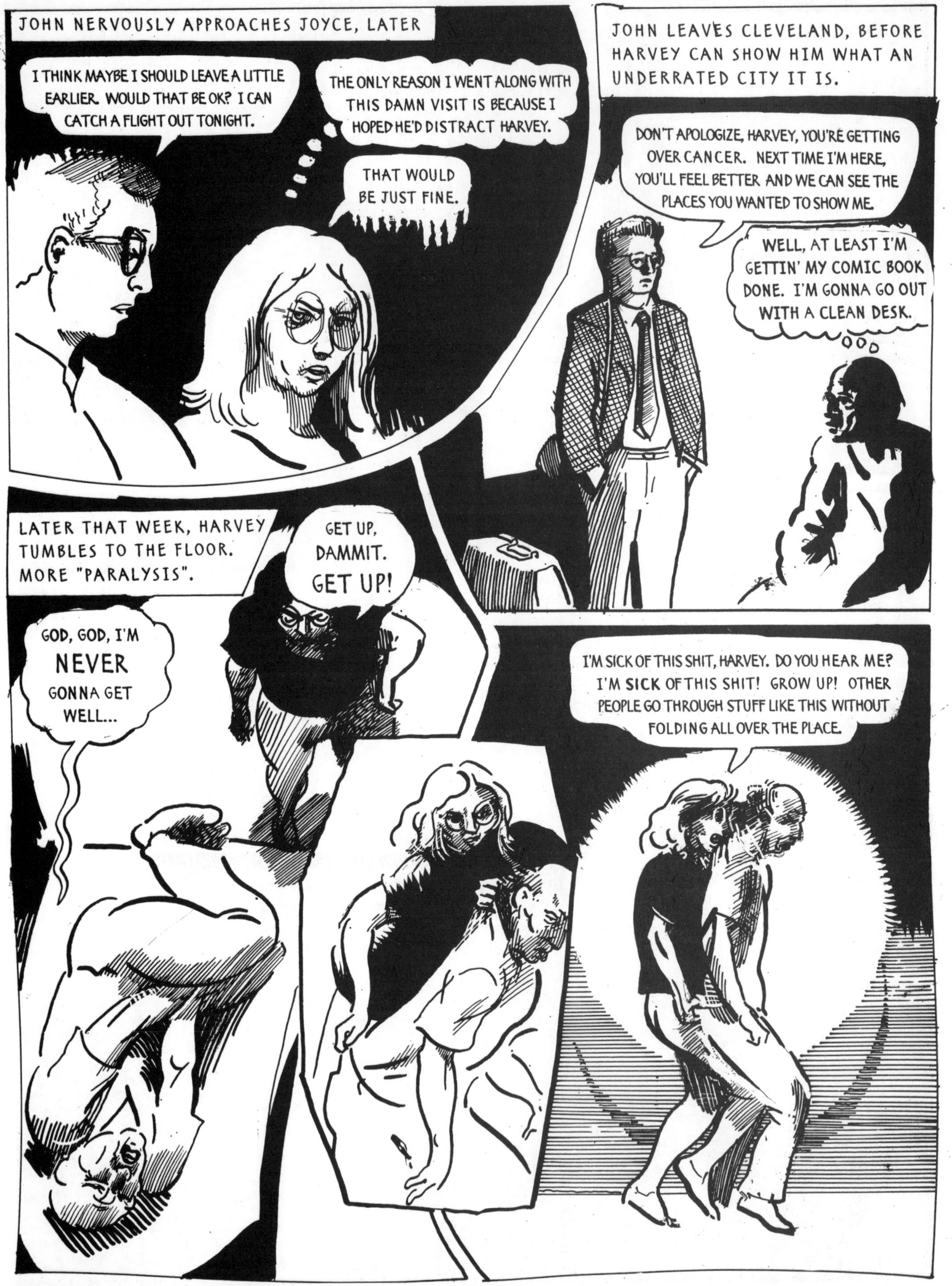

JOHN NERVOUSLY APPROACHES JOYCE, LATER
I THINK MAYBE I SHOULD LEAVE A LITTLE EARLIER. WOULD THAT BE OK? I CAN CATCH A FLIGHT OUT TONIGHT.
THE ONLY REASON I WENT ALONG WITH THIS DAMN VISIT IS BECAUSE I HOPED HE'D DISTRACT HARVEY.
THAT WOULD BE JUST FINE.
JOHN LEAVES CLEVELAND, BEFORE HARVEY CAN SHOW HIM WHAT AN UNDERRATED CITY IT IS.
DON'T APOLOGIZE, HARVEY, YOU'RE GETTING OVER CANCER. NEXT TIME I'M HERE, YOU'LL FEEL BETTER AND WE CAN SEE THE PLACES YOU WANTED TO SHOW ME.
WELL, AT LEAST I'M GETTIN' MY COMIC BOOK DONE. I'M GONNA GO OUT WITH A CLEAN DESK.
LATER THAT WEEK, HARVEY TUMBLES TO THE FLOOR. MORE "PARALYSIS".
GET UP, DAMMIT. GET UP!
GOD, GOD, I'M NEVER GONNA GET WELL...
I'M SICK OF THIS SHIT, HARVEY. DO YOU HEAR ME? I'M SICK OF THIS SHIT! GROW UP! OTHER PEOPLE GO THROUGH STUFF LIKE THIS WITHOUT FOLDING ALL OVER THE PLACE.

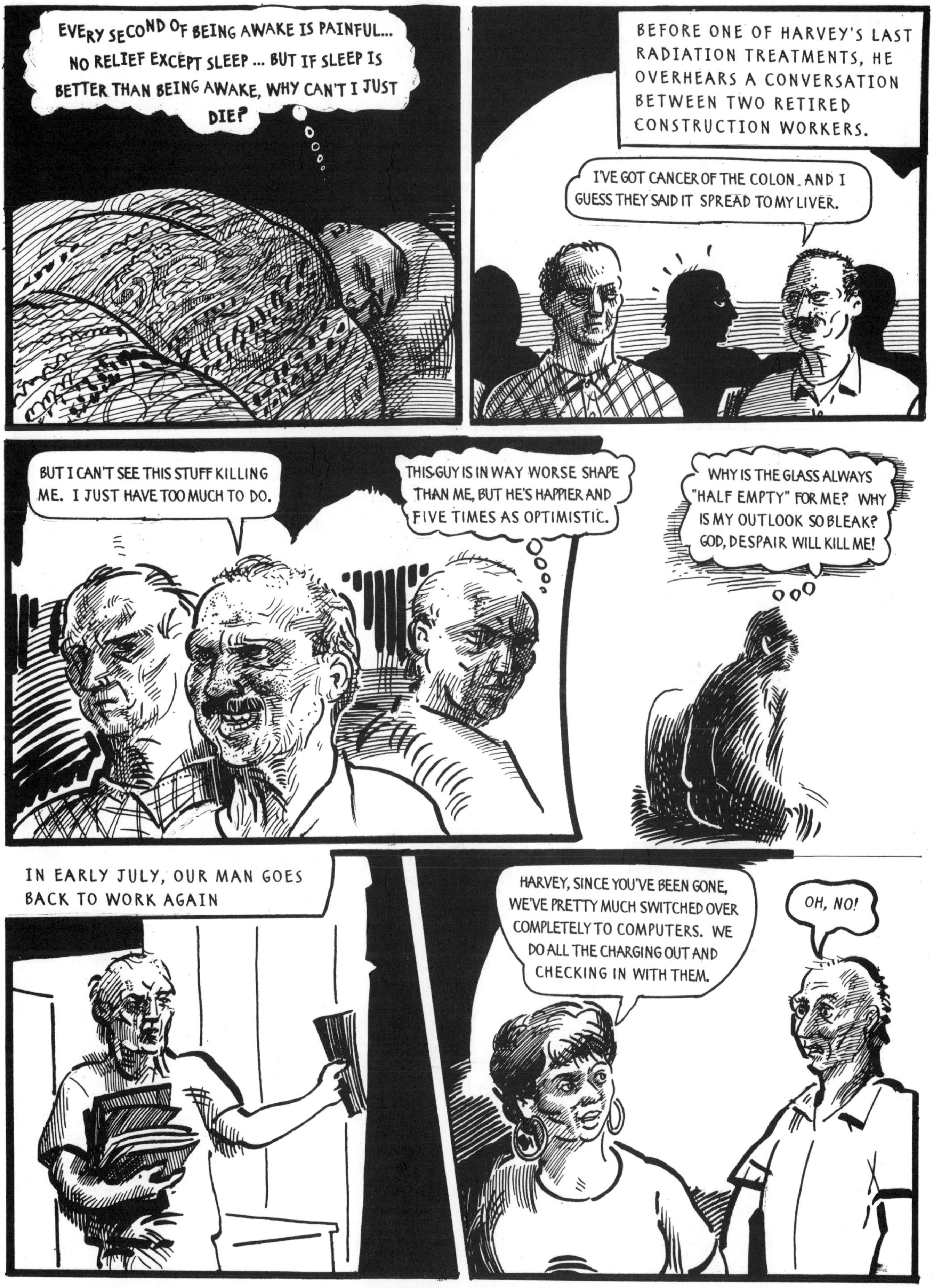

EVERY SECOND OF BEING AWAKE IS PAINFUL... NO RELIEF EXCEPT SLEEP ... BUT IF SLEEP IS BETTER THAN BEING AWAKE, WHY CAN'T I JUST DIE?
BEFORE ONE OF HARVEY'S LAST RADIATION TREATMENTS, HE OVERHEARS A CONVERSATION BETWEEN TWO RETIRED CONSTRUCTION WORKERS.
I'VE GOT CANCER OF THE COLON. AND I GUESS THEY SAID IT SPREAD TO MY LIVER.
BUT I CAN'T SEE THIS STUFF KILLING ME. I JUST HAVE TOO MUCH TO DO.
THIS GUY IS IN WAY WORSE SHAPE THAN ME, BUT HE'S HAPPIER AND FIVE TIMES AS OPTIMISTIC.
WHY IS THE GLASS ALWAYS "HALF EMPTY" FOR ME? WHY IS MY OUTLOOK SO BLEAK? GOD, DESPAIR WILL KILL ME!
IN EARLY JULY, OUR MAN GOES BACK TO WORK AGAIN
HARVEY, SINCE YOU'VE BEEN GONE, WE'VE PRETTY MUCH SWITCHED OVER COMPLETELY TO COMPUTERS. WE DO ALL THE CHARGING OUT AND CHECKING IN WITH THEM.
OH, NO!

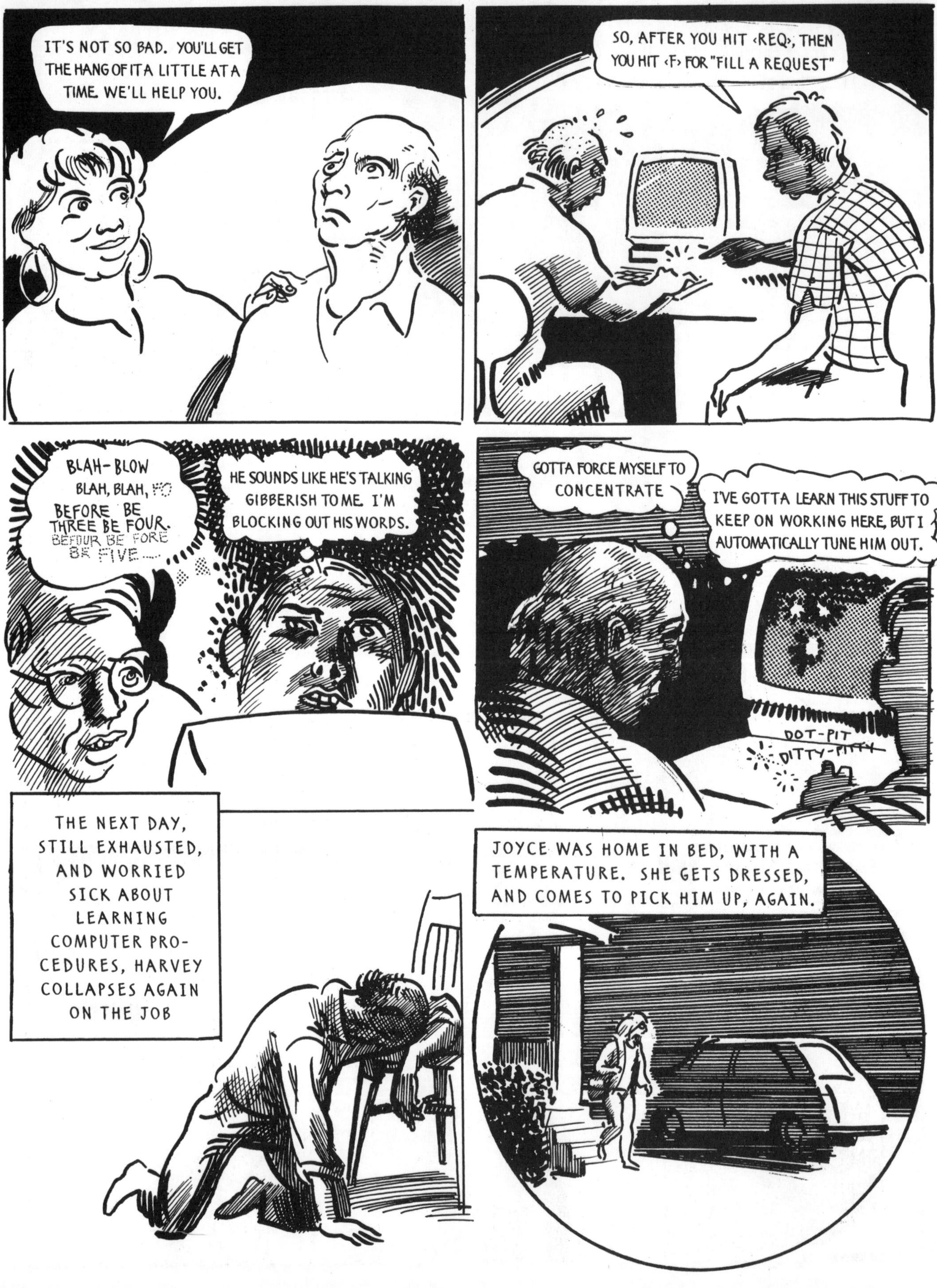

IT'S NOT SO BAD. YOU'LL GET THE HANG OF IT A LITTLE AT A TIME. WE'LL HELP YOU.
SO, AFTER YOU HIT ‹REQ›, THEN YOU HIT ‹F› FOR "FILL A REQUEST"
BLAH-BLOW BLAH, BLAH, FO BEFORE BE THREE BE FOUR. BEFOUR BE FORE BE FIVE...
HE SOUNDS LIKE HE'S TALKING GIBBERISH TO ME. I'M BLOCKING OUT HIS WORDS.
GOTTA FORCE MYSELF TO CONCENTRATE
I'VE GOTTA LEARN THIS STUFF TO KEEP ON WORKING HERE, BUT I AUTOMATICALLY TUNE HIM OUT.
DOT-PIT
DITTY-PITTY
THE NEXT DAY, STILL EXHAUSTED, AND WORRIED SICK ABOUT LEARNING COMPUTER PRO-CEDURES, HARVEY COLLAPSES AGAIN ON THE JOB
JOYCE WAS HOME IN BED, WITH A TEMPERATURE. SHE GETS DRESSED, AND COMES TO PICK HIM UP, AGAIN.

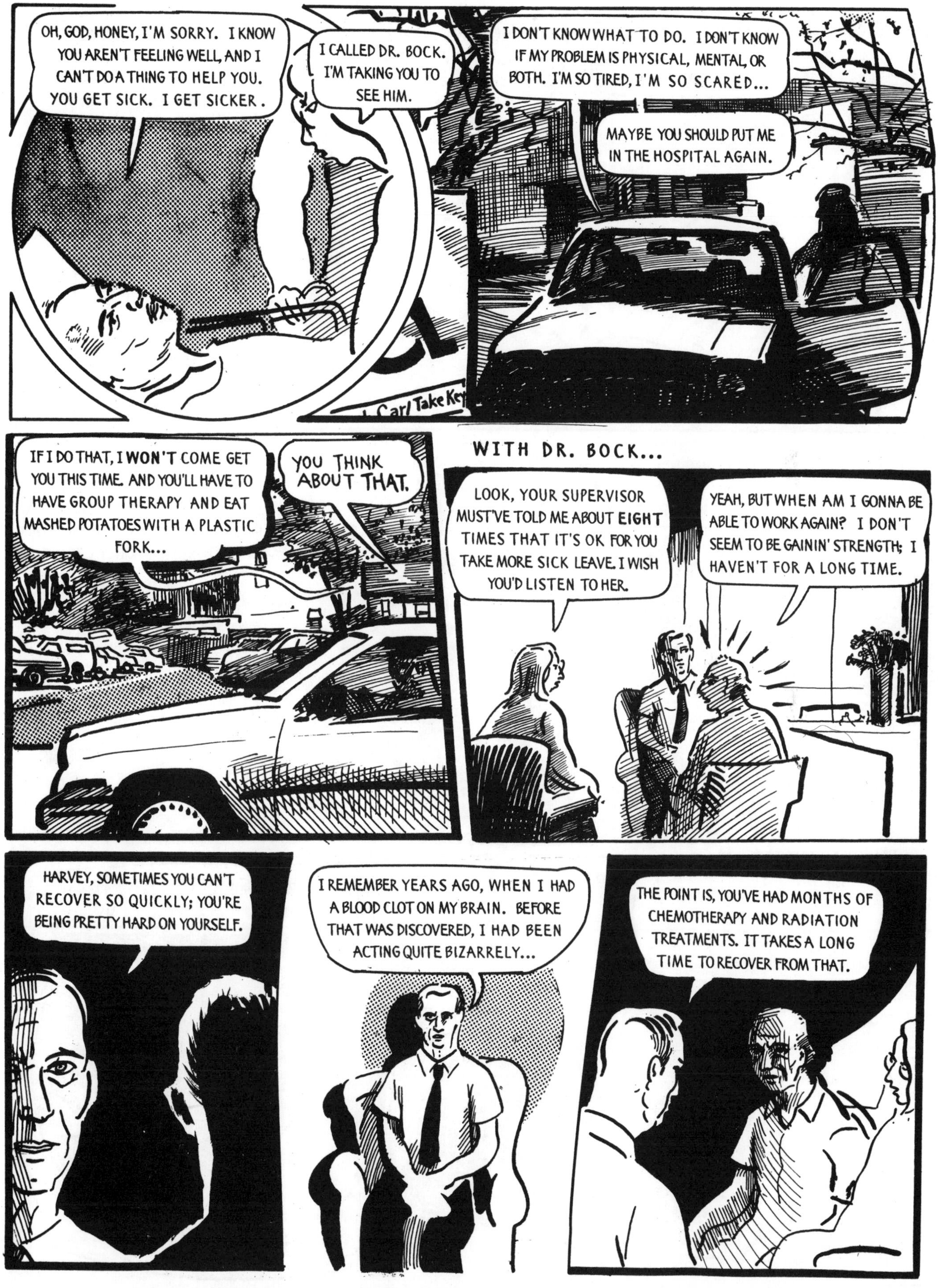
OH, GOD, HONEY, I'M SORRY. I KNOW YOU AREN'T FEELING WELL, AND I CAN'T DO A THING TO HELP YOU. YOU GET SICK. I GET SICKER.
I CALLED DR. BOCK. I'M TAKING YOU TO SEE HIM.
I DON'T KNOW WHAT TO DO. I DON'T KNOW IF MY PROBLEM IS PHYSICAL, MENTAL, OR BOTH. I'M SO TIRED, I'M SO SCARED...
MAYBE YOU SHOULD PUT ME IN THE HOSPITAL AGAIN.
IF I DO THAT, I WON'T COME GET YOU THIS TIME. AND YOU'LL HAVE TO HAVE GROUP THERAPY AND EAT MASHED POTATOES WITH A PLASTIC FORK...
YOU THINK ABOUT THAT.
WITH DR. BOCK...
LOOK, YOUR SUPERVISOR MUST'VE TOLD ME ABOUT EIGHT TIMES THAT IT'S OK FOR YOU TAKE MORE SICK LEAVE. I WISH YOU'D LISTEN TO HER.
YEAH, BUT WHEN AM I GONNA BE ABLE TO WORK AGAIN? I DON'T SEEM TO BE GAININ' STRENGTH; I HAVEN'T FOR A LONG TIME.
HARVEY, SOMETIMES YOU CAN'T RECOVER SO QUICKLY; YOU'RE BEING PRETTY HARD ON YOURSELF.
I REMEMBER YEARS AGO, WHEN I HAD A BLOOD CLOT ON MY BRAIN. BEFORE THAT WAS DISCOVERED, I HAD BEEN ACTING QUITE BIZARRELY...
THE POINT IS, YOU'VE HAD MONTHS OF CHEMOTHERAPY AND RADIATION TREATMENTS. IT TAKES A LONG TIME TO RECOVER FROM THAT.

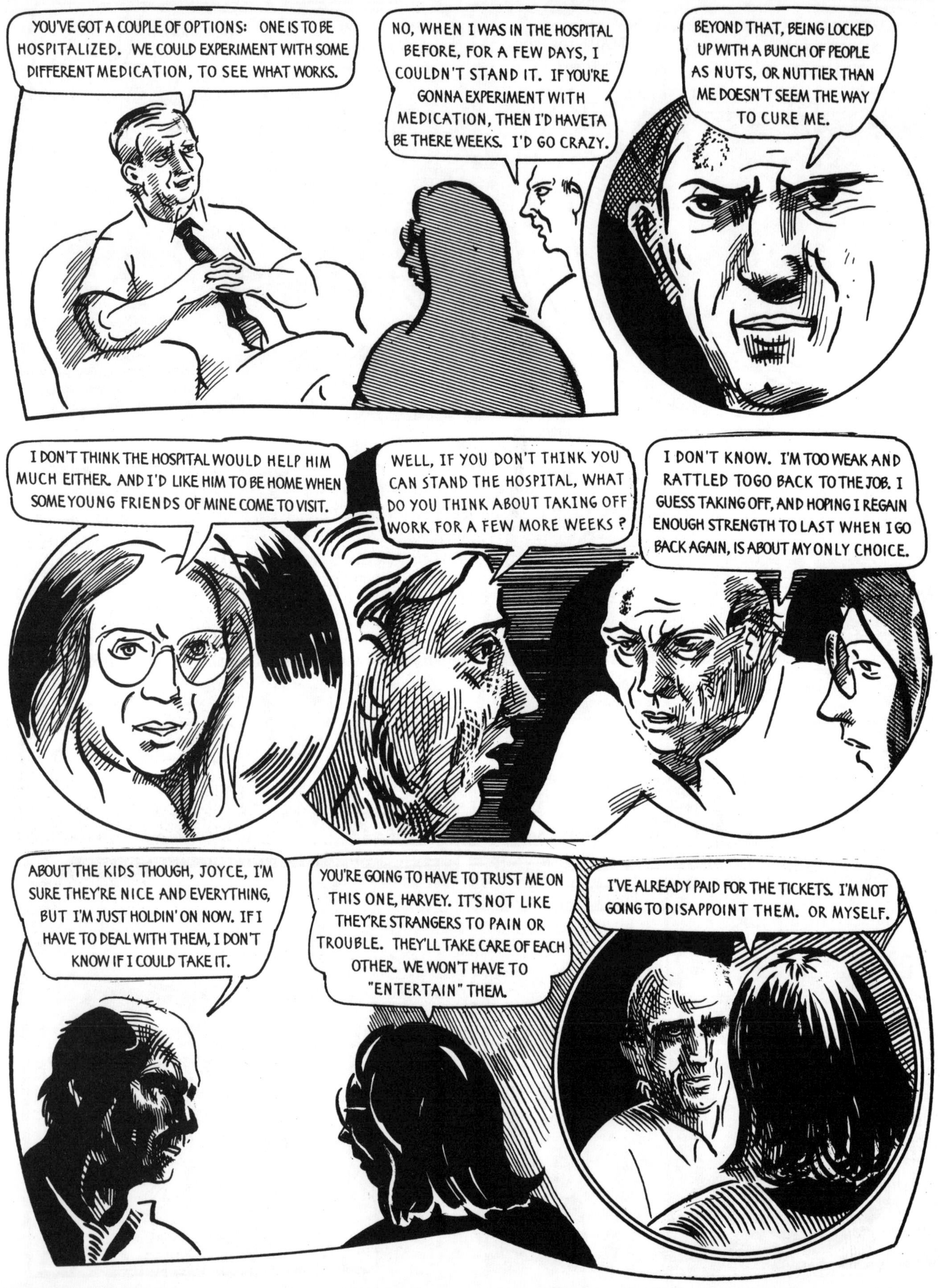
YOU'VE GOT A COUPLE OF OPTIONS: ONE IS TO BE HOSPITALIZED. WE COULD EXPERIMENT WITH SOME DIFFERENT MEDICATION, TO SEE WHAT WORKS.
NO, WHEN I WAS IN THE HOSPITAL BEFORE, FOR A FEW DAYS, I COULDN'T STAND IT. IF YOU'RE GONNA EXPERIMENT WITH MEDICATION, THEN I'D HAVETA BE THERE WEEKS. I'D GO CRAZY.
BEYOND THAT, BEING LOCKED UP WITH A BUNCH OF PEOPLE AS NUTS, OR NUTTIER THAN ME DOESN'T SEEM THE WAY TO CURE ME.
I DON'T THINK THE HOSPITAL WOULD HELP HIM MUCH EITHER. AND I'D LIKE HIM TO BE HOME WHEN SOME YOUNG FRIENDS OF MINE COME TO VISIT.
WELL, IF YOU DON'T THINK YOU CAN STAND THE HOSPITAL, WHAT DO YOU THINK ABOUT TAKING OFF WORK FOR A FEW MORE WEEKS?
I DON'T KNOW. I'M TOO WEAK AND RATTLED TO GO BACK TO THE JOB. I GUESS TAKING OFF, AND HOPING I REGAIN ENOUGH STRENGTH TO LAST WHEN I GO BACK AGAIN, IS ABOUT MY ONLY CHOICE.
ABOUT THE KIDS THOUGH, JOYCE, I'M SURE THEY'RE NICE AND EVERYTHING, BUT I'M JUST HOLDIN' ON NOW. IF I HAVE TO DEAL WITH THEM, I DON'T KNOW IF I COULD TAKE IT.
YOU'RE GOING TO HAVE TO TRUST ME ON THIS ONE, HARVEY. IT'S NOT LIKE THEY'RE STRANGERS TO PAIN OR TROUBLE. THEY'LL TAKE CARE OF EACH OTHER. WE WON'T HAVE TO "ENTERTAIN" THEM.
I'VE ALREADY PAID FOR THE TICKETS. I'M NOT GOING TO DISAPPOINT THEM. OR MYSELF.

SO, HARVEY TAKES OFF WORK ANOTHER FIVE WEEKS. NOW, HE'S GOT SOMETHING ELSE TO WORRY ABOUT.

ARE YOU SURE YOU CAN'T POSTPONE THE KIDS' VISITS? CUZ...

YES, I'M SURE I CAN'T POSTPONE THEM.

HARVEY, YOU'RE NOT GOING TO BE WELL UNTIL YOU'RE ABLE TO THINK ABOUT SOMEONE BESIDES YOURSELF.

BUT, HARVEY'S NOT THE ONLY ONE WORRIED ABOUT JOYCE'S PLANS...

THIS IS GREAT. THANKS.

YOU'RE LOOKING MUCH BETTER, BUT...

KARSTIN HAS KNOWN HARVEY FOR A LONG TIME. SHE'S A HIGH SCHOOL PSYCHOLOGIST. EVERY SO OFTEN SHE SENDS HER SON OR DAUGHTER OVER WITH SOME OF WHATEVER SHE'S BEEN BAKING. TODAY, KARSTIN COMES BY HERSELF, WITH A QUICHE.

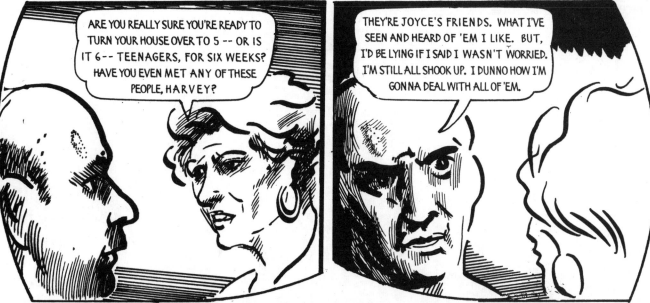

ARE YOU REALLY SURE YOU'RE READY TO TURN YOUR HOUSE OVER TO 5 -- OR IS IT 6-- TEENAGERS, FOR SIX WEEKS? HAVE YOU EVEN MET ANY OF THESE PEOPLE, HARVEY?

THEY'RE JOYCE'S FRIENDS. WHAT I'VE SEEN AND HEARD OF 'EM I LIKE. BUT, I'D BE LYING IF I SAID I WASN'T WORRIED. I'M STILL ALL SHOOK UP. I DUNNO HOW I'M GONNA DEAL WITH ALL OF 'EM.

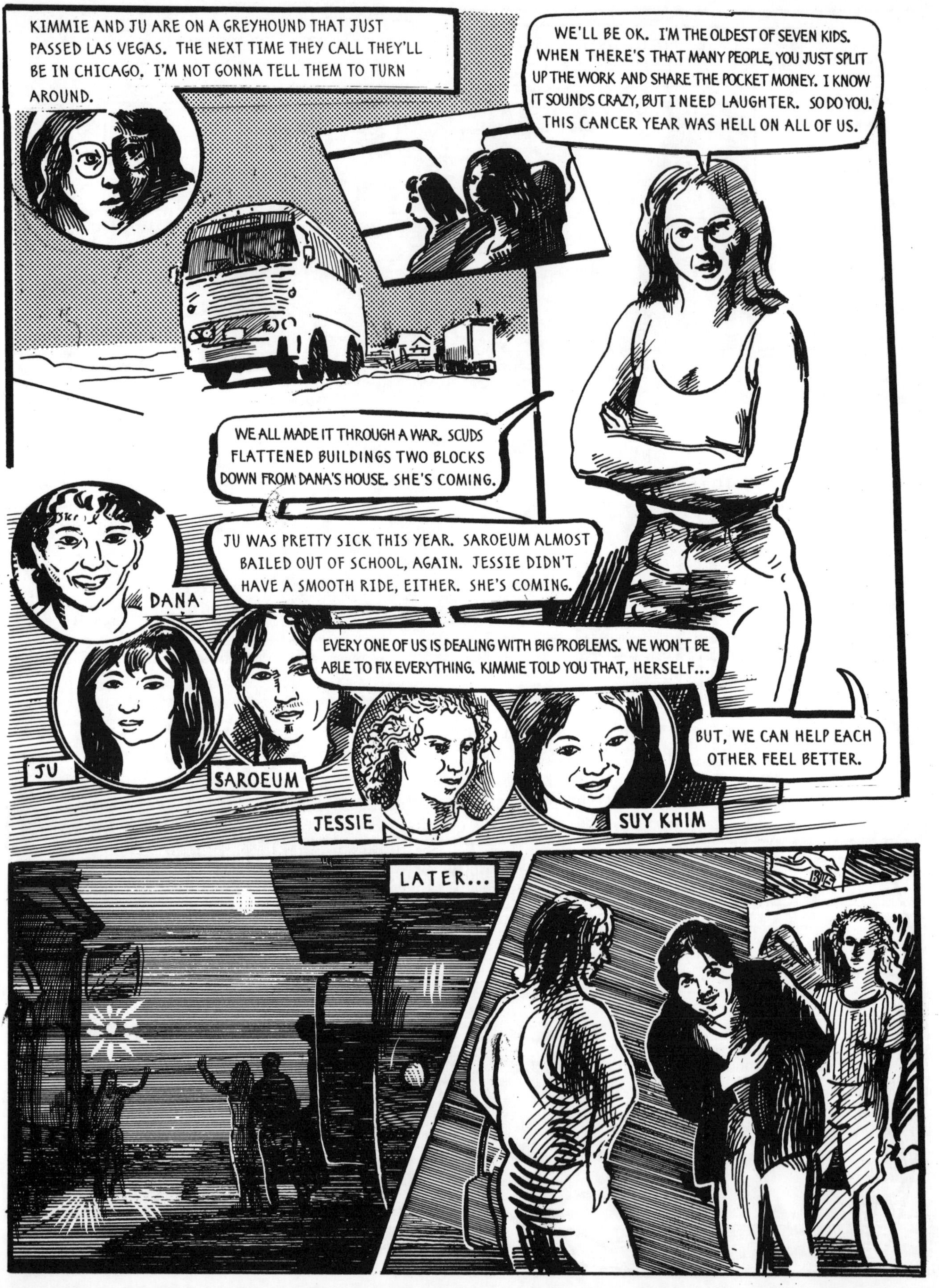
KIMMIE AND JU ARE ON A GREYHOUND THAT JUST PASSED LAS VEGAS. THE NEXT TIME THEY CALL THEY'LL BE IN CHICAGO. I'M NOT GONNA TELL THEM TO TURN AROUND.
WE'LL BE OK. I'M THE OLDEST OF SEVEN KIDS. WHEN THERE'S THAT MANY PEOPLE, YOU JUST SPLIT UP THE WORK AND SHARE THE POCKET MONEY. I KNOW IT SOUNDS CRAZY, BUT I NEED LAUGHTER. SO DO YOU. THIS CANCER YEAR WAS HELL ON ALL OF US.
WE ALL MADE IT THROUGH A WAR. SCUDS FLATTENED BUILDINGS TWO BLOCKS DOWN FROM DANA'S HOUSE. SHE'S COMING.
JU WAS PRETTY SICK THIS YEAR. SAROEUM ALMOST BAILED OUT OF SCHOOL, AGAIN. JESSIE DIDN'T HAVE A SMOOTH RIDE, EITHER. SHE'S COMING.
EVERY ONE OF US IS DEALING WITH BIG PROBLEMS. WE WON'T BE ABLE TO FIX EVERYTHING. KIMMIE TOLD YOU THAT, HERSELF...
BUT, WE CAN HELP EACH OTHER FEEL BETTER.
DANA
JU
SAROEUM
JESSIE
SUY KHIM
LATER...

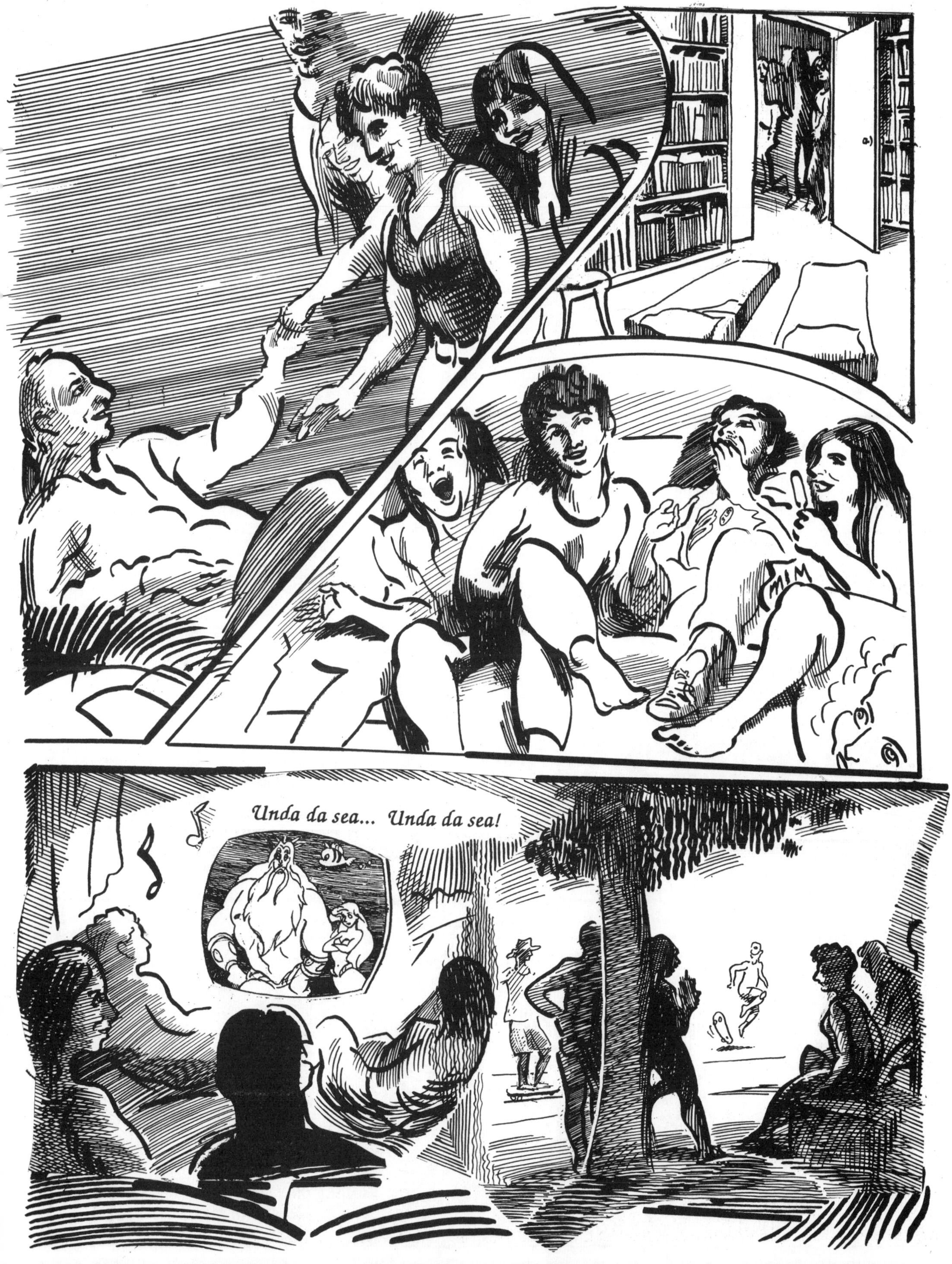
Unda da sea... Unda da sea!

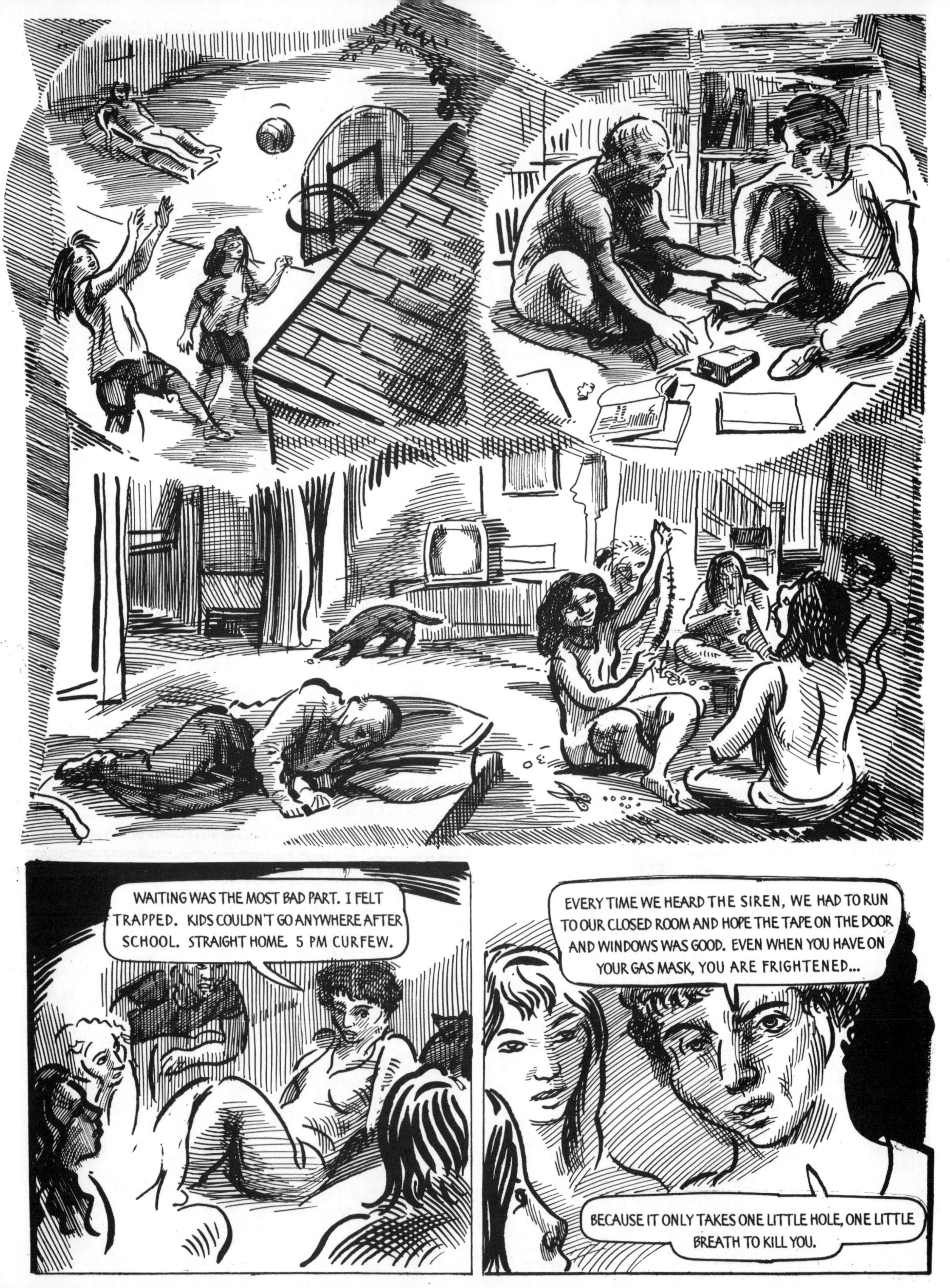
WAITING WAS THE MOST BAD PART. I FELT TRAPPED. KIDS COULDN'T GO ANYWHERE AFTER SCHOOL. STRAIGHT HOME. 5 PM CURFEW.
EVERY TIME WE HEARD THE SIREN, WE HAD TO RUN TO OUR CLOSED ROOM AND HOPE THE TAPE ON THE DOOR AND WINDOWS WAS GOOD. EVEN WHEN YOU HAVE ON YOUR GAS MASK, YOU ARE FRIGHTENED...
BECAUSE IT ONLY TAKES ONE LITTLE HOLE, ONE LITTLE BREATH TO KILL YOU.

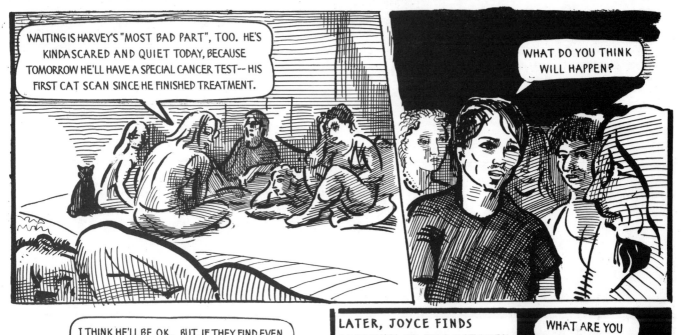

WAITING IS HARVEY'S "MOST BAD PART", TOO. HE'S KINDA SCARED AND QUIET TODAY, BECAUSE TOMORROW HE'LL HAVE A SPECIAL CANCER TEST-- HIS FIRST CAT SCAN SINCE HE FINISHED TREATMENT.

WHAT DO YOU THINK WILL HAPPEN?

I THINK HE'LL BE OK. BUT, IF THEY FIND EVEN THE TINIEST SPECK, JUST A TRACE OF CANCER, HE'LL HAVE TO GO THROUGH A WHOLE NEW TREATMENT, ALL OVER AGAIN.

LATER, JOYCE FINDS SAROEUM IN THE KITCHEN.

WHAT ARE YOU DOING?

MAKING SOMETHING FOR HARVEY'S BREAKFAST, TOMORROW. IT'S CAMBODIAN FOOD. TO GIVE HIM COURAGE AND HELP HIM FEEL BETTER.

SEVERAL ANXIOUS DAYS LATER, THE PHONE RINGS...

HARVEY'S NAPPING UPSTAIRS, BUT, GET HIM UP. WAKE HIM AND GET HIM DOWN HERE.

WHAT IZZIT?

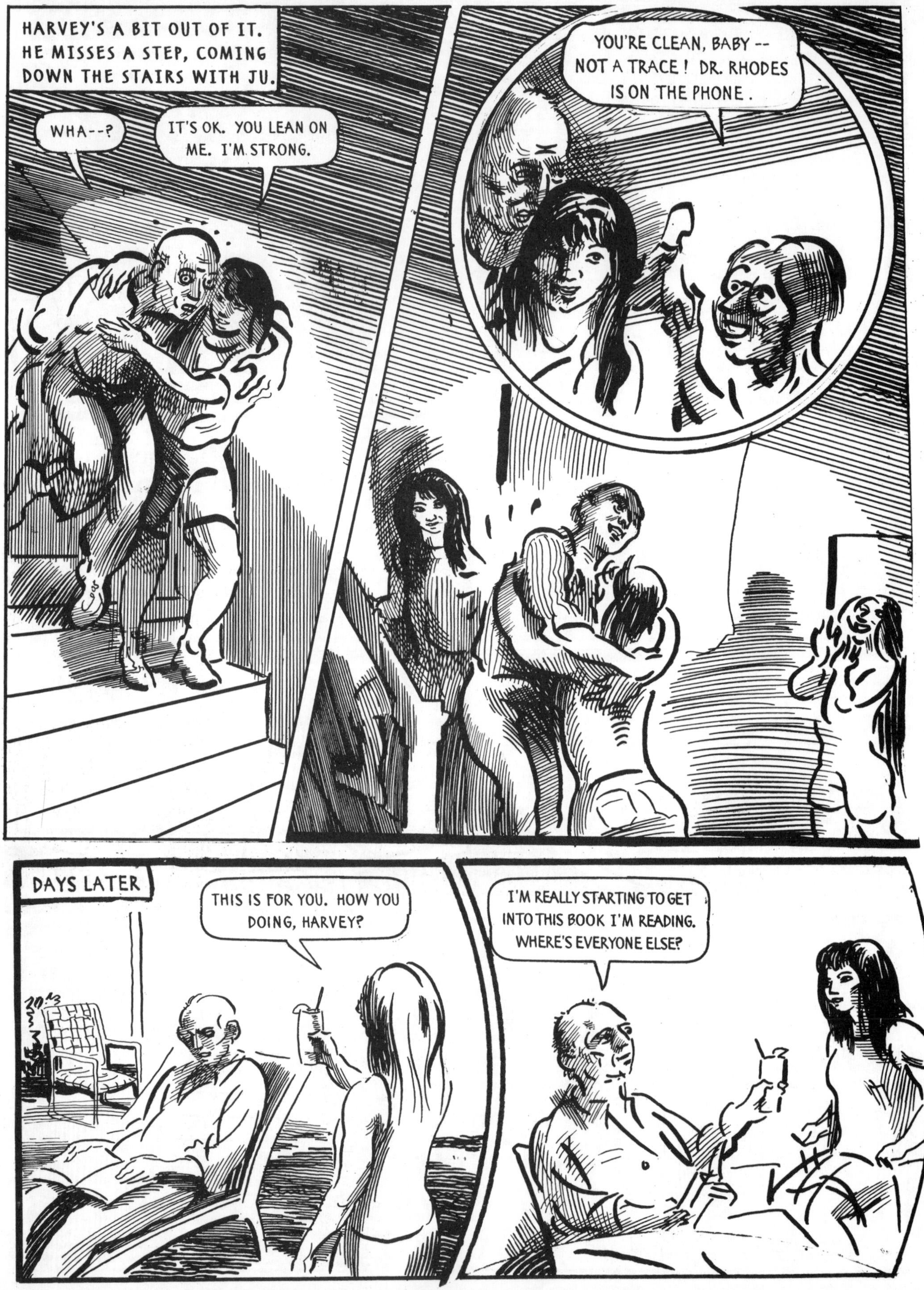
HARVEY'S A BIT OUT OF IT. HE MISSES A STEP, COMING DOWN THE STAIRS WITH JU.
WHA--?
IT'S OK. YOU LEAN ON ME. I'M STRONG.
YOU'RE CLEAN, BABY -- NOT A TRACE! DR. RHODES IS ON THE PHONE.
DAYS LATER
THIS IS FOR YOU. HOW YOU DOING, HARVEY?
I'M REALLY STARTING TO GET INTO THIS BOOK I'M READING. WHERE'S EVERYONE ELSE?

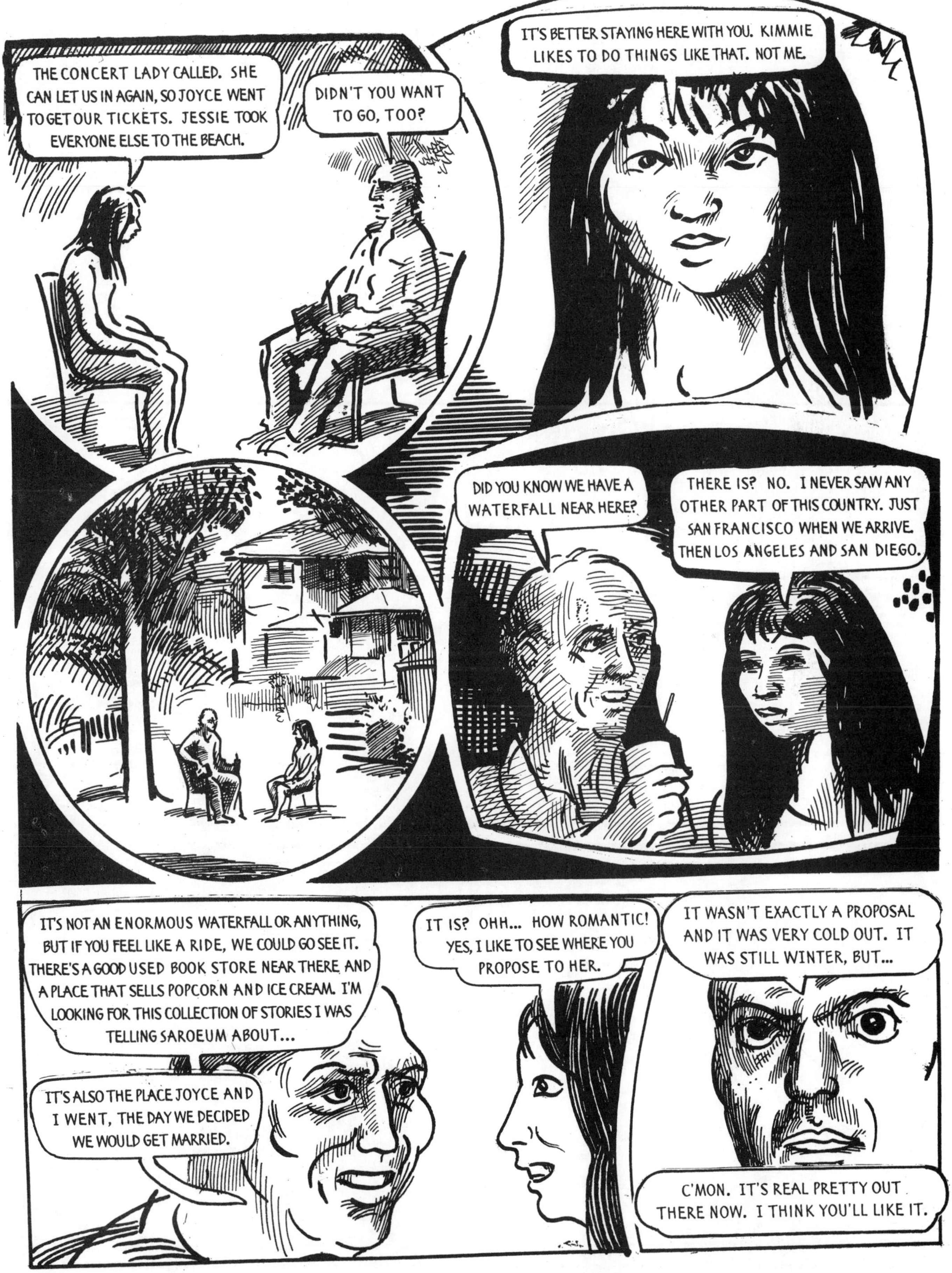
THE CONCERT LADY CALLED. SHE CAN LET US IN AGAIN, SO JOYCE WENT TO GET OUR TICKETS. JESSIE TOOK EVERYONE ELSE TO THE BEACH.
DIDN'T YOU WANT TO GO, TOO?
IT'S BETTER STAYING HERE WITH YOU. KIMMIE LIKES TO DO THINGS LIKE THAT. NOT ME.
DID YOU KNOW WE HAVE A WATERFALL NEAR HERE?
THERE IS? NO. I NEVER SAW ANY OTHER PART OF THIS COUNTRY. JUST SAN FRANCISCO WHEN WE ARRIVE. THEN LOS ANGELES AND SAN DIEGO.
IT'S NOT AN ENORMOUS WATERFALL OR ANYTHING, BUT IF YOU FEEL LIKE A RIDE, WE COULD GO SEE IT. THERE'S A GOOD USED BOOK STORE NEAR THERE AND A PLACE THAT SELLS POPCORN AND ICE CREAM. I'M LOOKING FOR THIS COLLECTION OF STORIES I WAS TELLING SAROEUM ABOUT...
IT'S ALSO THE PLACE JOYCE AND I WENT, THE DAY WE DECIDED WE WOULD GET MARRIED.
IT IS? OHH... HOW ROMANTIC! YES, I LIKE TO SEE WHERE YOU PROPOSE TO HER.
IT WASN'T EXACTLY A PROPOSAL AND IT WAS VERY COLD OUT. IT WAS STILL WINTER, BUT...
C'MON. IT'S REAL PRETTY OUT THERE NOW. I THINK YOU'LL LIKE IT.

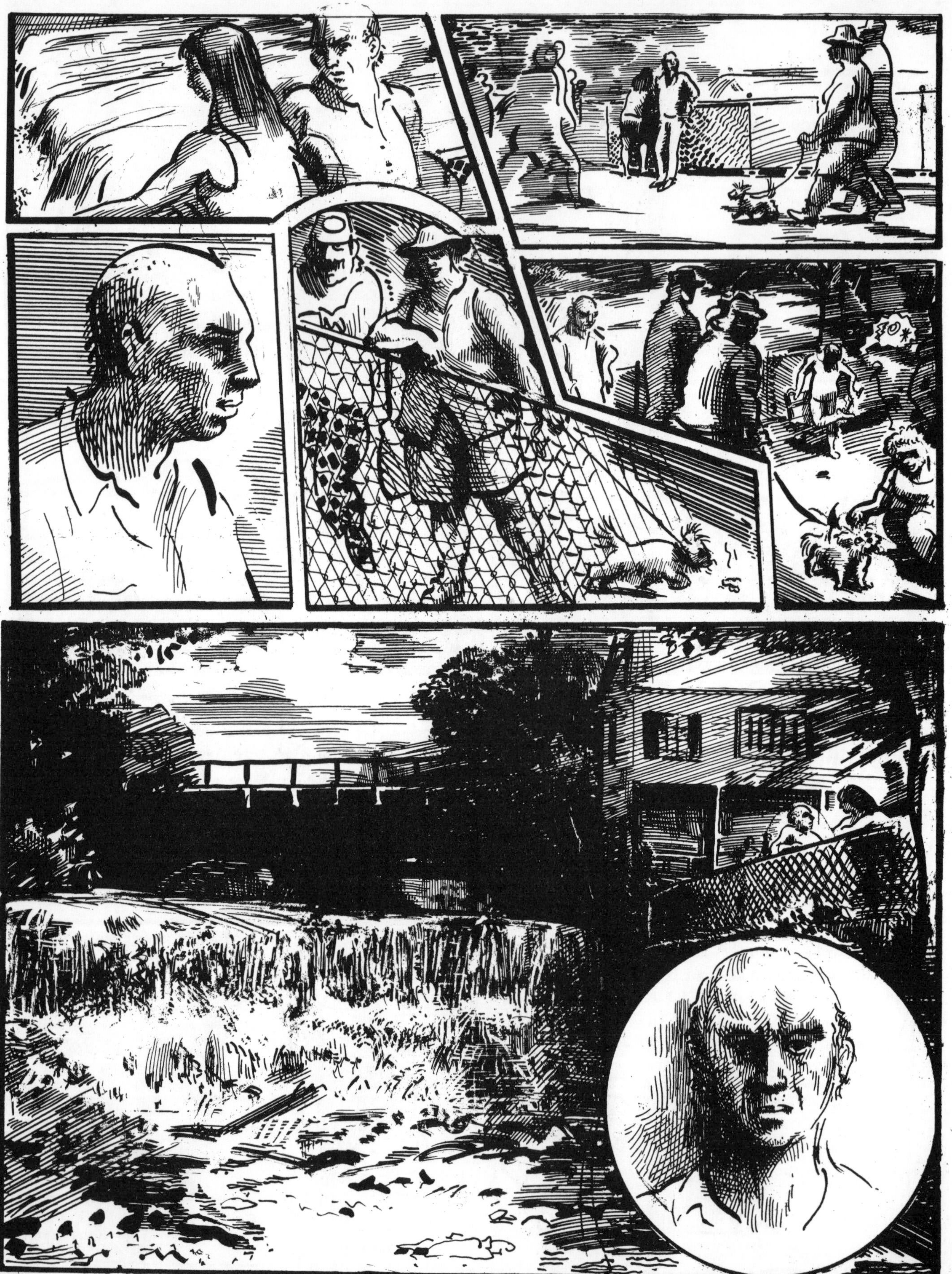